AF576509

THE CHIEFS OF NAVAL OPERATIONS

THE CHIEFS OF NAVAL OPERATIONS

EDITED BY ROBERT WILLIAM LOVE, JR.

NAVAL INSTITUTE PRESS
ANNAPOLIS, MARYLAND

Library of Congress Cataloging in Publication Data
Main entry under title:

The Chiefs of Naval Operations.

Includes bibliographical references and index.
1. United States. Office of Naval Operations—
History. 2. United States. Office of Naval Operations
—Biography. 3. Admirals—United States—Biography.
I. Love, Robert William, 1944-
VA58.C47 359.4'092'2 [B] 80-12253
ISBN 0-87021-115-3

Printed in the United States of America

To
My Mother and Father

CONTENTS

ACKNOWLEDGMENTS

The editor of a multiauthored work owes a primary debt to his contributors for taking his conception and executing it. In this instance, I am grateful for the care, patience, and punctuality of my coauthors, and for their cheery willingness to listen to my suggestions. Paolo Coletta's work on the *American Secretaries of the Navy* provided the inspiration for this book and he has my thanks. Earlier in my career, Donald Swain, Dennis Harris, and Wesley Frank Craven encouraged me to study naval history and bureaucracy and I am thankful for their tutelage. Editing this book was an education, for I had the enviable opportunity of working with Mary Veronica Amoss of the Naval Institute Press, a delightful but demanding critic whose defense of the purity of her mother tongue is indefatigable. My colleagues in the History Department of the U. S. Naval Academy have been invariably helpful in ways large and small. And my wife, Rose, and my precious children, Robert and Kirstie, have lived with this book for more years than they want to remember. For their forbearance and good humor, they have my love and affection.

INTRODUCTION

During the age of sail, the administration of the U. S. Department of the Navy underwent only two significant changes, despite repeated expressions of dissatisfaction with the prevalent forms of management. Various committees of the Continental Congress managed the naval forces of the national government during the Revolutionary War, but the navy was disestablished following the Treaty of Paris in 1783. Several attempts to re-create a naval force under the Articles of Confederation failed. In August 1789, President George Washington assigned naval affairs to the new Department of War, but no forces were afloat or ashore until Congress authorized six frigates to deal with the Barbary pirates in 1794. Four years later, during a crisis with revolutionary France over maritime rights, President John Adams, who always considered himself the preeminent American navalist, agreed with Congress to create an independent Navy Department headed by an appointed secretary of cabinet rank. This arrangement continued throughout the Quasi-War with France, the Tripolitan Wars of Thomas Jefferson's presidency, and the War of 1812 with Great Britain. In general, the secretary and a few clerks directed operations in consultation with a small number of senior ships' captains. Shipbuilding and manning policies were settled by the political secretary through compromises with Congress. All recognized that the configuration and use of naval forces were highly charged issues of partisan or sectional consequence.

This system worked modestly well in peacetime, but poorly when a major war erupted in 1812. Secretary William Jones, a former merchant and sea captain who headed the department throughout most of that conflict, admitted in 1814 that he was overburdened and needed professional assistance. Jones proposed, and Congress enacted on 7 February 1815, a law creating a Board of Navy Commissioners. President James Madison appointed three captains to the panel; they quickly tried to gain control of strategy and squadron deployments, but the new secretary, Benjamin Crowninshield, objected, claiming that these were his prerogatives, and Madison upheld him. A classic confrontation over civilian control of the military ironically left the commissioners with authority over "the civil functions of the department" and the secretary in charge of military matters. Navalists have since condemned this as being "the reverse of what it should have been."

However, the movements of the squadrons during the Jacksonian Era were inherently political, and their control had to be political. Visits to Liberia in the 1820s and 1830s, for example, or the half-hearted enforcement of the anti-slave-trade provisions of the Webster-Ashburton Treaty of 1842 were the by-products of domestic partisan or sectional politics. Nevertheless, the growth in number of the station squadrons and the increasing complexity of the shore facilities forced a thorough reorganization of the Navy Department in 1842. At the behest of the administration and the commissioners, Congress abolished the board and created five bureaus, each charged with one facet of "civil administration" and each headed by a uniformed or civilian chief responsible directly to the political secretary, who retained immediate control over strategy, deployments, and personnel.

For over a century, the bureau system enshrined the principle of dual administration of the navy. This "bilinear" form existed alongside an old habit of naming ad hoc boards or committees of experts to consider special issues of a unique or transitory sort. Almost from its inception, navalists criticized the bureau system. They claimed that it suffered from inefficiency and vulnerability to partisan political influence. Actually, Jacksonian politicians prized neither efficiency nor apolitical administration. They distrusted the expertise and latent elitism that the officer corps claimed to embody. The navalists therefore achieved little in the way of change until the Jacksonian model was challenged by the Progressives.

Contrary to the charges made against it, the bureau system exhibited remarkable flexibility. When sectionalism erupted into the Civil War in 1861 and the mission of the Union Navy grew in scope and diversity, Congress created three more bureaus and an assistant secretary to direct operations. A strategic planning council was assembled and the bureau chiefs gathered regularly to coordinate their war efforts. In contrast to the War Department, wartime naval administration—for reasons having perhaps less to do with the system than with the managers—proved to be a paragon of efficiency. Thus, early postwar proposals by line officers for a board of admiralty to direct fleet operations and make naval policy failed to attract the approval either of successive secretaries of the navy or of Congress.

The decline of the postwar navy resulted from the obvious purposelessness of maintaining a large peacetime naval establishment with no evident mission of consequence. This lack of purpose was aggravated by slow rates of promotion, which rankled career naval officers and tended to drive talent from the officer corps. For fifteen years after Appomattox the service languished and grew restive; but it was then revived with a spurt of intellectual enthusiasm.

At the core of this new navalism was a struggle to change American foreign policy from continentalism and nonentanglement to imperialism. Navalists played a significant role in that process. An ancillary feature of the expansionist movement involved an effort by the officer corps to gain greater control over the Navy Department; changing the form of administration—especially with regard to war planning and peacetime strategy—was one way of inching toward the more profound goal. While proposals to achieve this secondary aim of greater professional control of the fleet continued without abatement during the Gilded Age, they were given new credence by the success of the Prussian General Staff in the wars with Austria and France. For American navalists, some of the attractive features of the Prussian system were detailed prewar policy and strategic planning and preparations, and operational control of the forces in the field by a centralized agency staffed by the officer corps with a head who enjoyed immediate access to the chief political executive.

In the latter part of the Gilded Age, agitation among naval officers for establishment of a general staff coincided with demands for a battleship fleet that would enhance American prestige and advance a new foreign policy of expansionism. Pressure from imperialists, a federal surplus derived from protective tariffs, and the inception of a national steel industry provided the political stimulus for the battle fleet, but navalists failed to acquire the substantive control of their department that a general staff would provide. The American concept of direct political control of military forces was in opposition to such a reform. Thus, although navalists made a marked contribution to a new American foreign policy, they failed in their attempt to obtain more exclusive and unified control over their own institution.

Indeed, the very success of the bureau system combined with ad hoc boards during the Spanish-American War in 1898 served only to weaken the case for reorganization. At the onset of belligerency, Secretary of the Navy John D. Long created the Naval War Board to direct operations against the enemy's squadrons. Reporting to the board on 9 May, Captain Alfred Thayer Mahan, the preeminent navalist of his day, proposed that Long disband the panel and create, in the midst of war, a naval general staff. In reply, Long inquired, "Has the Board . . . made any mistakes that you can point out?" Mahan admitted that it had not and Long dropped the matter. After the peace, Mahan wrote to Rear Admiral Stephen B. Luce that "one man—a chief and his subordinates—is needed; but I fear we can't get him because the service and the Department don't want him." Ironically, while the blunders of the army in the war with Spain led directly to the acceptance of a general staff under the reforms of Secretary of War Elihu Root, the victories of the American fleet at Manila Bay and Santiago undercut the movement toward centralization of naval control.

The only important organizational change to result from the Spanish-American War was the formation of the General Board, a rather weak substitute for a naval general staff, which had been forcefully proposed by Capitan Henry Clay Taylor. When established in March 1900, the General

Board consisted of Admiral of the Navy George Dewey, the president of the Naval War College, the chief of the Office of Naval Intelligence, and the chief of the powerful Bureau of Navigation. To assist in its principal functions, war planning and advising the secretary on shipbuilding policy, the board was assigned a number of junior officers. This was, however, hardly the "nucleus of a general staff . . . created through the efforts of naval officers" as some have suggested. The General Board was purely advisory, never directed operations in wartime, enjoyed no authority over either the fleet or the bureaus, and had no special access to the chief executive. It also failed to sate the appetites of the militants in the officer corps for a true general staff.

Whereas the legacy of the political ideology of Jefferson and Jackson thwarted military centralization in the navy in the nineteenth century, the new doctrines of Progressivism injected renewed life into the issue after Theodore Roosevelt became president in 1901. A former assistant secretary of the navy, he was a self-conscious expansionist and navalist who intended to employ his fleet as an arm of Great Power politics. Although he distrusted Germany's political motives, he admired her standards of efficiency—as did many Progressives—and, when Congress approved a general staff for the army based on the Prussian model, Roosevelt notified Capital Hill that he agreed with the report of a board headed by Navy Secretary William H. Moody and Mahan that called for an analogous organization for the navy.

Opposition sprang both from the bureau chiefs, who, with justification, worried that their prerogatives would be curtailed and thus jealously guarded their authority, and from Assistant Secretary of the Navy Charles H. Darling, whose resistance killed the bill in the House. As Darling trenchantly pointed out, "the effect of this measure will be to make the Secretary . . . an ornamental figurehead. . . . The measure savors too much of militarism to be consistent with the spirit of our institutions."

Roosevelt tabled this idea until the end of his term, then he renewed his call for a naval general staff in his annual message of 1908. Shortly thereafter, he named two commissions within two months to study the problem; they submitted three reports, all ignored by Congress. However, an interesting feature of the last report, issued on 26 February 1909, was the inclusion of a "Chief of the Division of Naval Operations" to be the "principal military advisor to the Secretary." He was to be "without administrative functions" and would "supervise war plans; naval policy; the War College; the Office of Naval Intelligence; and kindred subjects." Here was the fetus of a supreme naval executive to which the proponents of a general staff had so long looked forward.

Shortly after this report was issued, William Howard Taft succeeded Roosevelt and named George von L. Meyer as his secretary of the navy. A Progressive, Meyer soon appointed yet another board in the summer of 1909, which endorsed the works of its predecessors. Meyer then waited until Congress was out of session to implement some of the proposals by Navy Regulation rather than by legislation. He divided the Navy Department into four divisions, each to be headed by an aide to the secretary. Each aide was an advisor whose authority over the functions of his division was tinged with more than a touch of ambiguity. The principal aide headed the Division of Operations of the Fleet and was charged with advising the secretary "as to strategic and tactical matters," "operations of the vessels of the Navy," and "the movement of vessels." However, the attorney general warned Meyer that "aides cannot . . . exercise supervisory authority over chiefs" of the contending bureaus.

This structure remained intact until after the outbreak of World War I in Europe, when many naval officers began to complain that Secretary of the Navy Josephus Daniels was not adequately preparing the fleet to enter the war, which they wanted to fight. Against Daniels's opposition, the aide for operations, Rear Admiral Bradley A. Fiske, connived with Congress and persuaded it to pass a bill establishing a chief of naval operations "charged with the operations of the fleet and with the preparations and readiness of plans for its use in war." However, Daniels's pleas that such a post was but the first step towards the "Prussianization" of the officer corps focused sufficient concern on that issue that Congress gave the first chief of naval operations no authority over the bureaus and enjoined him to work under the direction of the political secretary. Nonetheless, it was clear that the issue had been raised not so much because naval officers wanted greater control of their own department, but because they were unhappy with the national policy of neutrality and believed that it was necessary to prepare for American entry into the European war. Daniels was restrained on the preparedness issue because he opposed entry into the war.

With the creation of the chief of naval operations in 1915, the function of war planning was transferred from the General Board to the new office. A typically Progressive measure, the act that created the chief of naval operations was passed during a national crisis, advocated on the grounds of modernistic efficiency and preparedness, and triumphed over the objections of an older aristocracy of Jacksonian politicians who struggled in vain against the new elitist gradations of an increasingly pluralistic society.

The complaints of the Progressives against Daniels's policies and methods intensified during the war, and surfaced after the armistice when Rear Admiral William S. Sims, who had commanded U. S. Naval Forces in Europe, charged that the secretary and his first chief of naval operations, Admiral William S. Benson, had failed to prepare for the war or to support the Allied campaign against the U-boats. One of the obvious problems was that many of the services not easily categorized under the older bureau system, such as aviation, had been given to the chief of naval operations, who, because of Daniels's opposition to a general staff, had few assistants. Admiral Robert E. Coontz, Benson's successor, recognized the extent of the problem and, in 1921, agreed to the creation of a new bureau, Aeronautics, to handle air matters theretofore divided among his office and four bureaus.

The Republicans who governed in Washington during the 1920s had less fear of losing civilian control over the military than did the Democrats of the

New Freedom, as demonstrated by Secretary of State Charles Evans Hughes's cavalier treatment of the navy's General Board before and during the Washington Conference. In 1916, Assistant Secretary of the Navy Franklin D. Roosevelt worried that it would be "fatal" to civilian dominance "to give the chief of operations administrative powers," but in 1921 the Budget and Accounting Act established a centralized accounting system for the national government and required that each department appoint a budget officer. For the navy, that job was given to the chief of naval operations. However, this authority was short-lived and the chief of naval operations ceased to be the budget officer after 1923. Nonetheless, the next year he received an even more important writ when Congress revised Article 233 of Navy Regulations and ordered him to "coordinate all repairs and alterations to vessels and the supply of personnel and material thereto."

Because he controlled war planning, against which all shipbuilding proposals were tested, and because he had the authority to coordinate the work of the bureaus, the chief of naval operations emerged from the 1920s with enhanced but still limited authority in the professional service. Daniels and Roosevelt in 1915 perceived a possible competition for supreme power in the navy between the CNO and the political secretary. However, almost from the inception of the office, the chief of naval operations and the navy secretary formed a bureaucratic alliance, working in relative harmony to subjugate the bureaus or to defend the navy's interests against exogenous opponents. The civilian secretary found that the technical expertise of the chief of naval operations was indispensable to him in his dealings with the rest of the navy; as chiefs of naval operations recognized this, they began to frame policy questions in technical terms, thus gaining the advantage in most disputes. However, between the wars, few secretaries opposed their chiefs of operations on major issues of policy. Indeed, the chief of naval operations had become such a critical executive by 1930 that Congress provided for an assistant chief, who could replace the incumbent in his absence or disability.

Daniels had prophesied that a chief of naval operations would supplant the political secretary and, to an extent, this proved to be true in the 1930s. Claude A. Swanson, who served as navy secretary during the New Deal, was in poor health, and Congress provided that the chief of naval operations could serve as acting secretary when the political appointee was incapacitated. Indeed, when Admiral William D. Leahy was CNO, he so often served as acting secretary that one critic wrote of the "curious and rather ominous development" of the "evolution of the Chief of Staff [sic] as a *de facto* Secretary of the Navy. . . . due to the continuing ill-health of . . . Mr. Swanson."

Although the real authority of the chief of naval operations increased under Franklin Roosevelt, the president refused to permit any formal reorganization of the Navy Department to accommodate this fact until World War II had started. For example, in 1933 Chief of Naval Operations Admiral William H. Standley pressed for control over the bureaus and was rebuffed not only by the bureau chiefs, who dominated the board that considered the request, but also by the president, who wrote on 2 March 1934 that "the orders to the bureaus and offices should come from the Secretary." Likewise, when Representative Carl Vinson, chairman of the House Naval Affairs Committee, introduced a bill in 1933 calling for an end to the independent authority of the bureau chiefs, it never got out of committee because of presidential opposition. Four years later, FDR warned Swanson "to pass word down the line through Operations and Navigation that anyone caught lobbying for a General Staff will be sent to Guam." Despite Roosevelt's affection for Daniels's practices, the responsibilities of the chief of naval operations continued to grow, especially during the tenure of Admiral Leahy, whose skill as a military bureaucrat was near legendary. Nonetheless, even Leahy could not persuade FDR to restructure the Navy Department's command: for example, on 26 May 1939, he proposed to abolish the General Board and absorb its functions into his office, but the president again refused to permit alterations in the older system.

International tensions developed into war just as Admiral Harold R. Stark took over from Leahy, and Roosevelt's interest in naval affairs heightened before Pearl Harbor. Stark was a cautious traditionalist, but he wanted the United States to enter the war in Europe in a greater hurry than FDR was willing to admit was necessary. The frenzied pace of naval activity in 1940 and 1941, however, gave Stark no opportunity to put forward and press for major administrative reform proposals—perhaps he knew they had no chance for passage, given the president's attitude.

Many erroneously believed that poor cooperation between army and navy leaders had contributed significantly to the defeat by the Japanese at Pearl Harbor, and this widely held opinion may in part account for Roosevelt's decision in December 1941 to make Admiral Ernest J. King commander in chief of the U. S. Fleet. King's dynamism, Stark's shell-shocked weariness, and the latter's decision to leave office resulted in FDR's decision in Executive Order 9096 of 12 March 1942 to give King additional authority as chief of naval operations. Acting under spoken orders from the chief executive and mindful of the thorough reorganization of the army that had just begun, King issued a series of orders in May that formalized the practical control the CNO had already gained over the bureaus and offices. The keynote was King's directive ordering the chief of the Office of Procurement and Management, who worked for Undersecretary of the Navy James V. Forrestal, to serve simultaneously as assistant chief of naval operations for material. As justification for the order, King cited the presidential directive that charged him as chief of naval operations with the "direction of effort . . . of the bureaus and offices of the Navy Department." However, Roosevelt ordered King to rescind the directive. In reality, the whole scrap mattered little. Throughout the war, King regarded his billet as Commander in Chief, U. S. Fleet, as more important than his billet as CNO, and he retained real control over logistics and procurement through his membership on the Joint Chiefs of Staff, created in 1942 by Roosevelt to direct grand strategy during the war. Even so, at the end of the conflict King insisted on dismantling the system that he had used and leaving to his weaker successors the single supreme post, chief of naval operations.

During the war King had wrangled with Forrestal over the exact authority of the chief of naval operations. When the war ended, the executive order giving him control over the bureaus was canceled, some of their activities were consolidated under an assistant secretary, and the status quo ante bellum seemed to prevail, the only distinction being in the severely diminished role of the General Board, which was phased out in 1951. Again, substance belied form, because a primary role of the postwar Joint Chiefs of Staff was to review and adjust the budget of each branch of the armed forces. Within that context, the chief of naval operations as a member of the Joint Chiefs had a powerful lever to manipulate monies to fit the ends of his policies. The "CNO Act" of 1949 did not significantly alter the practical functioning of the office.

In the 1930s the main argument was over the CNO's control of the bureaus; in the 1950s it concerned his role as director of fleet operations. This was a sore point in 1934 between Admiral Standley and the commander in chief of the U. S. Fleet, Admiral John M. Reeves, but after 1937 there was little doubt that the CNO had the authority to deploy the fleet and direct its strategy. However, the postwar struggle over military unification and the "Revolt of the Admirals" in 1949 suggested to many that service parochialism guided many of the policy decisions of the increasingly important Joint Chiefs of Staff. This was a powerful argument, although by focusing on the disruptions of unification in the areas of roles and missions it missed the more profound agreement that had emerged around strategic war plans. Nonetheless, by the outbreak of the Korean War some had come to view the chief of naval operations as being more important in his role as a member of the Joint Chiefs of Staff than in his function as a service manager. For example, Admiral Forrest P. Sherman's achievements as chief of naval operations were the result not of his talents as a military administrator, but of his influence among his fellow chiefs.

President Dwight D. Eisenhower accepted this thesis, and his efforts at reorganizing the military command structure reflected his belief that the Joint Chiefs should serve as an advisory body on broad issues of policy for the commander in chief and his political secretary of defense. Following the president's orders, a committee headed by Thomas S. Gates reviewed the Navy Department's organization in 1954 and found it "basically sound." However, in that year the secretary of the navy relieved the chief of naval operations of his command authority over the marine corps, and, four years later, Eisenhower made a major assault on the operational authority of all the service chiefs. Since World War II, each of them had acted as the "executive agent" for the Joint Chiefs in charge of the joint commands that were assigned to flag officers of his service. In Eisenhower's Defense Department Reorganization Act of 1958, he placed the joint commands directly under the political defense secretary, thereby eliminating the service chiefs from the operational chain of command.

Practice remained divorced from the rule, however, because the naval joint commanders' dependence upon the chief of naval operations for support, plus the increasingly integrated character of strategic war planning, meant that these operational commanders' subordination to the chief was complete. Practical control of assignments of flag-rank officers, the prerogative of the chief of naval operations since 1942, alone gave him enormous power over the fleet commands.

Still, the chief of naval operations had little control over the management of procurement and material. In fact, in 1958 Secretary of the Navy Franke chaired a board that proposed to merge the two bureaus but specifically rejected a general staff for the department and smugly recommended a "continuation of the present bilinear system, with its definite division of military and non-military duties." What was hailed by the Franke Board as a beneficent division in 1958, however, became an unhealthy fragmentation four years later, when a new emphasis on systems analysis as a management tool for evaluating defense programs was introduced by Defense Secretary Robert S. McNamara. These means demanded centralized sources for planning and budgeting which the navy's older, conservative organization lacked, and so in 1963 a chief of naval material was created and ordered to report to the political undersecretary. Within three years this billet was placed under the control of the chief of naval operations, and the old bureaus, except the Bureau of Personnel and the Bureau of Medicine and Surgery, were abolished and replaced by six "systems" commands, also under the principal naval executive.

The prewar arguments over civilian control of the military melted away after World War II. Postwar American strategic planning, for example, was no longer the exclusive purview of military officers; control of war planning and the accompanying technological expertise were diffused among politicians, uniformed planners, and civilian defense intellectuals. Moreover, rapid communications strengthened the grip of the chief executive over the instant activities of even the most distant units. Thus military control over material management was perceived as less of a threat to control of the establishment by civilians than had been the case when the old Orange Plan was known to only a few members of the naval hierarchy.

During the Cold War and the era of detente the trend was for chiefs of naval operations to gain more internal control of their institutions but to lose authority in the wider defense community. The growth of the importance of the office of the secretary of defense after 1961 for example, tended to degrade not only the authority of the service secretaries but also of the service chiefs; Admiral David L. McDonald was rarely consulted about naval operations during the Vietnam War and admitted that his advice counted for little. Although, by law, the chief of naval operations remained the president's principal adviser on naval affairs, Admiral Elmo R. Zumwalt got to see President Richard M. Nixon only twice to discuss policy during his term of office.

Thus, although the goals of those who had argued in favor of a naval general staff were achieved in 1942, at the end of the war the system reverted to its earlier, less-cohesive status. The prevailing attitudes of the 1970s subsumed the chief of naval operations into a larger body of "military opinion" to which many said too little attention was being paid. But if this was so it had ever been thus, for it was what the original agitators had really been saying one century earlier.

THE CHIEFS
OF NAVAL OPERATIONS

WILLIAM SHEPHERD BENSON

11 May 1915–25 September 1919

DAVID F. TRASK

Even William S. Benson, who became the first chief of naval operations on 11 May 1915, expressed amazement at his selection for that billet. "I never sought the position . . . and was possibly the most surprised person in Washington when the Secretary of the Navy sent for me and told me he had decided to appoint me to the position. It was my first knowledge that any such thing was contemplated."[1] Others were equally taken aback. Rear Admiral Bradley A. Fiske, who was then the aide for operations in the Navy Department and aspired to the job, summarized the reaction of the navy. "Benson was a handsome dignified gentleman of thoroughly correct habits, very religious and conscientious, and an excellent seaman; but I had never heard that he had ever shown the slightest interest in strategy or been on the General Board, *or even taken the summer course at the war college.*" What was needed, Fiske maintained, "was a clear comprehension of strategy and a fine mind. Benson, so far as I knew, had devoted no attention whatever to strategy, and his mind, while good and sound, was such that he had never been reckoned one of the 'bright men' of the navy."[2]

Fiske was certainly disingenuous; better than most he understood that Benson was chosen precisely because he was not one of the "bright men" of the navy. For many years reform-minded officers such as Fiske had advocated a powerful naval general staff, one that would place the fleet in the hands of naval professionals and minimize the influence of civilian amateurs. Writing to Secretary of the Navy Josephus Daniels in 1913, Fiske cited Prussia's victory over France in 1870 to support the case for military organizations being directed by skilled professionals. Why had the French suffered a crushing defeat? "The reason was simply that the Germans, under the direction of Von Moltke, had organized a general staff which had made such perfect plans of mobilization and subsequent operations that, on the outbreak of war, the German Army was ready immediately." All nations recognized the need for a general staff, Fiske continued, and, although the U.S. Army had adopted such a system, the navy had not followed suit.[3] The service afloat lacked a leader such as Elihu Root who, as secretary of war, had brought about basic reforms in 1903.

Certainly the naval reformers had no confidence in the incumbent secretary of the navy, Josephus Daniels of North Carolina, an old-line Democrat of Bryanite persuasion. Even after the outbreak of war in Europe in August 1914, he showed no inclination to improve the administration of the Navy Department. The frustrated Fiske summed up the reformers' feelings about their civilian superior: "To bring up a subject in connection with the [enlisted] men or something like that, would secure his interest, but if you brought up anything in connection with the efficiency of the Navy and its part in the war, why that was not good. We must avoid that subject. . . . It was very difficult as a rule to get him to take any action whatever."[4]

From the viewpoint of many naval leaders, Secretary Daniels was all too efficient in certain ways. He abolished the officers' wine mess, thereby depriving the wardroom of spirits while at sea, and, whereas he showed great interest in the welfare and education of the enlisted men, he showed no interest in creating a naval staff or in building ships. Whatever might be the opinions of naval officers, Daniels was fully in accord with the desires of his chief, the president of the United States. One authority summarizes Woodrow Wilson's outlook succinctly: "The President wanted no militant demonstrations to tarnish his vision of a peaceful America as mediator of the world's disputes."[5] Wilson, a near pacifist, hoped to avoid involvement in the European conflict by facilitating a negotiated peace between the contending coalitions rather than by building up the nation's defenses.

At length Fiske took matters into his own hands. On 9 November 1914, he addressed to Daniels a memorandum that castigated the Navy Department's failure to prepare for war, noting three cardinal deficiencies: the navy was under strength; the navy had no general staff; the navy was not adequately trained. When this appeal failed to stir Daniels, the disgruntled admiral entered into secret negotiations with a friend in the Congress, the redoubtable naval hero of 1898, Richmond Pearson Hobson. The two drafted a bill that created, under the secretary of the navy, a chief of naval operations who, with the help of fifteen assistants, would assume responsibility for the readiness of the navy and for its general direction.[6] When Secretary Daniels learned of the proposed legislation, he proved more than equal to the challenge. Convinced that Fiske and his associates wanted to "prussianize" the navy, thereby violating the principle that the military should be subordinate to civilian leaders, Daniels managed to influence the wording of the law so that the chief of naval operations would not acquire the plenary power desired by Fiske. In its final form, the act passed on 3 March 1915 specified:

> There shall be a Chief of Naval Operations, who shall be an officer on the active list of the Navy, appointed by the President, by and with the advice and consent of the Senate, from among the officers of the line of the Navy not below the

> grade of captain, for a period of four years, who shall, under the direction of the Secretary of the Navy, be charged with the operations of the fleet, and with the preparation and readiness of plans for its use in war: *provided,* That if an officer of the grade of captain be appointed Chief of Naval Operations he shall have the rank, title, and emoluments of a rear admiral while holding that position. During the temporary absence of the Secretary and the Assistant Secretary of the Navy, the Chief of Naval Operations shall be next in succession to act as Secretary of the Navy.[7]

Daniels later explained the difference he discerned between the reformers' plan and his own. "But you do not want a military officer in control of the Navy Department. It is contrary to all the principles of American Government." Hobson's plan made the chief of naval operations "responsible for the readiness of the Navy for war and in charge of its general direction." The revised text assigned to the chief of naval operations not the "general direction" of the navy, but simply the tasks of guiding the operations of the fleet and preparing war plans. Daniels, proud of his success in frustrating the reformers, later remarked, "We saved the American system and destroyed this Von Tirpitz system."[8]

Surely Daniels exaggerated the differences between the two proposals, although no one can doubt that the language of the act, as finally passed, placed limits on the CNO's freedom of action. He could not act without the assent of the secretary of the navy; he did not have direct authority over the bureau chiefs; he had no staff; and he held a lesser rank than the officer commanding the Atlantic Fleet. And yet a truly significant change had been made in the administration of the navy. Even in its truncated form, the arrangement establishing the billet of chief of naval operations, as William R. Braisted notes, "was the most important institutional innovation in the Navy Department since the creation of the new bureaus in 1842 as well as the outstanding achievement of the preparedness movement during the winter of 1914–1915."[9] Much would depend on the early evolution of the new office, given its uncertain origin.

The sailor who assumed the office of chief of naval operations had behind him a successful but hardly brilliant career—one that was scarcely distinguishable from those of numerous other officers at the time. Born in Macon, Georgia, on 25 September 1855, William Shepherd Benson completed his studies at the Naval Academy in 1877. In 1879, after his first tour of duty at sea in the steam sloop *Hartford,* flagship of the South Atlantic Squadron, he graduated from the Naval Academy and served a series of assignments in various ships. His first promotion, to the rank of ensign, came in 1881. The second, to the rank of lieutenant, junior grade, occurred in 1888. In that year he began a round-the-world cruise in the dispatch vessel *Dolphin.* Shortly after his return in 1890, Benson went as an instructor to the Naval Academy, where he remained until elevated to the rank of lieutenant in 1893. For many years thereafter, he alternated between periods of sea duty and assignments at Annapolis. Gaining a solid reputation as a skilled seaman, he slowly rose in rank, becoming a lieutenant commander in 1900, a commander in 1905, and a captain in 1909. Although he held responsible command and staff positions in the fleet, he did not attend the regular course at the Naval War College and spent very little time in the Navy Department. After commanding the battleship *Utah,* he was assigned as commandant of the navy yard in Philadelphia with duties as supervisor of the Third, Fourth, and Fifth Naval Districts.[10] He was detached from this assignment in May 1915, and ordered to the Navy Department as the first chief of naval operations with the rank of rear admiral.

Benson is sometimes depicted as totally unqualified to be head of operations, surely an unwarranted view, but many other officers seemed better equipped for the task than he, especially those who had served in a broader range of assignments and received specialized training at the Naval War College. He never identified himself with the reformers of Fiske's stripe, a number of whom were prime contenders to be named the first CNO, but that fact surely was one of the reasons why Daniels selected him. The secretary of the navy, anxious to preserve his prerogatives and thoroughly alienated from officers such as Fiske, whom he deemed bent on undermining civilian control of the military, found in Benson an officer whom he could trust and who would not challenge civilian leadership. Benson later described his responsibilities as being "to coordinate all the technical work of the Navy Department as represented by the different bureaus and offices, see to the proper disposition and handling of the fleet and all floating material and the preparation of plans, and all the munitions of war that would be used by the fleet in its operations." Surely a modest job description by comparison with the dreams of Fiske.[11]

It is important that Benson secretly shared the reformers' adverse view of Secretary Daniels. Some years after the war, he penned his mature assessment of his former chief:

> It was unfortunate that at this period we had as Secretary of the Navy a man who, while he was honest, earnest and sincere in his efforts to do the best with the situation, due to a very meager experience and lack of knowledge of international affairs, could not appreciate the fact that we could be drawn into the European struggle, and in addition to that, was more or less suspicious of military and naval men, believing their principal effort was to do things that would redound to their military glory [rather] than to the best interests of the country. He was honestly and firmly of the opinion that we could not be drawn into the war, consequently when requests were made upon him for increased appropriations, more officers or material, he often could not see his way clear to give full and whole-hearted cooperation and sometimes even refused consent. He was at times suspicious of changes in organization and things of that sort.[12]

Daniels apparently never guessed that Benson harbored such views of him. He was sufficiently impressed by the discreet naval officer, during his early months in office, to permit some helpful improvements in the arrangements for the chief of naval operations. A law of 29 August 1916 specified the rank of full admiral for those serving as CNO and authorized fifteen assistants in the rank of lieutenant commander or above.[13]

When Benson reported to the Navy Department on 11 May 1915, he realized that a difficult task lay ahead. "I found absolutely nothing . . . that was of any service to me. Even the office to which I came was not in proper condition . . . for an officer of my rank and the position I held. That was about all there was to it; a room in the Navy Department, and I think one or two small rooms outside for clerical help."[14] The admiral's agenda soon became apparent. He must clarify his position and function, in particular developing good working relationships with the secretary of the navy and the bureau chiefs. He must contribute to expansion of the navy. He must reorganize the fleet in preparation for possible action. During the first two years of his service, he worked energetically to accomplish these purposes.

In June 1915, Daniels took a significant step towards coordinating the work of the Navy Department by creating an Advisory Council. It included the assistant secretary of the navy, then Franklin D. Roosevelt, the chief of naval operations, eight bureau chiefs, the commandant of the marine corps, and the judge advocate general of the navy. Although Benson never acquired the power to appoint bureau chiefs or give them direct orders, his tactful leadership combined with the exigencies of a great international crisis raised him gradually to a position of considerable influence within the Navy Department.[15] As he gained the confidence of other naval officers in the department and also of Daniels, he took a number of major initiatives. One was to order the General Board to study fleet organization, a step of importance in preparing the navy for war. Another was to develop his own administrative support, the Office of the Chief of Naval Operations, which benefited considerably when Congress granted him fifteen assistants in 1916. He also arranged for merchant ships to be inspected so that their use as auxiliaries in time of war would be facilitated.[16]

Although the principal operations of the fleet during his first two years as CNO took place in the waters around Haiti, Santo Domingo, and Mexico, where President Wilson undertook major interventions to restore stability and encourage democracy, Benson could not ignore the threatening developments in Europe. He became convinced that Germany would defeat the Allies unless the United States entered the war, but he gave no hint of favoring intervention. His stress lay rather on being prepared to deal with Germany *after* that country emerged victorious from the European conflict. "I came to the office [of CNO] . . . fully realizing that the U.S. Navy was not prepared for the ordeal which I felt absolutely certain she would eventually have to go through."[17] He did what he could to get ready for the challenges ahead, but much remained undone when the day of reckoning came in April 1917.

By far the most important reaction of the Navy Department to the crisis in Europe was the great naval construction program of 1916. President Wilson executed a dramatic about-face in his attitude toward the size of the navy after the failure of his efforts in 1914 and 1915 to bring about what he later called "peace without victory"—a negotiated peace in Europe resulting from the mediation of the United States. He came to realize that diplomatic initiatives usually stood little chance of success without the sanction of force. This realization coincided with considerable public agitation for "preparedness." Thus, both domestic and international influences account for Wilson's decision to place the navy "on an equality with the most efficient and practicably serviceable [foreign navy]." The Naval Act of 1916 provided for a fleet of sixty capital ships by 1925. The first phase of the building program, to be undertaken between 1916 and 1919, was to provide 10 battleships and 6 battle cruisers. During the same period, 146 vessels of lesser types were to be built.[18]

Admiral Benson exerted his influence in measurable ways as the building program came to fruition. He emphasized construction of capital ships, a course that led away from submarines, antisubmarine vessels, and auxiliaries. Of equal significance was the General Board's view, to which Benson subscribed heartily, that the three-year program should be designed "for a later contest in which the United States might face a coalition attacking in both oceans," rather than for participation in the struggle taking place in Europe.[19] What if Germany should triumph in Europe and later ally itself with Japan? This bogey influenced naval policy from 1916 to the end of 1918.

Although Admiral Benson made considerable progress in strengthening the Navy Department and Congress finally authorized a navy second to none, the United States was far from ready for the naval war it fought during 1917 and 1918. Many units of the fleet were not prepared to go to sea in April 1917, because they were not fully manned and were lacking in armament, equipment, and essential supplies. Well-trained, competent flag officers were in exceedingly short supply. Nothing had been done to achieve close liaison with the navies of the Allied powers. The naval war plans of the United States, for which Benson was responsible, envisioned a defensive battle against an enemy battle fleet in Caribbean waters. The navy had been built, organized, and trained for a type of warfare that did not materialize, i.e., full-fledged engagement between battle fleets. Preoccupation with capital ships led to a shortage of the types most in demand during the decisive phase of the war—antisubmarine ships capable of thwarting Germany's unrestricted submarine campaign against merchant shipping. That campaign, which began in February 1917, was designed to win the war for the Central Powers by interdicting the maritime communications of the Allied nations.[20]

Admiral Benson persisted in his view of the European conflict, even during the events that culminated in the American intervention of April 1917, consistently counseling against provocative actions. In October 1916, he expressed concern about American vessels stationed in the Mediterranean Sea. He told Frank Polk, an official of the State Department, that reports from that region confirmed a view he had held since the outset of the war, namely, "that the presence of our vessels in European waters was accompanied by great danger—a danger that to me seemed entirely unnecessary in view of the fact that the presence of our vessels in those waters could not [possibly] render adequate service to warrant the risk taken."[21] In February 1917, when the possibility of war could no longer be ignored, Benson instructed Daniels on how to respond to the emergency stemming from Germany's undersea warfare. It was important, he said, to proceed strictly in terms of the national interest: the United States must "not only . . . act quickly but . . . act with a full realization that we may eventually have to act alone." Obviously Benson still worried that Germany might defeat its enemies in Europe. Given this consideration, the basic naval missions were three in number. The nation must develop naval forces as quickly as possible; it must employ its forces to build up independent fighting power; it must render maximum support to the Allies as soon as possible. The third mission had first priority, but the others Benson deemed essential to the future security of the republic. He proposed to employ the fleet against enemy submarines in American waters, but he opposed plans that might interfere with the development of the big-ship building program. Once again the bogey of the long-term, rather than the imperatives of the immediate, crisis determined his outlook. "We may expect the future to give us more potential enemies than potential friends so that our safety must lie in our own resources."[22] This estimate of the situation dictated the prewar plans and preparations of the Navy Department. Benson was interested principally in defensive measures in the Western Hemisphere. Even as late as 13 March 1917, he showed himself unwilling to contemplate antisubmarine warfare in European waters, where the German U-boats had begun to take a terrible toll of merchant vessels supplying Britain, France, Russia, and Italy with essential assistance.[23]

Admiral Benson was not the only one responsible for the state of affairs in April 1917. In a postwar apologia, he offered a good explanation for naval deficiencies as the president took the country into the war. Benson claimed, "as a naval officer I would have had the fleet mobilized and I would have had many more vessels and would have had everything ready for anything we were called upon to do, if I had known that it was the intention of the people to go to war." Such knowledge, of course, was not vouchsafed to him. "Under the general conditions that existed, of our strict neutrality and the necessity for maintaining that attitude which had been made so evident by the people of the country, I felt then, and I still feel, that the fleet as it was distributed, under the circumstances and taking those things into consideration, was about as well as we could do."[24] He also argued that the situation might have been different, had he, as chief of naval operations, had the authority to make it so, a comment that revealed more than passing sympathy with the outlook of such naval reformers as Bradley Fiske. When, after the war, he was asked whether his organization was fully prepared for combat, he answered negatively, stating: "The office of the Chief of Naval Operations should have the responsibility for the preparation of the Navy as a whole. He should be strictly responsible for that, but he should have the authority that enables him to discharge that; all, of course, under a civilian Secretary of the Navy. . . . He should have the authority to coordinate all the technical activities of the Navy Department [the bureaus], and he should be held responsible for their efficient coordination and cooperation." Benson added that there ought to be arrangements to keep the CNO "fully informed as to the policies of the Government—I mean the political policies of the Government; what international problems were pending, what the international policy of the administration is at the time, any changes that might involve the distribution of forces."[25] In other words, he considered it essential not only that proper authority be lodged in the Navy Department, but that the navy grasp the political objectives to be supported by the application of sea power.

Nothing was more damaging to the navy than the constraints that flowed from the president's desire up to the very last moment to avoid belligerency. Only during the dark months of February and March 1917, after the German submarine offensive had begun, did Woodrow Wilson come, most reluctantly, to the conclusion that the only means of achieving his kind of peace was to accept belligerency on the Allied side.[26] The armed forces had to adjust to a truly remarkable political reversal, something they could not do overnight. Captain William V. Pratt, who served as assistant chief of naval operations in 1917 and 1918, noted the consequences of the reversal for the fighting services. It was not simply a matter of making the great technical transition from peace to war; it was a case of ideology. "I doubt whether we will ever be prepared to wage effective war at the instant of its declaration," Pratt maintained in 1920, "as I do not believe that our democratic form of government lends itself to the same instant readiness to strike other nations that an autocratic form of government does."[27]

Just before Wilson asked Congress to declare war on the Central Powers, Benson decided to send Rear Admiral William S. Sims abroad to ascertain the naval requirements of the war. The circumstances of Sims's departure reinforced a grossly oversimplified interpretation of Admiral Benson's outlook, i.e., that he was intensely Anglophobic, a prejudice that supposedly dictated his every action. Sims claimed that, upon his departure for London, Benson said to him: "Don't let the British pull the wool over your eyes. It is none of your business pulling their chestnuts out of the fire. We would as soon fight the British as the Germans." Questioned on this point after the war, Benson did not deny that he had said something of the sort, but he argued that the constraints of neutrality rather than anti-British sentiment accounted for his warning: "I endeavored to impress upon him [Sims] as emphatically as I could that he must not say or do anything which would embarrass the United States in its then position of neutrality." His concern stemmed from an incident that took place in 1910. It was because "I recalled Admiral Sims' indiscretions, " Benson wrote, "particularly his famous Guildhall speech which displayed his intense pro-British tendencies resulting in a reprimand by President Taft, that I cautioned him as I did."[28]

While Benson loyally enforced decisions of his civilian leaders that he may have privately questioned, it took some time to make the necessary adjustments to war. There was some truth in the picture of him transmitted to Paris by the French admiral, R.A. de Grasset, who visited Washington soon after the declaration of war. Although Benson and Daniels showed great cordiality to visitors from Britain and France, they lacked war plans and demonstrated no real grasp of what was going on in Europe. The Americans seemed lethargic, and none more so than Benson. De Grasset thought that "his spirit is slow and he does not seem possessed of the moral authority that comports with his rank and functions; he is, besides . . . a bureaucrat who arrived at the grade of admiral through political changes happening at the ministry."[29] It was not until Admiral Sims reported extensively on the situation in Europe that the Navy Department concentrated effectively on its wartime tasks.

In London Sims soon reached the conclusion that the United States should use its navy in European waters principally to frustrate Germany's hopes of starving Britain and France into submission before American power could become effective. To this end he urged the immediate dispatch of all available antisubmarine ships, particularly destroyers, to the submarine zone. When the British Admiralty finally decided to provide naval escorts for convoys of merchant ships through dangerous waters, Sims became an enthusiastic supporter of this approach. Of great long-run significance was Sims's belief that the United States should suspend construction of capital ships in favor of a crash effort to supply large numbers of antisubmarine and merchant ships.[30]

Admiral Benson demonstrated a strong proclivity for opposing Sims's recommendations, which were pressed upon the Navy Department with increasing urgency during the desperate spring of 1917, when the Allied land offensives in France failed miserably and the German submarines were taking a frightful toll of merchant shipping. The teachings of Alfred Thayer Mahan played a role in Benson's thought, and that of others in Washington. Mahan insisted that the nation should build and deploy a balanced and unified battle fleet in time of war, but Sims was recommending that the screen of the battle fleet be detached and used to reinforce British antisubmarine units. But probably of far greater import than Mahanian theory was Benson's continuing concern about the long-term future. What would happen after the war, if the construction of capital ships were deferred during the emergency in favor of antisubmarine vessels and merchant ships? Astute British observers accurately gauged Benson's concern. For example, Lord Northcliffe, the publisher who led a British mission to Washington during 1917, cabled home: "If war ends in compromise that leaves German fleet intact or in defeat of Allies, danger to U.S. [is] so great that utmost battleship and battlecruiser strength would be necessary in view of possible S. Atlantic and Pacific developments."[31] Northcliffe had in mind America's interest in enforcing the Monroe Doctrine and in curbing Japan's expansionist tendencies.

There was still another negative influence on the CNO; Benson wondered whether the Royal Navy had not adopted an unduly defensive outlook. He early showed an interest in mounting assaults against Germany's naval bases at

Heligoland and on the Channel coast at ports such as Ostend and Zeebrugge. Why not attack them? He was also attracted by proposals to lay mine barrages across the narrow waters through which Germany's submarines had to travel, if they wished to enter the Atlantic—especially the Straits of Dover and the North Sea between Norway and Scotland. President Wilson shared the suspicion that the British had not taken advantage of all their opportunities. On 11 August 1917, in an address to the officers of the Atlantic Fleet, he complained about the ineffectiveness of naval action against the submarine. "We are hunting hornets all over the farm and letting the nest alone." The fault lay with the British. "Every time we have suggested anything to the British Admiralty the reply has come back that virtually amounted to this, that it had never been done that way, and I felt like saying, 'Well, nothing has never been done so systematically as nothing is being done now.' " For a near pacifist, the president revealed a remarkable affinity to the offensive spirit of the country. "Please leave out of your vocabulary altogether the word 'prudent.' " He favored "audacity of method" rather than "circumspection and prudence," arguing the belief that "there are willing ears to hear this in the American Navy and the American Army because that is the kind of folks we are. We get tired of the old ways and covet the new ones."[32]

Changes in naval strategy had already begun—on both sides of the Atlantic—and others followed in due course. In July 1917, the United States made the difficult decision to suspend its big-ship program in favor of building destroyers and merchant ships. The British turn to the convoy system responded correctly to Wilson's just criticisms about hunting hornets all over the farm, but unsuccessful efforts to attack Ostend and Zeebrugge in 1918 confirmed the view that it was usually impossible for naval forces to overwhelm strong fortifications on land. One of Benson's pet projects, which did not find favor in Britain, the mine barrage in the North Sea, became feasible in 1918, when a workable marine mine was invented in the United States, but the war ended before the barrier had time to prove itself.[33]

The early differences between Sims and Benson, however apparent, were not so considerable as they have been painted by some authorities. The Navy Department wanted to respond quickly to the submarine menace, but not at the expense of what it deemed to be the nation's long-term naval interests, whereas Sims concentrated exclusively on the immediate task of defeating unrestricted submarine warfare, leaving the future to take care of itself. The Anglophile admiral discerned no long-range danger because he was convinced that British and American interests were complementary. Together, the two great maritime powers could ensure their security for the foreseeable future, especially after the destruction of the German High Seas Fleet.[34]

The differing outlooks of Sims and Benson brought to the fore the enduring possibility of disagreements between a theater commander with local concerns and a general staff saddled with problems of overall coordination. Sims was sent to London in search of information to guide American naval activity, and, when naval forces were sent across the Atlantic, he was given command of them. His principal function, however, according to Admiral Benson, was to act as "an assistant to the Chief of Naval Operations, with an office in London, simply coordinating and keeping a general supervision of the forces over there, seeing that the policies that the department decided on were properly executed, and as far as possible keeping in thorough touch with the whole situation in Europe and keeping the department informed in order that it might be able to formulate policies and give proper instructions." Benson had no doubt of the proper relationship between himself and Sims: "I feel that as Chief of Naval Operations I was responsible for the policies carried out in all parts of the world, in Europe as well as elsewhere, and I looked upon Admiral Sims simply as my representative to carry out those policies in European waters."[35]

Although Sims accepted Benson's view of his assignment in theory, in practice he sought considerable autonomy and constantly tried to head off orders from the Navy Department that were contrary to his desires.[36] By the end of the war, he had become thoroughly incensed at the course of action prescribed by the Navy Department. During the latter months of 1917 he grew particularly irritated at the department's refusal to assign certain officers to his staff and its reluctance to dispatch a section of battleships to serve with the British Grand Fleet in the North Sea. The department argued that it could not meet all of Sims's requests for personnel because of competing requirements, especially those of the fleet. Moreover, some experienced and competent naval officers had to be retained to train recruits. Benson resisted the departure of American battleships to European waters, in deference to Captain Mahan's injunction not to divide the battle fleet.[37]

Some of the tension between the London headquarters and the Navy Department dissipated after Admiral Benson visited Europe late in 1917 as a member of an American mission sent to improve inter-Allied coordination. Edward M. House, high in the confidence of the president, led this group. Sims had earlier claimed that visits by high-level American leaders to Europe would contribute measurably to the war effort, and in this belief he proved correct. After consultations with Sims and naval leaders in both Britain and France, Benson made a number of important decisions. He authorized the dispatch of four American battleships under Rear Admiral Hugh Rodman to reinforce the Grand Fleet. He expedited the development of mine barrages in the North Sea and the Straits of Dover. He arranged for Sims to serve as naval attaché in London. He helped establish in Sims's London headquarters a planning section that would work closely with the British Admiralty. And finally, he assisted in the creation of the Allied Naval Council, an organ set up to coordinate the naval operations of the Western coalition. These actions reflected growing American awareness that the Allied and Associated powers faced a great crisis in 1918; the outcome of the great war hung in the balance. Benson thought that the Entente powers were now prepared to accept "the sincerity and unselfishness of the United States; and feeling thus, they are not only willing for the United States to take the lead in matters which affect our common cause; but they are really anxious that we should dominate the entire allied situation." Benson had finally gone to war. "I believe that no time should be lost nor should any effort be spared to assist all the allies at the earliest possible date and to the utmost extent by any means which will help toward the prosecution of the war," he wrote in his report on his activities in Europe.[38]

Sims was pleased at the outcome of the CNO's visit to the war zone. "When Admiral Benson finally arrived in England," he noted later, "it took him only a few days to convince himself of the necessity of establishing a real advanced headquarters of the Navy Department abroad, with an adequate staff to make possible full cooperation with the Admiralty, to prepare plans for future operations, and adequately to cooperate with the Allies in coordinating all activities."[39]

But all was still not well between London and Washington. From Britain, Sims continued to decry decisions made in the United States that he thought impinged on his prerogatives as a theater commander. Writing to Captain Pratt in April 1918, through whom he communicated indirectly with Benson, he argued: "Of course you know this is something which should be resisted as much as possible. The responsibility for local dispositions, and for their success must necessarily be on this side; we would of course be blamed for any failure."[40] At the same time Benson retained his suspicions of the British, particularly concerning their presumed desire to dominate global commerce after the war, a reflection of Captain Mahan's view that trade rivalry was the prime cause of international disputes. To Secretary Daniels he wrote firmly in January 1918: "It should be clearly and constantly borne in mind that a fixed and continuous aim of British diplomacy and British negotiations is to further the interests of British commerce at the expense of the commerce of every other nation, whether friend or foe."[41] Clearly disposed to view Sims as unduly pro-British, Benson kept a wary eye out for signs of this propensity in the behavior of his deputy abroad.

Certain petty disputes between Sims and Daniels at this juncture of the war tended to poison relations between the Washington command post and the London outpost. In a truly unprecedented expression of Anglo-American solidarity, Great Britain proposed to make Sims an honorary member of the Board of Admiralty—and Benson also. The secretary of the navy refused to permit this honor, a piece of small-mindedness that humiliated Sims. The Navy Department was equally adamant in its opposition to the award of foreign decorations to American naval personnel, despite Sims's recommendations to the contrary.[42] Although Benson supported Sims in preventing Admiral Henry T. Mayo, the commander of the Atlantic Fleet, from taking his ships to Europe, a course that would have undermined Sims's authority, relations between the two leading naval officers were far from good as the war approached its end.[43]

During 1918 the Navy Department dedicated itself principally to the task of protecting troopships carrying American soldiers to France, whereas Sims remained preoccupied mostly with the protection of merchant ships carrying vital food and other supplies to Britain and France. Dean Allard has emphasized this important distinction between Sims's mission and that of the Navy Department. Rather than accept Sims's view that the U.S. Navy should concentrate on assistance to the Royal Navy, the department, "often reflecting the personal views of President Wilson . . . gave priority to establishing and supporting an independent American Army in France, an effort that was entirely separate from the defense of the mercantile convoys serving Great Britain." Allard shows that the Navy Department assigned about 450 ships to escort and transport American troops, whereas only about 350 ships and 15 per cent of the navy's personnel worked on other tasks in European waters.[44]

Admiral Sims was justly proud of the organization he built up in London during the war, but Admiral Benson might have made just as much of the remarkable improvements within the Navy Department. The CNO assumed that what was needed was not to reform the bureau system but to facilitate cooperation between the bureaus. His Office of Naval Operations, according to his coadjutor Captain Pratt, set out to break down barriers to internal cooperation. By 1 August 1918, when the war was nearly over, a relatively mature administrative arrangement had been completed. To accomplish one of the CNO's two prime responsibilities—the making of war plans—the Office of the Chief of Naval Operations included a Plans Division. To carry on the other main responsibility—guidance of fleet operations—the CNO or his assistant supervised an entity known as the Division of Operating Forces. Other administrative elements included the Intelligence Division, the Material Division, the Naval Districts Division, the Communication Division, the Gunnery Exercises and Engineering Performances Division, and the Files and Records Division.[45]

How did the Office of the Chief of Naval Operations conduct its work? In a directive on the subject, Benson explained the process:

> Certain conditions are known to exist, let us suppose, through information obtained from force commanders and detailed information obtained through Naval Intelligence. The information, with the objects to be obtained, is sent to the Planning Division. The Planning Division makes a study of the subject and calls a meeting of a certain plans committee. This committee deliberates on the information at hand and on the mission. It then prepares definite recommendations of what it proposes in order to insure the success of the mission. The matter is then taken up with the Chief of Naval Operations, and if approved by him (or the Secretary if required) is referred to [appropriate divisions.] These divisions proceed with the preparation of the material and personnel which may be necessary to make the approved plan effective.

When this procedure had been completed, the Division of Operating Forces issued the necessary orders, and the plan was put into effect at the direction of the CNO or his assistant. Here was a well-conceived system at work, a far cry from the haphazard methods of the prewar years. Perhaps the most distinctive innovation was the emphasis on planning. As an aspect of this trend, the Joint Army and Navy Board was revived in 1919, and it played an important role during the interwar years.[46]

Much to the chagrin of officers assigned to the Navy Department, Secretary Daniels did not change his ways, persisting in his concentration on what naval officers deemed small matters at the expense of critical ones, a habit that often subverted the process of making decisions. After the war, Captain Harris Laning testified that Daniels usually gave but a few minutes to important questions and then asked for a report—which usually disappeared later on. "We always considered it much easier to get up a sound plan or policy," Laning reported, "than it was to get permission or authority to carry it out." It took longer to process a request for action than to formulate it. "This condition finally became so bad," he concluded, "that officers used every means to put their plans and policies through without obtaining the required authority."[47] Given this circumstance, it was fortunate that Benson had as an assistant the indefatigable and competent Captain Pratt, who did much to expedite decision-making during the war.[48]

When, in October 1918, it became apparent that victory was near, Admiral Benson once again accompanied Colonel House to Europe, taking part in the pre-armistice negotiations in Paris. Intensive discussions with the leaders of the victorious coalition late in October and early in November turned on two great issues. President Wilson's Fourteen Points, drawn up 8 January 1918, included a commitment to freedom of the seas, and Benson did his best to force recognition of this traditional American fixation. The other naval issue that arose was the disposition of the German fleet. During the pre-armistice negotiations the British were unwilling to endorse freedom of the seas, and the Americans succeeded in getting a decision about the German ships postponed until the forthcoming peace conference. In the meantime, the German High Seas Fleet languished in internment at Scapa Flow.[49]

Admiral Benson spent much of his last year as CNO in Europe, helping to negotiate the naval aspects of the armistice and later advising the president on the naval terms of the treaty of peace with Germany. After the war ended, the Navy Department expended much of its energy on demobilization, but the General Board, the London planning section, and senior officials concentrated on the future shape of the navy. Benson's activities in connection with the postwar settlement reflected his conviction that the utter defeat of Germany had reestablished Great Britain as a potential future enemy. He made up his mind to oppose political agreements that might confer undue advantages upon the Royal Navy.

Even before the armistice went into effect, naval cooperation between the United States and Great Britain began to give way to competition. Reinforcing this tendency were suspicions rife in each nation that the other sought naval and commercial predominance during the postwar era. Sir Eric Geddes, first lord of the Admiralty, became convinced that the Americans had planned their shipbuilding program to give their merchant marine an advantage over that of Britain. Nothing alarmed the British Admiralty more than indications that the United States might complete the suspended three-year building program undertaken in 1916, a step that by itself would make the American fleet the most powerful in the world. And what if the United States should also embark on another comparable program as a supplement beginning in 1919? Benson became more and more vehement in denouncing British commercial aspirations. Stephen Roskill summarizes the American concern, which reflected a resurgence of the views that Benson had expressed before the American intervention of 1917. "It was obvious to the American naval planners that if the war-time alliance between Britain, France and Italy were continued, and if the Anglo-Japanese alliance of 1919 was extended when it fell due for renewal in 1921, the United States might be faced by an overwhelming preponderance at sea."[50]

As the war came to an end, American naval planners viewed the first postwar building program with an eye to considerations such as Roskill notes, most especially a possible combination of the British and Japanese fleets. At length Secretary Daniels recommended a three-year program that called for 10 battleships, 6 battle cruisers, 10 scout cruisers, and 130 other craft—all this in addition to the three-year program authorized in 1916. It is of great importance, however, that President Wilson viewed this proposal primarily as a club to be used during negotiations in Paris and dropped after concessions had been extracted from the British. He recognized that the proposed league of nations would have to have some means of enforcing its desires on recalcitrant nations, and the most logical force to place at its disposal would be an international navy. He was willing to settle for American participation in a league navy equal to that of Great Britain. Benson voiced the Navy Department's rationale for such a navy: "In order to stabilize the League of Nations, it is vitally necessary that no one power included in it should dominate in military or naval strength. There should be at least two powers of equal Naval strength." Obviously the two countries were Britain and America. In advocating such a policy, however, Benson placed the two nations on a collision course. The leaders of Britain were not reconciled to the idea of an American navy equal to the Royal Navy.[51]

Discussion of naval questions at Paris began with a contretemps. When Secretary Daniels arrived at the peace conference, Admiral Sir Wester Wemyss, the first sea lord, called upon him and questioned the need for the large American building program then before Congress. Benson, who was present, thereupon became quite angry. He later claimed to have said to Wemyss: "By what authority do you presume to come over here and ask such a question of our Secretary?" Daniels recorded the incident in his diary: "Benson talked very straight to Wemyss who wanted us to agree to a larger Navy for G.B. than America should build." Many years later, in 1937, he recalled that the two men nearly came to blows. In a meeting shortly thereafter between Daniels, Benson, Wemyss, and Walter Long, the new first lord of the Admiralty, the secretary of the navy made it plain that the United States would not attempt to outbuild the British if the "League was firmly established and all nations agreed to reduction of armament," a statement that implied Anglo-American parity at sea. Daniels thus played the American trump card. Long answered that the British prime minister, David Lloyd George, "could not support League of Nations if U. S. accompanied it by big building programs, for GB could not consent to any other nation having the supremacy of the sea." Benson later explained his reply to Long and his reasons for desiring naval parity. "Being in that position, we would be able to meet Germany possibly allied with Japan or some other nation, and . . . we felt strongly the danger to be apprehended from such a situation." Long later summarized his reaction to the chief of naval operations: "Admiral Benson is a man for whose honesty and straightforwardness I have the greatest respect, but he is a man of mulish character and not very quick at grasping any ideas other than his own."[52]

An impasse appeared unavoidable, but cool heads ultimately took over in the persons of Sir Robert Cecil and Edward M. House, who managed to work out a settlement. Recognizing that no definitive naval agreement could be reached in Paris, the two conciliators agreed upon a modus vivendi. On 10 April they decided that Britain would support the League of Nations, and in particular a clause in that organization's covenant that established the Monroe Doctrine in international law, while the Americans would postpone the construction scheduled for 1919 and after.[53] Seth P. Tillman justly considers that the "naval battle of Paris" stemmed from "false premises on both sides." The British had no basis for their fear that naval parity with the United States, or even U.S. superiority, would endanger the security of the British Empire. The Americans should have realized that British supremacy at sea did not pose a threat to their national security.[54] In any event the outcome that Benson sought in 1919 was delayed until the great naval conference met in Washington during 1921.

What came of the other naval issues that surfaced at the Paris peace conference, especially freedom of the seas and the disposition of the German fleet? President Wilson later explained why the question of freedom of the seas lapsed into unimportance during the course of the negotiations. The principle was intended to preserve the right of neutrals to use the high seas in time of war, but, he continued, "under the League of Nations there are no neutrals, and, therefore, what I have called the practical joke on myself was that by the very thing I was advocating it became unnecessary to define freedom of the seas." The lesson was obvious: "All . . . nations being comrades and partners in a common cause, we all have an equal right to use the seas."[55] As to the German fleet, its fate was not resolved by diplomacy. Both the British and the Americans wanted to destroy the German ships, but the French and the Italians, who coveted some of them, refused to accept this solution. The question became academic when, on 21 June 1919, German Vice Admiral Ludwig von Reuter's order that the ships interned at Scapa Flow be scuttled was successfully carried out.[56]

Admiral Benson returned to the United States convinced that Great Britain had no intention of accepting a reasonable naval settlement. "The outstanding fact throughout these negotiations," he insisted in 1921, was "the determination of Great Britain to maintain a position of dominance in world affairs, and a determination to so manipulate the interests of the minor powers as to secure the sympathy of sufficient nations to out-vote and block the United States in any efforts which might in any way interfere with British domination."[57] As he approached the end of his service as chief of naval operations, he must have felt considerable bitterness over the outcome in Paris.

During the Paris negotiations Japan greatly improved its strategic position in the mid-Pacific, especially by the acquisition of the Marshall, Caroline, and Gilbert islands from Germany. To counter the Imperial Japanese Navy, Benson devised a plan to deploy separate, self-contained battle fleets in both the Atlantic and Pacific oceans. Each fleet included sixteen battleships, but the Pacific Fleet was much stronger, mounting ninety-four 14-inch guns to twelve of that caliber for the Atlantic Fleet. At long last the U. S. Navy departed from the Mahanian dogma that the battle fleet should never be divided.[58]

The position of the chief of naval operations came into existence during a period of remarkable change in the U. S. Navy. By 1919 the United States had achieved virtual parity with Great Britain. The defeat of Germany and the wartime association with the British combined with the rise of Japan as a Pacific power to alter the list of possible naval antagonists. Technological innovations of great importance—especially the introduction of submarines and aircraft—forced notable changes in strategy, tactics, and logistics. Long before the armistice, the political import of naval planning and operations became very much present to the senses, especially as an aspect of a type of conflict with which Americans were not familiar—general warfare by contending coalitions. To deal with these unprecedented circumstances the navy had to be reorganized, and no part of this process proved more important than the appointment of a chief of naval operations. This new position allowed sufficient scope to naval professionalism to play its part without endangering the vital principle of civilian control.

Admiral Benson has received less credit than is his due in the naval history of the First World War. He has suffered from the fact that historians have given most of their attention to other personalities, notably Admiral Sims and Secretary Daniels, both of whom wrote influential memoirs. Benson kept silent, but part of the record has recently been corrected by scholars and more of it will be.[59] Sometimes Benson put himself on the wrong side of policy issues, particularly in the cases of wartime fleet disposition and naval construction, but he managed the early development of his office very well, and by the end of his tour he had presided over a remarkable improvement in the administration of the Navy Department. He did so in times made difficult not only by the great European war but by the cast of civilian characters with which he had to deal—particularly President Wilson and Secretary Daniels. It is of interest that he appears to have gotten along with Colonel House better than did most others in Wilson's administration. Many historians treat Benson merely as a rabid Anglophobe, an unjust characterization. His policies and activities can be treated properly only by those who recognize that the admiral reflected a well-established brand of American nationalism and that he had recourse to it in a time of truly unprecedented challenges. Surely it is reasonable to insist that Benson belongs on the list of those officers who have made truly important contributions to the development of the office of chief of naval operations.

After retirement on 25 September 1919 at the statutory age of sixty-four, Benson remained active for another decade, serving three presidents. Wilson immediately made him chairman of the U. S. Shipping Board, and Harding and Coolidge retained him as a commissioner on the board from 1921 to 1928.[60] This position afforded him many an opportunity to encourage the growth of the American merchant marine, a cause for which he had fought doughtily during his tour as chief of naval operations. On 20 May 1932, the first CNO and the man who had led the U. S. Navy in the First World War died in Washington, D.C.

ROBERT EDWARD COONTZ

1 November 1919–21 July 1923

LAWRENCE H. DOUGLAS

In 1928, as his two-star flag slipped down the flagstaff at the Naval Operating Base in Norfolk, Virginia, Rear Admiral Robert E. Coontz looked out on the waters of the Chesapeake and thought of the moment, almost fifty years earlier, when, from virtually the same spot, he had seen the sea for the first time. As an eager midshipman he had hurried to the *Constellation* and climbed to her main topgallant yard so that he might see the ocean as soon as possible.

A descendent of early settlers from Pennsylvania and Maryland's Eastern Shore, Robert was born in Hannibal, Missouri, on 11 June 1864 to Benton and Mary Brewington Coontz, who were classmates and neighbors of Samuel Clemens. One might surmise that whatever impact that great humorist had upon his parents was not lost upon young Coontz, who was known throughout his life for his sharp wit and sense of humor.

Robert studied at Ingleside and Hannibal colleges and worked briefly until, at the age of seventeen, he received an appointment to the Naval Academy, which he entered in 1881. During his years as a naval cadet, he displayed characteristics with which he was to be identified throughout his life. His interest in politics, his mature behavior, and his tact probably accounted for his nickname, "Senator." During his second year at the academy, he appeared before the Naval Committee of the House of Representatives to present the cadets' view of officer-promotion policies, which dictated that only a handful of graduates—the top 25 percent—would receive a commission at the end of six years in the service.[1] Later, he and other cadets petitioned Congress for an exemption from the Act of 1882, which had established a system that they felt was detrimental to both the service and their individual careers. In 1887 he was elected—only two years after his graduation—as secretary of the Ensigns' Committee and "took a leading part in the work . . . of all committees of the line officers."[2] His concern for the welfare of officers and enlisted men was succinctly expressed when, as chief of naval operations, he said, "Men fight, not ships."[3]

Following his graduation from the Naval Academy in 1885, Coontz was given the rank of passed midshipman and received pre-commissioning training in the steam sloops *Mohican* and *Juniata*, the screw steamer *Galena*, and the protected cruiser *Atlanta*. For a brief period before he was commissioned as an ensign in 1887, he assisted in the development of the first modern code used by the Navy Department.[4] He then selected an assignment in Alaskan waters in the gunboat *Pinta*, whose primary mission was policing commercial fishermen and Indians to ensure their compliance with sealing and fishing regulations. During his six years in the *Pinta*, Coontz became adept at coast-survey work and earned a license as a qualified pilot. While he was in Alaska, he married Augusta Cohen, of Sitka, in October 1890. Of their three children, a son and a daughter survived to adulthood.

Following a brief tour of duty at the Naval Observatory in Washington, D.C., in 1891 Coontz reported aboard the Great Lakes side-wheel steamer *Michigan* which was home-ported at Erie, Pennsylvania. An early fascination with man's attempt to fly moved Coontz to construct a pair of wings for his arms and, on several occasions, while the *Michigan* was surveying the Detroit River, he attempted to take to the air from a small island across from Amherstburg, Ontario, Canada. Needless to note, the local inhabitants thought he was a bit crazy.[5]

In November 1894, Coontz was ordered to Washington for duty with the Bureau of Navigation to correct the department's long-neglected officer records and update the error-ridden naval registers. During this tour he continued to lobby for changes in the navy's personnel policies. His efforts and those of many other officers culminated in the passage of the Personnel Act of 3 March 1899, which rectified many of the inequities that had caused widespread discontent among junior officers. Upon promotion to lieutenant, junior grade, in 1896 he was assigned to the flagship of the Pacific Station, the cruiser *Philadelphia*. Following that duty and a period with the Coast and Geodetic Survey, he reported to the protected cruiser *Charleston* in 1898.

In the 1890s Alfred Thayer Mahan's theories about sea power and maritime states won many advocates among the junior officers of the American navy, and Coontz was one of them.[6] He completely supported the war against Spain and, while assigned to the *Charleston*, participated in the seizure of Guam, saw action during the final bombardment of Manila, and fought in several operations during the Philippine Insurrection.

The territorial cupidity of Germany and the United States regarding Samoa eventually led to the partition of the islands by treaty in 1899, as well as to anti-German sentiment in America which indirectly affected Coontz. The excitement and uncertainty generated by the Samoan confrontation moved the navy to prepare a list of officers whose names were of German extraction. Coontz, of course, was on the list. His indignation at this action is described in his autobiography. A similar reaction to other Americans with German names took place during the First World War and, according to Coontz family lore, this emotionalism plus the admiral's apparent friendship with the kaiser may explain the fact that he was not given command of a combatant vessel during the conflict. Not surprisingly, no evidence has been found to substantiate this belief.[7]

Coontz, promoted to lieutenant, returned from the Philippines in the protected cruiser *Boston* and then served as executive officer of the Massachusetts Maritime School ship *Enterprise*. Assigned to the *Philadelphia* during the disturbances in Panama in 1902, he returned to the Pacific coast of the United States for duty in the screw gunboat *Adams* and, subsequently, the gunboat *Wheeling* and the auxiliary cruiser *Buffalo* from 1902 to 1904. Promoted to lieutenant commander the next year, Coontz completed a tour of inspection duty in the Seattle area with the Bureau of Equipment and then became executive officer of the new battleship *Nebraska*, which participated in the world cruise of the "Great White Fleet" in 1908 and 1909. As a result of this experience, he became an ardent proponent of "showing the flag" and demonstration cruises by the fleet.[8]

Promoted to commander in 1909, Coontz was next assigned to the Naval Academy, where he was commandant of midshipmen until 1911. His even temperament, insight, and understanding were clearly evident in his dealings with the midshipmen. During his last year at the academy, he commanded a midshipmen's summer practice cruise that went to Germany, and it was during this visit in July 1911 to Kiel that he became acquainted with Kaiser Wilhelm II. Coontz was impressed by the German ruler and they exchanged some formal correspondence for a few years.[9]

Following an assignment with the Board of Inspection and Survey of Ships, Coontz was appointed governor of Guam in April 1912 and, two months later, received his captain's stripes. As governor, he favored strengthening the administration and exacting discipline to correct what in his view was the poor management and limited imagination of previous governors. In his first address, he warned the native leaders that he planned to be a "hanging governor."[10] In spite of this rather grim and militant beginning, Coontz's administration was both just and beneficial and he made good use of his fine talents as a manager. His term as governor was characterized by local commentators as being efficient and enlightened, and he was described as one of the best executives in the navy. When Coontz departed for the mainland, one local chief noted that the captain "always had the interests of Guam at heart" and was "one of the best governors Guam has ever had."[11]

Coontz then assumed command of the battleship *Georgia*, which was in Mexican waters during the disturbances in Veracruz and Haiti in 1914. Under his command the *Georgia* moved from last to first place in the annual fleet gunnery competitions. On completion of this tour of sea duty, Captain Coontz anticipated assignment to the Naval War College; instead, he was ordered to the West Coast as commandant of the Puget Sound Navy Yard and the Thirteenth Naval District. Although he regretted not being able to attend the War

College, he relished returning to the Northwest and took up his new responsibilities with his customary enthusiasm.[12]

It was his performance in this assignment throughout the First World War that earned him promotion to rear admiral and placed him in contention for the navy's top billet. His modus operandi at the Puget Sound yard is evidence of his abilities both as an administrator and a leader. Upon assuming command in July 1915, he "found conditions somewhat unsatisfactory." There was "general dissatisfaction and apathy" among his staff, and the small, limited plant usually repaired only one ship at a time. Furthermore, the townspeople protested his appointment because they preferred an officer of flag rank. Coontz set about winning the confidence of the town by sharing his plans for the yard with the city fathers and involving leading citizens in overall strategy sessions. His ease in dealing with politicians worked to the benefit of his command and of the navy in general, for he soon had the state's entire congressional delegation giving him valuable assistance in Washington in getting the facilities of the yard expanded.

Before and during American belligerency in the First World War, activity at the yard increased considerably. The Puget Sound yard was charged with the construction and repair of merchant vessels and submarine chasers, the repair of American and British warships, and the reconditioning of seized German freighters. Coontz was also responsible for processing, equipping, and assigning the hundreds of naval volunteers and reserves who reported for duty, and for manning all ships built in Seattle and Portland shipyards. His yard even entered the munitions-manufacturing business for the government by making shells at half the contract rate charged by civilian firms. All these tasks were accomplished with efficiency and economy, two hallmarks of Coontz's administrative style.

His tour at the yard was punctuated by problems with radicals, and his handling of these affairs brought the attention and approval of his superiors in Washington. Industrial disruption from labor agitation was common in wartime America and the Bremerton yard was hardly immune to it. The governor of Washington State accepted a proposal that he name an advisory Committee of Safety on labor issues, and the radical Industrial Workers of the World, known popularly as the "Wobblies," were determined to gain control of the panel. Alarmed at this prospect and by their campaign, which he believed would undermine war work at his yard and elsewhere, Coontz organized a number of prominent local businessmen to oppose the Wobblies. At a crucial juncture in the statewide deliberations, he and his colleagues made a dramatic midnight trip to the state capital, Olympia, woke the governor, successfully pleaded their case, and won control of the important committee.

Coontz bolstered his reputation as a defender of the status quo in a second series of incidents. It was widely believed that agents from Bolshevik Russia were agitating in America, and, on one occasion, one of Coontz's aides captured a man suspected of stirring up worker discontent at the yard. During this same era of the "Red Scare," Coontz seized a number of Russian ships that had been taken over by Soviet committees of sailors and were sailing off the coast. He justified the seizures on the grounds of international law, and the practical effect of his actions was to enhance his reputation as a trustworthy, antiradical officer. Coontz completed his assignment in Bremerton as a rear admiral, and with the apologies of those who had first opposed his appointment.[13]

In late 1918 Secretary of the Navy Josephus Daniels offered him command of Battleship Division 7, which was considered the best in the fleet.[14] However, since Admiral William S. Benson, the first chief of naval operations, and his assistant, Captain William V. Pratt, were needed in London at the end of the year and Coontz was in Washington briefly, Daniels decided that he should serve as acting CNO during the absence of the other officers. In this capacity, Coontz worked with the General Board to prepare a demobilization plan for the navy, which was based on the assumption that a League of Nations navy would be created and, as Coontz later pointed out, would be "sufficient to control the nations of the world."[15] Relieved by Pratt on 1 January 1919, he finally took command of the battleship division, which was deployed with the Atlantic Fleet.

The *Arizona* served as his flagship for the first six months of 1919, but in July Coontz shifted his flag to the *Wyoming* to escort the dramatic transatlantic flight of the N-C flying boats. In September, he went to the *Nevada* as second in command of the Pacific Fleet under Admiral Hugh Rodman. Later that month, Daniels, who was inspecting naval facilities on the West Coast, offered Coontz the billet of CNO.

The personal qualities that favored Coontz's selection for the navy's most prestigious post were evident: his talent for administration, his record of efficiency and accomplishment, and his skill in human relations; other attributes included thoroughness, attention to detail, and a remarkable memory. Rear Admiral E. B. Rogers, supporting Coontz's selection, wrote to Senator Truman H. Newberry that Coontz

> has the very qualities needed in Washington: infinite tact, sound judgment, quiet decision, pleasant personality and a remarkable facility for getting things accomplished rightly.[16]

Although talented and enterprising, Coontz had not been as visible as, for example, the wartime commander, Admiral William S. Sims, who in 1919 became president of the Naval War College. However, because of his easy personal relationships and relatively low profile, he—unlike Sims—had no enemies who might have adversely affected his chances for selection.[17]

Coontz became CNO on 1 November 1919 and immediately faced one of the navy's most pressing issues: the ambiguous authority of his own office. He was sufficiently shrewd to recognize that this was a delicate matter and that Secretary Daniels was intent on retaining in his own office all the symbolism of "civilian control" of the military. The central controversy in 1919, and thereafter, involved the degree of authority the CNO could exert to coordinate and dictate the work of the various bureaus. Coontz had no inherent antipathy for the bureau system nor any desire to concentrate all control in his office. However, in the bureaus he had to deal with a "strongly entrenched" staff corps and the powerful bureau chiefs, whose opposition could frustrate the execution of his policies.[18]

To restrain rivalries, Coontz moved carefully. First, he assumed responsibility for delineating precisely the duties of each bureau.[19] Second, he formalized a Bureau Chiefs Council, at which he presided and which he hoped would lend direction and coherence to the activities of the bureaus.[20] He was careful not to approve projects that duplicated work already under way and he often deferred the implementation of programs until agreement on their administration had been reached. The weekly meetings of the CNO and the bureau chiefs were real "clearing houses" and, wrote Coontz:

> When the bureau chiefs sat around a table and threshed out questions, face to face, they got much better action than by running to the Secretary individually, with matters in their respective divisions. There is scarce a financial question arising in any bureau that is not, to some extent, dependent upon one or more of the bureaus.[21]

Secretary Daniels, however, preferred to deal directly with each bureau chief. As Lieutenant Harry W. Hill, a close friend of Coontz and one of his staff officers, wrote: "These two conflicting views dominated much of the first two years of his administration, but gradually, through his persuasive presentation of the many angles of the problem, his views prevailed."[22] The key, of course, was control of finances and, at his insistence, Coontz was appointed budget officer of the navy in 1921. The CNO's appointment of an assistant to fill this billet thereafter placed the financial control of the department more directly in his hands.

Coontz's efforts to reorganize the operations and functions of his office and increase his control over the bureaus culminated in the Revised Orders of Organization for the Office of the Chief of Naval Operations, which were approved in the summer of 1923. These orders incorporated parts of the 1915 and 1916 orders and included many of Coontz's ideas about the authority and responsibility of his office.

Another pressing problem that Coontz faced when he took office was postwar demobilization. Animated by public concerns for economy in government, cutbacks for the navy were implemented rapidly, so rapidly, in fact, that, in Coontz's opinion, little attention was paid to remaining national commitments that the navy would have to uphold. These complex matters were further tangled by the foremost fact that reductions in personnel made it extremely difficult adequately to man the ships of the fleet. Coontz's policy was to eliminate a number of shore facilities in order to maintain units afloat. Much of his time in 1920 was spent making inspection trips around the country in order to decide "what station complements could be reduced, which stations could be closed down, and possibly sold, and what property could be transferred, and disposed of."[23]

Inevitably, and despite his ability to persuade and manipulate men, Coontz's relations with Congress rapidly deteriorated. Every reduction at a shore station and every closing of a naval facility earned him the enmity of another senator or congressman whose constituency suffered from the policy. Indeed, several attempts were made to persuade the secretary of the navy to remove the admiral from his post. They all failed but, after a particularly vigorous attack on Coontz in the Senate, the assistant secretary of the navy, Theodore Roosevelt, Jr., wrote to Secretary of the Navy Edwin Denby:

> The trouble lies in a personal dislike for Coontz among many of the Congressmen. This is thoroughly unreasoned and based almost entirely on ingrained lack of respect, if not dislike, of ninety percent of the Congressmen towards anyone who wears a uniform.[24]

Coupled with demobilization were budget difficulties generated by what was to be a long-term reluctance on the part of Congress to provide the appropriations that naval leaders considered necessary to maintain the fleet, build replacement ships, and provide the required number of officers and enlisted men. By the end of 1920 no funds had been approved for new construction and barely enough for work to proceed at a reduced pace on the 1916 battleship building program. With a Republican president elected by a large majority in 1920 and Republican control of Congress, and because that party was committed to fiscal economies, opposition to naval expansion gained momentum.

Coontz was, of course, in the middle of the budget and appropriation controversies and he often appeared before the naval and appropriations committees of both houses to explain and defend expenditures, budget requests, construction plans, personnel policies, and his demobilization policies. In April 1921 he wrote an article for the *American Legion Weekly* in which he explained some aspects of his political philosophy. After analyzing the relationships between the military and the legislature, he observed that the military was but an instrument of, and must conform to, national policy. Continuing reductions in appropriations for the army and the navy, he surmised, resulted from differences of opinion as to the probability that force would have to be used to achieve the objectives of the nation's foreign policy. He concluded that the variance existed because the military were not adequately informed about foreign policy, and had, therefore, to interpret it as best they could. Coontz suggested that this gap could be filled if the State Department were represented on the Joint Army and Navy Board and cautioned against allowing economy to prevent the making of reasonable preparations for war, a policy that could result in national ruin.[25]

Although there was profound disappointment that the First World War had not immediately produced a world "safe for democracy," the ideas of achieving security through international agreements and economy through imposed limitations were actively pursued. In 1921, President Warren G. Harding invited delegates from Britain, France, Japan, and Italy to meet in Washington at the end of the year to address the problem of naval disarmament and the balance of power in the Far East.

Before the conference, Coontz and Assistant Secretary of the Navy Theodore Roosevelt, Jr., worked with the General Board to fashion an arms-limitation proposal that Harding and Secretary of State Charles Evans Hughes would accept. Most members of the General Board distrusted the whole idea of arms limitations and offered a plan for small reductions which was promptly rejected. Instead, Hughes introduced the concept of "stop building now," and instructed Coontz, Captain William V. Pratt of the General Board, and Roosevelt to translate the concept into proportional sea forces.[26] From these efforts the three men came up with the famous 5:5:3 ratio, by which American, British, and Japanese naval strength was to be measured and then restrained. Coontz described this proposal as the "last stand of the Navy."[27]

When the conference got under way in Washington in December 1921, bargaining and the political sense of the civilian delegates "took charge" and American naval leaders, including Coontz, were excluded from the key negotiations. The conferees had as their objective the limitation of all classes of warships, but they were soon restricted to dealing only with capital ships because the other issues were too complex. Although the essentials of the American proposal, which Coontz had worked diligently to frame, were finally accepted, his situation was quite awkward. As Roosevelt noted:

> Admiral Coontz, of course, is in a very difficult position for he has got to divorce himself from the traditions of a lifetime in relation to a strong navy, and place himself where he will unquestionably meet with active antipathy from a large number of commissioned personnel.[28]

Coontz regretted his role in the conference and the limitation agreements. In his autobiography he claimed that the American people were deceived as to what it all meant. He agreed with Frank Simons, of the *Washington Sunday Star*, who wrote, "Hughes had to choose between facing the political consequences of failure or agreeing to . . . a bad bargain." Roosevelt was also disappointed at the results but understood that Hughes "acquiesced in the hope that it would all turn out right in the end" and that it would "lead to better things."[29] Of one thing Coontz was sure: in the future, professional naval men should not be excluded from the negotiating table. Of this country's failure to maintain the ratio throughout all classes of vessels and the insertion of the non-fortification provision, Coontz observed that, as rich and powerful as this nation was, she was always too "niggardly and too slow acting upon matters pertaining to the Navy." Americans, he wrote, "play safe" and are unduly influenced by the "sicky sentimentality" of those who believe the nation should not be prepared at all.[30]

The "better things" that Hughes hoped would come from the conference did not appear immediately. In fact, the Washington experience seemed to restrict further appropriations for both material and personnel. In early 1922, Coontz requested authorization for 120,000 officers and men because shorter enlistments were causing more turnovers and a shortage of manpower. The House Naval Affairs Committee wanted to allow the navy only 67,000 men which would have practically nullified the 5:5:3 ratio. In the political maneuvering that surrounded the fight to retain an effective number of enlisted men, Coontz made bitter enemies of the chairman of the House Appropriations Committee, Congressman Martin B. Madden, and the head of the Naval Subcommittee, Congressman Patrick H. Kelly. A compromise figure was eventually reached, and the navy was allowed 86,000 men. It was effected primarily by Coontz's resourcefulness in obtaining a copy of the House committee's negative report and then writing and distributing to other congressmen and to the press minority views that upset the majority's plan to present a prejudiced report of the navy's manning needs. This fight to "save the Navy" was won when the Senate and later the House passed the Vare Amendment, which authorized the 86,000 figure. Coontz identified this victory as one of his major accomplishments during his tenure as CNO.[31]

Although a battleship sailor and considered by some not to be very "far-seeing" in relation to the development of naval aviation, Admiral Coontz supported attempts to create an effective air arm for the navy. One of the continuing threats that he and other supporters of naval air power had to address grew out of efforts to reduce spending by organizing a single air force or a unified air service. This concept was strongly supported by Brigadier General William "Billy"Mitchell of the army air corps but opposed by the CNO.[32] As early as March 1920 Coontz and his bureau chiefs began urging Secretary Daniels to formulate legislation regarding a separate naval air arm. The impetus to move with dispatch was provided in November of that year when level aerial bombing in a demonstration against the old battleship *Indiana* seemed to suggest that air power was effective against capital ships. In the summer of 1920 the Senate came close to giving the army air service control of all aircraft operations from land bases. The first draft of legislation that was eventually passed by the Congress was reviewed by a four-member group which Coontz appointed in March 1921; when three of the four members opposed the creation of a Bureau of Aeronautics for the navy, Coontz disbanded that group and convened a board composed of himself and two other flag officers. This new panel favored the new bureau and its report was instrumental in getting this position adopted by the secretary of the navy.[33]

In April 1921 Coontz appeared before the House Committee on Naval Affairs and testified that he was "strongly in support of . . . . having a Bureau of Aviation in the Navy Department. . . . Neither I nor any human can properly handle it as it stands now. . . ." In his concluding remarks, he noted:

> This is one case where the Chief of Naval Operations is willing to give up something. He is glad to have someone take the burden off him; he is not reaching for any other fields to conquer, but he wants to give this thing up where it will be efficiently and economically administered.[34]

That same month a special session of Congress passed an act establishing a Bureau of Aeronautics and the bureau became a reality in July. Coontz strongly and successfully pressed for the appointment of Rear Admiral William A. Moffett as its first chief.

According to his autobiography, Coontz "felt that aviation had grown to be too important for the small amount of consideration which it was receiving in the department, and that a strong and experienced man was needed to develop it to its proper sphere in the Navy."[35] He was opposed, however, to those who wanted to do away with the battleship in favor of aircraft. The bombing trials on naval vessels that were conducted in the early 1920s gave rise to a great deal of speculation regarding the usefulness of the battleship. Coontz observed that such experiments were "absolutely inconclusive" because true battle conditions were not simulated. There was no defensive maneuvering, antiaircraft fire, or damage control. It was not possible, claimed Coontz, "to get anything out of such one-sided affairs."[36] By contrast, the admiral was pleased that the conversion of the collier *Jupiter* was authorized and completed during his term as CNO: when she was commissioned the *Langley* in March 1922, she became America's first aircraft carrier. Coontz also sponsored the conversion of two uncompleted battle cruisers to carriers, and they became the *Lexington* and the *Saratoga*.

The major scandal of the 1920s, the "Teapot Dome" affair, rocked the Harding administration while Coontz was chief of naval operations. Secretary of the Navy Denby transferred the leases on naval oil reserves to the Interior Department under Secretary Albert B. Fall, who then made them available to private companies. Instead of insisting on Navy Department approval for any transfer of the leases, Denby told Fall that all the Navy Department would require was a signed copy of any lease the Interior Department saw fit to make, thus nullifying an important safeguard on these vital oil reserves.[37]

It was late April or early May of 1921 when Coontz first heard of the leases being transferred to the Interior Department. He and Assistant Secretary of the Navy Roosevelt objected strenuously, but Secretary Denby told them that the transfers had already been concluded, that the subject "was not open to discussion," and "the rights of the Navy would be conserved." Both Roosevelt and Coontz assumed that the transfers were the result of a decision reached at a cabinet meeting or of a specific presidential order, but subsequent disclosures, of course, proved this assumption unwarranted. In October Denby transferred all matters relating to fuels from Coontz's office to the Bureau of Engineering, and after 1 November, Coontz "abandoned all hope of the Navy controlling the oil situation."[38] Later, when the transactions were investigated, Coontz was called before a grand jury to testify. He supported Denby's claim of innocence and observed that the secretary's "integrity was so pronounced that he never suspected any one in high authority of being venal."[39]

In December 1922 Coontz completed one of the major tasks of his term as CNO; he considered it a major restructuring of American sea power. Following almost three years of planning and controversy, he established a combined U.S. Fleet. In fact, Admiral Benson had done this, on paper, in January 1919 simply by changing the designation of the Atlantic Fleet, but Secretary Daniels reverted to two fleets within six months. Coontz was concerned about the different practices of the two fleets in such matters as the interpretation of standing orders and the use of signals. Indeed, he believed that some officers in the two fleets considered themselves to be members of two distinct naval organizations.[40] Coontz abolished the Atlantic and Pacific fleets and reorganized the sea forces into four major commands: the Battle Fleet, the Scouting Fleet, the Control Force, and the Fleet Base Force. He also created type commands and a controversy about this form of organization that lasted into the 1930s. He argued that, with the defeat of Germany, the major naval threat to American interests was from Japan. By consolidating American naval forces in the Eastern Pacific, Admiral Coontz furthered the intense and suspicious scrutiny of Japanese sea power that was to characterize U.S. naval strategy between the world wars.

Throughout his tour as CNO Coontz was concerned about making improvements at the Naval War College. It would have been difficult for him to forget that institution for he was continually reminded of problems and plans by its president, Rear Admiral William S. Sims. The major difficulties centered on staffing and curriculum. One of Sims's complaints was that the college did not receive necessary staffing, but in the early 1920s Coontz was hard pressed to fill the seagoing billets in the fleet, let alone increase the size of the staff and the length of the courses at the war college. He pointed out to Sims in December 1921 that all temporary and reserve officers were going off the active list and that he would then be faced with a shortage of some 2,300 line officers.[41] Before Coontz left Washington, however, he was able to satisfy Sims by expanding the staff of the college, assigning more students to the school, and arranging for longer courses.

By the summer of 1923, Coontz was weary of the capital and ready for a change. Postwar shocks had stunned the navy and its CNO, who believed that the service was "at rock bottom and from now on will slowly but surely come up." The "stormy times" with Congress had taken their toll of Coontz, but he did not intend to retire. On 21 July 1923, he was relieved by Admiral Edward W. Eberle, and accepted a new billet as commander in chief of the new U. S. Fleet. He had not asked for this assignment and felt highly honored. Former Secretary Daniels wrote to him that the nomination was "a deserved distinction to you, because it gives you an opportunity to carry out policies and tactics you have studied all your life." "I felt," he concluded, "like congratulating the Navy rather than congratulating you." Coontz replied that he was tired of Washington and "ready to go to sea."[42]

The two most important events of Coontz's tour in command of the fleet were maneuvers in Hawaiian waters and a cruise to Australia and New Zealand. The maneuvers of 1925 were the largest held theretofore in the history of the American navy and involved 145 ships and 45,000 men. "For the first time in our history," wrote Coontz proudly, "the U. S. Fleet was actually deployed."[43] The cruise to Australia and New Zealand, which took place in the same year, was the culmination of Coontz's efforts to increase the presence of American naval forces in foreign waters. According to a New Zealand newspaper, the fleet, which included 45 ships and 23,000 men, gave the "impression of effective power" and was the "mightiest armada ever seen in New Zealand waters": its visit threw the "light of security on the future of the world in general and of the Pacific area in particular."[44] Coontz wrote an extensive report sharply criticizing certain deficiencies brought to light during the cruise, such as the lack of a uniform speed for ships. His report created a sensation and resulted in a general inquiry whose conclusions supported his observations.

Coontz left the fleet in October 1925 and on 30 November took up his last duty, which was commandant of the Fifth Naval District and commanding officer of the base at Norfolk. He wrote that during these last few years of his naval career his duties were routine and business at Norfolk was conducterd smoothly and with dispatch. However, the loss of his son, Kenneth, a naval lieutenant, in September 1926 was a staggering blow that he felt for the rest of his days.

Throughout his last assignment Coontz was actively involved in the continuing fight for a "treaty fleet" based on the limitations of the Five Power Treaty of Washington. Following the debacle of the Geneva Naval Disarmament Conference in 1927, he wrote to Congressman Patrick H. Kelly that it was just as well that it failed: "Every hour that passes, " he claimed, "puts us more and more into an inferior position as regards naval strength." He argued, "We're the ones that talk peace and do nothing, the others talk peace, but build on just the same, in spite of their great indebtedness."[45]

In May 1928 Coontz wrote to Franklin D. Roosevelt, urging him to include a preparedness plank in his party's platform for the upcoming election. Roosevelt replied that he would, and mentioned that he had plans for the navy and thought he could do a great deal to restore the nation's confidence in the navy.[46] Coontz actively supported the Democratic candidate, Alfred E. Smith, for the presidency that year.

After retiring in June 1928 Coontz remained active in the Veterans of Foreign Wars and was named its national commander in chief in 1932. He also continued his long activity in the Masonic organization, which he joined during his service in the Pacific Northwest. In 1930 he was recalled to duty for a brief period to assist a senate committee that was investigating Alaskan railroads, and in 1932 he served as a delegate from Alaska to the Democratic National Convention in Chicago which nominated Franklin D. Roosevelt for the presidency. Coontz's last public appearance was at the national encampment of the Veterans of Foreign Wars in Lexington, Kentucky, in October 1934.

It is difficult to evaluate Coontz as CNO for several reasons. The years directly following the First World War do not stand out in our naval history and, except for the Washington Conference, international affairs were relatively calm. He was cut from rather common cloth and had no readily apparent eccentricities for the press or a biographer to chronicle. He was a solid, predictable performer who was energetic in the discharge of his duties and had a deserved reputation as an able organizer and efficient administrator. But he was not beyond human frailty and peccadilloes and he made enemies and bore grudges. Coontz family lore recounts that a feud he had with Franklin Roosevelt early in their relationship was responsible for the naming of a combatant ship after the admiral—as was the custom— being delayed until 1958.[47]

It is clear, however, that Coontz served as CNO at a very difficult time for the service and that, in spite of widespread antinavalism, he accomplished many things. Under his leadership, cuts in numbers of officer and enlisted personnel were held to an acceptable level and lost ground was eventually recovered. Reorganization of the Operations Department and the concomitant strengthening of the position of the chief of naval operations vis-à-vis the bureau chiefs were long overdue and led to improved management within the Navy Department. Naval aviation and the submarine service also received new direction and emphasis, as did the scientific effort of the department through the establishment of the Naval Research Laboratory in 1921. However, Coontz was not an innovator and many of the changes that the navy experienced during his term were the product of his leadership and management rather than his direct sponsorship of specific projects. Notable exceptions to this generalization were the formation of the combined U. S. Fleet and the increased deployment of American naval forces to "show the flag," strategic programs for which Coontz deserved credit. In other areas, however, Coontz effectively encouraged experimentation and supported change, despite the constraints of the budget, politics, and the national mood.

Following a series of heart attacks in late 1934, Admiral Coontz died at the Bremerton Naval Hospital on 26 January 1935. He was buried in the family plot in Mount Olive Cemetery in Hannibal.

EDWARD WALTER EBERLE

21 July 1923–14 November 1927

RICHARD W. TURK

The third chief of naval operations, who took office on 21 July 1923, was Edward W. Eberle. He was born on 17 August 1864 in Denton, Texas, to Joseph and Mary Stemmler Eberle.[1] A Swiss immigrant, Joseph served as a colonel in the Confederate Army and, at the end of the Civil War, the family moved to Fort Smith, Arkansas, where Edward grew up. He received an appointment to the Naval Academy from the representative of the Third Congressional District of Arkansas in 1881 and, four years later, graduated in the middle of his class.

The 1880s were a time of transition for the U. S. Navy from a small and intimate service to a modern bureaucratic institution, from sail to steam technology, and from wooden to iron and steel ships. Slowly, the officer corps was dropping the gentlemanly standards of the antebellum years and adopting new, professional codes, a phenomenon that paralleled developments in other learned occupations. But the excessive number of officers in all ranks produced by the Civil War, plus the archaic system of promotion on the basis of seniority, meant that advancement for entering officers was quite slow. Although Eberle's career was enhanced by the policy of naval expansion after 1883, it took him twenty years from the time of his graduation to earn the rank of commander.

The first decade of his naval service was unremarkable, but in 1896 the Bureau of Navigation assigned him to the battleship *Oregon* and he was placed in charge of her forward gun turret. Two years later, when America declared war against Spain, the ship made her famous voyage from Puget Sound to the Caribbean in time to join the North Atlantic Squadron in the blockade of Cuba. In the ensuing Battle of Santiago, Eberle's skill in directing fire from his turret against the Spanish cruiser *Cristóbal Colón* caught the eye of the captain of another American battleship, Albert Sydney Barker. Later, while the *Oregon* was recoaling at Guantánamo Bay, Cuba, Eberle sighted a group of Spanish soldiers massing at Caimanera, five miles distant. Standing on the fore-topmast and using a navigation chart to estimate the range, he directed fire from his turret against the enemy and scattered them.

In 1899, Eberle became an aide to the superintendent of the Naval Academy. During this tour he applied his interest in ordnance technology and practical learning and wrote a drill manual for guns and torpedoes which was later adopted by the navy for training. His interest in technology never waned. He later was instrumental in installing the first wireless telegraphs aboard American warships and wrote an instruction manual for their use. After leaving the Naval Academy, he served on the staff of the commandant of the New York Navy Yard, saw brief duty at sea, and then was asked by the commander in chief of the Atlantic Fleet, Rear Admiral Albert S. Barker, to become his flag lieutenant.

An intense professional, Eberle was also an innovator who tried to adapt new ideas to solve practical problems in the fleet. For example, during his command of the newly formed Atlantic Destroyer Flotilla from 1911 to 1913, he developed smoke-screen tactics that proved effective in the fleet maneuvers of 1912. And, in the winter of 1913, during exercises off Guantánamo Bay, he deployed aircraft to locate submerged submarines, probably one of the first uses of air and surface forces in antisubmarine operations. Despite the fact that Eberle was proud of his work with the destroyer flotilla, his relief, Captain William Sowden Sims, wrote to colleagues that until he took command "it had not been taken very seriously." Referring to Eberle, Sims complained that "one old indifferently trained man cannot do it all."[2] However, there is no evidence that these complaints reached Eberle, who remained on good terms with Sims until a dispute arose some years later.[3]

Promoted to captain in 1915, Eberle received the superintendency of the Naval Academy, where he remained for the next four years. American belligerency in World War I brought great pressure on the academy to accelerate the commissioning of midshipmen and to train naval reserve officers. For this work Eberle was awarded a Distinguished Service Medal and promoted to flag rank. Between 1919 and 1921, he commanded Battleship Division 5 and Battleship Division 7 of the Atlantic Fleet and continued to demonstrate his old skill in battleship gunnery. For instance, he was accorded a commendation on his record when, during one target practice, every vessel in his division achieved a better score than any other battleship in the fleet.

It was this sort of accomplishment that brought Eberle, in July 1921, nomination as commander in chief of the Pacific Fleet and, when the two ocean fleets were combined, of the U. S. Fleet. His principal achievements in these billets were to perfect a fleet tactical system and to increase the use of naval aircraft for gunnery spotting and fire control. During this period, he enhanced his reputation as an admiral who was concerned about the welfare of his enlisted men. Soon after he took command of the Pacific Fleet, he began to receive reports that the city of Long Beach, California, was harassing sailors from his ships. What particularly annoyed him was a local judge's statement to the effect that he expected to build a new jail from the fines he was going to levy on the enlisted men. Eberle promptly sent Captain William H. Standley from his staff to warn the mayor of Long Beach that, if the local officials did not show a "different attitude," the town would be declared "off limits" for both officers and enlisted men. Standley recorded that the warning had the desired effect.[4]

At the pinnacle of his naval service, Admiral Eberle was still a gunnery officer. Much of his career had revolved around ordnance in one form or another, and his major contributions to naval science concerned improvements in accuracy and rate of gunfire and in the development of tactical systems to optimize its use against an enemy battle line. However, he recognized sooner than did many of his contemporaries the need to exploit major technological innovations in naval warfare: the mine, the submarine, and the airplane. A safe choice of all who had a say, Eberle in early 1923 agreed to a request from Secretary of the Navy Curtis D. Wilbur, a Naval Academy classmate, that he relieve Admiral Robert E. Coontz as the chief of naval operations.

The announcement of Eberle's appointment brought forth a broadside from Rear Admiral Sims, the bête noire of those he considered to be the agents of conservatism. Sims unleashed a public blast at both Coontz and Eberle, calling it a "crime" and a "scandal" that a graduate of the Naval War College had not been made CNO. "The service is disgusted with the situation, disgusted that the same old game of service politics is being played. It believes that the best place is a seat next to the dealer in Washington. Personal influence brings greater rewards than War College training."[5] The charge had the ring of truth, given the fact that both Coontz and Eberle were classmates of Secretary Wilbur, but it was not entirely fair because in 1905 Eberle served briefly as an instructor at Newport and eight years later completed the short course for the War College. Sims never repented of his remarks, which had no effect on Eberle's nomination. Taking almost all of his staff to Washington, Eberle relieved Admiral Coontz on 21 July 1923.

The major strategic problem with which Eberle had to wrestle during his tour as CNO concerned the defense of the Philippine Islands and Guam in the event of a war in the Pacific between the United States and Japan. This had been, of course, the paramount military problem for naval officers since 1905, and Eberle had first dealt with it in detail in 1913 in his War College paper, "Policy—Its Relation to War and Preparation for War." The paper was pedestrian, but it demonstrated that on the eve of World War I Eberle was particularly concerned with the threat that Japan posed to American supremacy in the Pacific Ocean. Bemoaning the lack of a combined army-navy plan for military operations, he stated that the United States must be the dominant power in the Pacific:

> Our position in the Pacific is now assailed by the naval activity of [Japan], and up to date we have engaged in diplomatic exchanges, in evasion of the issue at hand, and in [a] reduced building policy for the Navy. If we showed plainly that we were not to be trifled with either in our Island possessions or on the Pacific

> Coast of the two Americas, we should command much higher respect and dignity as a World Power.[6]

Ten years later, the Five Power Treaty signed at the 1921–1922 Washington Conference had made the defense of the Philippines more difficult for the navy, since the Japanese agreed to a 5:5:3 ratio for capital ships only because the United States and Great Britain in return promised not to fortify their possessions in the Western Pacific. Furthermore, Japanese control of the mandated islands, the Marshalls, the Carolines, and the Marianas, blocked the direct route of the American fleet from the West Coast to the Philippine Islands. Therefore, as did his predecessors and his successors for years thereafter, Eberle endorsed a policy that would "give priority to those elements" of the navy "which are essential to readiness for war with Japan."[7]

However, since public perceptions of Japan as an enemy of the United States were less acute than those of naval strategists, the CNO encountered his most vexing problem in maintaining a "treaty fleet." Under the Five Power Treaty, the U. S. Navy could deploy eighteen battleships, but many of these vessels had been laid down before World War I. Prevented by the building "holiday" clause of the treaty from replacing these ships, Eberle doggedly urged a modernization program for the units of the battle line.[8] As he edged this program along, he faced a Congress dedicated to economy in government and he often remembered Admiral Hilary P. Jones's earlier warning to him that the navy was "laboring under economy run wild."[9]

Admiral Eberle encountered analogous problems in maintaining subordinate classes of combatants. Destroyers, for example, did not fall under the provisions of the Five Power Treaty, but congressional stringency forced the navy to decommission or sell a large number of the hundreds of "four stackers" that had been built during World War I. Eberle did his best to limit this loss to the fleet. With cruisers, the problem was more complex. They were also outside the limitations of the treaty and, during his tour as CNO, Eberle sought to meet the challenge posed by Japan's decision in 1922 to lay down seven ships of this type and by the announcement in 1924 that the Royal Navy would build five 10,000-ton cruisers carrying 8-inch guns. At his urging, in December 1924 Congress authorized the construction of eight cruisers with 8-inch guns which would each displace 10,000 tons. Eberle in September of that year wrote that the United States was "not a warlike nation. We do not want war and we seek in every honorable way to avoid it, but we must be prepared, for unpreparedness is a potent invitation to war."[10]

The cruiser-building programs re-ignited the naval-arms race among the Pacific powers at the same time that diplomatic tensions between Japan and the United States heightened. Coincidentally, repeated demonstrations of aircraft sinking or seriously damaging capital ships put the navy under intense public pressure. In September 1923, for example, bombs dropped by aircraft put the old battleships *Virginia* and *New Jersey* out of commission. However, a year later it took a combination of bombs, mines, and naval gunfire to destroy the more modern battleship *Washington*. These seemingly contradictory results, plus Army Air Corps Brigadier General William "Billy" Mitchell's sensationalized criticism of the navy's reliance on the battle line, convinced Navy Secretary Wilbur to appoint Admiral Eberle as chairman of a special board to consider American naval policy with emphasis on the role of naval aviation.

Given the CNO's background in gunnery, the Eberle Board's conclusion that the battleship would continue to be the supreme arbiter of naval warfare was not surprising. Of all the weapons used at sea—the gun, the bomb, the torpedo, and the mine—they believed that the first was by far the most important. They largely discounted the sinkings of the *Virginia*, the *New Jersey*, and several former German warships by level aerial bombing because, when attacked, they were not under way, did not return antiaircraft fire, and had no damage-control parties aboard. Moreover, the most recent test, the one against the *Washington*, showed that the hull of a post-Jutland battleship could withstand aerial attack "to a remarkable degree."[11] Eberle believed that this experiment demonstrated that "the battleship of the future can be so designed . . . that she will not be subject to fatal damage from the air." Therefore, "it cannot be said . . . that air attack has rendered the battleship obsolete."[12]

In contrast to those officers who were coming to see aircraft as a striking arm within the fleet, Eberle believed that the airplane would scout, maintain command of the air over an opposing fleet, and spot gunfire for capital ships. However, he was no unreconstructed reactionary on the subject. In an article for the *U. S. Naval Institute Proceedings* in 1924 he called for a "broad definition of the word *navy* to assure command of the sealines of communication in wartime. "The tools required," he wrote, "are surface ships, submarines, and aircraft."[13] And, in another indicator of his views on the use of air power, Eberle endorsed the annual "Estimate of the Situation" prepared by Captain William R. Shoemaker, head of the War Plans Division, which claimed that

> the importance of the use of aircraft in a Pacific campaign promises to be such that every effort should be made to attain and maintain an advantage in this respect. This is of particular importance, because Japanese aircraft can operate in the probable theater of operations from shore bases; whereas our aircraft must operate from carriers in the initial stages of the campaign.[14]

Thus, some naval officers in the 1920s, Eberle among them, were beginning to realize that, to be successful, an American offensive westward in the Pacific against the Japanese-held Mandates would demand the use of carrier-based planes and the seizure of islands for the employment of land-based naval air power. Indeed, the Eberle Board concluded that "the operations of aircraft in battle may be so important that among the first objectives of attack are the enemy's aircraft carriers."[15]

However, Admiral Eberle was no visionary like Billy Mitchell or Rear Admiral William A. Moffett, chief of the Bureau of Aeronautics. He elaborated his views on naval air power in testimony he gave in September 1925 before the President's Aircraft Board, which was chaired by Dwight W. Morrow. The

CNO stressed the need to maintain an independent naval air arm rather than have all American military aviation incorporated into a single department. He echoed the recommendation of the Eberle Board, which had rejected the establishment of a separate Department of Aeronautics because of the cost involved, the difficulty there would be in coordinating its operations with the army and the navy, and, most importantly, the loss of control by the navy of its air units in wartime.[16] To the Morrow Board Eberle repeated the same ideas of his own panel, that "unless naval aviation is under naval control, works under the same discipline, acts in accordance with navy plans under precisely the same conditions as naval gunnery or naval engineering, it will not give the best results in battle." He emphasized the fact that an air arm that was to serve the navy could not operate at a distance from the fleet or independently of it. Eberle did not believe that the airplane was the ultimate weapon of warfare, and recalled that claims made in the past by supporters of the ram, the monitor, the torpedo boat, the submarine, and the mine about theirs being the "ultimate weapon" were similar to those being put forth in the 1920s by advocates of aerial bombardment:

> To the threat of each new weapon an answer has been developed, and the ultimate sea power has remained in the capital ship, with its better armor distribution, its improved underwater protection, its greater accuracy of fire, its increased speed and maneuverability, and with its own defending aircraft and other units. Aviation is in its infancy and has great possibilities and also limitations. The present state of its development and its achievements do not warrant all the extravagant claims set forth.[17]

In a sense, the state of military aircraft technology justified Eberle's hesitations. Neither the fighter nor the level bomber seemed to pose much threat to battleships, the torpedo plane was in its infancy, and the dive-bomber had not yet appeared. During his tenure as CNO, the capital ship did hold the upper hand over the airplane.

This is the theme that the Eberle Board repeated in the report it made to Navy Secretary Wilbur in late 1924. On air policy, Eberle hoped to press Congress to hurry completion of the large carriers *Lexington* and *Saratoga*. As Captain Shoemaker pointed out earlier in the year, "it is important that our two aircraft carriers now under construction be steadily proceeded with [and] our aircraft carrier tonnage be brought up to treaty ratios."[18] In addition, the CNO wanted Congress to approve a program of aircraft construction that would ensure the fleet a supply of modern planes and replacements, extend aeronautics courses at the Naval Academy, and encourage graduates to enter naval aviation "insofar as the other requirements of the service will permit." However, the major point of the report was the need to maintain at least the 5:5:3 ratio in all types of warships, not just in battleships and aircraft carriers, which were so limited by the Five Power Treaty. Here, of course, the key was authorization of the eight 8-inch-gun cruisers. In addition, the board recommended a sweeping modernization program for thirteen of the eighteen battleships in the U. S. Fleet. The major element of this program was conversion of the propulsion systems from the use of coal to oil, since this would increase range and speed and allow the fleet to operate more effectively in the Western Pacific. Other elements were greater use of electrical rather than manual systems and the elevation of main batteries, both of which enhanced the fleet's fighting power. Eberle urged that this vital program be funded by Congress "as soon as possible."[19]

The cost of the entire naval building program proposed by the Eberle Board was high and the fate of the recommendations provided an example of the CNO's difficulties with Congress and with President Calvin Coolidge. Upon receipt from Wilbur of the report, the chief executive returned it to the board, requesting a supplemental report listing the navy's priorities. Replying to Coolidge, Eberle recommended, first, modernization of the six coal-burning battleships; second, quick completion of the *Lexington* and *Saratoga*; third, modernization of the seven oil-burning battleships; fourth, the building of eight 10,000-ton, 8-inch-gun cruisers; fifth, the building of three fleet submarines; and sixth, the construction of one 23,000-ton carrier.[20] Paring these proposals, the president sent to Congress in 1925 a program that included only the conversion of three of the coal-burning battleships, completion of the two large carriers and authorization for their aircraft complement, and the building of two large cruisers. To add insult to injury, he added a request to build six gunboats for the Yangtze Patrol which Eberle had not even requested and which attested to the early political power of the "China lobby."[21]

The Eberle Board's report remained the objective for the CNO's naval policy throughout his term, although the requests the president sent to Congress in 1925 were about all he was ever able to get. Although eight of the large cruisers were authorized, Eberle was able to lay down only two, the *Salt Lake City* and the *Pensacola*, before he left office. The two new carriers were completed in 1927, but were not ready to enter the fleet until 1929. To Eberle, the conversion of the battleships seemed a slow process, although all thirteen had been modernized by 1931, only four years after he left office. However, the navy was able to persuade the Morrow Board not to propose the creation of a new and independent air department and to recommend a building program for the navy of 1,000 aircraft over the next five years. While this was mostly the work of Admiral Moffett, the CNO's willingness to integrate aviation into the fleet unquestionably eased the doubts of some about the navy's acceptance of aviation technology.

As with funds for building, Eberle had difficulty during his term as CNO convincing Congress that it should appropriate sufficient operating monies. Proposals to decommission older ships promised to save the operating budget for the rest of the fleet.[22] If one battleship were decommissioned, he protested during a budgetary battle in 1926, it would invite disaster, should an international crisis occur, "because it takes a considerable period of time to commission ships and train their crews to the [required] point of efficiency in gunnery, steaming, tactics, and communications."[23] Moth-balling more World War I destroyers, already undermanned, would be equally crippling, Eberle argued. That would deprive the fleet of the means for training officers and enlisted men to provide skeleton crews for other decommissioned vessels which the navy planned to bring into service in the event of a war. An additional worry for Eberle was the failure of Congress to provide an adequate appropriation for fuel for fleet operations. At one point during his tenure, he complained that the fuel ration was not sufficient to move the fleet from one operating area on the West Coast to another.

Eberle also pointed out that while Congress reduced the fighting strength of the fleet it maintained unnecessary bases, yards, and stations on the East Coast. He recommended to the secretary that the Great Lakes naval training station and the Boston and Charleston yards be closed, but Wilbur, perhaps wiser than the CNO in the politics of Congress, ignored the suggestion.[24] Despite these vicissitudes, the navy of Eberle's day somehow managed to stay afloat.

Allied to Eberle's other budgetary problems was the constant deficiency in manpower for the fleet. This had largely been fought out with Congress in 1922, before he became CNO, and the compromise that had been reached allowed the navy roughly 86,000 enlisted men. Even Congress agreed in 1922 that this figure was too low, but Eberle—and his successors—failed, despite constant pressure, to get the legislature to increase manning levels in the fleet and shore establishment. However, the CNO did endorse a campaign mounted in 1924 by his director of naval districts, Captain Charles F. Preston, to provide a nucleus of trained reserve officers and enlisted sailors. Preston proposed to recruit future officers at colleges and offer them parts of the Naval Academy's curriculum in addition to their regular courses. Helped by public pressure from the Naval Reserve Officers Association and by Admiral Eberle's support, Preston's proposal was accepted by Congress in 1925 and the modern Naval Reserve Officers Training Corps was born. The CNO also sponsored another of Preston's suggestions: with the help of organized labor, to bring skilled machinists into the navy as reserve petty officers. Although the goals of this program were somewhat less specific than the plan for NROTC, Eberle's support of both schemes illustrated his strong commitment to increasing naval manning levels, a problem he never really solved.[25]

Admiral Eberle's last year as chief of naval operations was clouded by uncertainty over the future of the navy's building program because of the Coolidge administration's commitment to extend naval arms limitation to types subordinate to capital ships. Indeed, the navy in 1924 had been able partly to convince Congress to authorize eight heavy cruisers of the *Salt Lake City* class on the grounds that American building would force Britain and Japan to come to an agreement on ceilings for this type of ship. From the CNO's standpoint, however, the American fleet was behind the British and Japanese navies in numbers of modern cruisers. Therefore, he wanted tonnage-limitation figures set relatively low, but high enough to provide for a "balanced fleet." This would give it some prospect of building up to "treaty strength." At the same time, the navy was wedded to the 8-inch-gun cruiser which displaced 10,000 tons, for Eberle and his fellow admirals believed that it best met their tactical requirements for a future war in the Pacific. Britain, on the other hand, wanted a much higher total tonnage limit, and a "standard" cruiser of 6,000 tons with 6-inch guns.[26]

Eberle's direct contribution to the Geneva Conference on naval armaments, which convened in June 1927, was minimal. Although the senior American naval delegate, Admiral Hilary P. Jones, encouraged Eberle to "not fail to keep us fully advised as to your ideas on the subject . . . and the stand we should take both as to unalterable decisions and those admitting of arguments," the CNO only urged the American representatives to hold firm on one point.[27] There had been widespread speculation that the Japanese would agree to cruiser limits only in return for an extension of the Five Power Treaty's "non-fortification" provisions for the Canal Zone, Pearl Harbor, and Singapore. As the senior member of the Joint Army-Navy Board, Eberle opposed any concession on this issue, and asked that the delegates reject any limitation on improving American base facilities and defenses at Pearl Harbor or in the Canal Zone, which the Japanese had tentatively proposed. "A fully developed naval base in the Hawaiian Islands," the CNO insisted, "is essential to the operation of our fleet in defense of the Philippines and Guam, and for the protection of our interests in the Western Pacific."[28] On this matter Eberle had his way. Secretary of State Frank B. Kellogg subsequently wrote that the American delegation in Geneva had received "specific instructions" to the effect that the status of the two American bases was not even "subject to discussion."[29] Likewise, the British refused to consider restricting their base at Singapore.

Nonetheless, the main issue at Geneva was between the United States and Britain and concerned cruiser tonnage. There was little flexibility in either delegation due, in retrospect, to the dominance of each party by its naval members. Many American naval officers were still smarting over the terms of the Washington treaties and wanted the Geneva negotiations to fail; the status quo, they reasoned, was better than further erosion of the fleet's strength. Eberle probably agreed with this consensus. British and Japanese naval leaders shared somewhat similar views and, consequently, the conference ended with no agreement.

Admiral Eberle was relieved as CNO by Admiral Charles F. Hughes on 14 November 1927. Secretary Wilbur, who later wrote that he could "count myself fortunate to have had the services of Admiral Edward W. Eberle," appointed his friend to chair the executive committee of the General Board.[30] Eberle served for less than a year, and retired in 1928, when he reached the mandatory retirement age of sixty-four, after forty-seven years of naval service.

Naval historian Waldo H. Heinrichs, Jr., observed how important doctrine, precedent, routine, and habit were to the navy in peacetime, when its most pressing engagement was the battle of the budget. In this environment, intra-bureaucratic contests were endemic and, to be successful, leaders required the qualities of the diplomat and politician. The navy's leadership in such times, he argued, was inclined to play safe "and rely exclusively neither on the weapons of the last war nor on new, untried ones."[31] These characteristics, with some modifications, describe the American navy during Eberle's tenure as chief of naval operations.

Eberle brought to the position of CNO a predilection for the gun, proven administrative competence, and a personality that inspired the respect, rather than the affection, of subordinates. The navy's budget declined during his tenure but he found the funds to complete the carriers *Lexington* and *Saratoga,* to modernize the battleships, and to lay down the cruisers *Salt Lake City* and *Pensacola.* What, in historical terms, raises Eberle above the ranks of other skilled naval bureaucrats is his willing acceptance of technological change—particularly of the airplane—and a suprising degree of receptivity to new techniques and ideas. As early as 1913, for example, he advocated the use of aircraft to drop free-floating mines and saw no reason to follow slavishly the reliance that the European navies placed on permanent minefields.[32] His support for naval aviation in its formative years was steady if unspectacular. If he seldom questioned national policy and prevailing naval doctrine, neither did he let it dominate his own thinking.

Eberle's health may well have been declining for several years before he retired, because Admiral Jones wrote to him in August 1926 and expressed the hope that Eberle was "steadily improving" from an operation.[33] The admiral was hospitalized in the spring of 1929 and died on 6 July. According to one report, the cause of his death was an infection, or abscess, that stemmed from an injury he had suffered more than thirty years earlier when he was struck by the tiller of a small boat and the shaft of his eyeglasses was driven into his right ear.[34] Admiral Eberle was buried with full military honors in Arlington National Cemetery.

CHARLES FREDERICK HUGHES

14 November 1927–17 September 1930

WILLIAM R. BRAISTED

"In the years to come, a score or more naval officers will recall the day they bade farewell to Adm. Charles F. Hughes, the Chief of Naval Operations, and watched a real man walk out of the room and out of active service." So observed the *Army and Navy Journal* of the devoted group that crowded the "top side" of the Main Navy Building on 17 September 1930 to honor the old sea dog as he gave up the helm. Among those present were brother officers who had grown gray with their chief, "juniors who had served under him and affectionately damned him with profoundest respect," and civilians who had worked "for, but with him." A hush fell as the tall, white-haired elder with walrus moustache and sad blue eyes fought back emotion to announce in husky voice: "Gentlemen, I just want to say good-bye and to thank you for your loyal and cheerful assistance, and I trust it will continue."

Tears were in the eyes of seasoned warriors as Hughes stepped back to receive an affectionate pat from Secretary of the Navy Charles Francis Adams III. Embarrassed for words, the old man's successor, Admiral William V. Pratt, affirmed: "I have nothing to say except that I am sorry to see Freddy go."[1] Secretary Adams perhaps best summed up Hughes, the man and his career, when he closed the admiral's official record that day with the single word "splendid."[2]

Charles Frederick Hughes had indeed demonstrated the qualities of "a real man" throughout his forty-six years of naval service. A stern disciplinarian, an indefatigable worker, a man not given to unnecessary verbiage or self-promotion, he was known by his intimates to conceal a heart of gold behind the somewhat forbidding exterior. "Fidelity, loyalty, and courage" were the qualities attributed to Hughes by a former classmate, Secretary of the Navy Curtis D. Wilbur.[3] Occasionally, Hughes would show frustrated impatience with those who failed to serve the navy as he did. But while he probably drove himself to a breakdown, he respected his subordinates' need for relaxation. Admiral William H. Standley, Hughes's choice to serve with him as assistant chief of naval operations, recalled how he once mustered the courage to tell Hughes that he, Standley, had to have his midweek golf game. Thereafter, although not a devotee of golf or bridge, the favorite recreations of his contemporaries, Hughes was punctilious in seeing that Standley did not miss his golf on Wednesday afternoons.[4]

In many respects, Hughes's life was the story of virtue rewarded that many of his generation were fond of accepting as typically American. He was born on 14 October 1866 in Bath, Maine, where his father, John, a Welsh immigrant, was reputed to have labored in local shipyards. His mother, Lucy, was a Delano and hence a distant cousin of the Roosevelts of Hyde Park.[5] Charles Hughes studied in public schools and sold newspapers on the train that ran between Bath and Portland. Just short of his eighteenth birthday, in 1881, he secured an appointment to the Naval Academy from Congressman Nelson Dingley, of Maine. The navy's official records contain a characteristic note from young Hughes to Secretary of the Navy William E. Chandler. Writing in a round, boyish hand on common, lined, tablet paper, Hughes explained that it would be a useless expense for him to report at the academy for a physical examination in May, rather than when he was to enter in the following September.[6] The Naval Academy's Cadet and Conduct Book reveals that Hughes was a fine seaman, a middling scholar, and a young man guilty of many minor indiscretions common to cadets—tardiness, untidy gloves, shoes adrift. Only thirty-five of the ninety cadets in Hughes's class received commissions, and Hughes stood somewhat below the middle of those commissioned.[7]

From his earliest service, Hughes was commended by his superiors as a sober, hard-working, and independent-minded officer of considerably more than average ability. While he was serving in the steam sloop *Mohican* on the Bering Sea patrol, his skipper and future father-in-law, Captain Charles E. Clark, commended him for volunteering for extra duty to assist with the patrol's extensive correspondence, a job that sometimes required him to work around the clock.[8] Somewhat later, when Hughes and Clark were shipmates in the monitor *Monterey*, Clark reported Hughes for being too free in expressing dissatisfaction when his ideas of duty were not met. It appears that Hughes used words that bordered on insubordination when a superior ordered the *Monterey*'s engineers, wearing dungarees, to man the third cutter.[9] Potentially far more serious for Hughes's later career was the accidental shooting in 1894 of a man in his command after target practice with revolvers. A court of inquiry found Hughes negligent because he trusted a subordinate to check the revolvers of his division after completion of the practice.[10] To a man with Hughes's deep sense of duty, the thought that his negligence might have caused the death of one of his men could only have been a source of great pain. The incident may explain his well-known reluctance to share responsibility in later years. Fortunately, Secretary of the Navy John D. Long decided in 1898 that the incident should not prevent Hughes from being promoted to lieutenant.[11]

Hughes's junior to middle years in the navy were marked by repeated displays of initiative. In 1898, during the Spanish-American War, he crossed the Pacific in the *Monterey* to join Admiral George Dewey before Manila, and the following year he led a landing party that captured Olongapo, on Subic Bay, from the Philippine insurgents.[12] Two years later, he was commended for his "excellence in all things, especially in coolness and presence of mind," after he helped steer the torpedo boat *Bailey* around Cape Hatteras in a perilous storm.[13] Again, when the battleship *Massachusetts* grounded in Bar Harbor in 1903, it was Hughes who led the crew into the depths of the great ship, and worked twenty-four hours a day, waist-deep in water, until the ship was safe.[14] At Coquimbo, Chile, in 1909, he headed a party of thirty that saved the waterfront from devastating fire by tearing down a house next to a burning hotel.[15] Hughes was also in command of the cruiser *Birmingham* when she was ordered on the first North Atlantic ice patrol after the sinking of the *Titanic* in 1912. After the Mexican revolution that overthrew President Porfirio Díaz, Hughes was ordered to Tampico and Veracruz in command of the gunboat *Des Moines*. The appearance of the *Des Moines* caused misgivings among the Mexicans, but Hughes's sincerity and unvarying courtesy won praise from both Americans and Mexicans.[16]

In his first major fleet assignment, Hughes served as chief of staff to Admiral Charles J. Badger, the commander in chief of the Atlantic Fleet, during the American landing at Veracruz in 1914. Badger was delighted by the "great judgment and discretion" demonstrated by Hughes during an operation that involved seventy ships of the fleet.[17] From the fleet, Hughes moved to the prestigious General Board in Washington, whose president, Admiral Dewey, found the younger officer "calm, even tempered, and forceful."[18]

For his captain's cruise, Hughes won the prize then sought by every line officer, command of a battleship. His clean and efficient ship, the *New York*, was designated flagship of the American division that, under Rear Admiral Hugh Rodman, served with the British Grand Fleet during World War I. After crossing to Britain through a storm that was the most terrifying in Rodman's experience, the admiral affirmed that Hughes was "as fine and efficient a seaman as any officer in the Navy, bar none."[19] Probably to Rodman must be ascribed the story, possibly apocryphal, that Hughes commanded the *New York* when she was rammed by a German submarine. The submarine was presumed sunk, but Hughes has been credited with missing three torpedoes as he navigated the *New York*, minus her starboard propeller, safely to port.[20] To Hughes's terrible disappointment, he was forced by his promotion to rear admiral to leave his ship and the war zone in September 1918.[21] "For exceptionally meritorious service in a duty of great responsibility," President Woodrow Wilson awarded Hughes the Distinguished Service Medal.[22]

Hughes continued to drive himself hard after reaching flag rank. His relief in the billet, Rear Admiral William V. Pratt, was delighted to find that Hughes had made Battleship Division 4 the finest division in the Battle Fleet during his two years in command, 1921-1923.[23] It was while serving as director of Fleet Training in the Office of Naval Operations that Hughes supervised the sinking of the hull of the fine new battleship *Washington* under the terms of the Five Power naval armaments treaty concluded in Washington in 1922. After withstanding aerial bombing, charges exploded in the water, and torpedo attacks, the *Washington* finally went down under a two-and-one-half-hour barrage from the 14-inch guns of the battleship *Texas*. The reticent Hughes left the publicity for the affair to Secretary of the Navy Wilbur and Admiral Edward W. Eberle, the chief of naval operations. Weeks later the press learned that Hughes had sat unperturbed on the after deck of the great ship during several of the key experiments.[24] For Hughes the experience with the *Washington* simply confirmed that the battleship was the backbone of the fleet.

After directing fleet training, Hughes served in quick succession in the navy's two top commands afloat: commander in chief of the Battle Fleet, from 1925 to 1926, and commander in chief of the U. S. Fleet, from 1926 to 1927. It was probably during these years that he was first really impressed by the potential of naval air power. When he commanded the Battle Fleet, one of his juniors, Captain Joseph Mason Reeves, organized a mock dive-bombing attack on his flagship, the battleship *California*, by eighteen planes in two successive waves. Hughes and his startled staff on the *California*'s bridge ducked as the planes hurtled toward them and then passed overhead, but Hughes came through this pioneer dive-bombing attack a warm supporter of naval air.[25] In his 1926 annual report, he especially urged construction of several smaller carriers to supplement the *Lexington* and the *Saratoga*, which had not yet joined the fleet. He wanted to liberate naval air from land bases so that it could freely operate with the fleet. As fleet commander, he also stressed the critical need for cruisers, a type that the navy had seriously neglected for many years.[26]

Just as he hated to leave the war zone in 1918, Hughes resisted the summons in 1927 from Secretary Wilbur to move from the fleet to the job of chief of naval operations. Assistant Secretary of the Navy T. Douglas Robinson and the chief of the Bureau of Navigation, Rear Admiral Richard H. Leigh, visited Hughes in his flagship, the armored cruiser *Seattle*, and insisted that he accept the navy's top billet. According to Hughes's chief of staff, Captain Yates Stirling, Jr., the modest Hughes doubted that the navy thought him the man for the CNO's seat. It seems that the admiral had been shaken by a heated argument with his old friend Rear Admiral Noble E. Irwin, then commanding destroyers with the Battle Fleet. Irwin confessed to Stirling that Hughes was right, but he was damned if he would provide the "old walrus" with the satisfaction of knowing. Told by Stirling that Hughes did not want to be CNO, however, "Bull" Irwin exclaimed: "There's no better man for the job. He's the one man I know who can keep those stuffed-shirted Bureau chiefs in line." Stirling then sat Irwin down with pen and paper, and Irwin wrote the note that finally convinced Hughes that he was the navy's man for the job. Hughes may have loathed leaving the fleet for Washington, but Secretary Wilbur needed his classmate's strength and integrity to bolster his administration, and there was a queue of admirals waiting to fly their flags as CinCUS.[27]

From the November day in 1927 when he relieved Admiral Eberle as CNO, Hughes's first objective was to promote the "sea-going navy" by advancing the efficiency of the fleet. Although he assured his new subordinates that he would be happy if they carried on as before, the admiral was known to favor strict rotation of officers between sea and shore and invariable application of the Navy Department's rule that the powerful bureau chiefs should serve only one four-year term.[28] His total commitment was to his job as he labored at his desk to keep abreast of all the navy's activities. The most junior officer on the most distant station could assume that, if he received an order from the Office of the Chief of Naval Operations labeled "by direction," it really came from the old man himself. Hughes limited his social life mainly to required official functions such as the White House receptions for the services on New Year's Day, when, resplendent as an aging Viking, the towering admiral headed the navy line.[29]

By statute, Hughes was responsible for the operations of the fleet and for the preparation of plans for its use in peace and war. In practice, he was the secretary's closest service adviser and helped him to integrate the rival bureaucracies within the department as well as to represent the navy outside. Not the least of his problems were the department's semiautonomous bureau chiefs, especially Rear Admiral William A. Moffett, the especially influential chief of the Bureau of Aeronautics. Although the secretary signed the letters to the powerful Bureau of the Budget, Hughes was the naval officer upon whom the burden of presenting the navy's total needs to Congress fell most heavily. He was also drawn into foreign affairs relating to such matters as policy on naval arms limitation, intervention in Nicaragua, and the protection of Americans in China. As senior member of the Joint Army and Navy Board, he was the naval officer ultimately responsible for the joint war plans and other major policies common to both services. For guidance in policy matters, he relied more heavily than any of his successors on the General Board, of which he was ex officio chairman.

The navy was under something of a cloud when Hughes arrived in Washington. Two months before, Rear Admiral Thomas P. Magruder, then commandant of the Philadelphia Navy Yard, had caused a minor sensation by publishing an article in *The Saturday Evening Post* in which he charged the navy with gross mismanagement and waste. The article sparked a congressional inquiry and, without a judicial hearing, the offending admiral was kept on the inactive list for several months after Secretary Wilbur had left office.[30]

Far more harrowing to the nation and to Hughes personally than the Magruder affair was the loss on 17 December 1927 of the submarine *S-4*. As she came to the surface at the submarine testing area near Provincetown, Massachusetts, she struck the coast guard cutter *Paulding* and sank. As soon as he learned of the accident, Hughes ordered Commander Ernest J. King to assist with the rescue operations and the raising of the submarine. The admiral and Secretary Wilbur went to Provincetown to observe the heroic efforts being made, under terrible winter conditions, to save the crew of the sunken craft.[31]

Coming after other naval disasters, the *S-4* tragedy provoked a whole series of inquiries by the navy, the coast guard, and the Congress. It was even suggested that President Calvin Coolidge should find a new naval secretary.[32] Hughes vigorously defended the navy against charges of negligence or incompetence, and recommended King for the highest decoration possible in recognition of his untiring energy and determination during the long, difficult task of raising the submarine.[33] The *S-4* was later designated an experimental vessel for testing devices that might prevent a similar tragedy. Hughes followed these experiments closely, and made the resulting technology available to the world.[34]

In Hughes's day, the War Plans Division occupied a key position in the Office of Naval Operations since, in addition to making war plans, it prepared the annual estimate of the situation upon which the navy's budget and policies were based. The war plans director during two of Hughes's three years as CNO was Rear Admiral Frank H. Schofield, a bruised veteran of several battles in naval diplomacy with the British. In his first annual estimate following the Anglo-American confrontation at the Geneva Naval Conference of 1927, Schofield observed that, whereas Britain had learned that the Americans were not "prepared to acknowledge the sea supremacy of Great Britain," the Americans now knew that Britain had "no intention of surrendering supremacy of the sea." Moreover, Schofield noted that the British and the Japanese had a disturbing tendency to reach agreements they did not share with the Americans. In light of this situation, Schofield held that the navy should prepare for eventualities against two enemies: Britain in the Atlantic and Japan in the Pacific. Believing that Japan alone would never attack the United States, he assumed that the most probable conflict between the United States and Japan would be a war in which Japan fought with a European ally, Britain. Japan, in Schofield's estimate, was in a position to force war on the United States in the western Pacific, and the United States could compel Britain to fight in the Atlantic by attacking Canada. The navy, therefore, should be ready "for a strategic offensive in the Pacific and a strategic defensive in the Atlantic." To Schofield, it was of utmost importance that the navy remain constantly alert to the changing international scene so that the U. S. Fleet could be concentrated in good time either in the Hawaiian Islands or in Narragansett Bay.[35]

Although perhaps somewhat extreme in his suspicions of Britain, Schofield certainly represented strong sentiment in the navy that Britain should not be ruled out as a possible enemy. Hughes warmly commended Schofield's estimate. He approved "constant watchfulness" to ensure timely concentration of the fleet, should an emergency arise, and he favored regular concentrations in peacetime in both oceans so that the fleet could be assembled in either the Atlantic or the Pacific without provoking public comment. He also endorsed completion of new plans for war against Japan, designated Orange, and against Britain, designated Red, as well as a full revision of the navy's Basic

Readiness Plan.[36] Perhaps Hughes's Welsh antecedents moved him to keep an eye on the Atlantic. His family cherishes a story of an Anglo-American occasion during which Hughes alone failed to rise for "Rule, Britannia!" Asked to explain, he grumbled that he did not believe Britannia ruled the waves.[37]

When Hughes took his seat on the Joint Army and Navy Board, that body was engaged in the preparation of a series of war plans against Orange, Red, and a Red-Orange coalition. Its first Orange Plan, that of 1924, incorporated the naval General Board's strategic thinking that called for a vigorous offensive to rush the American fleet, designated Blue, to the Philippines before its capture by Orange. Army planners came increasingly to regard the scheme as heroic in concept but unsound in expectation: the timetable it established was based on the assumption that the civilian authorities would warn the services of an impending zero day; it called for a fleet that Blue did not possess; it assumed that Manila Bay could be held as a base for the Blue fleet; and it left to the commander in chief of the Blue fleet the decision as to "*when* and *how* and *whether* Manila shall be relieved."[38]

Under pressure from the army, therefore, the Joint Board's planning committee devoted 1927 to the preparation of an eighty-one-page estimate of the situation that served as the basis for an entirely new Joint War Plan Orange. As finally accepted by Hughes and the Joint Board, the new plan, which was issued to the services in 1929, still called for a transpacific offensive to isolate and exhaust Japan, but with important modifications to meet army objections: the movement across the Pacific would await authorization by the president of the United States rather than depend on the commander in chief of the Blue fleet; an offensive would be directed toward securing an advanced base at Manila *or elsewhere* in the Western Pacific before an advance was made to Japanese home waters; and mobilization schedules were based on a firm M-day not related to any warning from the civilian authorities.[39]

In the course of drawing up the plan, the Joint Board, with Hughes in the chair, adopted a compromise mission for the services in the Philippines. Whereas army planners wanted to concentrate on holding the small, heavily fortified islands at the entrances to Manila Bay that could deny the bay to the enemy, naval men wanted to defend the entire bay area for use by the Blue fleet. Under pressure from the navy, the Joint Board accepted as a primary mission for Blue "To hold the entrances to Manila Bay" while retaining a secondary mission to hold the Manila Bay area so long as the primary mission was not compromised.[40] Clearly not satisfied with the qualifications imposed by the army, Hughes distributed the new Joint Orange Plan to the navy with the caution that it was "necessarily a compromise between divergent opinions, ideas and viewpoints of the Army and Navy."[41] Nevertheless, the plan, with amendments, survived until the army forced adoption of a far more defensive Orange Plan in 1938.

From a possible war with Japan, Hughes and the Joint Board turned to study a conflict with Red, the British Empire. Whereas in an Orange campaign, the Blue fleet would strive to establish its superiority in the Western Pacific before its territories in the area fell to the enemy, in the Red Plan of 1930 its initial objective would be to seize Red positions in the Western Atlantic before the Red fleet and other relieving forces could reach them. The Red Plan was far more important to the army than the predominantly naval Orange Plan because it assigned to the army such meaningful roles as the invasion of Canada and the capture of Halifax.[42] The army was never able seriously to interest the navy in a Red-Orange plan, probably in part because Hughes's successors in the Office of Naval Operations regarded a war with Britain as improbable.

Another of Hughes's prime responsibilities as CNO was to win congressional support for naval building, maintenance, and operations during peace, when the public was apathetic, if not hostile, to any naval buildup. Worked out before Hughes arrived in Washington, the navy's proposals to Congress for fiscal 1929 predictably reflected the sudden cooling in Anglo-American naval relations that followed the breakdown of the Geneva Naval Conference. Since the Washington naval treaty of 1922 had imposed a ten-year holiday on battleship construction and a total-tonnage lid on aircraft carriers, cruisers had become the symbol of competitive naval power. American naval men were appalled when they learned at Geneva that, whereas the United States had eighteen modern cruisers built and building, Britain claimed to need between sixty and seventy of this vital type. The Washington treaty limited individual cruisers to a maximum of 10,000 tons mounting 8-inch guns. Whereas the British sought strictly to limit the 8-inch-gun heavy cruisers favored by the United States but reserved to themselves the right to build numerous 6-inch-gun cruisers, the Americans wanted freedom to build as many heavy cruisers as could be accommodated within the cruiser-tonnage limitation. Secretary Wilbur was convinced that the navy had to complete without delay the cruisers then authorized, and he called on the General Board to formulate a five-year naval program to match developments in other navies.[43] Guiding the General Board's deliberations was Rear Admiral Hilary P. Jones, a formidable veteran of the Geneva talks.

The heart of the General Board's program was a request for twenty-five 8-inch-gun heavy cruisers, to be laid down at the rate of five each year, that would bring the number of modern cruisers to forty-three and the total tonnage to 396,000. Although that program was designed to give the United States parity in cruisers with Britain by 1936, the board insisted that it fell short of the estimates from the War Plans Division and the Naval War College. In addition to the cruisers requested, the board wanted to resume the building of battleships in 1931 and lay down five small aircraft carriers, thirty-seven destroyers, thirty-five submarines, and a floating dry dock.[44] President Coolidge, after deleting the battleships, the destroyers except for nine destroyer leaders, and the floating drydock, accepted the board's program. He assured the nation that the United States was building only to balance the fleet, not to compete with any other power.[45]

In his first appearance before the House Naval Affairs Committee in January 1928, Hughes declared: "All I know is that I want ships for the

Navy. . . . I depend upon you to get them. I want ships for the Navy." The picturesque old seaman warned that, while the program would not assure "command of the sea" to the United States, it would provide a balanced fleet that he deemed sufficient to defend the nation's coasts and commerce and to preserve relations with other countries. It would provide "reasonable" but not "adequate" force with which to deal with any other power. According to Hughes's lexicon, a "reasonable force" would assure that the Navy had "a fair chance of doing something," whereas an "adequate force" would provide a "sure chance of doing it."

Hughes assured the committee that the General Board's recommendations corresponded exactly with the requirements that he had determined independently when he was a fleet commander. Of the forty-three cruisers, he said, he would assign twenty-six directly to the battleship fleet, nine to guard coastal points and the Panama Canal, six for convoy work, and two as flagships for the destroyer squadrons. He would build only 10,000 -ton, 8-inch-gun cruisers, the largest allowed under the Washington naval treaty. Hughes did not say so but he obviously wanted heavy cruisers with sufficient range for distant operations against Japan in the Western Pacific, and he wanted them to mount large guns because they would be able to deal with a host of smaller, less heavily gunned British units. He claimed that substituting 6-inch for 8-inch guns would concede cruiser predominance to the British, since Britain had a five-to-one superiority over the United States in merchant ships convertible to 6-inch-gun cruisers.

Along with cruisers, Hughes called for completion of the full carrier force of 135,000 tons allowed by treaty. Since the *Saratoga* and *Lexington* absorbed nearly 50 per cent, or 66,000 tons, of this allowance, Hughes proposed to divide the remaining tonnage among five 13,800-ton carriers, the smallest ship then deemed capable of providing a stable landing platform. He denied the assertion by Rear Admiral William S. Sims that air power had displaced the battleship, but he also insisted that a commander must first win control of the air in any fleet action so that he could use his planes freely in "bombing enemy combatant ships, strafing attacks against heavy and light forces, torpedoing capital ships, laying smoke screens, tactical scouting, and observation of gunfire." Apart from fleet actions, Hughes saw important roles for naval aircraft in advance scouting, defense of sea communications, and attacks on enemy shore facilities. He also wanted the nine large destroyers to serve as leaders for the navy's eight destroyer squadrons, and thirty-five intermediate-sized submarines of 1,400-1,700 tons each with sufficient range for oceanic operations. All these ships he would lay down within five years and complete in eight.

Presiding Chairman Frederick A. Britten declared that he could not recall in his sixteen years on the naval committee "any other officer who has made the impression on the committee, who has been frank with the committee as well as imformative, as you have Mr. Admiral."[46] That Hughes impressed the committee was confirmed by the long summary of his views that the committee included in its report to the House. Nevertheless, the committee reported in favor of laying down but fifteen cruisers in three years, rather than twenty-five cruisers in five years, and it deleted all other vessels from the administration's program save one small carrier, later named the *Ranger*, to be started the first year. Even the reduced program, however, was an alert that the United States was not prepared to accept less than parity with the strongest naval power.[47] After passing the House, the bill, by then popularly known as the Cruiser Bill, was held up behind the Hoover Dam Bill in the Senate and not acted upon before Congress recessed for the summer.[48]

During the summer of 1928, the Cruiser Bill received an unexpected boost when it was learned that Britain and France had agreed that new naval limitations should be imposed only on the 8-inch-gun cruisers and long-range submarines desired by the United States. In some service circles, this accord was seen as evidence that perfidious Albion was lining up friends against the United States.[49] President Coolidge and Secretary of State Frank B. Kellogg were clearly suspicious of the accord, and Kellogg sought counsel with Hughes and other members of the General Board.[50] The president, in an unprecedented display of cordiality toward his naval friend, summoned Hughes to visit him at the summer White House in Superior, Wisconsin. While historians may never know what the two taciturn New Englanders said to each other in the northern woods, contemporaries conjectured that they conferred on the inner meaning of the Anglo-French agreement.[51] Kellogg fell in with the naval view that the United States must not accept a naval-arms agreement that would limit only the long-range, heavily gunned ships favored by the United States,[52] and he advised the president that the best response to the British was quick passage of the Cruiser Bill.[53]

Hughes reinforced the navy's position by having the General Board revise its 1922 statement on "United States Naval Policy," which called for superiority of armament and radius of action in all types of American fighting ships. As approved by Secretary Wilbur and presumably by the president, the new "Fundamental Naval Policy of the United States" specified that the navy would construct only cruisers of 10,000 tons' displacement mounting 8-inch guns, and that no smaller cruisers would be laid down.[54] Senate passage of the Cruiser Bill in early 1929 was probably the high point in Hughes's tenure as CNO. He continued to hope, however, that Congress would eventually provide for the other ships that he deemed essential for a well-rounded fleet.[55]

Hughes, like most of his naval contemporaries, regarded the battleship line as the single most important element in American naval power. Since the United States was committed by the Washington treaty to a ten-year holiday in capital-ship construction, the navy had engaged in the 1920s in a long-term program to modernize the thirteen oldest of its eighteen battleships so that its battle force would be closer to parity with the British, be able to meet the challenge of air power, and have better steaming qualities. This involved converting the coal-burners to oil, raising the elevation of the big guns to increase their range, and adding "blisters" to the hulls, deck armor, and antiaircraft guns. Congress had approved the modernization of the first eight before Hughes became CNO and added the *Pennsylvania* and the *Arizona* in 1929. But in 1930 Hughes tried and failed to secure authority to go ahead with the *New Mexico*, the *Idaho*, and the *Mississippi*—the last three of the thirteen—partly because modernization was one of the naval programs interrupted by the London Naval Conference, which convened that year.[56]

Hughes also expected to embark on a program to replace the older battleships at the conclusion of the naval holiday. Probably with President Herbert Hoover's approval, he announced in April 1929 that the Navy Department would ask Congress to authorize construction of two battleships as replacements for the *Florida*, *Wyoming*, and *Utah*.[57] This replacement program, however, was halted by the London Naval Treaty, which extended the building holiday for five years. Hughes believed that the delay would eventually prove uneconomical, but conceded that the scrapping of old battleships required by the treaty would leave the American and British battle fleets closer to parity.[58]

Hughes retained the existing organization of the U. S. Fleet throughout his term, in spite of agitation for change. Political interests required the navy to maintain extensive shore facilities on the Atlantic coast while navy yards on the West Coast were not adequate to service the entire fleet. Since 1922 nearly all the navy's forces had been theoretically brought together in the U. S. Fleet, which in turn was broken down into the Battle Fleet, the Scouting Fleet, the Control Force of submarines, and the Fleet Base Force. The heavy units of the Battle Fleet were customarily kept in the Pacific to deter a Japanese advance against Hawaii; the Scouting Force, in the Atlantic to apprehend a hostile British fleet and to escort army and marine expeditionary forces to Halifax, Bermuda, Trinidad, and Jamaica. The two forces operated separately except during fleet concentrations, when they came together under the commander in chief of the U. S. Fleet. The system did tend to cluster at the top several admirals each of whom guarded his prerogatives as a fleet commander.[59]

Admiral Henry A. Wiley, Hughes's successor in command of the U. S. Fleet, proposed a sweeping reorganization in which most of the fleet would be concentrated in the Pacific. His aim was to unite the fleet in fact as well as in theory and bring it more directly under the control of a single commander in chief. He also wanted to reorganize the ships into forces according to types: battleships, aircraft carriers, cruisers, destroyers, and submarines. Under the commander in chief, a four-star admiral would command the forces in the Pacific; a vice admiral, those in the Atlantic.[60]

Wiley was outraged that Hughes refused to publish his plan, much less approve it.[61] Concentration of the fleet in the Pacific was contrary to the War Plans Division's recommendation, approved by Hughes, that the fleet should move between the oceans so that it could more readily concentrate in either. It was also held in the Office of the Chief of Naval Operations that political and strategic considerations required the navy to maintain its yards on the East

Coast and that it would be most impractical to schedule overhauls in these yards for ships in the Pacific. Moreover, the navy had too few ships, especially cruisers, to allow it to be organized by types.[62] Admiral William V. Pratt, commander in chief of the Battle Fleet, at first inclined to these views. When he had "fleeted up" to relieve Wiley as commander in chief of the entire U. S. Fleet, however, he pressed for a fleet organization similar to that recommended by Admiral Wiley.[63] By the time Hughes retired, enough new units had joined the fleet to make organization by types feasible. Moreover, the easing of naval tensions with Britain that followed the London Naval Conference made the concentration of naval forces in the Pacific more logical and desirable.

Naval aviation expanded considerably during Hughes's tour as CNO, largely because of the implementation of policies already adopted. The five-year program to acquire 1,000 planes, approved in 1926, was nearly completed when Hughes retired, and the commissioning of the first large carriers, the *Lexington* and *Saratoga,* really got naval air out to sea.[64] The value of naval aviation was dramatized by the famout Fleet Problem IX, in which the *Saratoga,* escorted by the light cruiser *Omaha,* escaped detection by large sea, land, and air forces and launched a suprise air attack on the Panama Canal. The exercise vindicated naval airmen in their view that coast defense could not be left safely to the army air corps.[65] The operation was conceived by Hughes's good friend, Rear Admiral Joseph Mason Reeves, whom Hughes may well have brought to the General Board to balance Moffett, who was brilliant but difficult.

Much of the early success of naval aviation must be attributed to Moffett. Independently wealthy, he did not hesitate to use influence outside the service to win for naval aviation and for himself what he could not achieve through bureaucratic channels. The judicious, fair-minded Hughes inevitably disappointed the partisan Moffett, even as the volatile Moffett must have been a trial to Hughes. As CNO, Hughes was concerned when aviation increased its share of the naval cake at the expense of other branches of the navy. Every year, for example, citing figures to demonstrate that expanding naval air was draining the fleet of personnel, Hughes begged for more enlisted men. While the enlisted force remained fairly constant at about 85,000, men assigned to naval air duty increased from 4,247 in 1923 to 10,771 in 1930. Without a personnel increase, the fleet would be only 86.1 per cent manned in fiscal year 1931.[66]

Moffett suspected Hughes because of his devotion to Admiral Leigh, the chief of the Bureau of Navigation, and fought bitterly with Leigh over whether the Bureau of Navigation or the Bureau of Aeronautics should control the assignments of naval air personnel. Indeed, Admiral King later recalled that he was relieved as assistant chief of the Bureau of Aeronautics when he disagreed with Moffett's stand toward the Bureau of Navigation.[67] Aeronautics was even affronted when Hughes rejected its candidate to serve as air officer in his own Office of Naval Operations.[68]

Hughes was established on Moffett's enemy list when he and Leigh decided that Moffett, having served two four-year terms as aeronautics chief, should move on. Moffett viewed his detachment from the bureau as an attack on himself and on naval aviation. He enlisted such influential friends as William Wrigley, the chewing-gum king, to intercede at the White House, and was elated that his "rather active campaign" won him reappointment to an unprecedented third term.[69] Hughes and Leigh, he claimed, had suffered "one of the most severe jolts" of their lives. While Hughes is not likely to have been jolted, as Moffett supposed, he may very well have been disappointed that a fellow officer had employed outside influence to override a principle, a limit of one term for bureau chiefs, that to Hughes was manifestly for the good of the service.[70]

Furthermore, Hughes failed to lend enthusiastic support to several of Moffett's pet projects. He was cool to Moffett's campaign for large numbers of small carriers and flying-deck cruisers, apparently because he doubted whether such small ships could provide adequate landing platforms.[71] He also had reservations regarding Moffett's affection for rigid airships.[72] Hughes's judgment proved sounder than Moffett's. After building the *Ranger,* the small carrier authorized in the Cruiser Bill, the navy shifted to larger carriers. And it halted the construction of rigid airships after Moffett was killed in the crash of the *Akron* in 1933. Hughes's friends on the General Board, if not Hughes himself, also opposed Moffett's plan to establish the navy's West Coast airship base at Sunnyvale, California, because they believed Camp Kearney, near San Diego, was more convenient in relation to the fleet's main anchorages.[73]

Hughes supported those elements of naval aviation that, in his eyes, proved themselves. He praised the achievements of naval aviation in Fleet Problem IX,[74] and he and the Office of Naval Operations vigorously opposed pressure to decommission either the *Lexington* or the *Saratoga* because they had proved so expensive. To the Naval Subcommittee of the House Appropriations Committee, he declared that those were the last two ships that he would remove from the active list.[75] Still, Moffett looked forward to the appointment of a new CNO and, a year before Hughes's scheduled retirement, he was boosting Admiral Pratt for the billet. It is doubtful, however, whether Pratt was really far ahead of Hughes in recognizing naval air. Nonetheless, Moffett and Pratt were friends, and Pratt was an open-minded officer whose star was rising in official circles.[76]

When Herbert Hoover entered the White House on 4 March 1929, Admiral Hughes was at the high point of his term as CNO. He surely shared with others in the service the expectation that Hoover would provide the navy with strong leadership, and he established close relations with Charles Francis Adams III, the navy's popular new secretary, who could match Hughes himself as a true man of the sea. The old admiral was probably wholly unprepared for the disappointments, hurt, and illness that were to darken his final year in the navy.

Although, in his campaign, Hoover had endorsed a strong national defense, he and his strong-willed secretary of state, Henry L. Stimson, were determined to break the impasse with Britain on naval-arms limitation, to halt any loose talk of war between the two great English-speaking powers, and to check wasteful arms expenditures. Hoover was alerted by the budget director, Herbert M. Lord, to the fact that the navy's proposed building program, which included fifteen battleships, would cost the nation the then-staggering sum of $1.1 billion.[77] To avoid a ruinous naval race and to bring naval expenditures under control, therefore, Hoover and Stimson sought an agreement with England establishing parity between the two greatest navies while assuring each a fleet that would meet its particular needs. They hoped to achieve agreement by keeping the formulation of policy in their own hands and consulting the naval experts only on technical details.[78]

The Hoover administration's flexible approach to naval-arms limitation was unveiled in late April 1929 by Delegate Hugh S. Gibson at a Geneva meeting of the League of Nations' Preparatory Commission on Disarmament. Whereas the American government had previously insisted on strict limitation of naval tonnage according to categories, Gibson now spoke of searching for a formula to correlate equivalent tonnages based on such factors as displacement, age, and gun caliber. He clearly had in mind a formula that would permit the Americans to build heavy cruisers and the British to have their smaller cruisers and still achieve parity between their two fleets.[79] On Memorial Day, the president himself proposed to break the naval impasse by finding a "rational yardstick" for making reasonable comparisons between naval units of different characteristics so that an "agreed relativity" could be established between the world's navies.[80]

It appears that Hoover suggested his "yardstick" without detailed advice from Hughes or the navy's General Board. The following day, Secretary Adams forwarded to the board copies of Gibson's speeches at Geneva with a directive to "make such recommendations as [the board] considers advisable and pertinent in the premises."[81]

Whereas he usually attended only the monthly meetings of the full board, Hughes chaired all of these discussions and signed the board's key reports on naval limitations in 1929. The board's initial response was a grudging admission that Gibson's formula for computing "equivalent tonnages" was an expedient means for reaching agreement on cruiser limitation only. With some obvious reluctance, they conceded four possible ways to approach naval limitation: first and best, establishing total-tonnage limits according to categories; second, allowing small transfers of tonnage between categories; third, creating a formula based on unit displacement and age; and finally, devising a formula embracing unit displacement, age, and gun caliber. They clearly disliked the last two approaches because their fairness depended on the values attached to the constituent factors.[82] What Hoover wanted was what Hughes and the General Board were most reluctant to supply, a formula, or "yardstick," in which tonnage, age, and gun caliber were accorded values that could be used in establishing parity between dissimilar American and British cruiser forces.

Secretary Adams accordingly ordered the General Board to determine what values it judged equitable, just, and acceptable.[83]

Fortunately for Hoover, the new Labour prime minister of Great Britain, Ramsay MacDonald, was as determined as was the president to reach a naval agreement. Through the early summer, as Hughes and the General Board searched for a "yardstick," the president pressed the prime minister to reduce British cruiser requirements to a level that the Americans might match. By early August the General Board had completed a complex formula, or "yardstick," by which the relative strengths of cruisers could be determined in terms of values applied to displacement, age, and gun caliber,[84] and MacDonald had reduced the British cruiser needs to a level that the Americans regarded as reasonable. Hughes and the General Board held, however, that the "yardstick" should be applied in such manner as to allow the United States to retain its twenty-three 8-inch-gun heavy cruisers, and they insisted that the United States should not be forced to build any small "police" cruisers just to fit the "yardstick."[85]

Relations between Hoover and the General Board reached a climax when Hughes and the board were called to the White House on the morning of 11 September 1929 to recommend a response to Prime Minister MacDonald's latest proposals. The British wanted fifty cruisers totaling 339,000 tons, including fifteen 8-inch-gun cruisers, fourteen new 6-inch-gun cruisers averaging 6,500 tons, and twenty-one old 6-inch-gun cruisers averaging less than 5,000 tons. The board members were most upset by the British plan to build fourteen replacement cruisers and by a plea from MacDonald for the Americans to reduce the number of their heavy cruisers from twenty-three to eighteen. It was MacDonald's contention that, if Japan pressed for 70 per cent of the twenty-three big American cruisers, Britain's heavy cruiser force would be inferior to Japan's.[86]

On orders from Hughes, the board's secretary read to the president an eight-page opinion that reiterated support of heavy cruisers. Claiming that the British had abandoned the "yardstick," the board recommended that the United States demand twenty-one heavy cruisers, ten completed 6-inch cruisers of the *Omaha* class, and eight new 6-inch-gun cruisers.[87] Both the president and Secretary Stimson refused to admit that the British had abandoned the "yardstick." And when Hoover ordered Commander Harold C. Train to apply the "yardstick," Train came up with a cruiser allowance for the Americans of only 305,000 tons, including four or five new 6-inch-gun cruisers.[88] There is some evidence that the meeting broke up after Hughes bluntly told the president that the General Board had completed its last study of the cruiser question.[89] After the meeting, the president sent Stimson a short note in which he set forth his understanding of the "yardstick":

> At my request to know what the yardstick applied to the British fleet would represent in the equivalent of the American fleet, I was told it would represent

> 21 large ships, 10 Omahas, and 4 new 6-inch cruisers. I repeated three different times to make sure that my understanding was accurate and I received direct confirmation from Admiral Hughes, Admiral [Hilary P.] Jones and I think one other admiral. The figures were checked and handed to me in writing.[90]

That afternoon at the Navy Department, when Secretary Adams tried to win the General Board's acceptance of but four 6-inch-gun cruisers, he was told that that number would not ensure parity with Britain, even though it represented a fair application of the "yardstick." The debate continued to early evening, as Hughes conceded cruisers one by one. Finally, after visits from Stimson and Assistant Secretary of State Joseph P. Cotton, Hughes signed an amended version of the board's report accepting five new light cruisers. For Hughes the final reply was undoubtedly a bitter pill since it sacrificed two heavy cruisers from the navy's existing program and called for six light cruisers that the board did not want. Equally important, the twenty-one cruisers demanded by the General Board still exceeded by three what Prime Minister MacDonald was willing to allow.[91]

After the confrontation at the White House on 11 September, Hughes and the General Board were, for the most part, bypassed as Hoover and Stimson turned for advice to Admiral William V. Pratt, then commander in chief of the U. S. Fleet. Eight years earlier, Pratt had helped the State Department to find the formula for success at the Washington Conference. Whereas Hughes's total loyalty was to the navy at all times, Pratt held that the State Department's views should control during peace. Unlike Hughes, who accepted Britain as a possible antagonist, Pratt was dedicated to Anglo-American understanding. He found entirely reasonable the British proposal that the United States accept a reduction to eighteen heavy cruisers in exchange for a larger allowance of light cruisers.[92] Hughes himself recalled only one meeting with Pratt during which Pratt was somewhat embarrassed to explain his views on naval limitation. Hughes's fullest information came from Rear Admiral Hilary P. Jones, a seasoned veteran of arms conferences who, with Pratt, was named technical adviser to the American delegation to the London Naval Conference.[93]

Something of the pathos of Hughes's isolated situation may be sensed from a note he wrote to the wife of Secretary Adams:

> I wish you to know that there is to-day a much more cheerful atmosphere in the Department. There is a general and enthusiastic approval of your husband [sic] appointment to the Commission to meet in London, the Navy feels its interests are safeguarded.
>
> I have a divided feeling [.] For while I believe that the appointment is a most wise one [,] I know that the Secretary is going to be greatly missed in Washington during the months of January and February [.][94]

Hughes's doubts about Britain surfaced briefly when Prime Minister MacDonald visited the United States in October 1929. Hoover favored a naval division of the world in which Britain would refrain from building bases in the

Western Hemisphere while the United States would keep its naval power out of the Eastern Hemisphere. MacDonald was friendly to the idea, but he insisted that existing British positions were no menace to the United States. Hughes and the General Board conceded that British bases at Halifax, Bermuda, and in the West Indies were not "an appreciable menace" to the United States, but held that a threat was "inherent in their position and physical characteristics." Objections from the British Admiralty and Canada finally ended Hoover's happy thought.[95]

After Adams's departure for London in January 1930, Hughes necessarily shouldered much more of the burden of presenting the navy's requests to Congress, running the department, and caring for the fleet. Excluded from the negotiations in London, the old admiral later testified that the only information he had about the conference came from the press.[96] He once more demonstrated his detailed mastery of the navy's operations during the House budget hearings,[97] but in February 1930 he suffered a stroke, presumably brought on by overwork. Admiral Standley recalled that, thereafter, Hughes became increasingly irritable as he suspected that he was being bypassed. Hoping that the sea air would revive him, his friends arranged to have the admiral ordered to take a cruise to Panama in the new cruiser *Pensacola*.[98]

Hughes was back in Washington by late April, in time to review the London Naval Treaty with the General Board.[99] As did the General Board and most of the navy, he opposed the treaty because it allowed the United States only eighteen heavy cruisers and granted to Japan higher ratios in cruisers, destroyers, and submarines. His testimony on the treaty before the Senate committees was in the moderate tone of a loyal subordinate who disagreed profoundly with his superiors. He insisted that the United States should retain the freedom to build the ships best suited to its needs. Holding that the 8-inch-gun heavy cruiser was generally more versatile than the 6-inch-gun light cruiser, he contended that, by accepting an excess of light cruisers, the United States had tailored the navy to the specifications of others. He also believed that the treaty had increased Japan's predominance in the western Pacific. His testimony was a statement of conscience that had no influence on the Senate's ratification of the treaty.[100]

Hughes's position at the Navy Department became more difficult as he awaited retirement in November 1930. Perhaps with his own ill health in mind, he endorsed a bill that provided for an assistant to the chief of naval operations authorized to perform the duties of the CNO in the event of the latter's death, resignation, absence, or illness.[101] He accepted the logic of Pratt being designated as his successor, notwithstanding their disagreement on disarmament and on fleet matters. Pratt praised Hughes as "a blunt, frank seaman, thoroughly reliable, one of the hardest workers I have ever known, a splendid character." But he was enraged when, at their first meeting following the London Conference, Hughes rejected Pratt's elaborate rules for the operation of the fleet. Pratt lost patience and told Hughes that he would be a candidate for the job of CNO. Eventually Standley intervened to secure Hughes's approval of some of Pratt's rules, with which succeeding commanders in chief struggled, until Standley became CNO and discarded these regulations.[102]

As he learned of budget cuts, the typically considerate Hughes decided that he should pass the helm to Pratt so that Pratt would have time to prepare for the difficult decisions ahead. The president acceded to Hughes's request. On 17 September 1930, Hughes was placed on the retired list.[103] Something of Hughes's somber feelings may be sensed from his note to Admiral Charles B. McVay, commander in chief of the Asiatic Fleet:

> The Navy may be a little bit down now but it has been there and it has always come up; I have confidence if all hands put their shoulder to the wheel and work.[104]

After his four-star flag had been hauled down from Admiral's House, the old house on Observatory Circle that Admiral Leigh had resurrected for Hughes's use, Hughes moved to the Washington suburb of Chevy Chase. As was the rule in those days, he reverted in rank from full admiral to rear admiral. One man who surely appreciated the poignancy of Hughes's departure was Secretary Adams, who wrote the admiral on the day he retired from forty-six years of service: "Our days together were all pure joy to me. I miss you sadly, and want to express to you again my sincere affection."[105]

Charles Frederick Hughes will always remain one of the lesser-known chiefs of naval operations. Partly this is because he held the navy's highest commands during a period when he was called upon to fight only unglamorous battles in defense of the navy against the ravages of peace. It is also because he was a reticent, conservative person whose dedication was to the navy rather than to himself. Far more than for any publicized deeds, he was respected by his fellow officers for the fact that he was "a real man" of integrity, commitment, and humanity. Hughes died at his home on 28 May 1934. The navy's affection for him was perhaps most touchingly expressed to his widow by Admiral Reeves, then commander in chief of the U. S. Fleet: "I cannot tell you how fond I was of the Admiral. He was the best friend I had in the Navy. I owe to him, more than to any other one individual, what I have learned of the naval service."[106]

WILLIAM VEAZIE PRATT

17 September 1930–30 June 1933

CRAIG L. SYMONDS

Admiral William V. Pratt was sworn in as the fifth chief of naval operations on 17 September 1930. The occasion capped a professional career spanning forty years and should have been cheerful, but the simple ceremony in "Main Navy" was, instead, solemn and tense. The retiring CNO, Admiral Charles F. Hughes, was correct but abrupt. Pratt remembered later that following the change of command, Hughes "told me I would find the Secretary [of the Navy] in the office, and left the room without further demonstration."[1] From this comment many historians have concluded that Hughes, bereft of dignity, refused to shake the hand of the new CNO.

This may or may not have been the case, but it is a certainty that Hughes had come to dislike and distrust Pratt, despite their friendship of nearly half a century and their common home state, Maine. In this distrust, Hughes joined many others both in the service and in civilian life who believed that Pratt did not have the navy's best interests at heart. They saw him as the unprotesting agent of an administration, headed by an avowed pacifist, that was antipathetic to the navy. To Pratt's detractors, his lack of sympathy with their views was tantamount to treason.

In retrospect, however, Pratt's independence from the trends of prevailing naval opinion emerges as his greatest strength. Instead of adding but another voice to the chorus of navalist complainers, he contributed to the formation of military policy a keen perception of the issues of national and international defense. This broad perspective allowed him to sympathize with interests beyond those of his own institution and it was this breadth of vision that, in fact, led many of his colleagues to question his fundamental loyalty to the service.

Above all, then, Pratt was his own man. Although in his love of the sea and his faith in the primacy of battleships he was a typical naval officer of the early-twentieth century, at the core, he was atypical. "I have never been any man's man," he wrote in 1939, and that might as well have been his motto. He was intensely loyal to his country and to the navy, but he was unwilling to accept traditional doctrine as dogma.[2]

Like many naval officers of his generation, William Veazie Pratt was born into a family with a nautical heritage. Both his father, Nichols Pratt, and his maternal grandfather, William G. Veazie, commanded merchantmen in the China trade. Indeed, on the day William was born, 28 February 1869, his father was at sea off the China coast. In 1871, when William was less than two years old, Nichols Pratt decided that his future was in China and he moved his family to Shanghai, the teeming center of Western influence in the Orient. Not until six years later did William return to America in order to attend elementary school. His parents, however, remained in China and from the age of eight until he entered the Naval Academy at sixteen, young Pratt was reared by his maternal grandmother, Charlotte Hutchings Veazie. From her he learned discipline and a Congregationalist doctrine that he did not take very seriously, while from private and public schools he learned Latin and arithmetic.

Pratt's mother planned for him to go to the Massachusetts Institute of Technology, a curious choice since arithmetic was his particular bête noire, and it was apparently a chance suggestion from a visiting naval officer that led him to inquire about Annapolis. Whatever the reason, he secured an appointment as "first alternate," and was accepted when the principal failed the spelling portion of the entrance examination.

At the academy, Pratt compiled a satisfactory academic record and a reputation as a good baseball player. Throughout his life, he was an avid sports fan, and he later made many serious attempts to recruit good ball players for his ships' teams. But Pratt also compiled far more than his fair share of demerits. He was not a stickler for the details of dress or conduct—neither then nor later—and he was fond of illicit after-hours poker games.

Following graduation with the class of 1889, Ensign Pratt's first regular tour of sea duty was in the *Petrel,* a 900-ton gunboat on the Asiatic Station. There were at least two distinct advantages in this assignment: first, with such a small wardroom, he had ample opportunities to exercise responsibility; and, second, he could spend time with his father who was still piloting steamships on the Yangtze. After four years in Asian waters, Pratt returned to the Naval Academy as an instructor in mathematics. For the next fifteen years, his tours in "the Yard" were interspersed with tours at sea, as he moved up the promotion ladder from ensign to commander. Throughout those years he continued to combine thoroughness and dependability in his professional duties with a certain casualness in regard to the fine points of service etiquette. He was prone to bypass established procedure and invent new ways of accomplishing assigned tasks. As a young lieutenant, for example, he used a whistle to issue orders to the deck crew when at sea, where strong winds would carry off shouted commands. Chided for his unorthodox procedures, he imprudently responded: "But she went about didn't she?" Even then, he reported, "I was not a Department favorite."[3] Despite his iconoclastic tendencies, his fitness reports reflected consistently superior performance.

Pratt's first year as a student at the Naval War College proved to be a major turning point in his career. There, Professor William McCarty Little, an instructor in war-gaming, prodded him to seek original answers to old questions. "All my life," Pratt wrote, "I had been groping for an answer knowing there was one, but not knowing where to find it." Little encouraged his student to grapple with complex situations of political as well as naval significance and to appreciate the intimacy between international politics and naval affairs. "Ultimately," Pratt noted, "and little by little, some of the answers I had been seeking came to me, not at sea, but as a student at the Naval War College." His experience at Newport reinforced his growing distrust of "fixed, preconceived notions."[4]

Following his course at the War College, Pratt was sent, in 1913, to the staff of the destroyer commander, Rear Admiral William Sowden Sims, another officer whose nonconformity was notable. Perhaps because of their similar temperaments, they enjoyed one another and worked well together. Pratt was disappointed when he was denied permission to go to London with Sims after the United States entered the Great War in 1917. Instead, Pratt returned to Washington as the assistant chief of naval operations. "I entered upon my work without a gray hair on my head or a nerve in my body," he wrote, and "left with both . . . and with a resolve never to enter that cursed hole again."[5] He described his tenure as assistant to Admiral William S. Benson, the raspy wartime CNO, as a "nightmare" and recorded his elation in January 1919 when the war was won and he was "free, free to go to sea."[6]

Throughout his career, Pratt preferred service at sea to duty ashore. Nevertheless, after an altogether-too-brief tour in command of the battleship *New York,* which was followed by his promotion to flag rank, and an equally satisfying tour as commander of the Destroyer Flotilla, Pacific Fleet, he received orders to report to Washington to serve as a member of the General Board. A residual legatee of the struggle for a naval general staff, the board had as its primary function the responsibility to advise the secretary of the navy on naval policy, particularly the shipbuilding program. For a new selectee for flag rank, membership on the prestigious panel would bring high visibility, and Pratt wrote to his wife that he welcomed the opportunity and his increased influence over the essentials of naval policy.[7]

Pratt's being ordered to the General Board cast him into the midst of a conflict that was to define the character of naval politics for the next two decades. In the hope of limiting the huge expenditures for battleship construction that had been authorized in 1916, President Warren G. Harding had invited the powers, some great and some small, to Washington in the waning days of 1921 to discuss naval arms limitation. In preparing an American position for the upcoming conference, most members of the General Board insisted that completion of the 1916 building program was essential. Some believed that the security of the United States required a naval force equal to the combined strength of the Anglo-Japanese Alliance and superiority over the navy of Japan by a margin of at least two to one. Allied to these positions was the contention that any agreement that left the Philippines and Guam unfortified would be unacceptable to the navy.[8]

Most congressmen considered these demands excessive. Few men in Congress were so naive as to believe that the Allied victory had actually made the world "safe for democracy," and a number of them recognized that America's rejection of the Versailles Treaty meant that, in a crisis, the United States would have to rely on its own means of defense rather than on collective security. Nevertheless, they believed that the General Board's insistence that the entire prewar shipbuilding program be completed was based on parochial considerations rather than on national interest. Moreover, the public mood demanded cutbacks, not continued expenditures.

Studying these issues, Pratt found his own views to be closer to those of the Republican administration than to those of the General Board on which he served. While he shared his colleagues' concern over Japan's ambitions in the Pacific and East Asia, he did not agree with their contention that Britain posed a threat to the United States. He argued that continued Anglo-American cooperation was the key not only to a successful conference on naval armament, but also to a lasting peace. Whereas the General Board insisted that the U. S. Navy retain nearly one million tons of battleships, Pratt concluded that total tonnage meant less than the *ratio* of tonnage among the British, Japanese, and American navies. In the event, Secretary of State Charles Evans Hughes forced the naval powers to accept a limit of 525,000 battleship tons for Britain and the United States, and 315,000 tons for Japan—the famous 5:5:3 ratio. This was written into the Five Power Treaty along with a provision that prohibited the fortification of Guam and the Philippines, a quid pro quo for Japanese acquiescence to naval inferiority.[9]

Most members of the General Board were disappointed, even outraged, by the terms of the Five Power Treaty, but Pratt defended them in a series of articles. To "naval men" he addressed an essay in the *U. S. Naval Institute Proceedings* in which he argued that the development of a practical naval policy required more than consideration of the needs of the navy: international political relations should not be ignored, and domestic public opinion could not be ignored. Nevertheless, wrote Pratt, the opponents of the Five Power Treaty visualized conditions as they believed they ought to be rather than as they were. The ambitious proposals of the navalists to complete the 1916 building program were based on what they perceived to be the needs of the *navy* and not necessarily on the needs of the *nation.* While admitting that it was natural for naval officers to adopt this position, Pratt dismissed it as a "strictly technical viewpoint." He claimed that the statesmen who drafted the treaty based their agreement "on a just and discerning estimate of all conditions."[10]

Pratt's view of the Washington agreements was pragmatic. He insisted that the issue was not disarmament, but naval limitation. It is significant that he criticized not only the "technicians" in the Navy Department, but also civilian idealists who called for complete disarmament. In an article published in the more liberal *North American Review,* he directed his comments to this other group of extremists: he pleaded for an American navy capable of sustaining the balance of power that had been established in the Pacific at the Washington Conference. If the United States failed to make an effort to maintain the ratios contained in the Five Power Treaty, he warned, it would "stultify the purposes which the conference strove to achieve."[11] Thus, though he denied the practicality of complete disarmament, Pratt insisted that naval arms limitation could be "a practical, progressive way of handling the problem of armaments in the endeavor to eliminate the competitive and aggressive features and to reduce the financial burdens which huge armaments entail."[12] In a laconic ending to his *Proceedings* article, he guessed that few people in the navy would accept his conclusions. He was right, and his position on this issue was the single most important decision of his career.

Pratt's defense of the Five Power Treaty alienated him from many of his fellow officers, and he found it difficult to live down this "heresy." His exemplary service record in the 1920s helped as he served as a battleship division commander, president of the Naval War College, and Commander, Battleship Divisions, Pacific, and worked his way up the fleet ladder. In each of these commands, he attempted to introduce some reform or non-traditional methodology. As president of the Naval War College, for example, he required the officer-students to spend less time re-fighting the Battle of Jutland on wooden table tops and more in studying logistics, coordinated air-sea operations, and amphibious landings. Though the experience of war later proved such courses invaluable, they were unpopular with the students, and after Pratt left the college, his successors dropped them from the curriculum.

Despite his independent spirit, or perhaps because of it, in 1929 William Veazie Pratt achieved a long-desired goal, when he reached the highest fleet command available to an American naval officer, commander in chief of the U. S. Fleet. The secret of his professional success was a simple one. He was, in the words of Rear Admiral Josiah S. McKean, "A very good sailor man."[13] Though he was remembered as a supporter of naval-arms limitation, he was also known as a superb shiphandler and an effective leader and, for those qualities, he was much admired by his men as well as by his fellow officers.

On 16 August 1929, President Herbert Hoover sent Pratt a message to come to the White House on the next afternoon to discuss American policy on naval-arms limitation. At this meeting, Hoover asked him to join the U. S. delegation to the London Naval Disarmament Conference, which was to open the following year and where the sea powers would attempt to extend the ratios of the Five Power Treaty to include auxiliary warships. The attempt to do this at the Geneva Conference in 1927 failed because of the obstructionism of the "technical advisers," and Hoover hoped Pratt's moderate influence would prevent a repetition of this in London. In effect, the president wanted Pratt to counterbalance the conservative views of Admiral Hilary P. Jones.[14]

The assignment annoyed Pratt, who hoped to erase from the memories of his naval colleagues "some of the stigma attached to being on the Washington Conference."[15] Nevertheless, he accepted it at the personal request of the president.

The specific point of disagreement at Geneva in 1927 and in London three years later was the number of 10,000-ton cruisers the United States needed. These vessels were called "treaty cruisers" because they were the largest ships that escaped being typed as battleships under the guidelines established in Washington in 1922. It was the opinion of the General Board that, given the vastness of the Pacific Ocean, the United States needed a minimum of twenty-one of these long-legged scouts to protect American interests in the Far East. In the Cruiser Act of February 1929, Congress had authorized the construction of fifteen "treaty cruisers" which, when completed, would give the United States a total of twenty-three. The British were disturbed by these developments. With dozens of naval bases scattered over the globe, they preferred to rely on 4,000–5,000-ton cruisers, and Prime Minister Ramsay MacDonald had already announced that Britain would never acquiesce in an agreement that allowed the United States as many large cruisers as the General Board demanded.

Faced with this impasse, the chairman of the American delegation, Secretary of State Henry L. Stimson, called the delegation together in London in February. He asked the American admirals present, in particular Pratt and Jones, how many of these ships the navy would have to have to meet its commitments. Jones insisted that the General Board's figure was the absolute minimum, but Pratt conceded that eighteen large cruisers plus five small ones would be sufficient.[16]

With the proposal to accept a limit of eighteen, the impasse was broken. Once again, however, Pratt had placed himself on the opposite side of official naval thinking. Several of the more obdurate navalists accused him of treachery for abandoning the General Board's position on the cruiser issue. On close examination, however, it is clear that his position reflected a more realistic analysis of the balance of power in the Pacific than did the views of Jones and most members of the General Board. Whereas they continued to view Britain, as well as Japan, as a potential enemy, Pratt recognized that Anglo-American cooperation was much more likely than Anglo-American conflict, and was also more desirable. He believed that it would be foolish to destroy all chances for a naval agreement because of a dispute between the United States and Great Britain. Such an event would play into the hands of Japanese militarists, the only group that could gain from a split between the Western nations.

When Pratt returned to the United States after the London conference, he reported to Admiral Hughes, the CNO. "The reception," Pratt noted, "was not cordial," but perhaps to be expected. Not only did Hughes believe that he had been betrayed, but the two men had exchanged unfriendly words before. In October 1929, Pratt had approached Hughes on the subject of implementing a new organization in the battle fleet. Pratt recalled:

> To this request of mine a flat refusal was given. It was inferred, or so I thought, that I wished to put over some of my own personal ideas and this was not to be allowed. I lost my patience then, and replied to this effect. "Very well, then, if this is the case, my hat is in the ring. I will relieve you when your term of office expires." I then went out and put in a personal request that my name be considered when the office of CNO was vacated.[17]

Hoover and Secretary of the Navy Charles F. Adams III were happy with Pratt's request, and knowledgeable naval officers expected Pratt to relieve Hughes in October 1930. Indeed, the *Army and Navy Journal* referred to his elevation to CNO as a "foregone conclusion" as early as November 1929. But Pratt's orders came sooner than anyone expected, because Hughes's health deteriorated and in September 1930 he asked to be relieved. His request was motivated by more than poor health, however. It had become clear that the CNO would soon be called upon to preside over massive cutbacks in the navy's operating budget. "In order that authority . . . accompany responsibility," Hughes considered it most fitting that Pratt, the champion of arms limitation, assume the burden of that thankless task.[18] It is not surprising, then, that Hughes did not want to prolong the simple change-of-command ceremony by offering his successor any fond wishes for success.

The new chief of naval operations was a handsome man. His thinning hair was snow-white and only a touch of gray in his small, brush moustache kept it from being white as well. His demeanor, however, spoiled what could have been a distinguished appearance. He was extremely casual about his attire: he frequently wore a rumpled uniform, and an ever-present cigarette or pipe dropped ashes on his lap or about his feet while he worked or talked. His tie was seldom "two-blocked" and he often discarded it altogether when he was in the office. Moreover, what was good for the old man was good for the sailors as well. "I dislike salutes and side boys," he wrote, "and never cared much at what angle Jackie wore his white hat . . . ."[19] To Pratt, appearances were simply not as important as results. He worked hard and expected others to do the same. Once, when he was assistant CNO, as he rushed from one office to another in his working "uniform"—no coat or tie—he accidentally bumped into a typist, nearly knocking her off her feet. "I looked so disheveled," he wrote, "that turning to a companion she said 'If that carpenter bumps into me again I will tell him where he gets off'."[20]

As CNO, Pratt encouraged his subordinates to handle routine administrative questions at the lowest possible level. Only papers that required the personal attention of the chief of naval operations were to come to his desk. He encouraged the bureau chiefs, as the experts in their own particular areas, to make the daily decisions on all but questions of broad policy.

Partly because he promised them maximum independence, the bureau chiefs welcomed Pratt as the CNO. He got along particularly well with the chief of the Bureau of Aeronautics, Rear Admiral William A. Moffett, an old friend. Like Pratt, Moffett was an innovator, and a maverick. He was a champion of naval aviation in general, and of lighter-than-air craft in particular. His interest in the latter was his undoing, for he was killed in the crash of the dirigible *Akron,* one of a series of tragic accidents that led the navy to discontinue the construction of dirigibles, much to Pratt's regret. Ironically, Pratt might have been a victim of that crash himself. Before Moffett left on the ill-fated flight of the *Akron,* he dropped by Pratt's office to invite him along, but the CNO begged off because of a heavy work load. Pratt recalled that he was probably "the last person in Washington to see Moffett alive."[21]

Another close friend during Pratt's term as CNO was Secretary Adams, whom Pratt affectionately described as a "seaman at heart."

> Sometimes coming into his office to discuss the work of the day, he would look up with a merry twinkle in his eye and ask, "How is the climate down in Maine this morning?" It usually brought the retort, "It is better than that of Boston anyway." Who couldn't work with a man like that?[22]

But not all of Pratt's professional relationships were as friendly as these. If the bureau chiefs found him tolerant and thus tolerable, most members of the General Board viewed him as an ideological enemy because, regardless of his professional competence and administrative efficiency, he was, after all, the man who had twice "sold out" the navy at naval-arms limitation conferences. To them, Pratt's support of those policies smacked of disloyalty. At least Hoover had the excuse of ignorance, but Pratt, they believed, should have known better. His elevation to CNO was especially disturbing because in September 1930 the navy's prospects were as grim as they had been at any time since the naval retrenchment following the Civil War.

The vast majority of the navy's senior officers believed that the Washington and London treaties had weakened the navy's ability to protect American interests in the Pacific. Moreover, the nation was presided over by a chief executive who was a firm believer in disarmament and who distrusted military force. As if these burdens were not enough, the nation was just entering the critical phase of what was only then coming to be recognized as the Great Depression. The advocates of naval expansion could only wring their hands in despair that the Japanese threat was apparently to go unanswered.

The General Board's opposition to Pratt's support of Hoover's naval policy was not based solely on parochialism for, tasked with the heavy responsibility of national defense, they tended to base their calculations on "worst case" analyses. That is, they calculated principally on the basis of a potential enemy's *capabilities,* rather than his intentions. The latter, they argued, could change any time with national mood or a shift in cabinets. For this reason, the General Board continued in the late 1920s to consider the possibility of a war with Great Britain. By contrast, Pratt relied more heavily on analyses of national *intentions* and came to the not illogical conclusion that a war between the United States and Great Britain was virtually impossible. He was not even convinced of the inevitability of a naval war with Japan. While many naval officers harped on the Japanese threat in order to increase naval appropriations from Congress, Pratt always refused to do so. In fact, he often warned that constant predictions of war with Japan could eventually become self-fulfilling prophecies.[23] Given these differences in viewpoint, it was not long before the CNO and the General Board clashed on one of several issues.

The first open conflict concerned the role of the board itself. Though Pratt did not want to eliminate it, he did feel that its influence had grown to the point where, instead of advising, it had come close to making policy. He believed that the board's role was to provide the civilian authorities with advice that reflected the professional expertise of its members. Ideally, this advice should be given in the form of alternatives—perhaps majority and minority reports, with the arguments of each side presented fully, so that the administration could reach a sound decision. Traditionally, however, the General Board submitted its findings in such a way as to suggest unanimity among its members. Its reports began with the words: "The Board finds . . . . " Moreover, the fact that the CNO was a member of the board added the prestige of his office to these reports. Such unanimity could be intimidating to a congressional committee, and this is, no doubt, what many board members wanted.

This hope Pratt soon dashed. One of his first official acts was to resign from the board. He explained that this move was designed to provide the secretary of the navy with at least two sources of independent advice—the board's and his own—but the members of the board interpreted it as an attempt to demean the board and weaken its influence. The fact that Pratt's "independent advice" would undoubtedly often be contrary to the board's recommendations added to their distress.[24]

The second issue that divided Pratt and the General Board concerned the relationship of the Washington and London treaties to the maintenance of a "treaty fleet." The board saw the levels established in London as minimum requirements. In fact, it was not sure that those levels were adequate even for national security; the 180,000 tons of heavy cruisers allowed, for example, were less than the board claimed as a safe minimum. But, having been forced to accept those limits, board members believed that the government now had a moral obligation to initiate legislation to build up to treaty limits, and it developed a fifteen-year program designed to do exactly that.

President Hoover and the Republican majority in Congress, however, viewed the agreements reached in London as *maximum* limits up to which nations were allowed to build. As one congressman put it: "It is a limitation beyond which we must not go; but whether we should go so far depends on the exigencies of the situation year after year."[25] Hoover, in particular, thought that if the United States exercised its option and built its navy up to treaty limits quickly, other nations would feel compelled to follow suit. If, on the other hand, America demonstrated restraint, the British and Japanese might do the same.

The condition of the U. S. fleet in 1930 was not as desperate as many naval expansionists claimed. The Battle Fleet consisted of fifteen battleships, two new aircraft carriers plus the converted *Langley,* and two heavy cruisers. The battleships represented 460,000 tons, the upper limit for this class allowed by the London treaty. The three carriers, plus the *Ranger* which was under construction, gave the fleet 80,200 of the 135,000 tons allowed for this type under the Five Power Treaty. Finally, although only two heavy cruisers were operational, thirteen more were in various stages of construction and, when they were completed, the country would have 150,000 of an allowed maximum of 180,000 tons. The last three heavy cruisers, needed to reach the treaty limits, could not be laid down until 1933, 1934, and 1935 because of an agreement with the Japanese, a provision they had insisted upon as the price for their signing the London agreement. In short, in 1930 the United States had in operation or under construction ships that would give the fleet the maximum tonnage for all major combatants except carriers. But, would Congress appropriate the funds necessary to complete the ships under construction and to build the new carriers?

The Hoover administration supported a bill introduced in the House by Republican Congressman Frederick A. Britten of Illinois, to appropriate $50 million for the construction of one carrier, three light cruisers, continuation of the thirteen heavy cruisers, and six submarines. It was an impressive request coming from an administration that was supposed to be anti-navy. But Congress was not receptive. The recent signing of the London Treaty led many congressmen to expect cutbacks, not more expenditures. As one of them put it: "It would be a perversion of the magnificent work of President Hoover and Prime Minister MacDonald to transform a limitations agreement into a mandate for expansion programs."[26] Hoover did not strongly support Britten's bill and it died in committee.

Many naval officers felt that Hoover had betrayed them. They had agreed, albeit reluctantly, to severe limits on the fleet, and now the Congress appeared unwilling to build up even to those limits. Professor Gerald Wheeler, Pratt's biographer, has suggested that Pratt fully expected the administration to support naval expansion up to the authorized levels. Certainly Pratt sympathized with those who argued that America's security, as well as her position at future naval-arms conferences, would be enhanced by the adoption of a naval construction program designed to bring the U. S. Navy to treaty levels immediately, but he was also realistic enough to realize that the mood of the people, and of the Congress, made such an event unlikely. Moreover, he supported the administration in London not because of any implicit "deal" or expectation of reciprocity by President Hoover, but because he believed that Anglo-American amity was worth giving up American "rights" to three heavy cruisers. Though disappointed by the failure of the Britten bill, he did not charge betrayal, but instead set to work outlining long-range policies necessary to maintain fleet efficiency with reduced appropriations. In this, as in most things, Pratt's approach was pragmatic: he would support construction programs that had a chance of passing, but he would not jeopardize the navy's credibility by demanding the impossible.[27]

Pratt's first priority was to improve the Battle Force. As did most senior naval officers of his generation, he persisted in viewing the battleship as the queen of war. As late as 1939, he was still arguing strongly for the construction of more battleships. Undoubtedly, much of his loyality to the dreadnought derived from his long experience as a battleship commander. Indeed, he seems to have been guilty of a certain amount of parochialism himself on this issue. The battleship fleet was already at maximum limits in the fall of 1930, but he wanted to modernize the old ships. His support of the modernization program was unrelenting and the 1931 budget called for an expenditure of nearly $7 million to overhaul the *Pennsylvania* and the *Arizona*. Overhauls of this sort would continue through 1936—the expiration date of the London Treaty.

Of almost equal concern to the CNO was new carrier construction. The ancient *Langley* could no longer be considered a fighting unit of the fleet, and carriers were the only type of ship for which the United States had not already embarked on a program designed to attain treaty levels. Aviators such as Admirals Harry E. Yarnell and William A. Moffett, thrilled by the performance characteristics of the two 33,000-ton carriers *Lexington* and *Saratoga,* urged that the administration ask for two more large, fast carriers to use up the 55,000 tons "available" under the treaty system. Instead of many smaller carriers like the *Ranger,* they wanted a few large combatants, and were willing to give up a battery of 5- or 8-inch guns in favor of increased speed. To an old battleship captain like Admiral Pratt, this was a foreign concept. He suggested the possibility of raising the tonnage of each carrier in order to allow a battery of 8-inch guns to be included. In the end, however, he allowed the aviators to determine the specifications, and the next generation of carriers went to sea without a heavy battery. Pratt also urged the construction of two new carriers at 20,000 tons, and one at 14,500—a sister ship to the *Ranger*. His plan seemed to be based on the desirability of having two 33,000-ton ships, two at 20,000, and two at 14,500, for a total of 135,000 tons—the maximum limit allotted the United States by the London Treaty. Pratt's support was important, but in this case it was not sufficient to persuade Congress to adopt the plan immediately, and another decade passed before the "fast carriers" put to sea.[28]

Congressional support was also crucial if the thirteen heavy cruisers were to be completed. Though work on these 8-inch-gun ships continued throughout Pratt's term as CNO, it did so at a very slow rate, mainly because of limited funding. This was in marked contrast to Japan's frenetic efforts to expand its cruiser fleet. Indeed, although on paper the United States held an advantage over Japan by a ratio of 10:7, by 1932 the actual balance of forces in the Pacific was 10:7 in Japan's favor, as far as heavy cruisers were concerned.

Limited funding led Pratt to adopt drastic economy measures. In the late fall of 1930, he announced a "reorganization" of the fleet. He planned to establish "type commands" to facilitate training—it was this proposal that led to his tiff with Admiral Hughes a year earlier. But his announced reorganization involved more than that; it also called for reducing the authorized enlisted total by some 4,800 men and decommissioning one battleship, sixteen destroyers, twenty-five submarines, and five miscellaneous light vessels. These reductions, Pratt explained, were made necessary by the provisions of the London Treaty.

To the members of the General Board the reorganization was scandalous. Admiral Hughes had warned in his last annual report that the then-authorized enlisted total was inadequate.[29] Now Pratt was calling for reductions below those "inadequate" numbers. Clearly the navy's ability to man its ships would be affected. One solution was to keep all ships on active duty with smaller crews, but Pratt proposed a "rotating reserve" system in which one-third of the fleet would be kept at pierside with maintenance crews only. That would mean fewer active battleship commands, which, of course, was unpopular.

The Great Depression and Hoover's inability to deal with it added to Admiral Pratt's difficulties in 1931. Frustrated, Hoover sought to leave the world with a heritage of peace, and was moving away from attempts to achieve mutual and balanced arms reductions toward a policy labeled by his opponents "disarmament by example." Indeed, rumors circulated in Washington that he planned to impose a total "holiday" on all American warship construction. This was not a policy that Pratt could support, and the rumors led the CNO to address to the secretary of the navy an official and confidential memorandum in which he clearly stated his opposition to such a move.

The very term *holiday* bothered Pratt. It implied a complete cessation of effort and that, he maintained, was simply not practical. He admitted that it was not possible to build the navy up to treaty levels by 1935—a claim that the General Board would hotly contest—but he contended that it was also not possible to halt construction altogether. What the nation needed, he suggested, was "A steady even program spread out over a greater number of years. . . ." To stop construction now would not only make the London Treaty a sham, but would deprive the navy of sufficient hulls for training. Thus, once again the CNO found himself arguing against both the belligerent navalism of the General Board and the compassionate, if unrealistic, idealism of the administration. He summed up his own views in his memorandum to the secretary, when he wrote: "The man of practical common sense tries not to be carried away by any extremist views, but to walk the road which lies somewhere between the extreme navalist point of view and that of the pacifist." According to Pratt the nation should:

> a) Continue building on all ships which have been authorized, or are under construction, or for which contracts have been let. [This would include the thirteen heavy cruisers.]
>
> b) Continue the modernization of battleships . . . .
>
> c) Lay down three new aircraft carriers . . . .
>
> d) Lay down each year not more than seven new destroyers . . . .
>
> e) Lay down each year not more than three submarines . . . .

Pratt's forthright remonstrance was only one of a host of complaints from the navy. Even the *Army and Navy Journal* had its say: it argued that the president's proposal was the product of "abysmal ignorance" about the navy. Stung by the accusation, Hoover appointed a committee to look into the charge, of which, naturally, he was exonerated. However, there was widespread suspicion that Pratt had cooperated with the committee and widespread belief that, secretly, he favored the idea of a building holiday.[30]

Despite his opposition to a "stop-now" naval program, Pratt could do little to stem continued reductions in funds. During his years as CNO, naval appropriations declined from a high of $403 million in fiscal 1931 to a low of $333 million in fiscal 1933. Though the decline in real dollars, based on the price index, was less than 3 per cent, the smaller appropriations had an impact on the navy's ability to maintain a high state of efficiency. Pratt's reorganization of the fleet, which he implemented in 1931, helped stretch those meager funds, but the result was still what many naval officers had feared, a smaller Battle Fleet. The most serious result of the economic cutbacks was the lack of funding for new aircraft carriers. Most of the money that was available went into the modernization of the battleships which, for Pratt, and for the General Board, had first priority. The result of the lack of funds was that as early as 1931 the navy's official "Estimate of the Situation" concluded that Plan Orange could not be executed with any real hope of success and that this was "due to failure to initiate and carry on a well-balanced program of new construction."[31]

To remedy the situation, Congressman Carl Vinson, of the House Naval Affairs Committee, introduced a bill in January 1932 to appropriate $616 million for naval expansion, but the House failed to act on it. As noted by historian Ernest Andrade: "During the last months of the Hoover Administration, the navy's fortunes sank to their lowest point in this century."[32] By 1933 Pratt was regularly protesting in public and in private that the fleet had been dangerously weakened. In his annual report for that year, he claimed that maintenance of the forces afloat had been cut to the lowest point consistent with national security, and that it was difficult to see where further cuts could be made without impairing the navy's efficiency. In private letters and newspaper articles, he described the navy's condition as "appalling," especially in the Pacific. In January, he claimed that the nation had to begin to build immediately or it would be too late. His growing concern was underlined by a mounting crisis in the Far East.[33]

Besides naval-arms limitation, the most serious foreign-policy issue that arose during Pratt's tenure concerned the emerging Sino-Japanese War. The crisis began in September of 1931, when the Japanese army used an explosion at Mukden, on the Manchurian railway, as a pretext for occupying the entire province. American reaction to this blatant aggression was mixed. The American people, strongly influenced by sympathetic portrayals of honest Chinese peasants in Pearl Buck's *The Good Earth*, published that year, and by the cherished myth of the richness of the China market, were heavily pro-Chinese. Others, such as Rear Admiral Montgomery M. Taylor, commander of the U. S.

Asiatic Squadron, thought that the anarchic Chinese would be better off under Japanese rule. Pratt's own view was characteristically both moderate and pragmatic. He had no exalted dreams of Sino-American partnership, but neither did he support Taylor's view that the Chinese deserved to be defeated because of their weakness and lack of organization.

President Hoover and his secretary of state, Henry L. Stimson, hoped to stop Japanese aggression but not at the risk of American military or naval involvement. Instead, they relied on the force of moral sanctions. They first invoked the Nine Power Treaty under which the signatory nations, including Japan, pledged to respect the territorial integrity of China. But, at the same time, the administration carefully avoided the appearance of threatening to use force and Stimson ordered all American warships to keep clear of the area, in spite of the fact that a long-planned and routine visit was imminent.

Despite the military title of which he was so fond, Colonel Stimson clung firmly to the policies of moral sanctions. During an incident in Shanghai in January 1932, when Japanese brashness threatened to bring on a full-scale war, though he authorized Pratt to send the cruiser *Houston* to Shanghai, Stimson's principal hope for a solution to the crisis was not gunboat diplomacy, but "non-recognition," the doctrine that still bears his name. The presence of the *Houston* in Shanghai made some "face" for the United States, but she compared poorly to the Japanese naval force there: one carrier, four cruisers, seven destroyers, and several lighter ships. The *Houston,* after all, was not there to deter Japanese aggression, but to protect American lives and property.[34]

In mid-1932, Stimson finally became convinced that American protests to Japan might be taken seriously if a large American naval force were operating in the Pacific. The Scouting Force, consisting of a few old battleships, light cruisers, and several destroyers and submarines, was already in that ocean on a training cruise. Pratt, Secretary Adams, and Stimson all urged that the Scouting Force be retained on the West Coast. The official reason given for this decision was a desire to test facilities on the West Coast, but many in government and naval circles hoped that the Japanese would be impressed. Unfortunately, this demonstration of naval strength was either unconvincing or else the Japanese were determined to go ahead regardless, for they continued to consolidate their hold on Manchuria, ignored the subtle warning, and accepted Pratt's "official" explanation.[35]

Pratt's role in the Far Eastern crises of 1931 and 1932 was personal as well as professional. On the evening of 29 January, while he was hosting the Japanese ambassador and his naval aide at Admiral's House, he was called to the telephone. He was informed that Rear Admiral Shiozawa had landed a force of Japanese marines at Shanghai and a crisis of enormous proportions was about to break. Pratt returned to the dinner table and informed his guests. "Why don't you send Nomura down there?" he suggested. "He will clear things up." Pratt had known Admiral Kishisaburo Nomura since the Washington Conference and knew that he had the tact and diplomatic skill necessary to smooth over Shiozawa's precipitate action. Forty-eight hours later, Nomura was in Shanghai, pouring oil on troubled waters.[36]

Most historians characterize the American reaction to Japanese aggression in Manchuria and China as essentially fatuous. Reliance on "moral forces" was naive, they say, and realistic men should have known that bullies respect only strength. This view is compelling, especially considering the events that took place between 1941 and 1945. But in 1932, the Western World was impressed not by America's timidity, but by her forthright and open stand against aggression. Compared with British and French reactions to the crises in Manchuria and Shanghai, the American response seemed to verge on recklessness. Pratt's role throughout this period was an important one: he served as a conduit of information from Admiral Taylor to Secretary Adams on the situation in the Far East; he supported increases in American naval strength in the Pacific to underscore U. S. diplomatic efforts; and he encouraged the Japanese to send the moderate Admiral Nomura to Shanghai to forestall an even more serious crisis. Without vigorous support from the chief executive, neither Stimson nor Pratt could have done more than they did.[37]

If Pratt was not as alarmist as many of his naval colleagues, he was hardly naive. In an article published in 1933, he claimed that Americans were too willing to rely on paper agreements for their security. If other nations were determined to adopt "the policy of the mailed fist," he warned, solemn agreements were "but idle gestures, scraps of paper." His conclusion was that if the Japanese "do not accept our terms because they will not, or dare not, there is nothing for us to do except to meet them on their own terms."[38]

In November 1932, Franklin D. Roosevelt won election to the presidency with an overwhelming mandate from the country for change. Pratt had known FDR for many years. As assistant secretary of the navy, Roosevelt had visited the *New York* when Pratt was her skipper and the two men had enjoyed several long conversations. They found that they liked and respected one another.[39] But in November 1932, it seemed unlikely that their professional relationship would last much longer because, while Roosevelt was to be sworn in on 4 March, Pratt was to reach the mandatory retirement age of sixty-four in February.

Roosevelt's election and Pratt's impending retirement led to a great deal of speculation in the service about who Pratt's successor might be. The admiral naturally communicated with the president-elect; he recommended four men as possible successors. But Roosevelt apparently asked Pratt if he could not stay on the job himself, at least temporarily. Pratt was not opposed to the idea of staying on. Perhaps he hoped that Roosevelt would live up to his reputation in the service as a big-navy man and naval appropriations would soon increase. In any case, he answered favorably, noting that the sixty-four-year age limit did not apply to admirals and vice admirals. Ironically, therefore, and despite a minor flood of congratulatory letters and eulogistic editorials, Pratt's retirement orders were rescinded on 28th February, his sixty-fourth birthday and the day he was scheduled to retire.[40]

If Pratt did hope that his days of penny-pinching would be over after Roosevelt's inauguration, he was wrong. Despite the new president's affection for the navy, his first priority was the national economy, and initially at least, his solution was the conventional one of cutting expenses. Indeed, many of the "emergency employment measures" initiated by President Hoover were dropped by the Roosevelt administration. Appropriations for projects in the Bureau of Yards and Docks increased more than threefold between 1930 and 1933, but they dropped again in the first year of the Roosevelt administration and the new secretary of the navy, Claude A. Swanson, noted in his first *Annual Report:* "Because of reduction in funds available for general maintenance purposes, only the most essential repairs of public works were permitted during the first fiscal year." Funds were so scarce, in fact, that Pratt announced the implementation, at long last, of his rotating-reserve system in which all naval vessels would spend one-third of their time at pierside with only 60 per cent of their crews to maintain them. Fortunately for the navy, but unfortunately for Pratt's reputation in the service, the outcry against this scheme was so great that it was canceled.[41]

Admiral Pratt served four unhappy months under Franklin Roosevelt. His job remained what it had been under the Republicans: keeping the navy as efficient as possible with the smallest possible amount of funding. Ironically and sadly, it was only after he left office on 30 June 1933, that the first emergency employment measures involving new ship construction were approved by the administration.

Pratt retired amidst lukewarm good wishes from such periodicals as the *Army and Navy Journal.* In fact, he received little applause or gratitude from his own peers or from either of the administrations he served. He is not remembered in the annals of naval history as a great leader and the perception that he did little for the navy still lingers. Nevertheless, his role was a crucial one. For most of his three years as CNO, he was a pragmatist among extremists. Between the abiding faith of Herbert Hoover in the utility of moral sanctions and the complete lack of faith in them of most members of the General Board, Pratt was both physically and philosophically the man in the middle.

It would have been easy and the popular thing for Pratt to blame the parsimony of the civil government for the navy's decline in fortunes. He could simply have refused to accept responsibility for the nation's safety since the administration did not build the ships that the navy wanted. But he did not invoke the "needs of the service," nor was he merely the unwitting stooge of Hoover, Roosevelt, or anyone else. Instead, he studied the alternatives from a diplomatic as well as a technical point of view and came to his own conclusions. "The broadminded naval man," he wrote, "must learn to consider all sides of a question and to weigh and balance the evidence very carefully before he passes judgment."[42]

The admiral's own claim—that he had never been any man's man—was honest. He took an unpopular but realistic stand on naval-arms limitation at a time when career-oriented officers decried any limit on naval construction. He was politically experienced enough to realize that adding his own voice to the cacophony of naval protests would not bring about a change in the direction of the administration's policies; and, moreover, that doing so would be likely to alienate completely an administration already distrustful of naval and military professionals. Finally, Pratt was convinced that the psychology of Americans—and not just of Hoover—rebelled against the idea of large naval expenditures in peacetime. History convinced him, he wrote, that in a crisis, the vast latent potential of American strength could be roused to meet any challenge.[43] In the event, he was proved right. Meanwhile, he did what he could to keep the fleet at an efficient level with the meager operational budget he was allowed.

Given Hoover's views and congressional parsimony, the most enthusiastic supporter of naval expansion could have done little more that would not have polarized even further the schism between policy-makers and the naval officers. If Hoover was too sanguine in his trust in the rule of law and the efficacy of the Kellogg Pact and the Stimson Doctrine (which he always thought should have been called the Hoover Doctrine), the General Board was overly alarmist in its calls to "build now." Pratt kept the two sides from polarizing completely. He was aware of his role as middleman. In an article published near the end of his tour as CNO in April 1933, he wrote:

> The two extreme paths open to us in the march ahead of world progress are the way of arbitration, conciliation and compromise, and the path of war. Based on the history of the past the latter road seems inevitable and perhaps it is. Almost all military and practical men of this day feel somewhat this way about it. The idealist and the dreamer feel otherwise; they think that a ban can be placed on all war and that it will be effective. Not so until the moral and intellectual planes of the world are much higher than they are today. Yet these idealists are not wrong . . . . Neither is the extreme military reactionary entirely wrong. Each is right from his own point of view, but it is only the practical, constructive mind which can furnish adequate solutions in the step-by-step process of real world progress.[44]

Pratt had that "practical, constructive mind."

William Veazie Pratt enjoyed a long retirement. Despite FDR's adoption of naval construction as a partial cure for the economic crisis, Pratt grew increasingly distrustful of the chief executive. After Roosevelt announced that he planned to modify the Supreme Court, Pratt poured out to his wife his disgust in one of the bitterest letters he ever wrote: "I knew this man when he was Assistant Secretary of the Navy, and liked him though I never trusted him . . . today I see under this mask of geniality which he wears, not the great man, not the strong man, but the weak faith . . . petulant when he does not have his own way."[45]

Nevertheless, when the Japanese attacked Pearl Harbor, though Pratt was then nearly seventy-three years old, Roosevelt called him back into uniform and the former CNO again went to work. He studied methods for protecting convoys in the North Atlantic and strongly recommended both escort carriers and lighter-than-air craft to improve their air cover. Both suggestions were adopted. No doubt his old friend Moffett would have approved.

Pratt died on 25 November 1957 at the age of eighty-eight. His place in American naval history is not as distinguished as those of Farragut, Dewey, or Halsey, all of whom served at sea in naval wars and won great victories. But if Pratt's contribution was less flamboyant, it was at least equal in importance. A man who loved the sea, Pratt was destined to make his greatest contributions from behind a desk. He was denied the opportunity to serve in Europe in World War I because his job as assistant chief of naval operations kept him in Washington and he was denied active participation in World War II because he was too old for sea duty. But he could be justly proud of his accomplishments. In 1922 he wrote, "The true naval statesman, in peace, thinks less of what he will do in war, than of the part the navy should play to keep our country out of war."[46]

WILLIAM HARRISON STANDLEY

1 July 1933–1 January 1937

JOHN C. WALTER

Admiral William H. Standley became the sixth chief of naval operations on 1 July 1933. Born in Ukiah, California, on 18 November 1872, son of Jeremiah and Sarah Jane Standley, William enjoyed a typically Western adolescence and showed no inclination or aptitude for a naval career. His father, a sheriff of Mendocino County, had no contact with the navy, and it was only at the suggestion of a deputy sheriff that William's plan to attend the Naval Academy developed. At first, the suggestion was not particularly attractive to the boy. After all, he recalled, "I had never been to sea, taken practically no interest in naval life, and hardly knew where the Naval Academy was situated."[1] But in time he became fascinated with the idea, and persuaded his father to allow him to take the entrance examination. As it turned out, he was the top applicant and, in 1891, he entered the academy from the First District of California.

At the academy, Standley did not distinguish himself as a naval cadet. He later reflected that his preparatory schooling was not equal to that of the Eastern schools, nor did he know how to study. He had difficulty with the extensive assignments and his scholastic standing, which began low, had reached only midpoint by the time he graduated.[2] Later in life he remarked, "In retrospect I can't help but wonder as to the motive which actuated me in my urge to make satisfactory marks and remain in the Naval Academy."[3] Yet he found time to play football and in his senior year was captain of the baseball team. Because of his low grades and mediocre class standings, the likelihood of Standley obtaining a commission in the navy was slim, because at the time of his entry it was the law that only the first ten graduates could receive commissions. Luckily, Congress rewrote this legislation before his graduation and his entire class of 1895 was commissioned.

The young passed midshipman went to sea and was serving in the Far East during the Spanish-American War and the Philippine Insurrection. For leading scouting operations in the latter conflict, he was commended by the Navy Department.[4] Thereafter, he rose steadily in rank and, in 1915, was given his first command, the cruiser *Yorktown*, the ship in which he was serving at the time of the Philippine Insurection. Late in October 1916, Commander Standley returned to the Naval Academy as the officer in charge of buildings and grounds. Again, war hastened his career for, on 15 October 1917, he received the temporary rank of captain with his appointment as commandant of midshipmen. In this billet—as well as in others—Standley did well. The characteristics of leadership that he displayed had superseded his unremarkable academic background. He left the academy in July 1919 to assume command of the battleship *Virginia* and earned the rank of permanent captain within four months. The next year he attended the Naval War College, where the subject of his thesis was "Principles of Command," in which he urged an understanding of modern psychology as a means of improving leadership.[5]

On leaving the college in July 1921, Standley became assistant chief of staff to the Commander in Chief, Battle Fleet, and served in that position for two years. This was advantageous because the commander in chief was Admiral Edward W. Eberle, who was destined to be the next chief of naval operations. Indeed, by the time Eberle was appointed CNO in 1923, he was so impressed by Standley that he designated him assistant to Rear Admiral William R. Shoemaker, the director of the War Plans Division. When Shoemaker left the division, Standley moved into his billet and became, as well, head of the naval section of the Joint Army and Navy Planning Committee. This latter post enabled him to develop early and important contacts with officers from the War Department; it also gave him the opportunity to travel extensively through the fleet. "These interruptions in the ordinary tour of my shore duty," he noted, "brought me into contact with many high-ranking officers and eventually stood me in good stead when my name came before the Selection Board for [Rear] Admiral."[6]

But when Standley left Washington in February 1926, he was despondent about his chances of achieving flag rank and so, sentimentally, he asked for command of the ship that bore the name of his home state, the battleship *California*. His despondency was unfounded because Admiral Eberle and Admiral Robert E. Coontz, a former CNO and Standley's friend, sat on the selection board, and Standley's chances were bright. He assisted his own cause, however, when the *California* won the fleet gunnery trophy for 1926, and the president cited him and his ship for highest performance in the gunnery and engineering exercises later that year.[7] Thus, his selection as rear admiral in 1927 over several officers higher on the list was not entirely due to the influence of his former chiefs, but also to the very steady professional competence he had demonstrated since leaving the academy.

It was this competence that prompted the new CNO, Admiral Charles F. Hughes, to invite Standley to become his chief of staff. As fleet commander,

Hughes had seen Standley's performance when the latter commanded the *California*. Standley reported for duty in October 1927 and held the billet until May 1928 when he became Hughes's assistant chief of naval operations. He got along very well with Hughes and filled his unpublished memoirs with anecdotes illustrating the interest that Hughes took in him and the efforts of the CNO to further Standley's career.[8]

In September 1930, at the end of Hughes's term as CNO, Standley left Washington to take command of the destroyers of the Battle Force. While assistant chief of naval operations, he helped Rear Admiral Frank B. Upham to become chief of the Bureau of Navigation. In turn, Upham began to further Standley's career and in 1931 persuaded the CNO, Admiral William V. Pratt, to give Standley command of the cruisers in the Scouting Force, a billet that brought three-star rank. Standley was now one of the senior commanders in the fleet. When Pratt's obvious successor, Admiral Joel R. Pringle, fell ill in 1932, speculators began to mention Standley as the next CNO, and Upham confided to Standley that he had pressed for the appointment.[9] In early 1933, Pratt engineered Standley's selection as commander of the Battle Force so that he would have four-star rank, and then proposed to President Franklin D. Roosevelt that Standley come to Washington as his relief. As Pratt explained to Standley:

> As regards your coming in as my relief, you have my approval. There is just one point. In my mind there was a question between you and Hepburn, I suppose largely because Hepburn had been with me a good deal. I never pushed the matter actively, because I felt that the scales were so delicately balanced that I preferred to let the matter more or less adjust itself. When Hepburn decided he wanted to go abroad, I thought there was no more question but that you should have the appointment.

In the same letter, Pratt also noted,

> There was a purpose in having you made Commander-in-Chief of the Battle Force. For one thing, I wanted you to have had the Fleet and the rank of Admiral before you took over this job. I felt it would not hurt you in the matter of prestige and influence on the Hill and elsewhere.[10]

Standley became CNO in July 1933 with President Roosevelt's assurance that he favored increases in naval appropriations.[11] Standley apparently believed the president. This was understandable; in June Roosevelt had given the Navy Department $238 million from the appropriations for public works under the National Industrial Recovery Act. In addition, Congressman Carl Vinson, chairman of the House Naval Affairs Committee, planned, as he had done in previous years, to introduce legislation to build the American fleet up to "treaty strength." Also, Standley was under the impression that Roosevelt, during his tenure as assistant secretary of the navy in the Wilson administration, was a "big navy" man; consequently, he expected that FDR would encourage naval expansion.

Roosevelt created two immediate problems for Standley when he appointed a former senator, Claude A. Swanson, as secretary of the navy, and a distant relative, Harry Latrobe Roosevelt, as assistant secretary. An old man, Swanson was taken ill in early 1933 and was incapable of carrying out the full functions of his job for the rest of that year, part of 1934, and, again, virtually all of 1936.[12] As a result, the admiral frequently had to fill in as acting secretary when Harry Roosevelt was too busy. Standley's relations with the assistant secretary were poisonous; the two men simply did not get along. On the other hand, the president wanted to be his own secretary of the navy. Although his relations with Franklin D. Roosevelt were good, Standley was never on intimate terms with the president, as were many of his contemporaries. He recalled that he was persona grata at the White House but not a frequent guest and, during his tenure as CNO, he did not enjoy the kind of camaraderie with Roosevelt that his successors did.

Moreover, Standley failed to persuade the president to approve changes in the authority the chief of naval operations had over the activities of the bureaus. Roosevelt's consistent refusal to give the CNO command authority over the bureau chiefs stemmed from FDR's involvement in the origins of the office and the disputes in 1915 between Rear Admiral Bradley A. Fiske and Secretary Josephus Daniels, under whom he had served as assistant secretary. And, when Standley attempted to put across his plan in 1933, he failed in part because of the combined opposition of two vigorous and powerful bureau chiefs, Rear Admirals William D. Leahy and Ernest J. King.[13] Standley used the occasions when he served as acting secretary to advance his policies, but he suffered from the insecurity of knowing that he lacked the absolute confidence of an ambiguous and unpredictable president.

One of Standley's first priorities as CNO was to increase the number of naval personnel, sharply reduced during the cutbacks of the Hoover administration. FDR had given Standley assurances on this point before the admiral took his oath of office. In later years Standley claimed that the president subsequently promised an increase for 1934 of 10,000 men but that, when the CNO asked for funds for the increment, an official of the Bureau of the Budget just laughed at him because he had nothing in writing confirming the chief executive's pledge. In the event, Roosevelt granted an increase of 5,000 men for the navy and another 1,000 for the marines, but the episode alerted Standley to the ease with which the president made promises he later disowned.[14]

Standley and the chief of the Bureau of Navigation, Rear Admiral Leahy, paid close attention to other personnel matters in 1933 and 1934. For a year they lobbied Congress to restore the 15 per cent pay cut that had been imposed on naval officers and enlisted men by the Hoover administration. In 1934 the legislature restored all but 5 per cent of the reduction. Standley and Leahy successfully retrieved more than half of about 400 line and medical officers who had been detached from the Navy Department for duty with the Civilian

Conservation Corps.[15] Standley also persuaded Congress to authorize commissions for all the graduating midshipmen in the Naval Academy's class of 1934. This ended the brief practice, begun in 1933, of commissioning only the upper half of the class, which, in Standley's opinion, threatened in a short time to reduce dramatically the number of junior line officers.[16] On the other hand, Congress refused to reopen the Great Lakes and Newport naval training stations, and Standley could not get the increased number of line officers that would soon be needed to man the new ships.[17] Despite deficiencies in manpower, the CNO decided in late 1933 not to retire any ships in the fleet in anticipation of new construction.[18]

The major achievement of Standley's first year in office was the drafting of the Vinson-Trammell Act. Sponsored by Congressman Vinson and Senator Park Trammell, the bill aimed at expanding the navy toward "treaty limits." In Standley's view, his problem was to create a program of orderly naval expansion with the funds available through the National Industrial Recovery Act and annual appropriations for new construction. As he wrote to his friend, Admiral Edward C. Kalbfus: "I'm going to do my darnedest to put through a building program which will not only provide for our present obsolescence but will take care of future decay." The latter point, of course, was significant, since the American fleet was rapidly aging by comparison with the naval forces of other sea powers. The CNO considered this job so vital that he told Kalbfus, "If I do no more than put across this one, I will feel that my work here will not have been in vain."[19] He actively sought public support for the bill in Congress. In October 1933, in a radio address sponsored by the Navy League, he claimed that naval expansion "can only be accomplished by the adoption of a sound, businesslike annual program which will not only provide for replacement of ships as they become obsolete, but will keep our Navy modernized and up-to-date." Standley was not oblivious of the fact that, to many, one of the major attractions of naval expansion was that shipbuilding created jobs. "In addition" to the strategic benefits, he told his audience, "such a program will . . . have a very great stabilizing effect upon the economic and industrial activities of this country."[20]

The Vinson-Trammell Act was passed by Congress in 1934 and committed the government to the "construction of vessels and aircraft to bring the Navy to the prescribed treaty strength, and to replace ships as they become overage." The act, whose passage was impelled by Japan's seizure of Manchuria and by the fact that Japan had built her navy up to 95 per cent of treaty strength, as compared with 65 per cent for the American sea force, was the U. S. response to a renewal of the naval arms race among the Pacific powers.[21]

Although he signed the Vinson-Trammell Act, Roosevelt was more committed to naval arms limitation than he was to expansion, and he intended to contain an arms race by extending the lives of the Washington and London treaties. However, Japan had announced her demands for major changes in the terms of those treaties in the spring of 1933 and threatened to withdraw unless Britain and America made significant concessions. FDR hoped that some accommodation could be found, and, at Swanson's insistence, sent Standley to London in October 1934 for talks with the Japanese and British preparatory to a larger conference to be held the following year. Standley's instructions were to offer the Japanese compromises but to reject their demand for a "common upper limit" on fleet tonnage, which would destroy the ratio system. Roosevelt and Swanson hoped that Standley would put the Japanese admirals at ease and smooth the way for subsequent negotiations. Indeed, Standley and Admiral Isoroku Yamamoto, one of the Japanese delegates, got along well—so well, in fact, that Standley later speculated that this may have been why Tokyo withdrew the admiral from their negotiating team. The pace of the talks in London was too slow for Standley, but after a while he settled down and seemed to learn that in diplomacy doing nothing is sometimes useful. He found time to indulge his passion for golf, and enjoyed trips into the English countryside. However, because of the rigidity of all parties' positions, the negotiations stalled and Standley returned to Washington in December, in time to learn that the Japanese had denounced the treaties altogether.[22]

While Standley was in London he kept in touch with Leahy concerning the "admirals' slate" for 1935. The correspondence opened a recent wound. In July 1934 Standley witnessed the annual fleet exercises and came away with a high opinion of Admiral Joseph M. Reeves. Shortly thereafter, he prevailed upon Roosevelt to name Reeves as the next commander in chief of the U. S. Fleet. He regretted that action for the rest of his career. Reeves proved to be a very independent man who, after he took command of the fleet, resisted the CNO's authority. A year later, Standley's confidant, Rear Admiral Joseph K. Taussig, reported that the general feeling in the fleet was that Reeves was a poor commander who was openly critical of Standley and his policies. It is not surprising, then, that in November 1934, when Standley wrote Leahy from London, he agreed with most of his proposals for flag-rank billets but added: "I am not sure I would want to keep Reeves. He seems to be running wild with the schedules, etc., and his attitude towards War Plans [Division of the office of the CNO] was rather disturbing."[23] His objections notwithstanding, when Standley returned from London he learned that the president had kept Reeves as fleet commander for a second year of a tour that normally lasted twenty-four months.

In early 1935, Standley discovered that much of the enthusiasm for naval expansion had quieted down. Although the annual appropriation appeared to be quite generous, the CNO warned Admiral Upham that "last year we found naval appropriations and naval matters easy going. Everybody seemed to be in favor of a big Navy. Today, however, I sense a reaction, the extent of which it is impossible to perceive."[24] While Standley obtained authorization in 1935 for additional destroyers and submarines to balance the capital ships approved in 1934, he rediscovered that President Roosevelt was restraining the growth of the fleet more than was Congress. And manning remained a persistent concern for Standley. The fleet was manned only to the extent of 81 per cent of complement and each new ship created pressures on the inadequate manpower pool. However, Standley and Leahy finally persuaded Congress to restore the last 5 per cent of the pay cut made by the Hoover administration, to reinstate longevity credits, and to authorize reenlistment allowances for enlisted men, although the funds to implement the allowances were not made available immediately. These measures probably improved the overall caliber of the navy's manpower, which was high anyway because of the depression. But the reenlistment program was illustrative of New Deal naval policy: the seeds of growth that it contained were poorly tended by political leadership.

Throughout 1935 Standley was closely involved in the development of the positions that the United States would take at the upcoming London Naval Conference, which he attended. At the conference, the refusal of Britain and the United States to give Japan parity caused the Japanese delegation to withdraw early in the proceedings, and the rest of the meeting was devoted to an attempt to bring about an accord between the British and the Americans in the hope that eventually other naval powers would join. Standley took an active part in these talks and seems to have gotten along famously with Admiral Ernle Chatfield, the British naval representative.[25] Four days after the first round of conversations with the British delegation had taken place, Standley wrote to the assistant chief of naval operations, Admiral Taussig, and confessed: "We seem to have gotten all tangled up in the qualitative limitation details. I suppose everybody is like I am, and I feel like the old Indian when they asked him if he was lost, and he said, 'No, but the teepee is lost'."[26] The CNO felt that much of the talk was wasted because, with the Japanese gone, "Anything we may arrive at now is bound to be an acceptance of increase in armamemts."[27] Britain, the United States, and France signed the 1936 London Naval Treaty which extended the ration system but contained escape clauses that could be invoked in the likely event that Japan's shipbuilding exceeded limits set in the earlier pacts.

In 1935, the British had announced their intention to replace overage battleships and, in view of Japan's withdrawal from the treaty system, Standley wanted the United States to follow suit. When he returned from the London Conference in early 1936, the CNO, in his capacity as acting secretary of the navy, asked the president for authority to request two new battleships from Congress in 1937, none having been built since 1921. FDR agreed and Standley scheduled the *North Carolina* and the *Washington* to be laid down in the next year. Almost immediately, the General Board began to urge the construction of another pair of battleships for 1938, but, again as acting secretary, Standley vetoed the proposal. He warned the board that "the President has told us that he does not want us to talk about battleships until after the election" in November 1936.[28] More importantly, the General Board's plan represented the sort of haste that the CNO opposed on the grounds that it would be unwise to start building any more ships before there had been time to take advantage of any lessons in design and construction that could be learned from the first two. Such an approach would not be orderly and therefore was not part of Standley's program.[29] On the other hand, for 1938 Standley wanted to emphasize the construction of destroyers and submarines and to seek funds for a complete program of auxiliary-ship construction.

As chief of naval operations, Standley became reconciled to the fact that Roosevelt intended to make very personal choices for the key fleet billets. In fact, one of the appointments Roosevelt made while Standley was in London in late 1935 was the nomination of Admiral Arthur Japy Hepburn to relieve Admiral Reeves as commander in chief of the U. S. Fleet. The finality of the "slate" drawn up at that time and the inability of Standley, who opposed the selection of Hepburn, to change it were underscored when Swanson had Hepburn and other nominees confidentially informed of their new posts. "The slate for chiefs in the high command were what I expected," Standley despaired, "although . . . the Secretary knew full well in some respects my preferences were otherwise."[30] Typically, Standley congratulated Hepburn but told him that he would have preferred Admiral Harry E. Yarnell. In reply, Hepburn expressed his appreciation for the "gracious and square-dealing instinct which led you to express yourself." Hepburn also assured Standley that he could in the future expect much closer cooperation from the fleet than had been the case under Reeves.[31] This promise was kept.

Standley was also stung in June 1936 by a presidential order requiring all government departments to set up "substantial reserves" of funds already appropriated which would be liable for cuts. From an initial minor cut of $10 million, the amounts the navy had to reserve increased in the fall to a dramatic total of $75 million for 1937 and 1938. Standley protested to the Bureau of the Budget but it availed nothing and he was compelled to order a series of economies in fleet operations over the next two years to achieve the necessary savings. He began to worry that his carefully constructed policy of moderate expansion was on the verge of falling apart. Although funds for shipbuilding were adequate, more operating funds were needed if the new ships were to be integrated into the fleet in an orderly fashion.

Standley's frustration in 1936 was exacerbated by his failure to get his ideas on the organization of the fleet accepted by his colleagues. Hardly a new idea, the concept of "type" commands had been advocated in 1934 by King, then chief of the Bureau of Aeronautics. Simply stated, the idea was that ships and aircraft be organized by type and, for training, deploy in groups composed of various types of ships as well as groups of single-type ships. This approach Standley opposed on the grounds that it gave tactical responsibility for detailing task assignments to the fleet commander, whose time he felt would be better spent developing fleet strategies. Furthermore, in his opinion, the system would undermine the initiative and authority of the permanent force commanders and hurt task-group training.

Unfortunately, Admiral Hepburn, the new fleet commander, favored organization by type. This greatly annoyed Standley, and in September he told Taussig:

> I am endeavoring during the short time remaining to me to get this question of organization and command so straightened out that my successor will not have the difficulties which I have had, and so that the Fleet may have the cooperative rather than the controversial effort of both the Commander-in-Chief and the Chief of Naval Operations.[32]

Standley favored organization by task force and lamented Reeve's persistent attempts to change it. Noting that "Hepburn also has ideas of a Type Command," he commented:

> I cannot favor such an organization for I believe that the Commander-in-Chief should be free to study the broad strategic situation and to perfect his plans which must be executed immediately upon mobilization. Thus, because of these varying schools of thought, I decided to give the General Board a whack at it.[33]

To bolster his case, Standley asked Captain Royal E. Ingersoll, director of the War Plans Division, to prepare a study of the matter for presentation to the General Board; not surprisingly, the report Ingersoll wrote favored in essentials maintenance of the task commands. But King, who had left the Bureau of Aeronautics and was serving in the fleet, now actively supported the type system. In October 1936, Standley judiciously wrote him:

> I have gone over your organization recommendations and I note that you have endorsed the Reeves-Hepburn idea of a type command with no permanent assignment of type commands to either advance force, main body or any other particular force. In other words, you leave it to the Commander-in-Chief, U.S. Fleet, to make special details every time two type commands operate together, and thus tie the Commander-in-Chief down to the detailed organization and handling of fleet operations which is exactly the thing I object to in this organization.[34]

The problem was not solved while Standley was CNO, but the attempt to solve it taxed him severely. Combined with the increasing interference of the president, the formation of a coterie of officers who seemed to Standley to be excessively influenced by Roosevelt, and the cutback in operating funds, the effort aggravated the fatigue of this principled man. He therefore decided to retire on his sixty-fourth birthday, although as CNO he could have remained in the navy for another six months. Perhaps the last bitter pill was that Taussig, his friend and assistant CNO, did not receive a major fleet billet from Roosevelt, whom Taussig had once antagonized. Standley recalled that Roosevelt was not too pleased about his plan to retire, and reminded him he could remain in office until the next year. Standley refused to change his mind, however, and ended his naval career.

On 20 December 1936 the Navy Department hosted a dinner for Standley, and the president's naval aide told Roosevelt that he had "never been present at a more outstanding tribute to anyone."[35] On the dinner program was printed a list of six "Standleyisms." Probably the one that best summed up his career as

CNO was, "Confirm by appropriations through regular channels an orderly program to bring our Navy up to treaty strength and to maintain it there."[36] To this the president added his "sincere personal appreciation" for Standley's "long and distinguished service."[37]

Although he retired from the navy in 1936, the admiral got no chance to rest. He chose to accept a job with the 1939 World's Fair. During this employment, Congress passed an act that gave him the permanent rank of admiral. Resigning from the fair in late 1939, Standley became a director of and consultant to the Electric Boat Company. He held these posts until 1941, when, as he was about to resign under duress, he was recalled to active duty and assigned to the Planning Board in the navy's Office of Production Management. In late September 1941, he was appointed a member of the Beaverbrook-Harriman lend-lease mission to the Soviet Union and this assignment was a factor in his appointment the following year as ambassador to Russia. Between 1941 and 1942 he served in the navy's Public Relations Office and was a member of the Roberts Board, which investigated the Pearl Harbor attack. In February 1942 FDR sent Standley as ambassador to Moscow, where he remained until he resigned in a furor in October 1943. Nonetheless, Roosevelt assigned him to the Planning Group in the Office of Strategic Services, and he stayed in that post until October 1946, when he retired and returned to California.

In retirement Admiral Standley was very much in demand as a paid speaker. Because his sojourn in Russia convinced him that the Soviet government was dangerous and aggressive, the tone and content of the speeches he made throughout the country invariably reminded the American people of the necessity for them to be always on their guard against the Russians. He was a man of strong constitution. Even in his seventies he continued to play golf, a game he had played throughout his years in the navy. He became active in Republican politics in California. In 1947 Governor Earl Warren named him to head a commission to investigate organized crime in the state, and the admiral became an early supporter of Richard M. Nixon. Although he became much less active as the years went by, as late as 1959, when he was eighty-seven years old, he asked the city fathers of San Diego to remove a red star from atop the civic center because it reminded him of Russian communism![38]

As CNO, Standley faced problems that were unique by any measure, and his tenure was marked by sharp reversals in American naval policies. He assumed office when naval retrenchment had ended and modest expansion had begun under the National Industrial Recovery Act. Standley encouraged the trend by his vigorous support of the Vinson-Trammell Act of 1934. These programs created new problems in fleet organization, construction, engineering, and ordnance, and it fell to Standley as CNO to try to give order and design to the whole. In doing so, he found the debility of the secretary to be both an asset and a burden, for while Standley often had the advantage of making decisions as acting secretary he often had to bear the workload of two jobs, and, after the death of the assistant secretary, of three. Standley lacked the absolute confidence of the president but he was shrewd enough not to challenge sharply the chief executive's prerogatives; with Congress, he achieved considerable success despite his lack of political acumen. Nonetheless, his failure to influence the president on the issue of the fleet command, he believed, resulted in the efficiency of the seagoing forces being reduced during his tour as CNO. He was an able representative of American interests at two important international conferences, although his negotiating skills were never really put to the test, given the gulf that by 1934 separated the aims of the Pacific naval powers. Clearly his most outstanding achievement was the orderly, businesslike manner in which naval expansion proceeded. His refusal to be rushed precipitately into a shipbuilding program that would have had the defects of haste ultimately led to the creation of a superior naval establishment.

After a rich life in the best traditions of American naval leadership, William Harrison Standley, at the age of ninety-one years, died on 25 October 1963.

WILLIAM DANIEL LEAHY

2 January 1937–1 August 1939

JOHN MAJOR

William D. Leahy was born on 6 May 1875 in Hampton, Iowa, the son of third-generation Irish-American parents, Michael and Rose Leahy. He grew up in the small town of Ashland, Wisconsin, where his father practiced law and dabbled in local politics. Having aimed first for the Military Academy at West Point, he entered the Naval Academy in 1893 and graduated in the middle ranks of the class of 1897. In 1904 he married Louise Tennent Harrington; they had one child, William Harrington Leahy.

Leahy's entry into the navy coincided with the years of America's emergence as a world power, and his first seagoing assignment could not have been more dramatic. Detailed as an ensign to the battleship *Oregon,* he was on board during her celebrated dash from the Pacific Coast to Cuba at the opening of the war with Spain in 1898, and witnessed the destruction of the Spanish fleet off Santiago. From Cuba he went on to take part in the suppression of the nationalist rebellion in the Philippines and then in the international expedition that crushed the Boxer movement in China. Later, Leahy was to have firsthand experience of American intervention in Central America and the Caribbean, first in 1912, when he was chief of staff to the commander of American forces in Nicaragua, and then in 1916, when he was commanding officer of the dispatch boat *Dolphin,* which operated off Haiti, the Dominican Republic, and Mexico. These episodes confirmed him as a thoroughgoing American nationalist, steeped in the conviction that the power of the United States was a necessary and beneficial force in world affairs. At the same time—unusual for a man of his parentage—he was a devotee of Anglo-American partnership and in 1917 was strongly in favor of America's entry into the war on Britain's side.

During the war, Leahy first commanded the converted German liner *Princess Matoika,* ferrying troops to Europe, and for this was awarded the Navy Cross. He ended the conflict as inspector of gunnery and shortly afterwards was given command of the cruiser *St. Louis,* which saw service in the Aegean Sea during the Greco-Turkish war. By this time, Leahy was being singled out as a man of promise, and recognition came in 1926 when he was given command of his first battleship, the *New Mexico*. The following year, he attained flag rank as chief of the navy's second most powerful bureau, the Bureau of Ordnance, where he remained until 1931, when he took over as Commander, Destroyers, Scouting Force. In 1933 he was appointed head of the foremost bureau, Navigation, where he was influential in having battleship officers of the so-called Gun Club assigned to key posts, notably Admiral Arthur J. Hepburn, as commander in chief of the U. S. Fleet. Most of 1935 and 1936 he spent at sea, first as Commander, Battleships, Battle Force, then as Commander, Battle Force, until he succeeded Admiral William H. Standley as chief of naval operations on 2 January 1937.[1]

Leahy thus brought to the office of CNO an intensely conservative naval background, with no service, for example, in either submarines or aircraft carriers. This orthodoxy made it seem unlikely that he would make any dramatic impact on national affairs. Offsetting it, however, was his great skill in securing congressional sympathy for the navy's objectives, developed during his time in the bureaus of Ordnance and Navigation. He also was determined to put the navy's point of view before the public at large. This determination led to his being the first CNO to hold a formal press conference, which he did less than two months after relieving Standley.

A number of other factors lent Leahy a more than ordinary significance. First and foremost was the rapport he enjoyed with the president, whom he had come to know when he, Leahy, had command of the *Dolphin* and Franklin D. Roosevelt was assistant secretary of the navy in the Wilson administration. This rapport was to stand Leahy in good stead while he was CNO and led him on to even greater responsibilities after his retirement from the navy. His position as CNO was further strengthened by the fact that the elderly secretary of the navy, Claude A. Swanson, was almost continuously ill, which often made Leahy acting secretary, in preference to the civilian assistant secretary, Charles Edison. He was also undoubtedly lucky in not having to contend with an army chief of staff as prestigious as General Douglas A. MacArthur, as his immediate predecessors had done. His army counterpart, General Malin Craig, had none of MacArthur's glamour, did not have Leahy's contact with the White House, and was rarely the man to put the navy in the shade. Finally, Leahy was helped by the mounting international crisis that dominated his years as CNO. With the crisis came a long-awaited measure of naval expansion and this inevitably enhanced the status of the navy's senior representative. So Leahy became a prominent figure, the spokesman for a service that had long been neglected, but was commanding increasing respect as America's first line of defense in a world moving inexorably to war.

The gravest issue facing Leahy when he took over as CNO was Japan's refusal to accept naval arms limitation, which had resulted in the expiry of the Washington and London treaties on 31 December 1936. On 8 January 1937

Roosevelt announced that two new battleships, the *Washington* and *North Carolina,* each of 35,000 tons, would be laid down to replace the over-age *Arkansas* and *Texas;* however it was not clear how much further in new construction the president was prepared to go. The question was given extra urgency in mid-February, when Britain proclaimed a significant program of new construction, which included three battleships of the *King George V* class, to add to the two she had begun in 1936. Leahy immediately responded with a public call for parity with the Royal Navy, a view shared by the State Department at a conference with Leahy and his advisers on 12 March. The president, however, was not convinced. Indeed, he had already ordered a $75-million cut in the naval estimates for fiscal year 1938, and on 7 April he demanded reductions in current expenditures. He went on to deny the navy more than six auxiliary vessels and to reject its pleas for new dry docks and for modifications to capital ships. It is true that Leahy secured Roosevelt's agreement to having 16-inch guns mounted in the new battleships, but the overall prospect for a U. S. Fleet that could keep abreast of its rivals was bleak, an irony under a president reputed to be ardently pro-navy.[2]

The sudden explosion of Japanese power in the Far East soon changed the tempo of Roosevelt's policy. On 7 July 1937 fighting broke out near Peking between Japanese and Chinese forces and, according to Undersecretary of State Sumner Welles, Roosevelt at once drew up a plan for a trade embargo against Japan, to be enforced by the British and American fleets acting in concert. As Welles recalled, the idea was supported by Leahy, and though there is no other evidence for this, the CNO's feelings certainly ran high. By mid-August the undeclared war had spread to Shanghai and on 20 August an American seaman was killed when the flagship of the Asiatic Fleet commander, Admiral Harry E. Yarnell, was caught in the crossfire. Leahy reacted strongly. "If it were possible," he wrote in his diary, "to obtain an equitable agreement with Great Britain to share the effort and expense, this appears to be a wonderful opportunity to force Japan to observe Treaty agreements, and to depart from the mainland of Asia which would ensure Western trade supremacy in the Orient for another century. The cost of accomplishing this purpose at a later date will be enormously increased, and it does still appear inevitable that a major war between the Occident and the Orient must be faced at some time either now or in the future."[3]

At the same time, the CNO backed Yarnell's loud protests to Washington, together with his request that cruisers be sent out to Shanghai to evacuate American citizens. When Leahy saw Roosevelt at Hyde Park on 1 September, however, his request was denied for fear the ships might be lost. Yarnell, for his part, confided in a letter written to Leahy from the Yangtze on 12 September that "a few squadrons of our carrier planes would clear this river of Japs in 24 hours." In addition, there is little doubt that Leahy sympathized when Yarnell issued statements that he had ordered his ships to fire if attacked by Japanese aircraft. But Leahy was obliged by a nervous State Department to order Yarnell to refer all subsequent communiqués to Washington for clearance, and the CNO could express his support for the commander of the Asiatic Fleet only by forwarding to the president copies of Yarnell's letters.[4]

One of these included a plan for a "naval war of strangulation" against Japan, to be fought in conjunction with Britain, France, the Netherlands, and the Soviet Union. This was no doubt designed to implement Roosevelt's famous "quarantine" speech of 5 October 1937, in which he called for the isolation of aggressor states by the peace-loving nations of the world. The plan certainly bore a striking resemblance to what Welles wrote that Roosevelt had on his mind in July 1937, and Leahy at once interpreted the speech as "an invitation to the nations to take consolidated action against Japan in the present Oriental war." But whatever the president intended, the State Department had the final say. Early in November the United States took part in an international conference in Brussels to discuss ways to end the Far Eastern crisis. Before leaving for Brussels, the head of the American delegation, Norman H. Davis, was instructed by Roosevelt to take up the possibility of some form of concerted action if all else failed but, when Davis raised the issue of sanctions with Secretary of State Cordell Hull, he was told that they were out of the question.[5]

However, on 27 November the British ambassador in Washington proposed that Britain and the United States together put on "an overwhelming display of naval force" in the Far East and that Anglo-American staff conversations be held to prepare the ground. The navy's War Plans Division, according to one historian, had already called for staff conversations in mid-November and Leahy clearly favored such a move. The State Department, on the other hand, well aware of the possible implications of this commitment, held back, and it was not until another crisis erupted that Anglo-American naval cooperation was given further impetus.[6]

On 12 December 1937, during their offensive on Nanking, the Chinese capital, Japanese aircraft sank an American gunboat, the *Panay*. Leahy's answer to what was unquestionably a deliberate and unprovoked attack was "to get the Fleet ready for sea, to make an agreement with the British Navy for joint action, and to inform the Japanese that we expect to protect our Nationals." After a cabinet meeting on 17 December, Secretary of the Interior Harold L. Ickes wrote that the aged secretary of the navy, Swanson, wanted war "and undoubtedly he is talking for the admirals." Welles later recalled that Leahy, alone of Roosevelt's senior advisers, was urging trade sanctions against Japan, going well beyond the demand made on 13 December for an apology and compensation. Certainly Leahy was contemptuous of the State Department which, as he saw it, was "interested principally in getting the written record of this incident so complete as to provide defense against criticism."[7]

Roosevelt, however, now seemed prepared to take an initiative. In a conversation with the British ambassador on 16 December he sketched out a plan for a "peaceful blockade" of Japan, to be mounted by an Anglo-American cruiser force. At the same time, he agreed to the renewed British call for staff talks, and on 26 December the director of war plans, Captain Royal E. Ingersoll, was sent to London for discussions with his counterpart at the Admiralty. He was instructed to explore the possibilities of collaboration "after the next grave outrage." In other words, no immediate rejoinder was being considered. The upshot was negligible and, as Ingersoll recalled, "we found that there was not a great deal that could be done." As for Roosevelt: "He was perfectly satisfied. Of course, he realized how shallow the whole thing was."[8]

The precise limits of Roosevelt's intentions were revealed early in January 1938, following Japanese encroachments on the international settlement in Shanghai. After conferring with Leahy on 10 January, the president intimated that, provided the Admiralty announced that it was completing preparations short of mobilization, he might order the fleet to dock its ships for the purpose of cleaning their bottoms, advance the date of the spring fleet problem, send the fleet out to Pearl Harbor, and dispatch a division of light cruisers to attend the opening of the new British naval base at Singapore. All this fell far short of his earlier vaporings, and London could be forgiven for thinking that it placed the Royal Navy in the front line with no solid guarantee of American support. So Anglo-American cooperation in the Far East came to nothing, and the "sharp remonstrances" Leahy envisioned failed to materialize.[9]

Nonetheless, in other ways the administration's response to the Japanese challenge was less inert. Most importantly, the army and navy set about revising their war plans. Leahy described current strategic thinking to the president only a few days after taking over as CNO. In the Atlantic, the navy's approach was defensive, "primarily . . . in support of the army's efforts to protect the continental United States, with naval operations to dominate the Western Atlantic and Caribbean." In the Pacific, on the other hand, an all-out offensive was called for; "This Plan requires the maximum effort on the part of the Navy. Its conception is that if the United States is attacked . . . the war can only be terminated and a decision reached by carrying the war to the Western Pacific." Naval strategists confined practically all of their work to this plan—known as the Orange Plan—since the Joint Army and Navy Board had decided that war with a Pacific power was more likely than war with any other major naval power.[10]

Japan's successes in China placed a large question mark over this offensive strategy, and on 6 November 1937 came the news that Italy had joined Nazi Germany and Japan in the Anti-Comintern Pact. This at once raised the specter of a combination of forces that could weaken America's power to respond promptly to Japan in the Pacific. Thus, a full-blooded reply to a Japanese threat could be made impossible if, at the same time, Germany—already building up its influence in Latin America—made a move in the Western Hemisphere. Consequently, Roosevelt ordered a review of strategy, and on 10 November the Joint Board instructed its planning committee to work out a new Orange Plan because the existing one was "unsound in general" and "wholly inapplicable" to the changed world situation.[11]

Within weeks the committee reported itself deadlocked between army and navy views. The main stumbling block lay in the question of who was to provide manpower for the assault forces scheduled to storm Japanese-held beaches. In 1934 the Fleet Marine Force had been set up as the nucleus of the navy's amphibious landing operations, but reinforcements from the army would be indispensable. As Ingersoll reported to Leahy in July 1937, however, the army did not take part in the fleet landing exercises and the dispute over the Orange Plan showed that it was most concerned with the security of the so-called strategic triangle of Alaska-Hawaii-Panama. The army refused point-blank to give naval planners the 40,000 men they demanded to reinforce the Philippines and to seize bases in the Western Pacific.[12]

On 7 December Leahy suggested a compromise whereby the army would take up "an initial temporary position of readiness" on the points of the strategic triangle while the navy undertook "offensive operations against ORANGE armed forces and the interruption of ORANGE vital sea communications while protecting our Pacific Coast and outlying possessions from a major attack." As can readily be understood, this suggestion changed nothing fundamental and the plan finally agreed on in February 1938 embodied radically different concepts. The army had given way to the extent of promising 20,000 men and 150 aircraft for the naval task force, but would deploy no extra troops to the garrison in the Philippines. Service rivalries, rather than international circumstances, still determined American strategy.[13]

The navy was more successful in getting acceptance of an expanded building program. On 2 August 1937 construction for fiscal year 1939 was set at two battleships, two light cruisers, eight destroyers, and eight submarines. Just three days earlier, however, Norman Davis had written to Roosevelt advocating the building of two or three extra battleships so as to keep pace with Japan and Britain. Then, on 9 September, after hearing that the Japanese Ministry of Marine refused to communicate details of its naval estimates, the State Department urged Leahy to ask for an accelerated schedule of battleship replacement. On 10 November the CNO told the president that the navy intended to request two more battleships and, in a letter to Roosevelt on 15 December, he added two light cruisers to the list. No more carriers were needed, claimed Leahy, the navy had enough—three built and three building—and "in consideration of the increasing efficiency in both offense and defense of flying boats as compared with carrier based planes."[14]

But expansion was to go well beyond this. On 28 January 1938 Roosevelt asked Congress to approve an increase of 20 per cent in the navy's authorized under-age combat tonnage. In his testimony before the House Committee on Naval Affairs soon afterwards, Leahy explained that this would mean three more battleships, two more carriers, nine more light cruisers, twenty-three more destroyers, and nine more submarines. At the same time, the total authorized number of useful naval aircraft was to be raised from 2,050 to no less than 3,000. Appropriations to implement what was envisioned as a ten-year program were estimated at just under $1,100 million.[15]

During the House committee hearings, Leahy came under considerable fire from isolationists, alarmed that naval expansion signaled greater American involvement on the world scene. As recently as 10 January, the Ludlow Resolution, which provided for a national referendum before the United States went to war, had only narrowly been defeated in the House, and isolationist feeling there ran high. These flames were fanned when news of the Ingersoll mission was leaked in *The Daily Telegraph* (London) on 28 January, and suspicions were rampant that Roosevelt was about to join forces with Britain to carry out his "quarantine." The committee chairman, Congressman Carl Vinson, pointed out to Leahy that critics of the program believed it meant that "we intended to join with the British and French navies to police the world," while one congressman declared his opposition to the U. S. fleet acting "as a subsidiary to some concern that wants to exploit people on the other side of the globe." As the minority of the committee put it, in its report on the authorization bill, America was not going to enter "another war to make the world safe for democracy or to make the Yangtze safe for Standard Oil tankers."[16]

The CNO was at pains to refute this kind of accusation. "There is nothing in this program," he told the committee, "that will permit of aggressive action, of policing the world, or of projecting an attack against the territory of any naval power. It would require at least three times the projected increase to prepare for aggressive action with any prospect of success." In other words, far from being the spearhead of interventionism, the navy was the best guarantee of American neutrality. The argument was convincing, and the Expansion Act went into the statute book on 17 May 1938.[17]

At this same time, the program for fiscal year 1939 went through, including the four capital ships Leahy had asked for, the *Alabama, Indiana, Massachusetts,* and *South Dakota,* all of 35,000 tons; in addition, Vinson managed to secure a single carrier, the *Hornet.* The tonnage of the battleships raised problems. Although the Japanese kept the tonnage of the capital ships they ordered in 1937 a closely guarded secret, it was assumed that the vessels they were building were bigger than allowed by treaty and would make even the newest American battleships obsolete before they were completed. Therefore, after Japan refused to give a satisfactory reply to an American note of 5 February asking for tonnage details, Roosevelt invoked the "escalator" clause for the 1936 Anglo-American Treaty. This gave the signatories the right to build capital ships in excess of 35,000 tons. After consultation, Britain agreed to a new ceiling of 45,000 tons. Leahy planned to ask for two ships of this size in the program for fiscal year 1940.[18]

The tonnage issue had relevance not only to America's own construction. Since November 1936 the Soviet Union had been trying to have a battleship built in the United States, and in April 1937 Leahy had received the Russian agents, Messrs. Wolf and Carp. He described Wolf as "a typical argumentative, plausible advocate"; Carp as "a sinister appearing person who looks exactly like the conventional international villain of the stage." What followed over the next two years certainly came close to melodrama, if not to farce. Leahy, it is clear, opposed the scheme from start to finish, motivated in part by an antipathy to communism that was to become his guiding principle in the late 1940s. He was, however, faced with the awkward fact that, for diplomatic reasons, his president approved the transaction, as did the State Department. The CNO was therefore constrained to bring into play all the many bureaucratic stratagems at his disposal, saying nothing that could be interpreted as prejudice, but allowing his subordinates a free hand to run the project into the sand.

At one point the project was undoubtedly grandiose. Early in 1938 the naval architects, Gibbs and Cox, produced plans for a 62,000-ton monster of a battleship with a speed of 34 knots, armed with twelve 16-inch guns, and carrying its own miniature air force of thirty-six planes. It was to cost $150 million, two-and-a-half times more than the American 35,000-tonners. With its escorts, it was described as forming a unit "comparable with 'the Queen of the Chessboard' " which could "operate with impunity everywhere in the ocean." When the 45,000-ton limit was decided on, however, Moscow was told it could not have its leviathan, and, in January 1939, settled for one 45,000-ton ship and two model destroyers. Even then, and in spite of Roosevelt's continued support for the deal, Leahy's resistance continued. Scott Ferris, another member of the Soviet agency, spoke nothing but the truth when he claimed that the Navy Department had tried to "pile up difficulties by which action was continually being delayed and might eventually be prevented." It was. Shortly after Leahy was relieved as CNO, the Nazi-Soviet Pact and the outbreak of war in Europe ensured the death of the scheme. The tactics of obstructionism paid off.[19]

Anticommunism was not the only reason for Leahy's opposition to building up the Soviet battle fleet. Also at work was a profound concern lest scarce American resources should be diverted from the U. S. Navy at a time when it was coming under increasing international pressure. During the hearing in 1938 before the House committee, he was careful to point out that even the new authorization would not give America complete security. He claimed that "the proposed increase is not sufficient to guard against attack on both shores at one time." Here he was touching on the contingency implicit in the current revision of the Orange Plan, namely, a Japanese onslaught in the Pacific coupled with German penetration of South America. Though he did not declare it, there is no doubt where the CNO's preference lay. Asked what would be the repercussions in the Pacific if part of the fleet were ordered to prevent a German attempt to establish military and naval bases in Brazil, Leahy replied that the units remaining in the Pacific would be "very definitely reduced below what we consider necessary." In his opinion, splitting the fleet in two was no answer. He told the committee that the fleet should "remain in strategic concentration and . . . not be divided between the two oceans." In other words, it should stay in the Pacific. Since alliances were formally ruled out by the national policy of neutrality, the only alternative for an isolationist America was a two-ocean navy to defend the Atlantic as well as the Pacific. Otherwise, it seemed as though the government would have to choose whether or not to uphold the Monroe Doctrine. Although two members of the committee argued for an Atlantic fleet, Leahy knew that this was not necessary as long as the British and French navies stood guard against Germany and Italy. Since it was politically impossible to admit this publicly, he could only agree that, in principle, a two-ocean capability was a sound proposition.[20]

Leahy also displayed his political sensitivity over the issue of bases. Expansion in ship and aircraft construction had to be accompanied by the development of base facilities in the continenal United States, in the Caribbean, and in the Pacific. In January 1938 Captain Charles M. Cooke and Commander Forrest P. Sherman were sent to survey possible sites for naval air bases on Midway, Wake, and Guam, the American stepping-stones in a westward advance against Japan. But the State Department's fear of provoking Japan was widely shared in Congress, and on 18 March Leahy wrote to the commander in chief of the U. S. Fleet telling him that the time was not yet ripe to press for funds for Guam and Wake. Instead, the Expansion Act that was passed on 17 May set up a board of inquiry under Admiral Hepburn, who was to prepare a report for Congress by the end of the year.[21]

In certain areas of naval expansion, then, the CNO had to tread warily. He was on strong ground, however, when he faced the challenge from the army air corps, which claimed that strategic air power had eclipsed sea power and the bomber had become master over the battleship. Thus, one of the most fanatical members of the corps, Colonel Hugh G. Knerr, could write of "the necessity of developing of Air Power so that it can control any situation that may arise from Alaska to Cape Horn and from Guam to Nova Scotia-Bermuda." The commander of the general headquarters air force, Major General Frank M. Andrews, lecturing to the Army War College in October 1937, asserted the right of the corps to undertake missions "beyond the sphere of influence of ground or naval operations," that is, against a hostile expeditionary force aimed at some point in the Western Hemisphere and when "our Navy is occupied elsewhere." Andrews was speaking at precisely the time he took delivery of the first squadrons of four-engined B-17s, the Flying Fortress, which the corps saw as a war-winning weapon. In a submission to the adjutant general the same month, Andrews urged the manufacture of an even more powerful bomber, capable of making attacks 700 miles out at sea. In other words, the key army air corps leaders intended to take over the navy's mission of long-range coastal defense.[22]

Needless to say, the navy adamantly refused to accept these arguments. "If the Army GHQ Air Force cannot find enemy objectives except in going to sea, then that force (or its equivalent) does not belong in the Army, but in the Navy," wrote a leading naval aviator, Vice Admiral Ernest J. King. For his part, Rear Admiral Arthur B. Cook, chief of the Bureau of Aeronautics, told Leahy that an enlarged bomber program for the army could cause serious damage if it bit into the navy's funds for patrol planes. The rapid westward advance across the

Pacific envisaged in the Orange Plan depended heavily on patrol planes being available in quantity and, if bombers were to feature in the campaign, the time taken to construct their airfields would rob the fleet of its impetus.[23]

Fortunately, Leahy had allies in the War Department. Majority opinion in the army demanded an air corps with strictly tactical functions, acting in close support of ground commanders. If it were allowed to act as a strategic force, it would gobble up appropriations at the expense of the infantry and the artillery and unbalance the fighting structure of the whole army. For this reason, in April 1937 Secretary of War Harry H. Woodring was utterly opposed to a bill to give the air corps independent status, and dismissed the bid for a role in sea defense because it would "lead to conflict with the Navy." In July the War Plans Division drafted a letter for the army chief of staff's signature denying that the cruiser *España* was sunk by air attack in the Spanish Civil War and stating that she was destroyed by a contact mine. In October Woodring directed that the air corps' estimates for fiscal year 1939 be based exclusively on the procurement of two-engine planes, while he joined Swanson in playing down the significance of a recent exercise in which the target ship *Utah* was hit by army aircraft.[24]

Leahy naturally welcomed this support and was particularly grateful to General Craig, the army chief of staff, for gagging air corps lobbyists who had been hard at work on the Hill attacking the naval expansion bill. A good deal of testimony before the Senate Naval Affairs Committee in April was taken up with the bomber-versus-battleship question and, as a staunch battleship man could be expected to do, Leahy put up a vigorous defense. Battleships were "the backbone . . . of naval power"; land-based aircraft would never be a substitute for naval aircraft; aviation alone could not ensure control of the seas. When asked whether planes carrying powerful bombs could supplant capital ships, the reply was terse: "No; they cannot." The Army, for its own reasons, could not have agreed more, and on 29 June 1938 Craig together with Leahy expressed a Joint Board opinion that there would probably not be any future need for a bomber larger than the B-17.[25]

Even so, the battle was not yet over. In hammering away as it did at the theme of hemisphere defense, the air corps was echoing the concern of no less a figure than the president and his powerful confidant in the State Department, Sumner Welles. In April 1938 it was Welles who promoted the formation of the Standing Liaison Committee, comprising himself, the army chief of staff, and the chief of naval operations, and designed to foster military and naval cooperation with Latin America. Leahy did not display high enthusiasm. In November 1938, for instance, Welles told the committee that the president wanted legislation that would allow the supply of ships, aircraft, guns, and ammunition to the Latin-American republics; the Navy Department, he understood, objected. Leahy's answer is reminiscent of his poker-faced reaction to the State Department's pleas for naval aid to Russia. The navy was "experiencing great difficulty in supplying the needs of its fleet from its limited manufacturing facilities," but the policy was desirable and he would do what he could. As might have been expected, this did not amount to much, though the CNO continued to pay lip service to the idea.[26]

When the question of hemisphere security came to a head in the fall of 1938, the air corps gained at the navy's expense. At Munich, on 30 September, Britain and France gave way to Germany over Czechoslovakia, and Roosevelt was convinced that the strength of the luftwaffe made a German triumph possible. He was equally persuaded that the air corps must be given the leading role in the defense of the Americas which it so persistently claimed. At a White House conference on 14 November he demanded the production of no less than 10,000 army aircraft in the next two years. The new chief of the air corps, Major General Henry H. Arnold, was exultant. "The policy of the War Department of the United States changes as of this date," he minuted. "National Defense on a passive basis ceases. This country responsible for this hemisphere, from pole to pole. Coastal patrol will be undertaken by the Army." When a $500-million request for defense funds was sent to Congress in January 1939, the air corps was allocated $300 million. The navy, which had asked for $86 million to make good its deficiency of more than 1,000 planes, was given only $19 million.[27]

At the same time, as Arnold had indicated it would, the air corps made inroads into the navy's responsibility for coastal defense. On 4 November 1938 Craig told Leahy that he was directing army aviators who were participating in joint exercises off New York City to restrict their operations to 100 miles offshore. It will be remembered that Andrews wanted bombers powerful enough to operate 700 miles out to sea, and Leahy recorded his gratification at Craig's helpfulness in discouraging this "long continued encroachment on the Navy's responsibility for the sea defenses." In January 1939, however, the navy, no doubt prompted by the knowledge that the air corps now had presidential patronage, agreed informally to relaxation of the restriction and, by the summer, the concession had become permanent. A week after Leahy left office, the army's War Plans Division reported that on the Joint Planning Committee "at no time during recent months has there been any indication on the part of Navy members to challenge the uses of Army aviation proposed by Army members." What was more, the recommendation that no more heavy bombers should be developed was now disavowed: "A comparable situation would have been for the Navy to have put up to the Joint Board the problem of whether future battleship construction should be in excess of 35,000 tons." In short, the army had performed an abrupt about-turn and the navy had prudently done the same.[28]

Leahy was also forced to take the defensive after the Hepburn Board's report on naval bases was transmitted to Congress. Handed to the CNO on 1 December 1938, it called for the expenditure of $287 million, 80 per cent of it on air bases in the United States, the Caribbean, and the Pacific. With the long-term future in mind, the report was clearly looking to a two-ocean navy and providing for a spread of base facilities in both theaters. Its short-term emphasis, though, lay on the Pacific. No less than six of the nine bases described as being of "immediate strategic importance" were in that ocean: Kaneohe Bay, Midway, Wake, Guam, Johnston Island, and Palmyra, the staging-posts for an Orange war. Of these, the strong point was to be Guam, which Leahy had rightly described the previous February as having "nothing but a colonial government and a few marines." To construct air and submarine bases on the island, $39 million were called for, and the board went even further in calling for the transformation of Guam into a major advanced fleet base. In the words of the report, it was "practically defenseless against determined attack by any first-class power based in the western Pacific." Captain Cooke argued that, if the Japanese took Guam and strongly defended it, 60,000 men would not be able to retake it until it had been isolated. Given the continued apprehensiveness over Japan, this was strong meat for Congress to stomach. Aware of this, the board incorporated their proposals concerning Guam in such a way as to permit their being taken out of the report without destroying its continuity. It is a measure of Leahy's dedication to a Pacific strategy that he decided to keep them in, and he fought hard for Guam over the coming weeks.[29]

First, he had to persuade Roosevelt, who told him that he would ask only $20 million for the first year's work on priority bases, including Guam. The CNO succeeded in raising this to $27 million but, in a conference on 5 January 1939, Welles objected to the development of Guam on the grounds that it would tend to prompt a Japanese thrust against the Philippines. Hepburn's report made no provision for the Philippines, whose vulnerability had certainly increased since the recent Japanese conquest of south China. To Leahy, however, Welles's objection was just more proof of the cowardice of the State Department, which showed "every indication of being afraid to take positive action in the affairs of the Orient." Yet he did recognize the folly of spending large sums on Guam unless the administration were ready to defend it against air attack in force. By the end of the month, faced with continued apprehension from the State Department and a critical House Naval Affairs Committee, Leahy agreed with Roosevelt to request no more for Guam than authorization to develop harbor facilities for handling seaplanes. Even this was too much, and in the bill signed by the president on 25 April 1939 Guam was conspicuous by its absence.[30]

The debate on Guam coincided with the formulation of the construction program for fiscal year 1939. To Cooke, writing to the director of War Plans on 20 October 1938, carriers were the major deficiency in the fleet. Only seven were built or building, and Cooke called for two more "as soon as the designs can be drawn." Vinson, too, pressed Leahy for several carriers, but no more were laid down as long as Leahy was CNO. The central items in the coming program were the first two 45,000-ton battleships, the *Iowa* and the *New Jersey.* These ships presented problems in that they would be too broad in the beam to transit the 110-foot-wide locks of the Panama Canal. The solution was to construct a third set of locks, 140 feet wide, and the appropriation for it was made in the summer of 1939. But, since the locks could not be completed by the time the battleships went into commission, the logic of a two-ocean navy became more and more compelling: with a fleet in the Atlantic as well as a fleet in the Pacific, the canal would cease to matter. Although an Atlantic squadron of seven heavy cruisers and seven destroyers had been formed on 1 September 1938 and although Vinson, late in October, urged Leahy to discuss authorization for an Atlantic fleet, the CNO did not respond. His faith was still pinned on Britain and France as the deterrents to German sea power.[31]

Instead, still another strategic reappraisal was called for, to clear the ground for a decision. On 7 October 1938 Cooke pointed to the need for a revision of war plans for the Atlantic, and on 9 November Leahy and Craig directed the Joint Planning Committee to examine the contingency of "(a) violation of the Monroe Doctrine by one or more of the Fascist Powers, and (b) a simultaneous attempt to extend Japanese influence in the Philippines." Since no allies were in view, this was a summons for the United States either to choose between the Pacific and the hemisphere or to make ready to fight a two-front war single-handedly.[32]

As seen by the director of war plans, Rear Admiral Robert L. Ghormley, in a report to Leahy of 15 February 1939, the navy could do only one of three things. It could defend the Western Hemisphere, the west coast of the United States, and Hawaii; or it could wage war against Japan, while defending the east coast and the Panama Canal; or it could defend both coasts and the canal. What it could *not* do was undertake "an offensive naval war simultaneously in the Atlantic and the Pacific." For Cooke, in the light of a recent buildup of German and Italian submarines, the crucial need was for antisubmarine measures along the Atlantic coast and in the Carribbean. The planners' report, when completed in April 1939, acknowledged the limitations Ghormley had posited and came to much the same conclusions as had Cooke. In the event of a two-front war, the fleet in the Eastern Pacific would be held on the defensive, at three-quarters the strength of the Japanese Navy, and the country should be prepared to sacrifice Guam and the Philippines. Priority should go to the hemisphere, where U. S. objectives should be the security of the Panama Canal, the prevention of an Axis lodgment in South America, and the protection of American shipping in the Atlantic. For this last task, the navy should develop a large antisubmarine force of aircraft and patrol and escort vessels. In brief, it should be prepared "to carry out the operations of an Atlantic War." To provide the necessary resources for a two-ocean defensive, Vinson asked Leahy to make a study of the expansion required to meet simultaneous attacks in the Atlantic and the Pacific.[33]

The report had come down in favor of hemisphere defense, and challenged the old American emphasis on strategy in the Pacific. However, it by no means reflected a unanimous view in the Navy Department. The preference for a Pacific-first strategy remained strong. Thus, the CNO's annual estimate of 15 April 1939 spoke, as previous estimates had done, of the "greater danger of

War with Japan than with any other nation." As for the Atlantic, the role of the British and French fleets was made explicit. It was thought unlikely that Germany and Italy would "make a venture in the Americas unless Great Britain and France are disposed of in some way." On that assumption, the tiny Atlantic Squadron was considered quite enough to cope with violations of the Monroe Doctrine and to enforce neutrality. Similarly, Ghormley, writing to Leahy on 12 April, urged a concentration on the Pacific, advising that twelve battleships and four carriers be stationed there, as against four battleships and one carrier in the Atlantic.[34]

The pull of the Pacific was, moreover, intensified at this very moment in the wake of another crisis in Europe, the German seizure of Czechoslovakia on 15 March. Four days later the British asked for a renewal of naval staff talks, emphasizing that, if they had to go to war in Europe, they might not be able to reinforce the Royal Navy in the Far East. The same anxiety over their strength east of Suez underlay their request on 22 March for the early return of the U. S. Fleet to the Pacific from the Atlantic, where it had been carrying out the annual fleet problem. The request was urgently renewed on 10 April, after the Italian invasion of Albania, when the French faced London with the threat that they would come to terms with Germany at once if Britain transferred ships from the Mediterranean to the Far East. In consultation with Hull and Leahy, Roosevelt agreed to acquiesce and orders for the transfer were given on 15 April.[35]

The president, even so, had his mind on the Atlantic. On 20 April, Secretary of the Treasury Henry Morgenthau, Jr., noted that Roosevelt was planning a naval patrol of the Atlantic approaches in order to guarantee the neutrality of the hemisphere in the event of war in Europe. Indeed, he personally ordered the fleet problem in 1939 to be held in the Caribbean for the first time since 1930, and part of its purpose was the development of patrol techniques. During King George VI's visit to Washington in June, Roosevelt pursued his objectives by telling the king that he had been thinking of trying to acquire bases on British territory to give extra range to the patrol. He took up the question with the British ambassador on 30 June in the presence of Leahy, Hull, Welles, and others. On 17 July Welles told Leahy that the British had agreed to let the navy use seaplane-landing facilities in both Bermuda and Trinidad.[36]

Leahy's sights, meanwhile, were firmly set on the Pacific, as the staff conversations with Britain showed. On the American side, the talks were conducted by Leahy himself, aided by Ghormley, and were held in conditions of the strictest secrecy in Leahy's house. He believed that, if the two countries found themselves in a two-front war, the U. S. Fleet should operate in the Pacific while the British and French navies saw to the Atlantic and the Mediterranean. He considered that in the Pacific the U. S. Fleet should "move to Singapore in sufficient force to be able to engage and defeat any Japanese Fleet it met with on passage," but this was dependent on the Royal Navy's sending out an "adequate token force" at the same time. As for the Atlantic, if the neutrality patrol were activated, there was a possibility that it might pass on to the Admiralty information on the movements of German shipping. If the United States itself entered the war, it would assist in the escort of convoys, as it had done in the First World War.[37]

By the time the staff talks took place, Leahy was coming close to retirement. He had one more achievement to record as CNO, however. During May and June, in the aftermath of the strategic review, a series of plans was sketched out to replace the old "color" plans which were designed to meet the contingency of war between America and individual opponents. The new plans—code named Rainbow—were based on the concept of multiple threats, not all of which could be tackled by the United States alone. On 30 June the Joint Board outlined the plans in the following order of priority:

Rainbow-1 envisaged a single-handed defense of the Americas north of latitude 10 degrees south, that is, north of the "bulge" of northeastern Brazil, where the Germans were thought most likely to try to establish bases. Its purpose was thus to implement the conclusions of the April report. Rainbow-2 contemplated a war in the Western Pacific, fought in association with Britain and France, the United States exerting its maximum effort in this theater and participating on only a small scale in the Atlantic and Europe. Rainbow-3 was designed for a war in the Western Pacific fought without allies, in other words, the old Orange Plan. Rainbow-4 looked to a unilateral defense of the Americas extended to incorporate the area south of the Brazilian bulge—that is, the remainder of South America—as well as the Eastern Atlantic. Rainbow-5 presupposed a war in Europe fought in association with Britain and France in which American forces would be sent into the Eastern Atlantic and to Europe or Africa, "in order to effect the decisive defeat of Germany, or Italy, or both." Under this last plan, a strategic defensive would be maintained in the Pacific until major reinforcements could be transferred there from Europe for an offensive against Japan.[38]

Not surprisingly, the navy concentrated on Rainbow-2, in spite of the fact that Rainbow-1 had precedence as the plan that was to incorporate the president's Atlantic patrol. So, though Rainbow-1 was rushed to completion as war in Europe loomed, Rainbow-2 was given the focus of the Navy Department's attention over the coming months, proof yet again of the navy's tenacity in clinging to its cherished Pacific strategy.[39]

The service was to do so without Leahy. He retired at the age of sixty-four on 1 August 1939, handing over the navy to the successor he chose, Admiral Harold R. Stark. Leaving high office is a wrench at the best of times, but for Leahy it must have been particularly hard. With the onset of a second world war, the navy stood on the brink of one of the most momentous challenges in its history, and he was about to fall into obscurity as governor of Puerto Rico, a post that Roosevelt had chosen him for in March.

The president told Leahy, however, that, if war broke out and the United States entered it, he would need him as his aide and adviser. When in November 1940 Roosevelt found himself in need of an ambassador to Vichy France, he offered the position to Leahy, who served there from January 1941 to May 1942. During that time, Leahy strove to persuade Marshal Pétain to keep collaboration with Germany to a minimum, but he could not prevent the return to power of the pro-German premier, Pierre Laval. Leahy was recalled to Washington soon after the death of his wife, and it seemed that his long career was over at last. In fact, his greatest opportunity yet was awaiting him.

In February 1942 the army chief of staff, General George C. Marshall, had suggested to the president that the admiral serve as a neutral chairman of the Joint Chiefs of Staff, with the task of acting as intermediary between the service chiefs and the White House. Roosevelt agreed, and, at the same time, made Leahy his own chief of staff. Consequently, Leahy enjoyed a unique position at the center of affairs, standing at the president's side and presiding over the making of many of the highest strategic decisions of the war. In addition, he provided invaluable liaison between the services and the civilian agencies of the government.[40]

Leahy's influence on wartime strategy is difficult to gauge. Perhaps his most important achievement was to moderate conflicts between army and navy, and to encourage their acceptance of each other's primary roles: the army in Europe, the navy in the Pacific. He did so as a man with a name for sound, impartial judgment. "Whether he was right or wrong," wrote Roosevelt's secretary, Grace Tully, "the Boss knew that Bill had no personal axe to grind and meant only to serve the national interest." Thus, he could support the landings in North Africa against both Marshall and King, and oppose the official policy of unconditional surrender as well as the projected invasion of Japan. He also chalked up his fair share of aberrations: he favored Spain as the springboard for a second front in Europe; he predicted a revolution in liberated France; and he refused to believe the atomic bomb would work. Like Roosevelt, he was deeply hostile to General Charles de Gaulle, whereas he admired Prime Minister Winston Churchill and deplored the loss of his leadership in 1945. Stalin he considered an unwelcome but indispensable ally in the struggle for Europe.[41]

By the time of Roosevelt's death, Leahy was a formidable figure, then holding the newly created five-star rank of fleet admiral and with the status of chief presidential adviser on foreign affairs. The inexperienced Harry S. Truman leaned on him heavily, and the first advice Leahy gave the new president was to take a strong line with the Russians on Poland. Though Leahy recognized that it was necessary to make concessions to the Soviets at the Yalta Conference, he was convinced it would be dangerous to be conciliatory in the postwar era. He emerged as the doyen of the "cold warriors," even taking up the lost cause of Chiang Kai-shek in a vain effort to save China from communism. Although the administration did not share his views on the Far East, it took up most of his recommendations concerning Europe. By the time he finally retired, in March 1949, the United States had passed the test of the

Berlin blockade and was poised to enter an alliance system dedicated to the containment of Soviet influence.[42]

In 1950 Leahy brought out his war memoirs, *I Was There,* covering the years 1941–45 and based on his secret diary, later deposited in the Library of Congress. He died on 20 July 1959 at the age of eighty-four. By any reckoning he must rate as one of the most significant chiefs of naval operations, maintaining the interests of his service at an increasingly critical period in its development, and establishing a reputation that was to return him to the highest councils of state as the American power he had always venerated burgeoned and came to full flower. It was a fitting climax to his remarkable career.

HAROLD RAYNSFORD STARK

1 August 1939–26 March 1942

B. MITCHELL SIMPSON III

The twenty-seven months that intervened between the German attack on Poland in September 1939 and the Japanese attack on Pearl Harbor in December 1941 gave the U. S. Navy a golden opportunity to prepare for the coming war. At first there was a possibility that the United States might be able to stand aloof from the European war. In the Pacific the Japanese were recognized as the primary threat to American interests in Asia, but in 1939 armed conflict with Japan was seen as only a possibility. Clouds were gathering, however, and it soon became clear that it was only a matter of time before the United States would become actively involved in war.

In this period the U. S. Navy under the leadership and direction of its chief of naval operations, Admiral Harold R. Stark, embarked on a shipbuilding program that would give America worldwide supremacy at sea. In addition, the fundamental strategic decisions that were successfully applied during the war were made at this time and the machinery for their implementation was created.

When Stark relieved Admiral William D. Leahy as CNO on 1 August 1939, it seemed that he had reached the culmination of his naval career, which stretched back to 1899 when he entered the Naval Academy. The forty years in between were full and productive. The next seven years were to be filled with dramatic events as Stark, in Washington, prepared the navy for a world war, and later, in London, commanded U. S. Naval Forces, Europe, and served as Roosevelt's personal military representative in London.

Born in Wilkes-Barre, Pennsylvania, on 12 November 1880, Harold was the youngest of the five children of Benjamin Franklin Stark and Mary Francis Warner Stark. A bright student, he entered the Naval Academy in 1899 and did well as a naval cadet. Throughout his naval career he was known by and used the nickname "Betty" which he acquired at the academy. In his first year there, an upper classman erroneously informed him that General John Stark reportedly said at the Battle of Bennington in 1777, "We will win today or Betty Stark will be a widow." (The lady's name was Molly.) Harold was required to come to attention and repeat that phrase on appropriate and sometimes inappropriate occasions for sometime thereafter.[1] What began as undergraduate fun stuck for life.

Upon graduation in 1903, Stark requested assignment to the China Station, a remote but romantic post for a passed midshipman. Instead, he was sent to the South Atlantic. As a boy, he learned to sail on Lake Carey, Pennsylvania, and was particularly pleased when he was assigned in 1904 to the steam sloop *Hartford,* Admiral Farragut's old flagship and the last full-rigged ship in the U. S. Navy. He finally got to the Far East in the Battleship *Minnesota* when the Great White Fleet made a world cruise from 1907 to 1909. His thrill at making one of the great cruises of the century was tempered by the fact that it entailed a long separation from his bride of only five months. Ensign Stark married Katharine Adelle Rhoads of Wilkes-Barre, Pennsylvania, on 24 July 1907, and in due course they had two daughters, Mary and Katharine.[2]

At the end of the great cruise, Stark had earned his first command, the torpedo boat *Porter.* He moved on to increasingly responsible billets and by 1914 commanded the destroyer *Patterson.* During one passage Assistant Secretary of the Navy Franklin D. Roosevelt came aboard as a passenger. When they came to a particularly hazardous stretch of water off the coast of Maine, Roosevelt asked to take the conn, but Stark refused to abdicate his command and, with a show of bravado, increased speed and deftly brought his ship to a safe anchorage.[3] Roosevelt and Stark formed a close friendship which survived great trials without impairment.

When the United States entered World War I Lieutenant Commander Stark was en route to the Asiatic Fleet, where he was to command a torpedo flotilla. Almost as soon as he arrived in Manila, he asked Admiral Austin M. Knight, commander in chief of the Asiatic Fleet, to let him take the destroyers of his flotilla to the European war zone where they were needed for escort and patrol duty. A month later, Knight was directed by the Navy Department to send at once as many destroyers as he could spare to European waters. He then granted Stark's request. Commanding a division of five old, small, coal-burning destroyers, Stark left Manila on 1 August 1917 for the 12,000-mile voyage to Gibraltar. Having crossed the Indian Ocean at the height of the monsoon season, the ships arrived at Gibraltar in good material condition and were put to work almost at once, a feat for which Stark received his first Distinguished Service Medal. He was transferred to the staff of Admiral William S. Sims, who commanded American naval forces in European waters, and spent the remainder of World War I in London working on the problems of patrols, escorts, convoys, and coordination of American naval efforts with the British Admiralty. The experience served as an apprenticeship for Stark's duty in London during World War II.[4]

In the years immediately following World War I, Stark had various sea and shore duty and in 1923 attended the Naval War College. In 1930, by which time he was a captain, he was appointed aide to Secretary of the Navy Charles F. Adams, a billet he kept when Adams was replaced in 1933 by Claude A. Swanson. Later that year, Stark received orders to take command of the battleship *West Virginia.* He returned to Washington for a tour as chief of the Bureau of Ordnance from 1934 to 1937 before returning to the fleet as Commander, Cruiser Division 3. While at sea in 1939, he was appointed by President Roosevelt to succeed Admiral Leahy as chief of naval operations.[5]

The navy's lack of preparation in World War I colored Stark's opinions on American military policy from 1939 to 1941. Closely associated with Sims in World War I, he was all too familiar with the postwar controversy between the admiral and the secretary of the navy, Josephus Daniels. Indeed, Sims sparked a congressional investigation in 1920 when he charged that, under Daniel's leadership, the navy was ill prepared for the war and that lack of preparation extended the war by at least six months.[6] But, in 1939 when Stark became CNO, a modest but promising naval rearmament program was already under way. In 1934 Congress had authorized the construction of enough warships to build up to a "treaty fleet" by 1942, but, when the naval disarmament system collapsed in 1936, it was clear that the United States had fallen behind Japan in the arms race. Therefore, in 1938 Congress authorized a 20-per-cent expansion of the fleet beyond "treaty" standards to maintain the 5:5:3 ratio of the Five Power Treaty with Britain, France, Italy, and Japan.

Stark did not believe that this was enough. Following extensive consultations with Congressman Carl Vinson, chairman of the House Naval Affairs Committee, and with the approval of the president, he requested in November 1939 that the navy be expanded by another 25 per cent. As soon as Congress convened in January 1940, Vinson's committee held hearings on the bill, with Stark as the lead witness. He claimed that expansion was necessary if the United States intended to maintain the 5:5:3 ratio, especially in regard to such possible enemies as Japan, Germany, and the Soviet Union. But he added an ominous note, one not previously heard as a justification for naval expansion: instead of facing one belligerent, the United States might face a coalition of enemy powers. Stark contended that, should this be the case, even a 25-per-cent increase in ship construction would not guarantee national security. He forecast that, in the beginning, the United States would suffer sharp reverses, but was confident of eventual American victory.[7]

Nonetheless, Congress in early 1940 was in a mood to economize. Vinson decided that political discretion demanded an expansion of no more than 11 per cent. However, this change was more apparent than real, because the original bill applied to a five-year period, whereas the new version was for only two years. And, in the original version of Vinson's bill, the amount of expansion of the fleet in the first year totaled 11 per cent. This way, the navy could return to Congress in the next year and ask for another increase.[8] Stark and the bureau chiefs naturally favored the bill that called for 25 per cent, primarily because it would permit naval and private shipbuilders to plan more carefully for the entire program. Nevertheless, they agreed to accept whatever Congress would authorize.

When the naval expansion bill was introduced in January 1940, the "phony war" was going on in Europe. It appeared to most that the stalemate in the West was complete. Indeed, as late as March, Stark doubted that an attack by either Germany or Britain and France on the western front could succeed.[9] In April, however, Adolf Hitler occupied Denmark before seizing Norway, and in May he turned to the west. First the Netherlands, then Belgium, and finally France fell victim to the stunning tactics of the German blitzkrieg.

The fall of France in June 1940 shocked and dismayed American military strategists. For nearly nine months the Anglo-French forces had seemed sufficient to confine Hitler to central Europe. Until France unexpectedly sued for peace, her navy was allied with the Royal Navy as a maritime bulwark protecting the Western Hemisphere. The weakening of this shield created anxiety in Washington. After the surrender of France, the fate of the French fleet was a critical issue to U. S. Navy leaders. Its control by Germany, they believed, would pose a substantial naval challenge to Britain and, indirectly, threaten the Western Hemisphere. Also, American naval planners questioned whether Britain had the will or the means to face Hitler's forces alone. Thus, it was clear to Stark that the United States could no longer rely on other navies to keep the war away from America. The United States needed a navy second to none and the adoption of this policy could no longer be delayed.

Even before the president signed the act calling for an 11-per-cent expansion, Stark and his staff had begun to fashion an even larger building program. With Roosevelt's approval, Stark went before the House Naval Affairs Committee and asked that the navy be expanded by 70 per cent. Stunned by the fall of France and extremely sympathetic to the request, Vinson and his colleagues wanted to know whether Stark had asked for enough. Within one week the House approved the bill, the Senate followed, and within another month the president signed into law what became known as the Two-Ocean Navy Act.[10] By the summer of 1940 most of the navy that would wage World War II had been authorized and construction work was under way on some of the ships. The two authorization measures enacted in 1940 provided for an impressive fleet of 326 combatant ships, including 10 new carriers and 26 cruisers, 2 battle cruisers, 218 destroyers, and 70 submarines. In addition, the 185 ships that had been authorized in the 1930s would enter the fleet for wartime service.

Although Congress had authorized new ships, construction could not begin until funds had been appropriated. Therefore, besides seeking authorization to expand the fleet, Stark had to request monies to build the ships already approved. But shipbuilding was not the only area of expansion. Stark went to Congress in 1939 and obtained funds to refurbish and operate old destroyers that were laid up after World War I. Although these ships were well past their prime, he planned to deploy them in the Atlantic Neutrality Patrol. Immediately after the outbreak of war in Europe, Roosevelt directed Stark to institute a patrol extending 200 to 300 miles off the east coast of the United States. The mission of this Neutrality Patrol was to keep German U-boats away from American shores, but shortage of ships, a lack of trained personnel, and limited support facilities inhibited its prompt and effective operation. Stark saw the shortage of ships as the greatest of these problems. He pleaded with Congress for additional funds to modernize the old destroyers, emphasizing the need to defend the continental United States.[11]

At the same time, the French fleet's withdrawal from the war added to Britain's need for more ships, particularly destroyers, to keep open the Atlantic sea lanes from North America to the British Isles, since the British war effort depended on massive imports. If German U-boats could interrupt these sea lanes, Britain would be unable to continue as a belligerent. In the late spring of 1940, the British began to suggest that the United States should transfer some destroyers to the Royal Navy. Complicated negotiations between Roosevelt and Churchill concluded an arrangement for the transfer of fifty old American destroyers to Great Britain in exchange for ninety-nine-year leases on several British bases in the Western Hemisphere.[12]

In the meantime, Congress had specified that no ships could be transferred or otherwise disposed of unless the chief of naval operations certified that they were not needed for the defense of the United States. This legislation put Stark in the position of having to rule on the propriety of an international agreement made by the president. Although he was under great pressure from both the White House and the new secretary of the navy, Frank Knox, to make such a certification, Stark believed it was wrong for him to do so. When he was asking Congress for funds to refurbish the same destroyers, he used the argument that they were necessary for the national defense, and he was still of that opinion. He felt so strongly about the matter that he planned to ask to be relieved if Roosevelt directly ordered him to sign the certification. Compliance with such an order would compromise his reputation with Congress; he concluded that he could not change his position overnight and still serve as chief of naval operations.[13]

Fortunately, before that test arose, a solution to the impasse was found. After lengthy discussions with Roosevelt, Knox, and others, and a legal opinion from Attorney General Robert H. Jackson, Stark decided to certify the transfer on grounds that did not compromise his integrity. Essentially, he determined that, while the destroyers were necessary for national defense, trading them for the bases would result in a net advantage to the United States. With his conscience as well as his professional judgment satisfied, Stark made the certification. Within a month of the conclusion of the "destroyer deal," the first ships had been turned over to the Royal Navy.[14]

Navy Regulations required the chief of naval operations to provide general direction to the U. S. Fleet and to prepare plans for its use in war. Thus, from Washington, Stark was responsible for providing guidance to the commander in chief of the U. S. Fleet, then in Hawaii. The efficacy of this arrangement depended in large measure upon the relationship between the two men concerned. The events of 1940 strained that relationship between Stark and his fleet commander, Admiral James O. Richardson. Before 1940 the fleet was home-ported in San Diego and San Pedro, California. After the annual exercises in May 1940, it entered Hawaiian ports for a few days before returning to the West Coast. As part of his policy of deterring Japanese aggression, Roosevelt ordered it to remain in Hawaii temporarily. Stark transmitted the order to Richardson. At first it appeared that the stay would be only a few days and little more than an inconvenience, but FDR left the fleet in Hawaii for days and then weeks, and Richardson confronted major difficulties. Among these were the absence of support facilities, which at the time were on the West Coast. Indefinitely retaining the fleet in Hawaii meant unanticipated logistical problems involving not only the repair and overhaul of ships but also the creation of stocks of fuel, ammunition, and replacement parts. Stark knew that he had barely enough ammunition ships and tankers to transport needed shells and fuel to Hawaii even for the traditional fleet visits.

Stark told Roosevelt plainly what Richardson's problems would be if the fleet were not sent back to the West Coast, but FDR remained intractable.[15] The president insisted that the fleet stay in Hawaii because he hoped that its forward deployment would deter Japan from taking advantage of British and Dutch weakness in Europe to move against their empires in Asia. Richardson believed that the combat readiness of the fleet would be adversely affected by remaining in Hawaii, and that its deterrent effect would be enhanced by returning to its bases on the West Coast.[16] Stark, whose sympathies were with Richardson, was caught between his fleet commander and the president.

Although he tied Stark's hands with regard to the deployment of the fleet, the president in 1940 provided little policy guidance for the preparation of war plans. Until May, of course, there was little he could do. Within weeks, however, the fall of France fundamentally altered the balance of power in Europe. Both Stark and General George C. Marshall, the army's chief of staff, had grave doubts that Britain could hold out alone. Later in 1940, when it became clear that Britain could remain in the war at least for a while, the chiefs continued to lack specific policy guidance from the president. Part of the reason was that 1940 was a presidential-election year and Roosevelt was running for an unprecedented third term. Regardless of his personal inclinations, he was evidently uncertain as to what foreign policy the American people would support. Thus, in 1940 and 1941, the president tended to follow public opinion rather than to lead it. For Stark, this ambivalence created enormous problems.

When Stark became CNO he inherited the navy's basic interwar plan, the Orange Plan, which dealt with a conflict with Japan and called for the U. S. Fleet to launch an offensive in the Central Pacific when war broke out. The authors of the Orange Plan assumed that the Royal Navy would restrain any aggressor in the Atlantic. But the fall of France showed the urgent need for new strategies and war plans and, before these could be drafted, a statement of fundamental American objectives in the war. Britain, of course, was the key to any American strategy. Stark was frankly pessimistic about her ability to survive in the summer of 1940 but Roosevelt was more guarded. In June, he asked the directors of army and navy intelligence to give him an estimate of the situation, based on the assumptions that Britain would remain a belligerent and eventually would receive active American naval and air assistance against Germany. This latter assumption contained political dynamite and the intelligence directors passed the problem up to Stark and Marshall, who produced a document giving top priority to hemispheric defense. Roosevelt tacitly accepted it.[17] Of course, the soundness of a strategy of hemispheric defense could not be questioned, but it was both an irreducible minimum and a palliative because it did nothing to remove the real threat.

In November 1940 Roosevelt won election to his third term, thus both assuring the continuity of his administration and removing the most immediate political obstacles to making new decisions on foreign policy. Stark seized the opportunity. A week after the election he submitted to Knox and Roosevelt a memorandum in which he reviewed the world strategic environment. It was a paper he had worked on for several weeks and which he drafted with consummate skill. He maintained that an adequate defense of the United States required the survival of Britain as a belligerent. Since Germany posed the greatest threat to Britain and the Western Hemisphere, she presented the greatest danger of the Axis Powers to the United States. Stark reasoned that American interests in the Pacific, while important, were not vital to the security of the continental United States. The survival of Britain was. He reviewed four basic alternative courses of action that would be open to America in the event she became involved in the war. He labeled the alternatives A, B, C, and D, and recommended "D," or Dog, in the military alphabet; thus, his paper became known as the Plan Dog Memorandum. This alternative called for a defensive strategy in the Pacific and an offensive strategy in the Atlantic to defeat Germany first. Roosevelt read the memorandum but did not comment on it.

Stark set forth clearly and concisely the basis of the strategy eventually adopted by the Allies during World War II. He expressed a consensus among military and naval planners which was tacitly accepted by the president. Since the plan required a degree of collaboration with the British, Stark recommended Anglo-American staff talks.[18] In response to a question by Knox at a cabinet meeting on 29 November, Roosevelt said that he had no objection to military discussions with the British.[19] This was enough authorization for Stark, who invited the first sea lord, Admiral Sir Dudley Pound, to send a delegation to Washington. The British, who had sought staff talks for some time, readily accepted the offer. Only after he had issued the invitation did Stark tell Roosevelt what he had done.[20]

The talks, conducted in great secrecy, began at the end of January 1941 and continued until early March. Stark and Marshall attended only the opening session, but monitored the conference's progress closely. The Americans predicated all their positions on the contingency that the United States might "be compelled to resort to war." For this reason they made neither commitments nor binding agreements, but the foundation was laid for future bilateral cooperation. The product of the conversations, known as the ABC-1 Agreement, established, among other things, that the defeat of Germany would be the first strategic objective and proposed command relationships in the event of American belligerency.[21] Stark, Marshall, and the service secretaries read and approved the report of the conference. Roosevelt also read it, but again took no action. Nonetheless, the ABC-1 Agreement laid the military groundwork for the wartime Grand Alliance and, in so doing, facilitated Anglo-American strategic cooperation when the United States went to war in December 1941.

The most immediate effect of ABC-1 was that it provided the necessary assumptions for the strategists to revise their existing war plans. The result was Rainbow-5, or Navy War Plan 46, which provided essentially for a defensive strategy in the Pacific and an offensive strategy in the Atlantic in order to defeat Germany first. Stark approved this plan and sent it to his fleet commanders in May 1941.[22]

Throughout 1940 and 1941 Admiral Stark constantly urged Roosevelt to temporize in the Pacific and to be more aggressive in the Atlantic, despite the fact that the United States still was not at war. He was opposed to any action being taken in the Pacific that might provoke the Japanese to respond with force against British, Dutch, or American interests in Asia. He feared that involvement in Asia would be an unwise defense of clearly secondary American interests and would inevitably detract from the Atlantic, where the main American effort should be to ensure the survival of Great Britain as an active belligerent. Although for the same reason he opposed Roosevelt's schemes for deploying parts of the Pacific Fleet to the Southwest Pacific, a few combatants did visit Australia and New Zealand. He opposed the imposition of the oil embargo in July 1941 because he was afraid the Japanese would go to war to obtain oil from the Dutch East Indies. Despite his advocacy of a defensive strategy in the Pacific, he, along with General Marshall, took some steps to reinforce the Philippines and Guam. As late as 1940 Congress refused to appropriate funds for the defense of Guam, but in 1941 some monies were made available for that purpose, too late, however, to repair years of neglect. Stark rightly believed that the possibility of losing naval forces in East Asia was too great to justify the risk of dividing the fleet at Pearl Harbor. Therefore, no substantial reinforcements were sent to Admiral Thomas C. Hart, commander in chief of the Asiatic Fleet.[23]

The Atlantic theater posed different problems. Stark felt that, by escorting convoys across the Atlantic from North America to British ports, the United States could render significant assistance to Great Britain. When the Lend-Lease Act became law in March 1941, he proposed that the U. S. Navy ships begin escorting transatlantic convoys. However, Roosevelt was reluctant to take such a positive step at that time and the rather innocuous patrol and report operations continued. In July 1941 U. S. marines were landed in Iceland as part of an arrangement to relieve the British forces there so that they could be used elsewhere to greater advantage. With the marines, who were later joined by U. S. Army troops, in Iceland, it was clear that some escort of convoys would be necessary. Shortly afterwards, the navy was authorized to escort American-flag ships to Iceland. By this time, appropriate plans had been prepared and distributed to the Atlantic Fleet, and all the fleet commander, Admiral Ernest J. King, had to do was execute them on signal from Washington.[24]

At long last, in August 1941, President Roosevelt met with Prime Minister Churchill at Argentia, Newfoundland. Both men brought their principal military and diplomatic advisers, including Stark and King. The British sought to obtain commitments for more American involvement in the Battle of the Atlantic, but none were made. The chief benefit of the meetings was that Roosevelt and Churchill and high-ranking American and British military and naval officers got to know one another and close cooperation in the near future was greatly facilitated by these personal contacts.[25]

Meanwhile, Hitler had given his submarine commanders specific orders to avoid incidents with American warships. But it was not long before American and German naval forces met. The destroyer *Greer* tracked a sonar contact for several hours before the submarine turned and fired two torpedoes. Fortunately, both missed. Although it was a somewhat slim reed, Roosevelt used the "*Greer* incident" to issue his "shoot on sight" order. In early September 1941 the Atlantic Fleet was authorized not only to escort convoys but also to fire on sight at German submarines and surface raiders. For all practical purposes, the United States was involved in an undeclared war in the Atlantic. The belligerency was not made official until Hitler gratuitously declared war on the United States on 11 December 1941.

In the Pacific it was quite a different story. While the Atlantic Fleet was actively engaged in combat operations, the Pacific Fleet was a "fleet-in-being," a deterrent to Japanese expansion. Stark had finally persuaded Roosevelt not to divide the fleet for marginally important purposes, but to permit the CNO to keep it concentrated so that it would retain its maximum striking power. In the year since the fleet had been in Hawaii, considerable effort had been made to turn Pearl Harbor into a base capable of supporting the fleet. By the time war broke out in December 1941, it had become a major base from which the U. S. Navy could conduct the Pacific war.[26]

In the last few months of 1941, as diplomatic relations deteriorated before the Japanese attacked Pearl Harbor, a stream of information and warning messages went out from Washington to the principal army and navy commands in Asia, in the Pacific, and in the Atlantic. American cryptographers had broken the Japanese diplomatic code, and as a result Stark and other officials in Washington were able to read the messages that were flowing between Tokyo and the Japanese embassies in Washington, Berlin, and elsewhere. This information gave the Americans an incalculable advantage in their negotiations with the Japanese.

Since 1940, in his personal correspondence with the fleet commanders, Stark had constantly warned them that it was only a matter of time before the United States would be at war. Every day of peace was another day in which to prepare for war, he told them.[27] Then, on 3 July 1941, he informed them by top-secret message that Washington deduced from radio intelligence that the policy adopted by the Japanese government would involve war with the United States in the near future. Although he did not anticipate immediate hostile military action, Stark told the fleet commanders of the American oil embargo on Japan one day before it was imposed so that they might take "appropriate precautionary measures against possible eventualities."[28]

Throughout the summer of 1941, the Japanese ambassador in Washington, Admiral Kichisaburo Nomura, attempted to reach some sort of an agreement with the United States, but without success. The Japanese had occupied both northern and southern Indochina in an attempt to conclude their war in China successfully. In so doing, they threatened the stability of the Western Pacific in general, and, in particular, of British and Dutch sources of colonial support for their war effort in Europe. The United States had long opposed Japanese incursions into China and actively supported the Chinese. Given the irreconcilable positions of Japan and the United States, there was little hope for peaceful accommodation.

Events took a turn for the worse in mid-October when prowar General Hideki Tojo replaced Prince Fumimaro Konoye as prime minister of Japan. The fleet commanders were informed by Stark in official and private communications of the increasing gravity of the situation. In a personal letter to Admiral Husband E. Kimmel, whom Roosevelt had chosen in February 1941 to relieve Richardson as commander in chief of the Pacific Fleet, Stark doubted that the Japanese would "sail into us." However, as the crisis worsened, Stark advised Kimmel of the possibility of war. On 7 November 1941 he again wrote to Kimmel about the steady move towards a showdown in the Pacific: "Just when it will break no one can tell. . . . A month may see, literally, anything."[29] Precisely one month later, Japan struck.

In November, both Stark and Marshall were pleading with Roosevelt and Secretary of State Cordell Hull to play for time so that they could send more reinforcements to the Philippines. Troops and aircraft were either in transit there or about to be deployed. The service chiefs reported that, by early March 1942, at the latest, the American buildup in the Philippines would be sufficient to pose a major threat to the flank of Japan, if she should move south towards the Dutch East Indies, Malaya, or Thailand.[30]

In fact, diplomacy was rapidly running its course. By 25 November Roosevelt and Hull had told Stark that a Japanese surprise attack was a real possibility but they were not certain where it would occur. Stark at once passed this comment on to Admiral Kimmel.[31]

By 27 November it was clear that Japanese-American diplomatic negotiations had broken down, and Hull told Stark that, thereafter, it was up to him and Marshall. On that day, following frequent and long meetings at the White House with Roosevelt, Hull, and some cabinet members, and after consulting with Marshall, Stark and his staff drafted a carefully worded, unequivocal message to the fleet commanders: "This dispatch is to be considered a war warning. Negotiations with Japan looking toward stabilization of conditions in the Pacific have ceased and an aggressive move by Japan is expected within the next few days. . . ." The commanders were directed to execute an "appropriate defensive deployment preparatory to carrying out the tasks assigned in WPL 46," the navy's current war plan.[32]

More dispatches were sent on 3 December informing the fleet commanders that Japanese diplomatic and consular posts around the world were destroying their codes, ciphers, and classified documents. On 6 December the fleet commanders were authorized to permit the destruction of classified documents in outlying Pacific islands.[33]

Stark expected the Japanese to strike somewhere. The great question at this time was where would they strike? A large convoy of troop transports had departed Shanghai and was proceeding south. So far as Washington knew, this was the main Japanese naval movement and all eyes were focused on it. Was its destination Indo-China? Thailand? The Kra Isthmus? Certainly Japan coveted those areas.

But another Japanese task force was at sea. It had departed home waters in late November in total secrecy and, taking a northerly route to avoid shipping lanes and possible detection, was steaming to a position north of Hawaii from which the carriers would launch dive-bombers and torpedo planes to attack Oahu. Skillful use of deceptive communications had led Washington to think that the carriers were still in home waters.[34] Neither Stark nor anyone else in Washington, and very few in Tokyo, knew that this task force was at sea, let alone knew its mission or destination.

One final diplomatic step was left before the rupture. Nomura had been joined in Washington by Saburo Kurusu, and Tokyo directed these ambassadors to present a long diplomatic note to Hull. Washington intercepted and deciphered the first thirteen of its fourteen parts on Saturday, 6 December 1941. There was nothing new in the note, which was only a rehash of what had been said before. Then, early on Sunday morning, the fourteenth part was sent and deciphered. Still, the Americans found nothing new, for it only confirmed that negotiations were at an end.[35]

However, another intercepted dispatch directed that the note be presented to Hull at precisely 1:00 p.m. on Sunday afternoon, Washington time. Officials in Washington were not sure of the significance of that instruction. Nevertheless, when Stark and Marshall saw it, they decided to send the information to the army and naval commanders in Hawaii. Stark had a hunch the Japanese might have something timed to coincide with the delivery of their dispatch: 1:00 p.m., Washington time, was 7:30 that morning in Hawaii. Stark offered to send the message from him and Marshall through the navy's communications system, but the chief of staff assured him that the army could get it there without delay. The message from Stark and Marshall left Washington at 11:52 a.m., when it was 6:22 a.m. in Oahu, and it arrived in Honolulu at 7:33 a.m., local time, but it was not delivered until after the Japanese attack had begun.[36]

The Japanese achieved complete surprise in their brilliantly planned, coordinated, and executed attack. It was a definite tactical success. However, its most important effect was that it united the American people in support of the war effort and galvanized them into action. Roosevelt now enjoyed maximum public support to wage war against the Axis. Frank Knox, the secretary of the navy, left Washington almost immediately for Hawaii, where he assessed the damage and, on his return, reported to the president that everyone had been caught off guard.[37]

Within days a major shake-up in the navy's high command began. Rear Admiral Chester W. Nimitz, chief of the Bureau of Navigation, was ordered to relieve Admiral Kimmel, and Admiral Ernest J. King, commander in chief of the Atlantic Fleet, was brought to Washington to assume operational command of the sea forces as commander in chief of the U. S. Fleet. However, Stark remained as chief of naval operations.

Even before the smoke had cleared at Pearl Harbor and the full extent of the damage had become known, Churchill agreed to come to Washington to meet with Roosevelt. He brought with him his principal military and naval advisers, who met with their American counterparts. The strategy that had been agreed upon in ABC-1 was implemented with the execution of Rainbow-5 on 7 December. To Churchill's great relief, this fundamental strategy, which gave first priority to the defeat of Germany, was confirmed. The conference also established the machinery for its execution by laying the foundation for the creation of the Combined Chiefs of Staff. In the years of war ahead, this group coordinated and directed the Anglo-American war effort under the ultimate authority of Churchill and Roosevelt.

Stark recognized King's abilities and had proposed his appointment to the important Atlantic Fleet command in 1940. Thereafter, they worked closely together. When King assumed duties as commander in chief, U. S. Fleet, or CominCh, late in 1941, that association continued. However, after the initial shock of Pearl Harbor had worn off and after the navy had more or less adjusted to being at war, Stark saw that the division between CominCh and CNO was confusing and unworkable. Since King had established his headquarters in Washington, it made good sense to merge the two offices. Stark met with Roosevelt on Saturday morning, 7 March 1942, and later that day submitted his resignation as chief of naval operations to the president and waited for new orders.[38] Two weeks after Stark left office, Roosevelt called him to the White House to present him with his second Distinguished Service Medal, this one in recognition of his service to the country in preparing the navy for war.

All the available evidence, including Stark's diary and Roosevelt's papers, suggests that Roosevelt did not force Stark to resign, despite a widespread belief to the contrary. Stark's resignation must be seen in the light of his own personality and of his relationship with Roosevelt. Stark was modest and self-effacing, remarkable characteristics for a man in such a high position. He sincerely believed that King as CominCh should also be CNO. His three months' experience after Pearl Harbor in a duumvirate with King was more than enough to convince him that that arrangement was not the best one possible. In addition, Stark was intensely loyal to Roosevelt, with whom he shared a long and intimate friendship. For this reason, it was natural that Roosevelt should choose Stark as his personal representative in London. There, Stark would have access to the highest levels of the British government and the establishment and would be able to keep Roosevelt informed of what the British were thinking without going through channels. By experience and aptitude, Stark was well qualified for a delicate politico-military mission. He had the requisite seniority and administrative skills. Roosevelt assigned him as the commander of U. S. Naval Forces in Europe, with headquarters in London. This was essentially the same post that Admiral William S. Sims had held a quarter of a century before, and Stark's appointment brought a warm and admiring letter from Mrs. Sims.[39]

Before the United States formally entered the war, she built destroyer and seaplane bases in Northern Ireland and Scotland under the Lend-Lease Act so that they would be ready for future American use. In 1943 bases were built in southern England and were earmarked for use by landing craft in the forthcoming cross-Channel operations. In 1944, after the invasion of Normandy, bases were built in western France to serve Allied ground forces operating against the Germans to the east. The planning and construction of these facilities gave rise to a whole host of new and different requirements that had to be met quickly. Repair facilities, fuel depots, and warehouses for repair parts, food, clothing, and other supplies had to be obtained or constructed and then maintained. The large influx of American naval personnel added familiar problems to the growing list of immediate and pressing material requirements. Solution of the logistics problems surrounding the massing and support of American naval forces was a necessary prerequisite to the successful prosecution of the war in Europe. Cooperation and liaison between Stark and the various members of his staff with the U. S. Army and with British and other Allied officials was a daily necessity, and Stark's success can be measured by the adequacy of the support that the Allied forces received.[40]

More importantly, Stark assumed various diplomatic and political duties. For example, in 1942 the United States maintained diplomatic relations with the French government under Marshal Philippe Pétain at Vichy. However, the Fighting French under General Charles de Gaulle controlled French territory in Africa and in the Southwest Pacific that the United States needed to use. It was therefore necessary to deal with General de Gaulle, whose headquarters were in London. At the request of Secretary of State Hull, Stark consulted with de Gaulle and got permission for the United States to use the territories under his control for a variety of purposes. In time, Stark became the de facto American ambassador to de Gaulle and his faction in London. Although he found de Gaulle could be exceedingly difficult, the admiral established a cordial and useful relationship with the French general. Indeed, Stark got along so well with de Gaulle that Anthony Eden, the British foreign minister, once jokingly asked Stark if he would handle British relations with de Gaulle as well. Stark dealt with politico-military problems involving the various European governments in exile in London on a case-by-case basis, usually at the specific request of Admiral King or the State Department, but sometimes on his own initiative.[41] He had particularly good rapport with the Norwegians, and developed a genuine friendship with King Haakon VII.

Stark's most important task in the area of politico-military affairs during the war was establishing harmonious relations with the British Admiralty and British naval commands. He had met and worked with Churchill, A. V. Alexander, first lord of the Admiralty, and Admiral Sir Dudley Pound, the first sea lord, at Argentia and in Washington in 1941. His seniority and prestige gave him easy access to the Admiralty and to Number 10 Downing Street. His friendship with President Roosevelt, his knowledge of how the Navy Department and the U. S. government functioned, and his own diplomatic and political skills made him particularly useful to Washington in dealing with the British. The ties Stark established in London endured and, in 1965, Queen Elizabeth II invited him to attend Churchill's funeral, not officially as a guest of the government, but privately as a guest of the royal family. He was ill at the time and both his doctor and his wife cautioned him against attending.

In August 1945 Admiral H. Kent Hewitt relieved Stark as commander of American naval forces in Europe and commander of the Twelfth Fleet. Stark, having passed the statutory retirement age of sixty-four in November 1944, returned to the United States and retired from the navy. He had been on continuous active duty since he entered the Naval Academy in October 1899. But before his retirement there was a major congressional investigation into the attack on Pearl Harbor and the "events and circumstances relating thereto."

Eight inquiries authorized by the president, the army, and the navy, had been carried out during the war, but this was the first public one. In 1944 Stark testified before a naval court of inquiry. To enable him to return promptly from Washington to his post in London, the court called him as the first witness, and he then departed, leaving his case in the hands of his friend and counsel, Admiral Hart, the former commander of the Asiatic Fleet. In its report, the naval court faulted Stark for failing, after he had sent the war warning message of 27 November 1941, to inform the fleet commanders that the diplomatic negotiations between Japan and America had broken down completely. The court also believed that Stark should have telephoned Kimmel on the morning of 7 December 1941 and told him that the Japanese ambassadors were to present a note to Secretary of State Hull at 1:00 p.m. that afternoon, Washington time. However, it also concluded that the Japanese attack on Pearl Harbor could not have been prevented.[42]

In 1944, in his capacity as CNO, Admiral King endorsed this report, faulting Stark for having failed to give Kimmel an adequate summary of the information then available in Washington. In his endorsement, King cited five points: (1) failure to inform Kimmel that the negotiations with Japan had collapsed after the war warning; (2) failure to inform Kimmel of Tokyo's request to her agents for information relating to the disposition of ships in Pearl Harbor; (3) failure to inform Kimmel of the order for the attack supposedly contained in the mysterious "winds" message; (4) failure to appreciate the significance of the instructions from Tokyo to the ambassadors to deliver the final note in Washington at 1:00 p.m. on 7 December; and (5) failure to convey to the fleet commanders by the tenor of his messages "the sense of intensification of critical relations between the United States and Japan." King considered these derelictions to be "faults of omission rather than faults of commission" that indicated a lack of the "superior judgment necessary for exercising command" commensurate with his rank and assigned duties. In 1945 King approved administrative action relegating Stark to a position in which "lack of superior judgment may not result in future errors," even though Stark had ably commanded American naval forces in Europe during the war and was due only for retirement.[43]

A conclusion as to the propriety and justice of King's actions, which received widespread and uncritical acceptance in the navy, depends on whether the war warning sent on 27 November, taken with other messages and personal correspondence, conveyed to Kimmel the gravity of the situation in the view of Washington officials. On 24 November Kimmel was warned by dispatch of the possibility of a Japanese "surprise aggressive movement in any direction." Three days later Stark told him, "This dispatch is to be considered a war warning" and informed him that negotiations with Japan had ended. On 3 December Stark told Kimmel that Tokyo had ordered Japanese diplomatic and consular posts to destroy their codes and ciphers. If these messages, coupled with extensive personal correspondence over several months were sufficient warning to Kimmel and the other fleet commanders to be on the alert for a Japanese attack somewhere, then one must conclude that Stark did all that was reasonably within his power to alert Kimmel. Any other conclusion would be based on hindsight and the application of an impossible standard of prescience.

Concerning King's specific points, Hull did not tell Stark that he sent one final note to the Japanese after 27 November. When Stark sent the war warning on 27 November, the latest and best information in the Navy Department was that negotiations had in fact ceased.[44] The subsequent Japanese response only confirmed what Stark had already told Kimmel. For some time Tokyo had been asking for all kinds of information from every conceivable source. There was nothing unusual about a request for data on the ships in Pearl Harbor, and when that request was coupled with Japanese movements into Southeast Asia, it seemed to be secondary.[45] No evidence has come to light that the execute order of the "winds message" was ever received, and the great weight of the evidence is that no such message was intercepted by the Americans prior to the attack on Pearl Harbor.[46]

King was correct in saying that Stark failed to appreciate the significance of the 1:00 p.m. message. But so did all the other officials in Washington who were privy to the secret intercepts, including Roosevelt, Hull, Knox, Secretary of War Henry L. Stimson, and Marshall. Moreover, even the Japanese ambassadors were ignorant of the attack on Pearl Harbor until Hull told them. The Japanese achieved such complete surprise that no one predicted it. Even afterwards, with the benefit of hindsight, no one claimed to have had such foresight. In retrospect, Stark certainly would have rested easier had he telephoned Kimmel on that fateful morning. But he could have told Kimmel little more than that he was not sure why Tokyo had directed Nomura and Kurusu to present the fourteen-part note at precisely 1:00 p.m. on Sunday.

The inescapable conclusion, based on a search of the voluminous public record, of the navy's files, and of Stark's personal papers, is that Stark kept the fleet commanders abreast of his own and of official thinking. Nothing that seemed important at the time was withheld. Washington expected an attack in "any direction, including the Philippines and Guam." This was the gist of the series of warnings. Whether Washington, in the absence of any evidence, should have expected an attack on Pearl Harbor is an entirely different question. It is still another question whether Stark's responsibility in the matter should have been absolute or whether it should have been tempered by the facts as reasonably known or knowable.

By 1948 King was having second thoughts about his endorsement, and wrote to Secretary of the Navy John L. Sullivan, attempting "to terminate, in so far as possible at this time, any continuing injustices" resulting from it. He told Sullivan that, "if I were writing the endorsement today, or had expressed myself more accurately at the time," he would have written simply that the "derelictions . . . were those of omission rather of commission—errors of judgment as distinguished from culpable inefficiency." King then urged the secretary to approve his recommendation that Stark be awarded a third Distinguished Service Medal in recognition of his services in wartime London.[47] It is ironic that King made this same recommendation in 1945, after he had endorsed the findings of the court of inquiry.

It is not clear why King wanted to change his harsh endorsement. Perhaps the leisure of retirement gave him time to think and to reconsider his actions. However, one thing is certain. King was in Stark's office several times on 26 November and again on 28 November 1941. King met with Stark and his principal assistants on both days.[48] Thus, King had firsthand knowledge of events, as seen from Stark's vantage point, and he undoubtedly participated in the continuous deliberations over the wording of the war warning. At the very least, King was an accessory before and after the dispatch of that message. Recollection of these events after his retirement may have animated his actions in 1948.

Acting favorably on King's recommendation, Secretary Sullivan presented with a great deal of pleasure a gold star in lieu of a third Distinguished Service Medal to Stark on 9 September 1948 in recognition of his services as Commander, Naval Forces, Europe, and Commander, Twelfth Fleet, during World War II. It was a belated reward by the navy for Stark's wartime achievements; in 1945, General Eisenhower had awarded Stark the army's Distinguished Service Medal.

After testifying before the Pearl Harbor hearings held by Congress, Stark retired from active naval service in April 1946. He maintained his home in Washington and a summer home in the Pennsylvania mountains where he grew up. He remained active and pursued a wide variety of interests after he left the service. His affection for the navy's bluejackets continued unabated and he devoted much of his considerable energy to the Navy Relief Society, which prospered as a result of his financial acumen.

In retirement he steadfastly refused to engage in public debate or even to comment on the substantive issues of his career. He had testified fully and completely about his participation in the events leading to Pearl Harbor, and it was all in the public record. He felt that no further justification was necessary. He had striven long and hard before the war to prepare the navy for the conflict that lay ahead. The ships, the planes, the bases, and the strategy that were put to the test in the crucible of war were ample testimony to his initiative and foresight. He saw no need to spend the rest of his life caught up in bitter recriminations and personal acrimony. He had served his country brilliantly and he had stated his case publicly and well. He left it to history to make the final judgment. He died peacefully at home in his ninety-second year on 21 August, 1972.

ERNEST JOSEPH KING

26 March 1942–15 December 1945

ROBERT WILLIAM LOVE, JR.

Ernest J. King became the ninth chief of naval operations on 26 March 1942. He relieved Admiral Harold R. Stark at the nadir of American fortunes in the Second World War. The U. S. Navy had been defeated at Pearl Harbor and evicted by Japan from the Western Pacific, and was incapable of defending the Atlantic coast of the United States against a devastating assult by German U-boats. From this depth, King galvanized the navy into a force that proved to be the major factor in the ultimate defeat of the Axis Powers at sea. He conceived and oversaw the most impressive series of naval campaigns in modern history. Not only did he wage victorious naval warfare, but he also shaped the primary Allied decisions on grand strategy that both crushed the Axis in Europe and Asia and defined the politics of the postwar world. When he surrendered his office after a tenure of 1,350 days, King emerged from the cauldron of global war as the greatest naval leader of his century.[1]

It was an unexpected conclusion to an odd naval career, punctuated by great success, devastating failure, and intermissions of torment. Born on 23 November 1878, Ernest was the oldest son of an immigrant, James Clydesdale King, a "practical Scot" of "upright and inflexible character," who worked as a foreman in railroad shops. Reared in the modestly comfortable lower-middle class of Lorain, Ohio, Ernest was "unusually close to his father," whose plain and stern Calvinism stamped a fixed imprint on the boy's temperament. Central themes of that ethic being hard work and practical learning, the elder King pressed Ernest to complete his high-school education, a rarity in a town of Republican workingmen. Valedictorian in a graduating class of thirteen students, Ernest addressed his audience on the "Values of Adversity," a theme of persistent influence not only for the boy but also for the man.

The young man was obviously bright and ambitious, and he personified the aspirations of his class and his community. Attracted to a career in the navy by an article in a boy's magazine, in 1897 King won an appointment to the Naval

Academy in a competitive examination. During his four years in Annapolis, he established part of the "service reputation" that followed him throughout his professional life. Above all, he was intelligent, and his marks were always high. King was an opportunist, but clever in achieving his ambitions. In the summer of 1898, he used the connections of a friend to obtain orders for duty aboard the cruiser *San Francisco* during which he saw some action in the Spanish-American War off Cuba. He excelled in the minutiae of "military performance" at the academy and served in his final year as cadet lieutenant commander, the highest military rank for a student at the time. But he had bravado, often unnecessarily endangering his hard-won achievements—and his temper was often uncontrollable. He stood fourth in his class when they received their commissions in 1901.[2]

King's early naval career was rather ordinary. Within five years of graduation, he served successively in the converted gunboat *Eagle* surveying Cienfuegos, Cuba; the protected cruiser *Cincinnati* in Asiatic waters during the Russo-Japanese War; the battleship *Illinois,* flagship of the European Squadron; and the battleship *Alabama* of the Atlantic Fleet. He earned a reputation for good seamanship and increasing willingness to stand up to eccentric superior officers. After being suspended from duty because of a misunderstanding with an admiral aboard the *Alabama,* King resolved to suppress his temper and independence. He did not always succeed.

In 1906, he returned to the Naval Academy as a drillmaster in infantry and artillery. The three years that he spent there allowed him to read widely—especially in history—and to write an essay on "Organization on Board Ship." Appearing in the *U. S. Naval Institute Proceedings* in 1909, the article proposed enhancing the authority of shipboard division commanders. It won him a gold medal and a reputation as a thoughtful and articulate junior officer.[3]

The next phase of King's professional life was marked by the patronage of two senior admirals. In 1909, Rear Admiral Hugo Osterhaus, about to take command of a battleship division in the Atlantic Fleet, asked King to serve as his flag secretary. After an interlude of engineering duty in 1910, in June of the next year King joined Osterhaus again when the admiral assumed command of the Atlantic Fleet. Another engineering tour was followed by his first command, the destroyer *Terry*, and, in 1915, command of a torpedo flotilla. Patronage again accelerated King's career in December 1915 when Vice Admiral Henry T. Mayo asked him to join his staff. A short, balding man with fire in his eyes, Mayo was known for his belligerent role in the Tampico crisis with Mexico in 1914. Two years later, he became commander in chief of the Atlantic Fleet. King regarded the quiet but intensely demanding Mayo as a model flag officer and he remained with the admiral throughout the First World War, moving up to become his chief of staff. From Mayo, King adopted in theory the principle of allowing his subordinates unusual initiative; in practice, his adherence to this principle varied according to the competence of the subordinates.

After leaving Mayo's staff, King reorganized the naval postgraduate school at Annapolis during the next two years. When an old antagonist was appointed to the superintendence of the Naval Academy in 1921, King was eager to escape to sea and, to avoid a clash, accepted command of a refrigerator ship.

At this time, King was a junior captain. He had been careful in developing his career. To further his plan to achieve flag rank, he decided to accumulate as much time in command at sea as he could. He had been uncomfortable during tours of temporary duty in the Navy Department and was determined to defer a full tour in Washington for as long as possible. Although he wanted to return to destroyers, in 1922 he accepted command of a submarine flotilla, and from 1923 to 1926 had command of the submarine base at New London, Connecticut. It was during this tour that he directed the widely publicized salvage of the sunken submarine *S-51*.[4]

With his eye on getting command of a deep-draft ship, King accepted the suggestion of Rear Admiral William A. Moffett, chief of the Bureau of Aeronautics, that he take the flight training required for carrier commands.[7] He completed a shortened flight course at Pensacola, commanded the seaplane tender *Wright* briefly, and became Moffett's assistant bureau chief in August 1928. Moffett, the father of American naval aviation, had shrewdly developed the autonomy of his bureau. He and King fought over this and other issues, and in May 1929, King left Washington and assumed command of the naval air base at Hampton Roads, Virginia. He bided his time and, in early 1930, asked for and received command of the new carrier *Lexington;* his captaincy of the "Lady Lex" proved to be a brilliant success. In 1932, to ensure his selection to flag rank, he entered the senior course at the Naval War College. His plan succeeded and he was selected for rear admiral the following spring.

On 3 April 1933, Moffett died in the crash of the dirigible *Akron* off the New Jersey coast. Hours after the funeral, King launched a bold and successful campaign to succeed the deceased bureau chief. He was not a skillful bureaucrat. He did not get on with the new CNO, Admiral William H. Standley. He was impatient—and often too honest—with congressional committees. He was tactless with subordinates and unnecessarily rude. Most junior naval aviators congregated around Captain John H. Towers, an early naval pilot. They regarded King, who was forty-seven years old when he went to Pensacola, as an unwelcome interloper in their ranks. Since King refused to continue many of the policies of autonomy that Moffett cherished, the gulf between King and his subordinates widened. Desperate to return to sea, King exacerbated the tension in the bureau when, in 1936, he ignored Towers and sponsored Rear Admiral Arthur B. Cook as his relief.[5]

King returned to sea in command of the seaplanes of the fleet's Base Force, and two years later assumed command of the carriers of the Battle Force as a vice admiral. In 1939, in Fleet Problem XX, he operated the carriers *Lexington* and *Enterprise* together and defeated his "opponent" in the annual war game, part of which President Roosevelt followed from the cruiser *Houston*. In the years that had passed since he left Lorain for Annapolis none of his ambition had subsided, and he wanted to succeed Admiral Leahy as chief of naval operations. He had achieved a naval record of unparalleled variety and accomplishment. Although his service in aviation and submarines was unintentional, he had, nonetheless, done well in those billets. Indeed, King's professional reputation was so outstanding that a rival, evaluating the "admirals' slate" for 1937, acknowledged that, despite his personality, King could not be ignored.[6]

One part of King's reputation in the navy concerned his unquestioned professional ability. Another concerned the private man, whose habits were less respectable. He married Martha Rankin Egerton of Baltimore in 1905 and they had six daughters before their only son, Ernest, Jr., was born. King maintained his permanent home in Annapolis, where his wife became an active socialite. As their marriage wore on, King's faithfulness to his wife eroded. In contrast to his behavior at work, in social gatherings he was charming and polished. He was handsome, intelligent, and considerate, and he enjoyed the company of women, especially beautiful women. "His appeal to women," one officer recalled, "was most unusual." He propositioned the wives of fellow officers and other men—often with the desired results. He seldom made much effort to conceal his liaisons, and these entanglements were the subject of sustained gossip, as was his drinking. He drank heavily—until the war. Sometimes these bouts with colleagues ended with harsh words being uttered in a stupor. King made it a practice to forget all that was said, but others often did not.[7]

On the job, he seemed always to be angry or annoyed. This was aggravated by a lack of patience with the shortcomings of others. On the bridge of a ship, one junior officer observed, "he was meaner than hell." Another wrote that King was the "only captain I have ever heard curse his subordinates" openly. Despised if respected by most of the younger officers with whom he had contact, King had few friends among his peers. "He was a man . . . who didn't go out of his way to make friends with people," one wrote; he seemed almost to pride himself on the fact that he had earned his rank solely on his merits as a professional naval officer, rather than as a result of the friendship of others.[8]

In the spring of 1939, King was sixty years old. For his dream of becoming CNO, it was "now or never." In fact, King lacked precisely those qualities that made Admiral William D. Leahy such a successful naval chief. Since it was against his nature to do so, King had failed to take several opportunities to befriend the president. Moreover, the delicacy of the balance of power in Europe and Asia and the important role of the navy in American diplomacy animated Roosevelt's search for a naval leader of consummate tact. Leahy, whose judgment FDR seldom questioned, recommended Rear Admiral Harold R. Stark as his relief. King was bitterly disappointed when he learned, in Stark's company, of the president's choice.[9]

Reverting to the rank of rear admiral, King left the fleet in June 1939 for duty on the General Board in Washington. Since its inception as a war-planning panel after the conflict with Spain, the board had degenerated into an advisory group of supernumerary admirals who dealt mostly with ships' characteristics. King specialized in cruisers and destroyers. Three years from the statutory retirement age of sixty-four, he feared that the General Board was "a bourn from which no traveler returns."[10]

He arrived in Washington in August 1939, a few weeks before Germany invaded Poland and drew Britain and France into the Second World War. The following May, Adolf Hitler's armies struck the Allies through Belgium, and France surrendered in June. From air bases in France, the luftwaffe waged the Battle of Britain, and from submarine bases along the Atlantic coast of Europe Admiral Karl Dönitz sent his U-boats against the Western Approaches of the United Kingdom. The British Admiralty did not have enough escorts to guard their merchant convoys, and Prime Minister Winston Churchill appealed to President Roosevelt for assistance from the navy of the benevolent neutral.[11]

In the "destroyer deal" of August 1940, FDR transferred to the Royal Navy fifty American escorts built during and shortly after World War I. After his reelection in November, the president proposed a program of arms transfers to anti-Axis belligerents. Congress passed the Lend-Lease Act on 11 March 1941 and the Admiralty quickly placed orders for a variety of antisubmarine vessels. Roosevelt remained cautious about committing American naval forces to the Battle of the Atlantic. The navy maintained a small Atlantic Squadron while most of the U. S. Fleet steamed in the Eastern Pacific. At the outbreak of the European conflict, FDR negotiated a Pan-American "neutrality zone" for the purpose of excluding U-boat operations from the Western Atlantic, and ordered Rear Admiral Hayne Ellis, commander of the Atlantic Squadron, to patrol this zone and report in clear language contacts with German submarines. By the summer of 1940, the CNO had grown dissatisfied with Ellis and decided to replace him.[12]

Stark counted himself among King's few friends in the navy. He was keenly aware of King's bitter discomfort on the General Board and tried to arrange a final billet at sea for the difficult admiral but failed. He canvased several officers in August 1940 about relieving Ellis, among them Captain Charles M. Cooke of the War Plans Division, who vigorously pressed for King as commander of the patrol force. King's year on the General Board was not wasted because his overt contempt with delay and incompetence impressed both Navy Secretary Charles Edison and his successor, Frank Knox. Together, Stark and Knox persuaded the president to send King to sea for one last tour.[13]

Admiral King broke his flag in the battleship *Texas* on 17 December 1940 at Norfolk. Committed to the strategy of "Germany first" and faced with the accelerating U-boat offensive, Stark in 1940 shifted major combatants from the Pacific to the Atlantic. To symbolize commitment to the defense of the Anglo-American sea lines of communication, Roosevelt re-created the Atlantic Fleet and King assumed command of it on 1 February 1941. By the summer, Stark had added three battleships and the carrier *Yorktown* to the Atlantic Fleet and the president had extended its mission to escorting American convoys to Iceland. This shift on 19 July from a scouting to an escort mission drew King's fleet into an undeclared war against the German U-boat force.

As a fleet commander, King showed that he had not lost his intense professionalism. With subordinates he trusted, he restrained his urge to interfere. His notion about the "initiative of the subordinate" stood as a fine principle—but was often less than a practical guide. His experience in submarines and aviation gave him insight into the complexity of antisubmarine warfare and his deployments reflected the most economical use of the limited forces at hand. His slogan, "do all that we can with what we have," became the watchword of the Atlantic Fleet. Experience and age had failed to dampen his temper, and blunt, tactless honesty remained the hallmark of his speech. After Fleet Landing Exercise 7 in February 1941 in Puerto Rico, his criticism of the marines convinced their commander, Brigadier General Holland M. Smith, that the admiral planned to relieve him. Instead, King sent him a letter of commendation. However, King's relations with army officers during the exercise quickly eroded and soured his first dealings with the chief of staff, General George C. Marshall, whose reserve and self-control contrasted sharply with King's fiery outbursts. Vigorous in defense of his subordinates and his command, King had contempt for those in other commands whose competence did not match his own.[14]

Under Admiral King, risk-taking become common for the Atlantic Fleet. He wanted to fight his ships and the escort strategy gave him his chance. Following his meeting with Churchill at the Atlantic Conference in Argentia, Newfoundland, Roosevelt ordered King to escort transatlantic convoys during the middle third of their voyage, beginning 1 September. Three days later, the *U-652* fired two torpedoes at the *Greer* and the destroyer counterattacked with depth charges. Six weeks later, off Ireland, the *U-568* torpedoed the new destroyer *Kearny* and, on 31 October, the *U-552* sank the old destroyer *Reuben James*. "There are grim facts to be faced," King wrote, and "the sooner the better." Tensions grew taut in the Atlantic Fleet.[15]

Throughout 1941 King visited Admiral Stark in Washington every three or four weeks. Although he had no hand in the evolution of prewar diplomacy or strategy, he remained in touch with the navy's problems as a two-front war approached. The American oil embargo imposed in July forced the Japanese to decide for war before the year ended. King was with Stark on 26 November when the United States rejected the final Japanese compromise. In all likelihood, before he returned to his seagoing billet, he read and agreed with the wording of a "war warning" that Admiral Stark sent to the commanders in the Pacific.[16]

Admiral King was at Newport in the cruiser *Augusta* when he learned that a Japanese naval task force had attacked the Pacific Fleet at Pearl Harbor on the morning of 7 December 1941. On the following morning, Stark ordered him to come to Washington where he remained for the rest of the week. The Navy

Department, stunned by an attack that no one had anticipated, seemed, in the words of one of King's staff, like "an ant hill of which the top had been kicked off." Knox left for Pearl Harbor to inspect the fleet. He returned on 14 December and met with Roosevelt at the White House at 10:00 that evening. Admiral Husband E. Kimmel, commander in chief of the Pacific Fleet, the secretary reported, "admitted" that he "did not expect it and had taken no adequate measures to meet it if it came." Knox proposed to relieve Kimmel, to create a board of inquiry to investigate the attack, and to separate operational control of all American naval forces from the chief of naval operations. FDR agreed to these proposals and to the secretary's nomination of Admiral King as commander in chief of the U. S. Fleet, better known CominCh. Knox and the president decided that this new command would be moved from Pearl Harbor to Washington. Concerning King's appointment, Knox wrote a few days later, "Lord, how I need him!" Knox believed that "one of my most important jobs is to transform the mental attitude of a good deal of the Navy from a defensive to an offensive posture," and that King was uniquely qualified to instill this "offensive posture" in the service. That opinion was shared by King's few friends. "King is a man of action," Captain Cooke wrote to Stark on 13 December. "Assisted by someone who advocates action, he could do things."[17]

Summoned back to Washington, King accepted the appointment from Knox on the morning of 15 December and both men met with Stark and Roosevelt at the White House in the afternoon. To establish the new office, King asked Admirals Walton R. Sexton and James O. Richardson of the General Board to draft Executive Order 8984, which gave CominCh "supreme command of the several fleets . . . and the operating forces." "Under the general direction of the Secretary of the Navy," King was to be "directly responsible to the President." Thus, operational control of the fleet plus the responsibility to "prepare and execute plans for current war operations" was taken from the CNO and given to CominCh. The president signed the order on 18 December and two days later announced King's appointment. Bureaucratic tidiness never appealed to Roosevelt, and the decision to carve the traditional planning functions of the CNO in half created an administrative nightmare. A measure of expediency in a terrible crisis, it ensured that the raiment of confusion would cloak the navy in the first few months of her new belligerency.[18]

King returned to Newport after FDR signed the order, transferred his flag to the gunboat *Vixen*, and sailed for the Washington Navy Yard. For his relief in the Atlantic Fleet, King selected Admiral Royal E. Ingersoll, and Stark named Rear Admiral Frederick J. Horne to succeed Ingersoll as assistant CNO. King named Rear Admiral Russell Willson as his first chief of staff, but they fell out and he turned to Willson's deputy, Rear Admiral Richard S. Edwards, who became chief of staff in August 1942. During King's first months in office, the functions of the War Plans Division under Rear Admiral Richmond Kelly Turner were gradually incorporated under CominCh. Meanwhile, at Pearl

Harbor, Kimmel surrendered his command to Admiral William S. Pye on 15 December.

Although Admiral King did not become CominCh until 30 December, upon his return to the capital he soon became immersed in the search for a new Allied strategy to check the Axis offensive. In this endeavor, the Americans were joined by Prime Minister Winston Churchill and some of his chiefs of staff, who arrived in Washington on 22 December for the Arcadia Conference. During these meetings, which lasted into the new year, both powers agreed to an unwritten but closely coordinated wartime alliance in which they would include other belligerents under the umbrella of the United Nations. The Americans reassured the British that they would adhere to the strategy of defeating Germany first, despite the crisis in the Pacific. To this end, they tentatively decided to mount Operation Gymnast, the Anglo-American occupation of French northwest Africa, which was administered by the collaborationist government at Vichy. In the Pacific, the Americans agreed that Singapore should be held, although they were not hopeful that it could be, and the British concurred that the Philippine Islands should be defended, although they were certain that its defense would fail.[19]

As King realized, the formula of "Germany first" meant little until it was translated into the deployment of forces. Before the attack on Pearl Harbor, Stark had agreed that, when the United States entered the war, three American battleships and the carrier *Yorktown* of the Atlantic Fleet would join the Royal Navy at Gibraltar as a support force. After the Japanese attack, Stark warned General Marshall that the "Hawaiian Islands are in terrible danger of early capture," and ordered King to send the Gibraltar support force into the Pacific to defend Pearl Harbor and the lines of communications in the Eastern Pacific. Stark also relieved the Pacific Fleet of any responsibility for defending British possessions in the Western Pacific, ordered Admiral Thomas C. Hart's small Asiatic Fleet to harass the Japanese assault on the Philippine Islands, and reluctantly approved Pye's plan to send a carrier task force to relieve the American garrison on Wake Island.[20]

When the latter mission failed, Stark got King to agree with his assessment that Wake was a "liability" and authorized the task force to return to Pearl Harbor. On 28 December, FDR complained to Stark and King that "the operations used a lot of oil and had accomplished nothing." The president insisted that the navy "take some offensive action." King saved Stark from further embarrassment by pointing to a new list of priorities for the Pacific Fleet. "The first," he said, "was holding the Hawaii-Midway line" and the second . . . was reinforcing the line Hawaii-Samoa." To these objectives, "all other projects must give way."[21]

In early December, naval strategists grimly forecast sweeping Japanese offensives against British positions on the periphery of Asia and in the Southwest Pacific, against the Dutch East Indies, and into the South Pacific. During the Arcadia Conference, the navy was the object of angry criticism because the

Asiatic Fleet had failed to thwart the Japanese campaign. On Christmas Day, General Marshall proposed a "unified command" with "one man in command of the entire theatre—air, ground, and ships." Of all the service chieftains on the Allied side during the war, none opposed "unity of command" with greater vigor than did Admiral King. "I have no intention whatever of acceding to any unity of command proposals that are not premised on a particular situation in a particular area at a particular time for a more or less particular period," he wrote. The concept was "not a panacea for all military difficulties," he cautioned, although he was aware that "amateur strategists," including the president and Secretary of War Henry L. Stimson, favored it.[22]

Nonetheless, Marshall's plan for an American-British-Dutch area command met with King's "lukewarm" approval, perhaps because the plan might apportion the blame for the disasters all knew were impending. To Marshall's scheme King appended restrictions on the theater commander's right to deploy national forces, but he supported the army chief of staff against stern opposition from the prime minister. Churchill was won over by the thought of American help for the British Empire in the East and by Marshall's nomination of Field Marshal Sir Archibald Wavell to take the ABDA Command. However, since Marshall had suggested that this organization would be a model for other theaters, the first sea lord, Admiral Sir Dudley Pound, proposed the adoption of a unified command for the North Atlantic. Despite King's direct rejection of this idea, Churchill agreed to Marshall's ABDA plan and to the appointment of an American naval commander for that area.[23]

The remaining issue that King had to settle was the extent of American naval responsibility for the defense of Australia and New Zealand. According to prewar agreements these waters were under British naval command and, until 8 January 1942, King refused to extend the responsibility of the Pacific Fleet beyond the defense of the Fijis and New Caledonia because the British wanted American ships to relieve their units for duty in the Indian Ocean. For reasons that remain obscure, he changed his mind and finally agreed both to put the Australian-New Zealand-American naval subarea under American command and to retain the remnants of the Asiatic Fleet in the Java Sea. However, he warned that in the near future the American contribution to the defense of ANZAC would be "token." Australian approval of the scheme was delayed, and neither the ABDA nor the ANZAC command was activated until late January.[24]

In the fury of the Japanese offensive, the ABDA command soon disintegrated. By the end of January, the enemy controlled the northern Solomons, New Britain, New Ireland, most of the Celebes and Borneo, southeastern Burma, and most of Malaya. On 15 February, Japanese forces landed on Sumatra, and, to the east, entered the fortress of Singapore. Aloof and difficult, but with few ships at his disposal, Hart failed to cooperate effectively with his allies. Beset with criticism of Hart from the White House, Admiral King relieved Hart and ordered him to return to the United States. Between 26 and

28 February, the Japanese defeated the remnants of Allied naval strength in the Southwest Pacific at the Battle of the Java Sea and, on 8 March, seized Lae and Salamaua in New Guinea and, to the east, accepted the surrender of Rangoon, Burma. ABDA, the first experiment in a unified, combined command, collapsed on 16 February.[25]

The trauma of Pearl Harbor, the disintegration of ABDA, and the fall of the Philippine Islands in May forced a reorganization of the American military high command in 1942. On 12 January, the War and Navy departments agreed on the creation of the Joint Chiefs of Staff, who would be directly responsible for military strategy and operations to the chief executive. Initially, the chiefs were Admiral Stark, Admiral King, General George C. Marshall, army chief of staff, and his deputy, Lieutenant General Henry H. "Hap" Arnold, chief of staff of the army air forces. At the same time, Churchill and Roosevelt agreed that the Joint Chiefs and the British Chiefs of Staff Committee would sit together during Allied conferences as the Combined Chiefs of Staff and would formulate grand strategy for the alliance.

There were only two changes on the Joint Chiefs of Staff during World War II. On 7 March 1942 Admiral Stark resigned as chief of naval operations. Since late December King had directed the fleet and Stark had continued to administer the shipbuilding program, logistics, and long-range planning. But the division of responsibility between CNO and CominCh was not clear and, in February, Stark urged FDR to give both jobs to King. Roosevelt rejected this idea until Stark voluntarily resigned on 7 March, an act that apparently surprised the president but was politically helpful to him because it made it appear that he was changing the watch in the Navy Department as a result of the recent debacles. Five days passed before FDR finally agreed to the wording of Executive Order 9096, which gave King "supreme command of the operating forces" and authority for the "coordination and direction . . . of the bureaus." Although King argued before March that CominCh was a subordinate of CNO, after he relieved Stark on 26 March 1942 he insisted on the reverse precedence.[26]

For the next three years, King quarreled with Secretary Knox, and his successor, James V. Forrestal, about the exact authority of his office, but the practical effect of the executive order was to give him unlimited control over nearly the entire navy. He personally assigned all flag officers, captains of capital ships, and holders of major shore billets, and the new chief of the Bureau of Naval Personnel, Rear Admiral Randall Jacobs, was his loyal lieutenant. Once or twice in 1942, FDR insisted on his choices for some key fleet billets; thereafter, he ended this practice entirely. Even before King learned of FDR's decision to make him CNO, he made a major personnel change: he ordered Rear Admiral Cooke to return from his command in the Pacific Fleet to Washington, relieve Admiral Turner, and take charge of strategic planning for the navy. Cooke, who was highly regarded by navy, army, and State Department officials as an extraordinarily able strategist, arrived in Washington in April, and remained there throughout the war, with various titles but with the same function: to prepare strategic plans and direct fleet operations. The addition of Cooke completed the team. Admiral Edwards, a fatherly figure and a man of great tact and forbearance, ran the CominCh staff and soothed the egos that King often bruised. As vice chief of naval operations, Admiral Horne was responsible for logistics, material, and shipbuilding. A ruthlessly efficient executive who built his empire as shrewdly as any corporate mogul, he became so powerful that King more than once accused him of intrigues with the civilian secretaries aimed at increasing his authority even more.[27]

The second change in the membership of the Joint Chiefs of Staff came in late July when FDR named Admiral Leahy, recently returned from Vichy France where he had been the American ambassador, as his personal military chief of staff and chairman of the Joint Chiefs of Staff. Throughout his career King had opposed a joint general staff system for both the army and the navy, a concept that Marshall favored greatly. However, during the first five months of 1942 it became evident that the lack of liaison between King and Marshall on the one hand, and the president on the other, was thwarting the plans of the chiefs by leaving Roosevelt vulnerable to excessive British influence. There was also public demands to bring General Douglas A. MacArthur, who had escaped from the Philippines after his army had been defeated, back to Washington as overall military commander. Both King and Marshall bridled at this prospect. As an alternative, the chief of staff proposed Admiral Leahy for the billet; since this would restore the balance of two naval officers and two army officers to the Joint Chiefs, and because Leahy was close to the president and might influence him towards the navy's views, King accepted the idea. Roosevelt agreed, but he gave Leahy none of the command authority that Marshall envisioned, and Leahy tried valiantly to be a neutral adviser, which King evidently had not anticipated.[28]

The entry of the United States into the war and the disasters of the winter forced King and Marshall to reorganize their overseas commands. At the Arcadia Conference it had been decided that the British would be responsible for the Middle East and the Indian Ocean, the United States for the Pacific, and both for the Atlantic and Europe. Marshall and King divided command in the Pacific: the Pacific Ocean Area under Admiral Chester W. Nimitz, and the Southwest Pacific Area under General MacArthur. Against Nimitz's advice, King directed ANZAC Area naval operations from Washington before and after ABDA collapsed. In late March, he redesignated ANZAC as the South Pacific Area, a subdivision of Nimitz's theater. Since FDR had decided to send Admiral Stark to London to command U. S. Naval Forces, Europe, Vice Admiral Robert L. Ghormley, who had been a naval observer in Britain since 1940, would be returning home. Roosevelt was favorably impressed with Ghormley's diplomatic work since the fall of France and probably ordered King to give him the new South Pacific command. Totally unfamiliar with the problems of the Pacific theater, Ghormley reached Washington in early April, but did not arrive at his headquarters at Nouméa until early May.

On 30 December 1941, shortly after he became CominCh, King explained the essentials of his Pacific strategy to Nimitz. He planned to block the Japanese offensive by "maintaining communications between the West Coast and Australia, chiefly by . . . holding the Hawaii-Samoa line." The Japanese had shelled Ocean and Nauru islands to the west of the British Gilberts and the American bases at Midway, Johnston, and Palmyra islands, and King thought these attacks presaged an advance against Samoa and the Ellice Islands. From Samoa, enemy air and submarine forces would be able to sever the American line of communication with Australia. By contrast with King's emphasis on the South Pacific, the attack on Midway heightened Nimitz's primary concern for the mid-Pacific axis.

To block the Japanese from the South Pacific, King proposed to garrison a chain of bases along the periphery of the enemy advance. To delay and bruise their offensive, he planned to launch a series of raids by carrier task forces against exposed Japanese ships and positions. On 6 January, the *Yorktown,* recently detached from the Atlantic Fleet, left San Diego to escort a convoy with 5,000 marines bound for Samoa; at the same time, King ordered Nimitz to send the *Lexington* to raid Wake Island while the *Enterprise* would join the *Yorktown* later in the month to attack the Gilberts and Marshalls. The sinking of the oiler *Neches* forced Nimitz to cancel the strike against Wake, but King refused to allow any postponement of the raid by the other carriers, and they hit the Gilberts and Marshalls on 1 February.[29]

Meanwhile, by 24 January, the Japanese had completed the seizure of Rabaul on New Britain Island, and the entire Bismarck Archipelago, New Guinea, and northern Australia were exposed. Two days earlier, a convoy had left the United States for New Caledonia, and on 27 January another got under way for Bora Bora. King ordered Nimitz to send the *Lexington* into the South Pacific to guard these convoys and thereafter to raid Japanese shipping. King explained that "the purpose will be to establish a system of groups of islands, whose air contingents will provide mutual support." Given the Japanese concentrations in the area, on 6 February King told Nimitz to leave one carrier task force in the South Pacific permanently. By the end of the month, King had thrown two-thirds of the striking arm of the Pacific Fleet into the South Pacific.[30]

This blocking-and-raiding strategy did not lack opponents. Nimitz tried to restrain the deployment of carriers into the South Pacific because it weakened the defense of Hawaii and Midway. And the army's strategists in Washington began to resist fiercely King's plan "to employ Army forces as occupational troops" while the marines became the shock forces for future strikes. "The Navy wants to take all the islands in the Pacific," complained Brigadier General Dwight D. Eisenhower, chief of the War Plans Division, and "have them held by Army troops, to become bases for Army pursuit planes and bombers. Then!

the Navy will have a safe place to sail its vessels." The long-term issue involved an offensive in the South Pacific. Before the war, naval strategists had plans for advancing on Japan through the Central Pacific, but such operations would require many more ships than were available in 1942 or 1943. An opportunist, King hoped instead to turn the tide in the South Pacific, where Allied land-based air power and sea power could first check the enemy offense, then seize the initiative, employing the garrisoned bases as staging points for their operations. The instant issue before the Joint Chiefs of Staff concerned the garrisoning of Tongatabu in the Tonga Islands and Efate in the New Hebrides. The offensive character of King's strategy appealed to President Roosevelt, who wrote on 18 February that "we must at all costs maintain our two flanks—the right based in Australia and New Zealand and the left in Burma, India, and China" and "plan for the more southernly permanent base to strike back from." Although on 2 March General Marshall agreed to reinforce Tongatabu and Efate, he bridled at the "suction pump" effect of Admiral King's strategy in the Pacific.[31]

King knew that the early carrier raids had inflicted little material damage on the enemy. Their major benefit was that they forced the enemy to redeploy forces in a hurry, which threw off the timing of his offensive operations. The American raid on Tokyo comported with these objectives. The idea was raised by Churchill at the Arcadia Conference and King discounted it as impractical. In January, it was resurrected by Captain Francis S. Low, of the CominCh staff, and the concurrence of General Arnold was sought. He readily agreed to a raid by B-25 bombers, which would take off from a carrier, strike the Japanese home islands, and then land in China. On 20 February, King decided to deploy the new carrier *Hornet* to the Pacific on this mission, to be accompanied by the *Enterprise* in a task force under the command of Vice Admiral William F. Halsey, Jr. They rendezvoused on 16 April in the North Pacific and launched the B-25s two days later. The tactical consequences were nugatory. The totally unexpected strategic results, however, altered the balance of power in the Pacific war.[32]

First, the Tokyo raid fell only nine days after the surrender of Bataan and blunted renewed criticism of the navy. Second, it forced the Japanese to redeploy their fleet and to renew the demand for a second strike into the Central Pacific against Midway Island. Third, King's decision to send two carriers into the Northern Pacific halved the force available to check combined operations by Japan against the Australian base at Port Moresby, on the southern edge of New Guinea.[33]

Because a large Japanese fleet entered the Indian Ocean for a brief series of raids in early April, CominCh intelligence rightly concluded that only two carriers were left to support the invasion of Port Moresby. On 19 April, King warned Nimitz to prepare to defend Port Moresby during the first week in May. At a conference in San Francisco on 25 and 26 April 1942, King and Nimitz agreed to challenge directly for the first time the enemy's fleet with their only available carriers, the *Lexington* and the *Yorktown*. During the ensuing Battle of the Coral Sea on 8 May, the Americans damaged one Japanese carrier, lost the *Lexington*, and turned back the invasion force. The engagement represented a major change in King's Pacific strategy from blocking and raiding to barring Japanese forces south of the Solomons.[34]

Four days after the clash in the Coral Sea, Admiral King warned General Marshall that "6 or 8 Japanese carriers . . . have been organized into a task force . . . for another . . . large operation to be initiated the last of May or the first part of June." Until 15 May, King continued to assume that the Japanese would "proceed with the Moresby Operation," but he admitted that "we have no information as to the nature or direction of this projected operation." By this date, Nimitz's intelligence officers had convinced him that the Japanese were about to attack Midway. After the raid on Tokyo, Halsey took the *Enterprise* and the *Hornet* into the South Pacific. On 16 May, without King's approval, Nimitz ordered him to return to Hawaii, then spent an uneasy day awaiting the reaction from Washington. The next day, King, however, agreed to Nimitz's plan, which was to concentrate his carriers off Midway; guessed that the objective of the Japanese was to destroy the American carriers to end their raids; and cautioned Nimitz "not to allow our forces to accept decisive action as would be likely to incur heavy losses in our carriers and cruisers," because they would be needed when the enemy renewed his offensive in the South Pacific later in June.[35]

As Nimitz organized his task forces to ambush the Japanese fleet off Midway, King persuaded the army air forces to deploy more bombers to Hawaii. He also asked the British Admiralty to employ their Eastern Fleet, then in the Indian Ocean, in diversionary operations against enemy positions from Rangoon to Singapore. King had sent the small carrier *Wasp* and the battleship *Washington* to join the Royal Navy's Home Fleet in April so that the British could reinforce Malta, seize French Madagascar, and strengthen their position in the Indian Ocean. Nonetheless, Admiral Pound refused King's plea for help. He claimed that the Eastern Fleet did not have enough destroyers and that, anyway, British intelligence had "no indication of an attack on either Alaska, Midway, or Hawaii."[36]

The Battle of Midway, fought from 4 to 6 June 1942, was the first unquestionable victory for American naval forces in the Pacific. From their loss of 4 carriers and 253 aircraft the Japanese navy never recovered. By contrast, King foresaw the *Yorktown*, which was sunk at Midway, being replaced within a few months, when deliveries of the first *Essex*-class carriers would begin. And, within four days of the sea fight off Midway, the president was pressing for limited offensive operations in the Pacific.

The Battle of Midway checked the Japanese offensive; it also served to illuminate unresolved issues of grand strategy that had occupied King's attention since March. On the second of that month the Joint Chiefs agreed that the cost of the British decision to reinforce the Middle East and India and the

American decision to defend Australia would be the cancellation of Operation Gymnast. General Marshall wanted to limit deployments to the Pacific and to give life to the concept of "Germany first." On 25 March, he proposed to the president that the Allies adopt his plan for an invasion from Britain by an Anglo-American army of German-occupied France. The first operation, named Sledgehammer, would be launched in September 1942, if it then appeared that Germany was about to defeat Russia or to disintegrate from internal exhaustion. The objective would be to secure a lodgment on the French coast. The second operation, Roundup, would be executed in the spring of 1943. The Allies would secure a lodgment—or exploit the position seized during Operation Sledgehammer—and engage and defeat the German army in the west. Either operation constituted a "second front" and would divert German divisions from Russia. At the White House on 1 April, Roosevelt extended his writ to the scheme. Asked by the president's Special Assistant, Harry L. Hopkins, if the operations were feasible, King nodded agreement of a qualified sort. Bypassing the new mechanism of the Combined Chiefs of Staff, Marshall and Hopkins flew to London, where the British, with reservations, also approved Sledgehammer and Roundup. To ensure American adherence to "Germany first," British qualifications were muted.[37]

Hopkins expected more opposition from Admiral King, since the army's plans promised to retard the development of bases in the South Pacific and to upset the navy's shipbuilding program. The key deficiency was in oceangoing landing craft. Specific requirements for a cross-Channel operation were somewhat vague. On 4 April President Roosevelt initiated the first landing-craft program by ordering the navy to build 8,200 craft of all types for the cross-Channel operations; about one-quarter of them were to be ready for Operation Sledgehammer in September. A month later, he instructed King to revise that program and build more oceangoing landing craft, in accordance with proposals made by the Admiralty. However, as King explained to the president on 16 May, making up shortages in these craft for Sledgehammer meant that the navy would have to stop building carriers and escort vessels and deliveries of all other ships would be delayed. Unwilling to pay this price, FDR nonetheless refused to abandon Sledgehammer. He put landing craft at the top of his precedence list for production, but refused to abandon the other programs.[38]

King had more confidence in Operation Roundup than he did in Sledgehammer, and the ambivalence that Roosevelt showed during their meeting on 16 May justified that point of view. Nonetheless, the president's failure to specify realistic priorities had widespread repercussions. In this same month, latent British opposition to Sledgehammer began to surface. In early June, Churchill sent Vice Admiral Lord Louis Mountbatten, head of Combined Operations, to Washington to discourage the Americans from the project. His brief interview with Admiral King was somewhat tense, but it did result in the CNO sending Rear Admiral H. Kent Hewitt to study British amphibious training. Churchill and his chiefs crossed the Atlantic in mid-month to elaborate other reservations. Thus, in June American plans for a Channel crossing in 1942 dissolved rapidly and no alternative was in sight.[39]

Into this vacuum King moved decisively. To army leaders, the victory at Midway justified an end to further deployments to the Pacific theaters. However, King had always planned to use the South Pacific bases as staging points for a limited offensive whose objective was to bar a renewed Japanese drive southward and, by 12 June, he had secured General Marshall's agreement to a campaign in the Solomons leading to the enemy air base at Rabaul on New Britain in the Bismarck Archipelago. King proposed that a marine division, covered by aircraft from three carriers of the Pacific Fleet, land on Tulagi and Guadalcanal in the lower Solomons. These islands were in MacArthur's Southwest Pacific Area, and Marshall and King spent the next three weeks debating the delicate issue of command. Hart's bitter experience with MacArthur in the Philippines had soured King toward the histrionic general and he refused to put the carriers under army command. At an impasse, King threatened to order the navy to mount the operation alone. This stunned Marshall into accepting a compromise in which the Joint Chiefs shifted the boundary of the South Pacific command slightly to the west and the operation was divided into three tasks. Task 1 called for the seizure of Tulagi and Guadalcanal under the overall command of Admiral Nimitz and the direction of Admiral Ghormley. Task 2 included the recapture of Lae, Salamaua, and the northern coast of New Guinea. Task 3 would conclude with an assault on Rabaul. General MacArthur was to assume command for Tasks 2 and 3. This agreement was reached on 2 July, and on the fourth King met Nimitz in San Francisco and explained the plan.[40]

In the meantime, British antipathy toward Operation Sledgehammer had intensified and, on 8 July, Prime Minister Churchill informed President Roosevelt that it was impractical. Furious, Marshall and King proposed to expand the Solomons campaign into a "Pacific alternative" to the strategy of "Germany first," if the British refused to mount Sledgehammer. King later claimed that he "supported Marshall's proposal in order to put pressure on the British," since he thought that "they had never been in wholehearted agreement with the operation." Marshall also claimed after the event that the alternative was a bluff. Roosevelt rejected it gruffly and demanded Allied operations against the German Army in 1942. He sent King, Marshall, and Hopkins to London in late July to explore the options. The British favored a revised Operation Gymnast, which had been renamed Torch. This plan called for the occupation of French Morocco and Algeria and a quick thrust against the Axis base in Tunis to assist the British in Egypt. Roosevelt's instructions having left them no alternative, the Americans agreed. The poisoned relations between Britain and Vichy France, whose deputies governed North Africa, meant that an American had to command the operation. King nominated General Eisenhower, who was already in London, and Marshall instantly agreed to this suggestion. King then named Hewitt to command U. S. naval forces in the landings.[41]

During August, discussions between Washington and London continued over how extensive the landings should be. The British wanted to drive deep into the Mediterranean; U. S. Army strategists insisted on seizing Casablanca, in case Fascist Spain closed the Strait of Gibraltar after the landings. King's staff suggested that political guarantees be offered to Francisco Franco, the Spanish dictator, in return for his neutrality. By the end of the month, Roosevelt and Churchill agreed to order Eisenhower to occupy Casablanca, Algiers, and Oran, and to move eastward with rapidity. Nevertheless, King's enthusiasm for Operation Torch was never more than measured. The American and British navies opposed Torch because the deployment of the U. S. Army in North Africa would open a new and exposed front in the continuing Battle of the Atlantic. And Allied successes against the U-boats of Admiral Dönitz prior to the summer of 1942 were limited and transitory.[42]

All interpretations of "Germany first" at the Arcadia Conference included the securing of the sea lines of communication across the Atlantic Ocean. In December 1941, King warned the conferees that they could expect Dönitz to attack the East Coast within a few weeks. To defend the seaboard King had few ships or planes: most of the Atlantic Fleet's destroyers were deployed in ocean escort groups to defend convoys from North America to Britain. The president's decision at Arcadia to send fresh American soldiers to Britain to relieve seasoned units for duty elsewhere inaugurated a new charge on these slim resources in the form of the troop convoys. The decision to defend Australia plus the need to escort shipping in the Eastern Pacific meant that King could not continue to shift escort vessels from that theater into the Atlantic. From new construction in 1942, he could expect few additions to his antisubmarine forces. The *Benson*-class destroyers were built for the storms and short voyages of the North Atlantic, whereas those of the *Fletcher* class, which carried more fuel but had less weather protection, were intended for the Pacific Fleet. Thus, decisions made in 1940 and 1941 had cast in iron the delivery schedule for escorts for most of 1942. The navy had few patrol planes on the East Coast and Vice Admiral Adolphus Andrews, commander of the Eastern Sea Frontier, which extended from Maine to Key West, had no authority to deploy army air force bombers. When the *U-123* sank the steamer *Cyclops* off Cape Cod on 12 January 1942 and opened the German offensive, King warned that he did not have enough ships to defend the Atlantic seaboard.[43]

Admirals King and Pound agreed that allied cooperation was essential in the Battle of the Atlantic. The Admiralty believed that it was "in the Atlantic alone that the vital interests of ourselves and the United States are identical" and the British could "expect direct assistance . . . which may enable us to release our own forces for service in . . . the Eastern Mediterranean and the Indian Ocean." To this end, throughout 1942 and 1943 Pound pressed King to accept British command in the Atlantic and to deploy more ships to the theater. King, however, wanted to retain a divided command with a minimum of mixed Anglo-American units. He wanted to draw more British ships into the Atlantic to reduce their operations in areas that he considered secondary. His control over ships transferred under the Lend-Lease Act proved to be a major lever in the long term; in the near term, Pound used his few surplus antisubmarine vessels to extract promises of future deliveries. For example, at the Arcadia Conference, he promised to transfer ten corvettes to the Eastern Sea Frontier and secured in return King's vague pledge under a "gentleman's agreement" that the Royal Navy could continue to expect deliveries of escort carriers, destroyer escorts, and oceangoing landing craft, but no fleet carriers, cruisers, or destroyers.[44]

King believed that the "only" solution to the U-boat offensive was the initiation of well-escorted coastal convoys. In mid-January, he persuaded Pound to shorten the transatlantic convoy route, a move that would, by April, release several American destroyers for Andrews's command. Nonetheless, as sinkings off the East Coast increased in February and March, the demands on Admiral King grew intense. For the first four months of 1942 the Admiralty pressured King to begin convoys. At Pound's urging, on 6 February Churchill asked Hopkins "to make sure that the President's attention has been drawn to the very heavy sinkings by U-boats in the Western North Atlantic." To hasten the start of coastal convoys, the British offered twenty-four more antisubmarine craft but, despite a series of British proposals, King consistently refused to reduce further the number of escorts on the transatlantic crossings. He persuaded FDR in March to reject Churchill's suggestion that destroyers be shifted from the Pacific to the East Coast. And he even allowed Andrews to try offensive patrolling, a strategy in which neither had any faith and that failed to check the losses.[45]

King was "firmly convinced that inadequately escorted convoys are worse than none" because they would concentrate targets for the U-boats without affording significant protection, whereas the British argued that their experience proved that convoys, even with minimal escorts, resulted in fewer sinkings. King had the better of the argument. Without adequate escorts, the forming of convoys was a slow process by contrast to the speedier, if more dangerous, tactic of independent routings. Although losses were greater for merchantmen steaming alone, over the short term the difference in port time meant that the premature introduction of coastal convoys in 1942 would have reduced gross carrying capacity far beyond the tonnage losses inflicted in the spring by the U-boats. King's failure to explain this carefully to the British exacerbated a relationship that was already acid.[46]

By contrast with British leaders, the president was restrained in his criticism of the navy's failure to defend the coast. He claimed that "my Navy has been definitely slack in preparing for this submarine war," for which he blamed the navy's opposition to building small escort vessels. He demanded that King undertake a large building program for patrol craft and submarine chasers and insisted that the navy convert nearly 4,000 privately owned pleasure craft for antisubmarine duty. King scorned this "faith in the efficacy of such small patrol craft," but these vessels allowed him, on 1 April, to inaugurate limited "daylight" coastal convoys with a total of 28 escorts. The system was an immediate success. On the following day, King agreed with an estimate that the guarding of continuous convoys between Halifax, New York, Key West, and Guantánamo, Cuba, would require thirty-one destroyers and forty-seven patrol craft or corvettes. New construction would make up the deficiency in patrol craft, but King believed that each convoy had to be escorted by at least two destroyers, and he could acquire these only by transferring them from the transatlantic convoys. Since he had refused to weaken the escort forces for oceanic convoys, the only alternative was to decrease the number of sailings. At King's urging, Roosevelt asked Churchill to accept this plan on 17 March, and the prime minister consented when the president agreed to make up in 1943 the consequent loss of imports to Britain.[47]

The quick success of the "daylight" coastal convoys forced Dönitz to concentrate his U-boats southward, against oil tankers in the Gulf of Mexico and the Caribbean. By 14 April, losses were so high that Churchill and Pound suggested to Hopkins, then in London to discuss a "second front," that all tanker sailings be suspended until King could protect the ships. FDR and Admiral King agreed, and the latter called all tankers into port. To begin Caribbean convoys, King needed about a dozen escorts and, to obtain them, he asked Admiral Pound to extend the range of the British destroyers guarding convoys in the Western Approaches of the United Kingdom. On 12 May Pound agreed reluctantly in face of opposition from his subordinates. Three days later, King ordered Andrews to begin escorting convoys from New York to Key West and losses soon declined. Over the next few months, as escorts became available, this interlocking convoy system was extended into the Gulf of Mexico and the Caribbean and sinkings in those waters declined dramatically.[48]

Although, in June, King had also convinced General Marshall that all army aircraft along the coast should be under naval command, he was not satisfied that the problem of the U-boats could be resolved until the Allies were able to deploy sufficient escorts. Since his days on the General Board, he had pressed for the rapid, mass construction of a simple destroyer escort which, unlike patrol craft, would be able to operate in bad weather and throughout the year. In June 1941, the Admiralty had ordered 300 destroyer escorts under Lend-Lease, but progress was slow and, because they were built in the same yards that built landing craft, the "first landing craft program" begun in April 1942 promised to delay construction of the antisubmarine ships until late 1943.[49]

The first modest American victory in the U-boat war was followed on 7 August 1942 by the unopposed landings of the marines on Tulagi and Guadalcanal. However, in the early morning of 9 August, Japanese surface ships sank one Australian and three American cruisers in the Battle of Savo Island. King excused Admiral Turner, who had tactical command, and blamed Admiral Frank Jack Fletcher, who had withdrawn his carriers before the attack. During the next weeks, losses began to multiply. On 31 August a Japanese submarine badly damaged the *Saratoga;* two weeks later another sank the *Wasp.* As the crisis mounted in the South Pacific, King's expectations for a rapid advance on Rabaul collapsed. MacArthur had checked an overland stroke only thirty-two miles from Port Moresby but seemed incapable of further exertion. The loss of the carriers left Nimitz with only the *Enterprise* and the *Hornet* in the entire theater, the landing-craft program having delayed the completion of the *Essex*-class carriers until early 1943.[50]

Moreover, the Japanese decision to accept an air war of attrition in the Solomons compelled King to press the army for accelerated deliveries to the Pacific air forces. These demands created a prolonged and complex dispute which centered around the relative priorities of Torch and the Guadalcanal operation. Willing early in the war to abandon Australia, General Arnold never favored the advance into the Solomons, and during August and September he refused to augment the army air force in the South Pacific. Admiral King argued that air reinforcements should be sent "to the extent necessary, regardless of interference with 'commitments' for the Eastern Atlantic." Nimitz complained to King along these lines when they met again in San Francisco on 7 and 8 September. Pleading with Marshall that he had "gone much beyond our commitments" toward meeting the requirements for Operation Torch, King continued to demand more army air force fighters and bombers for the South Pacific. From Marshall's standpoint, the blunt fact remained that "the reinforcements which you propose can only be effected by diversions from Torch."[51]

On the other hand, the president told the Pacific War Council on 15 September that he was "frankly . . . pessimistic at the moment about the whole situation," and warned that the loss of Guadalcanal would have a devastating effect on American public opinion. Press attacks on the navy reached such a pitch that Secretary of War Stimson compared their authors to "hounds on a hot trail." On at least one occasion, King personally pleaded with Marshall for help, but to no avail. On 3 October, he claimed that "the evidence is cumulative—and now seems positive—that the enemy is massing great strength of all types . . . to attack on either the Papuan Peninsula or the Tulagi Area or both" and, in the Battle of Cape Esperance on 11 and 12 October, the Japanese tried to sever the American supply line to Guadalcanal. Shortly thereafter, Nimitz admitted that Ghormley, the commander in the South Pacific, was "unable to control the sea in the Guadalcanal area," and King warned on 21 October that the Japanese concentration in the South Pacific "greatly exceeds our movement." Ghormley insisted that the forthcoming enemy strokes would find his "forces totally inadequate to meet [the] situation." By the middle of the month King had ordered Nimitz to denude the Central Pacific and reinforce the South Pacific command with his last carrier, the *Enterprise*.[52]

To inject greater confidence into that command, Nimitz asked King for permission to relieve Ghormley. On 16 October King agreed, and Admiral Halsey flew to Nouméa to assume the South Pacific command. King had great sympathy for Ghormley. Some weeks later, when they talked, he noticed

Ghormley's rotted teeth and concluded that his dental problems lay at the root of his difficulties. He ordered Ghormley to have his teeth treated and gave him an obscure billet. Command of the carriers also shifted during the crisis. Admiral Fletcher, whose timidity had often annoyed King, was injured when the *Saratoga* was torpedoed and King ordered him to return to Washington for a medical evaluation. To relieve Fletcher in the South Pacific, King sent Rear Admiral Thomas C. Kinkaid, an aggressive leader who was as determined as was Halsey to stop the Japanese.[53]

Admiral King's insistent pressure, the military crisis on Guadalcanal, and the firm calculation of the initial costs of Operation Torch forced Marshall and Arnold to concede two points on 16 October: air strength on Guadalcanal and Espíritu Santo would be increased to the full capacity of those bases; and Nimitz would be given complete freedom, previously denied, to shift army aircraft about within his theater. Despite his earlier concern, President Roosevelt did not intervene until 24 October. Prompted in all likelihood by intelligence reports of an enemy offensive, he wrote to Marshall and King that his "anxiety about the South Pacific is to make sure that every possible weapon gets in that area to hold Guadalcanal . . . even though it means delay in our other commitments. . . ."[54]

The president's decision, which ensured more cargo ships for the South Pacific, had a long-term effect; the deployment of the *Enterprise*, the infusion of aircraft, and the changes in commands produced immediate results. The *Enterprise* reached the area 24 October; two days later, in the Battle of the Santa Cruz Islands, she was damaged and the *Hornet* was sunk, but the Japanese fleet withdrew to Truk. Determined that a loss in the next battle would give "the enemy quite a free hand," King ordered Nimitz to hasten repairs on the *Saratoga* and send her back into the South Pacific. His plans called for her arrival by 22 November. At the same time, he shifted into the waters around Guadalcanal a battleship task force from the Atlantic and twenty-four submarines from the Southwest Pacific. Except for the submarines, none of these units had arrived by the time a cruiser-destroyer task force, in a melee on 12 November, turned back a line of Japanese battleships. Two days later, guided by radar, two American battleships stopped a Japanese convoy and sank a battleship and four transports. The naval Battle of Guadalcanal not only ended the crisis in the South Pacific, but also encouraged King to begin planning the next stroke against the Japanese. Indeed, because of the victory at Guadalcanal and MacArthur's defense of Port Moresby, the Joint Chiefs agreed "to maintain the initiative in the Solomons-Bismarcks-East New Guinea area. . . ." However, Admiral King by the end of the year had concluded that broad statements were pallid substitutes for agreements on exact allocations of forces and concurrence on specific operations.[55]

The pace of the campaign in the South Pacific maddened King, and in early December, when he conferred with Nimitz in San Francisco, he proposed a bold stroke to outflank Rabaul and strike far to the north, seizing the Admiralty

Islands. Tried by the struggle in the Solomons and more sensitive to the flaws of boldness than was King, Nimitz had no enthusiasm for the idea. He soothed King with the balm that operations at Guadalcanal would shortly be accelerated, but he insisted on approaching Rabaul in slow, deliberate steps which assured that the enemy could not sever his line of communications. To do this, Nimitz pleaded for more forces. King seemed to agree. To give the appearance of action, Nimitz proposed to retake Kiska in March 1943, an operation that would be of greater political importance than military necessity.[56]

The next year ignited King's resolve once again. In January he put his strategy of outflanking Rabaul and seizing the Admiralties before General Marshall. The chief of staff queried General MacArthur, who decried any offensive campaign in the foreseeable future. Marshall also refused to recast planned operations or to free Halsey's forces from the deadening hand of MacArthur's authority, under which they would fall as Halsey moved up the Solomons and into the Southwest Pacific theater. Although King claimed in mid-January that the Japanese could be evicted from Rabaul by May, he knew that this happy prospect grew more dim with each inactive day.[57]

Despite King's discontent, the campaign in Guadalcanal had ended the Japanese offensive in the Pacific. In December 1942 the Russians stopped the Germans before Stalingrad and counterattacked. Two months earlier, the British Eighth Army defeated the Afrika Korps on the El Alamein line, and a few weeks later Anglo-American amphibious task forces descended on French North Africa. This rapid improvement in their fortunes convinced Allied leaders to meet in January 1943 to plan their strategies for the coming year.

At that meeting, which took place in Casablanca, King and his fellow chiefs dealt with three main issues. First, he and Admiral Pound persuaded everyone that "the defeat of the U-boat must remain a first charge on the resources of the United Nations." This accord took into account the fact that the new convoy route from America to North Africa had created an additional drain on Admiral King's limited pool of escorts and that a new onslaught by the U-boats in the North Atlantic would begin when the weather improved in March.[58] The second issue involved a cross-Channel invasion of France in 1943, which Marshall advocated and Churchill and the chief of the Imperial General Staff, General Alan Brooke, had long opposed. The British wanted to continue the campaign in the Mediterranean by jumping from North Africa to Sardinia or Sicily. King was ambivalent on this key strategic point. He was impressed by the arguments of his advisers that control of Sicily would open the Mediterranean to Allied shipping and that the British and American navies could not redeploy their armies to Britain in time to invade France in the fall of 1943. On the other hand, he wanted to avoid prolonged operations in the Mediterranean and to end the European war quickly so that the war against Japan could be prosecuted with greater vigor. In the end, however, King failed to strongly support Marshall on the matter. Since Roosevelt did not object to continuing the Mediterranean strategy, the conferees decided to seize Sicily or Sardinia after the collapse of Tunis.[59]

The third issue concerned the war against Japan. Sharp divisions along national lines marked the discussions. Implying that the American victories at Midway and Guadalcanal had ended the threat from Japan, Pound proposed that the Allies mount no more operations in the Pacific, since they would be unnecessary and would disperse Anglo-American resources. King countered that failure to contain Japan would ultimately endanger the main effort in Europe and that the proportion of assets applied to the Pacific was already too low. To intensify the pressure on Japan, he explained, a naval drive across the Central Pacific would be more economical than operations in the North Pacific or in the South Pacific beyond Rabaul. Such a strategy, of course, would enjoy the added benefit that the main operations would be conducted in the Pacific theater where the navy was the dominant service and the army's hand in military planning was minimal. At one meeting, King exploded in rage when General Brooke refused to agree to a continuance of Pacific operations. The impasse was broken when the Combined Chiefs agreed that the campaign against Rabaul should be concluded and operations in the Marshall Islands, which would lead eventually to the Philippines, should be undertaken. At the same time, King pressed for some sort of British operation against Japanese positions in Burma which he believed would compel the enemy to divide his forces between South Asia and the Pacific. Pound demurred, citing lack of ships and landing craft. Despite King's offer to provide some of these from new American construction in 1943, the British refused to create a major diversionary effort to ease the path of the Pacific Fleet.[60]

King visited several naval bases and air stations on his way back from Casablanca to Washington. Anxious to act upon the compromise that had been reached with the British, he told Nimitz to meet him again in San Francisco in February to discuss strategy. Nimitz continued to oppose King's suggestion that bold flanking operations be mounted in the South Pacific. He preferred a slow and measured pace up the Solomons. Nonetheless, King made it clear he would no longer sanction a frontal attack on Rabaul. As an alternative to a prolonged campaign in the Southwest Pacific theater, he brought up his plan to shift the weight of the offensive to the Central Pacific in 1943 by seizing the Gilbert Islands. In theory, this idea appealed to Nimitz. In practice, he claimed that he could take the Gilberts in 1943 but his forces would be too thin to hold them against a Japanese counterattack from the nearby Marshall Islands. Part of the problem lay in the uncertainty over the exact costs of operations in the South Pacific. Another was the lack of seaborne air power, but King assured Nimitz that the shipbuilding schedule for 1943 would expand the fleet enough for an offensive in the Central Pacific.[61]

King had repeatedly asked Marshall to insist that MacArthur clarify his plans for operations against Rabaul. This timetable was clouded by conflicting interpretations of the vague language used by the Combined Chiefs in their agreements at the Casablanca Conference. At that meeting, Allied air force leaders started planning for a combined bomber offensive against Germany. By February 1943 naval planners were complaining that the army air force had reduced scheduled deliveries of aircraft to the Pacific for the remainder of the year in order to increase their forces in Britain for the coming bomber campaign, justifying the change on the grounds of "Germany first." Meanwhile, MacArthur refused King's request that he send heavy bombers from his Southwest Pacific theater to help Halsey check an anticipated Japanese attack against Guadalcanal. Although the attack did not take place, the episode highlighted the lack of coordination that plagued the Pacific campaign. To solve these problems, King and Marshall asked the Pacific commanders to send senior members of their staffs to Washington in March. The presence of the field commanders at the ensuing Pacific Military Conference lent weight to King's arguments that more land-based aircraft were needed in both Pacific areas and possibly induced the president to intervene on the navy's side. Marshall agreed and ordered the air staff to increase deliveries of aircraft in the Pacific for 1943. After the meeting, the Joint Chiefs decided that Halsey—under MacArthur's overall direction—would move up the Solomons to New Georgia and New Britain while MacArthur would edge along the northern coast of New Guinea, both advances converging on Rabaul. This decision tied the War Department to specific allocations of shipping and aircraft to the Pacific in 1943, and satisfied for the time being King's persistent objections to the Pacific theater being dependent on what was left over from the European theater. Nonetheless, for King, it was a spring of discontent and frustration because the continued indecision on strategy in Europe curbed his plans to step up the naval war against Japan.[62]

By the end of 1942, King had established routines that remained fairly constant throughout the war. With Admiral Cooke, he lived aboard the yacht *Dauntless,* which was moored at the Washington Navy Yard. His wife lived in the CNO's official residence at Naval Observatory Circle; they saw one another infrequently, although he occasionally visited for dinner on weekends. On Tuesdays King lunched with the Joint Chiefs of Staff at the Public Health Building, across Constitution Avenue from the navy's offices. On Friday afternoons, he and the other chiefs met in the same place with the British military representatives. Although he had always enjoyed an active social life, he avoided parties. When protocol required his attendance at them, he drank sherry or beer and tried valiantly to avoid hard liquor. He did not always succeed. He smoked constantly, his slender fingers inserting cigarettes into a long holder. His eyesight had worsened and he wore glasses to read, although he removed them to pose for photographs. As CNO, King's penchant for experimenting with uniforms had free rein. He wore a cap on which the eagle was reversed, a variety of sweaters under his coat, and a defiant white handkerchief in his breast pocket. He adopted a uniform cut from a gray cloth which naval officers in Washington had to wear—and failed to appreciate the joke when his chief of staff, who hated the color, as did most others, adorned the coat with a dazzling array of gold braid and odd decorations![63]

King reached the official retirement age of sixty-four in 1942 but FDR ignored the fact. Age had not dulled the sharp edge of his razorlike personality.

It often appeared that he "never excused a fault," a belief held throughout the navy. Most of all, he detested sloth. Captain Cato D. Glover, Jr., who served on his staff, admitted that King was "meaner than I can describe." "He was cold blooded," recalled Admiral Bernhard H. Bieri, his assistant chief of staff, "you either did your job or you got out." And "only the brave and the foolish crossed him," Glover somberly noted. Nonetheless, he seldom imposed his views on those he trusted, and both Edwards and Cooke consistently intervened to save from exile good officers who had aroused his ire. King's reputation often exceeded reality. He had a keen, if unusual, sense of humor, and he often calmed anxious subordinates by assuring them that "sometimes my bark is worse than my bite." His reputation for never forgiving a fault was not truly justified. To flag officers—and others—who were removed from active commands King often gave less demanding but worthwhile assignments. He made Admiral Fletcher commander of the North Pacific area in 1943 and, at the end of the war, gave Ghormley the important command of American naval forces in Germany. He unashamedly played favorites with his few friends in the navy. He kept Admiral Turner in command after the debacle off Savo Island and, against the best advice of his staff, left Admiral Robert A. Theobald in charge of naval forces in Alaska for six months after the disaster at Dutch Harbor. He refused to criticize Admiral Halsey after he bungled the Battle of Leyte Gulf and then ran the Third Fleet into a typhoon. "Any officer," he wrote, "can 'redeem' himself by outstanding and long-continued demonstration of professional capacity." However, he could be mindlessly cruel at the same time he tried to help someone. Many in the navy blamed Admiral Stark for the defeat at Pearl Harbor, but King, who evidently did not believe Stark's claim that he had resigned, felt that his friend had been mistreated by President Roosevelt. In 1943, he tried to arrange a separate American naval command for Operation Overlord and to give it to Stark, but the project failed. Shortly thereafter, he endorsed the report of a court of inquiry that held Stark in part responsible for Pearl Harbor, a view that King recanted after the war.[64]

King knew that he was unpopular and that he would have retired to obscurity had war not broken out. His authority as CNO depended solely on the president, who was one of his few unreserved admirers. Roosevelt viewed him with bemused affection. FDR loved the navy but often criticized it for being too conservative and "not a good hand at improvising." By contrast with those of other admirals, King's methods must have seemed to the president startling but effective. Although King was never Roosevelt's personal friend—as was Leahy—the two men got along well and, during the difficult days of the U-boat assault on the East Coast early in the war, FDR supported King completely in his dealings with the British. In late 1943, when Washington was alive with rumors that King would be replaced—rumors spread by Secretary Knox and Undersecretary James V. Forrestal—the president made a special point of applauding the admiral's work, along with that of General Marshall, on national radio, and told reporters that King's duties might even be increased. King and Roosevelt sharply disagreed on only one point: reorganization of the Navy

Department. During the war, King enjoyed ad hoc authority over the bureau chiefs and wanted to make the arrangement permanent. In early March 1942, FDR ordered him to make changes in the navy's organization but, when he found out what King planned, he rescinded the order and even pretended that he had never intended changes to be made. However, this was consistent with FDR's refusal to legitimatize other temporary wartime arrangements. He consistently refused, for example, to grant a charter to the Joint Chiefs of Staff.[65]

King and Secretary Knox also disagreed over reorganization of the Navy Department. An amiable, talkative, and impulsive man, Knox was quite unlike King in temperament and character. They clashed repeatedly over the extent of press coverage that naval operations should be given. Knox, a newspaper publisher, wanted reporters in the Pacific theater to have more freedom than the navy allowed, while King was constantly afraid that they would print information that would help the enemy. Shortly after the Battle of Midway, a newspaper article disclosed elements of the navy's radio intelligence operations. This and other episodes strengthened King's argument, and Knox never fully overcame it. In general, Knox stood in awe of King, and the admiral did nothing to create a working partnership such as existed between Secretary Henry Stimson and General Marshall in the War Department. Referring to Knox, Stimson recorded in his diary: "I am amazed again and again how little he knows about the plans of his own people."[66] By contrast to his correct relations with Knox, King's attitude toward Knox's successor, Forrestal, was unconcealed hostility. King and Forrestal detested one another, and King went out of his way to slight the secretary. By the end of the war, Admirals Edwards and Cooke were acting as emissaries between the two.[67]

Among the Joint Chiefs, King and Arnold engaged in acid dialogue that reflected old and poisonous differences between the navy and the army air force over military policy. Arnold was often the object of King's most colorful barbs. King and Admiral Leahy were old friends. Leahy kept his promise to stay out of Navy Department business and his guidance of the Joint Chiefs was indirect but sure. The hinge of the higher direction of the American war effort was the working relationship between Admiral King and General Marshall, two men quite different in tastes, personality, and background. The chief of staff was a man of great tact and breadth; the CNO was a man of blunt speech and agonizing precision. Marshall hid his temper under a cover of tremendous reserve; King was easily roused and often became so enraged that he was physically incapable of talking. Marshall was a superb conversationalist and public speaker; King had trouble engaging in small talk with men and hated public speaking. They probably did not like one another very much, and during the first few months of the war things did not go well with them, in part because their parochial interests were so intense. Both matured with the war, joined together by the bond of necessity and the fear that if they did not unite the British would exerise unwarranted influence over the president. And, as the war progressed, King, the greater strategist, often gave way to Marshall, the greater man. That King realized this essential fact was itself an illustration of his remarkable willingness to engage in remorseless self-examination.[68]

Marshall's greatest contribution to the war was his advocacy of a cross-Channel operation, and in 1943 King shared the general's faith in the plan but put little trust in the willingness of the British to concur or in the ability of the Americans to persuade the British to change their minds. One diversion, he feared, would follow another. As the British leaders sailed for Washington and the Trident Conference, which began on 12 May 1943, Allied armies entered Tunis, and Eisenhower began to plan Operation Husky, the amphibious descent on the island of Sicily. However, during two meetings with Roosevelt, on 2 and 7 May, Marshall and King finally persuaded the chief executive to support unswervingly the cross-Channel strategy for 1944.[69]

This united front, plus the fact that the western Mediterranean was nearly saturated with American ground forces, broke British resistance and the Combined Chiefs agreed to "a decisive invasion of the Axis citadel" by 1 May 1944. Thereafter King wanted to limit operations in Italy because he did not think the navy would be able to provide enough landing craft for the cross-Channel operation, should the occupation of Sicily be followed by more amphibious landings in the Mediterranean. British opinion was that operations on the Italian "boot" were necessary in order to draw German divisions from France and the Russian front and make a Channel crossing possible. The Americans consented to operations in the Mediterranean being continued so long as their costs did not detract from the main strategy. But Marshall explained to the British chiefs that their failure quickly to accept a strategy of concentration in 1943 meant that the war against Japan would be prosecuted more vigorously.[70]

Before the Trident Conference, the Joint Chiefs increased the number of their subordinate committees devoted to strategic and logistic planning. By early May, these planners, led by Admiral Cooke, had drafted a broad strategy for the Pacific, and Admiral King explained his interpretation of it to the British on 21 May. He foresaw that a combination of bombing, blockade, and invasion would lead to the defeat of Japan. Therefore, preliminary operations undertaken in 1943 and 1944 should be such as would lead to positions of readiness for the final attack. In the meantime, the Americans should exploit their material superiority by using attrition tactics and intensifying the pressure on Japan. King maintained that seizure of the Marianas and the initiation of a decisive fleet engagement with the enemy would sever Japan's lines of communications and be the key to the reoccupation of the Philippine Islands and to victory in the Pacific. In order to couple surplus American war goods with Chinese manpower, he pressed again for operations in Burma to open a road from India to China. To keep the Japanese uncertain as to the main thrust of the American advance, King favored the recapture of the Aleutians, the continuation of the campaign against Rabaul, and raiding operations by the fleet on points along the Japanese defensive perimeter. The British were unhappy with the scope of these projects but, given the American agreement on Italy, their objections were muted. They implicitly gave the Americans the right to control the campaign in the Pacific. They refused resolutely, however, to hasten the advance in Burma.[71]

Once his concept had been accepted by the Combined Chiefs at the Trident Conference, Admiral King unrelentingly pressed General Marshall to move in the Pacific before the year closed. MacArthur's failure in early 1943 to provide specifics about his coming operations lent weight to King's complaint that, unless the navy launched an operation against the Marshall Islands, nothing would be done in the Pacific that year. Admiral Leahy sided with King, and the army chief of staff reluctantly followed. With this agreement, King promptly summoned Nimitz to San Francisco for another meeting, which began on 1 June. There, he told Nimitz that MacArthur and Halsey were to continue their campaign in the South Pacific, and he, Nimitz, was to advance against the Marshalls within six months. King said that he planned to follow that operation with the seizure of the Japanese base at Truk, in the Carolines, in early 1944.[72]

During the next month, however, army strategists came out against the Central Pacific being made the primary front in the war against Japan. For the operation against the Marshalls, the 1st Marine Division, which was then in the Southwest Pacific, would be needed. Marshall's refusal to transfer this division to Nimitz's command forced naval planners to stretch out over time the costs of Central Pacific operations by taking the Gilbert Islands in November 1943 and to postpone the stroke into the Marshalls until February 1944. In any case, Nimitz wrote to King that, for somewhat different reasons, he wanted to seize the Gilberts first. Another element entered the picture in July 1943 when army air force planners proposed to mount a very-long-range bombing campaign with B-29s against Japan from the Central Pacific. King, suspecting that the air staff would thereafter support operations in the Central Pacific, assigned Cooke to explore this scheme with General Arnold.[73]

The pace of the offensive in the Southwest Pacific in 1943 tested Admiral King's limited patience. In January forces under MacArthur took Buna, on the coast of Papua. The air battles that ensued left the Americans in command of the air over eastern New Guinea and the Solomons and prevented the Japanese from reinforcing their remaining bases in the area. Halsey's units then took Rendova and Munda islands, and on 15 August seized lightly held Vella Lavella, outflanking the major enemy base at Kolombangara. This was too slow for King. "I am 'appalled' at the slowness of the progress in the area where you are working," he wrote to Halsey. "I do not think there has been sufficient will to 'do the best you can with what you've got.' " For this King blamed MacArthur, whom he liked less with each day of the war. When Marshall claimed that King's view of the general was colored by a "policy of hatred," he was near the mark.[74]

Convinced that the navy had to accelerate the pace of the offensive—and to be "so committed in the Central Pacific that the British cannot hedge" on the deployment of forces—King sent word to Nimitz to join him in San Francisco for another bi-monthly meeting at the end of July. He said that, although he hoped to limit the army's participation in the Central Pacific, Nimitz would have to use one army division, plus two marine divisions, in the Gilberts-Marshalls campaign. He "stressed the necessity of keeping pressure on the Japs," a concept lacking in American strategy in the Pacific since Guadalcanal. "In order not to set off an alarm" in Washington or London about the extent of the new commitment to the Pacific theater, King wanted Nimitz to hurry his planning and perhaps "start one operation before another ends." And King speculated that an entire amphibious command from the Mediterranean might be shifted to the Pacific if the British continued to thwart the cross-Channel operation.[75]

King's pressure to expand the Pacific war plus events in Europe were rapidly forcing a climax over the issue of a second front. On 10 July the Allies landed in Sicily and, by 17 August, had overrun it. Meanwhile the Italians ousted Mussolini, then pleaded with Eisenhower to allow them to change sides. The thought of occupying Rome entranced Churchill, who urged that the Allied forces in the Mediterranean move quickly up the Italian peninsula. Marshall half-heartedly agreed, and on 20 July the Combined Chiefs ordered Eisenhower to seize Naples and move north to take cheap advantage of the coming Italian surrender. All of this confirmed King's belief that the British commitment to the cross-Channel operation was weak. "The British have no intention of executing a cross-Channel operation unless it is a walk-over," Cooke noted, "yet they want to assemble all the material to be ready for a walk-over." Indeed, on 4 August, naval strategists, clearly acting with King's approval, proposed that the operation, now named Overlord, be relegated to secondary status. At the very least, they argued, this would allow the concentration of Allied forces against the Axis at only two major points: in the Mediterranean and in the Pacific. By early August King seemed quite willing to characterize Operation Overlord as a diversion from the main strategic effort. But Marshall had lost none of his passion for the great single stroke into France, despite his unfortunate approval of the Italian campaign.[76]

On the eve of another conference with the British, Marshall and King again secured Roosevelt's hearty support for the cross-Channel operation and his agreement to demand that Allied landing craft and several army divisions be shifted from Italy to Britain by the end of the year. However, King warned the president that a final decision had to be made quickly and that Overlord should be abandoned if the British withheld their approval or if it appeared that the operation would be delayed beyond the spring of 1944. King's reasoning was simple: he could not provide enough amphibious lift for Overlord without taking landing craft from the Mediterranean or reducing deliveries scheduled for the Pacific in 1944.[77]

King wrote that the Quadrant Conference, which opened in Quebec in August, "was the scene of two show-downs, . . . when I say 'show-downs,' I mean just that." The first concerned a Channel crossing. In the discussions, the position of the United States as senior member of the Grand Alliance was pressed openly for the first time. The British chiefs dutifully pledged allegiance to Operation Overlord and claimed that they only wanted to pursue the operations in Italy in order to assure its success. While they concurred in making Overlord the "main object" for 1944 in Europe, they refused to accord it absolute priority, which General Alan Brooke considered "too binding." Roosevelt and Churchill agreed that an American—most assumed it would be Marshall—should command the Channel crossing. With these conditions met, King promised to make up deficiencies in the number of landing craft for the great effort. It remains a mystery why he failed to act on this promise more quickly; in the event, landing-craft production was not greatly accelerated until the end of 1943. This delay disrupted not only the timing of Overlord but also the sequence of operations in the Pacific later in the coming year.

The second "show down" at Quebec was less decisive and more divisive. All the American leaders saw China as a valuable ally and hoped that she would fill the vacuum of power in East Asia after the war. They wanted to build a road through Burma to China for the transport of lend-lease equipment to arm the Nationalist Chinese forces. In early 1943 the Combined Chiefs had tentatively approved an attack against northern Burma by Chinese forces and a simultaneous one against southern Burma by British units from India. The British saw this operation as a diversion from their main effort in the Mediterranean, and they resisted American pressure to mount them. At Quebec they repeated their agreement with the strategic concept but continued to thwart the execution of operations by over-estimating the risks. Once again, the Americans left a conference with high hopes that the British had accepted their strategy only to be later shocked when the British laid out exact objections to precise military plans.[78]

King described these frustrations to Nimitz at Pearl Harbor between 25 and 27 September. He also heard Nimitz's plans for the operations in the Gilberts and the Marshalls. This meeting tested a process that King began after Guadalcanal: shifting the burden of theater strategic planning from Washington to Hawaii. Broadly, after the fall of 1943, King and Marshall would agree on a specific schedule of operations for each Pacific area, then Nimitz or MacArthur would complete the detailed planning. This allowed Nimitz to deploy his forces freely within his theater, although shifting units from one theater to another still required the consent of the Joint Chiefs.[79]

On the eve of the opening of the Central Pacific offensive, Admiral King could count yet another naval victory in the Battle of the Atlantic which was essential to the defeat of the Axis. After King introduced the inter-locking convoy system in the summer and fall of 1942, Dönitz shifted his wolf packs back to the main transatlantic convoy routes for a major assault on Allied shipping in the spring of 1943. Admiral King's major contribution to the defeat of the U-boat was his management of the escort program in the difficult months of late 1942 and early 1943. Most of the smaller craft, submarine chasers, and patrol craft that he put into service in the spring of 1942 to guard the coastal convoys were unsuited for transatlantic work. On the other hand, he did not have enough destroyers to provide adequate escorts for the North Atlantic convoys. He soon became convinced that the answer was the destroyer escort, which could be mass-produced and was capable of escorting convoys in the winter weather of the Atlantic Ocean. However, the first landing-craft program had completely disrupted the building schedule for destroyer escorts and it was not until the fall of 1942 that King was able to persuade Roosevelt to give these ships the highest priority. The program was disrupted twice again. The Maritime Commission had no interest in building destroyer escorts and preferred to building cargo shipping, and the War Production Board, at the end of 1942, assigned the synthetic-rubber program a higher priority than escort vessels. King surmounted both of these tremendous obstacles and the first of nearly 500 destroyer escorts completed during the war joined the fleet in early 1943.[80]

The destroyer escort proved to be the long-term strategic solution to the commerce warfare of the U-boats, but the major crisis erupted in March 1943 before these new ships were operational. King recognized when he became CominCh that American naval intelligence in the Atlantic was poor and in June 1942 he sent a team to London to study the Admiralty's methods of using radio intelligence in antisubmarine operations. Radio intelligence had been useless during the U-boat attacks on East Coast shipping because the boats communicated infrequently with their headquarters. Moreover, in February Admiral Pound told King that the British had been unable to crack the new code, Triton, that Dönitz had begun to use to direct his "wolf packs." In December the British did crack Triton and they shared the intelligence with King's new Convoy and Routing Section, which controlled all shipping in the Western and South Atlantic. And, when the climax of the Battle of the Atlantic came in March 1943, King's decision to deploy the escort carrier *Bogue* in the Atlantic played a major role in closing the "air gap" and decisively defeating the U-boat.[81]

Throughout 1942 and into 1943 King carried on an intensive effort to compel the army air force first to transfer control of its antisubmarine aircraft, and then to transfer the planes, to the navy. A system of dual command on the East Coast created in mid-1942 was complicated and inefficient and King pressed Marshall over the next twelve months to give the navy exclusive control over what was clearly a naval mission. In June 1943 the chief of staff and Secretary Stimson relented, although not without some rather hypocritical posturing about the navy's inability to deal with the U-boat menace. At the same time King had to deal with Pound's demands for a unified, combined command in the North Atlantic, a proposal that he consistently rejected. In March 1943 King did agree to reorganize the theater boundaries in the Atlantic, but the practical effect of this agreement seems to have been nil.[82]

Of more importance was King's decision to centralize the direction of antisubmarine operations in CominCh. In early 1943 he became convinced that too many commands were responsible for anti-U-boat activities. Moreover, radio intelligence, or "special intelligence," from the Admiralty was sent only to CominCh, and its source was highly secret. King had seen several instances in which this intelligence had been sent, without revealing the source, from CominCh to operating forces and there ignored. Since the source could not be explained, it was necessary to unite intelligence evaluation and command of the operating forces under the same roof, and that could only be CominCh. This arrangement ran directly counter to all of King's principles of command, but he could find no alternative. In May 1943 he assumed command of the Tenth Fleet, an organizational headquarters that had no ships and simply coordinated evasive routing strategies, intelligence evaluation, and operating orders for ships detailed to the Atlantic fleets. In practice, the Tenth Fleet was run by its chief of staff, Rear Admiral Francis S. "Frog" Low. Although there were several minor crises in the Battle of the Atlantic after the summer of 1943 when escort carriers and destroyer escorts began to join the fleet in large numbers, the U-boat had been defeated and the path across the Atlantic cleared.[83]

In November 1943 King sent major units of the U. S. Fleet into the Central Pacific, for the first time since the Battle of Midway, to seize the Gilbert Islands. The cost of the brief operation was high, especially on Tarawa Atoll where there were 3,301 marine casualties, but the Japanese outer perimeter had been breached and Admiral Nimitz had bases from which his aircraft could bomb the Marshalls. However, criticism of the operation in the United States was intense and MacArthur continually cited the staggering losses as evidence that his more leisurely campaigns were less costly and militarily preferable.

In the same month, before the fleet invaded the Gilberts, the president and the Joint Chiefs of Staff sailed for North Africa in the battleship *Iowa* for another conference with the British, this one in Cairo. The daily meetings among the American leaders exposed a degree of unity that had been forged at Quebec and remained unbroken. The agreed that they would insist on the execution of Overlord in the spring of 1944 and a simultaneous invasion of Southern France, named Anvil; propose a series of operations in the Central and Southwest Pacific against Japan, including the reduction of Truk and the seizure of the Marianas; and demand that the British mount an operation against Burma in conjunction with the Chinese.[84]

In addition to the British, the Chinese dictator Chiang Kai-shek and his American adviser, General Joseph W. Stilwell, attended the Cairo Conference. In 1943, the Americans urged the British and Chinese to mount Operation Anakim, which would combine a strike south from China into northern Burma by American-trained Chinese divisions, an attack by land from India by the British, and an amphibious assault from the Bay of Bengal on the coast of Arakan. Believing it would divert Japanese attention from the Pacific, King favored this operation, but he refused to provide the British with much assistance for it because he needed the shipping for operations in the Central Pacific and because "unilateral decisions" by the British Chiefs of Staff led him to the conclusion that they had not made "a firm commitment" to Operation Anakim. In Cairo, Chiang refused to send his army into Burma unless the British agreed to undertake the amphibious operation. Churchill wanted to seize Sumatra instead, and the British chiefs were reluctant to do anything. The dispute was the watershed in Anglo-American military relations with the Chinese. On the afternoon of 23 November, Chiang's generals presented their plans to the Combined Chiefs. General Alan Brooke, who, like King, was very bright and could be very cruel, ripped them apart. Stilwell recorded that "Brooke got nasty and King got good and mean. God, was he mad. I wish he had socked him." Nonetheless, Stilwell admitted that the Chinese had put on a "terrible performance." That evening the Combined Chiefs celebrated Admiral King's sixty-fifth birthday; somewhat bemused, Brooke recorded that he "was as nice as could be and quite tranformed." One of King's suspicions was that the British would demand American landing craft to execute Operation Anakim and then use them for operations in the Aegean Sea which the Americans opposed. Churchill put these fears to rest, for the moment, when he reluctantly agreed to Operation Buccaneer, an amphibious invasion of the Andaman Islands, off the coast of Burma. Although King thought a strike against Rangoon would have made more sense, Buccaneer met Chiang's requirements and Roosevelt promised that some American naval support for the operation would be forthcoming.[85]

From Cairo the Americans and British flew to Teheran for their first meeting with Soviet dictator Josef Stalin and his advisers. They were somewhat surprised that he gave strong backing to the Overlord concept and characterized most other operations against Germany as "diversions." He did, however, support Marshall and King in their demand for Operation Anvil against southern France, which the Joint Chiefs considered necessary to establish a secondary supply line from America to the major Allied army in the north. The British bitterly opposed Anvil because it would inhibit operations in northern Italy and the eastern Mediterranean, and claimed that the resources for it were not available. Overnight, Admiral Cooke and Major General Thomas T. Handy, the army's chief planner, drafted a detailed plan for Anvil, and at least part of the British opposition was temporarily overcome.[86]

When they returned to Cairo on 3 December to discuss the war against Japan, the Combined Chiefs hastily approved King's proposal for operations in the Pacific against Japan in the coming year. In the Central Pacific, Truk, in the Carolines, was to be taken in mid-July and the Marianas in October; in the Southwest Pacific, operations were to center around MacArthur's slow westward advance along the north coast of New Guinea and to be climaxed by an attack on the Vogelkop Peninsula before mid-August. Not only did the British agree to this plan without argument, they offered to deploy heavy units of their fleet in the Pacific by June 1944 and to increase this commitment in 1945. King was uneasy about this offer, both because he was afraid it would give the British some measure of control over the Pacific campaign and because the Royal Navy lacked the logistical and base support required to operate at sea for extremely long periods.[87]

More disturbing was the British refusal to undertake Operation Buccaneer on the grounds that Stalin had indicated that he would declare war on Japan after Germany surrendered and, therefore, Allied attention should, in Brooke's words, "concentrate on the European front." Although King wanted the Russians to enter the war in Asia, he did not see this as a panacea for the problem of defeating Japan. After two days under constant pressure, which King described as a "hammering," Roosevelt and Marshall accepted the British position, but the admiral was "obdurate." On the afternoon of 5 December FDR overruled King and wrote to Chiang that Buccaneer had been canceled. It was, King wrote, "the one instance during the war in which he felt that the President had gone against the advice of his Joint Chiefs of Staff." To King it was another example of British perfidy and thoroughly justified his untrusting attitude toward his allies.[88]

Barely two weeks separated King's return to Washington from Cairo and his next conference with Nimitz in San Francisco, which began on 3 January. The basis of the decisions on Pacific strategy reached at Cairo, he told Nimitz, rested on the compromise of continuing a dual advance on Japan from New Guinea north to the Philippines, and from the Gilberts, Carolines, and Marianas to either the Philippines or Formosa. The schedule of operations for 1944 would lead the American forces to the edge of the Philippines-Formosa-China triangle, and they would then have to decide where to place the weight of the assault. King's idea was that the seizure of either Luzon or Formosa would cut Japan's sea communications and her supplies of oil and raw materials from the Netherlands East Indies and Southeast Asia; thereafter, the Americans could secure bases along the Chinese coast from which to bomb Japan preparatory to an invasion of the home islands. The key to all of this, however, was the conquest of the Marianas, because, when that had been accomplished, the fleet would be able to roam freely throughout the Western Pacific.[89]

The conference in San Francisco in January 1944 showed how far King had come in delegating responsibility for theater strategy to his Pacific commanders. Flown in from the South Pacific for the meeting, Admiral Halsey described his next moves to encircle and neutralize the Japanese bases at Rabaul and Kavieng. Nimitz then outlined his plans to send the Fifth Fleet under Vice Admiral Raymond A. Spruance to the Marshalls in February in order to exploit the new air bases constructed in the Gilberts and, after that, to send the new fast carriers and battleships on a raid against Truk. King approved all these plans. His confidence in Nimitz was at its height. Early in 1943 he was uneasy about Nimitz's refusal to move aggressively and he planned to send his most trusted assistant, Admiral Cooke, to Pearl Harbor as deputy commander in chief. Now, in January 1944, he readily agreed to let this new billet go to a longtime antagonist, Vice Admiral John H. Towers.[90]

King knew that the compromise on the dual advance on Japan was fragile and was sure to be challenged by MacArthur. Following the Cairo Conference,

General Marshall and Admiral Cooke visited MacArthur in the Southwest Pacific and listened to his complaint that operations against the Carolines and Marianas would delay the invasion of the Philippines. In late January MacArthur sent Lieutenant General Richard K. Sutherland, his chief of staff, and his air and naval commanders to Pearl Harbor for a conference with Nimitz concerning operations for the rest of the year. With Tower's help, they persuaded Nimitz to propose to King that the Marianas operation be abandoned and the weight of the offensive thrown against the New Guinea-Mindanao line. MacArthur dispatched Sutherland with this recommendation to Washington and Nimitz sent Rear Admiral Forrest P. Sherman.

King exploded with rage when he read the minutes of the Pearl Harbor conference. His reaction, he wrote Nimitz, was "indignant dismay." The "idea of rolling up the Japanese along the New Guinea coast . . . and up through the Philippines to Luzon, as our major strategic concept, to the exclusion of the Central Pacific . . . is to me absurd." Nor did Sutherland and Sherman find a welcome reception for their ideas when they presented them to the Joint Chiefs. General Arnold now backed King's strategy because the army air corps wanted to use the Marianas as bases for B-29 raids against Japan. Sherman was soon "educated" about King's plans and began to debate with Sutherland before the Joint Chiefs over the issue of the Central Pacific! However, Marshall forced a delay on a decision for another month.[91]

In the meantime, on 1 February the Fifth Fleet under Admiral Spruance attacked Kwajalein, in the Marshalls, and by 3 February had taken Roi and Namur atolls. And, at the end of the month, Eniwetok Atoll was occupied. Tactics had been considerably improved since the landing on Tarawa, and the casualty rate in the Marshalls was about one-third that sustained in the Gilberts, a fact that took some of the edge off MacArthur's argument. On 17 February Vice Admiral Marc A. Mitscher took Task Force 58, consisting of three carrier task groups, into the Central Pacific to raid Truk. Although the Japanese fleet escaped, the attackers damaged the base and ended its use as an anchorage. This raised the prospect of bypassing Truk and the Carolines altogether, a strategy that King began to press with increased confidence. Just before the raid, King worried that Nimitz "seriously contemplate[d] taking Truk by assault." Thereafter, the issue was moot.[92]

Confusion reigned in Washington over the shape of the Pacific offensive in 1944 and the Joint Chiefs asked Nimitz and MacArthur to return to the United States to clear the air. MacArthur declined but Nimitz arrived in Washington in early March. King was relieved to hear Nimitz urging the chiefs to bypass Truk and strike into the Marianas in the summer. MacArthur, realizing that the Pearl Harbor agreement between Nimitz and Sutherland had come unglued, submitted another proposal. In September 1943 his forces had retaken Lae and Salamaua. These operations began a series of strokes, including the seizure of Bougainville by Halsey's units on 1 November, which aimed at concluding the American conquest of northern New Guinea and the Solomons in mid-1944. On 5 March MacArthur told the Joint Chiefs that he would occupy

Hollandia in the middle of April. King's planners then proposed a compromise on the greater issue. King pointed out that invasion of the Luzon-Formosa-China triangle could be staged from rear areas, such as the Marianas, but that New Guinea was not suitable for this purpose. Since Nimitz wanted to jump directly into the Marianas, naval strategists suggested that Central Pacific forces do this in June and seize the Palau Islands in September. Bowing to MacArthur, they then proposed to mount a major effort to take Mindanao at the end of the year. This compromise left open the key issue of whether the next operation would be against Luzon or Formosa but, on the grounds that it increased the pace of the offensive, King urged that it be accepted and a decision on the other issue left until later. Leahy supported King, and Marshall finally assented on 12 March. It was a major victory for King because it gave operations in the Central Pacific a clear priority for most of 1944 and assured that the Japanese defense perimeter would be broken, once American naval forces were able to operate from the Mandates.[93]

However, in the spring of 1944 all the major operations projected for the coming year—including Overlord—faced severe shortages in cargo shipping and landing craft, and the solution of this problem became Admiral King's principal task in the next few months. The victory over the U-boats in the fall of 1943 allowed King at the end of the year to halve the navy's order for 1,000 destroyer escorts, and at the same time to accelerate production of LSTs for the Channel crossing. Complicating this arrangement was the decision Eisenhower made in February 1944 to broaden the attack on the beaches of Normandy, because this in turn required even more landing craft. Most of the production of large landing craft for the first five months of the year was assigned to Europe and, thereafter, to the Pacific. At Marshall's request, King agreed to let Eisenhower have an additional month's production so as to ensure that the main effort would have sufficient lift. A second problem involving Overlord concerned American naval combatants. At the Cairo Conference British agreement to simultaneous invasions of Normandy and southern France was reluctant and Eisenhower was forced to recommend in the spring that Anvil be postponed until August. King's first plan was to limit American naval participation in Overlord to providing landing craft, and to provide the major units required for Anvil. In February 1944 he sent Cooke to London to discuss these propositions with the Admiralty and with Rear Admiral Alan G. Kirk, whom King had named to command the limited American forces in the operation. Kirk and his assistants were bitter about the small amount of offshore gunfire support that the British planned for the landing and pleaded with Cooke for more heavy combatants, a request to which King acceded. The old battleships that King sent to support Overlord proved vital when the Americans landed on 'Omaha" and "Utah" beaches on 6 June 1944.[94]

Six days after the landings in Normandy King and Marshall visited the beachhead. At the same time, half-way around the world, Spruance was assembling the Fifth Fleet, which stormed into the Marianas, landed troops on

Saipan on 15 June, and destroyed Japanese naval air power in the Central Pacific in the naval-air Battle of the Philippine Sea four days later. These two great campaigns were the culmination of two-and-one-half years of military diplomacy and the product of repeated compromise and opportunism. They were also complementary, for Marshall's idea of crossing the Channel would have been politically impossible had King not insisted on maintaining momentum in the Pacific campaign. It was no accident that within a month of the seizure of Saipan the war government of Hideki Tojo in Tokyo resigned and a group of German generals tried to kill Hitler. After the landings in Normandy most of the decisions on the European front were the province of Generals Marshall and Eisenhower. When the Combined Chiefs returned from France to London in mid-June, they agreed to mount Anvil at the end of July. Shortly thereafter, Churchill did his best to get Anvil canceled in favor of operations against the Balkans, which Marshall and Eisenhower opposed. King's position was oddly ambivalent: at one point he supported a plan to attack Istria, but, at another, resisted fiercely any more forays into the Mediterranean. He finally supported Marshall on the grounds that a major port in the south of France was necessary for the support of Eisenhower's armies in the north. In the event, this view won out and Operation Anvil was launched on 15 August 1944.[95]

At their meetings in London in mid-June, the Combined Chiefs discussed briefly the next moves in the war against Japan. A combined British-Chinese-American operation against northern Burma had gotten under way on 3 March and on 17 May culminated in the capture of Myitkyina airfield, the key to control of the region. Subsequent progress, however, disappointed Marshall and King, as did a Japanese offensive in China which threatened all of their plans for further operations with the Nationalist government. From London the Joint Chiefs queried Nimitz and MacArthur for their recommendations on the next phase of the Pacific war. MacArthur was adamant: the Americans had a moral duty to liberate the Philippines and the invasion of the islands of Leyte and Luzon had to follow the conquest of Mindanao. Nimitz was less sure of himself, as King discovered when they met in Pearl Harbor in July. Moreover, when King and Nimitz visited Saipan, Spruance and Turner urged King to agree to the Luzon operation before the assault on Formosa. Nimitz wanted Manila Bay because it was the only good anchorage, a line of reasoning that King rejected. "If we get busy and set our minds to it," he said, "with facilities in Saipan and Guam for supplies and Eniwetok for berthing, we could do a great deal to maintain the fleet in advanced bases." He refused to accept Nimitz's idea that the seizure of Luzon was a necessary prerequisite to a stroke against Formosa. The meeting reached no conclusions, nor did Roosevelt when he met with Nimitz and MacArthur at Pearl Harbor shortly after King had left.[96]

As had been the case before, an unexpected issue influenced the final decision on the Luzon operation. MacArthur wanted to jump from Mindanao into the central Philippines and assault Leyte Island before he launched his attack against Luzon. One of King's assistants commented that the advantage of the idea was that MacArthur would "be stuck down there slogging it out for the rest of the war!" but King opposed the plan because he saw it as just another step on the road to Luzon. However, in early August, Sherman detailed the deficiencies in army service units and shipping for the Formosa campaign and it became clear to King that they could not be made good early in 1945. On 8 September, with great reluctance, he agreed to the Leyte operation.[97]

After the Cairo Conference Admiral King told Nimitz that, when operations in the South Pacific area ended, he would transfer Admiral Halsey back to the Pacific Fleet, where he would alternate with Admiral Spruance as commander of the striking and landing forces. When Spruance commanded these forces they would be designated the Fifth Fleet, but when Halsey assumed command the same units would be called the Third Fleet. In early September Halsey led carrier task forces in raids against enemy bases on Mindanao and Leyte and discovered that the opposition was light. In the meantime, King and the other chiefs had flown to Quebec for another conference with the British. As the sessions began, King received a message from Nimitz endorsing a suggestion by Halsey to cancel the Mindanao operation and land on Leyte instead in late October. MacArthur concurred and the Joint Chiefs approved a revised directive incorporating Halsey's proposal. As Marshall later wrote, "it was not a difficult decision."[98]

King and Marshall had fenced for over two years about the divided command in the Pacific and had been unable to resolve the question. Every time King proposed that Nimitz be named supreme commander for both theaters Marshall replied that MacArthur should have the job. Therefore, the ground forces for the Leyte Gulf landings were provided by MacArthur and the major naval forces remained under the command of Nimitz, who assigned them to Halsey. Also participating were units of the Seventh Fleet, which was commanded by Vice Admiral Kinkaid and under MacArthur. It was a confusing arrangement for all concerned. Three days after the first landing in Leyte Gulf on 20 October the remnants of the Japanese fleet sortied and divided into several groups. A decoy task force of carriers drew Halsey and all the fast carriers away from the beaches. The transports, thus left undefended, were approached by enemy surface forces, which were driven off by Kinkaid's small carriers and other units. King was furious at Halsey when he heard the first reports of the Battle of Leyte Gulf but he calmed down and withheld comment. Early in 1945, he sent Cooke out to the Pacific to discuss the battle with Halsey and Kinkaid. Cooke reported that Halsey's tactics had endangered the landing. However, King did not mention the incident until he wrote in his memoirs in 1952 that Kinkaid failed to take sufficient precautions, a judgment that clearly missed the point of the controversy.[99]

Nonetheless, the landings at Leyte Gulf succeeded and the last vestiges of Japanese sea power were destroyed in the naval actions. And once the decision had been made by the Joint Chiefs to take Leyte the argument over the Luzon operation lost intensity. King continued to insist that MacArthur's thesis that the United States had to liberate the Philippines was specious since, once Japan had been defeated, the islands would be free in any case. Moreover, he contended that the Luzon operation would merely delay the necessary operations against Formosa and the coast of China before the final assault on Japan could be launched. In his view, Formosa, a powerful enemy air base, had to be taken. But, until Germany surrendered, scarcity continued to hamstring operations in the Pacific: King simply could not find the army service units or shipping that Nimitz claimed he needed to conduct a campaign against Formosa. Still, he asked, "What would we do after Luzon? We cannot remain idle [until the end of the war in Europe]." Nimitz provided a partial solution when he met King in late September 1944. Instead of making a frontal attack on Formosa, he wanted to neutralize it with air attacks and seize Iwo Jima and the Bonins in early 1945. Thereafter, he proposed to launch a major assault on Okinawa, which would provide better airfields than would Formosa for attacks on the Japanese homeland. Coupled with Halsey's proposal that the date for the Leyte landings be advanced, the evidence was overpowering that the Formosa operation could not be launched. King relented and agreed to the Luzon operation, on the understanding that it would be followed in early 1945 by strokes against the Bonins and Okinawa. It was a major reversal of his strategy and he regretted the decision for the rest of his life.[100]

King lost another argument at the second Quebec conference in September 1944, this one concerning British naval participation in the Pacific war. The issue had a tortured history. In 1942 King had requested British naval assistance and diversions in the Indian Ocean and the Southwest Pacific, and the Admiralty had refused. The British had also refused, on the grounds of lack of resources, to undertake Operation Anakim, which King wanted, and their reversal on this point at the Cairo Conference in November 1943 infuriated him. "The seeming 'helplessness' of our cousins strikes me as amusing when it is not annoying," he wrote to Stark in November of that year. "I am sure that what they wish in their hearts is we would haul down the Stars and Stripes and hoist the White Ensign on all of our ships. . . . I cannot be expected to agree to help them to cling to tasks that they themselves say they are unable to do unless we lend them our ships and other forces." King's attitude toward the British, in other words, evolved from suspicion to profound distrust and near antipathy. In early 1944, before Task Force 58 raided Truk, the Japanese moved their heavy units to Singapore. As an alternative to Anakim and to keep the British Indian Ocean Fleet active, King sent the carrier *Saratoga* and escorts into the Indian Ocean, but only a few desultory air raids were made. Although at the Cairo Conference the Combined Chiefs had initialed a paper that approved British naval participation in one of the Pacific theaters, King twice assured Nimitz in early 1944 that he could limit British naval activity to MacArthur's area in the form of an Empire Task Force, a notion the general opposed as firmly as did the Admiralty.[101]

By September 1944, however, it was clear that the British would be able to release most of their heavy units for the Pacific in 1945 and Churchill, who had never favored the idea but who had been brought around to it by the Admiralty at the last moment, offered his fleet to the president. In all likelihood, before the conference Hopkins prevailed on FDR to accept such an offer, which he did, to King's chagrin. Although King tried to persuade the British chiefs to send their fleet into the Southwest Pacific, they refused on the obvious and correct grounds that the area was fast becoming a backwater in the war against Japan. At Quebec King bluntly told the British that "the American Navy had carried the war all the way from Honolulu to the West and it would carry it to Japan," a statement that seemed to encapsulate his complex views on the issue. Despite King's reservations, the decision had been made and a British Pacific Fleet joined the Central Pacific forces in February 1945, staying with them until the end of the war. King's fear that their ships could not operate at great distances was justified, but his worry that the British Chiefs of Staff would demand a hand in Pacific strategy was not.[102]

On the third anniversary of the attack on Pearl Harbor, Allied forces stood poised to assault the inner defenses of the Japanese Empire, but their leaders had reached no conclusions as to how the final defeat of the oriental enemy was to be brought about. On 24 November 1944 B-29s based in the Marianas had opened a strategic bombing campaign against the Japanese home islands, but King had no faith that bombing alone would force the enemy to surrender. The end of the year also saw the climax of a great campaign against Japanese shipping by American submarines guided by radio intelligence. In the early months of 1945 the last links between Japan and the East Indies were cut and shipping in the waters around Japan was decimated to the point that the boats began to have difficulty finding targets, but King realized that there were still large ground forces in the home islands and in occupied China and that the sea traffic between the mainland and the islands could not be severed completely. Roosevelt relieved Stilwell in November 1944 and, thereafter, faith in the strategy of linking up the Pacific Fleet with the Nationalist Chinese dwindled among King's staff. Although King continued to hope that a lodgment on the Chinese coast could be secured, the wisdom of this strategy became less and less evident. King and Marshall shared the belief that it was essential to encourage the Soviet Union to declare war on Japan after Germany surrendered so as to engage the large Japanese army in China and prevent its transfer back to Japan. They pressed this opinion on Roosevelt before and during the Yalta Conference with the Russians and British in February 1945, King being less adamant about it than the army chief of staff. The controversial agreements reached at Yalta between Roosevelt and Stalin on the terms for Soviet entry into the war in Asia three months after the defeat of Germany involved neither Marshall nor King, although there is no evidence that King had strong objections to the territorial concessions made to the Russians to obtain their belligerency. Indeed, King was a bit surprised that the Soviets delayed their entry as long as they did, but he later commented that he had "no first hand knowledge of decisions reached" on the terms for Soviet entry into the war against Japan. This statement was, however, contradicted by Rear Admiral

Oscar C. Badger, a logistics planner, who claimed that the chiefs received the news of the settlement "with considerable relief as being the lesser of three evils."[103]

Stalin's pledge to enter the conflct inevitably shaped the subsequent discussions by the Joint Chiefs concerning the final operations against Japan. American support for the Chinese now became less critical. In addition, carrier strikes by Halsey's Third Fleet against Japanese installations in the Gulf of Tonkin and the South China Sea were so successful that the need to land on the Chinese coast became problematical. However, when King and Nimitz met in Washington on 6 March 1945, King clung to the hope that Chu Shan Archipelago might be seized, despite the fact that his staff questioned the number of sites for air bases in the area. Army planners had long favored bypassing the coast of China and invading Kyushu, the southernmost of Japan's home islands, and the landings on Iwo Jima on 19 February and the beginning of the Okinawa campaign on 1 April thrust the American forces in that general direction. Moreover, King acknowledged that, when Okinawa was in American hands, the fleet would have enough anchorages near Japan and an abundance of airfields from which attacks could be launched against the home territory. Finally, his own key advisers were sharply divided over the idea of an operation against the Chinese coast and Nimitz was ambivalent. While he insisted that the Chu Shan strategy remain under consideration, in May King agreed that the invasion of Kyushu would follow the conquest of Okinawa. The Joint Chiefs issued a directive to that effect on 25 May, naming Nimitz as commander during the naval and amphibious phase and MacArthur as commander of ground operations. After the war King claimed to have believed that "the defeat of Japan could have been accomplished by sea and air power alone, with the necessity of actual invasion of the Japanese home islands by ground troops." However, no contemporaneous evidence supports this assertion. It is true that he favored the China coast operation before a landing on Kyushu, but no documentary record indicates a conviction that the Kyushu campaign was unjustified. Indeed, his statements on the fanaticism of the Japanese and their unwillingness to surrender despite great hardship strongly suggest that his approval of an invasion of Kyushu was not as grudging as he later claimed.[104]

This issue was more important in the postwar debate over strategy than it was in April 1945, when Franklin D. Roosevelt died and Harry S. Truman became president. Truman disliked admirals, especially King, and later wrote that he was "a martinet" and "an old crustacean." King's influence in the White House clearly ended with the change in incumbents. Shortly after Truman was sworn into office, Secretary Stimson told him about the Manhattan Project to build an atomic bomb, on which the army had been working for several years. King kept in close contact with this effort, despite his later claims to the contrary, and was fully aware of its progress on 18 June when the Joint Chiefs first discussed it with Truman in the Oval Office. Marshall and King insisted that both an invasion of Kyushu in November 1945 and, possibly, a subsequent landing on the main island of Honshu in 1946 would be necessary to defeat Japan. When Truman asked whether he should employ the atomic bomb, which had yet to be tested, to preclude an invasion of Kyushu, King and Marshall said he should. And when Assistant Secretary of War John J. McCloy protested that the destructive power of the bomb should first be demonstrated to the Japanese, King supported Marshall's objections that such a scheme offered no assurance of success and would use up one of the three bombs that would be available in 1945.[105]

With the prospect of the atomic bomb being used, King became less convinced that the Russians should be encouraged to enter the war and warned Truman in early June that their contribution to the defeat of Japan now might be minimal and not worth much of a price. In general, this was the attitude that the new president adopted at the Potsdam Conference in mid-July, where he received word that the first test of the bomb was successful. After Japan rejected the warning that the Allies issued at Potsdam, Truman ordered that one bomb be dropped on Hiroshima and one on Nagasaki in early August. Japan sued for peace on 10 August and signed the instrument of surrender in Tokyo Bay aboard the battleship *Missouri* on 2 September 1945.[106]

King's role in the development of Allied grand strategy in World War II was significant. Unlike Stark, he was not firmly committed to the absolute priority of "Germany first" to the exclusion of the Pacific. He willingly backed Marshall's strategy of concentration on a cross-Channel invasion, but insisted that some attention be paid to the war with Japan. In 1942 and 1943, when the British refused to be drawn into a Channel crossing, King used their position to demand a series of compromises that increased the resources available to the commanders in the Pacific. This insistent pressure forced a dilution of "Germany first" and allowed American material superiority to be used to the greatest advantage in a two-front war. King was an impatient opportunist but he also had great fixity of purpose: after the Guadalcanal diversion, he reverted to the strategy of the old Orange Plan and insisted on the centrality of the Marianas to a victory in the Pacific.

King's influence on the U. S. Navy was no less significant. For one thing, he personally selected most of the new admirals who rose through the ranks during the conflict. More importantly, he sensed the need as did few others after Pearl Harbor for a restoration of the willingness to take risks—and he rewarded risk-takers, even if they sometimes failed. His vision was narrowed by his intense parochialism, and his pettiness when he believed long-term navy interests were at stake was unmatched, but this spirit of pride and jealousy served the navy well although it often embittered fellow service chiefs. A poor military diplomat, he was a war leader of the first rank.

Admiral King disliked the division of authority between CominCh and CNO and abolished it before he left office. He nominated Nimitz as his successor and, when Forrestal objected, took his case to Truman and won. The nomination was a parting shot at an old adversary. Honors followed after King left office, including a special resolution by Congress praising him for his part "in formulating and executing the global strategy that led to victory in World War II" and an honorary degree from Oxford University. Promoted to the five-star rank of fleet admiral in December 1944, he never retired, and remained on the active list of the navy after Nimitz became CNO. King kept an office in the new Pentagon building and was given a title as adviser to the secretary of the navy, but he was supernumerary and frustrated. The navy had been his whole life and each day he learned that his professional career had truly ended. He stayed on the margin during the fight over unification, appearing once before Congress in 1948. Unification of the services was not a good step for the navy, he claimed, and "any step not good for the navy is not good for the nation." He began to write a history of his family and his naval life but in 1947 a massive brain hemorrhage halted the project until it was taken up by Walter Muir Whitehill, an archivist who had worked in the Navy Department during the war. The book, *Fleet Admiral King: A Naval Record,* was published in 1952 and received generally poor reviews.[107]

The effects of the stroke lingered and King spent his winters in Washington and summers at the Portsmouth Naval Hospital. One day in late June 1956 he suffered acute heart failure and lapsed into a coma. His only son, Ernest J., Jr., was at his side when he died the next morning, 25 June 1956.

A naval plane flew the body to Washington where it lay in state in the National Cathedral, before being placed on the same caisson used for President Roosevelt, and drawn down Constitution and Pennsylvania avenues to the Capitol. After a brief ceremony, a procession left for Annapolis, where King was buried on the grounds of the Naval Academy. An old friend, Admiral Emory S. Land, wrote simply that King was "the greatest naval officer the United States ever produced." While clearly true, King surely would have preferred the parting salute from another admirer, military commentator Hanson W. Baldwin. The admiral was, he said, "a man too rare in any age, a man who could not be had."[108]

JAPAN SEA

CHESTER WILLIAM NIMITZ

15 December 1945–15 December 1947

STEVEN T. ROSS

Executive Order 9635 of 29 September 1945, transformed the chief of naval operations into the senior uniformed officer of the U. S. Navy. The CNO was to act as the chief adviser to the president and the secretary of the navy, command operating fleets and the shore establishment, coordinate the programs and activities of bureaus and departments, and supervise war plans, fleet readiness, and logistics. The order went into effect on 10 October 1945. It was the culmination of a process designed to unite the posts of commander in chief, U. S. Fleet, and chief of naval operations. On 18 December 1941, Executive Order 8984 directed the commander in chief to operate the fleet and the CNO to control war planning, logistics, and construction. Executive Order 9096 of 12 March 1942, combined the billets of commander in chief and chief of naval operations in the person of Admiral Ernest J. King. Each billet, however, retained its own staff. Admiral King favored a single service chief, and the navy adopted his view after the war.[1] On 15 December 1945, Fleet Admiral Chester W. Nimitz became the first postwar CNO and the first holder of the post to be the head of the navy. For Admiral Nimitz, it was the climax of a long, varied, and successful career.

The Nimitz family traces its origins to German knights who conquered and settled in Livonia, on the Baltic Sea. When the Swedes took Livonia in the seventeenth century, some Nimitzes joined the Swedish army. After the Thirty Years' War, one of them settled near Hannover. This branch of the family all became merchants until the admiral's great-grandfather, having squandered the family fortune, broke the pattern and joined the merchant marine. The admiral's grandfather, Karl Heinrich, also went to sea, but in 1844 he joined other members of his family who had settled in South Carolina a few years earlier. In 1846, he migrated to Texas where, with other German immigrants, he helped found the town of Fredericksburg. He became a hotel-keeper, and one of his sons, Chester Bernard, married Anna Henke, the daughter of a local butcher, in 1884. Chester Bernard died before his son, Chester William was born on 24 February 1885.[2]

When Chester was almost five, his uncle married Anna, and the family moved to Kerrville where Chester attended grade school and high school. He also worked as a clerk in a hotel owned by his aunt. In 1900 he met two West Point graduates who were on their way to their first post. Impressed by the two officers, who were, after all, only a few years older than himself, he decided to apply to West Point and pursue an army career. He discovered that there were no vacancies, but his congressman suggested that he apply instead to the Naval Academy. Nimitz agreed and, on 7 September 1901, was sworn in as a naval cadet.[3]

The new cadet—students at Annapolis were not at this time known as midshipmen—did quite well and in 1905 graduated seventh in a class of 114. As his first assignment, he joined the battleship *Ohio* and sailed in her to the Orient. In 1906, he visited Japan and met Admiral Togo, father of the navy that the American fleet would ultimately fight for control of the Pacific.

The American navy in the first decades of the twentieth century was still small. The officers formed a close-knit, homogeneous group and knew well each other's strengths and failings. Officers also gained a wide range of experience by serving aboard a variety of ship types on many stations. Nimitz was no exception, and after his Far Eastern tour, he commanded a gunboat, a base, and then a destroyer in the Philippines. He was also commissioned as an ensign and court-martialed for running his destroyer aground. He escaped with a simple letter of reprimand because of his previous record, which was quite good.

Returning to America in 1909, Nimitz spent the next four years serving in submarines. He commanded several boats and eventually took command of the Atlantic Submarine Flotilla. One of the navy's early submariners, his expertise was recognized in 1912 when he was invited to lecture at the Naval War College on submarine tactics. Professional advancement coincided with personal happiness: while serving in the United States, he married Catherine Freeman in 1913.[4]

Nimitz was determined to expand his knowledge of the new diesel engines. Shortly after his marriage, the Navy Department sent him to Germany to study this technology and, upon his return, ordered him to supervise the installation of two large diesel engines in a new oiler. He remained as engineer and executive officer of the oiler until 1917 and gained valuable experience with under-way refueling. With American entry into World War I, Nimitz returned to submarines and during the belligerency served first as engineering aide, and later as chief of staff, to the commander of the Atlantic Fleet's Submarine Force, Captain Samuel S. Robison.[5] After the war, he served in the office of the CNO with special duty as the senior member of the Board of Submarine Design. This duty was followed by a tour as executive officer of the battleship *South Carolina* and, in 1920, he was put in charge of building a submarine base at Pearl Harbor and given command of an inoperative cruiser and of a submarine division.

Two years later, he went as a student to the Naval War College. Of his year in Newport Nimitz later wrote; "The enemy of our games was always Japan—and the courses were so thorough that after the start of World War II, nothing that happened in the Pacific was strange or unexpected."[6] In his courses at the war college he studied the logistics of a naval war in the Pacific, replenishment at sea, and the practicality of circular formations in task groups. Although he spent a great deal of time studying the Battle of Jutland, and even wrote his thesis on it, he later claimed that he learned so much about the Pacific and the problems of moving across that vast ocean that when he had to fight there, he found it easy to devise strategies and tactics. Only the kamikaze attacks came as a real surprise.[7]

After graduation, Nimitz returned to the West Coast to become aide to Admiral Robison, his former chief, who had risen to command the Battle Fleet. When Robison became Commander in Chief, U. S. Fleet, Nimitz continued to serve under him. In 1926, Nimitz went to the University of California at Berkeley and organized the first NROTC course there. Three years later, by this time a captain, he received command of a submarine division and, in 1931, took command of a tender and more than thirty decommissioned destroyers in San Diego. In 1933, he assumed command of a heavy cruiser and deployed to the Far East for two years. He returned to Washington to become assistant to the chief of the Bureau of Navigation, a billet in which he learned the ins and outs of naval bureaucracy. In 1938, Nimitz became a rear admiral and obtained command of a cruiser division. The need to undergo surgery forced him to give up his command but, upon recovery, he received an even more desirable one—a battleship division. In 1939, after a brief tour as commander of a task force that included an aircraft carrier, President Franklin D. Roosevelt ordered him to return to Washington as chief of the Bureau of Navigation.[8]

The Bureau of Navigation handled officer assignments, and Nimitz found himself faced with the task of finding competent men for a rapidly expanding navy. He enlarged the classes at the Naval Academy and increased the number of NROTC units. He also introduced a program, known as V-7, for the rapid training of officers.[9] Thus, by the time of the attack on Pearl Harbor, Nimitz had enjoyed a varied career, at sea and ashore, and had experienced almost every aspect of naval life, both operational and bureaucratic. His superiors had chosen him for higher command, and on 16 December 1941, Secretary of the Navy Frank Knox informed him that he was to take command of the Pacific Fleet.

Taking over during the darkest days of the war, Nimitz had the difficult missions of halting the Japanese onslaught, rebuilding and expanding the American fleet, and devising strategies to defeat Japan. He brought to his new job a number of advantages, including experience, a detailed knowledge of his brother officers, and a sense of inner balance and calm that steadied those around him. He had the ability to pick able subordinates and the courage to let them do their jobs without interference. He molded such disparate personalities as the quiet, introspective Raymond A. Spruance and the ebullient, aggressive William F. Halsey, Jr., into an effective team.

In the modern war, few, if any, strategic decisions are the product of one man's vision. Scores of individuals contribute to the formulation of strategy. Nimitz had his own staff and received advice and direction from Admiral King and his staff, and from the Joint Chiefs of Staff and the Combined Chiefs of Staff. President Roosevelt also had an effect on Pacific Ocean strategy. Nevertheless, had America lost the war in the Pacific, Nimitz would probably have been held responsible.

During the first months of 1942, the navy had few assets. Nimitz, however, insisted on using them aggressively. Despite the risks to his handful of carriers, he decided to resist the Japanese advance into the Coral Sea. He lost one of his carriers, but he forced the enemy to retreat. In May, he accepted the assessment of his intelligence staff that the Japanese fleet would attack Midway in June and persuaded Admiral King to let him concentrate his carriers in mid-Pacific. Nimitz's plan for an ambush worked, the Japanese fleet was defeated, and their Pacific offensive was halted.[10]

After the victory in the Battle of Midway, the Americans began the long and difficult counteroffensive. Nimitz acted as a conduit between King and the Joint Chiefs and his force commanders in the field, periodically imposing his own views on the strategic conduct of the war against Japan. In 1943, he persuaded King that the Gilbert Islands should be attacked before the Marshalls were invaded, and in 1944, he insisted on striking at the heart of the Marshalls, Kwajalein Island, instead of first attacking the outer islands. Nimitz also came to agree with General Douglas A. MacArthur concerning the merits of invading Luzon in the Philippines as opposed to King's preference for a leap to Formosa. He was instrumental in arranging a compromise in which MacArthur seized the Philippines while Nimitz's forces took Iwo Jima and Okinawa.[11]

Nimitz then turned his attention to organizing the invasion of Japan, but before he had to launch this operation, atomic bombs and a Soviet declaration of war led the Japanese government to surrender. On 2 September 1945, on board the battleship *Missouri,* the Japanese signed the articles of capitulation. MacArthur represented the Allied powers and Nimitz signed the documents for the United States. Nimitz had borne his immense responsibilities with calm efficiency and he looked forward to completing his naval service by succeeding King.

Nimitz wanted to be the next chief of naval operations, but his appointment was opposed by Secretary of the Navy James V. Forrestal, whose relations with King had been poisonous and who may have viewed Nimitz as a no more pliable figure. Forrestal's exact motives are uncertain, but he met with Nimitz on 6 October 1945 and urged the admiral not to ask to be chief of naval operations.

Nimitz refused, and King pressed Nimitz's claim to the billet in the letter of resignation he wrote to the president on 10 October. King also asked his friend, Congressman Carl Vinson, who chaired the House Naval Affairs Committee, to help Nimitz, and Vinson arranged to have presidential adviser Edwin Pauley recommend to President Harry S. Truman that he name Nimitz as the next CNO. Truman agreed to do so but Forrestal exacted a price. He accepted Nimitz's appointment on the condition that Nimitz would serve only one term of two years. Affronted by Forrestal's rather mysterious resistance to his appointment and by the limit placed on his term of office, Nimitz managed nonetheless to establish a harmonious relationship with the secretary. However, his tour as chief of naval operations began on a sour note.[12]

One of Nimitz's major problems as CNO was the army's proposal to unify the armed forces. Army leaders were wedded to the general staff system and believed that the navy should adopt it. The navy wanted to keep its decentralized command structure, with the bureaus and fleet commands enjoying wide lattitude in their policies and procedures. The army also expected that the ground forces would suffer the most of any of the services due to postwar cuts in their appropriations and manpower. Unification of the services was seen as being one way for the army to get a larger share of peacetime budgets. On the other hand, the admirals realized that they had always done relatively well in the fight for peacetime appropriations, and they feared that a merger with the army would probably undermine this tradition. Army air force leaders were reasonably secure about postwar funding, but they backed the army's proposals for unification in return for army support for an independent air force. However, naval leaders feared that an independent air force would try to absorb all land-based aviation. Thus, they wanted to maintain the status quo with separate services, civilian secretaries, and congressional committees.[13]

On 15 May 1945, Senator David I. Walsh, chairman of the Senate Naval Affairs Committee, wrote to Forrestal suggesting that if the navy opposed consolidation, it should prepare a constructive alternative.[14] Forestal, who opposed unification, was already thinking along the same lines. He moved quickly and on 19 June asked Ferdinand Eberstadt, a management specialist and a long-time friend, to examine the unification issue within the broader context of a general reorganization of the nation's defense structure. The Eberstadt Report, issued on 25, September 1945, accepted air force independence, but rejected the idea of a single chief of staff and a single civilian secretary. It called for keeping separate service secretaries under the overall supervision of a secretary of national defense. Instead of a single service chief, the report advocated continuing the Joint Chiefs of Staff and, to obtain coordination of the entire defense effort, called for the creation of a National Security Council, a National Security Resources Board, and a Central Intelligence Agency.[15]

President Truman, however, favored unification and in December 1945, sent a message to Congress calling for the creation of a single defense department and a single chief of staff. Both houses of Congress then held hearings at which the service witnesses again asserted their various positions. Some air force spokesmen claimed that carriers were obsolete, that the navy was no longer the nation's first line of defense, and that the air force should control all aircraft operating from the land. Army witnesses noted that the marine corps duplicated army functions and should be drastically reduced. The navy then in addition to worrying about being reduced to a subordinate arm within a unified defense structure also worried about being deprived of its air and amphibious missions.[16]

Nimitz found himself thrust into the middle of this battle even before he became CNO. One of his most important tasks was to defend the navy's position before Congress and the public. On 2 October 1945, in a speech in San Francisco, he noted that sea power was vital to the defeat of Japan and that America had to maintain her naval power in the postwar world. On the same day, the Veterans of Foreign Wars heard a recording, made on 17 September, of the admiral's assertion that sea power was vital to American security, as it had been during the war. Three days later in Washington, D.C., Nimitz pointed out that the atomic bomb, which in fact had been brought to the air force by ship, did not defeat Japan. It simply hastened Japan's recognition of its hopeless situation. On 5 October, he repeated similar views before the Congress.[17]

On 17 November 1945, Nimitz testified before the Senate Military Affairs Committee. He noted that in 1944 he had been in favor of unification, but since then he had changed his mind. Autonomous services, he said, could work together smoothly and efficiently, and independence enabled the services to check on one another. Coordination rather than unification was the admiral's goal, and he advocated retaining the Joint Chiefs of Staff. Merging the services, he argued, would create a large bureaucracy, produce internal friction, and probably be less efficient than the system already in existence. He ended his testimony by suggesting that Congress provide the services with a large degree of autonomy.[18]

After he became chief of naval operations in December 1945, Nimitz took the navy's case to the press. In one article, he noted that even in an atomic age the navy was important. Submarines might be the capital ship of the new era and might be equipped with atomic missiles. The carrier would still be important, and the navy of the future would still be the nation's first line of defense. In case of war, America would strike at her enemy with atomic weapons, but the navy and the marines would first have to seize and maintain forward bases. Basically, Nimitz argued that "the function of the navy will not be obsolete as long as men are inclined to fight."[19] Weapons might change, but the need for a navy with a global reach would not. On 3 May 1946, Admiral Nimitz again testified before Congress. This time he defended the Eberstadt report. He noted that the navy needed a balanced fleet because of the variety of missions it had to perform. He pointed out that land-based air resources were important for the navy's mission of antisubmarine warfare.[20]

As the hearings continued, tempers frayed and a number of witnesses began to take extreme positions. Some admirals, for example, opposed both unification and a separate air force. Others asserted that the army and the air corps wanted to take over all naval aviation and reduce the marine corps to a corporal's guard.[21] Nimitz, however, always kept his dignity. Like Forrestal, he realized that a completely negative attitude towards unification would sit badly with the president, the Congress, and the public. Therefore, he backed the Eberstadt report as an alternative to outright unification. Nevertheless, he developed an especially good relationship with President Truman. He kept his lobbying to a minimum but, in response to presidential questions, noted that during the war the navy had successfully used land-based aircraft for antisubmarine warfare. Since the Soviets were building a large force of modern submarines, the navy continued to need land-based aviation under its control if it was to cope with that increasingly dangerous threat.[22] Nimitz also seems to have persuaded the president that the navy's resistance to unification was not simply a matter of narrow-minded parochialism.

The unification question dragged into 1947. The navy, fearing the loss of its air and amphibious missions, continued to advocate coordination, as opposed to unification. In May 1946, Nimitz, Forrestal, and Eberstadt met with Secretary of War Robert P. Patterson: all agreed that there should be no single chief of staff. They also agreed that, although there would be a secretary of national defense, the services should retain their own civilian secretaries.[23] By September, the parties to the controversy had ironed out most of their differences, and a defense reorganization bill went to Congress in 1947. Passed in July of that year, the National Security Act basically followed the recommendations of the Eberstadt report.[24] It was a victory for the Navy Department, which kept most of its autonomy, its marines, and its air arm intact.

The National Security Act did not end interservice rivalry. Competition for budget allocations and the debate over the roles and missions of each service continued. Nevertheless, the navy kept its independence. In addition to speaking *for* the navy, Admiral Nimitz had to speak *to* the navy and convince his fellow officers that the act protected the navy's interests. Many high-ranking officers were suspicious of it, but Nimitz assured them that the act was reasonable and that the navy could and should live with it. Forrestal later told Truman that the navy would not have gone along with the act had Nimitz not endorsed it.[25]

Besides struggling with the issue of unification, Nimitz had to supervise the demobilization of the wartime navy, organize a peacetime naval force, plan for new ships and weapons, and, with the other service chiefs, prepare strategies to deal with the emerging cold war with the Soviet Union. Under pressure from Congress, naval officers and enlisted men, and their families, Nimitz ordered that demobilization be carried out swiftly. Despite fears among naval strategists and others that the rapid reductions of the forces would hamper American diplomacy, the navy not only brought the army and army air force home, even pressing battleships and carriers into service as transports, but cut its own strength from more than four million men in July 1945, to a little more than one million by June 1946.[26] Within another twelve months, it had 447,000 officers and men, plus 92,000 marines. Material stocks also shrank rapidly. By late 1947, the navy had cut the number of its airplanes from 43,000 to 27,000, and the number of its shipyards from 117 to 33; it had sold 3,875 vessels as surplus and placed 2,051 in "mothballs." And no new ships were built in 1947.[27]

Meanwhile, Nimitz and his fellow chiefs worked on plans to deal with a conflict with the Soviet Union. In late December 1945 American military strategists began to draft the Pincher Plans, which formed the basis for Joint War Plans Committee plan 432/7, dated June 1946. These plans all concerned American strategies in the event of an all-out attack on the West by Russia. The planners assumed that a war with the Soviets would follow the pattern of World War II in that it would be global and total, and would start with a Soviet offensive in the Middle East and Europe. The Americans would mobilize, launch a strategic bombing campaign against Russian war industries, and then counterattack against a weakened foe.[28] Nimitz took the lead in the complex process of defining the navy's part in the overall war plan. He believed that the United States had to react to a Soviet attack and he restrained some of his more aggressive admirals who called for a preemptive strike against the Russians.[29] Once the attack from Russia occurred, Nimitz maintained, the navy would bear the brunt of the first phase of the war while the army and air force mobilized. At the start of hostilities, American forces in Germany would retreat to the Rhine and then to Antwerp, from where the navy would evacuate them to Britain. At the same time, the navy would have to evacuate American forces from Italy. In the Far East, the Pacific Fleet would be responsible for transferring American troops from Korea to Japan. Thereafter, the navy would have to defend the British Isles, secure bases in Iceland and the Azores, and keep open the Atlantic sea lanes. In addition, Nimitz believed that the fleet would need to hold Suez, Crete, and Cyprus, and to secure Bahrein Island to guard the oil resources of the Middle East and provide bases from which to launch an aerial blitz against Russia.[30] Nimitz and his naval planners emphasized the importance of Middle Eastern oil in a war between the United States and the Soviet Union and assumed that the main Soviet military objective in such a conflict would be to capture those resources. Consequently, he concluded that the eastern Mediterranean was to be the major theater of concentration and naval operations at the start of any general war. Naval planners assumed that the Soviet naval effort would consist of a defense of their homeland, a submarine offensive against American lines of supply, and operations in support of their ground forces.[31]

It was clear to Nimitz that, to accomplish its wartime missions, the navy required a large, balanced fleet, including twenty-four aircraft carriers. These carriers, his planners maintained, could and and should take part in the launching of any attack with atomic bombs against Russia, especially since, in the early days of a conflict, the Soviets would probably overrun the forward bases of the air force. Naval experts believed that tests conducted with atomic bombs and American warships at Bikini Atoll in 1946 proved that combatant vessels could survive in a nuclear environment. By 1947, there was widespread agreement among American strategists that atomic weapons would be used by both sides in a general war. Therefore, Nimitz and other naval plnners were convinced that aircraft carriers could, indeed, retain their traditional strategic mission. Although American war plans changed considerably after 1947, by then the navy had, under Nimitz's leadership, staked its claim to participate in strategic atomic warfare.[32]

The essential step in Nimitz's postwar strategy was the forward deployment of his forces that would, in a general war, absorb the first blow of any Soviet offensive, and secure the areas from which American counteroffensives could be launched. Two crises in the Mediterranean provided the opportunity to implement this strategy in that area. In 1945 and 1946 the Russians pressed Turkey to grant them joint occupation and control over the Dardanelles. At the same time, Stalin supported Greek communists in a civil war with the central government in Athens. The Truman administration opposed Soviet occupation of the strait and favored the rule of the Athens regime in Greece. After a period of indecision, in April 1946 Nimitz, with the agreement of the president and the State Department, sent the battleship *Missouri* into the eastern Mediterranean to visit Istanbul. The visit demonstrated American support of Turkey as well as American resolve to defend her interests in the region. In August, a small American task force entered the Mediterranean, and in September, a carrier visited Greece. The following month, Forrestal announced that the navy would permanently deploy a carrier in the Mediterranean. This was an essential step in the execution of the strategy of forward deployment that Nimitz had adopted earlier.[33]

To give his forward-deployed force an atomic-strike capability, Nimitz moved quickly during his first few months as chief of naval operations to begin a research program on the uses of nuclear technology at sea. With his experience in engineering, he rapidly grasped the implications of atomic power. In his last days as CNO, Admiral King had created a division of special weapons to study atomic bombs; although this unit was later abolished and its functions split between two other groups, the navy had committed itself to respond to the military implications of the atomic age.[34] On 17 January 1946, Nimitz informed Secretary Forrestal that he had endorsed a report calling for a naval program of nuclear research. Three weeks later, after a conference of submarine officers had discussed at length desired improvements in submarine design, the General Board recommended that the navy conduct research on ways to improve submarine performance, including the use of nuclear propulsion. At Nimitz's urging, on 26 March Forrestal asked Truman to order the Manhattan Project to work with the navy. And, on 4 April, the General Board issued an important report which concluded that nuclear propulsion was essential to the navy's future.[35]

Thereafter, the exploratory studies moved at a rapid pace. In June, the navy sent a team of officers, including Captain Hyman G. Rickover, to inspect the Clinton laboratory at Oak Ridge, Tennessee, where the world's first nuclear-power reactor was being built. Rickover soon became a strong advocate of nuclear propulsion. He wanted to design and build a nuclear submarine, for which purpose he sought to establish a special office, fearing that if the project were made a bureau responsibility, it might get lost in a maze of competing programs.[36] In August the Submarine Conference recommended to Nimitz that future research in the area should be aimed at the development of submarine-launched ballistic missiles which would carry atomic warheads. And, in December, the conference endorsed research on nuclear propulsion. This last conclusion must have finally convinced Nimitz that the project was feasible, for on 10 January 1947 he approved a policy of planning a submarine with nuclear-power plants to provide unlimited, high-speed submerged endurance. He also agreed that design studies for nuclear-powered submarines carrying atomic missiles should be made.[37] These studies went forward in 1947, but Rickover was concerned over the lack of a clear priority for the project and, in October 1947, wrote to Nimitz, requesting his approval to build a nuclear-powered submarine. Nimitz agreed, endorsed the letter on 5 December, and sent it on to Secretary of the Navy John L. Sullivan, who also approved it and forwarded it to James Forrestal, now secretary of defense.[38] Thus, when Nimitz left his billet a few days later, he had helped to commit the navy to the development of the fleet ballistic-missile submarine, a weapon system that has become one of the most vital elements in America's strategic deterrence.

Just before leaving office, Nimitz summarized, in a letter to Secretary Sullivan, his views on the future of the navy. He noted that in peacetime it acted as a force for stability and in war it controlled important sea lines of communication. In any future conflict, land powers with extensive human resources would be America's most probable enemies. In such a war, the navy would bear the initial weight of an enemy attack; thus, his strategy of forward deployment of the fleet in peacetime was vital to success in a general war and useful in the absence of a conflict. Nimitz forcast the general outline of the arms competition in the cold war, maintaining that the United States could achieve military superiority over the Soviet Union, despite the latter's tremendous advantage in manpower, by exploiting her own more advanced technology. For the naval forces, of course, he expected that a key result of this technological superiority would be the development of atomic-powered submarines that could fire missiles with atomic warheads against an enemy's homeland.[39]

When Nimitz was relieved by Admiral Louis E. Denfeld as chief of naval operations in December 1947, he moved to Berkeley, California, where he relaxed from the pressures of command. In 1949, he accepted an offer, arranged by Truman, from the United Nations to supervise a plebiscite in the disputed territory of Kashmir but, because India and Pakistan failed to negotiate a preliminary agreement, the elections were never held. In 1952, after performing some goodwill missions for the United Nations, Nimitz resigned.

Meanwhile, Nimitz had become indirectly embroiled in the "admirals' revolt" of 1949, which erupted when Secretary of Defense Louis A. Johnson fired Denfeld, who had criticized Johnson's policies during congressional hearings. On 31 October, Truman called Nimitz and asked him to return to Washington for a second tour as chief of naval operations. The president clearly hoped that Nimitz's enormous prestige within the navy would calm the opposition in the service to the administration's defense policies. Nimitz declined the request on the grounds that he was too old to return to an active billet and he persuaded Truman to name Admiral Forrest P. Sherman to succeed Denfeld.[40]

Nimitz did accept a call from the president to head a federal board to consider how to deal with alleged subversives in the civil service while, at the same time, protecting their civil liberties. However, conservatives in the Senate prevented the establishment of the board and Nimitz again returned to Berkeley and retirement. His inclinations on the issue were demonstrated some years later when he became a regent of the University of California and fought against the imposition of a loyalty oath upon the faculty.

Nimitz enjoyed a peaceful and dignified retirement, watching his children's progress, refusing to become involved in wartime controversies, and co editing a textbook on sea power for use at the Naval Academy. He died on 20 February 1966.

Nimitz was a man who wielded enormous power without arrogance or ostentation. He led the navy in the Pacific campaign against Japan and then guided it through the first difficult years of the cold war. As chief of naval operations, he developed an American naval strategy to deal with the threat of Soviet power, defended the interests of the navy within the defense establishment, and helped to move the service into the nuclear age. A quiet man, who loved to tell stories to his friends and who never sought the public eye, Admiral Nimitz served the navy and his country well.

LOUIS EMIL DENFELD

15 December 1947–1 November 1949

PAOLO E. COLETTA

Louis E. Denfeld was born on 13 April 1891 to Professor Robert E. and Etta May Kelley Denfeld at Westover, Massachusetts. His early education, however, was acquired in Minnesota, and he was appointed to the Naval Academy by Congressman J. Adam Bede, of Duluth, in the Eighth Minnesota congressional district. After graduating in 1912, Denfeld served in battleships. He married Rachael Metcalf in 1915; they had no children.

Following service in a destroyer out of Queenstown, Ireland, during World War I, he went to his first tour in personnel work, a field in which he excelled. Additional duty in destroyers and in command of a submarine was followed by his becoming the aide and flag secretary to Admiral Richard H. Leigh, Commander in Chief, U. S. Fleet. After a tour in command of a destroyer squadron and a tour as aide to the chief of naval operations, Admiral William D. Leahy, Denfeld returned to destroyers and, for a while, was on the Neutrality Patrol. He negotiated some naval issues in London in March 1941, then became aide, and later chief of staff, to the commander of the Atlantic Fleet Support Force.

For most of World War II, however, he was an assistant to the chief of the Bureau of Naval Personnel. After commanding a battleship division that supported the Okinawa campaign and serving as chief of the Bureau of Naval Personnel, he assumed command of the Pacific Fleet on 28 February 1947.

In October of that year, the chief of naval operations, Fleet Admiral Chester W. Nimitz, told Secretary of the Navy John L. Sullivan that he would leave office on 17 December. Sullivan asked Nimitz who should succeed him and Nimitz suggested Admirals William H. P. Blandy, Dewitt C. Ramsey, Richard L. Conolly, Charles M. Cooke, or Louis E. Denfeld. Fleet Admiral Ernest J. King strongly supported Cooke, but President Harry S. Truman's confidant, Fleet Admiral William D. Leahy, the chairman of the Joint Chiefs of Staff, recommended Denfeld.[1] When Truman sounded out James V. Forrestal, the secretary of defense proposed Ramsey, Blandy, or Denfeld. He was "somewhat concerned about Denfeld's political activity," but since it was obvious that the president would find Denfeld the easiest of the lot to work with, Forrestal raised no objection to his appointment.[2] Many surface line officers preferred Blandy; aviators, Ramsey. On 12 November, Truman named Denfeld, a compromise candidate, to a two-year term. On 15 December, when he became chief of naval operations, Denfeld chose an aviator, Vice Admiral Arthur W. Radford, as his vice CNO.

Neither the press nor the officer corps of the navy regarded Denfeld as a brilliant man, but there were many predictions that he would do well as CNO because of his experience in personnel work. However, Denfeld had not spent much time in "joint" billets dealing with the other services, and some believed that "the in-fighting in the Joint Chiefs of Staff . . . was something foreign to his nature."[3] Upon becoming chief of naval operations, Denfeld took his first step along a path of frustration that led to the premature end of his career.

Rapid demobilization and a small defense budget had made a shambles out of the great American navy of World War II. The National Security Act signed by President Truman on 18 July 1947 created a national military establishment headed by a secretary of defense, but it failed either to "unify" the armed services or to define satisfactorily their strategic roles and wartime missions. A lingering and especially important issue for the navy was where naval aviation fitted into plans for the employment of strategic and tactical aviation.

Moreover, the president's defense policies were certain to cause problems for any naval chief. Truman fondly recalled his days in the National Guard in World War I, disliked most professional military officers—especially admirals—and favored the air force in his budgetary decisions. Indeed, the fact that the air force received the highest percentage of the budget for fiscal year 1948 caused some naval leaders to charge that Truman was letting dollars determine his military strategy. A major issue for the next fiscal year's budget concerned the request of the air force to build up to seventy air groups, or a total of 6,869 planes, of which 988 would be heavy bombers. This proposal was in part reinforced by a report issued by the president's Air Policy Commission headed by Thomas K. Finletter. The panel concluded that, for the next two years or so, the United States would continue to enjoy a monopoly in atomic bombs and recommended that the "military establishment . . . be built around the air arm."[4] This clearly meant that both land-based *and* naval aviation units should be increased, but the air force used the report to justify its demand for seventy air groups, the number it claimed would be needed to wage a general war with the Soviet Union.

Denfeld and other naval leaders disputed that claim. They pointed to the facts that most American air bases in Europe had been closed after World War II and that the air force still lacked an intercontinental bomber able to deliver atomic bombs on Russia from bases in the United States. On the other hand, an aircraft carrier could place its planes within 1,700 miles of any target on earth in addition to commanding the air and sea where it cruised. Therefore, Denfeld decided that the navy had to build a supercarrier that would be able to handle heavy bombers carrying atomic bombs. Without such a ship, he worried, the development of naval aircraft would cease. With one, the navy would be able to break the air force's monopoly on the delivery of atomic weapons. A supercarrier, labeled Project 6A, appeared in the navy's shipbuilding program for fiscal year 1949. With a budget of only $4.35 billion for that year, however, no more than $6 million, a small amount, could be allotted toward its construction.[5] But the need for a supercarrier was acute, Denfeld believed, because Rear Admiral Daniel V. Gallery, director of the navy's guided-missile program, had warned him that the air force wanted heavy atomic bombs that only its bombers could deliver and opposed the production of lighter bombs that naval aircraft could carry.[6]

Since 1945 the Joint Chiefs of Staff had completed a series of war plans to deal with a general war between the West and the Soviet Union. The service chiefs were in broad agreement about Soviet strategy in such a war and on the outlines of American strategy. They believed that the large Russian Army would drive from the Elbe River to the English Channel with ease, strike into the Middle East to deny Britain and the United States the oil resources of that region, and, in Asia, throw American forces off the Korean Peninsula. American naval forces would evacuate Allied armies from Europe and Asia and defend the English Channel, the Mediterranean, and both major oceans. Meanwhile, the United States would mobilize and launch a counterattack against Russia with atomic bombs. It was on this point in their planning that the chiefs could not reach agreement because the air force demanded the sole right to deliver atomic bombs and the navy disputed this demand. Thus, the issue of strategic roles and missions directly concerned the way in which the United States would wage a total war against the Soviet Union.[7]

When Denfeld became chief of naval operations, the Joint Chiefs had been struggling with the question of roles and missions for some time. During World War II, General George C. Marshall and Admiral King set a precedent by agreeing that all recommendations of the Joint Chiefs would be unanimous. However, by early 1948 unanimity on roles and missions seemed so far away that Secretary of Defense Forrestal asked the chiefs for a final report on the thorny matter by 8 March 1948, "with a split paper if necessary." This spurred the chiefs into day-long sessions on 3 and 5 March, but the army and air force lined up against the navy and there was no agreement.[8] As Denfeld told Secretary Sullivan: "The Army-Air Force party line is that the Unification Act is wrong and needed to be amended. The attack is on the Marine Corps and the role of naval air."[9] By supporting the army's demand that the size of the marine corps be reduced, air force leaders had assured army support for their demands for control over strategic aviation.

Forrestal believed that this deadlock had to be broken before he could propose a military budget to the Congress for fiscal year 1949, and he called the Joint Chiefs into conference at Key West, Florida, for three days beginning 11

March. The debate that took place was heated, but Denfeld and his colleagues finally drafted a paper entitled "Functions of the Armed Forces . . . ," which assigned disputed duties as the "primary" responsibility of one service and "collateral" functions of other services. Strategic bombing, for example, was a primary function of the air force, and a collateral function of the navy and marine corps. Forrestal further refined this point by stating that the navy would not be prohibited from attacking any target whose elimination was necessary for the accomplishment of its mission but that the weapon it used would have to be approved by the Joint Chiefs of Staff on the "basis of its contribution to the over-all war effort."[10] The agreement reached at Key West allowed the navy to proceed with its supercarrier and with its program for atomic weapons.

Not only had the Joint Chiefs been unable to reach unanimity over roles and missions before the Key West conference, they had also found it impossible to agree on a unified defense budget. Forrestal decided that, until they did, he would divide the forthcoming budget equally among the army, navy, and air force. The army supported his "balanced" program, but both the air force and the navy opposed it in principle. The air force continued to insist on funds to expand their fighting units from fifty-five to seventy air groups. Denfeld, of course, balked at this increase. The air force's retort was that there was no need for a large American navy because the Soviets did not have sizable naval forces, and it hinted that eventually naval aviation should be absorbed into the air force. Denfeld claimed that an increase in strength of the land-based air forces would have to be met by the expansion of naval aviation until the two elements had achieved approximate parity. More practically, he warned that the proposed increase in the number of air groups inevitably meant that the army and the navy would need more money or that American bases for heavy bombers would have to be built overseas.[11] Unable to agree upon a division of the budget, Denfeld and his fellow chiefs established a board of three deputies to study the question and propose a solution.

Meanwhile, Denfeld and Sullivan decided that the supercarrier program was to have priority over several other shipbuilding projects. To ensure that the supercarrier would be completed, Denfeld agreed to Sullivan's decision to cancel the completion of thirteen other ships and to shift the funds for them to Project 6A. He defended the decision in early June 1948 before the Senate Armed Services Committee. The supercarrier, he told the committee, had been approved "all along the line" and was needed in order "to work out the capabilities of a ship of this type" and of the new jets she would carry.[12] Although Denfeld's problem concerned simply getting one supercarrier built, others had greater hopes. Vice CNO Radford, for example, favored building four ships of this type, as did the chief of the Bureau of Ships, Vice Admiral Earle W. Mills, and the powerful chairman of the House Naval Affairs Committee, Congressman Carl Vinson.[13]

The issue of the supercarrier was so important that the president discussed it with the Joint Chiefs of Staff. Denfeld defended the project vigorously.

General Carl Spaatz, chief of staff of the air force, opposed it but told Truman that he would support the decision of his commander in chief to go ahead. Nonetheless, Spaatz maintained that the carrier had to be approved by the air force, which had primary responsibility for strategic bombing, or by the Joint Chiefs of Staff. Since the army chief of staff, General Omar N. Bradley, supported Spaatz's idea that the ship had to receive the approval of the Joint Chiefs, Denfeld asked for a formal vote by the chiefs on the project. The count was three to one in favor of the supercarrier, the negative vote being cast by Spaatz's relief, General Hoyt S. Vandenberg.[14] So the matter stood when Congress approved a "balanced" budget for fiscal year 1949 of $4.9 billion for the navy, $4.7 billion for the air force, and $4.2 billion for the army. Despite his victory in the vote of the Joint Chiefs, Denfeld had to defend the supercarrier against air force opposition throughout 1948. Forrestal ended the argument, for the time being, when he decided that the ship would be built. The chiefs then went along by agreeing to Denfeld's proposal that it be equipped to bomb strategic targets within an area of naval operations.[15] In the first week of August 1948, a contract for the construction of the supercarrier was finally let.

The struggle for the supercarrier, to be named the *United States*, was far from over. In contrast to Vandenberg's vote against the ship, on 5 February 1948 Denfeld agreed with his fellow chiefs that the air force should acquire more B-36B heavy bombers. Forrestal concurred, and Truman released funds on 4 May for the purchase and modification of the bombers. The air force also pressed its case for seventy air groups and persuaded Congressman Vinson to introduce into the House a bill authorizing a force of this level. At the same time, the air force persistently attacked the *United States* as being a wasteful "effort to duplicate unnecessarily a proved and experienced land-based organization."[16] Stung by these charges, Denfeld established in his office the Organizational and Policy Section to defend the navy's position and named a brilliant captain, Arleigh A. Burke, to head it.[17] During the year the contest became increasingly bitter, and Forrestal grew so weary and tense that Attorney General Tom C. Clark claimed he was "as nervous as a whore in church."[18] Forrestal was caught between the rising prices of an inflationary period and the incessant demands of the services for more funds. At one point, he stunned Sullivan and Denfeld by requesting that the carrier strength of the fleet be reduced from eight to six and budget cuts of over $100 million be accepted. Denfeld, who appealed the cuts without success, ascribed them to the air force's "unscrupulous" and "unjustified" attacks on the navy.[19]

Although Denfeld was frustrated by Forrestal during 1948, the secretary of defense was his valuable ally on several important issues. On the other hand, Truman never liked Forrestal and, after his own re-election in November, was determined to replace him. On 1 March 1949 the two men met in the White House, a meeting that Forrestal found "shattering," and he resigned.[20] As the new secretary of defense Truman appointed Louis A. Johnson, who had successfully raised funds for the president's recent campaign. A quarrelsome, efficient, and ambitious executive, Johnson had served as assistant secretary of war during Roosevelt's second term but was replaced in 1940 for feuding with the secretary. By 1949, he had come to hate the navy and, as secretary of defense, adopted two primary objectives: to merge naval aviation with the air force and to merge the marine corps with the army. Congress planned to pass amendments in 1949 that would give the secretary of defense more direct control over the military departments, and with this increased authority Johnson intended to "crack heads" and force agreement with his policies.[21] As chief of naval operations, Denfeld stood directly between the new secretary and his goals.

Johnson took office on 28 March 1949, the same day on which the North Atlantic Treaty was signed. Within a month he decided to cancel the construction of the *United States*. During the Berlin airlift in 1948 the air force had deployed to British bases bombers that could deliver atomic bombs against the Soviet Union. The NATO alliance meant that the air force would, in the near future, be able to deploy land-based bombers in Europe. To supply these aircraft, the budget for fiscal year 1950 allowed the air force to increase the number of its air groups from forty-eight to fifty-eight. Moreover, Truman had ordered Johnson to cut defense expenditures. The air force's ability to forward-base heavy bombers undercut some of the navy's earlier arguments in favor of the supercarrier, which, for this and other reasons, must have seemed to Johnson a perfect target for economy.[22]

On 23 April, Johnson, without consulting or informing either Denfeld or Sullivan, publicly announced the cancellation of the *United States*. The secretary of the navy was in Texas when he heard the news. He flew back to Washington, discussed the situation with Denfeld, and wrote an angry letter of resignation. Denfeld, too, was furious, but there was little he could do. If he raised the issue in the Joint Chiefs of Staff again, Bradley would vote with Vandenberg, the chiefs would issue a "split paper," and Johnson would be able to disregard the matter. In addition, there was no likelihood that either of the armed services committees in Congress would interfere. But, for Denfeld the decision carried the more disturbing portent that, by a vote of two to one, the army and the air force could veto the acquisition of any weapons the navy needed to execute its assigned strategic mission. And, as Burke warned Denfeld, Johnson would merely wait for the furor over the scrapping of the carrier to die down, then transfer naval and marine corps aviation to the air force.[23]

More and more the dispute between Denfeld and the leaders of the air force turned on comparisons between the capabilities of the supercarrier and the B-36B heavy bomber. At one point, for example, the air force proposed tests between its bomber and one of the navy's fighter-bombers. This was reminiscent of the experiments in bombing battleships conducted during the early 1920s, the results of which confused the prewar argument over the proper role of aviation in warfare. Denfeld rejected the idea, maintaining that the tests could hardly compare the value of the aircraft in executing strategic bombing missions. Oddly enough, in the midst of the debate, the very value of strategic bombing against the Soviet Union in a general war came into question when a joint board, which had studied the matter, concluded that bombing alone would not force the Russians to capitulate. Since this conclusion damaged the air force's case, Vandenberg tried to have it changed, but Denfeld prevented the move.[24]

In the summer of 1949 Denfeld did his best to accommodate Johnson and the new secretary of the navy, Francis P. Matthews. Another Democratic party fund-raiser, Matthews was a friend of the defense secretary and knew little about naval affairs. Nonetheless, Denfeld apparently persuaded him that many of the air force's arguments were invalid and Matthews wrote a strong memorandum shortly after he took office defending the modernization of two *Essex*-class carriers and expressing concern over the veto power the army and the air force could exercise over naval weapon systems. On 5 June 1949, Denfeld and Matthews saw Johnson and complained that policies which restricted the expansion of naval aviation would reduce the navy's ability to execute its assigned strategic and tactical missions. However, Johnson had made up his mind. In several moves aimed at giving the air force a virtual monopoly over atomic bombing, he cut naval and marine corps aviation funds and transferred the monies to the air force. Besides scrapping the supercarrier, he slashed the navy's budget for aircraft research and development, thus placing a ceiling on the level of technical improvements in naval planes. He also reduced the Fleet Marine Force by one-fifth and marine aviation by one-half, making a shambles out of the quick-response forces of the corps. Denfeld slowly came to the conclusion that naval aviation faced the greatest crisis in its turbulent history.[25]

Despite Denfeld's obvious differences with Johnson and his policies, Matthews was pleased with his chief of naval operations. He told Truman that the admiral "has worked with me in fullest harmony and cooperation from the day I was honored with this office. His experience as Chief of Naval Operations, coupled with his outstanding administrative abilities, makes him most valuable to me, the Navy, and the National Defense Establishment." This ringing endorsement was followed by an ironic citation of Denfeld's value as a member of the Joint Chiefs of Staff, where he was consistently pummeled by the alliance of the army and the air force. "The wisdom of his reappointment is emphasized by the importance of the continuity of the members of the Joint Chiefs of Staff, of which Admiral Denfeld is senior member, in dealing with the numerous long range problems with which that body has been laboring."[26] Johnson evidently agreed with this assessment and so did Truman, who announced on 10 August that, when Denfeld's term expired on 15 December 1949, he would be appointed for another two-year tour. At the same time, however, Truman announced that he was naming General Bradley to replace Fleet Admiral Leahy, who had stepped down earlier in the year, as chairman of the Joint Chiefs of Staff. Whereas Leahy was neutral in the interservice feud, Bradley was a partisan of the army-air force alliance.

All of this set the stage for the "revolt of the admirals," an episode that began when Congressman James E. Van Zandt, a member of the House Naval Affairs Committee and a captain in the naval reserve, charged that there were irregularities in the air force's procurement of the B-36B and demanded an investigation by Congress. Since the inquiry involved Secretary of Defense Johnson, who was a director of the company that manufactured the bombers, Vinson decided to chair the hearings, which he intended to expand beyond the conflict-of-interest charges into a full-scale investigation of American defense policy. Asked by Vinson for his comments on the committee's agenda, Denfeld suggested that the committee address the issues of the cancellation of the supercarrier, a yearly modernization program for the *Essex*-class carriers, and the protection of naval and marine corps aviation from merger with the air force. He also told Vinson that the committee should address a cut made by Truman in the defense budget for fiscal year 1951 from $14.1 billion to $13 billion, because it primarily affected naval aviation, which would be unable to carry out its missions. Vinson's final agenda covered most of these points.[27]

The hearings were divided into two parts. In the first part, the conflict-of-interest charges against Johnson were not proven when the committee investigated the procurement of the B-36B. Nonetheless, an acerbic debate developed in testimony between the devotees and the opponents of the air force's strategy, and this dispute was aired during the second part of Vinson's inquiry.

Unfortunately for Denfeld, he had to spend most of the summer of 1949 in Europe dealing with the organization of a NATO defense command. Seemingly simple matters of convincing the new allies that they should subordinate their armed forces to combined ground, air, and naval commands in Europe proved to be complex, and they consumed Denfeld's time when many in the navy believed that his presence in Washington was necessary. Instead, Denfeld left Burke and his unit to prepare much of the navy's testimony for the Vinson hearings. Dissatisfaction within the navy over Denfeld's performance as chief of naval operations was growing for several other reasons as well. Many officers believed, wrongly, that he, along with the other service chiefs, had a hand in the cancellation of the *United States*. Others opposed Denfeld's refusal to allow a test between a naval fighter-bomber and the B-36B. He was also accused of being passive when Secretary of the Navy Sullivan resigned and of agreeing with the decision of the Joint Chiefs to allow the air force to procure their new heavy bomber. Indeed, some even charged that, as the price of being offered a second term as chief of naval operations, Denfeld agreed to de-emphasize naval aviation and stress antisubmarine warfare and surface operations! In Denfeld's absence during the summer of 1949, Admiral Radford, the new commander in chief of the Pacific Fleet, stayed in Washington for the hearings and became the spokesman for the navy. Because Denfeld, who should have represented the service, was less articulate and more conciliatory than Radford, he began to lose the confidence of Radford's following of "radical" naval aviators.[28]

In late September, Denfeld endorsed and sent on to Matthews a secret letter written by Vice Admiral Gerald F. Bogan claiming that unification was not working well and that "the morale of the Navy is lower today than at any time since I entered the commissioned ranks in 1916."[29] Denfeld warned Matthews that "sea power will not be accorded adequate recognition, because the [unified] organization contemplated would permit reductions of that sea power by individuals who are not thoroughly familiar with its potentialities." Unification had been enacted into law and Denfeld claimed that he was trying to make it effective. "In this effort," he wrote, "I am fully supported by a large majority of Naval personnel."[30] A navy partisan, Captain John G. Crommelin, leaked Bogan's inflammatory letter to the press along with Denfeld's endorsement. Johnson was furious and warned Matthews to keep Denfeld "in line" or the admiral's reappointment as chief of naval operations would be disapproved. Denfeld tried to calm the situation by publicly stating that his endorsement of Bogan's letter did not signify his agreement with Bogan's opinions and that, as chief of naval operations, he had wholeheartedly supported unification. Nonetheless, Matthews decided that Denfeld had to be replaced. He suggested that if Conolly would "pull his punches" in his testimony before the Vinson committee he, Matthews, would support Conolly as Denfeld's relief. Conolly rejected the bribe. Matthews then turned to Admiral Forrest P. Sherman as a possible successor to Denfeld.[31]

Vinson opened his crucial hearings on 5 October and Secretary Matthews was the first to testify. He claimed that morale in the navy was good, except among "insubordinate," "faithless," and "guilty" officers, most of whom were aviators. He had high praise for Johnson. In answering questions, he revealed that he had blocked the promotion of some officers who wanted to strengthen national security and that he did not know of the fear, widely held in the navy, that Johnson's budget cuts, especially in naval aviation, would make it impossible for the service to accomplish its assigned missions. Furthermore, he dismissed the possibility that Denfeld's solitary position on the Joint Chiefs of Staff had affected morale in the navy.[32]

During the night of 5 October, Matthews obtained a copy of the testimony that Radford intended to deliver the following day. In it, Radford directly attacked the air force, and, implicitly, Johnson's defense policies. Worried that Radford's testimony might inflame the situation, Matthews persuaded Denfeld that they should ask Vinson to hold an executive session to listen to Radford. Vinson refused, and Radford took the oath before the committee on 6 October. His testimony was dramatic. He claimed that air power, which he said was the sum of the air, sea, and land forces of the country, was the dominant factor in American military security. Although he admitted that strategic bombing was properly the primary mission of the air force, he maintained that bombing alone would bring no "cheap and easy victory" in a general war: it was, in other words, no short cut to military triumph, as the air force insisted. Additionally, Radford directly attacked the B-36B on its technical performance, which he argued was deficient; in adopting the bomber, he said, the air force had made a "billion dollar blunder." He contended that his views were supported by almost every experienced active and retired naval officer and that it was very difficult for them to get their views across to "our sister services" and "some of the civilian secretaries." A galaxy of naval and marine corps leaders from World War II followed Radford and upheld his charges.[33]

For Denfeld, the question was whether he would continue publicly to support Matthews or whether he would defend Radford and his "radicals." Matthews, who was being hounded by the press about the contradictions between his testimony and that of Radford, asked Denfeld to "get him off the hook." Denfeld was under intense pressure from all sides. For example, Truman's naval aide, Captain Robert L. Dennison, was ordered to help him prepare a statement that would not oppose "the President's policy."[34] Denfeld was torn between his obligations as a member of the Joint Chiefs of Staff and his duties as chief of naval operations. He had to balance his responsibilities as a spokesman for the navy before Secretary of Defense Johnson and his loyalty to Secretary of the Navy Matthews. The tragedy of Denfeld's position was that a vigorous defense of Radford would diminish his own stature among the Joint Chiefs and ruin his relations with Matthews; this, in the long term, would harm the navy. He had long hoped that the interservice dispute could be resolved amicably, without his being forced to take a rigid position in public and to say things about the other services that he would have normally left unspoken. But Burke and Radford both favored an airing of the dispute and a strong statement by Denfeld, and their influence probably inclined him to make a more forthright case than he might otherwise have made.[35]

Despite his earlier attempt to keep Radford's testimony secret, Denfeld decided—much too late—that he could no longer play the part of conciliator, that he had to bluntly defend the navy's position, and that this meant that he had to support Radford's charges. Denfeld asked Captain Charles D. Griffin to prepare a draft statement for him. Although Griffin was not an aviator, as he was working he kept in close touch with Radford, but he was surprised that Denfeld did not call him into the CNO's office until 8:00 a.m. on 7 October, the day before Denfeld was scheduled to testify. There, Denfeld, Griffin, and others used Griffin's basic paper to prepare the opening statement to the committee. That evening, Hanson W. Baldwin, a reporter and former naval officer, dined with the Denfelds and then read the paper. Baldwin found it "very much stronger than anything he'd said before, very much stronger, and the first time he'd really come down hard." Later that night, Denfeld met in his office with Radford, Burke, and Dennison to review the statement. Before dawn, they had hammered out the paper Denfeld would read at 10:00 a.m.[36]

At the hearing, Denfeld began by stating that he "fully supported the broad conclusions presented to this committee by the naval and Marine officers who have preceded me." The navy supported unification, he insisted, but the concept of unification was being ignored because the Department of Defense was excluding the navy from consultation on issues of high policy and from full partnership with the other services. He cited the department's decisions to cancel the construction of the *United States*, allow the air force to increase its stock of B-36Bs, and cut the navy's budget. He added:

> The entire Navy . . . is gravely concerned whether it will have modern weapons, in quality and quantity, to do the job expected of the Navy at the outbreak of a future war. We have real misgivings over the reductions that are taking place in the Navy today. . . . It is not so much the reduction in congressional appropriations that worries us. . . . Our concern is with arbitrary reductions that impair, or even eliminate, essential naval functions. It is not so much a question of too little appropriated money, but how we are allowed to invest that money. . . . Limitations are imposed without consultation, and without understanding of the Navy's responsibility in defense of our maritime nation.
>
> I am an advocate of air power. . . . I am also a proponent of strategic air warfare.
>
> There has been no objection raised by the Navy to the development of the B-36 to the point where its value as a weapon might be thoroughly evaluated. . . . However, it is illogical, damaging, and dangerous to proceed directly to mass procurement without evaluation to the extent that the Army and Navy may be starved for funds and our strategic concept of war frozen about an uncertain weapon.
>
> The procedure leading up to the cancellation of the carrier *United States* is another exemplification of the improper operation of unification.[37]

Denfeld's statement was vigorous but more moderate than Radford's. However, because he had supported Radford, Denfeld expected to be the butt of subsequent criticism.

As his fellow officers congratulated Denfeld when he finished his testimony, Matthews, visibly flushed, hurried from the committee room. The next day he told Denfeld that he was "stunned" by the admiral's presentation. On 14 October Matthews complained to Nimitz that he "was the victim of a conspiracy in which the Chief of Naval Operations, Louis E. Denfeld, was the principal conspirator." Matthews believed that "something was going on" in Burke's policy unit which involved Radford and "had to do with the B-36 and the unification of the services." Referring to Denfeld, Matthews complained that "he tells me nothing . . . . Is that right?" In fact, Denfeld's preoccupation with NATO and other administrative problems had partly blinded him to the fact that much of the testimony that Burke had written for naval witnesses before the Vinson committee was far more antagonistic than Denfeld believed necessary. In the event, Matthews was determined to relieve Denfeld but he did not seem to know how to go about it and he asked for Nimitz's advice. Nimitz admitted that Denfeld had erred in failing to keep Matthews informed of Burke's activities and suggested that the secretary tell Truman that he could no longer work with the chief of naval operations.[38] Matthews then wrote to the president. He complained that Denfeld had not been loyal to the secretary of the navy or to the concept of unification and he claimed that he could not satisfactorily perform his duties as secretary unless Denfeld were relieved. Truman, who seemed to take a certain delight in firing government officials, promptly agreed that Denfeld should be dismissed "as a move to restore discipline."[39]

Denfeld learned of his relief from a radio newscast. Although he must have expected something, he was justifiably aggrieved that Truman had not been courteous enough to call him and tell him in person that he had been fired. On 1 November 1949, Matthews detached Denfeld from duty as chief of naval operations. As Denfeld left the Pentagon, a large number of naval officers and civil servants, some of them in tears, offered their chief a parting salute. As Vinson put it, although Johnson had promised that there would be no reprisals for forthright testimony given before Congress, Denfeld was made to "walk the plank" because he claimed that the navy was not granted full partnership in the new national defense organization. There was a brief furor in the press between those who wanted to impeach both Johnson and Matthews and those who defended civilian supremacy over the professional military and the need to maintain the unity of the armed forces. But moves in both houses of Congress to investigate Denfeld's ouster failed. There were other reprisals as well which affected Bogan, Conolly, Burke, and others.[40]

Matthews offered Denfeld the post of Commander in Chief, U. S. Naval Forces, Atlantic and Eastern Mediterranean, but Denfeld declined, saying that the "embarrassment" he had suffered would place an "undesirable restraint" upon him in his dealings with other governments. He retired from the navy on 1 March 1950.

It was ironic that the report of the Vinson committee was issued the next day. It generally supported Denfeld's position and urged that the National Security Council give the Joint Chiefs of Staff clear statements of American foreign and defense policy on which the chiefs could base their strategic planning. The authors of the report stressed that the views of one or two of the services should not be imposed on a third and criticized the air force as being unbalanced in favor of bombing forces. They specifically castigated Johnson for "summarily" canceling the *United States* and maintained that a supercarrier should be built when the budget permitted. Last, with respect to Denfeld's ouster, the committee was

> convinced that this act was a reprisal—that the frank and honest testimony of Admiral Denfeld in respect to national defense planning and the administration of the unification law, not some more distant cause, produced his removal from office . . . . The removal of Admiral Denfeld unquestionably tends to intimidate witnesses from the executive branch. It greatly aggravates the ever-present difficulty of obtaining uninhibited testimony upon which to base legislative decisions. The committee is convinced that the removal of the Chief of Naval Operations . . . violated promises made to witnesses by the committee and the Secretary of the Navy, and by the Secretary of Defense . . . .[41]

Upon retiring after forty years of naval service, Denfeld struck back at Johnson and Matthews in articles published in *Collier's*, a popular magazine. In one, which he titled "Reprisal: Why I Was Fired," Denfeld asserted that he knew he would be the first target of reprisals by Johnson and Matthews but he did not expect the "contemptuous treatment" he had received. Loyalty should work down as well as up, and loyalty included "politeness." Denfeld argued that his firing and the cancellation of the supercarrier were done in such an arbitrary way that they justified his fear that control over national defense might pass from the electorate's representatives. Matthews and Johnson, and Vinson, had promised that there would be no reprisals, but he had "offended the secretariat." Denfeld then listed Matthews's reprisals against Burke, whose promotion to flag rank the secretary tried to thwart, and Bogan and Blandy, who were edged into early retirement by the secretary. Denfeld hoped that Radford, "this splendid officer," would not also be the object of Matthews's ire.[42]

The purpose of Denfeld's second article was clear from its title, "The Only Carrier the Air Force Ever Sank." He claimed that army and air force officers, especially Bradley and Vandenberg, lacked professional knowledge of the navy's role in the Pacific in World War II. Indeed, until 1949, neither Bradley nor Vandenberg had even been aboard an aircraft carrier at sea! Denfeld concluded that they were ignorant of the way in which a naval war would be waged in the future, yet they had consistently disapproved the construction of large carriers. He disputed the claim of some air force leaders that the supercarrier was intended to participate in the atomic bombing of enemy cities. "Strategic bombing was never a factor in the plans for the carrier *United States*," he insisted. However, air force generals imagined that it posed a danger to their primary function of strategic air warfare, and they gathered enough supporters to "sink the *United States*." Moreover, the supercarrier was canceled without either Secretary Sullivan or the chief of naval operations being consulted—by a purely "dictatorial ukase." Finally, because of the alliance between the air force and the army on the Joint Chiefs of Staff, the navy had been continually outvoted by two to one.[43]

Ironically, the supercarrier for which Denfeld fought so hard was approved again by Congress on 25 April 1950 after a request by his successor, Admiral Forrest P. Sherman. And, in mid-May, the navy revealed that it had deployed two squadrons of AJ-1s, attack aircraft which weighed only half as much as B-29s but could carry atomic bombs. In effect, this breakthrough achieved one of Denfeld's major goals as chief of naval operations—it ended the air force's monopoly on atomic bombing. The Korean War that followed proved Denfeld right in his insistent demands for balanced and flexible forces and exposed the faults of a military philosophy of reliance upon a single weapon system or doctrine.

At the end of Denfeld's tour, civilian authority triumphed over the military, but low morale in the navy demanded a successor who could raise that morale and still accept the limits imposed by unification. There is no doubt that Denfeld's ouster was conducted in an utterly unfair manner, but the admiral, who was criticized by naval officers for his apparent weakness as chief of naval operations, appeared to be a much greater man after his "firing" than he did during his tour as CNO.

After the publication of his articles in *Collier's* in 1950, Denfeld made no further public comments on national security. In 1972, at eighty years of age, he died and was buried in Arlington National Cemetery.

FORREST PERCIVAL SHERMAN

2 November 1949–22 July 1951

CLARK G. REYNOLDS

The strategic crises, confusion, and international realignments of the early years of the cold war demanded a naval leader with the ability to provide intellectual and administrative direction for the navy and, indeed, for American defense policy. Happily, such a leader emerged with the ascension of Forrest P. Sherman to the post of chief of naval operations in late 1949. Not only did Sherman dominate American and Allied strategic planning during the next two years, but the cold war frontiers that he helped to establish proved to be so realistic that they remained basically unchanged over the next three decades.

Forrest P. Sherman was born in Merrimack, New Hampshire, on 30 October 1896. He was one of six children, and was raised in Melrose, Massachusetts, in the Episcopal faith. The fact that his father sold school textbooks for a living probably enlarged the reading material available at home to the son. When he was eight years old, Forrest visited the battleship *Kentucky*, and thereafter a naval career was his only ambition in life. While waiting for an appointment to the Naval Academy, he spent 1913 and 1914 at the Massachusetts Institute of Technology.[1]

In 1914 Sherman entered the academy. At Annapolis, his superior intellect, his businesslike attitude toward problems, his serious demeanor, and his impeccable manners set him apart from his classmates. So did his preference for horsemanship and fencing over more plebeian sports, and many of his peers regarded him as cold, aloof, and ambitious. However, many respected his clear ability, as the 1918 *Lucky Bag* noted, "Above all, Sherman knows his job; when he is given a thing to do he finds out all there is to be found about it and the job is well done."[2] Standing more than six feet tall, with a round face and ruddy complexion, "Fuzz" Sherman—the nickname being the verbalization of his initials, F.S.—led his class in theoretical and practical ordnance and gunnery. He stood second among the 199 midshipmen of the class of 1918, which was graduated early in June 1917 because of America's entry into World War I.

During the war, Sherman served in the gunboat *Nashville* which escorted convoys and patrolled for submarines in the Mediterranean. Just before the armistice of 1918, he was sent to the Atlantic in the destroyer *Murray*. His professional ability, his fine memory, and his knack for solving complex problems brought him to the attention of Rear Admiral Newton A. McCully, Jr., who commanded the postwar Control Force of escort ships in the Atlantic and who chose him in 1921 as his flag lieutenant and aide. But Sherman had already found a new love in naval aviation, which he discerned as holding the future of the navy. Six months of flight training culminated in his designation as a naval aviator in December 1922 . He was such a skilled pilot that in 1924 he returned to Pensacola for a two-year tour as a flight instructor, and from 1930 to 1931 he taught flight tactics at the Naval Academy. In the meantime, he had not only written several essays on aviation for the *U. S. Naval Institute Proceedings*, but he had attended the Naval War College in 1926 and 1927. He married in 1923 Dolores Brownson, by whom he had one daughter, Elizabeth Ann.[3]

The next phase of Sherman's career was dominated by service in large, fast aircraft carriers. In the summer of 1927 he joined the precommissioning detail as a ship's officer for the first one, the *Lexington*. However, most of his carrier duty was in the *Saratoga*, first as a pilot, then briefly as commander of Scouting Squadron 2 in 1929, and from 1932 to 1933 as commanding officer of her Fighting Squadron 1. His keen mind took him out of flying and into staff work and he served as flag secretary to the fleet's carrier commander, Rear Admiral Joseph Mason Reeves, and his successor, Rear Admiral Harry E. Yarnell. After heading the aviation ordnance section in the Bureau of Aeronautics from 1933 to 1936, Commander Sherman returned to the fleet as navigator for the carrier *Ranger* and then as aviation officer for Admiral Claude C. Bloch during his successive tours as commander of the Battle Force and commander of the U. S. Fleet from 1937 to 1940.[4]

Early in 1940, Admiral Harold R. Stark, the chief of naval operations, brought Sherman into the War Plans Division where he drafted plans for North American military strategy and served on the Canadian-United States Joint Board on Defense. The senior member of the board, Captain Harry W. Hill, recalled that Sherman's "tact and ability to mediate between Board members holding opposing views was instrumental in making the Board successful."[5] Sherman's abilities as a planner led to his inclusion in Stark's party which attended the Atlantic Conference summit off Argentia, Newfoundland, in August 1941. When the United States finally entered World War II, he was assigned in February 1942 to the Joint War Plans Committee where he remained for three months helping to draft the first plans for an American counteroffensive against the Axis powers.

Promoted to captain, in May 1942 Sherman took command of the carrier *Wasp*, which supported the landings on Guadalcanal in August and continued to cover that beachhead into the next month. On 15 September a Japanese submarine fired three torpedoes into the *Wasp*, turning her into such a blazing inferno that Sherman gave the order to abandon ship. He spent nearly two hours in the water and received internal injuries from concussions caused by exploding depth charges dropped by American destroyers attacking the enemy submarine. Although he received a Navy Cross for "extraordinary heroism" during his command of the *Wasp*, he suffered the stigma of any captain who loses his ship. He seemed fated never again to command at sea in combat.[6]

However, Vice Admiral John H. Towers, the newly appointed commander of the Pacific Fleet's air forces, needed a chief of staff. Not only was Sherman available, but the admiral believed that he was the ideal man for the billet. Sherman reported for duty with Towers at Pearl Harbor in mid-October 1942 and, over the next year, coordinated the deployment of the growing inventory of naval aircraft throughout the Pacific while the fleet shifted from the strategic defensive to the offensive. Sherman's ability and his tact in dealing with superiors impressed the commander in chief of the Pacific Fleet, Admiral Chester W. Nimitz; for example, Sherman eased a difficult relationship between Nimitz and Towers. Finally, in November 1943, on Towers's advice, Nimitz transferred Sherman to his own staff as assistant chief of staff for plans with the rank of rear admiral.[7]

"Ask Forrest" was a byword of the Pacific Fleet staff at Pearl Harbor from late November 1943 until the Japanese surrender in August 1945. Promoted to deputy chief of staff for plans and head of the fleet war plans division in March 1944, Sherman became Nimitz's alter ego. He often represented Nimitz in Washington, where Admiral Ernest J. King, commander in chief of the U. S. Fleet and chief of naval operations, gave Sherman a better hearing than most. Sherman played a key role in planning the bypassing of key Japanese strongholds, and he contributed materially to American grand strategy in the Pacific theater. Nimitz especially honored Sherman and Admiral William F. Halsey, Jr., both of whom stood beside him during the surrender ceremonies on the *Missouri* in Tokyo Bay on 2 September 1945.[8]

Sea duty continued to elude Sherman after the war. In December 1945, Nimitz, then chief of naval operations, promoted him to vice admiral and brought him to Washington as deputy CNO for operations. Sherman's new responsibilities included war planning, fleet operations, fleet training, and intelligence, and with these duties he moved into a new arena of interservice politics and national defense policy. The creation of an independent air force and unification of the armed services provided the first test of Sherman's bureaucratic acumen. In August 1945 he had argued that no independent air force be created; instead, he proposed to allow the army air force gradually to take over the army, just as he believed the air arm had gained control of the navy, and that both services should share the major postwar mission of strategic bombing. He stressed that any immediate war would have to be fought with the inventory of World War II weapons. Since military direction in another war would necessarily be similar to that of World War II, Sherman maintained that major changes in the War Department or the Navy Department should await the growth in stocks and deployment of atomic bombs.[9] These ideas found few adherents.

In November 1945 Secretary of the Navy James V. Forrestal, trying to arrange a compromise solution to the question of unification, ordered Sherman to meet with presidential adviser Clark M. Clifford and Major General Lauris Norstad of the army air force. During that winter, the three negotiated an agreement on unification that eventually formed the basis of the National Security Act of 1947. Both the agreement and the act provided for an independent air force and unification of the services under a secretary of defense.[10]

Sherman realized that the only effective way for the postwar navy to acquire an atomic capability, and thus equality alongside a new air force, was to demonstrate by example. Other admirals resented his cooperative participation in the unification effort, but he worked in 1946 and 1947 to persuade Congress to pass a bill that was advantageous to the navy. At the same time, he fostered the development of the navy's new AJ-1 Savage bomber, which would carry the atomic bomb from the decks of the three *Midway*-class carriers. Since the unification act was signed in the summer of 1947 and the capability of the AJ-1 was not demonstrated until the spring of 1948—and not deployed with atomic bombs until early 1950, he enjoyed little popularity within the navy during his tour as deputy CNO.[11]

But Sherman was not interested in personal popularity, only in doing his duty with intelligence, integrity, and loyalty, hoping that this was enough to earn more responsible posts. During his two-year tour as Nimitz's deputy, he began work on establishing America's strategic posture in the Atlantic and Europe. In 1946, he drafted the first postwar plan dealing with a war between the United States and the Soviet Union. He assumed that an attack by the large Russian army in Western Europe would meet with almost no opposition and that the Soviets could, at the same time, strike from Bulgaria through Turkey into the Near East to deny Arabian oil to Britain and America. This scenario, which Sherman outlined to President Truman, was in part responsible for the formulation of the Truman Doctrine and the program of aid to Turkey and Greece in early 1947. In March of that year, Sherman forcefully defended this policy in testimony before committees of both the House and the Senate.[12]

His sponsorship of the decision in September 1946 to deploy carriers permanently in the eastern Mediterranean made Sherman the logical choice to command American naval forces in that area. In December 1947 the new chief of naval operations, Admiral Louis E. Denfeld, named him as Commander, U. S. Naval Forces, Mediterranean, and in January he returned to sea after an absence of more than five years following the loss of the *Wasp*. During the next two years the Sixth Task Fleet supported the royalist regime in Athens against the communists in the Greek Civil War, and the presence of American naval forces in the area stiffened Turkish resolve against continuous Soviet pressure.

Sherman conducted an active policy of port visits and overflights by American naval aircraft in Italy to convince the Italians that the United States was prepared to defend the southern flank of Europe.[13]

During this time Sherman wisely remained far away from the "revolt of the admirals" that erupted in 1949 in Washington. After all, he was in part responsible for the unified system, and he knew that political imbroglios would hurt the career of an ambitious officer. Nonetheless, he anguished over this renewal of interservice conflict at home. In October 1949, however, when the dam of frustration over the cancellation of the supercarrier *United States* broke and the admirals poured out their fears before the House Armed Services Committee, even Sherman could not hold back. He flew back to Washington to testify, but Secretary of Defense Louis A. Johnson and Secretary of the Navy Francis P. Matthews persuaded him not to become involved, and he returned to his command to await the outcome of the hearings.[14] At the end of October, Congressman W. Sterling Cole, the ranking Republican on the committee, sent an open telegram to all the navy's admirals asking for their views on Denfeld's testimony criticizing the Truman administration. In answering, Sherman said that he agreed with some parts of the testimony, disagreed with other parts, and was ignorant of some of what had gone on, but he supported Denfeld and other admirals when they called for naval preparedness.[15]

In the meantime, Johnson and Matthews asked Truman to relieve Denfeld, whose first two-year term as chief of naval operations expired in November 1949. As Denfeld's relief, Johnson proposed Sherman, who could compromise and mediate and who had remained aloof from the political struggles over unification. Truman wanted someone he could personally trust, someone he knew: Nimitz. On the evening of 31 October he called Nimitz and asked him to succeed Denfeld, but Nimitz, who was sixty-four years old, refused on the grounds that returning an older officer to active duty in peacetime was an unsound practice. Instead, he suggested that Truman name either Sherman or his superior, Admiral Richard L. Conolly, commander of American naval forces in the Eastern Atlantic and Mediterranean. However, Nimitz pointed out, Conolly was involved in the recent unification disputes; with obvious satisfaction, he recommended Sherman. Truman concurred.[16]

Johnson had already ordered Sherman to return to Washington. On the afternoon of 1 November the latter arrived at the Pentagon, where he was told that he would relieve Denfeld. On 2 November 1949, just three days after his fifty-third birthday, Sherman became the youngest CNO ever appointed and the first who had devoted his entire career to aviation. Sherman was clearly an unpopular choice within the navy. A chief architect of unification, which was seen as the cause of the navy's troubles, Sherman was looked upon with suspicion by aviators, surface line officers, submariners, and marines alike, who were afraid that he would betray the navy's interests to Johnson, who was himself heartily despised. Many noted that Sherman had spent more time in Washington than at sea and that he appeared to be more of a political manipu lator than a sailor. Indeed, neither the senior admirals nor key congressmen or senators had been consulted about this appointment. Moreover, Sherman was supremely self-confident, an intellectual, seemingly unapproachable, and not a good team player—unlike the martyr, Denfeld, who had sacrificed himself for the good of the navy. The moment that Sherman became chief of naval operations this criticism began, and morale in the service, already low, plunged to new depths.[17]

As for Sherman, his appointment took him completely by surprise. He did not want the job, at least not under such chaotic conditions. He confided to Towers that "I have always set my sights high. . . . The developments which preceded my assignment were not to my liking and the assignment at this time was not of my seeking." However ambitious Sherman was before, he had now reached the top and his motives could no longer be questioned. His immediate task, he told Towers, was "to promote stability and harmony among the senior officers" and "to get on with the numerous tasks which confront us."[18] He quickly set about restoring the navy's influence in Congress, in the administration, and in the Joint Chiefs of Staff. Having favored Sherman's appointment, Johnson found it difficult to oppose his policies. Indeed, Conolly marveled that Johnson wanted Sherman as chief of naval operations because he was "not an especially malleable person." Interviewed only days after taking office, Sherman said that he was determined to see the navy maintained as a "vital force" in the defense establishment, but that "when the plays are called, there can be no doubt as to who is the quarterback." He would assert his command prerogatives, be nobody's "man," and play no favorites.[19]

He lost no time in establishing his authority. He tried to block further reprisals by Johnson and Matthews against officers who had participated in the "revolt of the admirals," but he would tolerate no further outbursts. A fiery partisan of the navy, Captain John G. Crommelin, who was deeply involved in the controversy that precipitated Denfeld's ouster, had been suspended by Secretary Matthews. Sherman had that order rescinded, issued Crommelin a reprimand, and returned him to duty. However, Crommelin continued to criticize Johnson and Matthews in public, although Sherman again ordered him to stop. Sherman then got Matthews to put Crommelin on the retired list as a "tombstone" rear admiral on the basis of his service in combat.[20]

At the same time, both Johnson and Matthews were angry at Captain Arleigh A. Burke, who had prepared parts of the navy's testimony during the Vinson committee hearings in 1949, and they refused to endorse Burke's selection for flag rank. Sherman appealed to President Truman to approve the promotion, and thus saved Burke. Since Burke was popular in the navy, Sherman's defense of the young captain made new friends for the CNO. However, Sherman quietly removed Vice Admiral Gerald F. Bogan, who had muddied his record during the unification controversy. He proposed to transfer Bogan to a two-star billet in December 1949; when Bogan learned of this, he voluntarily retired. In his first speech as chief of naval operations, delivered at the Naval Academy on 2 December, Sherman said that he envied younger officers who were "less marked by events of recent years which tend to obscure the broad view of the future." He advised the midshipmen to forget interservice controversies and obey their civilian leaders.[21]

The Senate confirmed Sherman's appointment without dissent on 12 January 1950, but he had already set about restoring morale in the navy and mending fences with congressional allies. For example, he maintained an active correspondence with his friend, Rear Admiral Richard E. Byrd, Jr., the famous polar explorer, and cultivated Byrd's kinsman, Senator Harry F. Byrd of Virginia. In return for the senator's support of naval appropriations, Sherman kept the shipbuilding and repair facilities in Norfolk busy. He also reestablished the longtime association between the navy and Congressman Carl Vinson, who had opposed the navy on several issues during the unification struggle. Shortly after he was confirmed, Sherman vetoed a proposal that officers not wear their uniforms in Washington. "The uniform carries considerable prestige on Capitol Hill," which was, he concluded, "the reason we do better in uniform." He recognized the need to heal the wounds of the unification battle, and one observer wrote that Sherman "intends to do all his fighting against foreign enemies."[22]

An early test of Sherman's authority came late in 1949 when Johnson, in an effort to save money, tried to mothball the last battleship in commission, the oil-guzzling *Missouri,* which was assigned to the Atlantic Fleet and was then undergoing overhaul at Norfolk. The ship symbolized the navy's role in the Pacific war, which ended on her decks. Johnson's way of eliminating the ship from the order of battle was to reduce the operating budget for the Atlantic Fleet, so Sherman simply transferred the *Missouri* from the fleet to training status at the Naval Academy. This small victory did a great deal to restore confidence in Sherman within the navy, especially among surface line officers, many of whom took it as a sign that Sherman sought a balanced fleet rather than one skewed toward carriers.[23]

The ineffectiveness of Secretary of the Navy Matthews, who had earned the nickname "Rowboat," posed a problem for Sherman from the start of his tour. Despite his inability to make decisions or defend his policies, Matthews complained during Sherman's confirmation hearings that he had been excluded from the operational chain of command by the "CNO Bill," which was passed in 1948 and made the chief of naval operations responsible through the Joint Chiefs to the secretary of defense. However, the old General Board, which decided questions about the shipbuilding program, still reported directly to the secretary of the navy and remained an instrument of his office. Sherman wanted to restore to the billet of chief of naval operations some of the power to direct the navy that Admiral King had exercised during World War II. In the autumn of 1950, he sounded out Congressman Vinson on the proposition that the legislation passed in 1948 had outmoded the board by delegating most of its functions to the CNO and his various deputies. Moreover, he claimed that the General Board wasted the time and talent of half a dozen flag officers. In November, Vinson and Congressman Cole agreed to Sherman's plan to replace the General Board with a Ships Characteristics Board in the office of the chief of naval operations. The General Board passed out of existence in March 1951.[24]

Sherman wanted to maintain some control by the CNO over the operational use of the marine corps and to be the sole spokesman for the Navy Department on the Joint Chiefs of Staff. After the war, many marines believed that the fact that the commandant of the marine corps did not have a seat among the Joint Chiefs of Staff hurt the ability of the corps to defend its budgets and amphibious mission. They also thought that the interests of the corps had been indifferently defended by Admirals Nimitz and Denfeld. Thus, by 1950, there was a strong movement among marine corps leaders and their allies in Congress to include the commandant among the Joint Chiefs. Sherman stoutly opposed this effort. When, in August 1950, Truman alluded to the corps as the navy's "police force," Sherman drafted for the president's signature a letter of apology to the commandant, General Clifton B. Cates, and used the opportunity to suggest that the corps' bid for representation on the Joint Chiefs was the result of "propaganda inspired by individuals who may not have in mind the best interests of our Naval Establishment as a whole." In the spring of 1951, a bill to give the commandant full membership on the Joint Chiefs of Staff was nevertheless introduced. Sherman testified before Vinson's committee against it. However, he conceded that the commandant might sit more regularly with the chiefs than he had in the past. In the event, Sherman retained operational command over his landing forces.[25]

The brand of leadership Sherman exercized as CNO was strictly personal. He exercised command by himself and had no need for a strong alter ego. Thus, he orchestrated the navy through his deputies. He personally inspected all the major commands, asked probing questions on the spot, and expected discussions to be followed up by arguments in writing from the discussants. And if things went awry, he would shrug it off with the remark to his aides, "Tomorrow is another day," and try a different approach. Sherman worked extraordinarily long hours every day to see that his plans worked out, and he kept his fears and hopes to himself until each task had been accomplished. In assigning admirals to fleet or shore billets, he tried to replace the aging commanders of World War II with younger blood, and he generally succeeded.[26]

The abrupt cancellation of the supercarrier *United States* in 1949 left the navy's shipbuilding policy in a shambles, and Sherman had to establish new priorities and seek funds to meet the most important of them. This meant challenging the retrenchment policies of President Truman and Secretary of Defense Johnson. However, five weeks before Sherman was appointed, the seeds of America's postwar military revival were sown when Truman, on 23 September 1949, ordered a reevaluation of the nation's defense posture because Russia had detonated its first atomic bomb. The resulting study, known as National Security Council Memorandum 68, not completed until mid-1950, called for a fourfold increase in defense spending. In the meantime, Sherman laid plans to end cutbacks in the fleet and to expand the naval forces of the future; his objective was to "modernize and revitalize the concept of sea power in the atomic age."[27]

He moved quickly to arrest mothballing, as in the case of the *Missouri*, by assuring Secretary Johnson that ships and aircraft marked for elimination could be retained by internally shifting appropriations. In November 1949 he asked that the antiaircraft cruiser *Juneau* be retained in the fleet in addition to the twelve other cruisers. Two months later he suggested that Johnson shuffle the marines' ground forces to increase the ratio of combat to service elements in the two active divisions. In February 1950 he persuaded the Joint Chiefs of Staff to request the retention in commission of a seventh aircraft carrier which some wanted to cut. And, between March and May, he urged the chiefs to keep sixteen rather than twelve marine combat air squadrons. On all of these points, Johnson and the Joint Chiefs supported him.[28]

Still, these were relatively limited measures, and in February 1950 Sherman went to the House Appropriations and Armed Services Committees for supplemental appropriations to prevent further reduction of the fleet and to begin expanding it. For example, he warned that if proposed reductions of patrol squadrons from 30 to 20 and of destroyers from 170 to 140 were implemented, the fleet would not be able to fulfill its antisubmarine warfare mission. He also looked to the future by asking Congress to approve the development of new ships on which research was well along. One such ship was a nuclear-powered submarine being designed by a naval group under the leadership of Captain Hyman G. Rickover. Sherman also hoped to convert a heavy cruiser into a guided-missile ship and to modernize six aircraft carriers. In the spring of 1950 he asked the Vinson committee for a $500-million increase in the navy's budget, but he settled for $350 million which the committee approved in May. Sherman decided to use this amount for modernizing ships, since modernization—more quickly than new construction—would reinforce NATO's posture in the Atlantic. However, he put part of the appropriation into development of the first nuclear-powered submarine, the *Nautilus*. Furthermore, on 25 April 1950, at Sherman's request, Congress authorized the construction of a supercarrier of the type canceled only a year before by the secretary of defense. It was an extraordinary achievement after only six months in office.[29]

The outbreak of the Korean War provided a catalyst for naval expansion not only to fight in the far Pacific but also to defend American maritime interests in the Western Hemisphere, the Atlantic, and the Mediterranean. In late June 1950 Sherman and his deputies went to work on a comprehensive and long-range plan to greatly expand the fleet. He received encouragement in September when Truman dismissed Louis Johnson and named General of the Army George C. Marshall as secretary of defense. Sherman's goal was a truly balanced fleet: antisubmarine vessels to counter the growing Soviet submarine squadrons in the Atlantic; attack carriers and escorting missile ships to command open sea lanes and project seaborne air power inland; and conventional weapons, such as those used in World War II, to fight the war in Korea. This program began to bear fruit in July 1950 when the Joint Chiefs approved Sherman's plan to increase the navy's manpower and keep the carrier *Leyte* in commission. It culminated in a congressional resolution and presidential authorization in July 1951 for a major shipbuilding and modernization program.[30]

The fast carrier remained the capital ship for all the navy's missions, and Sherman, an aviator, lost no time in restoring it to the preeminence it lost when the *United States* was canceled. Sherman's supercarrier was to be the *Forrestal,* a new class of 56,000-ton ships whose design was much superior to that of the *United States.* He also ordered Rickover's group to begin studying a design for a nuclear-powered carrier. He obtained authorization to increase the fleet from eight large carriers to twelve, plus another fifteen light and escort carriers. Naval and marine air squadrons and subordinate ship types were increased proportionately. Overall, Sherman believed that "the types of ships authorized for construction and conversion" during the first seven months of 1951 would prove "to be of far more importance in the future than any of the programs authorized by Congress in this field since 1938."[31]

The navy's shipbuilding program was part of a grand strategic blueprint developed by the Joint Chiefs of Staff, which Sherman dominated while he was chief of naval operations. After September 1950, the key figure in the Defense Department was General Marshall, on whom Truman leaned heavily. The second was General of the Army Omar N. Bradley, the chairman of the Joint Chiefs of Staff, who was also friendly with Truman and through whom all the recommendations of the chiefs had to be funneled. This was a procedure that Sherman believed held "obvious disadvantages to all concerned."[32] Nonetheless, Sherman's ability to think logically, to formulate practical solutions to complex problems, and dispassionately to explain his conclusions impressed Secretaries Johnson and Marshall and President Truman, who often bypassed the formal chain of command to seek Sherman's advice. Assistant Secretary of the Navy John F. Floberg noted the "obvious confidence" which the president and the defense secretaries

> manifested in Sherman and the well-known major responsibilities which they vested in him rather than the other members of the joint chiefs. [This caused] even the most skeptical senior Naval officers to realize that Sherman was a gem and that he was accomplishing by his quiet manner and his talent at intelligent persuasion infinitely more than all the bombast, Congressional hearings, and protest which the ablest of them could make.[33]

From the policy of containment of communism, which had been developed by the Truman administration and which Sherman accepted as correct, the chief of naval operations developed a supporting naval strategy. A student of naval history, Sherman adopted the traditional strategic goal of the dominant maritime power: achieving command of the seas and denying their use to the enemy in wartime.[34] This involved extending the strategy of forward deployment of the fleet, increasing naval aid to allied nations, convincing a proud Great Britain to accept its role as a subordinate sea power, neutralizing or winning over fascist Spain, and working with General of the Army Douglas MacArthur to prevent the United States from becoming involved in a hopeless ground war on the mainland of Asia.

Despite his alarm over the "reawakening" of Soviet maritime "ambitions," Sherman told the aged financier and presidential adviser Bernard M. Baruch that he was "inclined to believe that the significance of [the expansion of the Russian Navy] may be as simple as a Soviet intention to create sea-borne trade with China and Southeast Asia—undoubtedly paralleled by the development of naval forces in the same area." Although he realized that American naval "superiority over the Russian fleet lies in our carrier force," which was strengthened in February 1950 when AJ-1 Savage aircraft armed with atomic bombs were deployed with the Atlantic Fleet, Sherman admitted to Baruch that Soviet naval policy "leads me to wish that we might have a stronger Pacific Fleet. However, I still feel that Germany is the more critical spot, even though not so much a naval problem."[35]

Sherman's honesty about the primacy of the European theater where sea power played a subordinate role did not divert his attention from the growing problems in antisubmarine warfare, and he initiated a major program to improve the fleet's ability to deal with Soviet submarines both in the Atlantic and off the Pacific coast. Shortly after he became CNO, he asked Vice Admiral Francis S. Low, who directed anti-U-boat operations during World War II, to survey the entire American antisubmarine warfare effort. Low's report included a series of complex recommendations on deployment, strategy, tactics, and technology which Sherman implemented. For instance, since he had inadequate antisubmarine forces, Sherman used very-long-range flights by patrol planes—some launched from carrier decks—to impress Soviet naval leaders about American antisubmarine capabilities. These flights could be dangerous; in April 1950 , for example, Soviet fighters shot down a PB4Y over the Baltic coast at the cost of its crew of ten.[36]

Sherman believed that the political and economic rehabilitation of Western Europe was a stronger counter to Russian expansionism than an American military buildup, and he kept in especially close touch with Admiral Conolly, whose headquarters were in London, and with Admiral John J. Ballentine, who succeeded Sherman in command of the Sixth Fleet. Indeed, that fleet remained highly visible throughout most of the summer of 1950, and Sherman augmented the carrier task force when he sent the *Midway* into the Mediterranean for those months. A typical mission of these units was a fly-over of Beirut by eighty-four aircraft from both carriers in the task force, undertaken at the request of the Lebanese government to demonstrate its anticommunist stance.

However, the war in Korea forced Sherman to recall the *Leyte* and the marines from the Mediterranean later in the year, leaving the Sixth Fleet considerably weakened.[37]

The primacy of the defense of the West was partly responsible for American military leaders being unprepared for the Korean War. After 1945, Truman left MacArthur in Japan to reconstruct her government and politics on a democratic, pro-American model. MacArthur did an admirable job but, as in World War II, his theater soon became secondary to Europe. The victory of the communists in China and the evacuation of Chiang Kai-shek's forces to Hainan Island, in the Gulf of Tonkin, and Formosa in December 1949, and the alliance concluded two months later between China and the Soviet Union, required American leaders to make some difficult strategic decisions. The apparent success of the Berlin airlift plus the creation of NATO suggested that the Soviets might test American defenses in the Far East.

In February 1950 Sherman and his fellow chiefs flew to Tokyo to confer with MacArthur and Admiral Arthur W. Radford, commander in chief of the Pacific Fleet. For Sherman, the visit had nostalgic overtones; the last time he and MacArthur had been together was in Tokyo Bay for the Japanese surrender ceremonies, and the general greeted Sherman as "an old associate of the Pacific war."[38] For ten days MacArthur, Radford, and the Joint Chiefs discussed Pacific strategy, bases, and training. Although the chiefs had warned in December 1949 that a peace treaty with Japan at that time would be "premature," it seemed inevitable, and they now reached a number of agreements with their Pacific commanders on which bases to keep and which to close.[39] To allow MacArthur more authority in deterring Soviet moves in the Far East, the Joint Chiefs gave him control over fleet units whenever they were in Japanese waters. Previously, such control had been in effect only during emergencies. Sherman calculated that in a major war the Pacific Fleet would be able to defeat the roughly seventy-five Russian submarines in the Western Pacific, but Radford asked him to deploy more boats from the Atlantic to the Pacific. Turning to Korea, the Joint Chiefs of Staff agreed that, "from a military point of view, the U. S. has little strategic interest in maintaining troops and bases" there, but should support South Korea's small army and coast guard against the activities of North Korea. This sentiment was echoed by Secretary of State Dean Acheson, who announced that same month that America's defensive perimeter excluded the Korean peninsula and Formosa.[40]

The question of American involvement in the Chinese Civil War was more complex. In late 1946, Truman had decided to keep American support of the Nationalist government to a minimum. On 5 January 1950, shortly after the establishment of the People's Republic in Peking, he announced that the United States would not get involved in a military confrontation with that regime over Formosa. Sherman and the other chiefs explained this again to MacArthur and Radford; it was a policy with which none of them except Bradley fully agreed. However, the Joint Chiefs estimated that the communists could not mount an attack on Formosa before June and, because of the typhoon season and the lack of training of their amphibious forces, they would probably not strike before September. By then, Sherman guessed, the Nationalists, badly demoralized by their defeat on the mainland and short of spare parts, would not be able to defend their island.[41]

This assessment did not change after the Joint Chiefs returned from Tokyo to Washington. Indeed, in the spring of 1950, Sherman received a series of letters from Admiral Charles M. Cooke, Jr., who retired in 1948 after commanding the Seventh Fleet, and went out to Formosa in early 1950 as a technical adviser to the Nationalist government. Cooke sent Sherman reports of Russian military assistance to the mainland government, warned of the imminence of an attack across the strait, and urged American military aid for Chiang's forces. On 1 May, Sherman issued a warning to his fellow service chiefs to prepare for alternative strategies should Japan, Formosa, or the Philippines fall to the communists. The situation deteriorated during May, when the Nationalists, fearing Russian and Chinese air attacks, evacuated Hainan. In June the chiefs persuaded Acheson to support a proposal for military aid to the Nationalist government, a proposal which, near the end of the month, reached Truman's desk. Nonetheless, the primary focus remained on Europe during the spring of 1950.[42]

On 25 June the North Korean army crossed the 38th parallel and attacked South Korea. Despite many warnings, both the State Department and the Defense Department were taken by surprise. Sherman ordered Radford to make the Seventh Fleet ready to move north from the Philippines. In the evening, he attended a meeting between Truman and his key foreign policy and military advisers, during which the president closely questioned the Joint Chiefs of Staff. All agreed that the aggression had to be stopped. Sherman and General Hoyt S. Vandenberg, chief of staff of the air force, wanted to avoid committing American ground forces to the Asian mainland and argued that American naval and air forces alone should be used to support the South Korean army. General J. Lawton Collins, chief of staff of the army, saw that ground troops might have to rescue the weak South Korean divisions. Sherman recommended that the Seventh Fleet be ordered to deploy to waters off Korea and that it be reinforced by ships from the First Fleet in California. Truman approved this plan and authorized Sherman to order naval and air operations south of the 38th parallel.

The next day, during another conference, Truman vested overall command of American forces in Korea in MacArthur, sanctioned naval and air operations against North Korea, and ordered Sherman to send units of the Seventh Fleet into the Formosa Strait to prevent the Communist Chinese from attacking the Nationalists and thus enlarging the war. At the same time, Truman and the Joint Chiefs agreed to increase military aid to the French, who were fighting the communist Vietminh in Indochina, and to the Philippines, although these were proposals which the chiefs had earlier opposed.[43]

Meanwhile, the South Korean army broke and fled southward toward the port of Pusan. Sherman thought that the application of American sea power could arrest the debacle. Whereas the State Department opposed American participation in the defense of South Korea unless "the Russians should openly intervene," Sherman sought specific authority for naval air forces to attack targets in North Korea.[44] On 29 June, Truman agreed, and the strikes, launched from the carrier *Valley Forge,* began on 3 July. On the 29th the president decided to send "limited Army forces" to defend the Seoul government. The following day, Sherman persuaded him to declare a naval blockade of North Korea, but the admiral continued to point out the hazards of fighting Orientals on the Asiatic mainland.[45] Sherman's initial idea of exploiting the tremendous advantages of American sea power was vindicated as it became clear that it would take weeks to send a large number of American troops to the peninsula. But he was dissatisfied with the pace of the first attacks, and on 9 July he dispatched Rear Admiral Matthias B. Gardner to the Pacific to tell Radford to make "more energetic use of [his] naval forces."[46] MacArthur, however, had nothing but praise for his naval forces during the first weeks of fighting in Korea.

The command of the sea that Sherman sought and achieved in the waters off Korea included several political considerations. To implement a decision reached by the National Security Council in March 1949 to promote trade rifts between Russia and Red China, he urged in August 1950 an American embargo against Soviet allies "and that the U. S. [and its allies] adopt . . . stricter maritime trade controls and measures which would preclude shipment of strategic items in Western flag vessels to the Soviet bloc." To set an example, he had two American-flag merchant ships prevented from loading copper, tin, and armor plate bound for Communist China on the principle of the broken voyage. Sherman's sensitivity to the canons of international law led him to protest North Korea's use of floating mines but he allowed all non-North Korean warships, including some Soviet units, to enter blockaded North Korean ports.[47]

In the first months of the war, all eyes were focused on MacArthur, whom Sherman stoutly supported. On 10 August Sherman told Truman, Johnson, and the other chiefs that he was "confident that General MacArthur would make good use of the forces" he was being given. Although Sherman warned against "fighting Asiatics on the Asiatic mainland," he opposed MacArthur's plan to allow Nationalist naval and air forces to attack targets on the Chinese coast.[48] In Korea, MacArthur stabilized a perimeter around Pusan, reinforced it with U. S. Army and Marine Corps units, and planned to break out during the winter or spring. In mid-July, however, the general came up with a brainstorm to exploit his amphibious, naval, and air superiority: an assault on Inchon, gateway to Seoul on the western side of the peninsula, to outflank the communist forces surrounding Pusan. And he proposed to attack not in the winter or spring, but two months hence—in September.[49]

After receiving MacArthur's proposal on 23 July and studying it, Sherman and Collins decided to fly to Tokyo to discuss it with him. In particular, Sherman had serious doubts about the operation because Inchon had terrible tides which would affect the landing. MacArthur was convinced that the purpose of the visit was to dissuade him from the enterprise; he knew that they preferred a landing at Kunsan, which was closer to Pusan and had safer beaches.

Sherman and Collins arrived in Tokyo on 21 August and promptly conferred with MacArthur, who defended his Inchon plan, asked for more troops, and insisted that he was ready to go on the offensive. Sherman toured the front lines in Korea and discussed the plan with all the commanders who would be involved in the operation. On 23 August there was a general meeting at MacArthur's headquarters. Rear Admiral James H. Doyle, who was to command the amphibious forces, presented the navy's objections to the Inchon plan, most of which concerned the erratic tides. As Sherman summarized, "If every possible geographic and naval handicap [to a successful amphibious operation] were listed, Inchon has 'em all."[50] Then he and Collins presented the alternative case for a landing at Kunsan. Heavy discussion ensued and ended with MacArthur giving a passionate and eloquent address, forty-five minutes long, in which he stressed the advantage of the element of surprise and, thus, light opposition, and placed his faith in the navy to succeed in the operation, as it had always done in the past. Whereupon, according to MacArthur, Sherman rose and said, "Thank you. A great voice in a great cause."[51]

Since MacArthur had placed the burden of responsibility for the Inchon operation squarely on the navy, and because Sherman's opinion would probably be decisive among his fellow service chiefs, the admiral had to explore every angle and to play devil's advocate. His admiration for MacArthur could not be allowed to rule his professional judgment, which MacArthur appreciated when he recalled, "I sensed that Admiral Sherman's objections to the Inchon movement were largely animated by a sense of duty which necessitated the presentation in their most naked form of all professional difficulties and objections which could be foreseen."[52] Most of the others had been won over by MacArthur's arguments, but Sherman had to know more, and he remained in the room when the meeting ended. In his diary, he summarized the conversation that followed:

> Had a long talk with MacArthur alone. He praised the Navy and spoke in glowing terms of its future. Said the entire Pacific should eventually be commanded by a naval officer. He agreed to my proposal that in the event of general hostilities, Radford should move forward to wherever MacArthur is and take operational command of entire Pacific Fleet. Criticised Air Force and blamed them for poor support of troops. Told me Marines were superb, but had a tendency to gripe. I told him again that Inchon was a dangerous enterprise if any resistance developed. He agreed it could be done only if there were none.[53]

Before leaving Tokyo the next day, but after conferring again with the key commanders, Sherman approved the Inchon operation. After a final meeting with MacArthur, he remarked to Admiral C. Turner Joy, "I wish I had that man's confidence."[54] When he returned to Washington, Sherman noted in a letter to Truman "my principal impression . . . of confidence and offensive spirit wherever I went." He wrote to MacArthur that he "restrained my own optimism only because I feel that in Washington it is dangerous to be too optimistic. There are too many tendencies to cut down on readiness and to interpret optimism as a definite commitment for early victory." MacArthur more than anyone else appreciated the fact that Sherman became the guiding force in the decision, made on 28 August, by the Joint Chiefs of Staff to approve the Inchon operation.[55]

On 15 September the brilliantly executed assault against Inchon was made; the North Korean army reeled before the master stroke and retreated across the 38th parallel. MacArthur hastily organized another amphibious force to land at Wonsan, on the east coast of North Korea, but the detection of magnetic mines held up the operation until 10 October. This delay particularly disappointed Sherman. "They caught us with our pants down," he complained. "We've been plenty submarine-conscious and air-conscious. Now we're going to start getting more mine-conscious—beginning last week."[56]

More important, however, was the concern of the Truman administration that Russia or China, or both, might intervene to save North Korea. Truman did not agree with MacArthur over the use of Nationalist Chinese forces, and in mid-October he met with the general at Wake Island to discuss this and other issues. Flushed with his victory at Inchon, MacArthur assured Truman that the Chinese communists would not intervene. Indeed, neither the president nor the Joint Chiefs of Staff wanted to provoke a general war with either Russia or China, a fact which MacArthur discounted. One month later Chinese troops crossed the Yalu River. MacArthur had been wrong and unprepared, and his achievement at Inchon was completely neutralized. American strategy was torn asunder, United Nations forces fled south in a general retreat, and by the end of November MacArthur accepted the decision of the Joint Chiefs that he assume a defensive position "across the neck of Korea."[57]

Sherman feared Soviet intervention as well, and he decided to increase the number of fast carriers in the Seventh Fleet from two to four. Shortly thereafter, at the height of the withdrawal to the south of the peninsula, Sherman received a copy of the order from Admiral Joy, commander U. S. Naval Forces, Far East, to evacuate army and marine corps units of the Tenth Corps by sea from North Korea.[58] Sherman believed that American economic pressure could play a role in ending the crisis in Korea. He declared that "in view of the intervention of Chinese Communist forces in Korea, Communist China has for all intents and purposes become an enemy of the U. S. and that U. S. trade policy should be revised without delay to reflect this fact." Specifically, he urged an embargo on all trade between the United States and China which, in his opinion, would demonstrate America's resolve to her allies.

On 3 December 1950 the Joint Chiefs met with the principal civilian leaders in the Defense Department and the State Department. Sherman asserted that "the only issue was peace or war, that we had lost the campaign, but not a war, that we were not a defeated nation, and should tell the Chinese Communists to get out of Korea or face war." Sherman was not invited to the White House to discuss his plan for an embargo of Red China—which no doubt bothered him—and the National Security Council rejected it, although a halt to all American exports to China was approved. Two days later Sherman called this "unsatisfactory" and asked for a reexamination of the policy. Finally, on 16 December, Sherman prevailed, and a complete embargo on trade with Communist China was imposed. Not satisfied that the coast guard could enforce this embargo, Sherman persuaded Truman to order the navy to do it.[59]

In Korea, MacArthur tried to prevent a complete rout. On 29 December the Joint Chiefs told him to hold the peninsula if possible but to evacuate American forces if necessary. He replied the next day, calling for the use of Nationalist Chinese troops in Korea, air and naval attacks against Chinese war industries, more American troops for his command, a blockade of mainland China, and a political decision "to maintain the fight" or "to effect a strategic displacement." On 9 January the Joint Chiefs replied that there was no justification for reinforcements to Korea; that no blockade of China was yet necessary; that the use of Nationalist Chinese forces would not be decisive; and that, "should it become evident, *in your judgment* that evacuation is essential to avoid severe losses of men and material you will at that time withdraw from Korea to Japan." The chiefs had both reasserted their command authority over MacArthur and put the onus of possible retreat upon the man who was burned with the memory of Bataan and Corregidor.[60]

Incredulous at such an option, MacArthur asked for clarification; his query had its intended effect, which was to shift the responsibility back to Washington. Sherman considered this request, received on 10 January, to be a breach of command authority. The president refused to consider evacuation and his foreign-policy advisers inclined more and more toward "negotiation" and a "cease fire." On 11 January, the visiting British military chiefs met with their American counterparts; Sherman recorded that all "indulged in some very plain speaking," with the British "urging us to stay" in Korea and adding their lack of confidence in MacArthur. And, during the following week, MacArthur lost his credibility with the Joint Chiefs after Collins and Vandenberg visited Korea and discovered that American forces had already stopped the Chinese offensive.[61]

Since evacuation did not seem to be necessary, Sherman renewed his earlier call for a naval blockade of China which he had persuaded the Joint Chiefs to endorse on 9 January. To support this proposal, he submitted to the chiefs a study on a naval blockade that included the "belligerent right" of a maritime nation at war. However, after a few weeks Sherman modified his advocacy of a blockade because he reached the conclusion that its effect would be largely psychological, encouraging to friendly Asian nations, but weak unless the British cooperated. He also saw that Port Arthur and Dairen could not be blockaded without "severely straining relations with Russia and possibly bringing on hostilities." Worse, the Soviets would probably respect a naval blockade imposed by the United Nations, but not one imposed unilaterally by the United States. Finally, a naval blockade would not interrupt overland Sino-Russian trade. Believing that a blockade, "to be completely successful, should cut off all access to vital strategic materials or equipment," Sherman concluded that it was not the answer, at least until it was sanctioned by the United Nations, which was an unlikely prospect. However, he continued to advocate a stronger American policy to control trade between Western Europe and Red China, but he met with no success.[62]

Meanwhile, the battle in Korea had shifted against the communist forces, and in March the Allies reached the 38th parallel. On 19 March, Marshall and Secretary of State Dean Acheson decided that a cease-fire was the most acceptable objective of American policy. Sherman disliked this approach: "I went out for [the] arrangement to stop [the] conflict, stop aggression and solve [the] Korean problem with [a] 'cease-fire' as only an incident to [the] solution—not an end in itself because the Chinese want to stop fighting and stay while we want to leave." The Joint Chiefs debated the issue again on 28 March with representatives from the State Department. When Collins "argued for an armistice to get [American] troops out of Korea," Sherman recorded that "I said that it would go down in history as a military defeat and that [the] Chinese had pushed us south of the 38th parallel and kept us there." When some maintained that regaining the line of 25 June 1950, the day the war began, "was a victory," Sherman held that the Americans needed to retake the line of 21 November, when U. S. ground forces reached the Yalu River, the farthest point of advance. Thus, Sherman advocated containment from a position of real strength—a compromise between MacArthur, who wanted to bomb across the Yalu, and the proponents of the status quo, who were willing to accept an armistice.[63]

But any acceptable criticism of Truman's search for a peace settlement was made nearly impossible when, in early April 1951, MacArthur committed an act of outright insubordination by faulting the president's policy in Korea in a letter to Republican Congressman Joseph W. Martin. At Bradley's instigation, the Joint Chiefs of Staff met in special session on 7 April to consider what to do about MacArthur's letter. Although it was during this day that Sherman first noted a distinct possibility that MacArthur might be relieved, he counseled Bradley "to oppose acting on [the grounds of] a letter to a Congressman" and, in the meeting, the general and Secretary Marshall opposed firing the commander in the Far East.[64]

Finally, on the afternoon of 8 April, a Sunday, the chiefs met in Bradley's office and for two hours discussed the problem. Then they moved into Marshall's office, where the secretary of defense "asked each of us for our views concerning [the] relief of General MacArthur." Sherman later made notes of his answer to Marshall's question about the fate of a man whom the admiral had so long admired, an answer which in all probability strongly influenced Bradley, Collins, and Vandenberg.

> I based my reply on the future and said that if we are to be successful in the attempt to limit the conflict in Korea and avoid World War III, we must have a Commander in whom we can confide and on whom we can rely, and that General MacArthur has not been sufficiently responsive to the directives and policy given him. I added that from a military point of view, he should be replaced and that the political aspects were above my level.[65]

Sherman and his colleagues agreed that, if the Chinese or the Russians or both launched a major air strike, MacArthur probably would take it upon himself to hit not only Manchuria but China's Shantung Peninsula in retaliation. They therefore "agreed not to confide in General MacArthur our clearance to retaliate against [a] major air attack." Lastly, the chiefs worried that MacArthur's actions gave the American public the impression that the civilians in Washington were losing control of the war. The next day Marshall conveyed these views to Truman along with his reluctant agreement, and on 10 April the president ordered General Matthew B. Ridgway to relieve MacArthur. Sherman learned about it on the radio at 7:00 a.m. the following day.[66]

The public uproar generated by MacArthur's relief inevitably brought questions to Sherman because, as chief of naval operations, he had made so large an impact on the general's actions. On 18 April, the day after MacArthur returned to the United States, Sherman spoke out against the old warrior's critics: "I refuse to sanction criticism of General MacArthur by those who have never known him. If persons who really know him offer criticism it can be condoned as a matter of personal opinion. He is too much of a man to be handled by those who know little or nothing about his mentality."[67]

Congress convened hearings to review Truman's decision to fire MacArthur, to hear the general and the Joint Chiefs of Staff, and to provide a forum for the critics of the administration's foreign policy. These critics were surprised when the Joint Chiefs opposed MacArthur's desire to expand the war and when the lack of American troops to fight in mainland China or against Russia in the Far East was explained. Sherman testified before three committees of the House—Armed Services, International Affairs, and Appropriations—and withstood Republican attacks on his positions. He opposed a House resolution for an American declaration of war against North Korea and China on the grounds that it was not in the nation's interest to fight such a war alone. Last of the service chiefs to testify at the Senate hearings on MacArthur's relief on 30 and 31 May, Sherman exuded optimism which provided a marked contrast to the views of his military associates. He defended the change in command in Korea, but he also reaffirmed his faith that the American forces could win the war. He predicted that in a general war the United States would defeat the Soviet Union. To hasten victory in Korea, he called for the imposition of a naval blockade on China.[68] His testimony was received favorably by the press and radio, especially in the Midwest, where even the antiadministration, antinavy *Chicago Tribune* joined in the praise. The *Los Angeles Times* hailed his position as "a welcome change from the gloomy statements given by Defense Secretary Marshall and by other members of the Joint Chiefs of Staff." It was, the editors claimed, "the kind of talk Americans expect to hear from their military leaders—and it is more in accord with the facts than the worried and hesitant testimony given the committees by Sherman's colleagues."[69]

Sherman, in fact, now tried to develop a grand strategy for a general war in Asia. In such a war, he wanted to isolate the battlefield in Korea by the use of American sea and air power against Soviet or Chinese forces. On 1 June, therefore, the chiefs directed Radford to plan for a blockade of China in case of Chinese aggression outside Korea and to prepare, in that event, to evacuate American forces from Korea. Not ignoring MacArthur's proposals altogether, the Joint Chiefs directed Ridgway to develop plans for military action against selected targets outside Korea and for the use of Nationalist Chinese units. Sherman publicly warned that the outcome in Korea might determine the fate of the United Nations and that the United States might "possibly" have to fight a "series of relatively small wars—possibly a general war" to defend the Free World.[70]

In Korea, Ridgway initiated a number of small, successful operations to stabilize the front, and on 23 June the Soviet delegate at the United Nations proposed a cease-fire along the 38th parallel. The next day Sherman left Washington for Tokyo. While he was in the Far East, the North Koreans and Chinese accepted a proposal issued by Ridgway for armistice talks. Sherman discussed this with Truman on 5 July, five days before Admiral Joy opened the negotiations at Panmunjom. The seesaw war in Korea had come to a strategic end, although it dragged on with little movement for another two years. During the war, Sherman failed to get tight economic sanctions imposed on the Soviet bloc or a naval blockade imposed on China, and the cease-fire along the 38th parallel did not conform with his proposal for a treaty line near the Yalu. Nonetheless, he was a major force in giving direction and vigor to American war policy, and his strategy of forward deployment probably helped to convince the communists that their best course was to negotiate an end to the war.

While the Korean War focused public attention on Asia, Europe remained the primary front in the cold war, and Sherman kept in close touch with his principal commanders across the Atlantic. He was a relentless advocate of a strategy of forward deployment of American forces in Europe also and told a congressional committee that there were, in the struggle with the Soviet Union, only two choices: "to accept the necessity for deploying forces overseas—troops, ships and aircraft—and to fight overseas if necessary," or "to withdraw, abandon our allies, and later to fight alone. I believe that the first course offers the greatest prospect for survival." By favoring the basing of U. S. Army divisions in Europe, Sherman challenged such Republican conservatives as Senator Robert A. Taft and former President Herbert Hoover, who wanted to limit American commitments to NATO to sea and air power alone.[71]

One major issue with which Sherman had to deal as chief of naval operations concerned the new commands for the NATO military organization. Negotiations over these issues began in 1949, and most were completed during the autumn of the following year when the NATO powers agreed to accept General of the Army Dwight D. Eisenhower as the first supreme commander of their forces in Europe. The contest over the naval commands was between the United States and Great Britain. The latter had traditionally dominated the waters of Europe but was in a state of rapid postwar decline as a great power. In October 1950 Sherman persuaded the twelve NATO defense ministers to give the supreme allied command of the North Atlantic region to Admiral William M. Fechteler, who was also commander in chief of the Atlantic Fleet. He also persuaded Bradley to make this naval command separate from Eisenhower's command, which was quite a feat of persuasion since Bradley and Eisenhower were close friends and Bradley wanted his West Point classmate to control all NATO forces.[72]

But Sherman wanted more. Admiral Robert B. Carney, commander of U. S. naval forces in the eastern Atlantic and Mediterranean, should be appointed, in addition, commander in chief of Allied forces in the Mediterranean. The British first sea lord, Admiral of the Fleet Lord Fraser, whom Sherman knew during World War II, was especially unhappy that his government agreed to this arrangement. When Eisenhower assumed his post in February 1951, the other commands were made public, causing a storm of protest in Britain, led by Winston Churchill, the opposition leader, against Clement Attlee's cabinet. Sherman decided that personal diplomacy was in order, and he flew to Europe where he met with Eisenhower and Carney in Paris on 3 March. Eisenhower wanted to placate the British by giving them greater authority in the Mediterranean, but Sherman opposed any changes because they could not be justified by the small naval force that the Admiralty maintained there. Moreover, Sherman pointed out that even the British chiefs of staff would not want to rehash the negotiations that had led to the arrangements and that the label of "supremo" for Carney, which the British had inspired, was unfortunate. "Naval officers have managed to get their business done without such titles as 'supreme commander,' " he complained. However, Sherman finally suggested a face-saving compromise under which Carney would become commander in chief of a "Southern Region" based in Italy and be responsible to Eisenhower, while a British admiral would become Allied commander in chief in the Mediterranean and be responsible to Carney. Eisenhower finally agreed.[73]

Two days later, Sherman met in London with the British chiefs of staff—but Fraser was absent—and set forth his proposal. He found that they were so upset about both the Atlantic and Mediterranean commands that nothing could be done. Sherman just let them talk until, in Carney's words, they came to feel "that Sherman was in pretty general agreement with their views," which he was not. Indeed, the British were disconcerted by Sherman's remark "that we should consider what would remain to the British Supremo if he did not have the U. S. Naval striking force." When he returned home, Sherman agonized about the delays and complained that the whole matter was "moving very slowly." However, he would not retreat: "We have stuck to our guns in that we will not recede from our position concerning the Mediterranean." After constant pressure, the British government agreed to Sherman's proposal, at least to the extent that Carney be allowed to move from London to Naples and begin to organize NATO's southern flank. When Carney broke his flag on 21 June 1951, he had command over Italy, French and American air bases in North Africa, the Sixth Fleet, and all Allied forces assigned to him by Eisenhower. Left unresolved were the NATO commands for the North Atlantic region, the remainder of the Mediterranean, and the Middle East.[74]

Despite the frostiness between Sherman and Fraser, they kept in touch, and Sherman believed he had to strike a bargain with the British admiral before the problem could be solved. Thus, he welcomed "peace" feelers extended by Fraser in early July, especially after he learned that the British believed that Sherman had "slandered the Royal Navy" during the MacArthur hearings by his candid remarks about Britain's reduced naval strength. This charge irked Sherman, who told Carney: "No one has gone to greater lengths than I have for the last ten years in fostering Anglo-American friendship and cooperation. If I have been reserved in my recent attitude it has been because of my determination to uphold the dignity of the United States Naval Service and withdraw it as far as possible from a controversy which has an international political basis and which is inevitably damaging to both navies." Sherman also told Carney that he intended to "visit Europe some time this month but shall not visit England unless specifically asked by Fraser." Carney passed this word to Fraser and, shortly thereafter, Sherman received an invitation to come to London.[75]

In addition to the issue of the NATO commands, the question of American bases in Spain was on the agenda for Sherman's trip in July 1951. In early May Secretary Marshall recommended to the State Department that the United States "conduct initial military discussions of an exploratory nature with the Spanish military authorities." The idea of an American military relationship with fascist Spain offended many European governments, and in early July the British and French urged Washington to abandon such a policy on moral grounds. The London government "is deadly serious on this," warned the American ambassador to the United Kingdom, "It really means business and does not mean to recede to [a] compromise view." Despite the fact that the American ambassador in Madrid, Stanton Griffis, invited Sherman to visit Spain, Secretary of State Acheson strenuously opposed any military conversations with the government of Francisco Franco, a position that was supported by all the Joint Chiefs except Sherman. Queried during the MacArthur hearings in late May about including Spain in NATO, Sherman stated that he had "never recommended the inclusion of Spain, but that again is a matter of timing." Normal diplomatic relations between Spain and the NATO signatories would have to come first, but Sherman left no doubt that NATO's southern flank would be vulnerable without friendly Spanish and American naval and air bases there—alongside the British base at Gibraltar. Consequently, Truman agreed to Marshall's proposal and authorized Sherman to begin discussions with the Spanish during his trip to Europe. On 11 July Sherman met with the president and explained his proposals for setting up American bases in Spain.[76]

Considering Sherman's heavy schedule, continuous travel, and the onerous demands on his time, one can only marvel that his health stood up as well as it did. Although he had chronic low blood pressure, when he underwent his annual physical examination in October 1950 he even retained his clearance to fly. However, he began to suffer from insomnia, and his periods of intense fatigue increased. He recognized that he had social obligations as chief of naval operations and, in order to please everyone, never refused an invitation. In short, he never rested. Moreover, like all the president's key advisers, Sherman was not without his critics, particularly those who opposed "the questionable way in which the Truman administration has been utilizing honored military figures to achieve the political aims of an uncertain foreign policy." His appointment as a political emissary to Spain brought the charge that he had become "an instrument of the Truman-Acheson-Marshall coterie that has dictated our diplomatic and defense strategy" to the wrong ends.[77]

Deciding to combine the business of the trip with some pleasure, Sherman took along his wife, Dolores; they left Washington on 15 July and arrived in Madrid the next day. He talked to Franco and Ambassador Griffis that afternoon and began to lay the groundwork for establishing American bases in Spain. Franco had no faith that the neighboring French would ever fight the Russians, and after the talks Sherman concluded that "we will be asked for considerable military and economic aid." Nonetheless, Franco agreed in principle to Sherman's proposal for bases, and both sides planned to go ahead with detailed staff discussions. Sherman emerged from the lengthy meeting looking pale and tired. However, he attended a reception in the evening, held more talks with the Spanish the next day, went to two more receptions that night, and saw Franco again the following day before leaving for Paris.[78]

Arriving in the French capital on the nineteenth, he described the Spanish negotiations to Eisenhower, secured some valuable support for the basing plan from the French naval staff, and the following morning flew off to London. Bracketed between a luncheon and a dinner party, Sherman had his long-awaited conversation with Fraser, who continued to object to the NATO command arrangements but extended the wholehearted support of the British chiefs of staff for the American negotiations for Spanish bases. After midnight, Sherman flew on to Naples for another round of conferences with Carney and local officials.

Tired from his week-long ordeal, he took his wife to an opera one evening but was so exhausted that he slept in the car on the way back to their hotel. At about 10:40 the following morning, 22 July, in his hotel room he suffered a mild heart attack, which several doctors thought they had eased after two hours. His wife and Carney were with him when he passed into unconsciousness and died at 1:05 p.m., the victim of two massive heart attacks. That day his remains were piped over the side of Carney's flagship *Mt. Olympus,* and five days later his casket was buried at Arlington National Cemetery. He was only fifty-four years old.[79]

Reactions to Sherman's death were shock and a sense of loss. "He was able, he was a patriotic American, he was a fine gentleman," President Truman said, "The country's loss is great and so is mine." Marshall called Sherman "an outstanding leader, a great personality," and Bradley revered him as "a great statesman of outstanding ability." "For two years," wrote *The Detroit News,* "Sherman ran the Navy with an iron hand. The control was perhaps too tight, for it did not permit the emergence of a second strong man, which is now to be regretted." But the *Portland Oregonian* made the central point about Sherman's tenure as chief of naval operations: "There has been no anti-Sherman faction anywhere in the armed services." Even the British press, which had opposed his plans for the NATO commands, now mourned his death. One broadcaster commented that he "was a war casualty just as much as if he had been killed in battle. He worked himself to death."[80]

Sherman's achievements were extraordinary. He restored central authority in the navy, ended the chaos and depression he inherited from Denfeld, established a postwar shipbuilding program where his predecessors had failed, and brought affirmative and decisive leadership to American defense policy, which would surely have been in disarray without him. In the Pacific, he helped to stabilize the Korean confrontation. In the Mediterranean, he established American authority, and, within days of his departure from Spain, that country's cabinet suffered an internal shakeup partly to accommodate Sherman's proposals. Finally, the basic cold-war battle lines existing at the moment of his death have not changed since. The fact that World War III did not occur in his time and has not occurred to date may well be Forrest Sherman's most enduring monument.

WILLIAM MORROW FECHTELER

16 August 1951–17 August 1953

GERALD KENNEDY

When Admiral Sherman died in July 1951, Admiral William M. Fechteler was serving at Norfolk, Virginia, as commander in chief of the Atlantic Fleet. Fechteler considered his billet to be the high point of his naval service, which had begun in 1912 with his entry into the Naval Academy. Born in San Rafael, California, on 6 March 1896, William was the son of Lieutenant Commander Gustav Fechteler, whose naval career also ended in four-star rank. William's experience at the academy followed the usual pattern of heavy academic emphasis on nautical subjects within an atmosphere of strict discipline, traditional high jinks, and strong camaraderie. An evaluation by his peers upon commissioning revealed personal characteristics that changed little over the coming years. He was popular, "a strong favorite," because "he has always been unselfish, straight-forward, and independent." "He has applied his talents more earnestly to helping others than to fattening his own averages." From his father, William acquired a "thorough knowledge of the Navy" and "a very salty manner." A quiet boy, his speech was "well-charged with seagoing phrases" but he did "not talk for the music of it." Fechteler was bright, and graduated eighteenth of the 177 members of the class of 1916.[1]

Fechteler's first duty was in the battleship *Pennsylvania* where he served throughout the First World War, and it was this experience that whetted his appetite for battleship duty—an affection that characterized his entire naval career. Between the wars, he had a varied series of tours, as an instructor at the academy, in the Asiatic Fleet, and in the Navy Department in Washington. In 1928, he married Goldye Stevens Dobson, the widow of Lieutenant Rodney H. Dobson, who perished when the submarine *S-51* went down in 1925.[2]

When the Second World War erupted, Captain Fechteler was staff operations officer for Commander, Destroyers, Battle Fleet, in the Pacific, whom he later served as chief of staff. In August 1943 he received command of the battleship *Indiana* and participated in several engagements in the Central Pacific before earning a promotion to rear admiral and assignment as the commander of Amphibious Group 8 in the Seventh Fleet. When the war ended, he returned to the Navy Department as assistant chief of the Bureau of Naval Personnel.[3]

In January 1946, Fleet Admiral Nimitz sent Fechteler to sea again with the rank of vice admiral and the command of the battleships and cruisers of the Atlantic Fleet. After a year in that billet, he returned to Washington as deputy chief of naval operations for personnel, and it was from this duty that he was, in January 1950, promoted to full admiral and given command of the Atlantic Fleet.

Hostilities in Korea caused a change in American naval policy from retrenchment to expansion both in the Pacific and Atlantic areas. Not only did the navy have to conduct active operations in Korea, it had also to increase the deterrence strength of NATO's sea forces to prevent the "police action" from escalating into a wider conflict. With his command, Fechteler also had responsibilities as the American representative to NATO's North Atlantic Ocean Regional Planning Group and for the creation of an acceptable command structure for the naval units in the area. Indeed, he was assessing NATO operations when he learned of Sherman's unexpected demise.

The death set off a skirmish for nomination to the vacant office. The principal candidates were Fechteler; Admiral Lynde D. McCormick, vice chief of naval operations; Admiral Arthur W. Radford, Pacific Fleet commander; Admiral Robert B. Carney, commander of Allied Forces in Southern Europe; Vice Admiral Richard L. Conolly, president of the Naval War College; and Vice Admiral Donald B. Duncan, deputy chief of naval operations for operations. After the burial rites for Sherman, these men met with Secretary of the Navy Francis P. Matthews, who, to their surprise, took them immediately to the White House to meet with President Harry S. Truman. The conference lasted about ten minutes, and Fechteler believed that it was designed to give Truman a chance to look over the candidates. "We just sat around like schoolboys for inspection," he recalled, but he could not remember saying one word on the occasion. He claimed that he refused to "lift a finger" to improve his chances, on the grounds that "the job should seek the man rather than vice versa." He made no other contacts in Washington and returned directly to Norfolk.[4]

In fact, Fechteler's chances were quite good. Truman had passed over Conolly in favor of Sherman; Radford wanted to remain at sea while the war continued; McCormick loudly expressed "his desire for a fleet command." A major factor in the choice between Carney and Fechteler apparently was the effect that the departure of either man from NATO would have on that organization's new command structure, in which they were both involved. Moreover, Carney and Radford had been rivals in the recent and unforgotten struggle over unification. The appointment of either might well have rekindled old personal and professional animus. By contrast, Fechteler's steadiness and lack of fiery ambition may have appealed to a president who had often been troubled by his admirals.[5]

In the next few days, Truman forced Matthews to resign and accept the ambassadorship to Ireland. Matthews was replaced by the former undersecretary, Dan A. Kimball, who quickly called Fechteler, told him that he was to be the next CNO, and ordered him to Washington for another meeting with the chief executive. The president told Fechteler that the choice had been difficult but that he had been recommended by Fleet Admirals Leahy and Nimitz and Secretaries Matthews and Kimball. Truman announced his selection on 1 August 1951 and it was promptly confirmed by the Senate.[6]

Fechteler had no public following when he became chief of naval operations on 16 August, but he carried to the office a fine reputation within the navy. Fifty-five years old, he was "bulky and handsome" and "pleasant and easy of manner" and often wore his cap at a jaunty tilt. In the fall of 1951, he faced an unusual set of circumstances. While Sherman's leadership, which Fechteler described as "superlative," had restored the navy's morale and the Korean War had ended Truman's policy of contraction of the fleet, Fechteler still had to deal with sputtering hostilities in Asia and the confrontation between the West and the Soviet Union in Europe. "Unlike his predecessor," one report noted, the new CNO "begins with naval ideas and methods generally accepted. His job is to keep things that way."[7]

He enjoyed one asset that some of his predecessors lacked, however, and that was a good relationship with the secretary of the navy, Kimball. Fechteler considered his civilian superior to be "a fine individual"—a respect that was reciprocated—and the two worked in harmony over the next twenty-four months. Likewise, the admiral's dealings with the new secretary of defense, Robert A. Lovett, a former naval pilot, were always amicable. In addition, Fechteler and Truman got on well together, and the admiral's admiration for the president was enhanced "because you never had any difficulty getting a decision from him"[8]

Throughout his tour as CNO, Fechteler was plagued by the issue of the NATO command structure. Since the surrender of Germany, the British had been uncomfortable with American naval primacy in the Atlantic; and since the introduction of the first units of the Sixth Fleet into the Eastern Mediterranean, this anxiety had intensified. Early in his tour as CNO, Fechteler identified the "resolution of conflicts in command relationships between NATO and U. S. commands" at sea as one of his major missions. This was one of Sherman's objectives during his fatal visit to Europe, but Fechteler was unable to find any report or notes of his predecessor's trip. Thus, in October 1951, Fechteler took his wife and a few aides to Paris, Bonn, Nice, Naples, and London to "get a feel of the situation in NATO circles."[9]

Sherman had offended the British by demanding that American admirals take the NATO commands in both the Atlantic and the Mediterranean. The Admiralty finally agreed that Carney could break his flag as commander in chief of Allied forces in Southern Europe, but they demanded that a British admiral be named as the supreme commander for the Mediterranean, despite the few remaining Royal Navy units in the area. Fechteler's trip in October 1951 failed to resolve these matters and, during the next year, he met again in Europe with the Greek, Italian, and French chiefs of staff. By this time London had proposed another compromise which kept the British "supremo" but allowed Carney to direct all NATO forces in the region.

During Fechteler's second trip to Europe a small furor erupted over an article that appeared in *Le Monde,* a leading French newspaper, when the CNO was in Paris. The author alleged that, in a report to the National Security Council, Fechteler had predicted that a war between the United States and the Soviet Union would break out in 1960, that Western Europe would be overrun by the Red Army, and that the Americans would thus be forced to reenter the Continent from the Mediterranean flank. Various plans incorporating these possibilities had, of course, floated around the navy since the early days of the cold war. Despite the initial uproar, the entire episode faded a few days later when Albert Besnard, the naval affairs editor of the Amsterdam *Algemeen Handelsblad,* recognized the piece in *Le Monde* as a massively doctored version of an article that had appeared in the *U. S. Naval Institute Proceedings* in September 1950.[10]

One of Fechteler's principal concerns as CNO was the welfare of naval personnel, a field in which he had been intimately involved for some time. Not surprisingly, he lobbyed for important legislation to increase pay, provide incentive allowances, and broaden survivors' benefits. On the question of incentives, he explained that, although he had never drawn them in his career, the navy's experience with submarines in the 1920s had demonstrated that the caliber of the crews increased when volunteers were available for the duty. He observed that a submarine, which cost $25 million, could be put out of action by one inept crewman. Fechteler testified passionately on the matter of survivors' benefits. He told congressmen that he "had long been an advocate of legislation to grant personnel . . . the right to share their retirement compensation with their surviving widows and minor children." His pleas fell on deaf ears and the bill was still in committee when Fechteler left office. On these issues, the admiral summed up his attitude during congressional testimony in 1951: "Realization of the importance of the human factor in military operations has caused me to devote considerable energy to the welfare of personnel throughout my career. It might be said that this is the main reason why I am here today." Fechteler's fairness on these questions impressed Congress. Congressman Paul K. Kilday told him that "many times we saw you oppose items in a bill which could have resulted in personal benefit to you, but you opposed them in order to carry out the philosophy . . . that a just and equal pay distribution be made."[11]

Beyond his pay reforms, Fechteler proposed no new naval policies of any consequence. His shipbuilding program emphasized the expansion of a "balanced fleet" centered on the *Forrestal*-class aircraft carriers to ensure "minimal naval forces adequate to our basic military tasks in global or limited wars and capable of supporting U. S. foreign policy."[12]

Fechteler was an able advocate for the navy before Congress. Indeed, Congressman Carl Vinson, longtime chairman of the House Armed Services Committee, recalled that "I'd have put Fechteler close to the top of the list insofar as ability as a witness is concerned. . . . He always knows his subject well, doesn't attempt to give evasive answers, and speaks his mind when he happens to disagree with official Defense Department views." Nonetheless, in 1952 Congress made serious cuts in the entire request for defense money and this reduced the navy's appropriations. However, Fechteler saved the second *Forrestal*-class carrier by accepting other cuts. Under the circumstances it was difficult for him to plan for any significant expansion of the fleet beyond that already undertaken. Sensing that naval technology was in a transitional phase, he recognized that coming changes augered a different navy from the one in which he had grown up. On the other hand, he did not believe that the new weapons were panaceas; for example, he encouraged the development of shipborne guided missiles but was skeptical of claims that they would revolutionize naval warfare since the missiles could not discriminate between ship types. Fechteler was also very cautious about igniting the smoldering interservice rivalries of the recent past, and went out of his way to point out on more than one occasion that traditional naval functions did "not duplicate functions of other services."[13]

The stalemate on the Korean peninsula, reached before Sherman's death, meant that Fechteler's primary role in that war was to maintain American naval forces at levels already set during the height of the fighting. Barring unforeseen developments in Korea as a result of the prolonged truce talks at Panmunjom, or elsewhere in Asia, the CNO's strategy was to build up the forces of NATO. However, in July 1952 he decided "to go take a look" at American naval positions in the Western Pacific and Far East. After a stopover in Pearl Harbor, he visited the front in Korea, discussed Asian politics and strategy with Chiang Kai-shek in Taiwan, and inspected naval installations in Manila and Guam before returning to the United States. The trip evidently disturbed him, for he recalled that many of the demonstrations staged for his visits failed to convince him of the practical readiness of American forces, and the Nationalist Chinese leadership seemed naively anxious to begin a third world war. Fechteler's fondness for overseas travel took him to Brazil in December 1952 for a ten-day goodwill trip. He admitted that it did not entail much official business, but he found the country "extremely interesting" because he had "never been down the east coast of South America."[14]

One month earlier, Eisenhower had won the presidency and early in 1953 he began to assemble to new administration. He named Charles E. Wilson as secretary of defense and Robert B. Anderson as secretary of the navy. Although Fechteler's modest policy of limited fleet expansion seemed to fit nicely with the new administration's concept of "security with solvency," in May the president announced that all the Joint Chiefs of Staff, including the CNO, were to be replaced. While the others either planned to retire anyway or were ineligible for reappointment, Fechteler expected to stay on and his removal came as a surprise—particularly within naval circles. Editorial reaction was mixed. The *New York Times* claimed that the change would put the Joint Chiefs under stronger civilian control and "remove the military from the quicksands of politics into which the old chiefs had sometimes been forced as a result of postwar controversies." Since Fechteler had dutifully stayed far from interservice squabbling, this hardly seemed fair. The *Army Navy Air Force Register,* while claiming that the appointment of Carney as chief of naval operations and Radford as the chairman of the Joint Chiefs was "a great day for the Navy," complained that there was "a definite matter of principle in removing Admiral Fechteler as CNO without cause, at flank speed and without future assignment." Rumor had it that Fechteler was told of the change only eighteen hours before it was publicly announced.[15]

The rumor was close to the truth, for Fechteler learned of his relief when Anderson called him into his office shortly before the public announcement. He assured Fechteler that his "performance of duty had not been criticized by anyone in any respect," but that Eisenhower had decided to change completely the membership of the Joint Chiefs of Staff. Although Fechteler had hoped that his appointment might have carried him into the new administration, he was not surprised by the news. He told Anderson that he intended to retire as "there is no place in the organization of the U. S. Navy for an ex-chief of naval operations." Furthermore, the only precedents dated back to the 1920s—and involved Admirals Coontz and Eberle—and he "did not propose to repeat that." However, he changed his mind and asked for Carney's old command of Allied Forces in Southern Europe on the grounds that it "was not in the organization of the U. S. Navy." Fechteler's decision placated a number of Republican officials and friends who questioned his hurried removal from office. Of Secretary Wilson he demanded greater authority in his new billet than his predecessor enjoyed and the right to leave it if and when it proved unappealing. Wilson agreed and Fechteler left office on 17 August 1953, after a tour of duty of precisely two years.[16]

Although Fechteler took his disappointment well, he did not tarry long after the change-of-command ceremony. Within an hour, he and his wife left for London. For the next three years his headquarters was in Naples, where he enjoyed an attractive villa overlooking the bay, a steady stream of "visiting firemen" from Washington, and an active social life. He traveled frequently, and his job was enlivened by such contentious personalities as Ambassador to Italy Claire Booth Luce, NATO Ground Forces Commander Field Marshal Bernard Montgomery, and NATO Naval Forces Commander Lord Louis Mountbatten. Fechteler retired in July 1956.

Leadership requires diverse personal qualifications and performance standards, and these are modified by organization structure, a traditional modus operandi, and existing circumstances—internal and external, foreign and domestic. As a result of the interaction of these elements, the pattern of effective leadership may vary: under one set of circumstances innovation and creativity may be necessary, while under another custodial requirements may dominate. The former conditions are usually found during periods of major change, the latter during more stable conditions. In these aspects, the position of the chief of naval operations differs little from the presidency, the papacy, or any other important position of leadership.

Fechteler's custodial tenure as chief of naval operations during a period of stabilization followed long years of turmoil that predated the world war. Indeed, with respect to his tour, Fechteler confessed, "I don't know that I could say that I contributed anything of great significance to this thing ever" other than "to continue" programs initiated by Sherman. Conceivably, his appointment was a case of the job proving bigger than the man, but Fechteler could justifiably claim that "two years isn't very long to get your stamp on anything." Yet what was needed when he served as chief of naval operations was a respected skipper, capable of maintaining course and speed. Fechteler filled this need. He lacked the unvarnished ambition and drive that moved Sherman, Carney, and Radford, but this may have been his greatest asset as CNO. Unlike those men, he had no burning desire for the billet, possibly because he saw its thanklessness and increasing impotence, or because he realized that its demands fitted neither his personality nor his professional preferences. For, above all, Fechteler liked to command ships. In retirement, he often recalled a visit by Admiral John H. Hoover to the *Indiana* during the Second World War. After inspecting the ship, Hoover told Fechteler that he hoped Fechteler would go far in the navy but that he should always remember, "No matter if you get to the very top, you have got the best job now, command of a big ship, that you will ever have." To this, Fechteler reacted, "I think, perhaps, he was right."[17]

For a few months after his retirement, Fechteler remained on duty as a member of the Defense Advisory Committee on Professional and Technical Compensation. Known as the Cordiner Committee for its chairman, who headed General Electric, the panel's concluding report, strongly influenced by Fechteler, laid the foundation for the modern system of compensation of the American armed forces. Illustrative of the admiral's naval service, his work on this commission was unheroic, intelligent, dogged, and worthwhile. Cordiner was so impressed with Fechteler's efforts that he hired him to work at General Electric where the admiral remained until 1961 when he reached the age of sixty-five. He died of a heart attack in Bethesda Naval Hospital on 4 July 1967, and was buried in Arlington National Cemetery.

ROBERT BOSTWICK CARNEY

17 August 1953–17 August 1955

PAUL R. SCHRATZ

Robert B. Carney was born in Vallejo, California, on 26 March 1895, the son of Lieutenant Commander Robert Emmett Carney and Bertha V. Bostwick Carney. The younger Carney entered the Naval Academy in 1912 and graduated with distinction four years later. His early career was unexceptional. During World War I, he served in the destroyer *Fanning,* based at Queenstown, Ireland, and he assisted in the sinking of the German *U-58* and the capture of her crew. When he returned to the United States, he married Grace Stone Craycroft of Aquasco, Maryland, on 7 September 1918. They had two children, Robert Jr. and Betty.

Between the wars, Carney commanded four destroyers, served as gunnery officer in the cruiser *Cincinnati,* executive officer in the battleship *California,* and in the office of the secretary of the navy. In February 1941 he helped to organize, under the command of Vice Admiral Arthur L. Bristol, Jr., a special surface-air convoy escort force which, from September 1941 to April 1942, established the remarkable record of escorting more than 2,600 ships in the North Atlantic with the loss of only six. As Bristol's operations officer and later his chief of staff, Carney earned the Distinguished Service Medal for his contributions to antisubmarine warfare. Commanding the light cruiser *Denver* from October 1942 to July 1943, he was twice decorated for heroic conduct in the Solomons Islands campaign.

Promoted to rear admiral on 26 July 1943, Carney became chief of staff to Admiral William F. Halsey, Jr., Commander, South Pacific Area, and later Commander, Third Fleet. From this vantage point, he participated in the planning and execution of many of the major operations in the South Pacific and Central Pacific. He was decorated for his contributions to overall strategy and to the logistic support of Allied forces in the South Pacific, for actions against Japanese forces in Leyte Gulf, and for the planning of the first proposed landing on the Japanese mainland.

Carney arranged for the entry of the Third Fleet into Tokyo Bay, accepted the surrender of the Yokosuka Naval Base, and attended the surrender ceremony aboard Halsey's flagship, the battleship *Missouri,* on 2 September 1945. Promoted to vice admiral in 1946, he served as deputy chief of naval operations for logistics, during which time he chaired a joint committee to develop a budget structure that would be applicable, and acceptable, to all the services.[1]

Following command of the Second Fleet, Carney was advanced to the rank of admiral, and, on 1 October 1950, became Commander in Chief of U. S. Naval Forces, Eastern Atlantic and Mediterranean, headquartered in London. On 18 June 1951, General Dwight D. Eisenhower, Supreme Allied Commander, Europe, named Carney as commander in chief, Allied Forces, Southern Europe. Carney set up his headquarters in Naples with a combined staff responsible for American naval units in the Eastern Atlantic and Mediterranean as well as NATO units in Southern Europe. Once, during Carney's service in this billet, the general hinted to him that he could expect new responsibilities after Eisenhower returned to Washington.

In November 1952 Eisenhower won the presidential election, and succeeded Harry S. Truman in the White House in January 1953. During Truman's presidency, Republicans charged that the Joint Chiefs of Staff had become "politicized." For example, General of the Army Omar N. Bradley, the chairman of the Joint Chiefs, heaped public scorn on the "Gibraltar theory of defense" espoused by the powerful Senator Robert A. Taft. When he became president, Eisenhower agreed to the demands of congressional Republicans and of his secretary of defense, Charles E. Wilson, that he name an entirely new set of service chiefs. Fortuitously, the terms of all of the chiefs would expire by the end of 1953 except that of the CNO, Admiral William M. Fechteler, who expected to serve until 1955. But Eisenhower and Wilson decided that Fechteler also had to go.

On 13 May 1953, the president announced that he had selected Carney to relieve Fechteler as chief of naval operations. Under the circumstances, Carney was in some ways an unusual—but superb—choice for the navy's highest uniformed office. Before becoming CNO he had served for ten years as a flag officer, longer than any of his predecessors. He and Eisenhower had worked closely together in Europe and the new president was clearly impressed with the quality of the admiral's work. Also, Eisenhower evidently believed that Carney was his best selection to ease the tension within the navy caused by the premature relief of Fechteler and to mediate a nasty quarrel in the service over control of the development of nuclear-powered submarines. Carney and Fechteler were Naval Academy classmates and lifelong friends but Fechteler was deeply disappointed and refused to retire. The only assignment available was the billet Carney was leaving. Thus, when Carney became CNO, Fechteler went to Naples to command NATO forces in Southern Europe.

But Eisenhower's choice of Carney was unexpected. Carney, Fechteler, and Admiral Arthur W. Radford were top candidates for the office when Forrest P. Sherman died in 1951. Fechteler, a favorite of Congressman Carl Vinson, had not been a part of the struggle over military unification, whereas Carney had served from 1945 to 1947 with Radford and Sherman on Navy Secretary James V. Forrestal's Committee on Research and Reorganization, the "brains trust" that prepared the navy's position and strategy for the congressional battle.

When Eisenhower became president in 1953, Radford was a strong contender for leadership in the Department of Defense. The general toured the Pacific before his inauguration and Radford, commander in chief of the Pacific theater, favorably impressed both the president-elect and the secretary-designate, Wilson. Radford's persuasive views on military aviation and strategic bombing and his strong orientation toward Asia earned him appointment as the chairman of the Joint Chiefs of Staff—even though he would have preferred, initially at least, to be CNO. As events soon proved, Carney had far less in common with Wilson than did Radford.

Nonetheless, in 1953 from Eisenhower's standpoint, Carney had outstanding qualifications. He had a superb record and, in particular, was highly regarded for his wartime performance as Halsey's chief of staff. Slight of figure, reserved in manner, and not widely known on the Washington scene, he was a skilled planner and administrator who was experienced in the ways of the bureaucracy. Driven by strong ambition, he maintained a reasonably low profile and, amid considerable elbowing by contemporaries for the national limelight, remained frank and fearless in expressing his views.

One of Eisenhower's criteria in selecting the new chiefs was breadth of experience in both geography and command. All of the new chiefs in 1953 had served in both the European and the Pacific theaters. The president sought men with "global outlooks," at least by contrast to their predecessors, who were identified primarily with Europe. In addition, all the men chosen in 1953, except General Nathan F. Twining, the new chief of staff of the air force, had headed large commands. They were expected to reflect Eisenhower's own strong preference for centralized organization with minimal service bias.

Pending Fechteler's arrival in Naples, Carney turned over his duties to his deputy and returned to Washington. On 17 August 1953 he was sworn in as the fifth chief of naval operations in six years. However, before he and his fellow chiefs took office they were briefed by President Eisenhower in the White House in early July on the global commitments of the United States. The president complained that under the Truman administration military planning had proceeded from the assumption that American strength had to be directed to successive "periods of maximum danger," one such being 1954–1955. The chief executive rejected this basis for planning and fought instead to insulate the defense budget from both crises in foreign affairs and discontent at home. He wanted to terminate the alternating peaks and valleys in defense allocations that had plagued American preparedness in the past, and at the same time immunize the domestic economy against the vagaries of international politics.

Eisenhower and Wilson asked the new chiefs to draft a complete survey of the nation's military capabilities in light of these assumptions. They were to consider military policy in all its aspects—weapons, systems, strategic doctrine, service roles and missions, force and manpower levels, and the military role of the allies—and to relate the whole not only to foreign policy but also to the stringent fiscal policy of the new administration. The Joint Chiefs were given to understand that they were dealing with the president's "great equation": how to strike the proper balance between a strong military posture and the risk of "bankruptcy." Borrowing an idea from his friend, Winston Churchill, Eisenhower directed the chiefs to design the new program without the benefit of a staff. He wanted not a long, exhaustive study, but the personal views of the chiefs based on their great collective experience.[2]

The four men began their study on 13 July 1953 in a conference room near the office of the chairman. A single aide provided pencils, large, yellow scratch pads, and an occasional pot of coffee. They alternated their study and discussion with brief inspection trips to military installations within the United States. Carney's services were particularly valuable in the task of matching strategy with resources. As a principal strategic planner during World War II, he was appalled by the great piles of excess equipment rotting on Pacific islands at the end of the hostilities. As deputy chief of naval operations for logistics after the war, he sought better ways to manage the navy's resources and, in 1947, was one of those who drafted the first unified military budget.

By early August 1953, the new Joint Chiefs were making progress but were finding it difficult to isolate themselves from the pressures of service demands and the distractions of other business in the Pentagon. To escape these interruptions, Radford asked to borrow the secretary of the navy's yacht *Sequoia.* The chiefs went to sea on 6 August, anchored across from Quantico, Virginia, and were sequestered there until they reached an agreement on the general outlines of future strategy.

Planning for the indispensable long-term balance between external defense and domestic liberty, they hammered out the basis for Eisenhower's "New Look." The term, attributed to Admiral Radford, was taken from an advertising slogan that season which highlighted changes in women's dress styles and may have suggested far more radical changes in defense policy than was actually the case. As a military policy, the "New Look" placed its major emphasis on a strategy of using nuclear weapons as a deterrent to war between the United States and the Soviet Union. Secretary of State John Foster Dulles later popularized this concept as a strategy of "massive retaliation" which, he claimed, was the new cornerstone of American defense policy.

The appeal of the "New Look," even to traditional supporters of the navy in Congress, was that it promised to avoid a long series of limited and frustrating wars. The vivid and unpleasant aftertaste of the stalemate in the Korean War tended to stigmatize a strategy of limited conflicts fought for specific political objectives well short of the unconditional, ideological crusades of both world wars. Admiral Carney took a typically broad, pragmatic view of the "New Look." "The policy was a single, unified plan to counter a centralized Communist strategy rather than a succession of minor strategies to cope with brush fires." However, he later added that the nation had to "hedge our strategic bets" and be "ready to rush into the future but also [be] prepared to rely on the methods of the recent past."[3]

The product of the chiefs' planning effort in the summer of 1953 was a statement of American forces and weapons that they believed would be necessary by 1957. However, Carney lent strong support to the insistence of Army Chief of Staff General Matthew B. Ridgway that the Joint Chiefs' approval of this new policy be qualified since it was based on several important assumptions. The more critical of these assumptions were that there would be no outbreak of war in Korea; that the political situation in Korea would stabilize and that South Korean armed forces would be armed and trained on schedule; that the creation and rearmament of West German and Japanese forces would proceed according to plan; that the civil war in Indochina would turn in favor of the French; and that other international conditions would not deteriorate in favor of the Soviet Union.[4] What the chiefs agreed to they called the "Interim Look," an agreement on future requirements conditioned by immediate reality. The implications of their agreement became a matter of bitter contention both among themselves and between them and the secretary of defense.

Carney partly supported Ridgway's view that the 1953 agreements on forces for 1957 were "ceilings." To the other chiefs, these levels were "targets." Carney and Ridgway agreed to the "ceilings" only to the extent that none of Ridgway's assumptions were invalidated. These points were important since the conventional forces of the army—and to a lesser extent of the navy—were to bear the brunt of the reductions in defense expenditures that would follow the Korean War. If an easing of world tensions did not precede the decreased budgets and new force structures necessitated by a concentration on strategic air power and nuclear weapons, then national security would be in jeopardy. The Joint Chiefs' agreement, although strongly qualified, thus implicitly supported lower levels of conventional forces and the assumptions attached to that agreement were soon forgotten.[5]

Potential reductions in their conventional forces made the navy and army partners in disaster. In his approach to this problem, Carney differed from Ridgway in a subtle but important degree of emphasis. Ridgway believed that the Joint Chiefs should have based their estimate of force requirements on military factors alone. He believed it possible to make a "purely military" recommendation concerning the forces required by measuring enemy capabilities and American commitments. He did not think that "enemy intentions" were properly part of the military calculus, and,while he agreed that military recommendations should be "reasonable," he did not believe they should include nonmilitary considerations.

Carney, by contrast, was content with the role of neutral expert, merely pointing out the consequences of the changes civilian leadership made in his policy recommendations. The admiral realized fully that a rejection of his initial proposals may have been the result of applying legitimate considerations beyond military experience. Moreover, he was by nature a less tense and emotional man than Ridgway, and he refused to denounce, as did Ridgway, the administration's proposed reductions in the navy and the army which the general believed were motivated by considerations of domestic political advantage, and consequently he did not see them as legitimate. Carney thought that the administration's processes of making decisions were quite normal, although he believed that the chiefs had participated to a somewhat greater degree than was the case under Truman in developing the economic parameters for decisions.[6] Of course, a major contributor to this difference of opinion was the fact that Ridgway lacked Carney's experience with the budgetary process at high levels. But because of the disagreement, what should have been a natural alliance of army and navy interests in the drastic cutbacks in conventional forces and manpower necessary for the expansion of the air force failed to develop.

For Carney, the situation was even more complex. Ridgway badly needed the CNO's support, and Carney, though a strong advocate of naval aviation, could have used army backing against what many saw as the domination of the navy by air-power enthusiasts led by Radford. Not only was he chairman of the Joint Chiefs of Staff, but Radford also retained tremendous influence within the Navy Department and he actively cultivated the support of Secretary of the Navy Charles S. Thomas, who soon fell under his sway.

It was a tribute to Carney's strength of character that he maintained a relaxed and casual attitude despite the stresses under which he was operating. Both Carney and Radford endorsed the necessity for a policy anchored in the use of nuclear weapons at the beginning of hostilities between the United States and the Soviet Union. Radford, however, a prime architect of the strategy of "massive retaliation," had moved from earlier support of the carrier in a general war to all-out reliance on the employment of the atomic bomb because he had finally come to believe that the carrier was too expensive. He admitted that his views had changed and that he was a "little political," but claimed that he had to be in his job.[7] Carney and Radford were strong, forthright personalities, but Radford's forcefulness found quick rapport with the defense secretary, whereas Carney's support lay more with the president. The two admirals had long had a basic policy dispute, since Radford had pushed for the domination of the navy by aviators whereas Carney had resisted any compartmentalization of the service. During Carney's term as CNO, their differences were less fundamental but strains inevitably appeared between two strong-willed men, the most important of which concerned their relations with Secretary Wilson.

The differences on defense policy between Carney and Radford in the Eisenhower administration first appeared during the initial budget hearings for the "New Look" program in the fall of 1953. Radford's statement directly mirrored administration policy, stressing American technological superiority and limitations in manpower and suggesting that "the other Free Nations can most effectively provide in their own and adjacent countries the bulk of the defensive ground forces and local naval and air power."[8] Yet, the key to the ability of other Free World countries to provide for their own defense was increased foreign and military aid from the United States—which Radford and the other chiefs had been forced to reduce for reasons of economy.

On the other hand, Carney qualified his support for the administration's program with a disclaimer about the traditional role on the seas:

> The Navy will do its utmost to assure the effective accomplishment of its mission within our resources. Our plans for the future, as always, reflect our efforts to support the national policies. I should like to point out that the new emphases [on massive retaliation] have in no way altered the roles and missions of the Navy. It is still responsible for the accomplishment of its fundamental assigned mission: To gain and maintain control of the seas. . . . a task dependent upon two fundamental factors:
>
> a. On the one hand, maintaining forces-in-being best calculated to be an effective deterrent to war; and
>
> b. On the other hand, and equally important, these forces-in-being must have the peacetime capability of initiating on D-day, the tasks, both offensive and defensive, which will inevitably devolve upon us in the event of war.
>
> With regard to this second factor, we cannot accept the risk of restricting ourselves to one fixed concept of operations in war. To do so would be to invite the enemy to take the course that we would not be prepared to counter. The Navy that we are recommending for the coming fiscal year, therefore, is not tied to one fixed concept.[9]

The commandant of the marine corps, General Lemuel C. Shepherd, Jr., upon whom Carney may have leaned for support, was in an equally difficult position. The only surviving Truman appointee, he was at the close of his fourth year as commandant and planned to leave at the end of 1953. His statement stressed the continuing need for a ready amphibious capability, but its tone was futuristic, looking toward exploring in realistic terms the design of landing forces under atomic conditions. Both Carney and Shepherd in short, gave the "New Look" their loyal support, but indicated doubts about the wisdom of overreliance on nuclear weapons as the heart of defense policy. To sacrifice the mobile, ready forces upon which the nation's defenses had always rested nourished the germ of conflict with the new administration's program.

Eisenhower's emphasis on joint planning and budgeting required that Carney, in his early days as chief of naval operations, devote a major share of his energies to his duties on the Joint Chiefs of Staff. Meanwhile, in his role as the operating head of the navy, he was hardly free from problems. Incident to the major policy review that he and the other chiefs were required to draft, in July 1953 Carney had to visit several military installations within the United States. As soon as the final writing of the "New Look" program could be turned over to subordinates, each of the chiefs traveled separately to American installations overseas. Having recently returned from duty in Europe, Carney decided to make a tour of the Far East, two purposes of which were to see what economies he could make in operations and to explore the feasibility of reducing overseas deployments. Above all, this trip gave him an excellent opportunity to have a broad look at the operating forces, an experience which he found useful, stimulating, and in some ways, troubling.

The achievement of an armistice in Korea fulfilled one of President Eisenhower's major campaign promises. It did not, however, immediately reduce tensions between North Korea and South Korea and Carney believed that the frequent border incidents would not allow any major reduction of American forces in the Far East or any lessening concern with their state of readiness. However, on 26 December 1953 the president announced that some army units in Korea would be withdrawn and Carney was ordered to plan for a major redeployment of naval forces in the Far East in January 1954. However, with the Chinese no longer engaged in Korea, threats against Taiwan and Indochina seemed to intensify, and with heightening tension, plans to withdraw American forces from Asia were reconsidered. On 12 January 1954, in a major address, Secretary of State Dulles announced that the withdrawal of ground forces from Korea which the president had promised would be reduced, and he reaffirmed that American forces in the Far East would continue to feature "highly mobile naval, air, and amphibious units." Shortly thereafter, Carney shifted one battleship division and a destroyer division to the Atlantic Fleet, but he canceled the rest of the redeployments. In the same address, Dulles repeated the warning he had given on 2 September that open Chinese aggression in Indochina would result in "grave consequences which might not be confined to Indochina," but his simultaneous announcement of the "massive retaliation" strategy tended to obscure the message to the Chinese government.

The war between the French and the Vietminh in Indochina had dragged into its seventh year. The communist strategy of "long-term revolutionary war" was beginning to take its toll. In 1953, war-weariness had not reached crisis proportions in France, but American leaders were urging more aggressive French military action to achieve an early victory in the conflict. Shortly before his trip to the Far East, Carney had ordered a destroyer division to visit Saigon in October to give visible evidence of American interest and support for the French and the Associated States of Vietnam.[10]

At the same time, an increase in American military aid to France to fight the war in Indochina was approved, and Carney was authorized to lend the French Navy the light carrier *Belleau Wood,* which they rechristened *Bois Belleau* and which eventually arrived in Saigon on 30 April 1954. Carney, through the Joint Chiefs, also expedited delivery to the French of ninety-five amphibious landing craft of various types and seventy armored river craft under the Mutual Defense Assistance Pact of 1954. In addition, the CNO lent them four more landing craft which they could keep until the end of 1954. Through American aid, the French naval capability in Indochina was significantly enhanced. Repair and maintenance facilities were included in the form of major assistance to the French naval shipyard in Saigon, the repair facility at Haiphong, and the transfer of a repair ship and smaller vessels. Nonetheless, on the ground in Vietnam a crisis was approaching, and both the French and the Vietminh doubted whether they could hold out for much longer.

On his Pacific tour in October 1953, Carney met with Admiral Felix B. Stump, Commander in Chief, Pacific, whom he had recently directed to prepare plans in case of Chinese military intervention in Indochina. Should that happen, Stump planned to use the Pacific Fleet to blockade the coast of China and take action against the Chinese mainland "to destroy or neutralize the Communist air strength, to interdict lines of logistic support and, generally, to reduce the military potential of Communist China." Stump told Carney that Chinese ground forces then in position north of the Indochinese border, and their air forces either within combat range or capable of rapid deployment, could drive French forces out of Tonkin in a few weeks. Stump believed that an American naval task force to operate in Southeast Asian waters should be organized under Commander, First Fleet, and be based at Subic Bay. The "existence of such a force," he assured the CNO, "would be at least a deterrent to further Chinese Communist aggression and might be a controlling factor in preventing such aggression."[11]

In early February 1954, Carney advised Stump that he was considering recommending to the Joint Chiefs the deployment of two carriers and about six destroyers to the Subic Bay area for the "ostensible and announced purpose.... of fair weather training." Stump concurred, suggesting eight destroyers instead of six, and the inclusion of mobile logistic support capable of under-way replenishment of the combat ships with oil, provisions, and ammunition. Nine days later, the chief of naval operations transferred the operational control of two attack carriers and a destroyer division to Stump. Carney informed the Pacific commander that the purpose was "to conduct training exercises as a cover for possible operations to assist the French in Indochina if such operations become necessary." He added that the "task force should be ready to render prompt assistance during the time they are in the South China Sea."[12]

Carney kept two additional carriers in the Japan-Korea area under Vice Admiral Alfred M. Pride, Commander, Seventh Fleet, but he wanted the new Southern Force to be under another admiral for three reasons. First, Pride's fleet was under the operational control of the Commander in Chief, Far East, who was responsible for the Japan-Taiwan area, where Carney feared that a crisis simultaneous with the Indochina war might erupt. Second, because of the continuing Chinese threat to Taiwan a separate carrier force was needed in that area as a deterrent to an invasion attempt from the mainland. Third, Carney wanted the Southern Force to have a direct chain of command separate from the Japan-Taiwan area. He concluded that "the realism of the threat in the Pacific lends added importance to any thinking which involves the utilization of the Commander First Fleet as the tactical commander for special operations."[13]

Commander, First Fleet, Vice Admiral William K. Phillips, took command of the new "Fair Weather Training Force" on 28 February 1954. Since Carney had previously assigned him to coordinate and evaluate fleet readiness in the Western Pacific as well as off the West Coast, Phillips was prepared for his new mission. His force was to conduct training operations in the South China Sea, maintain itself in a high state of readiness, and evaluate the feasibility of using the Subic-Sangley area as an operating base. Carney also assigned Phillips the secret mission of maintaining readiness for combat operations in case it became necessary to employ his units against China or in support of the French Union forces.

In Indochina, General Henri-Eugene Navarre launched a new French offensive on 12 December 1953, which included amphibious landings at Nha Trang. In late January and early February 1954, General John W. O'Daniel evaluated the progress of the French campaign for the Joint Chiefs. He was generally optimistic, but suggested a liaison office in Saigon to expedite deliveries of military assistance and to inject American thinking on strategy and tactics into the French command at the highest levels. Navarre regarded the proposal as an attempt to undermine his control of the war and he opposed it. Meanwhile, near the Laotian border, part of his army was increasingly hard-pressed. Its fortified position at Dien Bien Phu lay in a valley and the French had left the high surrounding ground to the Vietminh, under General Vo Nguyen Giap. Armed with artillery, mortars, recoilless rifles, and flak guns, which his men had dragged through miles of dense jungle and swamp, Giap opened an all-out offensive immediately after the announcement in Paris that an international conference would convene in Geneva to help the French and Vietminh to end the war. The French position at Dien Bien Phu soon grew critical.

On 19 March Carney ordered Phillips to go on a twelve-hour alert and be prepared to steam to a point near the entrance to the Gulf of Tonkin and lend support to the French on three hours' notice. Carney told Phillips:

> Although there is no approved plan nor even a tentative plan for intervention in Indochina, authorities here including Secretary Dulles, are aware of the potential critical military situation in Indochina and the possible implications of serious French reversals. There is an approved expression of national policy recognizing the grave consequences that could result from loss of Indochina to the Communists.[14]

While he continued to emphasize that no decision had been made in Washington about American offensive operations, Carney followed this alert order by moving the Southern Force again to positions from which it could support the defenders of Dien Bien Phu. The French were not informed of the possible availability of this naval force, but Carney did authorize Stump to initiate with French authorities the technical preparations necessary to ensure effective air support, should American military assistance be approved. Carney issued a continuous stream of alerting orders, including those for logisitic support.

On Carney's orders, Phillips had formed a striking group of two attack carriers and they steamed at flank speed to an operating area about 100 miles south of Hainan Island on 22 March. Two days earlier, General Paul Ely, the chief of staff of the French armed forces, arrived in Washington for hurried talks with American officials. He carried with him an urgent request from Navarre for additional air power and airborne logistic support to break the tightening ring of fire around Dien Bien Phu. Ely laid this plea before the Americans. Three questions were involved in the ensuing discussions. The first concerned the advisability of providing American air support for French forces in the absence of Chinese aerial intervention. The second concerned the effectiveness of air strikes against guerrilla forces in the screening jungles around Dien Bien Phu and the possible consequences if American intervention did not produce the desired results. The third involved the use of atomic weapons to save the French.[15]

Carney believed that the commitment of American tactical air power by both the navy and air force would help the French, but he did not see it as being decisive in the battle. From his experience with jungle warfare in the South Pacific during World War II, he was convinced that air strikes with conventional ordnance would not be effective against jungle-covered troops. On the question of the use of atomic bombs, he soberly concluded that they would harm the defenders of Dien Bien Phu as much as the attackers. Finally, he cautioned that any tactical advantage had to be weighed against the potential political and military consequences of American involvement in the Indochinese war. To monitor Chinese activity, he supported a recommendation made by Stump that carrier aircraft be sent to reconnoiter the nearby Chinese airfields, assembly points, and critical roads and trails that had been used to send military supplies southward during the previous three or four months. On 31 March, Carney explained to Stump the substance of the discussions between the Joint Chiefs and Ely and directed him to review his plans and arrangements with Navarre. No commitments had been made, but Carney abandoned a planned trip to the Pacific because "time is in short supply."[16]

Nonetheless, neither Radford nor Dulles, who favored American intervention, could persuade Congress or America's allies to conur. In addition, Ridgway, who opposed intervention, reported to the Joint Chiefs that American bombing in Indochina would lead to ground action in which the U. S. Army would be the loser. He estimated that perhaps one million troops would be needed to hold Indochina and construction costs would be enormous. After he presented this report to President Eisenhower, the idea of American intervention was abandoned. Without help, Dien Bien Phu fell to the Vietminh on 7 May 1954, and with it the remnants of the French colonial empire in Asia. This disaster precipitated the fall of the government in Paris and its replacement by one that promised to bring peace within thirty days.[17]

At Geneva on 20 July, a cessation of hostilities was arranged by three accords, one each for Vietnam, Laos, and Cambodia. The first divided Vietnam along a demilitarized zone at the seventeenth parallel, roughly following the Ben Hai River. Up to 300 days was allowed from the signing date for French forces to move south and for Vietminh troops to withdraw to the north. Until the movement of these units was completed, civilians residing in one zone were free to migrate to the other. Because of the great number of Vietnamese who wanted to leave the north, the French asked again for American help before the civilians became subject to harassment as the communists gained control above the parallel. In addition, the French needed to move their troops and equipment from the north to the south. Ngo Dinh Diem, the new president of the government in Saigon, asked Eisenhower for help in this project and Carney was authorized to execute operation "Passage to Freedom." The French began a major effort on 5 August to move the refugees but, efficient as their efforts were, they could not handle all those who wanted to leave. Prior to the president's authorization, Carney had warned Stump to plan to assist the French and on 6 August he ordered the Pacific commander to execute his evacuation plan.[18] Stump sent Rear Admiral Lorenzo S. Sabin, Commander, Amphibious Force, Western Pacific, to Haiphong on 10 August to confer with French, Vietnamese, and American officials, and within a week refugees were being loaded aboard American vessels. When the task was completed nine months later, about 800,000 people had been carried to freedom in the south by American and French ships.

The crisis at Dien Bien Phu had rekindled the general debate in Washington over policy and strategy in Asia, a debate to which Carney added his own insight derived from his long experience as a strategist and from his grasp of Asian problems. But he had long been worried about strategic thinking in the navy. He was not pleased with what he had seen of naval officers' strategic thinking in preparation for World War II and he was quick to point out where improvements could be made. Addressing the class at the Naval War College in 1947, Carney claimed that:

> After World War I, the fascinating study of the battle of Jutland blinded many people to the importance of other facets of war. World War I had not produced many serious strategic problems for the United States Navy and consequently, much of our strategic thinking and study was channeled into tactical lines. The influence of this thinking was felt throughout the service, and throughout the

> years; tactical proficiency and service in the closely knit tactical fleet became a prime requisite for promotion, and there was a tendency to brush aside, as too academic, such things as planning, studying amphibious warfare, and the lowly business of supply and resupply of overseas bases. . . . We were wholly unprepared materially and spiritually for a long-drawn-out struggle.[19]

Carney pointed out that the navy and the nation had gone to war twice already in the century, both times victorious, both times unprepared, and both times grievously misreading the military lessons and political consequences of the conflict. Naval officers shared the typically American perception of the United States as a noble and righteous nation whose security was not likely to be endangered seriously by conflicts between other nations. This was the defect primarily responsible for "spiritual"unpreparedness for war.[20]

Carney believed that the writings and thought of Alfred Thayer Mahan, whose explanation of the nature of international politics and war was of doubtful validity in the 1890s, had become even more questionable as a result of changes in technology and in the political order during the twentieth century. Too few naval officers grasped Mahan's limitations and his teachings continued to be accepted, whereas a wholly new concept of maritime thought was needed. As chief of naval operations, Carney made a strong case for Secretary of the Navy Thomas to encourage naval officers to speak out on strategic issues, particularly in the pages of the *U. S. Naval Institute Proceedings*, but Thomas merely forwarded the memorandum to Defense Secretary Wilson and it had no effect.[21]

Carney's hope for new thinking about naval strategies was reemphasized when the Soviets exploded a hydrogen bomb, almost on the day that he took office as chief of naval operations. He believed that the navy had to develop new ways of thinking about the naval mission and to present these views forcefully to the American public, and he felt that little had been done to draft long-term objectives for the navy. To avoid ad hoc arrangements for dealing with crises, Carney created the Long Range Objectives Group in his office and named talented officers, such as Rear Admiral Charles D. Griffin, the first director, to this unit. The group examined major strategic issues—the mission of the aircraft carrier and the nuclear submarine, for example—after a careful analysis of future needs rather than on instinct, emotion, or "professional experience," which had too often marked such studies in the past. Experienced observers saw this as the fulfillment of a hope that "if naval officers could continuously maintain up-to-date studies of the nation's projected naval needs based on respectable research, perhaps the Navy could indefinitely avoid finding itself in the weak defensive position it had occupied during most of the years from 1944 to 1950."[22]

A mark of the planning group's success is the fact that it was continued and expanded by Carney's successors. In one important respect, however, it never fulfilled its promise. It could not be totally free from "the hampering aspects of day-to-day administrative problems." The enigma was that if it were to work in an ivory-tower world, away from involvement in immediate issues, its product might not be relevant; with involvement in those issues, it might be overwhelmed by detail. The caliber of the group's leadership, activist rather than contemplative, often guaranteed its involvement in key questions for which primary responsibility lay elsewhere. And, after Carney ceased to be chief of naval operations, this trend limited the number of long-range studies produced by the group and eventually compromised its mission.

The other prong of Carney's drive to stimulate the development of broad conceptual thought among the navy's leadership was an effective program of public information. In the area of public relations, the navy had not always done well. Its ultraconservatism prevented the public from being made aware of its wartime accomplishments. Public relations suffered from poor administration, and the unification struggle put the navy in a bad light. Carney found that public-relations officers took what he called a "refutation-defensive" approach. "These people were always trying to get the Navy off the hook," he complained, "rather than pursuing a positive selling program which would keep us off the hook in the first place." Carney attributed this attitude largely to the training that the navy gave its young officers which he believed encouraged them to be taciturn, "a psychological restraint" in public-relations work. He directed his public-relations officers to take a "positive educational approach" to their business, stressing the need for the navy to be strengthened to counter the increasing menace of the Soviet Navy. "A good program is worthless until it is sold," he said, and to do this with Congress, in 1955 he set up an Office of Legislative Affairs directly under the secretary of the navy. Even in its relations with the army and air force Carney found the navy too reluctant:

> As CNO and a member of the JCS I was under pressure to defend Navy interests against Army/Air Force proposals to preempt the major theater and unified commands. My staff spent too much time in defensive effort. Curiously, my combat-proven deputy was reluctant to generate comparable power-grab proposals, typical of a widespread mentality that was basically conservative, honest—and, I thought, naive.
>
> I instigated some outrageous command proposals that would in effect, put all theater and unified commands under Navy leadership. These were quite reasonable for the Navy was the only Service with sea, air, and ground (Marine) components and know-how. My staff found if difficult to stimulate conviction in presentations, but the initiative was shifted.[23]

Carney considered his attempt to reorient the navy's external relations, particularly the approach taken by public-relations officers, to be one of his most important accomplishments as chief of naval operations.

From the day that he became CNO to the end of his term, Carney had to deal with the president's hope to unify and centralize the military forces under the traditional army concept of a general staff. Eisenhower's first reorganization of the Defense Department brought unexpected difficulties. He sought, from the lessons of the Korean War, to strengthen civilian control in the department, to make the Joint Chiefs less vulnerable to partisan political influences, and to improve strategic planning by having the planners take into account "a wider range of political and economic factors" than they had before, "as well as the latest developments of modern science." Based on the recommendations of a committee headed by Nelson A. Rockefeller, Eisenhower gave the service secretaries more authority by making them "operating heads of their departments in all respects." They, rather than the service chiefs, became executive agents for the military unified commands and the Joint Chiefs were removed from the chain of command.

This scheme, known as Reorganization Plan Number Six, became effective on 30 June 1953. A board headed by Undersecretary of the Navy Thomas S. Gates studied it, examined proposed changes for the navy, but simply concluded that decentralization was correct for the Navy Department. However, the board overlooked an unintended consequence of the plan and the implementing legislation, which was to enlarge further the power of the secretary of defense and put the Joint Chiefs of Staff into a staff, as opposed to command, role. The service secretary, both by tradition and because of the political character of his appointment, was a manager, not a commander. Perhaps in recognition of this, the plan allowed him to delegate his military authority to the service chief, who could "act for the Department." The first test of the new organization came during the crisis over the Tachen Islands, when the secretary of the navy seemed content to leave town and allow Carney to make the necessary decisions.[24]

Another provision of Reorganization Plan Number Six directly affected Carney's duties as chief of naval operations. In his letter to Congress transmitting the plan, Eisenhower referred to the "legal responsibility of the Joint Chiefs of Staff to advise the President in military matters." Despite this reservation of authority for the service chiefs, both the secretary of defense and the secretary of the navy were sensitive about communications, the former about those between Carney and the president, the latter about those between Carney and the fleet commanders. In fact, Secretary of the Navy Thomas was so upset when he discovered that Carney, continuing a long-standing practice, had privately communicated with Stump, the Pacific Fleet commander, during the Indochina crisis, that relations between Carney and Thomas were strained for a period.

A more serious situation arose with the defense secretary, who was choleric about his own formal role in the chain of command. Both Carney and Ridgway had disagreements with him over the question of their bypassing him and communicating directly with the president. Carney maintained that, as the principal statutory naval adviser to the president, he could and should go directly to the chief executive on some issues, a responsibility he claimed had been preserved in Reorganization Plan Number Six. Wilson disputed this claim and, in December 1954, marched all the service chiefs to the White House for a decision. Eisenhower supported Carney's position, adding that he could "ring the night bell if necessary," and told Wilson that a civilian such as the secretary just would not understand the military command issue. But Carney realized that he had won a Pyrrhic victory. Wilson would not overlook the incident, and Carney knew only too well that the secretary intended to have advisers fully amenable to his views. Carney told his family that his "victory" would cost him reappointment.[25]

One of the most challenging tasks that faced Carney as chief of naval operations was to reconcile Eisenhower's austere defense budgets and reliance on strategic air power with the reality of the Soviet Union's threat to American naval supremacy. Most contemporary observers tie the Soviet drive toward maritime supremacy to events that occurred much later. Not until 1967 did Admiral Sergei G. Gorshkov, head of the Russian navy, reveal that it was in 1954 that the Soviet government decided to replace the Stalinist postwar naval plan with a new and more ambitious one. The objective was to build an "oceangoing fleet" capable of accomplishing tasks in a nuclear or a conventional war, and of protecting "state interests" at sea in peacetime. The immediate Soviet aim was a seagoing fleet by 1957. Carney was perhaps the first American leader to warn of the Soviet challenge, and his address to the Naval War College on 16 February 1954 almost coincided with the change in naval policy which the Soviets had yet to announce:

> Recently Soviet nuclear achievements have grabbed the stage and precipitated much sober thought—and a measure of hysteria. . . . But another development which merits our very serious consideration . . . is Russia's emergence as a maritime power. Suddenly and without fanfare it has risen to second strongest in terms of number of ships in commission. She is flooding the shipyards of our allies with orders for merchant ship tonnage and building formidable combatant types in her own plants. She recognized the importance of naval aviation . . . though land-based, [and] we cannot exclude that she will in time build carriers. The Russian Navy is the one Soviet service which is more heavily manned than in World War II.[26]

Carney worried about the inadequacy of the American shipbuilding program which was less than necessary to respond to the Soviet challenge: the American fleet, built during two years of World War II, was getting "old and pot-bellied." He participated in the dramatic launching of the nuclear-powered *Nautilus* at New London, Connecticut, a few weeks before he delivered his prophetic address at the war college. A still more revolutionary type of vessel, the nuclear-powered, missile-launching Polaris submarine, was already on the drawing boards. But research and development for nuclear propulsion and for ballistic missiles were extremely expensive, and in 1953 the secretary of defense had halted all work on a nuclear-powered aircraft carrier for reasons of economy. However, during Carney's tour as chief of naval operations there were some major improvements in the fleet: angled decks, steam catapults, mirror landing systems, and heavy arresting gear were added to the aircraft carriers; the cruisers *Boston* and *Canberra* were equipped with guided missiles; and the *Thetis Bay*, an escort carrier, was converted into an assault helicopter carrier, the first ship of this type. But new construction, except for submarines, languished, and only the *Carronade*, a fire-support ship, joined the fleet in 1955.

Carney was well aware that nations are sensitive to manifestations of power. For example, increased Soviet naval presence in the Mediterranean clearly influenced the nations of that region to think twice before granting preferential treatment to the United States. In August 1953, just as Carney completed his tour as commander of NATO forces in Southern Europe, the first plan for NATO defense, with allied forces assigned to exact missions, was finally approved. The American decision to produce tactical nuclear weapons for the army and to deploy them where they were needed was supplemented by a major change in NATO strategy in 1954. A year earlier, Carney began to urge the adoption of a nuclear strategy for NATO, and in July 1954 Supreme Headquarters, Allied Powers, Europe, recommended that tactical nuclear weapons be integrated into the defense of Europe. The North Atlantic Council in December of that year agreed to the plan, which brought NATO strategy into line with American strategy and included an authorization for the Supreme Commander to assume that nuclear weapons would be used in a future conflict with Russia. Coupled with the rearmament of West Germany, this strategic change righted the balance of power in Europe and brought stability and peace.

American policy was less fruitful in Asia. After the French collapse in Indochina, the Communist Chinese lost no time in renewing regional turmoil. During the summer of 1954 their naval and air units became increasingly aggressive, clashing with Nationalist forces at several points along the coast. On 23 July Communist Chinese fighter planes shot down a British commercial airliner south of Hainan Island. At the urging of Carney and Radford, two aircraft carriers were ordered into the area to conduct an armed search for any survivors. Three days later, two American jets shot down two Communist Chinese propeller-driven fighter planes only thirteen miles from the mainland. Two weeks later, Chou En-lai called for the liberation of Taiwan, but Eisenhower replied on 17 August that any Chinese offensive against Taiwan "would have to run over the Seventh Fleet."[27] However, on 3 September 1954, while Dulles was visiting Manila, Communist Chinese shore batteries near Amoy began to shell the Nationalist-held island of Quemoy, two miles across the harbor.

On 6 September Carney, Radford, and Twining recommended to Eisenhower that Chiang Kai-shek be allowed to bomb mainland China and that American aircraft should join in the defense of Taiwan if the Communists invaded the island. Of the chiefs, only Ridgway dissented. Dulles supported that recommendation, but Eisenhower, then hospitalized in Denver, decided to warn Chiang against any provocative operations, especially while the governments were negotiating a mutual defense treaty. Nonetheless, American policy with respect to Quemoy and Matsu islands, which lie close to the Chinese mainland, remained ambiguous. After the Central Intelligence Agency estimated on 9 September that both islands were vulnerable to capture and that, without active American military aid, Taiwan was in danger, the Joint Chiefs, with Ridgway again dissenting, sought to extend the shield of American protection across the Taiwan Strait to the Communist Chinese doorstep. Churchill wrote Eisenhower to express his support for the defense of Taiwan, but he did not favor holding onto the offshore islands.[28] The defense treaty between the United States and Nationalist China was signed on 2 December, but the attacks on Quemoy, Matsu, and other offshore islands held by the Taiwan government continued.

The crisis went on into the next year. American policy was partly clarified by the Formosa Resolution, which was passed overwhelmingly by Congress and signed by the president on 29 January 1955. It gave Eisenhower the authority to use force if, in his judgment, a communist attack on the offshore islands presaged an attack on Taiwan and the Pescadores. However, the shelling persisted. Carney flew out to the Far East to assess the situation and, while he was gone, at a meeting on 11 March with Eisenhower, he was quoted as having said that war might be "only weeks away."[29] Eisenhower and Dulles continued to threaten Peking, both suggesting in mid-March that tactical nuclear weapons might be used if war broke out in the Far East.

On Thursday, 24 March, after he returned to Washington, Carney invited a group of correspondents to dinner and gave them what was supposed to be a strictly off-the-record background briefing on the crisis. His guests asked his opinion about Communist Chinese intentions, but Carney steadfastly maintained that he could judge only their capabilities, with which the United States should be prepared to deal—a major difference. He did indicate, however, that the Chinese might attack Matsu in mid-April, to coincide with a meeting of the Afro-Asian Conference in Bandung, Indonesia, and might follow that with an all-out attack on Quemoy some weeks later, perhaps by the end of May. Carney added that the military advisers had recommended to the president that, if such attacks occurred, he should take action to destroy Communist China's industrial base and thus end its expansionist policies. One well-known reporter violated his pledge of secrecy and published Carney's remarks; the others quickly followed suit.[30]

A storm of protest over a possible American attack on China erupted. Carney was angered that his remarks had been published and disheartened that they had embarrassed the administration. Some of the reporters who leaked the story later apologized, but the apologies were not accepted. One admitted that Carney had been treated unfairly. On the same day that the newspaper stories appeared, Eisenhower wrote himself a note: "Hostilities are not so imminent as is indicated by the forebodings of a number of my associates. . . . Most of the calamities that we anticipate really never occur." When he was asked at a press conference on 30 March whether Carney would be reprimanded for his remarks, the president answered cryptically, "Not by me." However, the secretary of defense directed all military personnel to submit for clearance all speeches, press releases, and "other information" intended for the public.[31]

If Carney in adversity found support from his fellow Joint Chiefs, he got none from Secretary Wilson. In fact, relations between the defense secretary and the chief of naval operations had considerably deteriorated during the year. An army planner, General James M. Gavin, claimed that Wilson treated the Joint Chiefs of Staff like "recalcitrant union bosses," rather than as legitimate members of the Defense Department hierarchy.[32]

Yet the Carney "leak" may have been useful to the ends of American foreign policy. For some reason, Peking suddenly ended the bombardment of Quemoy and sought a relaxation of tensions in the Taiwan Strait and, at the Bandung Conference on 29 April, Chou En-lai stated that his government did not want war with the United States and did want to negotiate outstanding issues. With this crisis over Quemoy and Matsu ended, talks between the Chinese and American ambassadors began in Geneva a few months later.

For Carney, however, the damage was done. Secretary of the Navy Thomas notified him in May that he would not be reappointed. When his two-year term ended in mid-August, Carney requested retirement effective 1 September 1955. To his last day in office he was motivated by the hope that his decisions would meet the approval of his colleagues and family—and of the reflection in his mirror. In retirement, Carney served as a business executive, was twice president of the U. S. Naval Institute, sat for six years on the Naval Academy Advisory Board, and was elected president of the Naval Academy Alumni Association.

Carney served his nation well during a difficult postwar period. During his tour as chief of naval operations—indeed, throughout his naval service—his personal convictions echoed the philosophy he advocated to the students at the Naval War College:

> Be frank and fearless in your considered counsels. No valid exception can be taken to forthright and mature opinion; there need be no inconsistency between honest belief and loyal compliance with the dictates of constituted authority.[33]

ARLEIGH ALBERT BURKE

17 August 1955–1 August 1961

DAVID ALAN ROSENBERG

In March 1955, Rear Admiral Arleigh A. Burke, Commander, Destroyer Force, Atlantic Fleet, received a call from Admiral Arthur W. Radford, chairman of the Joint Chiefs of Staff. How soon could Burke arrange a trip to Washington, Radford wanted to know; Secretary of the Navy Charles S. Thomas and Secretary of Defense Charles E. Wilson wanted to meet with him. Burke, having just arrived at Key West in the frigate *Wilkinson*, was less than eager to leave his flagship, and asked if the meeting could be postponed. No, said Radford, come as soon as possible.

When Burke arrived in Washington, he could not see the reason for the urgency. Radford, Wilson, and Thomas all spoke with him briefly on a number of subjects, but he was unable to discover what the discussions were intended to accomplish. He sought out his long-time friend, Admiral Robert B. Carney, the chief of naval operations, to ask what was afoot, but neither Carney nor his staff knew what the secretaries had in mind. It was probably some sort of job interview, Burke was told, perhaps for a Joint Staff position. Burke traveled to his headquarters at Newport still mystified, but inclined to put the incident out of his mind. On 10 May he was again summoned to the Pentagon, this time by Thomas, and was offered the post of chief of naval operations.

Although Burke had heard rumors that he was being considered for CNO, he had not taken them seriously because he lacked the necessary seniority for the job. There were ninety-two admirals ahead of him on the navy register, more than eighty of whom had to be considered possible candidates for the service's highest uniformed post. The offer left him stunned and apprehensive. He was certain that he did not want the assignment. He disliked political maneuvering, and was deeply absorbed in his current billet, which was one he had wanted for years. In addition, he admired Carney, and was extremely reluctant to relieve a man whose policies he fully supported.

Thomas, however, was determined that Carney not be reappointed. He felt that the CNO was excluding him from key decisions, including those regarding appointments, and was not giving him full access to information about day-to-day developments within the service. Although the secretary liked Carney personally, he believed that Carney relied too much on old friends who lacked vigor and imagination and were reluctant to promote change. Thomas wanted a CNO who would reorganize the navy and assign greater responsibility to younger officers. He wanted vigorous, inspiring leadership that would revive the navy's sagging morale and restore its vitality and enthusiasm. He wanted a CNO who would promote new technology so that the navy could keep pace with the air force in innovative weapon systems. Finally, he wanted a CNO who would work closely with the navy's secretariat. In short, he was looking for a younger officer with a strong interest in new technology, a gift for leadership, and a willingness to coöperate with the civilian leaders of the navy. Did Burke know any reason, Thomas inquired, why he should not be given the job?

Still in a state of shock, Burke explained that there were a number of things that might stand in his way. First, he was not willing to accept the post if his taking it would discredit Carney or undermine the respect due to other senior naval officers. He believed that younger officers should be given greater responsibility, but that this should not be done in such a way as to disparage the contributions of those who had given a lifetime to the service. In addition, Burke declared, under no circumstances would he retract anything he had said in 1949 in the hearings on unification and strategy and, therefore, would bring with him to the office of chief of naval operations a certain measure of notoriety. Finally, he warned Thomas that the secretary might find him a very difficult man to work with because he had a bad habit of expressing his opinions freely, and sometimes loudly. Thomas assured Burke that he understood his position on all these matters, that he had no intention of discrediting Carney, and that he thought that he and Burke could work together very well.

As soon as he left the secretary's office, Burke, with his "heart in his boots," went to tell Carney what was being proposed. Carney had already learned he would not be reappointed and, although hurt and disappointed by Thomas's lack of confidence, he supported Burke. He admitted that he thought Burke was being given the appointment two years too early, and that he would have preferred a more senior officer such as Vice Admiral Robert P. Briscoe to serve in the interim. But he urged Burke to accept the responsibility that was being thrust upon him, whether he wanted it or not, for the good of the navy.

Riding home with Carney that evening, Burke poured out his misgivings to the older officer. Given the high casualty rate among CNOs, he would probably not last two years in the job. He did not have enough experience in matters of high policy, and was not sure that he could handle the assignment competently. Although the secretary had listened carefully to his reservations about accepting the post, Burke was not at all confident that Thomas fully understood his position. He did not know Thomas, or Wilson, or President Dwight D.

Eisenhower, who had selected him, and was afraid he had been chosen "because they thought I might be a push-over." If that was what they were thinking, Carney said, "they are due for a hell of a surprise."[1]

At the time of his appointment as CNO, Arleigh Burke was a 53-year-old career naval officer, with 32 years of commissioned service. He became chief of naval operations at the height of the cold war, and retired in August 1961. Despite his anxiety about accepting the appointment, it was a job for which he was eminently suited. He was already a naval hero as a result of his exploits in World War II and of his outspoken defense of naval weapons, strategy, and prerogatives in the postwar era. Although he was chosen as CNO with the expectation that he would shake up the service and change its generally conservative orientation, he was himself a conservative in his dedication to the ideals and traditions of the navy. Burke as CNO did advocate and sponsor innovation, particularly in weapons technology and in strategy. But the motivating force behind what he did was not a desire to initiate change and place his own personal mark upon the service, but rather a desire to preserve and improve the organization that he had made his life.

Burke's professional career was varied and somewhat paradoxical. The navy's most famous destroyerman, he began his service in battleships, maintained ties with the conservative "gun club" of the Bureau of Ordnance, and emerged from the war as a leading advocate of guided missiles, nuclear submarines, and attack aircraft carriers. Although he often claimed that any success he achieved was the result of hard work rather than intellectual ability, he nevertheless earned a master's degree in chemical engineering from the University of Michigan and sponsored much of the technological research and strategic planning that carried the postwar navy into the nuclear age. As CNO, he carefully preserved his public image as a plainspoken, hard-driving destroyerman suddenly thrust into the halls of power; but he approached his duties on the basis of broad knowledge and careful analysis of strategy, politics, and the dynamics of leadership. By virtue of his character, his intelligence, his training, and his experience, he was well prepared to take on the responsibilities of guiding the navy through a difficult and dangerous period in the nation's history.

Burke came from tough pioneer stock. August Burke, born Anders Björkgren, emigrated to America from Sweden in 1855 and traveled west as a cavalry cook to become the first baker in the frontier town of Denver, Colorado. His son, Oscar, worked as a cowboy, a hard-rock miner, and a homesteader, before marrying at the age of thirty-six and settling down to raise hay and other fodder not far from the farm his father had bought three miles east of Boulder. Arleigh Albert, the eldest child of Oscar and Clara Mokler Burke, was born on 19 October 1901. Four girls and a second boy followed.

Life on the farm was austere. The five-room house where Burke was born and raised was heated by a wood stove, and had neither indoor plumbing nor electricity. There was endless work to be done, and all the children were expected to do their share. Still, there was always enough food on the table, and time for play with friends on weekends or in the evenings when chores were done. Work was never allowed to keep the children from school, and Clara Burke made sure they had a constant supply of library books to read. Oscar Burke dominated the family. Strong, hard-working, and never satisfied, a taskmaster who offered no excuses and accepted none, he was nevertheless scrupulously just, and let his children know that they were equal and respected partners in the family's undertakings.[2]

Encouraged by his father to pursue his own ambitions, Arleigh decided early that farm life was not for him. He was repelled by the tedium and frustration of scratching a living from the land, and the dirt and smell of cattle. Inspired by the martial trappings of National Guardsmen called out to quell the 1910–1911 coal strikes, by books his teachers gave him, and later by the example of neighbors who enlisted to fight in World War I, he decided to try a military career. Ironically, it was the flu epidemic of 1917 that turned him in the direction of the navy. When the epidemic forced the closing of the Boulder high school during his junior year, Burke was too young for appointment to the Military Academy. He was, however, able to win an alternate appointment to the Naval Academy, which he entered on 26 June 1919.

Accustomed to discipline and hard work, and inspired by the spirit of the service, Arleigh quickly decided that a naval career was precisely what he wanted. He enjoyed competing "in just such an organization in which the rules were strict, known and observed."[3] During his first-class year he selected a commission in the marine corps, following a rousing address by Major General Commandant John A. Lejeune, but after a few months withdrew the request. Midshipman Burke was bright and ambitious, but painfully aware of the deficiencies in his Colorado education. He had managed to gain his appointment and then pass the academy entrance exams only after several months of intensive tutoring. But by applying himself to his studies with typical determination, he was able to compile a respectable academic record, and by graduation stood seventieth in his class of 412.

On 7 June 1923, Burke was commissioned an ensign in the U. S. Navy in the morning, and married Roberta Gorsuch in the academy chapel that afternoon. His bride, whom he met on a blind date during plebe year, was the Kansas-born daughter of a Washington businessman. Standing only five feet tall, but fully a match for her six-foot husband in intelligence and determination, she was to prove a loyal and energetic ally for more than fifty years of married life.

Like 80 per cent of his classmates, Ensign Burke was assigned to a battleship, where he could receive an "intensive education in the practice of [his] profession at sea."[4] As a junior officer in the *Arizona* from June 1923 to April 1928, he acquired a solid background in navigation and steam engineering, and demonstrated technical aptitude in gunnery as a turret officer and as head of the plotting room. Ambitious and eager to make his mark, he was not content with his steady progress, and decided that postgraduate specialization was the key to advancing his career. For a time he considered doing "p.g." work in an exotic field such as lighter-than-air aviation or aerology; but with the encouragement of his superior officers he decided to pursue his interest in gunnery, and to request postgraduate study in ordnance, a prestigious course in which he would be competing with the cream of the officer corps. In January 1929, while serving in the fleet auxiliary *Procyon*, he was accepted into the program.

Lieutenant, j.g., Burke spent fifteen months at the Postgraduate School in Annapolis, and another nine at the University of Michigan, studying chemical engineering, fuels, and explosives. In June 1931 the university awarded him an M.S.E. degree. Promoted to lieutenant, he spent the next year traveling the eastern seaboard visiting military and civilian installations involved in the design, production, and storage of explosives. Ordnance was a conservative specialty, tied to the battleship big gun, but Burke's advanced training did not limit his future career because engineering specialists did not form a separate corps within the interwar navy. More than half of all junior officers during this period received some postgraduate education; all were oriented toward the goal of command of a ship at sea. Burke's postgraduate training not only prepared him for shipboard gunnery duty, but gave him a theoretical groundwork in physics and chemistry which he later used in a variety of assignments.

During the next five years, he served in the heavy cruiser *Chester* as main battery officer; as assistant-officer-in-charge of the Battle Force Camera Party analyzing the results of fleet target practice; and in the Bureau of Ordnance in Washington, D.C., where he worked on the procurement and distribution of ammunition and research and development. In May 1937, he was ordered as prospective executive officer of the new destroyer *Craven*. The assignment was a propitious one. For eleven years, Burke had requested battleship duty, but in 1934 switched his preference to destroyers in order to broaden his experience. During his two years in the *Craven*, he gained an understanding of materiel, administration, logistics, and, most important, a mastery of shiphandling that his concentration on technical specialties had left undeveloped.

On 5 June 1939, Burke reported to his first command, the *Craven*'s sister ship *Mugford*, as one of five officers selected early for command of the new destroyers. The *Mugford* was the flagship of Commander Francis E. M. Whiting, commodore of Destroyer Division 8. "Red" Whiting was an experienced destroyerman, whose rigorous training and incessant drills made a lasting impression on the young skipper. Burke proved equal to the challenges of command, demonstrating himself to be, in Whiting's words, "a leader of the highest type."[5] Under Burke's command, the *Mugford* scored high in engineering and communications competitions, and earned an unprecedented perfect score in short-range battle practice, winning the coveted Destroyer Gunnery Trophy for 1939–1940. Years later Burke wrote to Whiting:

> Although you think I was pulling your leg when I said that the time I was skipper of the Mugford was one of the happiest times of my life, it is still true. It is always good when a man has duty where he knows the job is running

> smoothly and when he knows that he is learning a hell of a lot. I think that I learned some very important lessons under your guidance, the most important one being that when you have got anything to do, the time to do it is right now. If you've got power, use it and use it fast, and the time to make a decision is as soon as the problem presents itself....[6]

From July 1940 to December 1942, Lieutenant Commander Burke worked as inspector of antiaircraft and broadside gun mounts at the Naval Gun Factory in Washington, D.C., making frequent inspection trips to naval ordnance facilities and commercial plants as far west as Chicago. The assignment made full use of the training he had received as an ordnance design and production specialist, but he found the work confining. The day after Pearl Harbor, he requested sea duty in the Pacific Fleet, and renewed his request weekly for over a year, until Rear Admiral Theodore D. Ruddock, the assistant chief of the Bureau of Ordnance, reluctantly approved his transfer.[7]

From February to October 1943, Commander Burke commanded Destroyer Divisions 43 and 44, and Destroyer Squadron 12 in the South Pacific, the latter billet winning him a spot promotion to captain. Soon after seeing his first combat in March, he began to evolve new tactics for the use of a destroyer squadron attached to a surface task force as a spearhead in night engagements. He developed similar tactics for independent squadron actions, taking advantage of American radar superiority and destroyer speed and maneuverability. Because a critical shortage of destroyers in the war zone kept the units under his command scattered on escort duties, however, he had no opportunity to test his theories or use his ships as aggressively as he would have liked.[8]

On 22 October 1943 Burke was ordered to the command of Destroyer Squadron 23. The largest unit of new destroyers arriving in the Solomon Islands, DesRon 23 was assigned to Rear Admiral A. S. Merrill's Task Force 39. Made up of new *Fletcher*-class destroyers and commanded by skilled regular line officers, the squadron was nonetheless untested, having never operated as a unit before Burke took command. With the invasion of Bougainville only a week away, Captain Burke worked fast to organize his men into a fighting team. He began by giving the squadron a nickname—the "Little Beavers"—and by issuing a terse statement of doctrine.[9]

On the night of 1–2 November, DesRon 23 supported Admiral Merrill's cruisers in the battle of Empress Augusta Bay, repulsing a strong enemy force that was attacking the American beachhead. Twenty-four days later, in what a president of the Naval War College later called "an almost perfect action," Burke's five ships engaged an enemy force of equal strength off Cape St. George, New Ireland, sinking three Japanese destroyers without taking a single hit.[10] In these two actions Burke, by this time known as "31-Knot Burke" because he drove his destroyers as fast as possible while still reserving fuel for combat, was at last able to prove his concepts for destroyer operations. He served as commander of DesRon 23 until March 1944, during which time the squadron participated in twenty-two engagements and was awarded the Presidential Unit Citation, while Burke himself won the Distinguished Service Medal, the Navy Cross, and the Legion of Merit.

On 27 March 1944, Burke was ordered to report as chief of staff to Rear Admiral Marc A. Mitscher, the commander of Fast Carrier Task Force 58—the result of a directive from the chief of naval operations, Admiral Ernest J. King, that aviator commanders select nonaviators as their chiefs of staff. For Burke, the switch from destroyers to carriers was both unexpected and, at first, unwelcome. Although determined to serve effectively in his new assignment, he did not lose his interest in destroyer operations. He wanted a billet "where the bullets are a little thicker and the paperwork is a lot thinner."[11]

In the beginning, Burke's relationship with Mitscher was quite stormy. However, the two strong-minded officers gradually developed a deep respect and affection for each other. Burke served with Mitscher through July 1945, and participated in the planning and execution of all the operations undertaken by the First Fast Carrier Task Force (alternately Task Force 58 and Task Force 38), including the Battle of the Philippine Sea, the Battle for Leyte Gulf, and the invasions of Iwo Jima and Okinawa. In August 1944 Mitscher recommended his chief of staff for accelerated promotion to rear admiral, citing his leadership, his combat experience, and his mastery of carrier operations and naval warfare. Burke argued that such a promotion would not enhance his effectiveness as a commander, and thus would not be justified. As a compromise, in October 1944, he accepted a temporary promotion to commodore. However, Mitscher made the recommendation again in June 1945.[12]

Burke's service in World War II prepared him for high command better than any war college could have done. He took part in tactical and strategic planning, commanded groups of ships in combat, and, as Mitscher's chief of staff, maneuvered the largest naval force in history in some of its most crucial actions. Although a surface line officer, his service with Mitscher qualified him as a member of the increasingly powerful naval aviation community. In view of his wartime performance and the fact that Mitscher considered him "the most outstanding tactician and the most experienced officer in the American fleet today," Burke was clearly marked for high command.[13]

Burke himself, however, had no great expectations regarding his future. Before World War II he was frankly ambitious, but by 1945 he had begun to see his naval career as coming to a close. Painfully aware of the roles that circumstance and luck had played in his achievements, and tired from the strains and frustrations of combat, he expected to retire as a "tombstone" rear admiral soon after the war ended. He may even have been looking forward to such a future. As he wrote on the twenty-fifth anniversary of his graduation from Annapolis:

> I like this Navy, but I hope I can tell when I am no longer pulling my weight in the boat. At that time, when either I or the Navy believe I can't contribute anything more, I hope to be able to retire in some nice, peaceful, warm climate; but not on a farm. I had all the farming I wanted when I was a kid.[14]

Shortly after the Japanese surrender, Burke returned to the Bureau of Ordnance for three months as director of research. In this post he became familiar with the navy's early guided-missile programs, and gained access to the closely guarded secrets of the atomic bomb. In November 1945 he was recalled by Admiral Mitscher, and ordered to form a staff for the new Eighth Fleet, to be ready for operations in the Mediterranean by June 1946. Up until this time, Burke's experience in international relations was limited to a Naval War College correspondence course in strategy and tactics, which he took in 1928, and spare-time reading. Now he was expected not only to help organize the navy's first postwar striking fleet, but to study the international environment in which it would be operating. In the summer of 1946, he accompanied Mitscher, Vice Admiral Forrest P. Sherman, and Captain George Anderson on a fact-finding trip to Europe, which included prolonged stopovers in London, Berlin, Paris, Rome, and Naples. This three-week tour allowed Burke to get a firsthand look at strategic and political problems in Europe and greatly increased his awareness of the primary theater of the postwar world. In mid-September, Mitscher was appointed commander in chief of the Atlantic Fleet, and Burke once again accompanied him as his chief of staff.[15]

In January 1947, one month before Mitscher's death, Burke wrote a memorandum on the deteriorating morale among naval officers as a result of the growing prominence of the army air force in public and congressional perceptions of national defense, and the corresponding decline in the navy's prospects. He emphasized the dangers inherent in the proposed merger of all the services into a single, highly centralized department of defense, with consequent loss of the navy's control over naval aviation.[16] His memorandum caught the attention of Secretary of the Navy James V. Forrestal, who forwarded it to President Harry S. Truman's naval aide with the recommendation that it be shown to Clark Clifford, then handling unification matters for Truman. Forrestal also recommended that Burke be introduced to the president, since he appeared to be "one of the younger officers who have all the potential qualifications for CNO."[17]

The secretary even expressed an interest in having Burke serve as his aide, but decided instead to support his appointment to the General Board. The board, whose function was to advise the secretary of the navy on matters of high policy, had lost some of the considerable prestige and influence it enjoyed before the war, and Burke was one of a number of bright, younger officers assigned to it at this time in order to revitalize it. While serving there for the next fifteen months, he participated in such projects as an analysis of future shipbuilding programs, a study of the navy's shore establishment, and a projection of force requirements in connection with the first long-range war plan of the Joint Chiefs of Staff.[18]

By far his most important contribution, however, was a project he personally originated in January 1948: an in-depth analysis of the navy's potential contribution to national defense over the next ten years. At this time the president, the National Security Council, and the State Department had not yet developed guidelines for national-security policy. Given this lack of overall direction amidst unification and growing interservice disputes, Burke believed that the navy was drifting dangerously. His study covered political, economic, and military factors at home and abroad, and projected the effect that these would have on the navy's role in national defense. The final report was pessimistic. Because of declining defense budgets and the increasing threat of war with the Soviet Union, Burke foresaw that so many charges might be placed upon the navy for operations in all parts of the world "that fulfillment of all demands may well be beyond the capacity of the Navy in being."[19]

Although some of its prognostications were wide of the mark, this study was by far the most influential and realistic analysis of its kind undertaken by the navy in the early postwar period. In particular, it appears to have been a major factor in turning naval thinking away from politically attractive but strategically and operationally extravagant plans to use carrier task forces as bases for strategic nuclear attacks against Soviet urban-industrial targets. In contrast with earlier planning, it stressed that the Soviet submarine force was the most significant enemy of the U. S. Navy, and identified destruction of Soviet submarine bases as the prime objective of the carrier task forces.

Despite his success as a planner, Burke was eager to return to sea, and in July 1948 he jumped at the chance to serve as commanding officer of the light cruiser *Huntington*. The assignment came just in time to spare him from another desk job: James Forrestal, now secretary of defense, was on the point of making Burke his adviser on the allocation of funds under the tight ceiling Truman had imposed on the fiscal year 1950 defense budget.[20] Burke's sea tour, however, was extremely brief—less than six months. In December, he was detached and ordered immediately to Washington to head the newly established Organizational Research and Policy Division of the Office of the Chief of Naval Operations (Op-23).

Op-23's mission was to advise the CNO on "organization policy problems arising under the National Security Act of 1947 and other similar legislation proposed or enacted."[21] Through June 1949, Burke prepared the navy's position papers on the amendments to the National Security Act, which would transform the National Military Establishment into the Department of Defense. After the amendments became law, the office turned its attention to broader questions. In April, Defense Secretary Louis Johnson's cancellation of the aircraft carrier *United States*, then building, highlighted fears that had been growing in the navy as a result of increasing centralization in the defense establishment, the tight fiscal year 1950 defense budget, and the resulting over-reliance on the air force's atomic air offensive against the USSR as the central component of American war planning.

The navy's anxiety over its declining role in defense planning and opposition to the direction of American strategy surfaced in June when an overzealous civilian employee of the navy circulated an anonymous document that charged illegal conduct in the air force's procurement of its B-36 bomber. The resulting furor led the chairman of the House Armed Services Committee, Carl Vinson, to schedule hearings to investigate the charges and to allow the navy to present its concerns about the direction of defense policy. Burke's Op-23 was assigned to support a high-level task force that would prepare the navy's testimony.[22] The first set of hearings, the B-36 investigation of August 1949, resulted in a vindication of the air force's procurement procedures and a serious loss of the navy's credibility. Burke spent most of September working directly with Admiral Radford, commander in chief of the Pacific Fleet, who was in Washington to orchestrate the navy's presentation during the second round: the unification and strategy hearings in October. These hearings, at which Burke testified, were consumed with acrimony because the navy disagreed so strongly with Truman's national-defense policies.[23]

In the ensuing controversy, columnist Drew Pearson charged that, in violation of naval policy, Burke was running an anti-air force "rumor mill." In early October Secretary of the Navy Francis P. Matthews ordered the files of Op-23 impounded by the inspector general of the navy, and Burke's entire section was held incommunicado while those papers were examined. Although no improprieties were discovered, the office was disbanded by the newly appointed chief of naval operations, Admiral Forrest P. Sherman. The next month, the selection board for rear admiral voted unanimously to promote Burke to flag rank. All of his fitness reports since 1945, echoing Mitscher, had recommended him for accelerated promotion. Although the 1946 selection board had considered such action "a little premature," by 1949 the class of 1923 had reached the promotion zone.[24] Matthews, however, angered by Burke's part in the unification and strategy hearings, removed his name from the list, apparently with Johnson's concurrence. While Burke was reconciled to possible retirement, word of Matthews's decision provoked furious opposition in the press. Burke had many supporters in the navy, including Sherman and classmate Robert L. Dennison, the president's naval aide, who advised Truman that a serious injustice had been done. On 29 December, the president met with Matthews, Sherman, and Johnson, and that evening released a revised selection list, which included Burke's name.[25]

Burke's experience in Op-23 was significant in a number of ways. On a personal level, it reinforced his feeling that his time in the navy was coming to an end and that it would be pointless to depend on the prospect of future promotions. Professionally, it provided a crash course in the politics of national defense, and convinced him that the navy had a continuing need for politically adept and knowledgeable officers at the highest levels of the service. As CNO, Burke made sure that such men were available to provide advice and to state the navy's case to Congress and the nation.[26]

Following the controversy in Op-23, Burke was assigned to the prestigious post of navy secretary on the Defense Research and Development Board, where he was brought up to date on the latest advances in guided missiles, nuclear weapons, and various propulsion systems. Shortly after the outbreak of the Korean War, he became deputy chief of staff to Commander, Naval Forces, Far East, as Sherman's personal troubleshooter in the area. His most significant accomplishment in this post was helping to initiate the rebuilding of Japan's maritime strength. While negotiating with the Japanese Maritime Safety Agency for the services of its minesweepers to assist in clearing the North Korean harbor of Wonsan, Burke became convinced that a nation of Japan's stature needed a navy for defensive purposes. Subsequently, he served as a liaison between former Japanese naval officers and Sherman's staff in planning the new navy. Largely as a result of this experience, Burke became deeply committed to assisting American allies, particularly in the Far East, in building or rebuilding their naval forces, a commitment which he implemented as CNO.[27]

In May 1951 Sherman assigned Burke to the command of Cruiser Division 5 off the coast of Korea so that he could enjoy a choice sea command before returning to duty in Washington. Two months later, however, Burke joined the United Nations delegation to the truce talks in Korea. He worked on drawing up an agenda for negotiations, and then was one of two U.N. delegates on a subcommittee charged with defining the military demarcation line and demilitarized zone as a condition for the cessation of hostilities. Frustrated by procedural delays, propaganda, and the unwillingness of the Chinese and North Korean delegates to change their position while bloody battles were waged for territory under discussion, Burke felt trapped "in a conference which seems to have no ending."[28]

In November 1951, the Joint Chiefs of Staff and the National Security Council ordered the U.N. command to accept the communist position on the line of demarcation in the interest of reaching an early agreement. Burke felt that his usefulness in the negotiations had ended since he had "walked back the cat."[29] He departed for Washington in early December, convinced that

> the only thing the Communists pay any attention to is power. I believe that Americans have a great deal to learn, including those in the military services, in regard to this business. We now have the power. We still have to learn the next two steps, which are (1) how to use the power and (2) how to capitalize on the power. We've had power before but we don't know how to capitalize on it. We just let ourselves be talked out of the advantages we could have had. It looks like the old world is going to be in a really tough turmoil until we destroy the power of communism.[30]

Upon his return to Washington, Burke conveyed his frustration to President Truman and then reported as director of the Strategic Plans Division (Op-30) in the Office of the Chief of Naval Operations.[31] He took on this demanding post at a time when the nation's defenses were undergoing rapid change as a result of the rearmament program begun in 1950. He had to consider not only internal naval plans and programs, but how they related to the overall defense program and national policies being developed by the National Security Council and the Joint Chiefs of Staff. Because of his recent experience in Japan and Korea, he gave as much attention as possible to the Pacific region during his two years at Op-30, at a time when most American defense planners were focusing on building up U.S. forces in Europe.[32] Burke also assisted the CNO, Admiral Robert B. Carney, in preparing the navy's critique of defense policies being developed by the Eisenhower administration in its so-called new look at American military strategy.[33]

Carney believed that the younger officer "had to be considered a strong candidate" for high command, and that "it would be very advisable to send Burke to sea and get him dressed and ready for when the time came." In April 1954, he assigned Rear Admiral Burke to the Sixth Fleet in the Mediterranean for nine months as commander of Cruiser Division 6. Then in January 1955, Burke returned to his beloved destroyers as Commander, Destroyer Force, Atlantic Fleet. Carney expected that, following this service, Burke would be named to command of one of the navy's four numbered fleets as a vice admiral, and would thereby be fully prepared for a four-star command.[34]

Navy Secretary Charles Thomas, however, had other plans and Burke did not complete the apprenticeship Carney had mapped out for him. Once Burke had decided, with Carney's support, that he could not reasonably refuse to serve as chief of naval operations, events moved quickly. His meeting with Thomas on 10 May 1955 was followed by two days of discussion with the navy's high command, including Thomas, Undersecretary of the Navy Thomas Gates, and Secretary of Defense Charles Wilson. A meeting with President Eisenhower on 17 May completed the selection process.[35]

Burke's appointment was announced on 25 May. During the three months before he took office he was briefed extensively on the state of national security, and traveled both to the Pacific and Europe to discuss conditions with American commanders and foreign leaders. It was during his trip to the Pacific in June and July that he laid out his working philosophy for his two years as chief of naval operations. He knew that he could not afford to move slowly in designing and implementing his policies. Since he did not expect to be reappointed, and could not count on his successor to carry out projects left uncompleted, he figured he had about eighteen months to put forward policy initiatives. Burke was aware that his new power was strictly limited. He could not simply order those under his command to carry out his wishes; he would have to convince them that the policies he wanted implemented were worthy of their best effort. In some cases he would have to override his staff and make unpopular decisions, but such occurrences would have to be kept to a minimum if he was to be effective. He also knew that his accelerated promotion would be a special handicap. Nearly all of the officers he would have to rely on to carry out his policies would have been senior to him before the day he took office. He knew that he must give special attention to winning the confidence and support of these men.[36]

Burke relieved Carney as chief of naval operations at the Naval Academy on 17 August 1955. It was a time of relative quiet on the international scene.

The Indochina crisis in the fall of 1954 and the Taiwan Strait crisis in the spring of 1955 had ended. The problems he confronted were, therefore, not operational in nature, but were related to planning for and maintaining the navy in the long pull ahead.

Burke made it clear to Thomas from the first that he would not purge the high command of the navy, and in fact fired no one after taking office. He even kept on Carney's entire immediate staff, replacing them with his own people only when they were due to be relieved. He was careful to seek the opinions of his top officers, particularly Atlantic commander Jerauld Wright and Pacific commander Felix B. Stump, on appointments and other matters of importance, in order to lay the groundwork for a smoothly operating administration.[37] In addition, he personally wrote a monthly newsletter and had it distributed to all flag officers to explain what was happening in Washington and what he was trying to accomplish. By such methods, he soon succeeded in winning the respect of the navy's officer corps and consolidating his leadership.[38]

Burke's position among the Joint Chiefs of Staff was complicated by the presence of Radford as chairman. Burke worked closely with Radford during the unification and strategy hearings in 1949, and they remained in frequent touch. Radford's role in Burke's selection as CNO is not clear, but the two were known to be friends and were expected to work closely together. A problem arose, however, because Radford believed that he knew the needs of the navy as well as anyone and was inclined to speak for the service without consulting Burke. Although he succeeded in maintaining cordial relations with Radford, Burke was forced to insist repeatedly on his right and responsibility to be the navy's sole representative among the Joint Chiefs.[39]

One of the major policy decisions of Burke's first term was made during his first few days in office. Briefings during the summer of 1955 had convinced him that declining enlistments and retention rates had reached a critical level. Unless the draft for the navy were reinstated, the service would be unable to meet its manpower goals. When he explained this to Thomas, however, he was told that Eisenhower had only recently decided against this proposal and that the matter could not be reopened. Undaunted, Burke appealed to Wilson, and, when Wilson confirmed what Thomas had told him, he decided to take his case to the president. The idea of asking Eisenhower to reverse himself on a stand he had so recently taken caused Burke considerable anxiety, especially since he had been CNO for only three days and was hardly a seasoned policy-maker. Unwilling to back down from a position he believed in, however, he proceeded with his appeal, and was gratified when Eisenhower accepted his arguments and agreed to include the navy in the draft. Burke's persistence created a certain coolness between him and his superiors for a time, and the president expressly warned him never again to put his commander in chief in such an embarrassing position. Despite issuing this warning, which Burke took to heart, Eisenhower was impressed with Burke's frankness and forthrightness, and the two developed a good working relationship based on respect for one another.[40]

The navy of which Burke took command was moderately well prepared for war. Although overseas deployments in the Pacific resulted in a relative under-emphasis on the European theater—which, according to American war plans, was to be the major area of operations if war came—the navy-in-being was in general adequate for the tasks it was assigned. Fifteen attack aircraft carriers were in commission: six in the Atlantic, with two always forward deployed to the Sixth Fleet in the Mediterranean; and nine in the Pacific, with two or three always assigned to the Seventh Fleet in the Far East. The strength of this force increased in October 1955 with the commissioning of the *Forrestal.* A second supercarrier, the *Saratoga*, joined the fleet six months later, by which time three others were under construction or authorized. Nine ASW support carriers, 3 battleships, 17 cruisers, 249 destroyers, and 109 submarines were also in the active fleet. All the attack carriers carried atomic weapons, and four attack carriers, four cruisers, and one submarine could fire the Regulus-I surface-to-surface cruise missile. Within a year the navy's nuclear-strike capability had expanded, in line with the Eisenhower administration's policy of emphasizing the deployment of nuclear weapons. The first Douglas A3D Skywarrior heavy attack aircraft were delivered to fleet squadrons in March 1956, and A4D Skyhawk nuclear-capable light attack aircraft came into service the following September.[41]

In terms of materiel, the navy's most serious deficiencies when Burke took office were ships equipped with surface-to-air guided missiles to meet the Soviet air threat and forces to counter the growing Soviet submarine threat. From 1949 until at least the spring of 1955, air defense was recognized as the single most serious problem confronting the navy. In response, a concerted effort was mounted to build or convert cruisers and destroyers capable of launching Terrier, Talos, or Tartar missiles. Although some progress had been made in this direction—the Terrier-armed converted cruiser *Boston* was to be recommissioned in November 1955 and her sister ship *Canberra* the following June—the effort was far from complete. Through the end of 1957, orders were placed for nine more missile-cruiser conversions, ten new-construction missile frigates, and eight new-construction missile destroyers.[42]

Antisubmarine warfare had been defined as the navy's top priority from 1946 through 1949, but in 1950 it was decided that increased research and development and an adequate destroyer and escort building program would enable the navy to counter any foreseeable Soviet advances in submarines, including those based on German technology captured at the end of World War II. By 1955, however, the problem had become one of quantity as well as quality. The Soviet Union was in the midst of a massive submarine-building program, and, according to estimates of the Central Intelligence Agency, might be producing nearly one hundred submarines a year. Although none of these submarines was nuclear-powered and this rate of construction was not maintained, it was estimated that by 1956 the Soviet submarine fleet would pose considerable danger to American and allied wartime lines of communications. On the basis of such projections, in the fall of 1955 Burke reassigned antisubmarine warfare as his top priority. He encouraged investigation into new solutions for submarine detection, such as the Sound Surveillance System (SOSUS) then being placed in operation, and supported the development of new antisubmarine technology and tactics.[43]

Burke also moved to upgrade the United States's own submarine fleet. Following conclusions derived from conferences with Rear Admiral Hyman G. Rickover and other representatives of the Bureau of Ships, the interim recommendations of an ad hoc committee on shipbuilding, as well as his own studies, he announced in September 1955 that two more nuclear submarines would be included in the fiscal 1956 program and that thereafter all new submarines would be nuclear-powered. The nation's first nuclear submarine, the *Nautilus*, had been in commission since September 1954 and "underway on nuclear power" since January 1955. Building on that experience, Burke backed the construction of a sizable nuclear-submarine force, and directed that the use of nuclear power in frigates, cruisers, and attack aircraft carriers be studied.[44]

Burke's most significant initiative during his first term was his sponsorship, in the face of considerable opposition, of a high-priority program to develop a naval intermediate-range ballistic missile (IRBM). In February 1955, Eisenhower's Technological Capabilities Panel had reported to the National Security Council that by the late 1950s the United States might be extremely vulnerable to a Soviet multimegaton thermonuclear attack if present trends continued. The panel, headed by Dr. James R. Killian, Jr., president of the Massachusetts Institute of Technology, recommended that a concerted effort be made to strengthen U. S. continental defenses and stressed the importance of effective delivery systems. It urged that the air force's intercontinental-ballistic-missile (ICBM) program be given highest priority, and that a 1,500-nautical-mile IRBM be developed, with both land- and sea-basing options being considered. The Killian committee's recommendations were endorsed by the National Security Council in September 1955.[45]

Although the navy had sponsored research on the technical feasibility of a sea-based IRBM system, development of such a missile was not being seriously considered at this time: the liquid propellants then available were extremely difficult to use on shipboard, and a reliable solid propellant was estimated to be from one to three years in the future. The navy was already developing the Regulus-I subsonic cruise missile, the Regulus-II supersonic cruise missile, and the Triton ram-jet cruise missile. All three were designed for use against targets of naval interest—naval airfields, bases, and shipyards—rather than urban-industrial or counterforce targets within the Soviet Union. In October 1955, the director of guided missiles, the deputy CNO (Air), and the deputy CNO (Fleet Operations and Readiness), among others, formally endorsed the position that the navy should not give high priority to the IRBM. They argued that the three missiles then under development might be jeopardized if the navy committed itself to an additional costly missile program, and that it might be possible to satisfy the National Security Council by redefining the task of the cruise missiles to include targets of national as well as fleet interest. They pointed out that until serious technical difficulties had been overcome a sea-based IRBM system would not be practical, and suggested that the navy could leave preliminary design work to the other services and join the IRBM program once these difficulties had been overcome.[46]

Burke was unwilling to accept this advice. Not only was he certain on the basis of his own expertise that the technical difficulties could be solved, but also he was more concerned than many others with the political and strategic implications of the project. Since the late 1940s, he had been disturbed that the United States was "placing all its eggs in one basket" by relying on the land-based Strategic Air Command to provide a deterrent force. He was attracted to ballistic missiles because they would be difficult to intercept, and he believed that sea-based IRBMs could be a nearly invulnerable deterrent to war. Moreover, he was convinced that without naval participation from the outset, an IRBM that was unsuited for shipboard use would be developed and would never be successfully modified. Thus, the navy would be cut out of future funding if it did not assist in initiating the project.[47]

On 10 and 11 July 1955, while preparing to take over as CNO, Burke had visited the Heavy Electronics Division of the General Electric Company in Syracuse, New York, where he received an extensive briefing on current work on guidance for the air force's ICBM. The engineers who gave the briefing believed that their systems could be adapted to a sea-based "fleet ballistic missile task force" if the navy were interested in sponsoring such research. Within days of taking office, Burke rescinded the internal restrictions Carney had placed on the advocacy of an IRBM by the Bureau of Aeronautics, and urged the bureau to move rapidly to sell it to the navy. Fearing that the project would be given low priority if assigned to regular channels, he also began a search for a "brilliant, aggressive, hard working young flag officer" to direct a special development effort. On 19 October, rejecting the recommendations forwarded to him, he stated that without abandoning current missile development, the navy should proceed as rapidly as possible to achieve a sea-based IRBM. Secretary Thomas strongly supported Burke's decision.[48]

In early November, Burke and the army's chief of staff, General Maxwell D. Taylor, agreed that their services should collaborate on the development of the IRBM, and on the eighth Wilson ordered implementation of the plan. Code-named Jupiter, the development of an IRBM was administered by a Joint Army-Navy Ballistic Missile Committee, of which Thomas was chairman. It was assigned top priority by the two services, the Department of Defense, and subsequently, the president. On 17 November, Thomas, following Burke's recommendation, appointed Rear Admiral William F. Raborn to head a Special Projects Office that would oversee the navy's part in developing an IRBM and would report to the secretary through the Bureau of Ordnance. Pledging his vigorous support, Burke authorized Raborn to pick his own staff of forty officers. However, he also warned Raborn that unless a series of tight deadlines were met, the project probably would not survive.[49]

The first objective of the naval IRBM program was to develop a liquid-fueled ballistic missile suitable for use on a merchant-type hull. Its long-term goal was a solid-propellant missile for both surface and submarine use. The year following the creation of the Special Projects Office saw considerable progress made in both solid-fuel technology and the development of a 600-pound nuclear warhead suitable for a submarine-launched system. In November 1956, Thomas requested authority to withdraw the navy from the Jupiter project and to proceed directly with development of a small, solid-propellant missile designed exclusively for naval use. In early December, the Joint Army-Navy Ballistic Missile Committee was dissolved, a Navy Ballistic Missile Committee was established, and Special Projects was made responsible for all aspects of the naval version of the IRBM, the fleet ballistic missile (FBM) program, now code-named Polaris. Simultaneously, the Naval Warfare Analysis Group analyzed the FBM's mission and concluded that it was primarily a weapon of deterrence and could best be launched from a nuclear-powered submarine. This analysis paralleled conclusions Burke had reached earlier. In January 1957, he decided that the navy would aim to have ready by 1965 a solid-fueled, 1,500-nautical-mile Polaris ballistic missile capable of being fired from a submerged submarine.[50]

Burke's decision to develop the FBM on a priority basis was probably the single most significant action of his six years as chief of naval operations. It reflected both his commitment to enhancing the capabilities of the navy and his desire to integrate the service into the broader context of national defense. It was a risky decision, since Polaris would require a substantial allocation of the navy's limited resources and might ultimately prove unworkable. But, based on his technical experience, his confidence in the navy's ability to meet new challenges, and his deep concern about the current direction of American strategy, Burke was willing to gamble.

His shrewd approach to questions of national strategy made him a valuable member of the Joint Chiefs of Staff. Eisenhower warned him at their first meeting that his work on the JCS would have to take precedence over his responsibility for running the navy. In fact, Burke found that work with the Joint Chiefs regularly absorbed about one-third of his time. In addition to addressing current foreign policy, research and development, and organizational questions, the Joint Chiefs were responsible for the annual preparation of three interlocking plans: the Joint Long-Range Strategic Estimate, which provided a broad appraisal of long-term defense trends and options; the Joint Strategic Capabilities Plan, which provided war-planning guidance for the immediate future; and the Joint Strategic Objectives Plan, which dealt with the middle ground between the estimate and the plan. The Joint Strategic Objectives Plan was the most important of the three. It translated the National Security Council's annual statement of basic national security policy into military objectives and defined what forces would be "reasonably obtainable" to achieve them in a cold war, a limited war, and a general war, over a four-to-six-year period. It served as the framework for the Joint Chiefs' budget requests, and generally determined the mix of forces each service would have under the ceiling on defense spending established by the president and the secretary of defense.[51]

The basic national security policy that was in effect when Burke took office was first developed by President Eisenhower and Secretary of State John Foster Dulles in the fall of 1953. This was the strategy of "massive retaliation," which has been considered by historians to have been an inflexible strategy designed to take maximum advantage of American superiority in nuclear weapons. Massive retaliation did stress nuclear weapons: the United States was to maintain a nuclear retaliatory capability great enough to deter a general war or prevail in one. But the strategy also called for the maintenance of ready forces to deter or contain local communist aggression without recourse to a full-scale nuclear exchange. The language of the basic national security policy was general and ambiguous; it never specified a mix and balance of conventional and nuclear forces.[52] The policy of massive retaliation was motivated by the administration's desire to control defense spending in order to prevent serious damage to the American economy through inflation and the undermining of incentives. As implemented by Eisenhower, Wilson, and Radford, this required cutting back spending on manpower and conventional forces while maximizing American capabilities through the exploitation of advanced technology, particularly nuclear weapons. Consequently, the administration's defense budgets, beginning with fiscal year 1955, gave priority to the air force, which consistently received approximately 47 per cent of the defense budget, compared with 29 per cent for the navy and only 22 per cent for the army.

General Taylor was disturbed at how the ambiguous language of the basic national security policy was being interpreted so as to assign the army the smallest share of defense funds. In the spring of 1956, he expressed this concern in the Joint Chiefs' debates over the Joint Strategic Objectives Plan. He specifically questioned the concept that nuclear weapons should be used in local conflicts, and argued against channeling resources into strategic nuclear forces at the expense of conventional forces that could respond more effectively to limited wars. His position was strongly opposed by the air force, which held that any future war would be both general and nuclear, and by Eisenhower and Radford, who felt that use of nuclear weapons must be considered in any conflict, particularly if it involved a confrontation between Soviet and American troops.[53]

Burke was an early critic of massive retaliation. In December 1953, as director of Op-30, he prepared the navy's first full critique of that policy for Carney. In that report, Burke argued that the administration's policy of reliance on strategic nuclear forces should not be strictly interpreted, and that adequate ground and naval striking forces must be retained. He also warned that growing Soviet nuclear capabilities would eventually lead to an atomic stalemate and, when that point was reached, U.S. strategic nuclear forces would not be effective deterrents to local aggression.[54] Two years later, Taylor echoed his arguments.

In the Joint Chiefs' debates in 1956, however, Burke remained largely in the background. His reluctance to support Taylor's dissenting views is explicable on both political and philosophical grounds. He was a friend and supporter of Radford, who had helped design the administration policy, and he was the least experienced member of the Joint Chiefs of Staff. Thus, he was reluctant to split with the administration so early in his tenure as chief of naval operations. More importantly, he did not feel that revision of the basic national security policy would substantially improve the position of the navy. He knew that debates over statements of policy were likely to be inconclusive, and that, unlike Taylor, he could justify the forces his service needed within the context of the current policy. For example, although carrier striking forces were not designed primarily for nuclear war, they were nuclear-capable and thus came within the administration's funding priorities. In addition, Burke personally agreed with the administration's position that nuclear weapons should be available for use in limited conflicts whenever appropriate. Although he believed that the air force's strategic nuclear forces were too big and too vulnerable, he could offer no concrete alternative to the Strategic Air Command's bombers. The FBM program might eventually provide such an alternative, but not for some years.[55]

In May 1956, the Joint Chiefs of Staff promulgated their interpretation of the basic national security policy for war-planning purposes. This document stressed the importance of maintaining conventional forces, but, in contrast with Taylor's position, reaffirmed reliance on nuclear weapons in both general and limited wars. It also incorporated one of the arguments Burke had presented orally during the debates. He took issue with the air force's position that a general nuclear exchange would be decisive, and argued that such an exchange would probably be followed by a protracted period of struggle during which the opposing forces would try to win some semblance of victory. The military chiefs endorsed this concept and called for the United States to prepare to gain and maintain control of sea lines of communication and territory under dispute during that phase of any conflict.[56]

The debates over the Joint Strategic Objectives Plan in 1956 gave Burke his first experience as CNO in tackling national-security strategy. After this initiation and as his own thinking matured, he began to act with greater independence in defining his position on questions of national strategy. His first public statement at odds with administration policy came in June 1956 during the hearings on air power which had been convened by Senator W. Stuart Symington to investigate the possibility that a "bomber gap" had opened between the

United States and the Soviet Union. In the course of these hearings, Burke testified that the navy's aircraft carriers were not competing with the air force's bombers for either targets or funds, but that the navy sought to balance the air force's contribution by preparing "to deal with isolated danger spots during periods of cold war as well as limited or global war."[57] Then, in November 1956, he was advised by Secretary Thomas that Defense Secretary Wilson was planning to request $11 billion for the navy for fiscal 1958, much less than the navy anticipated. Burke responded quickly with a long memo to Wilson in which he not only argued that the proposed budget was too low, but laid out the navy's view of the demands of national security in the nuclear age.

All-out nuclear war, Burke maintained, was unlikely, since both sides now recognized that such a conflict would be tantamount to suicide. Although maintenance of a strong nuclear force was clearly necessary as a deterrent, he pointed out that the current level of that force was adequate "to destroy the USSR several times over, even accepting great attrition and large numbers of aborts for our delivery forces." Increasing the number of long-range bombers would neither increase the nation's deterrent power nor improve its chances of surviving a nuclear holocaust. This overemphasis on weapon systems suitable only for all-out nuclear war was draining funds away from aspects of the defense program that might prove more useful in achieving American aims. During the preceding decade, Burke noted, the United States had handled a series of local conflicts without recourse to nuclear weapons. Although such weapons might be used in the future to settle a local incident with the greatest possible speed, care would undoubtedly be taken to avoid a general nuclear exchange. Since such local conflicts were certain to recur, it was imperative that the United States be prepared to handle them quickly and efficiently.[58] During the next several years, Burke refined and expanded these concepts into a sophisticated philosophy of limited war.

His memo of November 1956 represented a major step in Burke's emergence as an advocate for change in official thinking about national power and defense policy. Although his analysis paralleled that of a number of academic strategists outside of government, he based his concepts less on abstractions than on the day-to-day problems of running the navy. He believed that the budget proposed for fiscal year 1958 would restrict the navy in almost every area of programming, slowing the installation of missiles to replace antiaircraft guns, causing large cuts in aircraft procurement, crippling research and development, and forcing reductions in shipbuilding which could mean that by 1965 the navy would have one-third less ships than it then had. Fear that the navy might be cut back to the point where it could no longer operate effectively forced Burke to articulate and justify the role he envisioned for the navy more fully than he had during the Joint Chiefs' debates on the basic national security policy.

One of the examples Burke used in his memo to Secretary Wilson to illustrate the dangers of reduced naval power was the British experience with the Suez Canal. Hampered by a defense posture based primarily on strategic nuclear deterrence, poor planning, and inadequate equipment, the Royal Navy was unable to act swiftly during the months following Egyptian President Gamal Abdel Nasser's nationalization of the Suez Canal on 26 July 1956. Burke warned that the United States might find itself similarly constrained in the execution of its foreign policy if adequate naval forces were not maintained.

As a member of the Joint Chiefs of Staff and commander of the navy's operating forces, Burke advised both President Eisenhower and Secretary of State John Foster Dulles on technical matters pertaining to the canal and the potential of American naval forces in the Eastern Mediterranean during the Suez crisis. He was convinced that "Nasser has to be shown that international thievery is unprofitable, that violation of international commitments is dishonorable and therefore cannot be looked on with approbation."[59] He urged that the United States support the British and French in actions against Egypt, even recommending that the navy loan some of its landing craft to the British for the planned amphibious landing at Suez in early November. Dulles, on the other hand, believed that the United States should do everything in its power to quell the crisis, and suggested that the navy might intervene to block the British and French invasion force, a course of action Burke strongly opposed.[60]

The situation in Suez was further complicated by the simultaneous emergence of a number of other conflicts, including political turmoil in Hungary and Poland, and the Israeli invasion of Egypt, as well as by a Soviet threat to intervene with "volunteers" on the side of Nasser. Unable to project what might occur in the Suez area in the midst of this confusion, Burke moved the combat-ready Sixth Fleet into the Eastern Mediterranean without fanfare or explanation. On 30 October he signaled the fleet commander, Vice Admiral Charles R. Brown, "Situation tense; prepare for imminent hostilities," to which Brown signaled back: "Am prepared for imminent hostilities; but which side are we on?" Burke's reply was classic: "If U. S. citizens are in danger, protect them: take no guff from anyone."[61] He also alerted the Atlantic Fleet to watch for Soviet submarine deployments through the Greenland-Iceland-United Kingdom gap, sent a carrier task force into the eastern Atlantic, and ordered an amphibious task group into the Indian Ocean.

Although the crisis was resolved without major clashes between the United States and the British and French, the lesson of Suez was clear to Burke: "as usual, only naval forces could take the military action that was required when the situation broke."[62]

The eleven months following the Suez crisis were relatively free of major international crises or domestic controversies about the military, aside from the ongoing battles over plans and budgets. Burke continued to argue the case he had made in his memo to Wilson in November 1956, that over-reliance on strategic nuclear power was counterproductive, that the United States should have enough conventional forces, particularly naval forces, to meet any situation, and that the current nuclear stockpile was demonstrably more than adequate for deterrence or massive retaliation. In the spring and summer of 1957, this argument was reinforced by the first naval analysis of the Strategic Air Command's targeting plans, which indicated that the air force was requesting airplanes and weapons for what Burke maintained was a militarily unjustifiable overkill capability against Soviet forces and industry.[63]

In 1957 Burke was appointed to his second term as chief of naval operations, thereby breaking the de facto postwar tradition that the CNO would serve only one two-year term. He accepted reappointment reluctantly. He was tired from two years of constant pressure and fourteen-hour working days, and felt that he had already done his best for the navy as CNO. In March 1957 he informed Radford and Air Force General Nathan F. Twining, Radford's relief as chairman of the Joint Chiefs, that he would personally prefer not to serve another term, and would appreciate their assistance in impressing this preference upon the president. Radford assured him that Eisenhower understood his position, but was almost certain to reappoint him, anyway. Burke accepted the call of duty, and took the oath of office as CNO for the second time in August.[64]

Burke's next two years in office proved even more challenging than had the first two, and were marked by a continuous stream of crises. In early August 1957, American intelligence learned that the USSR had successfully tested an ICBM, ahead of the United States. On 3 October 1957, five days before the CNO departed Washington for an inspection tour of the Western Pacific, the Soviet Union announced the launching of Sputnik, the world's first satellite. When Burke returned to the capital on 1 November, he found official Washington deeply concerned about the implications of the Soviet ICBM and its venture into space. In response to these developments, Secretary of Defense Neil H. McElroy, who had just relieved Wilson, requested the services to supply him with their proposals for the acceleration of their missile programs, including Polaris, which only that summer had suffered a 5 per cent cutback in funding.[65]

On 7 November, while those proposals were under consideration, the CNO attended a meeting of the National Security Council at which the report of the Security Resources Panel of the Science Advisory Committee, better known as the Gaither Report, was presented. That report concluded that Soviet economic and military expansion was far more rapid than had been anticipated, and that "by 1959 the USSR may be able to launch an attack with ICBMs carrying megaton warheads against which SAC will be almost completely vulnerable under present programs." It stressed the need for an early-warning system in order to allow the Strategic Air Command time to launch a counterstrike, and recommended that the development of current passive and active defense and missiles be accelerated to overcome this anticipated "gap" in deterrence.

The Gaither Report also emphasized the advantages of the Polaris system as a deterrent because of its relative invulnerability. It recommended that the initial operating capability of Polaris be accelerated and that the navy should triple its goal of having six Polaris submarines operational by 1965. The report also noted growing American vulnerability to attack by Soviet missile-armed submarines, and emphasized the need for increasing American antisubmarine warfare capability. Finally it recommended major changes in defense organization, particularly greater centralization of operational command responsibilities under the secretary of defense and more concentration of the activities of the military departments and of research and development. Although many of the Gaither Report's other recommendations were not implemented, those pertaining to missile development, antisubmarine warfare, and reorganization received serious attention from Burke and other Defense Department leaders.[66]

The Polaris program was accelerated at an even faster rate than had been recommended by the Gaither Committee. A proposal by the secretary of the navy in October 1957 that Polaris be developed as a 1,200-mile missile by December 1959 and that three FBM submarines be operational by 1962 was revised the following month to call for having the entire system operational by October 1960. The cost of this acceleration during fiscal years 1958 and 1959 was estimated at $389 million. In December 1957 Secretary of Defense McElroy approved the acceleration and, in early 1958, using funds "borrowed" from other naval programs, the construction of the first three FBM submarines was begun. By March 1958 long-lead-time funds had been allocated for the fourth and fifth Polaris submarines, and Burke had directed the responsible naval offices to begin detailed planning to place the Polaris system in operation in 1960.[67]

The antisubmarine warfare problem proved more difficult to solve than the "deterrence gap," which acceleration of Polaris was designed to alleviate. Although hard intelligence was lacking, the Soviet ICBM and Sputnik achievements convinced Burke that the Soviet Union could soon have in operation a nuclear-powered submarine capable of firing ballistic missiles armed with nuclear warheads. American ability to track and identify such submarines was still limited, and only one Soviet boat needed to slip through the defense screens to cause immense damage. Convinced that the nation had to improve its antisubmarine-warfare capability on a "crash basis," Burke urged the cognizant offices in the Pentagon and fleet units to explore aggressively new and unorthodox approaches. Additional funding was allocated to antisubmarine warfare: priority was given to the development of new sonars such as the AN/SQS-23; the Lockheed P3V Orion antisubmarine patrol aircraft, the Sikorsky HSS-2 Sea King antisubmarine helicopter, and weapons such as the Asroc and Subroc antisubmarine rockets. In the spring and summer of 1958 three task groups, Alfa, Bravo, and Charlie, were set up as semipermanent combat teams within the newly established Atlantic Fleet Antisubmarine Defense Force to test antisubmarine, hunter-killer, and convoy-escort tactics, respectively. To Burke the key remained not resources but new ideas and complete dedication, and he continued to stress these factors.[68]

Over the next three years, the massive, high-priority effort in antisubmarine warfare that the navy began in 1958 achieved significant results with regard to conventional submarine operations. By the time Burke retired in August 1961, it was estimated that, even without recourse to nuclear weapons or to strikes against Soviet submarine pens, the United States could "defeat any submarine operations which the Soviets are capable of mounting" against sea lines of communication. The danger posed by Soviet ballistic-missile submarines, which began to appear in 1960, however, continued to be serious and remains so to this day.[69]

While the recommendations of the Gaither Report pertaining to missile development and antisubmarine warfare posed difficult choices for the navy in terms of resource allocation, they generally reflected Burke's priorities for the navy. Its recommendation for greater centralization in defense organization clearly did not. The possibility that the Eisenhower administration would introduce legislation aimed at further consolidating decision-making in the Defense Department worried Burke throughout his first term as chief of naval operations. Reports and studies by a variety of individuals and groups, including Henry A. Kissinger, the Rockefeller Brothers Fund, and the U. S. Air Force, all recommended that the authority of the secretary of defense be increased and the power and prerogatives of the uniformed services and their chiefs be correspondingly decreased.

Burke did not oppose such redistribution of authority per se; but he did fear that it might misfire. He was concerned first of all that reorganization might be regarded as a complete solution to the problem of how to provide efficient, coordinated management of the myriad activities of the Department of Defense. He firmly believed that it was individual initiative and commitment that made any system work, not mechanical models of decision-making. Just as he was unwilling to place his confidence in any single concept or war plan, he refused to accept increased centralization as a panacea for existing and anticipated problems in defense management.

In addition, Burke worried that any new legislation might initiate an attempt—one the navy had feared since 1945—to merge the individual services into a single armed service. Although the Eisenhower administration did not favor such a merger, Burke was concerned that overzealous supporters of the single-service concept, particularly in the air force, would take advantage of the reorganization to win support and advance their position. Whether the merger were accomplished by new legislation or by administrative manipulation of loopholes in the law, the single service would almost certainly be modeled on the army and air force staff system, including a single chief of staff, a form of organization Burke believed could destroy the integrity of the navy and endanger the nation itself.

The existing structure of the Joint Chiefs of Staff, as a forum in which diverse views were presented and argued, represented for Burke a microcosm of the democratic form of government. The balance of this structure prevented "single-mindedness" and the domination of one concept; in the military context, the orientation toward "one interest, one strategy, one military posture, [or] one weapon." If a single school of thought were ever allowed to achieve dominance within the Joint Chiefs, either by merger or by subordination of the individual services to too much central control, Burke feared the result would be rigidity, loss of creativity and perspective, and failure to recognize the importance of diversity and flexibility in national defense.

Decentralization of decision-making, he argued, was also critical to the survival of the navy. Diffusion of responsibility was basic for the maintenance of service pride and morale. "Decentralization," he wrote,

> means we offer officers the opportunity to rise to positions of responsibility, of decision, of identity and stature—if they want it, and as soon as they can take it.
>
> We believe in *command*, not *staff*. We believe we have "real" things to do. The Navy believes in putting a man in a position with a job to do, and let him do it—give him hell if he does not perform—but to be a man in his own name. We decentralize and capitalize on the capabilities of our individual people rather than centralize and make automatons of them. This builds that essential pride of service and sense of accomplishment. If it results in a certain amount of cockiness, I am for it. But this is the direction in which we should move.[70]

On 3 April 1958, Eisenhower sent a special message to Congress on reorganization of the Defense Department: it included a series of recommendations that would, if legislated, consolidate and increase the power of the secretary of defense and reduce the authority of the civilian and military heads of the individual services. In particular, Eisenhower recommended that direct control of operating forces by the president and the secretary of defense be strengthened by removing the service chiefs from the operational chain of command. The Joint Staff was to be enlarged, the chairman of the Joint Chiefs was to have more power over it, and the role of the Joint Chiefs was to be redefined so that they would function as a unit, their principal responsibility being to act as joint advisers to the secretary of defense, rather than as heads of their respective services. Other proposals made by Eisenhower were that the service secretaries be relieved of direct responsibility for military operations so that they could devote themselves to questions of administration and logistics, and that a Director of Defense Research and Engineering be established.[71]

In general, Burke supported Eisenhower's recommendations. He thought the administration of the Defense Department would be more efficient if the responsibilities of the secretary of defense and the Joint Chiefs were clarified. Although he was reluctant to see the chief of naval operations deprived of direct control of the navy's operating forces, he realized that this might be necessary in the interests of coordination and quick decision-making. Despite his support of the president's intentions, however, Burke retained serious reservations about the possible implications of his proposals. He considered it essential that the CNO retain control over "details connected with operations," especially those relating to "support, logistics, communications and so on with which the JCS should not be concerned." As he saw it, an enlarged Joint Staff, under the auspices of the chairman, might assume responsibility for matters that could be handled better by the services themselves, and might in fact grow into a national general staff, opening the way for a merger of the services. He felt strongly that the legislation would have to be very carefully worded, so as to prevent abuse, and so as to assure naval officers that their interests were being considered.[72]

Shortly before Eisenhower sent his message to Congress, Burke, while offering his qualified support for the proposals, explained his misgivings to the president. Later that spring, he testified before both houses of Congress regarding the advantages of reorganization and the danger that reorganization might, intentionally or unintentionally, result in creation of a national general staff or merger of the services. His comments received considerable press coverage. When McElroy expressed disappointment that Burke had not supported the administration's proposals unreservedly, someone circulated the story that Burke had been rebuked for his stand. Although McElroy tried to make clear that no rebuke was intended, Burke was subjected to considerable public and political pressure, and there was some speculation that he would be forced to resign. Determined not to retire under pressure, Burke took a certain grim pleasure in riding out the storm. Having no particular political ambitions and not being averse to getting fired for defending the navy, "gives me a freedom of action which is quite a powerful asset," he wrote to a friend. "You are quite right that there will be a lot of subtle pressure put on to make my last year unpleasant, but I don't think it can be done. I am going to have fun this last year."[73]

When the dust settled, what had looked like a major defeat for Burke and the navy's supporters in Congress turned out to be a limited victory. The Defense Reorganization Act of 1958 was passed on 6 August, and measures for its implementation were worked out over the next year. Although the chief of naval operations was removed from direct control of the navy's operating forces—an outcome Burke was resigned to from the start—the legislation did not provide for the de jure or de facto establishment of a national general staff, nor did it lay the groundwork for eventual merger of the armed services.

Ironically, while congressional debates over whether the CNO would continue to command the navy's operating forces were still under way, Burke was exercising that power in two of the most significant naval actions of the postwar era: the landings in Lebanon and the crisis in the Taiwan Strait.

The Lebanon operation has been identified as one of the finest examples of gunboat diplomacy carried out by the United States since World War II.

During this crisis, American naval forces were used to implement foreign policy, specifically the Eisenhower Doctrine, which had been promulgated in March 1957 following the Suez crisis. That doctrine stated that the United States considered the independence and integrity of the nations of the Middle East vital to its national interest. As a result, Washington would be prepared to use armed forces to assist any nation in the area requesting such assistance against communist-inspired or communist-controlled armed aggression. During 1957, Burke was obliged to order the Sixth Fleet into the Eastern Mediterranean in the wake of an insurrection in Jordan, and again later when war threatened between Turkey, a member of NATO, and its southern neighbor, Syria, which at that time had begun receiving large quantities of arms from the Soviet Union. These incidents reinforced Burke's belief that the navy must be prepared to act quickly and in force in order to contain any crisis that might occur in the area, while at the same time avoiding any "unnecessary fights."[74]

In May 1958, the pro-Western president of Lebanon, Camille Chamoun, notified the United States that he might need help because of internal dissension and the threat of invasion by procommunist Syria. With Eisenhower's approval, Burke once more dispatched the Sixth Fleet to the Eastern Mediterranean and ordered it to stand by in case a request for an immediate landing were made. He also augmented marine strength by adding two battalion landing teams to the one already in the fleet. On 14 July, radicals toppled the government of Iraq and Chamoun requested armed assistance from the United States within forty-eight hours. That night Eisenhower ordered the marines to land.

The president's order allowed Burke only thirteen hours to get the operation under way, rather than the twenty-four hours the CNO had predicted he would need. Although much of the Sixth Fleet had moved out of the area by that time, Burke's precautions paid off. The marine landing team standing by off the Lebanese coast was able to begin operations on 15 July, and the other two were ashore by the eighteenth. The landings were conducted with few incidents; the marines, reinforced by army troops, remained in Lebanon until they were withdrawn by the president in October.[75]

Burke later identified a number of reasons for the smooth planning and implementation of the operation in Lebanon. With the example of British and French unpreparedness in the face of the Suez crisis fresh in their minds, both civilian and military leaders worked hard in the spring and summer of 1958 to ensure that the United States would not be caught in a similar situation. As in the Suez operation, Burke kept Eisenhower and Dulles informed of the navy's capabilities to carry out landing operations in Lebanon, and also kept American commanders on the scene informed of events and decisions in Washington so that they would be able to act quickly in case of an emergency. Preparations were made with full communication and real cooperation between the civilian and military leaders responsible for various aspects of the operation. In addition, those at the highest level on both the civilian and the military side were experienced and knowledgeable, and had respect for and confidence in each others' abilities. Finally, the command system operated very smoothly. "Since the CNO was in command of the Fleets," Burke wrote,

> I was responsible to the JCS and to the President for the readiness and movement of the Fleets. I followed President Eisenhower's and the JCS directives but it was up to me to have the Fleets positioned and ready for action whenever and wherever they were needed.
>
> So I moved the Sixth Fleet and made other necessary preparations including reinforcing it for any emergency—or at least for some of them. Naturally everybody was informed, but I did not have to wait until the end of weeks of debate before getting ready. It was a very flexible command system in which action could be taken very fast. It was a decentralized system.[76]

The crisis in Taiwan Strait followed on the heels of the landing in Lebanon. On 23 August 1958, the People's Republic of China launched a heavy artillery attack against the Nationalist Chinese-held Quemoy Islands, located less than twelve miles off the southeast coast of mainland China. Although this action was anticipated by some American officials, including the Joint Chiefs of Staff, it nevertheless created a dilemma for the United States. It was not clear whether the People's Republic intended to take the offshore islands, and, if so, whether this action would be the prelude to an invasion of Taiwan. Although the United States was committed to the defense of Taiwan, the Quemoy Islands themselves had no particular strategic value, and American intervention to defend them would involve serious risks; it might lead to war between the United States and mainland China, or, much worse, between the United States and the Soviet Union.[77]

Among the military, Burke and General Twining were the two most vociferous proponents of support for the Chinese Nationalists on Quemoy. Both believed that, with American help, the Nationalists could defend the islands, even during an extended siege. This position was strongly criticized by journalists and politicians who considered the islands too unimportant to be worth the risk of nuclear war. Burke and the Eisenhower administration felt otherwise. Although the offshore islands had little strategic importance, Burke believed that politically and psychologically their defense was critical to the United States. The important things in a conflict such as this, he pointed out, are often intangible:

> President Chiang [Kai Shek] can't give up those islands—and we can't ask him to give them up—without giving up one of the most important things in the world to him and to us—prestige, standing up under fire for principles, little things, intangible things. . . . If we retreat under fire and retreat under pressure, where does that leave us in the eyes of the rest of the world—and our own eyes?[78]

Equally important, he noted, "I think that any retreat from Communist pressures only renews the pressure at some other point . . . if we hold fast, the expense of the Communist bombardment will in time show them the futility of their approach to this problem. I hope we have the courage and stamina to see it through in this manner."[79]

As long as Peking was content to harass Quemoy from a distance, Burke believed it would be relatively easy for the United States to provide the Nationalists with the assistance they needed to resupply and defend the islands. If the People's Republic launched a full-scale invasion of Quemoy, however, the fighting was likely to be heavy and protracted. Because of continuing tensions in Europe and the Near East, including the presence of the marines in Lebanon, American forces were spread quite thin in the summer of 1958, and Burke doubted that the United States would be able to provide conventional resistance to such an invasion over the long term. He therefore joined other policy-makers in advocating that the United States be prepared to use tactical nuclear weapons against the artillery batteries, airfields, and troop concentrations of the enemy if an invasion from the mainland appeared imminent.

By the time the shelling of Quemoy began in late August, Congress had passed the law that deprived Burke of control over naval operations, but the legislation had not yet been implemented. He was, therefore, still in control of the navy's operating forces, and, with the approval of the Joint Chiefs of Staff, used his authority rapidly to redeploy ships and aircraft in order to reinforce the Seventh Fleet in the Western Pacific with three attack carriers, two cruisers, and supporting ships, and to increase the number of nuclear-strike aircraft on hand on those carriers. He also acted during the crisis as the "executive agent" of the Joint Chiefs for the Pacific unified command. In this role he was responsible for having the Politico-Military Affairs Division in the office of the CNO prepare position papers for the Joint Chiefs, which enabled him to exercise considerable influence in their deliberations as to how the crisis should be handled.[80]

During the two months that intensive bombardment of Quemoy continued, the Seventh Fleet assisted the Nationalists primarily by providing surveillance of Communist Chinese forces on the mainland and protective escort for Nationalist convoys resupplying the islands. On 3 September, the Joint Chiefs of Staff endorsed the concept that tactical nuclear weapons, which were already deployed in the area, should be used—by order of the president—in the event of an invasion from the mainland. A few days later, after intensive discussion of what its implications might be, this position was approved by Eisenhower. Fortunately, use of these weapons was not necessary; on 5 October, Peking announced a temporary cease-fire which signaled their intention not to precipitate a major war. Although the Seventh Fleet remained on alert through the end of the year, the crisis had passed.[81]

The crises in Lebanon and Taiwan Strait verified for Burke the truth of his contention that the conflicts the U. S. Navy was most likely to be involved in during the coming decades would be caused by local and limited communist aggression. As the Gaither Report had projected, and as Burke had foreseen, an atomic stalemate was steadily developing, in which the use of strategic weapons by either side would inevitably result in the destruction of both. In the spring of 1958, the army's General Taylor again presented his criticisms of the massive-retaliation policy to the service chiefs. His call for revision of that policy was endorsed by Burke and by the commandant of the marine corps, and went forward to the National Security Council as the majority position of the Joint Chiefs of Staff. Even Dulles had begun to express serious reservations about the policy with which he was so closely identified. He pointed out to both the Joint Chiefs and the Security Council that American allies in Europe and Asia were increasingly concerned that the United States would not risk nuclear holocaust in their defense, thus leaving them vulnerable to Soviet attack. Although the basic national security policy was not revised, in May 1958 Eisenhower did order that the sections dealing with limited war be kept under continuous review.[82]

Burke's endorsement of Taylor's views in the spring of 1958 indicated how circumstances had changed since the debates on national security strategy two years earlier. Not only had Burke established his authority within the Joint Chiefs of Staff, but the navy's position he was propounding had begun to take shape as an independent alternative approach to national defense. In the spring and summer of 1957, naval analysts had concluded that the Strategic Air Command had many more weapons than it needed to implement its mission, and had even prepared a study that suggested how the resources needed to support the strategic air offensive could be cut if lower-yield weapons and more selective targeting were used. Since the navy's estimates of the Strategic Air Command's force requirements carried very little weight, in the fall of 1957, the Long-Range Objectives Group (Op-93) followed them up with a more basic analysis of U. S. strategic objectives from the navy's point of view.

Ever since his service on the General Board, Arleigh Burke had believed that long-range planning would provide coherence and balance to the navy's developing goals and priorities, and would stimulate creative thinking about future problems and opportunities. As CNO, he upgraded the status of Op-93, appointed some of the navy's brightest junior flag officers to head it, and maintained it in his immediate office, where its influence would be most widely felt. From 1957 on, Op-93 prepared annual statements of the navy's long-range objectives, and studied the impact that important developments in technology and strategy might have. Its work on nuclear strategy from the navy's perspective was one of its most important contributions, and fully justified Burke's confidence in the value of long-range planning.[83]

Op-93's study of national strategy in an era of nuclear parity between the United States and the Soviet Union was completed in December 1957. Building on arguments Burke had been making since 1953, it offered a concrete alternative to massive retaliation and a justification for concentrating resources on preparations for limited war. The Strategic Air Command's bomber force was designed to be capable of either blunting a Soviet nuclear strike against the United States by attacking first, or of surviving a Soviet first strike and still having sufficient forces left to launch its own devastating retaliatory blow. Since many of its bombers would undoubtedly be destroyed on the ground during a surprise attack, it had to allow for high rates of attrition in order to assure a second-strike capability. It also had to have enough bombers available to carry out a preemptive mission, through destruction of a rapidly growing number of counterforce (Soviet nuclear threat) and military targets within the Soviet Union.

Op-93 argued that U. S. nuclear strategy would be greatly clarified if the preemptive-strike mission were separated from the retaliatory mission and each were considered separately. It would be extremely difficult, they pointed out, to wage a successful preventive war once the Soviet Union had an operational ICBM system; furthermore, such a war was inconsistent with U. S. policy. Deterrence was far more important, but did not require nearly as many weapons as were currently assigned to it. Given appropriate targeting, the deterrent capability of the large and vulnerable bomber forces of the Strategic Air Command could be duplicated by a comparatively small number of mobile weapon systems such as Polaris submarines because mobile systems were difficult to target and all but invulnerable to surprise attack. It was assumed that, because of the difficulty of locating them, Soviet ICBMs would be equally invulnerable. Thus there would exist a situation of "mutual deterrence" in which neither side could launch preemptive strikes and the threat of a general war would be greatly diminished. By relying on a small mobile deterrent force, Op-93 concluded, the United States could afford to redirect most of its defense funds to improving its capabilities for counteracting local and peripheral actions, which were the most likely form of Soviet aggression.[84]

The concept of "finite deterrence," with its dual emphasis on construction of mobile nuclear-strike systems and preparations for limited war, laid the groundwork for naval strategy and planning over the next several years. In January 1958, OP-93 promulgated a study of "The Navy of the 1970 Era," which was widely circulated and ultimately approved by Burke as a blueprint for future shipbuilding programs. It forecast that the primary mission of the fleet would be to deter or fight limited wars, toward which tasks most of the navy's forces would be oriented, while also addressing the continuing problem of antisubmarine warfare. It identified carrier striking forces, in particular, as the nation's "primary cutting tool" for limited war. Since Polaris was expected to be the nation's primary nuclear-deterrent system, supplementing or partially replacing the Strategic Air Command's vulnerable bomber fleets, it was proposed that a force of forty Polaris submarines be built rather than only eighteen, as called for by the Gaither Report. This figure was apparently developed by Burke himself, based on an assessment of Polaris's anticipated damage-effectiveness and how many targets would have to be hit in order to ensure an effective deterrent.[85]

By early 1959, naval strategists had further refined their concepts of the targets that should be struck under a strategy of finite deterrence. A retaliatory strategy, it was argued, could be most effectively implemented, not by targeting counterforce objectives, but by targeting political and military command-and-control centers and critical parts of the Soviet urban-industrial base. These combined "optimum" objectives could be totally destroyed by a relatively small number of low-yield, air-burst weapons. Since such targets were necessarily in densely populated areas, civilian casualties might reach one-third of the total population of the Soviet Union. That figure would be considerably lower, however, than would be the case if the Strategic Air Command bombed its much longer list of military targets, using high-yield, ground-burst weapons with their attendant widespread radioactive fallout.[86] In the summer of 1959, Burke introduced the navy's arguments regarding retaliatory strategy into the Joint Chiefs of Staff as guidance for a proposed "alternative undertaking" to supplement current nuclear-war plans. After lengthy debate, the Joint Chiefs accepted the navy's paper as a basis for planning, with the navy's second-strike guidance serving as an approved alternative to the air force's primary plan, which was based on first-strike counterforce targets. The new guidance was to be incorporated into actual plans in 1960.[87]

By this time, the navy's defense of invulnerable retaliatory systems had gone beyond the concept of finite deterrence. Invulnerable systems such as Polaris, Burke believed, not only reduced the resources that had to be devoted to the deterrent mission, but gave the United States an even more valuable advantage: flexibility in deciding when to use its retaliatory power. Since such systems were not in jeopardy, some or all of their weapons could be held back in a crisis. This would allow the president critical time for decision-making, thus reducing the danger of general war through miscalculation. It would also allow the president the option of launching missiles against only a few retaliatory targets in hopes of avoiding a full-scale nuclear exchange.[88]

Convinced of the advantages of mobile nuclear striking forces in terms of both finite deterrence and controlled retaliation, some officers and naval analysts optimistically proposed that the Strategic Air Command could be disbanded once the Polaris system was fully operational. Burke did not endorse this view. In his opinion, the United States should maintain a variety of mobile missile systems, both sea-based and land-based, so that a Soviet breakthrough in countering any one system would not undermine the entire U. S. deterrent capability. But he opposed any more stationary basing for strategic weapons within the continental United States, and used the navy's alternative strategic concepts in arguing against the building of an extensive system of protective silos for the Minuteman missile. He proposed as one alternative that Polaris missiles be placed on American surface ships, which would not only be as mobile as submarines but, since they would be indistinguishable from other military or merchant vessels, their actual mission would be concealed.[89]

Although Burke was able to make some headway in arguing in the Joint Chiefs for the navy's alternative strategy, he was aware that victories on the level of policy would be of little value if the navy could not acquire the numbers and types of forces it needed to carry out the missions it had defined for itself.

Moderate increases were made in the navy's budget in most years from fiscal year 1958 on, but not enough funds were allocated to support the research and development of new weapon systems and also cover the costs of basic maintenance and replacement programs. Burke calculated that an annual budget of $16-17 billion would be needed to replace outdated World War II hulls and produce a modern fleet by the 1970s. The navy's budgets of $10.9 billion in fiscal 1958, $11.7 billion in 1959, $11.6 billion in 1960, and $12.7 billion in 1961 were clearly too small. The need to reallocate available funds for the acceleration of programs such as Polaris forced even deeper cuts in other areas. Indeed, the fears expressed in 1955 that the cost of Polaris might result in the cancellation of earlier missile programs were borne out. The Triton program was canceled in August 1957 and Regulus-II was dropped in December 1958.[90]

Also destined for cancellation as a result of the low budget was one of Burke's favorite projects, the Martin P6M Seamaster long-range jet seaplane. The 600-mile-per-hour P6M, which was under development at the time Burke became chief of naval operations, was the centerpiece of a proposed Strategic Seaplane Force that would be able both to drop nuclear weapons on Soviet naval targets and to mine Soviet strategic sea lanes and waterways. Using the ocean as a base, and with specially modified surface tenders and submarines in support, the proposed P6M force offered great promise as yet another mobile, sea-based deterrent. Six test and twenty-four production aircraft were planned, but development was marred by two spectacular crashes, one in 1955 and the other in 1956, and the program was slowly cut back until in the summer of 1959 Burke regretfully canceled it.[91]

Lack of funds for new construction meant that many aging ships were kept in service long after they were due to be retired. In early 1959, as problems resulting from aging and deterioration within the fleet approached crisis proportions, Burke decided to divert available funds into a massive Fleet Rehabilitation and Modernization program (FRAM) that would extend the lives of 314—later reduced to 255—of the navy's ships of World War II vintage for a period of five to eight years. Although the FRAM program enabled the navy to maintain minimally acceptable levels, it was clearly a stopgap measure. In order to fund FRAM, during the rest of Burke's tour more money had to be diverted from new construction, which continued at only about half the level defined as necessary by long-range building programs. In addition, Burke was forced to decommission a considerable number of ships from the active fleet. Between July 1957 and July 1960, overall active force levels dropped from 967 to 812 ships.

Despite the cutbacks, certain naval programs continued to receive adequate funding. The Polaris missile and submarine program remained fully funded, and progressed ahead of schedule. The first FBM submarine, the *George Washington*, was launched in June 1959 and commissioned that December. The first successful submerged-submarine launch of a Polaris missile occurred on 20 July 1960, and the following November the *George Washington* departed on the first undersea-deterrent patrol. Between fiscal 1957 and fiscal 1961, nineteen Polaris submarines were authorized, along with twenty other nuclear-powered submarines. Generally satisfactory levels of aircraft and missile procurement were also maintained.

The construction of modern surface warships, however, was seriously affected by the budget crunch. Only three nuclear-powered surface ships were authorized during Burke's six-year tour: the missile cruiser *Long Beach*, the carrier *Enterprise*, and the missile frigate *Bainbridge*. An additional nuclear carrier was deferred in fiscal 1959 and 1960, and finally authorized as a conventional carrier in fiscal 1961. The dream of a modern 900-ship navy by 1970, which Burke endorsed in the winter of 1958, thus steadily faded, as long-term development was sacrificed to maintain force levels for the short and mid-term.[92]

Budget pressures at home increased Burke's interest in reinforcing the self-reliance and capabilities of America's allies as a means of strengthening her own position in the world. From the very beginning of his tenure as CNO, he paid special attention to building or rebuilding allied navies, particularly those of West Germany, Japan, Nationalist China, and the South American states, through loans or transfers of ships and technical assistance under the Mutual Defense Assistance Program. Believing that there was a professional bond between naval officers everywhere and that they shared a code of conduct that transcended nationality, Burke promoted the exchange of ideas between foreign and American naval officers. In 1956, he established the Naval Command College at the Naval War College to bring together outstanding captains and commanders from many nations so that they could work out problems together and develop bonds of trust and understanding. He also personally hosted visits by senior foreign naval officers—CNOs or high-ranking staff officers—of both allied and neutral nations so as to promote open communication regarding their expectations of the United States and his expectations of them. He formed particularly close ties with Japanese naval leaders, whose postwar navy he had helped establish; with Admiral of the Fleet Lord Louis Mountbatten, first sea lord of the Royal Navy; and with Vice Admiral Friedrich Ruge, the chief of naval forces of the Federal Republic of Germany.[93]

Burke's cultivation of allied powers was partly an outgrowth of his increasing anxiety that the United States might prove unable, or unwilling, to defend its interests in the face of communist aggression. Since the late 1940s, he had been concerned about the threat posed by communist expansionism, and his experience with the Korean truce-negotiating team had confirmed his worst fears. The failure of the American public to support intervention in the Quemoy Islands in the face of a direct challenge by the People's Republic of China forced him to conclude that the nation was in danger of losing the cold war not because of a lack of military preparedness, but because of a faltering of national will.

This concern, as well as his own evolving strategic philosophy, caused him to speak out publicly with increasing frequency after late 1958 on questions beyond the interests of the navy, as narrowly defined. He emphasized the need to persist in a long and difficult struggle against Soviet expansionism, and to defend and promote the values of freedom and individual enterprise, which were at the heart of the American system. "The USSR long ago declared cold war on us," he warned,

> and they have been working hard at it ever since. We cannot stay aloof from this challenge. We are engaged in a war of attrition in which the Communists intend to make each victory irreversible, no matter how minor it may seem to us. Taken together over the long haul, these victories could be decisive.[94]

Unless the entire American people recommitted themselves to maintaining a strong, free-enterprise economy, defending the values of democratic government, and taking a firm stand in international affairs, the cold war could easily be lost.

Burke's interest in and understanding of the broad issues of American foreign policy and economic and military concerns may have been one of the major factors that led Eisenhower in March 1959 to ask him to stay on for a third term as chief of naval operations. Although Burke openly disagreed with the administration on certain questions of national strategy, particularly its prevailing concepts on the usefulness of strategic nuclear weapons, he had gained the president's confidence, and demonstrated that he could see beyond the narrow interests of the navy in approaching questions of national security. By the end of Burke's second term, Eisenhower had begun to call him over to the White House to sound him out on questions of military or economic policy, often not directly connected with the navy. Burke also worked closely with Dulles, who, though seriously ill from a cancer that killed him in May 1959, remained the president's right arm in matters of foreign policy. Despite their clash over the Suez crisis during Burke's first term, he and Dulles found they had much in common, and Burke often visited the secretary on a Sunday morning to help him with speeches he was writing.[95]

Burke seriously considered refusing reappointment. He was not sure he would be able to keep driving himself at the pace he had been going, and was looking forward to retirement. As chief of naval operations, he explained,

> you get very tired. It takes a lot of stamina for that job. You work seven days a week and you're lucky if you can get seven hours sleep a night, and you have a lot of social work in addition to other work. Your personal life is nil. . . . I wanted to be home a little bit. I've got a nice wife; I want to keep her, and I was tired.[96]

In addition, Burke was afraid that he might be getting stale in the job. He suspected that he had been stereotyped by Congress and thus was probably becoming less effective as a spokesman for the navy and, more important, that he might be losing his creativity in dealing with the problems that confronted him from day to day, having dealt with them too often before. Despite the urgings of his advisers and his own gratification that Eisenhower wanted to reappoint him, Burke was not convinced that a third term would be in the best interests of the navy. What finally convinced him, he later explained,

> was when I went over to see President Eisenhower, and he didn't try to argue at all, he just said, "It's your duty". . . and that ended it.[97]

Arleigh Burke was sworn in as chief of naval operations for the third time on 17 August 1959.

When Navy Secretary Thomas first offered Burke the job as CNO, he wanted, he said, a leader who would integrate new technology into the navy; who would promote younger officers to positions of responsibility; who would reinvigorate the service and restore its enthusiasm and sense of purpose; and who would reorganize channels of communication and authority to improve coordination and efficiency. Measured against these goals, Burke's record during his first two terms was remarkable.

Although tight budgets limited the number of ships Burke was able to add to the fleet, an impressive array of new technology was ordered or brought into service between 1955 and 1959. Besides the Polaris system, and the guided-missile cruisers, frigates, and destroyers that were under development when Burke took office, these four years witnessed the authorization of the attack carriers *Kitty Hawk*, *Constellation*, and *Enterprise*, the *Skipjack* and *Thresher* classes of nuclear attack submarines, the first helicopter-equipped amphibious assault ships, and amphibious transports, dock. Among the new aircraft ordered were the McDonnell F4H Phantom-II fighter, the Grumman A2F Intruder and North American A3J Vigilante attack planes, and the Grumman W2F-1 Hawkeye early-warning plane. The last-named aircraft was part of a revolutionary computer-based combat information and evaluation system, the Naval Tactical Data System. In addition, Sidewinder and Sparrow air-to-air missiles, Terrier, Talos, and Tartar surface-to-air missiles, and the Bullpup air-to-surface missile were brought into the fleet. Installation of the worldwide Naval Command Communication System was begun during this period as well. Such innovation ensured the existence of a modern U. S. Navy into the 1960s.[98]

Burke's first four years as chief of naval operations also saw the navy forcefully identify a major role for itself in grand strategy, a role that had previously been overshadowed by the national debate over nuclear weapons and massive retaliation. Burke focused attention on the unique characteristics and capabilities of naval forces and clearly enunciated how they could and should be used to strengthen the national defense. He identified limited war as the primary task facing the navy in years ahead, and tried to prepare the service to confront that challenge. Furthermore, by promoting development of the Polaris missile and its submarine launching system, Burke sought not only to supplement existing deterrents to general war, but to lay the groundwork for redirecting strategic planning toward smaller nuclear weapons and a more deliberate, flexible approach to deterrence and nuclear retaliation.

These contributions in hardware and strategy were equaled by Burke's efforts in the less tangible fields of personnel policy and service morale.

Although he saw no need for a reorganization of the service, and never attempted such a move, he did want to see communication within the navy improved, service pride and vigor restored, and effective, innovative leadership encouraged. These concerns were rooted in his own deep commitment to the navy, but also in his growing fear that the service, and the nation as a whole, was losing its will to confront the challenges a continuing cold war would inevitably produce. He believed there was an urgent need to prepare the navy to meet those challenges with energy, creativity, and determination.

As Thomas wanted, Burke made a point of promoting younger officers to positions of greater responsibility within the service. When he became CNO in 1955, most of the top positions in the navy were held by officers from the Naval Academy classes of 1916 through 1921. Four years later, the leadership roles had passed to men ten years or more younger. This change resulted in part from the natural process of aging and retirement, but it was accelerated by Burke's selection of much younger flag officers for the important billets of those who did retire. By 1959, most of the navy's leadership came from the Naval Academy classes of 1923 through 1930.[99]

Burke also devoted considerable attention to instilling in the navy's leaders an understanding of the urgent nature of the challenges they faced. Each year he brought all rear admiral selectees to Washington for extensive briefings on the international situation and the special responsibilities of flag rank. He invited flag officers of particular promise for a brief stay with him at Admiral's House in order to expose them to policy-making at the highest levels. His concern for better leadership reached down the ranks. Recalling his own experience, and concerned about the challenge of Soviet technical achievements, he emphasized the importance of postgraduate work for all officers, and established a program that allowed outstanding graduates of the Naval Academy to go into Ph.D. programs after only a year at sea.[100]

Burke's most outstanding achievement in personnel policy was the Naval Leadership Program, which was established by Navy General Order 21 of 17 May 1958. Under this program, seven leadership training teams were dispatched to selected bases to instruct officers and petty officers in how to get the most from the men under their command. The training emphasized the need to develop a sense of individual responsibility and pride of accomplishment throughout the service, in part by involving enlisted men in a series of discussions that laid out the magnitude of the challenge facing the navy and the nation and the importance of their contribution toward meeting that challenge. Although the ideas conveyed were simple, the results were impressive. Officers who applied the principles they learned in the training found that rates of reenlistment and performance rose substantially, while disciplinary problems and accidents steadily declined. The navy's inability to retain highly trained enlisted men beyond their first tour of duty had long been one of Burke's concerns. The Naval Leadership Program did not resolve the problem of enlistment rates, which were too low, but it did have a positive effect, and was continued through the remainder of Burke's tenure as CNO.[101]

Burke tried in other ways to increase communication and establish a sense of common purpose within the navy. Deeply committed to the old naval adage that loyalty must extend both up and down the ranks, he encouraged all officers to share information with each other and with those under their command. He circulated high-level policy materials—including the navy's annual statement of its long-range objectives—as widely as possible to keep officers informed as to the current position and future direction of the navy, and encouraged similar efforts to "pass the word." Burke hosted a dinner at Admiral's House every two weeks for officers of all ranks, in order to sound them out and to express his own views and concerns. He also made it a practice to pick up hitchhiking sailors so that he could hear their gripes and suggestions. The qualities that made him an outstanding ship commander—energy, dedication, loyalty, compassion, and common sense—served him well as CNO, and were reflected in his handling of questions of personnel and morale.

Burke's third and final term as chief of naval operations was characterized by fewer victories and greater frustrations than had been the case during his first two terms. Through the end of the Eisenhower years, military planning was carried out under the shadow of the so-called "missile gap" between the United States and the Soviet Union. The Gaither Report of 1957 had warned that the Soviet Union might well be able to gain a critical edge over the United States through rapid acquisition and deployment of ICBMs. By 1959, based on available intelligence, many military and civilian officials within the Defense Department were convinced that this was in fact happening. Although such fears were later proved groundless, they forced the services into even greater competition with each other over funds to improve their capacity to oppose the supposed Soviet threat. The result was that the navy was forced to fight harder than ever to defend its programs and priorities.[102]

One bone of contention was the attack aircraft carrier. Despite air force opposition, the navy had succeeded in winning authorization for one new carrier in every fiscal year from 1952 to 1958, and hoped to continue this rate of construction in order to maintain a modern, active force of fourteen or fifteen attack carriers. Because of budgetary considerations, however, the administration did not include a new attack carrier in its defense program for fiscal year 1959, and its program for 1960, presented in January 1959, included a conventional carrier rather than the nuclear-powered ship the navy desired. Even so, the House of Representatives rejected the administration's request, while a contrary Senate voted funds for the more expensive nuclear-powered carrier. The final compromise which became law appropriated long-lead-time funds only for a nuclear ship. Determined not to build a nuclear carrier, the Eisenhower administration chose not to spend the money and the project was shelved.[103]

Under Burke's leadership, the role of the carrier had increasingly been defined during these budget debates in terms of its usefulness in peacetime deployments and limited war. Its potential as a mobile base for nuclear striking forces, however, was not forgotten, and the navy continued to maintain its carriers in readiness to carry out any necessary missions. As concern over Soviet missile deployments grew, Burke—always skilled in the politics of defense budgets—revised his defense of the carrier and reemphasized its usefulness as a supplementary deterrent system. The aircraft carrier, he pointed out, was a highly versatile weapon system, capable of carrying out a variety of missions, including those of nuclear retaliation.

Burke's renewed campaign for a new nuclear-powered carrier in the fall of 1959, during preparation of the budget request for fiscal year 1961, again met with serious resistance. Opponents argued that the expense involved could not be justified, given severe budget constraints, and suggested that the navy already had more than enough attack carriers for any likely contingency. Eisenhower privately stated that he had "lost faith" in the carrier and could not see allocating funds to a weapon system which the Soviets had not adopted and which, therefore, did not directly respond to the Soviet military threat. He did agree to request funding for a conventional carrier in fiscal 1961, based on its potential for use in limited conflicts. However, Eisenhower thought that the navy should consider building smaller, less expensive ships for this purpose, and was not convinced by Burke's argument that the carrier should be viewed as a multipurpose ship, capable of a wide diversity of uses.[104]

Renewed emphasis on the carrier's potential as a supplementary deterrent system was not the only response Burke proposed to the alleged missile gap. By the spring of 1959, the navy had raised its estimate of the number of Polaris submarines that should eventually be built from forty to forty-five. This new goal was based on a more precise targeting analysis than was available when Burke developed the original estimate in 1957, a more precise definition of the requirements of finite deterrence, and new information regarding the operational characteristics and prospective deployment schedules of the FBM submarines.[105]

Burke now also strongly pressed the idea that Polaris should be placed on surface ships as an additional supplement to the deterrent forces. In June 1959 he asked the Joint Chiefs of Staff to approve the placing of eight Polaris missiles on each of the six guided-missile cruisers—including the nuclear-powered *Long Beach*—being built or converted at this time. It was estimated that conversion of two cruisers to carry, between them, sixteen Polaris missiles would cost between $74 million and $86 million, while an FBM submarine with the same missile load would cost more than $100 million. Since the full force of six cruisers could be converted and deployed more rapidly than an equivalent force of new-construction Polaris submarines, it would provide a valuable deterrent until such time as the FBM submarines were fully operational.[106]

The concept of using cruisers for the deterrent mission was particularly attractive to Burke because it would help ease the navy's funding problems by taking advantage of the flexibility and versatility of naval forces. Unlike the FBM submarines, whose only capability was nuclear deterrence, the cruisers could simultaneously carry out a variety of other missions, including escorting task forces and antisubmarine warfare. Burke also believed that, once nuclear deterrent forces were fully deployed and the accuracy of Polaris had been refined, cruiser-based missiles could be readied for use against targets of tactical and naval significance. This would give the navy a level of flexibility in the use of its nuclear missiles that the CNO had long desired.

Neither McElroy nor the Joint Chiefs of Staff, however, were convinced by Burke's arguments. They questioned whether the cruisers could perform other missions and still serve as an effective deterrent force, and argued that, given other urgent needs, funds should not be allocated to any such marginal deterrent system. General Thomas D. White, chief of staff of the air force, took issue with Burke's position that the cruisers would be relatively invulnerable because of their mobility, and argued that Polaris-equipped cruisers, like aircraft carriers, could be put out of action more easily than land-based missiles in protective silos. Although the navy continued for the next two years to reserve space on the cruisers for the installation of missiles and Burke continued to fight for the program, it was never implemented.[107]

Some of the opposition to equipping cruisers for nuclear-strike missions grew out of the perception that such flexible, mobile forces were inherently incompatible with the tightly coordinated command, control, and targeting system needed to fight a general nuclear war. The need to create such a system, and how it should be organized, were subjects hotly debated in the Pentagon during Burke's third term. Air force officers had long wanted operations of the nuclear forces under tight, centralized control. During the early 1950s this belief was founded on the relative scarcity of atomic weapons and the determination of General Curtis E. LeMay, commander of the Strategic Air Command, to get maximum use out of the limited stockpile. Subsequently, with the advent of nuclear plenty and the development of thermonuclear weapons, such control and coordination was thought necessary in order to avoid mission duplication and the danger that American bombers might accidentally blow each other out of the sky while carrying out their missions. By 1959, conferences between the air force and the navy had permitted progress to be made in coordinating nuclear missions to avoid fratricide, but serious disagreements persisted between the services over what targets had highest priority, the yields of bombs to be used against them, and the damage those weapons were intended to achieve. The difficulty of integrating aircraft carriers into the Strategic Air Command's plans and Burke's insistence that the carriers must remain flexible in terms of definition of their missions, also remained sources of irritation.[108]

In April 1959, with the commissioning of the first Polaris submarine less than a year away, the new commander of the Strategic Air Command, General Thomas S. Power, submitted a paper to the Joint Chiefs requesting that he be given operational control of all Polaris submarines. This would be accomplished by assigning them to a unified strategic forces command under the control of the Strategic Air Command.[109] The *Washington Star* quoted the reaction of a "high ranking" naval officer to this plan:

> Polaris is perhaps the most attractive missile system under development. . . . Of course they want control of Polaris. But they will have to walk over a prostrate (Admiral) Arleigh Burke to get it.[110]

Over the next fifteen months, Burke stubbornly fought the proposal, not only within the Joint Chiefs, but before Congress and in the press. It would be inefficient and dangerous, he argued, to transfer control of any sea-based system to those who were not familiar with and not qualified to handle operations at sea. Turning Polaris over to generals with no experience in naval—much less submarine—operations would reduce the system's effectiveness, lower overall deterrent capability, and, most important, endanger American ships and lives. In addition, land-based and sea-based deterrent systems were basically incompatible. The Strategic Air Command, Burke argued, was organized around a strategy of immediate response because of its vulnerability to a Soviet first strike, whereas Polaris "will be relatively secure from countermeasures, capable of inevitable retaliation. It will be under positive and absolute U. S. control, capable of responding instantly, or with deliberation." The option of delayed response would be lost to the nation, Burke warned, if the Strategic Air Command were allowed to impose its control and thus its strategic concepts on the FBM submarine.[111]

In the spring of 1960, the navy presented the Joint Chiefs of Staff with its own proposal for command and control of Polaris submarines. The Submarine/Antisubmarine Warfare Division of the Office of the CNO (Op-31) originated the scheme, and developed it in cooperation with the staffs of Admiral Robert L. Dennison, commander in chief of the Atlantic Fleet (CinCLantFlt) and of the Atlantic unified command (CinCLant). Op-31's plan called for the Polaris submarines, which, until 1967, would be deployed only in the Atlantic, to be placed under the operational control of CinCLant, by redesignating Submarine Force, Atlantic Fleet, from an administrative "type" command reporting to CinCLantFlt to an operational command reporting to CinCLant also. Since CinCLant was a unified command, this arrangement would satisfy the desire of the Joint Chiefs for a line of control running directly from the secretary of defense. On the other hand, since CinCLantFlt had always simultaneously held the CinCLant post, the navy could be assured that Polaris would operate under a naval officer's control. In late July 1960, after heated debate, this command structure was approved by Thomas S. Gates, the former secretary of the navy, who had succeeded McElroy six months earlier as secretary of defense.[112]

This compromise did not close the issue. Gates appears to have accepted the air force's argument that the United States must have a coordinated plan for the use of its nuclear weapons in addition to an integrated command structure. In August 1960 he proposed that a Joint Strategic Target Planning Staff be established, with the commander of the Strategic Air Command as its director, and a vice admiral as deputy director. That staff would prepare a list of prospective targets for strategic nuclear attack in the event of war, and an integrated operational plan that would specify the delivery systems, timing, routes, yields, and designated ground zeros for all strategic nuclear weapons in the American arsenal, including those on Polaris submarines and on attack carriers deployed to the Mediterranean and Far East. Guidance for the preparation of the list and the plan would be contained in a national strategic targeting attack policy, prepared by the secretary of defense with the approval of the president and the National Security Council, which would define American goals in the event of nuclear war, set the plan's objectives, describe options to be developed, assign specific tasks to be performed, and identify the forces to be involved.[113]

Burke protested vigorously against creation of the Joint Strategic Target Planning Staff, first to Secretary Gates, and then to President Eisenhower. Giving the Strategic Air Command control over planning for the use of all strategic nuclear forces, he contended, would spell defeat for the navy's attempts to reduce the size of those forces and revise the existing concepts for their use. The president, however, was convinced that greater coordination was needed. In August 1960 the staff was formally established. Disappointed, but determined that the navy would have as much influence as possible within the new organization, Burke soon selected Vice Admiral Edward N. Parker to be deputy director, and dispatched forty naval officers, rather than the five that had been requested, to draft the target list and the operational plan.[114]

Although the creation of the joint planning staff was a major defeat for Burke, the first national strategic targeting attack policy issued by Gates may well have been developed in part out of the navy's proposals and arguments. Available evidence suggests that it called for the preparation of a plan that would be strictly retaliatory, rejecting the Strategic Air Command's longstanding preference for assuring first-strike capability as well. The guidance gave first priority in assignment of targets to urban-industrial areas, then to Soviet nuclear forces, and finally to other military forces. Unfortunately, it appears to have been sufficiently vague to allow the Strategic Air Command considerable latitude in developing target lists and, thus, in recommending bomber and missile force levels and nuclear-stockpile goals.[115]

Although Burke refrained from criticizing the decision to create the Joint Strategic Target Planning Staff once it had been endorsed by the president, he watched the development of the first integrated operational plan with considerable anxiety. He was particularly concerned that the Strategic Air Command might use the broad policy guidance on damage criteria to justify requests for more forces. Whereas, in calculating damage caused by nuclear weapons, the navy included "secondary" or "bonus" effects, the Strategic Air Command counted only the immediate or "primary" effects of a nuclear blast, a method that greatly inflated its estimates of how many weapons would be needed to achieve the requisite level of damage. Burke was also concerned that the joint planning staff was not attempting to differentiate between targets in the Soviet Union and those in the satellite countries, but was planning to attack all targets indiscriminately, if retaliation should become necessary.[116] He expressed his concern to Eisenhower, and in November 1960 the president dispatched his science adviser, Harvard professor George B. Kistiakowsky, to the Strategic Air Command's headquarters to review the first integrated operational plan.

Kistiakowsky returned to Washington convinced that the procedures adopted by the air command and the joint planning staff "may lead to less than optimum plans," and that "damage criteria in the directives to the planners are such as to lead to unnecessary and undesirable overkill." The president was "greatly interested" in Kistiakowsky's report, and took steps to ensure that it would be passed on to the newly elected Kennedy administration. In 1961 President John F. Kennedy ordered that a new integrated operational plan be prepared, presumably one that contained more specific guidance.[117]

Although this sequence of events was a victory for Arleigh Burke in that it resulted in tighter controls being imposed on the Strategic Air Command's planners, it did not reverse the long-term defeat inherent in the creation of the Joint Strategic Target Planning Staff. The integrated operational plan legitimized most of the air command's principles that Burke had been fighting against for five years. Despite Kennedy's subsequent commitment to expansion of the Polaris program, the opportunity had been lost to make use of the FBM submarine's unique capabilities to develop a national strategy based on the principles of finite deterrence and controlled retaliation. Such a strategy may have been politically impossible from the start; the establishment of the joint planning staff ensured that it would not be given further consideration.

Battles over budgets and war planning absorbed much of Burke's time during the final year and a half of Eisenhower's administration, but they were not the only problems he had to contend with. The tensions of the cold war continued unabated. Naval forces were put on alert when a crisis developed in Laos in 1959, and again the following year, while trouble in Europe over Berlin kept the Atlantic Fleet in a state of constant readiness. Closer to home, relations with Cuba steadily worsened after Fidel Castro seized power in January 1959, and in March of 1960 Burke attended a series of National Security Council meetings at which a Central Intelligence Agency plan for taking secret action to remove Castro from power was discussed and approved. Civil war in the newly independent Congo also required an American response. In the summer of 1960 an attack carrier was stationed off the mouth of the Congo River in order to deter threatened Soviet intervention in the region. Additional attack carriers were deployed to both the Sixth Fleet in the Mediterranean and the Seventh Fleet in the Far East to reinforce the American presence in those areas as well. Later that year, the first SoLant (South Atlantic) Amity force was organized by the navy to provide a friendly military presence in Africa as a part of Eisenhower's "people to people" program. These years also witnessed a series of pioneering undersea voyages by American nuclear submarines. Beginning with the passage of the *Nautilus* under the North Pole in August 1958 and climaxing with the *Triton*'s 84-day submerged circumnavigation of the globe in the spring of 1960, these cruises were used to gather scientific data, test the capabilities of nuclear submarines, and gain operational experience in preparation for Polaris-submarine deployments.[118]

In the fall of 1960, Burke let the president know that he intended to retire at the end of his current term. He had a number of reasons for making this decision. The strain of five years of continuous crises and controversy had at last taken its toll. Also, Burke was firmly convinced that for him to serve any longer would be detrimental to the best interests of the navy. Despite his efforts to improve communications and keep in touch with dissenting viewpoints, he was aware that he was becoming increasingly isolated from developments within the service. This was happening through no fault of his. He had made it his practice since the time he took office to surround himself with men whose views differed from his and who were not afraid to defend their ideas. During his third term, however, Burke's attempts to foster diversity of opinion among his staff had begun to lose their force. His long experience as CNO, his stature within the service, as well as his famous temper which, on the rare occasions when it was let loose, was an awesome thing to behold—all these deterred younger officers from approaching him with ideas or criticism. Captains and commanders coming into his office were often reluctant to bring problems or proposals to his attention because they assumed he had already considered such issues and did not need their advice. In addition, officers who had served with him for many years naturally sought to protect him from unnecessary irritations and interruptions, thus creating a wall between him and the rest of the service. Realizing that the navy needed a change as much as he needed a rest, Burke assured the president that he would serve out the rest of his term, but would under no circumstances consider accepting reappointment.[119]

On 20 January 1961, John F. Kennedy was inaugurated as president of the United States. Burke, who had favored neither Kennedy nor Richard M. Nixon during the 1960 election campaign, took the change of administration in stride. Although he had not dealt with Kennedy often before the election, he had no reason to suspect that the new administration would fail to respond to the navy's needs, and he was impressed by Kennedy's eloquent inaugural address. Any change of administration, however, necessarily involved a major disruption of established patterns of communication and decision-making, and the shift from Eisenhower to Kennedy was to be particularly disruptive for the armed services. In fact, Burke's last six months as chief of naval operations were the most difficult and frustrating of his entire naval career.

Over the course of five and one-half years as CNO, Burke had worked closely and harmoniously with President Eisenhower. They came from similar backgrounds and shared a similar philosophy and world view. Although they disagreed on particular points of policy, they were both military professionals, communicated easily and openly, and enjoyed a deep mutual respect. More importantly, Eisenhower's approach to administration was one that Burke understood and worked with comfortably. Under Eisenhower, channels of communication and areas of responsibility were organized along the lines of a military staff; operating procedures were carefully defined, and decision-making was clearly enunciated. Within this formal structure, Eisenhower promoted a spirit of teamwork and cooperation, and frequently brought his secretary of defense, the service secretaries, and the Joint Chiefs of Staff together for informal discussions of various problems.

Much of this changed under Kennedy, who had no close friends or advisers in high military posts at the time of his election and was not inclined to develop the kind of rapport that Eisenhower enjoyed with his service chiefs. Burke liked and respected Kennedy, but felt he had less access to him than to Eisenhower and was frustrated by his inability to find out precisely what the new president expected from him. Anxious to do away with what he regarded as unnecessary "red tape," Kennedy discarded many of the structures and procedures Eisenhower relied on, but failed to specify to his top military men just what would take their places. The confusion and poor communication that resulted had serious consequences.[120]

Determined to shake up the Defense Department by bringing in new people, Kennedy appointed as secretary of defense Robert S. McNamara, a brilliant and energetic executive of the Ford Motor Company with no experience in recent defense planning. His choice as secretary of the navy, John B. Connally, was also a businessman and new to the Pentagon, although he had served in the navy during World War II. "Breaking in a new secretary," Burke later noted, "is always difficult," and Connally presented a special challenge because of his lack of experience. Burke approached the problem with characteristic directness. The best way for Connally to learn about running the navy, he suggested, was for him to move into Admiral's House for about ten days, and to stay with the CNO day in and day out so that he could observe firsthand what the issues were and how they were being handled. Connally readily agreed, and Burke was pleased to find the new secretary quick, observant, and adaptable. After his intensive apprenticeship, Connally proved a committed and able advocate for the navy, using his considerable political skills to good advantage on behalf of the service.[121]

Burke was less successful in establishing a good working relationship with McNamara. Highly intelligent, impatient, sometimes insensitive, and overly concerned with detail, the new secretary of defense was more difficult for Burke to deal with than any of his predecessors had been. McNamara made little effort to promote the kind of easy civilian-military interaction that was encouraged in Eisenhower's Defense Department, and appeared indifferent to Burke's efforts to help such rapport along. Nevertheless, Burke kept trying. Observing that McNamara always arrived at his desk before 7:00 a.m., Burke, who also got to the Pentagon early, began stopping by the secretary's office for early-morning conversations. Although he seemed to appreciate Burke's willingness to offer advice and counsel, McNamara remained reserved. He was not antimilitary, Burke later noted, but he did not understand the military well.

Despite considerable effort, Burke felt that he was never able to find out just what it was that McNamara believed in or wanted to accomplish as secretary of defense.[122]

The impact of the new administration was quickly apparent within the Defense Department. As soon as Kennedy took office, Burke submitted for review a speech he was scheduled to give on 27 January 1961 as the recipient of the Silver Quill award from National Business Publications. The text focused strongly on the dangers of communist expansion in Laos, Cuba, and other parts of the world, and the need for a strong national commitment to stand up against this global threat and defend American principles and interests. Arthur Sylvester, the assistant secretary of defense for public affairs, found the speech completely unacceptable and refused to clear it for public release. Burke, who respected the administration's right to control the statements of its officials, had the speech rewritten in milder tone, whereupon it was cleared and delivered, as scheduled. Trouble erupted when this minor incident was leaked to the press. Sylvester was quoted as saying that he was displeased with Burke for having considered delivering such a speech. Burke was surprised and offended to see the matter, which he had discussed with no one, being used as the basis for a public rebuke. Sylvester, on the other hand, appears to have blamed Burke for leaking the story, and on a number of subsequent occasions made comments that seemed intended to discredit or embarrass the admiral. Although Kennedy took pains to let Burke know that he was not displeased and appreciated his courtesy in submitting the speech for review, this incident—which eventually resulted in a congressional hearing on censorship—left tensions that were never entirely resolved.[123]

Another source of tension, as far as Burke was concerned, was the new administration's effort to overhaul completely the procedures used in planning and budgeting the defense program. Under Eisenhower, much of the responsibility for developing the defense program was vested in the services themselves. The president would set an overall ceiling on defense spending, the secretary of defense would establish general guidelines as to how much of the budget would go to each service, and within those limits each service would formulate its own program requests, in line with the loose guidance provided by the basic national security policy. Since the services invariably asked for more funds than could be allocated, it was the responsibility of the secretary of defense to review and evaluate their requests and prepare an integrated defense budget.

By the close of the Eisenhower administration, the dangers of this system had become apparent. Conflicting service doctrines had produced a situation in which the air force was prepared only for a short, total, nuclear war, while the army was stockpiling supplies for a conflict lasting two years. The air force was not prepared to provide the airlift and tactical air support that was defined as necessary in army plans. Strategic nuclear forces were not balanced and were vulnerable to surprise attack, and counterinsurgency forces were practically nonexistent. Only the navy was prepared to contend with a broad spectrum of conflicts, even it suffered from some deficiencies. Naval planners had identified the need for greater amphibious sealift capability and more resources for counterinsurgency warfare to round out the navy's operational capability, but the CNO had not been able to win complete funding for such programs.[124]

The planning, programming, and budgeting system developed by McNamara's staff, by contrast, gave much greater leadership responsibility to the secretary of defense and his office. Under that system, McNamara's staff would prepare their own overall evaluation of defense needs, including an "open and explicit" analysis of program alternatives and costs. They would then develop a five-year force and financial plan that would provide a framework for more specific planning and budgeting. Throughout the process, programs would be categorized by function rather than by service of origin in order to avoid duplication and imbalance in the final defense program. Although the services would be consulted throughout the process, their freedom to choose the weapons and programs to which they would give priority was severely circumscribed.[125]

The system promised to provide a balanced, integrated approach to defense planning with many obvious advantages over Eisenhower's planning and budgeting process. However, it threatened to create a monolithic structure that would reduce the initiative of the individual services and allow less room for diversity and creative competition in defense planning. It posed particular problems for the navy whose flexible and versatile weapon systems could not readily be categorized by function. To Burke the entire exercise seemed to be inspired more by the desire to impose change for the sake of change than by any understanding of what the true requirements for defense planning were. He believed that, out of necessity, the navy had already adopted a balanced appproach to planning, which McNamara failed to appreciate and which would be effectively dismantled by the new system.

In addition, most of the officials who developed and implemented the system were bright young men who had little knowledge of or experience with the armed forces and were inclined to treat professional military men with suspicion or disdain. Many of them seemed to think, Burke later noted, that civilian control of the military meant that all civilian officials of the Defense Department were superior to all military officers, including the Joint Chiefs of Staff. They presented their proposed procedures in a manner that seemed to Burke to be arrogant and overbearing. Even under the best of circumstances, he would have found it a time-consuming and wearisome job to try to educate an entirely new administration regarding the navy's programs, philosophy, and priorities. Under these circumstances, he found it virtually impossible.[126]

After a rapid review of the budget for fiscal year 1961, which was already in effect, and the budget for fiscal year 1962, which had been proposed by the Eisenhower administration, McNamara recommended a number of revisions, the most significant for the navy being an acceleration of the Polaris submarine program. Five additional submarines were to be procured in fiscal 1961, raising the number from five to ten for that year. Another ten were to be procured in fiscal 1962, raising the total authorized to twenty-nine. Funds for the fiscal 1961 acceleration were to be borrowed from other naval new-construction programs already funded. Although Burke favored acceleration of Polaris, he considered it to be a "national" program that should not be funded at the expense of building programs intended to enable the navy to carry out its unique missions. Furthermore, Burke noted, not only would new construction be temporarily cut back under McNamara's funding plan, but personnel would have to be transferred into Polaris from other programs, forcing the decommissioning of more surface ships and the phasing out of such ongoing projects as the navy's lighter-than-air antisubmarine warfare program.[127]

In his last posture statement to the House Armed Services Committee in March 1961, Burke painted a gloomy picture of the future of the navy. If ship construction continued at the level of 22 ships per year, which had been maintained on average since 1948, he warned, the U. S. Navy would be reduced from the current active fleet of 817 ships to 440 within twenty years. Such a situation would be extremely serious, Burke noted, since the fleet had already "been squeezed down to the bare minimum which will do the jobs the Navy must do."[128] His warning proved accurate. New construction continued at an inadequate level, and within eighteen years the navy had only 439 ships in the active fleet, including forty-one Polaris submarines. Six of the submarines were authorized in fiscal year 1963 and another six in 1964, completing the program at four short of the navy's goal.[129]

In the spring of 1961, the CNO's anxiety about the long-range future of the navy was largely overshadowed by more immediate crises. In March 1960, the National Security Council had given the Central Intelligence Agency the mission of planning covert operations to overthrow the Castro regime, and the deputy director for plans, Richard M. Bissell, Jr., had proceeded to implement that policy. Initial plans called for the CIA to land Cuban exiles trained in guerrilla warfare, but by the summer of 1960 Bissell and his staff had concluded that Castro's growing control over Cuba would make small-scale guerrilla operations ineffective. A new plan was therefore devised to train the exiles for an amphibious assault which, it was hoped, would trigger a general uprising.[130]

The situation in Cuba had bothered Burke since at least the summer of 1958, when Castro's guerrillas kidnapped thirty sailors and marines from the American naval base at Guantánamo Bay and outraged Burke with their escalating demands for American concessions in exchange for the release of the hostages. After Castro came to power in January 1959, Burke frequently pointed to the new regime as a leading example of the kind of communist disruption the United States must guard against in order to avoid losing the cold war. His opposition to Castro became so widely known that the Cuban leader occasionally responded to Burke's comments in his own speeches.[131]

Burke had heard nothing about the intelligence agency's plans since the March meetings of the National Security Council, but suspected by November 1960 that "something was cooking" with regard to Cuba when naval intelligence uncovered the CIA's training operation for Cuban exiles in Guatemala. He continued to monitor these operations, but could not find out for certain what was going on. In early January 1961, unaware of what the CIA was then planning, but concerned about Castro's increasing political power and worsening relations with the United States, the Joint Chiefs of Staff developed an outline of possible American actions to undermine the Castro regime. Although this paper was shown to Kennedy, the new administration did not follow it up.

On 28 January 1961, President Kennedy, the National Security Council, and the Joint Chiefs received their first official briefing from the CIA on the proposed operation in Cuba. The presentation was given orally, and did not include operational detail. Because of the intense secrecy surrounding the plan, no documents were provided and no one was allowed to take notes during the meeting. The Joint Chiefs agreed not to discuss the operation with anyone, not even their immediate staff. The president asked them to review the plan and comment on it, but he made it clear that the CIA had the responsibility for the operation and the military chiefs would act in a strictly advisory capacity.

Burke disliked these ground rules. He had no confidence that a complex military operation of the sort the CIA proposed could be successfully executed under the direction of amateurs, and he was concerned that plans had been allowed to proceed so far without any military advice. In addition, he feared that the excessive secrecy that surrounded the project would ultimately prove to be a great disadvantage, since it would prevent the expert staffing and thorough coordination necessary to the success of the operation. Finally, he resented the implication that military officers of the highest rank could not be trusted to keep a secret.

Burke's misgivings were not allayed by the more complete description of the planned operation prepared in early February by a Joint Staff task force after a detailed oral briefing by the CIA. The CIA proposal appeared to him to be "weak" and "sloppy." Furthermore, it was impossible to assess it from a military point of view because it contained no logistics or communications annexes. The task force concluded, however, that the operation would have a "fair" chance of success, based on the information available, and the Joint Chiefs later transmitted that conclusion to the president. Unfortunately the precise definition of "fair" was never spelled out. Brigadier General David W. Gray, who headed the task force, later explained that he intended to convey the idea that the project had about a 30 per cent chance of success; Burke thought a "fair" chance was about 50 per cent, but many on Kennedy's staff may have interpreted the term with much more optimism.[132]

In late February, a team of officers from the Joint Staff visited Guatemala and reported to the chiefs that the CIA's training activities were so visible that it would be virtually impossible for the attack to achieve surprise. This posed a serious problem, since the Cuban air force—or even a single plane—could sink the entire invasion fleet. When the CIA presented its updated plan to the National Security Council on 11 March, it proposed a number of ways of dealing with this problem. The main invasion was to take place at Trinidad, an isolated village on the south coast that was known to be hospitable to anti-Castro guerrillas. It would be preceded by a diversionary landing to distract Castro from the main objective, and accompanying exile-flown air strikes against the Cuban air force would delay retaliation and allow the expeditionary force to establish its beachhead. If the landing force could not hold its position, it would disperse into the surrounding Escambray Mountains to engage in guerrilla activity.

Major objections to the proposed operation at Trinidad surfaced almost immediately. Kennedy was concerned that it was too "spectacular"—like a World War II amphibious assault—and suggested that a night landing would be more suitable. Secretary of State Dean Rusk objected that the proposed air strikes in support of the landing would inevitably implicate the United States in the operation, unless the exiles controlled an airstrip on Cuban soil at the time the strikes were launched. Unfortunately there was no suitable airstrip in the vicinity of Trinidad. Under pressure from the State Department, Kennedy agreed that an alternative site for the landing would have to be found. After a rapid review of available options, the CIA proposed three alternatives and subsequently presented them to the Joint Chiefs of Staff for review. The site the intelligence people were inclined to favor was the Bay of Pigs. A sparsely populated area surrounded by the Zapata Swamp, it had no harbor facilities, but was less readily accessible to Castro's militia than Trinidad. Furthermore, it had an airfield, which could be identified as the source of any necessary air strikes.

Burke and his fellow service chiefs were not happy about this change. On 15 March they cautioned McNamara that, while the Bay of Pigs was the best of the three alternatives proposed, none of the three was as good a place for the operation as Trinidad. McNamara, however, may not have clearly explained this cautionary note to Kennedy. He later stated that it was his understanding that the Joint Chiefs agreed with the Central Intelligence Agency in preferring the new site over Trinidad, a statement which is difficult to explain in the light of the memo he had received from the chiefs.[133] Believing that McNamara had explained their analysis to Kennedy, the Joint Chiefs of Staff, despite their misgivings, were not willing to challenge the president's decision to proceed with the CIA's Bay of Pigs plan. During the following month they collectively reviewed the new plan four times, and individually provided advice the CIA requested with regard to certain operational aspects, although they were not permitted to assign staff to this task.

As Burke later pointed out, the Joint Chiefs never approved the Bay of Pigs plan because they were never asked to approve it. They confined their comments to the plans they were presented with and the questions they were asked and, once the president's decision had been made, they did not propose arguments. Kennedy, however, despite his repeated admonition that the Joint Chiefs were to serve in a strictly advisory capacity with regard to the operation, apparently expected Burke and his colleagues to object if they did not like the options they were offered, and he interpreted their silence as endorsement. Misunderstanding and lack of communication fouled an already complex and difficult situation.

The invasion of the Bay of Pigs took place on the night of 16–17 April 1961; throughout, it was hampered by blunders and mishaps. Of these, the most serious were the failure of the diversionary force to carry out its landing on the far side of Cuba and the fact that Kennedy—pressured by the State Department and United Nations Ambassador Adlai E. Stevenson—decided, only hours before the main landings, to cancel the supporting air strikes, in order to remove the risk that the United States would be implicated in the operation. The Joint Chiefs were not informed of this decision and Kennedy was not told that it was likely to have disastrous military consequences. Not until the following morning did Burke learn that the air strikes had been canceled. By then, the Cuban air force was in the air and succeeded in sinking one supply ship which carried important reserves of ammunition, damaging another so severely that it had to be beached, and driving off the rest of the ships. Although the expeditionary force later launched air strikes from Nicaragua to cover the beachhead, it soon discovered that its slow B-26 bombers were no match for Castro's handful of speedier Sea Fury propeller-driven fighters and armed T-33 jet trainers. Without air support, the Cuban exiles' transports would not return to the invasion area, no supplies could be brought in over the beaches, and the expeditionary force was left isolated and vulnerable.

During the next two days Burke and General Lyman L. Lemnitzer, the chairman of the Joint Chiefs of Staff, tried to persuade Kennedy to intervene in support of the Cuban exiles, but as the invasion gradually crumbled under the pressure of Castro's military forces, the president firmly adhered to his original position that American forces would not become involved in any way. He had approved the operation with the understanding that the exiles' landing force could fade into the surrounding swamps to join other anti-Castro guerrillas, if the pressure became too great, an assumption that Burke and other Joint Chiefs shared. Only later did they learn that the CIA had not trained or equipped the exiles to turn guerrilla if the expected general uprising did not erupt and their hold on the beachhead became untenable. Finally on 19 April, after many requests, Burke received authority to order unmarked jets from the aircraft carrier *Essex* to fly cover for an air attack by the Cuban expeditionary force—a mission that was not completed because the exiles' planes were destroyed before they could rendezvous. Approval was subsequently given for destroyers to send boats in to the beaches to assist in evacuating what was left of the Cuban exile brigade.

The Bay of Pigs invasion was undoubtedly one of the most distressing episodes of Burke's service as chief of naval operations. The Joint Chiefs of Staff were not responsible for the operation, and Burke believed that they had discharged their obligations as advisers to the president in accordance with Kennedy's established procedures. Nevertheless, he regretted that he and his colleagues had not insisted more strongly that they be adequately informed and that their views be fully considered. He was convinced that the landing could have been successful if the Cuban brigade had had enough ammunition and air cover. Furthermore, he believed that establishment of a firm beachhead, combined with continued, visible control of the air by the exiles, could have started a chain reaction of defections and increasing support throughout Cuba, leading to accomplishment of the operation's ultimate objective.

Preparations for the Bay of Pigs landing were made in the midst of another cold-war crisis: the intensifying civil war in Laos. In March 1961 the Pathet Lao Army, equipped by the Soviets, launched a major offensive and began to gain ground against the Royal Laotian Army, armed and trained by the Americans and led by General Phoumi Nosavan. Kennedy, who believed that the Eisenhower administration had seriously erred by supporting the pro-Western Phoumi rather than a neutral coalition government, was nevertheless unwilling to see the Pathet Lao win control of the country. During his first few months in office, he devoted considerable attention to the question of how to support Phoumi while still laying the groundwork for the creation of a neutral government under the ousted premier, Prince Souvanna Phouma.[134]

During the third week in March, Burke, acting as the chairman of the Joint Chiefs of Staff in Lemnitzer's absence, briefed Kennedy on the situation in Laos. Burke had been concerned about the prospect of communist expansion in Southeast Asia since his service as director of the navy's Strategic Plans Division during the Korean War. Since 1958 he had advocated a national commitment to defend Laos against communist aggression, and his presentation to Kennedy stressed the need for the president to make a clear decision as to whether the United States would commit itself to supporting Phoumi against the Pathet Lao. He emphasized the point that, once such a commitment had been made, it could not be abandoned halfway through. Although training the Laotians to defend themselves would be far preferable to sending American troops to Laos, Burke argued, Washington had to be prepared to do whatever was necessary to fulfill its commitments if it wished to exercise any influence in the area. Recalling the lessons of the Korean War, he pointed out that Kennedy must be ready to approve any necessary intervention quickly, decisively, and in enough force to achieve a rapid military victory and avoid a protracted land struggle.

The president appeared convinced by the points Burke made, and in a news conference on 23 March used many of the latter's arguments as well as the maps he had prepared. Within a few days, however, Kennedy was again wavering. He did not want to provoke a confrontation with the Soviet Union and China, and was concerned about the difficulty of mounting a successful American military action in Laos. Since Laos was a landlocked country, troops would have to be flown in and then supported by long air and ground lines of communication. In the wake of the Bay of Pigs experience, Kennedy was even more reluctant to consider such an option, unless the Joint Chiefs could provide him with a plan that was guaranteed to succeed—a promise neither Burke nor the other chiefs could give.

On 27 April, Burke made a final plea to congressional leaders who had assembled for a special briefing at the White House for a national commitment to defend freedom in Laos. The question of how difficult an operation in Laos might be, he argued, was secondary to the question of whether the United States was morally committed to using its power to halt communist aggression. War is not a game to be dabbled in, he warned; it is a deadly serious business. Willingness to use all necessary military force might make the use of any military force unnecessary. Lack of commitment, on the other hand, would only encourage communist expansion, and make ultimate confrontation, or even ultimate defeat, inevitable.[135]

The congressional leaders listened to Burke's arguments, and some even sympathized with his position, but they were not willing to break with the president on the basis of such philosophical considerations. By this time, other members of the Joint Chiefs had also accepted the pragmatic argument that American intervention in Laos would be extremely difficult to carry out successfully, leaving Burke to stand almost alone in defense of the principle that the United States must be prepared to do whatever was necessary—no matter how difficult—to keep its promises and fulfill its commitments. In the event, no drastic action was required in Laos at this time. On 3 May, a cease-fire was announced, and verified within two weeks. Although the long-term crisis was not resolved, the imminent threat of a communist takeover had been averted.

On 22 April, just as the Laotian crisis was coming to a head, President Kennedy appointed a Cuban Study Group to review the Bay of Pigs operation and make recommendations as to how similar mistakes could be avoided in the future. Kennedy was impressed with the criticism of Eisenhower's defense policies that Maxwell Taylor made in his book *The Uncertain Trumpet*, and brought the former army chief of staff out of retirement to head the committee. He subsequently came to rely heavily on Taylor's advice, and appointed him as chairman of the Joint Chiefs of Staff. Kennedy also appointed to the study group Attorney General Robert F. Kennedy; CIA Director Allen W. Dulles; and Burke, who represented the Joint Chiefs. The committee met frequently over the next two months, collected testimony from dozens of participants in the Bay of Pigs operation, and prepared its analysis and recommendations.[136]

The final report of the Cuban Study Group, which was drafted mainly by Taylor, was presented to President Kennedy on 13 June 1961. It identified a number of factors that had contributed to the failure of the operation. Problems of logistics, communications, and coordination were analyzed, with particular emphasis on the decision-making in Washington. The basic problem, the committee concluded, was that an operation of such magnitude "could not be prepared and conducted in such a way that all U. S. support of it and connection with it could be plausibly disclaimed." The effort to keep the landing totally covert prevented adequate staffing; led to a lack of communication and to misunderstanding because there were no written plans, policy statements, and records of decisions; and imposed a crippling array of nonmilitary considerations on the entire operation.

The committee recommended that Kennedy form a Strategic Resources Group of representatives from the State Department, the Defense Department, and the Central Intelligence Agency to plan and execute the kind of paramilitary and cold-war operations which the United States must necessarily engage in to counter the threat of communist expansion. These undertakings, the committee emphasized, must be adequately staffed, properly coordinated, and, once begun, must be "carried through to conclusion with the same determination as a military operation." The Joint Chiefs, the report concluded:

> should be brought to feel as great a sense of responsibility for contributing to the success of the Cold War as to the conventional military defense of the country in time of war. They should be encouraged to express the military viewpoint clearly and directly before the President and other high officials of the government. The latter, in turn, should be aware of the need of getting the considered views of the Chiefs before taking important decisions affecting Cold War programs and operations.[137]

Kennedy accepted and implemented many of the recommendations contained in the report, particularly those relating to clarification of the responsibilities of his military advisers. Feeling that the Joint Chiefs had failed him badly during the planning of the Bay of Pigs, he met with them in May, while the report of the Taylor Committee was in preparation, to discuss his concerns and expectations. On 28 June, they were presented with a formal statement of their duties as the president's "principal military advisors." The Joint Chiefs of Staff, Kennedy stated, would be expected to take responsibility for both military and paramilitary operations. They were charged with ensuring that military factors were clearly understood before decisions were made, and would be expected to offer advice as well as respond to requests. They were to participate fully in discussions of economic and political as well as military affairs. The kind of misunderstanding between the commander in chief and the Joint Chiefs that had played so large a role in the Bay of Pigs operation could not be allowed to recur.[138]

The report of the Cuban Study Group, although it contained a number of compromise findings and conclusions, was nevertheless agreed to by all members of the panel. The overall tone of the report, with its emphasis on removing restraints from American prosecution of the cold war, clearly reflected Burke's own views. Implementation of the recommendations of the study group, however, would not be his responsibility. Discouraged by the events of the past spring, Burke was by this time greatly looking forward to retirement.

Shortly after his inauguration, Kennedy had offered to reappoint Burke as CNO, and renewed the offer on a number of occasions. Burke declined each time. His decision to retire was not politically motivated: he had submitted his request for retirement before the election of 1960. He thought the navy needed new leadership, and that his continued service as chief of naval operations would not be in the best interests of the service. He also preferred not to become involved in selecting his successor. He prepared a list of the fifty naval officers qualified for the post and, under pressure from Navy Secretary Connally, identified the six or eight he considered the leading candidates, but he strongly believed that his relief should not be burdened with the charge that he was "Burke's man."[139]

Burke also declined Kennedy's offer of the ambassadorship to Australia. He did not want to be an ambassador, Burke explained, and did not think he would be very good one. He spent his last two months in office carrying out the many tasks that had become so familiar over the past six years. He was tired, discouraged, and extremely glad that he had submitted his request for retirement nearly a year before. "I was completely frustrated," he later explained:

> I felt there was nothing that I could accomplish. I was spinning my wheels. I would submit recommendations, I would explain and explain and explain and nothing would happen. And what the hell, I could go out and grow roses or sugar cane or sit on the front porch, and at least I could watch the sun come up in the morning under pleasant circumstances. But of that job was nothing I wanted to continue.[140]

On 25 July, he was awarded a Distinguished Service Medal by President Kennedy at the White House. One week later, on 1 August 1961, he turned over the post of chief of naval operations to Admiral George W. Anderson. The ceremony took place at a time of grave international tension, as the United States stood on the brink of a major confrontation with the Soviet Union over the fate of Berlin. But Burke, who had led the navy through six years of crisis, was no longer at the helm. He was a private citizen once again, after forty-two years of naval service.

Following his retirement, Burke took several months to relax and consider his future. He was only fifty-nine years old, and had been used to hard work all his life. He knew that he would not enjoy being idle, and would have to find a new career for himself, starting from scratch. He sought the advice and counsel of a number of friends who knew and understood the business world. They advised him to divide his time equally between some sort of business employment and public service, and helped him to review the many job offers he received. Within a year, he had chosen many of the corporations to which he would devote his time. These included the Newport News Shipbuilding and

Drydock Company, the Chrysler Corporation, the Thiokol Corporation, where he was a member of the board of directors, and Texaco, Inc., where he served on both the board of directors and the executive committee.[141]

Burke's public service was also chosen with care. He served on the advisory committees or boards of directors of veterans' organizations, patriotic groups, educational institutions, and a host of others. Of particular interest was the Georgetown Center for Strategic and International Studies, which Burke helped to organize in the summer of 1962, and for which he served as chairman, counselor, and member of the executive committee for fifteen years, helping to build it into one of the nation's top institutions for the study of policy issues in international affairs. In connection with this work, he also organized conferences, promoted studies, and wrote articles of his own on questions related to the cold war, the Soviet threat, and military strategy. Never having had children of his own, he also derived particular pleasure from his work for the National Capitol Area Council of the Boy Scouts of America, for whom he served as president and member of the executive committee from 1962 to 1974. This service gave him an opportunity to expand in civilian life on some of the moral commitments that lay behind the Naval Leadership Program he instituted when he was CNO.

Burke also continued to take a strong interest in current questions of national security, making frequent speeches on political issues. In August 1963 he testified before the Senate Armed Services Committee in opposition to ratification of the nuclear-test-ban treaty, and in 1964 he was active in supporting Republican Barry M. Goldwater in his presidential campaign. In September 1973, Burke served as President Richard M. Nixon's representative and head of the American delegation to the funeral of King Gustav VI Adolf of Sweden. On 10 January 1977, in recognition of Burke's efforts on behalf of the United States in the period following his retirement from the navy, President Gerald R. Ford awarded him the nation's highest civilian honor, the Medal of Freedom.

In the spring of 1962, Burke was asked to deliver the Walter E. Edge lecture series at Princeton University. He chose as his subject "Power and Peace," and used the occasion to sum up much of his philosophy of world affairs. Power, he pointed out, was far more than the ability to exert physical force. It was "the capacity to induce others to behave according to patterns in one's own mind." The exercise of power, Burke argued, might involve anything from pure persuasion, to economic rewards and social sanctions, to the use of military might. Resources alone did not constitute real power; the exercise of power also required a clear sense of direction, a realistic understanding of human motivation, skill in applying different modes of influence, and the determination to impose one's will.

Ever since his experience with the Korean truce negotiations, Burke had been painfully aware of the expanding pressure of communism in the world, and deeply troubled by an apparent lack of will in the United States to stand against it. "Between the free West and the Communist movement," he told his

Princeton audience, "there can be no reconciliation, no real coexistence. The confrontation is absolute. . . . The defense of civilization is tantamount to the destruction of the communist movement throughout the world."

Faced with such a challenge, Burke concluded, the United States could not afford to be half-hearted or diffident in the use of its power. It could not afford to rely on "territory-centered" policies such as containment, or on the "last-ditch" concepts of massive retaliation and deterrence. The nation had to recognize that the cold war was more than a struggle for real estate, or a military confrontation. It was an ideological challenge that had to be met with all the varied and complex forms of power the nation was capable of wielding, backed by the will to use force if necessary, and the firm determination to win.[142]

As chief of naval operations, Burke devoted himself to preparing the United States to meet this crisis, and it was a source of frustration to him that he was not more successful in mobilizing a higher level of national commitment, which he felt was urgently needed. His political philosophy was apparent in many of his most innovative programs. His emphasis on developing the navy's capability for limited war, his critique of existing national strategies, his sponsorship of Polaris, and even his Naval Leadership Program were shaped by this vision of the cold war. Burke succeeded to a remarkable degree in charting an independent course for the navy in national defense, one that reflected traditional naval strategic tenets of flexibility, versatility, and the peacetime exercise of power, as well as his own understanding of the postwar world. He fought to maintain a well-rounded, flexible, innovative service, honed to a sharp edge of operational readiness, and prepared to meet a wide range of demands. The performance of the fleet in the October 1962 Cuban missile crisis and the early years of the Vietnam War was in part due to his significant success in achieving that goal.

Burke came to office at a time when the powers of the chief of naval operations were at their peacetime height. For his first two terms he maintained operational control of the navy's forces, and until nearly the end of his tenure had great influence in designing navy programs and budgets. He used these powers to the limit, applying his wide experience in weapons technology, planning, and operations, as well as his considerable political skill to enhance the prestige and influence of the navy within the Defense Department. He also demonstrated a remarkable ability to speak firmly and forthrightly for the navy's interests, while remaining a loyal and well-respected member of Eisenhower's defense team.

The legacy Arleigh Burke left the navy, however, was far more than the sum of his achievements in weapons innovation, strategy, and shipbuilding. His style of leadership embodied to a high degree the ideals of naval service: loyalty, integrity, and above all devotion to duty. A man of simple virtues, high principles, and great dedication, Burke committed himself totally to the service he loved, and having discharged his duty to the best of his ability, he left the navy stronger for his having worn its uniform.

GEORGE WHALEN ANDERSON, JR.

1 August 1961–1 August 1963

LAWRENCE KORB

George W. Anderson, Jr., the sixteenth chief of naval operations was born in Brooklyn, New York, on 15 December 1906.[1] The son of George W. Anderson, who ran a real estate agency, and Clara Green Anderson, George, Jr., was reared in the Roman Catholic faith and received his primary and secondary education in the parochial schools of the Diocese of Brooklyn. An exceptionally bright student, he graduated from the Jesuit-run Brooklyn Preparatory School at the age of sixteen and entered the Naval Academy in the summer of 1923. There, Anderson continued to excel in his studies. He graduated twenty-seventh in his class and received his commission as an ensign on 2 June 1927, six months shy of his twenty-first birthday.

After serving for three years as a surface-warfare officer in the cruiser *Cincinnati*, Anderson volunteered for flight training and was accepted. He received his wings in October 1930 and spent the next decade in a variety of aviation billets, afloat and ashore. In the first part of World War II he was in the Plans Division of the Bureau of Aeronautics, where his main function was to work on the development of naval aircraft. His responsibilities included liaison with all the wartime agencies charged with the production and allocation of military aircraft. He performed so effectively in this assignment that the War Department awarded him a letter of commendation and Brigadier General Dwight D. Eisenhower, then in the Army's War Plans Division, personally commended him.

In March 1943 he was assigned as navigator and tactical coordinator for the new aircraft carrier *Yorktown*. During the eight months he served in her, he participated in several air actions against the Japanese Navy and received a number of personal and unit decorations. From late 1943 to mid-1945, he served on the staff of the Pacific Fleet as plans officer and as assistant to the deputy commander in chief of the fleet, Vice Admiral John H. Towers.

From 1945 to 1948, Anderson was assigned to the Navy Department in Washington where he served in naval, joint, and international billets. These included deputy naval planner on the Joint Planning Staff, member of the American-Canadian Permanent Joint Board of Defense, and naval member of the Brazilian-United States Defense Commission. During the following five years, he commanded an escort carrier, the *Mindoro,* and an attack carrier, the *Franklin D. Roosevelt;* attended the newly established National War College; and, at the personal request of the new NATO commander, General Eisenhower, was assigned as the senior American officer for plans and operations on the staff of the Supreme Allied Commander in Europe. In 1953, when Eisenhower became president, he named Admiral Arthur W. Radford as chairman of the Joint Chiefs of Staff, and Radford, in turn, asked fellow-aviator Anderson to return to Washington as his special assistant. The appointment reflected an appreciation for the flexibility of Anderson's skills. It also assured him of selection to rear admiral, a rank he received in the summer of 1954.

Within three years, Anderson moved up to vice admiral. In 1955, he took the "double-hatted" billet of commander of the Taiwan Patrol Force and chief of the joint staff of the Pacific theater command. In May 1957 he was given the three-star billet of chief of staff to aviator Felix B. Stump, commander in chief of the Pacific theater. However, Anderson had not had command of a carrier task force and, in July 1958, he took the unusual step of reverting to rear admiral so that he could take command of Carrier Division 6 in the Mediterranean. The timing was fortunate. Immediately upon his arrival in the area, his force became involved in the landings in Lebanon and his work during those operations earned him command of the Sixth Fleet in 1959 and a return to his vice admiralcy. This tour did much to enhance Anderson's reputation as a shrewd military commander and naval diplomat.[2]

When John F. Kennedy became president in early 1961, he offered Admiral Arleigh A. Burke a fourth two-year term as chief of naval operations, but Burke refused to continue. Instead, he suggested the names of six admirals whom he felt were qualified to relieve him and it surprised no one that Anderson's name was on this list.[3] Essentially, there were three reasons why President Kennedy selected Anderson to become the first Roman Catholic and the third aviator to fill the billet of CNO. First, Anderson had an extremely broad operational background. As a junior officer he had served in both battleships and carriers and had flown with both patrol and fighter squadrons. The major commands he had held included both antisubmarine and attack carriers, a fleet air wing, and a carrier air division. Moreover, his operational assignments had not been confined to one theater. Second, Anderson had had extensive experience on naval, joint, and international staffs. He worked on three fleet staffs, in a bureau, in the office of the CNO, and with the Joint Chiefs of Staff. He had also had unusual experience with Allied military leaders in Europe and the Western Hemisphere. Third, Anderson had earned widespread support within the navy, the other services, and the civilian leadership of the national-security bureaucracy. His naval support was based not only on his comprehensive operational and staff experience, but also on his respect for the informal customs of the service, as illustrated by his willingness to give up a star so that he could comply with the tradition that an admiral's flag is not genuinely earned unless it is flown at sea. Anderson enjoyed the respect of army and air force officers because of his performance in the joint arena and his graduation from the National War College. Anderson was a skilled interservice diplomat who had great tact and seemed to be able to rise above naval parochialism. Moreover, most high-ranking army and air force officers were graduates of the National War College, a virtual prerequisite for key billets in both of those services but not in the navy, and Anderson was the first prospective CNO to have attended that school.[4]

For these reasons, both Navy Secretary John B. Connally and Secretary of Defense Robert S. McNamara recommended that Anderson be elevated over ten senior admirals to become the chief of naval operations. Kennedy agreed. However, because Anderson's qualifications were so diversified and unusual, the Kennedy administration proposed that he serve a two-year term as CNO and then, in 1963, move up to be chairman of the Joint Chiefs of Staff. In 1961, General Lyman L. Lemnitzer was beginning the third year of a four-year term as chairman, and it was generally believed that a naval officer should take over that job when the general retired in 1963. Given Anderson's record of interservice cooperation—which made him a logical choice—and the fact that his first two years as CNO would end when a relief for Lemnitzer would be needed, the plan seemed perfect. However, when the time came, Anderson was not promoted to chair the chiefs and did not even receive the customary second two-year appointment as CNO. Acknowledged as one of the best qualified men ever to hold the billet, he was fired. His two years as CNO proved to be the most frustrating and difficult in his forty years of naval service.[5]

Anderson's problems as CNO were primarily attributable to his difficulties with Secretary McNamara; indeed, his relationship with McNamara overshadowed his whole tenure as CNO. The two men had diametrically opposed views on the roles that the secretary of defense and the service chiefs should play in the process of making military policy. A former president of Ford Motor Company, McNamara made it a condition of his taking the post of secretary of defense that he could be an "activist manager."[6] Unlike his seven predecessors, he wanted total control of the defense establishment. He wanted not only to set policy but also to control its implementation—in some cases, down to the minutest detail. One of McNamara's proudest claims was that he personally made several thousand decisions every year.[7]

Primarily by introducing program budgeting and systems analysis into defense decision-making, McNamara created a revolution within the Pentagon. Defense policy and defense budgets were formulated within the Office of the Secretary of Defense (OSD). The military departments and the Joint Chiefs of Staff lost much of their previous authority. They could only comment on and try to make changes in OSD initiatives. Moreover, the contributions of the services and the Joint Chiefs to making decisions had to be based on cost-benefit analyses, and were often overruled by McNamara without consultation, explanation, or discussion. Military leaders believed that experience and intuition gathered over several decades of service in the field by professionals counted for very little in this "McNamara monarchy." Finally, once McNamara had made a decision, he expected everyone in uniform to support it unequivocally and enthusiastically both within the executive branch and before the legislature.[8]

Anderson had a completely different perspective on the proper relationship between the OSD and the services. In his opinion, McNamara's civilian analysts were working at the wrong echelon; they were operating above the professional military level rather than in an advisory capacity to the military.[9] Anderson did not question the value of cost-benefit analysis but he believed that it should be used to temper military experience, not to substitute for it. In his view, the specialists in that field endangered national security by extrapolating their judgments into areas in which they had no expert knowledge. Moreover, the OSD should content itself with laying down broad policy guidelines and allow the service chiefs latitude in implementing them. After thirty-six years of commissioned service, Anderson considered himself better qualified than a businessman or a scholar to decide questions concerning the specific characteristics of weapon systems and tactics for operational units. Finally, as a service chief and member of the Joint Chiefs, Anderson was responsible not only to the secretary of defense but also to the president and to Congress, and the chief executive and members of the legislature had a right to hear the opinions of their senior naval adviser, even when these opinions differed markedly from those of the secretary of defense. As Anderson noted on one occasion, the full force of recommendations made by the service chiefs to the president and Congress should not be "dulled in any way in transmission."[10]

During his seven years at the helm of the Department of Defense, McNamara's style of leadership frequently brought him into conflict with his military chiefs. However, for two reasons, the scope and intensity of his clashes with Anderson were unrivaled. First, his tight controls most heavily affected the navy, which had always been less hierarchical and more decentralized than the other services.[11] Second, Admiral Anderson was articulate, strong-willed, adamant in his convictions, and, like McNamara, somewhat autocratic and arrogant. None of the other chiefs who served during McNamara's tenure possessed this particular combination of traits.

Ironically, relations between Anderson and McNamara did not go badly in the beginning. Indeed, rapport at first between the two men was excellent. Anderson impressed the secretary by making a determined effort to dampen the interservice rivalries that had plagued the Pentagon during the Eisenhower administration: for one thing, he instructed his staff to be more accommodating in their dealings with the other services.[12] For McNamara's part, during his first year in office he raised the navy's budget by $2.6 billion, or 21.4 per cent, and provided more funds for programs such as the Polaris. Harmony was at such a premium that, in the fall and winter of 1961, Anderson even supported within the executive branch McNamara's decision to overrule Congress's resolution that the next aircraft carrier would have nuclear propulsion. In February 1962, Anderson somewhat casually informed Congress that a simple lack of funds had made it necessary to make the new carrier a conventionally powered ship.[13]

However, the honeymoon between the CNO and the secretary was short-lived. Well before the end of Anderson's first year in office, the Jesuit-trained naval officer and the Harvard-trained businessman were in open conflict. The most critical of the several issues over which they clashed were the B-70 bomber, the TFX fighter, and the conduct of the naval blockade during the Cuban missile crisis. These three controversies highlighted the dynamics of the McNamara-Anderson relationship, but their disagreements ranged over such disparate areas as military compensation and the terms of a treaty to ban nuclear testing.

Whether or not to develop the B-70 manned bomber was the first key issue about weapons that McNamara had to decide.[14] The air force wanted the B-70 to replace the aging B-52 as its principal strategic bomber. The B-70 was designed to fly at 2,000 miles per hour at an altitude of 70,000 feet and to drop nuclear bombs on designated enemy targets. In McNamara's view, it was not worth its estimated cost of $11.4 billion because it had the advantages neither of missiles nor of other manned bombers. It was slower and more vulnerable than a missile and less flexible than other bombers, that is, it would not, as the B-52 could, look for new targets or find and attack mobile targets whose location was uncertain. The secretary of defense preferred to put the same money into accelerating the programs for the Polaris submarine and the Minuteman missile.

Anderson, like his predecessor, Burke, agreed with McNamara's analysis of the B-70.[15] President Kennedy also supported the secretary's position and therefore the weapon was not funded in McNamara's defense budget for fiscal year 1963, nor would he agree to spend the extra funds voted for that purpose by Congress in fiscal year 1962. However, the system had strong support in the legislature, particularly among the members of the House Armed Services Committee. To prevent Congress from trying to force the administration to build a bomber that it did not want, McNamara needed support for his position from the Joint Chiefs. Anderson was the logical choice to lead the fight against the B-70. The chief of staff of the air force, General Curtis E. LeMay, a life-long supporter of manned bombers, was the principal advocate of the new plane.

In early 1962, McNamara sought public support from Anderson but the CNO refused because he believed that McNamara's attempt to play one service off against the other could set a dangerous precedent and would revive the interservice squabbling that he, Anderson, was working to eliminate.[16] In the absence of public opposition from the military, Congress approved the program in the spring of 1962, and only the personal intervention of President Kennedy prevented a minor constitutional crisis. As a result of a meeting between Kennedy and Congressman Carl Vinson, chairman of the House Armed Services Committee, Congress agreed to drop language in the Defense Department appropriation act "directing" the secretary of the air force to proceed with complete development of the B-70. However, in return for this concession, Kennedy agreed to allow the air force to build three prototypes of the bomber.[17] These planes eventually cost $1.5 billion, money that McNamara argued might have been saved had Anderson supported him.

While the B-70 was the first major weapon system to be killed by McNamara, the TFX (tactical fighter experimental), or F-111, was the first one to be initiated by him.[18] In February 1961, less than one month after he took office, he directed that a tactical aircraft should be built to fill the aviation requirements of all the armed services. He did this despite the facts that the TFX had been designed by the air force's Tactical Air Command as a replacement for its F-105 and that the navy was developing the F-6D Missileer to replace its aging F-4H. The air force needed a plane that could operate from sod fields, fly nonstop without refueling across the Atlantic, carry large quantities of ordnance, and operate equally well at high and low altitudes at speeds in excess of 1,700 miles per hour. On the other hand, the navy wanted a tactical fighter with long endurance and a very complex missile system.

On 7 June 1961, about two weeks before Anderson's selection as CNO was announced, McNamara ordered the air force to develop the TFX to replace both the F-105 and the F-4H. He instructed the air force to work closely with the navy in order to develop coordinated design specifications that could be issued to the aircraft industry in the fall of 1961. However, on 22 August, three weeks after Anderson took office, the navy and air force reported to the secretary of defense that they had been unable to work out an agreement. The air force wanted the plane to have a minimum weight of 65,000 pounds and a fuselage length of eighty-five feet. Aviator Anderson insisted that the plane weigh no more than 55,000 pounds and be no longer than fifty-six feet, so that it would be able to operate from a carrier.[19] McNamara then took matters into his own hands. He had Harold Brown, his director of defense research and engineering, unilaterally formulate requirements for the bi-service plane and issue requests for contract proposals from the aircraft industry. Brown completed these tasks in October 1961 and by December several companies had submitted proposals.

However, eleven months passed before McNamara selected a company to develop the aircraft. Admiral Anderson was responsible for most of this delay. In May 1962, after several reviews, the Source Selection Board and the Air Force Council recommended awarding the TFX contract to the Boeing Company.[20] Instead of endorsing this decision, Anderson, on the advice of the chief of the Bureau of Naval Weapons, pointed out that none of the proposals met the navy's requirements and once again suggested abandoning the project.[21] In June, after another review, the Selection Board and Council again recommended that the contract for the TFX be awarded to Boeing, but Anderson countered by contending that Boeing should be selected only to continue design studies. The CNO refused to commit the navy to development because he was not yet certain that the Boeing design met the navy's specifications.[22] Finally, on 10 November 1962, Anderson supported the decision of the air force chief of staff that a contract for the TFX be awarded to Boeing. He did this not because he had changed his mind but because the Boeing design had less commonality than other designs and more combat capability.[23] McNamara advised him that if the navy refused to buy the TFX it would not get a replacement for the F-4H. Two weeks after Anderson had given his endorsement to the Boeing design, McNamara announced that a consortium of General Dynamics and the Grumman Aircraft Company would get the contract for the TFX.

Anderson and many other military leaders were outraged at McNamara's choice. In awarding the contract to General Dynamics, the secretary had overruled the unanimous opinion of twenty-one flag and general officers from the navy and the air force. The CNO could not take his case to the president since Kennedy had approved the secretary's decision on 13 November, about one week before McNamara announced it publicly. However, in February 1963, when the Subcommittee on Investigations, chaired by Senator John McClellan, opened hearings on the TFX, primarily to allow Senator Henry Jackson to protest Boeing's loss of the contract, another opportunity arose, and Anderson planned to take full advantage of it to vent his discontent.

The hearings were supposed to last only five or six days; instead, they lasted for nine months and virtually destroyed McNamara's reputation as an objective leader who relied on scientific methodology. The testimony of Anderson, which Senator McClellan called the finest the committee received, played a large part in undermining McNamara's credibility.[24] Anderson explained why he disagreed with the concept of the TFX and with McNamara's choice of General Dynamics rather than Boeing as the prime contractor to build the plane.[25] He said that, in his opinion, combined development of the aircraft was not technologically feasible but that he had accepted McNamara's decision on that point in consonance with the military tradition of submission to civilian authority. He promised the committee that in the future he would be more contentious. He explained his reasons for opposing the choice of General Dynamics by pointing out that it was his responsibility to procure the best weapons possible for the navy and to provide the men under his command with the greatest possible margin of safety in carrying out their hazardous tasks. Anderson cited the many advantages of the Boeing proposal and belittled those who tried to quantify such intangibles as combat capability. He closed his testimony with the observation that two of his nephews were killed in naval aviation and his son was serving as a naval test pilot.

Strong as was the disagreement between Anderson and McNamara over the TFX, that controversy paled when compared with their dispute during the Cuban missile crisis of October 1962. The clash between the secretary of defense and the chief of naval operations in the navy's flag plot on the night of 24 October was so nasty that the two men never again enjoyed a decent relationship.

The Cuban missile crisis erupted when an American U-2 reconnaissance aircraft discovered that the Soviets were placing intermediate-range ballistic missiles in Cuba to overcome the advantage of the United States in the strategic balance of power. To force the Russians to withdraw their missiles, McNamara and his deputy, Roswell Gilpatric, proposed a blockade or quarantine of Cuba. By contrast, Anderson and most of the Joint Chiefs wanted to launch air strikes against the Soviet bases in Cuba but admitted that an invasion by American ground forces would have to follow. On Monday, 22 October, President Kennedy announced that a blockade would be imposed effective the next day at 10:00 a.m.

The conflict between Anderson and McNamara concerned the navy's conduct of the blockade. Although Anderson enthusiastically supported the decision to create a blockade, he found three aspects of its implementation disturbing. First, the blockade line was drawn too close to Cuba. Originally, the navy deployed its ships 500 miles to the east of Cuba so that they could be out of range of Russian MIG aircraft on the island. However, on Tuesday evening, Kennedy, at the urging of British Ambassador David Ormsby-Gore, drew the line much closer to Cuba. This move was urged on the president in order to give Soviet leader, Nikita Khrushchev, more time to decide whether or not to challenge the blockade. Second, the blockade was conducted in a manner that violated two sacred naval doctrines: going through the chain of command to convey orders, and the autonomy of the commander on the scene. Throughout the crisis, political leaders in the basement of the White House communicated with and gave direct orders to the ships stationed along the quarantine line. Third, the blockade was not enforced in accordance with standard naval procedures. On Sunday, 21 October, Anderson had described to the National Security Council the navy's plan and procedures for conducting the blockade. He told the president and his advisers that each ship approaching the quarantine line would be signaled to stop for boarding and inspection. If any ship failed to respond, a shot would be fired across her bow. If there was still no satisfactory response, a shot would be fired into her rudder to cripple, but not to sink her. Anderson was left with the impression that the president would permit the navy to conduct the blockade in this manner. Yet, when the first Soviet ships approached the quarantine line, the White House directed that they not be boarded. Moreover, one Soviet ship, the tanker *Bucharest,* was allowed to pass unchecked after merely identifying herself.[26]

Anderson's frustrations with the conduct of the blockade came to a head on Wednesday night, 24 October, when McNamara and Gilpatric came unannounced into the flag plot to explore the navy's procedures and routine for intercepting. Anderson reminded McNamara that he had outlined the procedures at the meeting of the Security Council on Sunday, and he saw no need to discuss the subject further. McNamara then asked a number of detailed questions about what the navy would do under certain circumstances. Anderson refused to be drawn into specifics and explained that the navy had longstanding regulations that covered blockades. This sequence angered both men and led to some harsh exchanges.[27] The sharp encounter ended when Anderson told McNamara that he and his deputy ought to go back to their offices and let the navy run the blockade.

Gilpatric informed the White House about what had happened and warned that the relationship between Anderson and McNamara could never again be one of mutual confidence and loyalty.[28] Shortly thereafter, the president agreed to allow McNamara to replace Anderson at the expiration of the CNO's first two-year term the following summer, but only on the condition that an attractive position were found for the admiral.[29] On 21 May 1963, the White House announced the appointment of David L. McDonald as the seventeenth CNO and the selection of George Anderson to be American ambassador to Portugal.

In retrospect it is not surprising that Anderson lasted for such a short time as a member of the Joint Chiefs under Kennedy. His fellow members did not fare much better, even though none of them had challenged the secretary to the degree he had. In October 1962, upon completion of his first year as chairman, General Lemnitzer was transferred to NATO. In the same month, General George H. Decker, who was completing his first term as army chief of staff, was summarily retired. Finally, General LeMay, who was appointed to the Joint Chiefs of Staff at the same time as was Anderson, received reappointment for only a partial term at the expiration of his first two years in office.

Indeed, it would have been surprising had Anderson been reappointed to a second term as CNO. This would have meant that he had failed in his first term. Many of the changes that McNamara attempted to make in civil-military relationships within the Defense Department and between the uniformed military and the president and Congress not only altered customs but also violated the spirit of the Constitution and the National Security Act of 1947 and its related amendments. For a chief of naval operations, or any other member of the Joint Chiefs, to allow these practices to go unchallenged would have been a disservice to the nation and to the military profession.

While Anderson's contemporaries also took issue with McNamara on occasion, none did it as consistently or as cogently as he did. Within the executive branch, in public speeches, and before the Congress, he forcefully articulated the real issues raised by McNamara's methods. Ultimately, Anderson was vindicated. The General Dynamics version of the TFX did not meet the navy's specifications. The role of systems analysts in the making of military decisions was downgraded by McNamara's successors. And, in 1967, Congress gave the service chiefs a statutory four-year term so that they could testify more freely. Lastly, in 1975, after the *Mayaguez* incident, Secretary of Defense James R. Schlesinger admitted that Washington had reached the point where it was overcontrolling the operational forces.

However, Anderson can be faulted for accepting the ambassadorship to Portugal. This lowered the political costs that the administration had to pay to fire him and prevented him from carrying his case to the public as an authoritative private citizen. In 1963, the armed forces and the nation needed a symbol and a spokesman. The only plausible explanation for Anderson's decision to accept the new job seems to lie in his rapport with John F. Kennedy, which was matched only by his lack of empathy with McNamara.[30] Perhaps because Kennedy was the first Roman Catholic president, Anderson, himself a very devout Catholic, respected him and was anxious to see him succeed. Therefore, he took the ambassadorship to remain on the Kennedy team and to avoid embarrassing his commander in chief.

After leaving the embassy in Lisbon, Anderson retired from government service and took up residence in Washington, D.C. However, he remained active in national security affairs. During the Nixon administration he served as chairman of the president's Foreign Intelligence Advisory Board, and from 1970 to 1974, served as the leader of a group of retired admirals who opposed many of Admiral Elmo Zumwalt's policies concerning personnel.[31]

DAVID LAMAR McDONALD

1 August 1963–1 August 1967

FLOYD D. KENNEDY, JR.

In 1963, for one of the few times in his naval career, David L. McDonald was fairly certain of what his next, and probably his last, duty assignment would be. He had just finished a tour as the three-star commander of the Sixth Fleet, had pinned on the fourth star of a full admiral, and was embarking on a tour as commander in chief of U. S. Naval Forces, Europe. At fifty-six, he had achieved his command ambitions, those of the Sixth Fleet and of the new London-based billet; moreover, it was then the pattern for the man in London, after a three-year tour, to go to Norfolk and become commander in chief of the Atlantic Fleet, with the dual NATO assignment of Supreme Allied Commander, Atlantic. This would be a highly desirable end to his distinguished thirty-eight-year naval career.

But future assignments had to await the completion of his three-year tour in London. This was a prestigious position, replete with diplomatic responsibilities for which by temperament and predilection this naval aviator was eminently suited. It was, however, his reputation for diplomacy and tact that was to cut McDonald's tour in London very short and prove the certainty he felt about his next duty assignment to be unwarranted.

One month after he relieved Admiral Harold P. Smith in London, McDonald was in Ankara, Turkey, on the first leg of an inspection tour of the facilities under his command in the Near and Middle East. His schedule called for subsequent stops in Teheran, Iran; New Delhi, India; Manama, Bahrein; and Asmara, Ethiopia. Very early in the morning of the day that he was scheduled to leave Ankara for Teheran, McDonald received a telephone call. As he related the conversation in his oral autobiography,

> it was a Commander in Washington calling to tell me that the Secretary of the Navy wanted me to be in his office at 7:30 Monday morning. By that time it was one o'clock Saturday morning in Turkey. So I said why. "I can't tell you."
>
> "What?"
>
> "I can't tell you," he repeated.

"Well," I said, "You obviously know where I am. I hope you know what I'm doing. You know, we spend a lot of money to make friends in this part of the world and tonight in Iran they're giving a big reception honoring me and my very good friend General Sunay. I'd like to come in about Wednesday or Thursday. This will not interfere with tonight's reception in Teheran and then I can give the people advance notice in other places. But just to summarily cancel tonight's affair like this, not even giving them an explanation, not only will the Iranians be upset but I think General Sunay will have his nose out of joint and I think he's a pretty important fellow in this part of the world."

"Well, there's nothing I can do about it," said the Commander.

"Who can?" I asked.

"The Secretary of the Navy."

I said, "Put him on."

"Well, Admiral, I can't. He's in San Juan."

I said, "If I contacted him, would it do any good?"

"Not a bit," he says.

I hung up the phone, and this is a very interesting thing. I hung up the phone and my wife said: "What was that?" I said, "They've fired George Anderson and, Goddammit, I'm going to be CNO."

She said, "What?" and I said, "No. I was just kidding."[1]

Admiral McDonald walked into the secretary of the navy's office on schedule the following Monday morning. He had been met in New York by an officer who told him unofficially that George W. Anderson had indeed been fired, or at least was not going to be reappointed, and he, David L. McDonald, would be the next CNO. Secretary of the Navy Fred Korth made the information official. McDonald's reaction was unexpected:

> When he informed me about the CNO job I told him I was highly honored but I was also highly embarrassed. I was honored about the job but embarrassed to tell him I didn't want the job; never had wanted it, didn't want it then.[2]

After explaining his reasons to Korth, McDonald repeated them to Deputy Secretary of Defense Roswell L. Gilpatric, who rebutted them, point by point, until the admiral interrupted and said:

> We're wasting our time. I thought we were going to discuss whether or not I was to be appointed. From what you've just said, President Kennedy has already approved it and I'm going to be CNO, unless I just say I won't take the job.
>
> And he said, "That's right." My reply then was, "Of course I'm not that big a fool."[3]

McDonald returned to London and then visited various naval establishments in the Pacific and the Far East while he waited for the term of his predecessor to expire on 1 August 1963. He was genuinely disappointed over his appointment. In addition, the manner in which he had been told about it was symptomatic of an issue that rankled him throughout his tenure as CNO, that of increasingly clumsy civilian control over the assignment and promotion of flag officers and the unprofessional manner in which the civilian authority attempted to interject itself into the selection process. This was, however, but one of many issues he had to face in the next four years.

Born in Maysville, Georgia, on 12 September 1906, to the Reverend William Benjamin and Mary (David) McDonald, David was reared in a variety of small Georgia towns. From the time he was ten, he wanted to be a lawyer, an ambition he did not abandon until he was well into his naval career. To attain this end, as a youngster, he swept out a dentist's office every night and eventually supplemented this income with a "laundry concession," which meant he had to collect dirty laundry on Monday and ship it by train into a distant city that afternoon. When it came back the following Saturday, he delivered it to its owners, clearing twenty-five cents on each dollar. He also took over a pressing establishment where he pressed the clothes of farmers who came into town to take a shower and visit the barber.

In 1923, a banker suggested to McDonald that he could do well by attending the Military Academy at West Point. There he would receive an excellent basic education and embark upon a rewarding and secure career; if he decided he did not like military life, he could resign from the service upon graduation. A congressman who was a close friend of his maternal grandfather agreed to give him an appointment to the academy, but he was two months and twelve days too young. The minimum age for the Naval Academy at that time was one year younger than that for West Point, so the congressman offered this alternative to McDonald. He suggested, however, that a year of prep school would provide him with an opportunity to weigh the decision more carefully and would give him the extra age he needed for West Point. McDonald agreed, and used his savings from his various business enterprises to prepare for entry to one of the two academies. During this year he made his choice between the two academies; as he described it,

> I discovered during the Fall that the cadets at West Point—in the summertime—went up the Hudson and drilled and the midshipmen went to Europe. So I said I wanted to go to the Naval Academy because I wanted to go to Europe. Honestly, that's the real reason I selected the Naval Academy.[4]

McDonald arrived at Annapolis in 1924, but he did not go to Europe until 1955. Between 1900 and 1939, only two academy classes did not have a summer cruise to Europe, and David McDonald's class was one.

Despite this disappointment, McDonald did well at the academy, winning the Battalion Commander Medal as outstanding rifleman, the DAR sword for excellence in practical and theoretical seamanship, and a third award for excellence in ordnance. However, he still wanted to pursue a career in law, and, upon graduation from the academy in 1928, he began making inquiries about legal opportunities. His first assignment as an officer was to the battleship *Mississippi,* where he was to serve the two-year obligation required under a recently enacted law.

In 1929, Ensign McDonald had lined up a civilian position and penned his resignation from the navy when he had an opportunity to enter the navy's flight program in Pensacola, Florida. His prospective employer urged him to accept the flight training and resign after he had completed that potentially exciting experience. McDonald agreed. However, he delayed entering the flight program until after his marriage to Catherine Thompson on 7 October 1930. He excelled in flying and, after graduation, went to Fighter Squadron 6 aboard the carrier *Saratoga,* where he flew Boeing F2B, F3B, and F4B fighters. In 1934, after three cruises in the *Saratoga,* he requested and received a transfer to the *Detroit,* a light cruiser, so that he could qualify as a watch-stander, a requirement for his next promotion. When he had finished a year aboard the *Detroit,* the navy sent him back to Pensacola as a flight instructor. It was during this tour that, having been seven years in the navy, he finally gave up his dream of a career as a lawyer. He enjoyed teaching others to fly so much that he never again spoke of trading the service for the bar.

After three years at Pensacola, McDonald returned to the fleet in Patrol Squadron 42, operating PBY flying boats out of Alaska and Seattle, Washington. In September 1941 he became aide and flag secretary to Rear Admiral Arthur B. Cook, who had command of a carrier group home-ported in Norfolk, Virginia. He was in this billet when America officially entered World War II.[5]

Rather than heading through the Panama Canal to fight the Japanese, Cook's force, centered on the *Ranger,* began operating out of Bermuda against German submarines. In March 1942, Cook was selected to establish the Naval Air Operational Training Command in Jacksonville, Florida, to train naval aviators in operational aircraft using real combat tactics. At Cook's request, McDonald accompanied him.

Seven years after he had retired from the navy's top uniformed job, David McDonald stated that the greatest contribution he made to the navy was the work he did in the Naval Operational Training Command.[6] He helped Cook establish a series of airfields along the east coast of Florida for the purpose of training aviators in the same type of aircraft they would be assigned to in the combat zone. In addition, an Aircraft Carrier Training Unit was established in Glenview, Illinois, to provide new aviators with practice in landing on carriers. Two Great Lakes coal-burning, paddle-wheel ferry boats were fitted with flight decks, and the student pilots were able to sharpen their skills in a training environment without tying up a desperately needed operational fleet carrier. McDonald allocated aircraft and instructors to the seventeen air stations in the program and then determined the student load that could be processed through the syllabus.

Cook and his successor, Admiral Andrew C. McFall, kept Commander McDonald out of the war until April 1944, when he went to the fifteen-month-old carrier *Essex* as air officer. Very shortly thereafter he was reassigned as executive officer and remained in that billet until June 1945. During his time in the *Essex*, she served under both Admiral Raymond A. Spruance and Admiral William F. Halsey, Jr., in the final battles of the Pacific War. She was hit by one kamikaze, which killed seventeen men, but the crew's efficiency was such that even this loss did not interfere with flight operations. McDonald received several awards for his performance as executive officer and was selected for promotion to captain.

Rather than assignment as commander of the Naval Air Station, Fort Lauderdale, Florida, which he had requested in order to be near his family, McDonald received orders to the staff of Commander, Naval Air Forces, Pacific, on Oahu. As plans officer on that staff, his original assignment was to assist in the planning for the invasion of Japan but, when Japan surrendered, his job became planning the phase-down of forces. As a result of a staff reorganization he received the concurrent assignment of operations officer. Captain McDonald remained in Hawaii until June 1947 when he left for his first tour of duty in Washington.

Many of the men with whom McDonald worked during the first twenty years of his career had a significant influence on his life, either as senior officers who thought highly of him, or as mentors who imparted certain aspects of their philosophy to him. Examples of the latter include Ensign McDonald's division officer in the *Mississippi*, an old lieutenant named Becker, who had worked up through the enlisted ranks. He told McDonald that the best officer in the navy is the one who can do the least but accomplish the most. Admiral Cook, for whom McDonald was aide, told him, "Young man, I'll very seldom ask for your advice, but when I ask you what you think, I want to know what you think and not what you think I'd like you to think." McDonald adopted both of the above attitudes. Another attitude he did not forget was that of a friend who had been promoted to rear admiral and who shall remain unidentified. This friend told him:

> Mac, it surprised a lot of people when I became a rear admiral, because you know a lot of them think I'm the dumbest rear admiral in the Navy. Maybe I am, but let me tell you, I'm also something else . . . I'm the most polite rear admiral in the Navy. If I'm dumb maybe I can't help it, maybe I was born that way, but even a dumbbell can be polite and don't you ever forget it.[7]

Armed with these various pieces of advice, Captain McDonald assumed his duties in Washington in June 1947 as director of military requirements in the Bureau of Aeronautics. His primary function in this capacity was drawing up the specifications for the aircraft that he and his staff felt the navy should have, and for an aircraft carrier large enough to handle them. The carrier concerned was the ill-fated *United States*, whose construction was abruptly canceled by Secretary of Defense Louis A. Johnson five days after her keel was laid on 18 April 1949. The *Forrestal*, completed in 1955, embodied many of the characteristics specified for the *United States* by Captain McDonald's office.

In 1948, McDonald was ordered as aide to the assistant secretary of the navy for air, John Nicholas Brown. The following year, Brown was replaced by

Dan A. Kimball, with whom McDonald established a very close working and social relationship. When Kimball was appointed to replace Undersecretary of the Navy W. John Kenney, who had resigned in protest over the cancellation of the *United States,* McDonald went with him. He later commented that he came closer to running the navy when he was aide to Undersecretary of the Navy Dan Kimball than he did when he was chief of naval operations.[8]

Captain McDonald left the Pentagon to study at the National War College in July 1950, one year before Kimball was appointed secretary of the navy. Upon completion of the college curriculum, in June 1951, he was given his first command, the *Mindoro,* an oil tanker that had been converted during World War II to an escort aircraft carrier. For the year that McDonald commanded her, the *Mindoro*'s mission was antisubmarine warfare.

From the *Mindoro* he went as operations officer to the staff of commander in chief of the Pacific Fleet, Admiral Arthur W. Radford, and from there, in December 1954, to command of the aircraft carrier *Coral Sea* in the Atlantic. It was aboard the *Coral Sea,* on his first deployment to the Mediterranean, in April 1955, that McDonald finally arrived in Europe. The prospect of going to Europe was, after all, the reason he had chosen the Naval Academy over West Point in 1924.

As commanding officer of the *Coral Sea,* visiting many ports on the Mediterranean littoral, McDonald had opportunities to cultivate the charm and diplomacy that were to serve him in more stressful situations in his later career. He had had command of his ship only six months when, in June 1955, he was selected for rear admiral, and in November of that year he returned to Washington as director of the Air Warfare Division in the Office of the Chief of Naval Operations.

His new job carried some of the responsibilities he had as director of military requirements for the Bureau of Aeronautics eight years earlier. Reorganization of the Department of the Navy had placed the determination of requirements for naval aircraft squarely under the aegis of the CNO. The work done in the Air Warfare Division while Rear Admiral McDonald was in charge of it resulted in the development of the McDonnell-Douglas F-4 Phantom II, still a front-line fighter for the navy, the marine corps, and the air force, and the Lockheed P-3 Orion antisubmarine-warfare patrol plane, presently being procured in its fourth major variant. As was the case with his billet in the Bureau of Aeronautics, McDonald's desk in the Office of the Chief of Naval Operations was also responsible for determining aircraft-carrier requirements. *Forrestal*-class carriers were already being launched at the time, so concentration was on the *Enterprise* and later designs. One of McDonald's collateral duties was as a member of the Military Liaison Committee to the Atomic Energy Commission. The primary reason for this assignment was that studies were then under way to determine the feasibility of atomic-powered aircraft.

McDonald's next assignment was as deputy assistant chief of staff at Supreme Headquarters for NATO in Europe. Air Force General Lauris Norstad, the commander for whom McDonald worked, was not a very popular individual with the majority of naval officers. McDonald, however, immediately established a smooth working relationship with him and with the other American and Allied officers on the staff of the Paris-based headquarters, despite the bitter interservice rivalry that then existed between the navy and the air force. So close did the relationship between Norstad and McDonald become that the former sent McDonald around Europe on many sensitive, unofficial missions. More than any other post he had held, this NATO billet permitted McDonald's tact and easy-going professionalism to be seen in a diplomatic setting, and his handling of it probably had a lot to do with his selection as chief of naval operations.

From Paris, in October 1960, McDonald reported to Mayport, Florida, as the commander of Carrier Division 6, and then returned immediately to the Mediterranean as commander of the striking force of the Sixth Fleet. At that time, the force was composed of three aircraft carriers and their escorts and comprised the primary American offensive power in southern Europe. This highly visible command, which was considered to be a stepping-stone to command of the Sixth Fleet, provided McDonald with more opportunities to polish his reputation as a congenial, confident flag officer.

It proved to be just such a stepping-stone for David McDonald who, in July 1961, pinned on his third star and followed Vice Admiral George W. Anderson in command of the Sixth Fleet. Anderson, in turn, pinned on a fourth star and relieved Arleigh Burke as chief of naval operations. Curiously, McDonald had followed Anderson on other occasions: both had command of Carrier Division 6, and McDonald relieved Anderson's successor as commanding officer of the *Mindoro*. The Sixth Fleet was not the last command held by both men.

McDonald was commander of the Sixth Fleet for twenty months. He relished the job, and delighted in the diplomatic functions his position required. He and his wife became well acquainted with heads of state and government, military leaders, and politicians from countries along the length of the Mediterranean. If being commander of Carrier Division 6 was a highly visible position, being commander of the Sixth Fleet was the limelight. McDonald saw 75 per cent of his work as diplomacy, and he "showed the flag" in a manner designed to reassure the governments along the Mediterranean of America's resolve to defend her own interests and those of her Allies.[9]

Command of the Sixth Fleet also gave McDonald the opportunity to be with his wife, a benefit seldom accorded a naval officer on sea duty. Catherine McDonald followed the fleet in naval aircraft in order to share the diplomatic responsibilities of her husband's position. Upon his relief from the Sixth Fleet and assignment to command U. S. Naval Forces, Europe, McDonald was looking forward to an even more idyllic shore-based existence in England to compensate for the many years he had spent at sea. It appeared that London would provide the McDonalds with the diplomatic benefits and pleasures he had enjoyed with the Sixth Fleet, but there would not be the concomitant necessity of going to sea.

On 9 April 1963, Admiral David McDonald became Commander in Chief, U. S. Naval Forces in Europe. Less than four months later, on 1 August 1963, he once again relieved Admiral Anderson, this time as chief of naval operations. McDonald was sincerely reluctant to accept the appointment; he wanted to see Anderson serve a second term as CNO because he and Anderson shared many of the same views on a variety of important subjects. In his opinion, Anderson had not been reappointed because his ideas collided with those of his civilian superiors. Anderson's problems, therefore, would be inherited by a successor with similar views. He was unhappy with that prospect. Also, as he explained to Secretary Korth upon notification of his selection, he had been in high-pressure jobs in the Sixth Fleet for two and one-half years and was ready for the "semi-relaxed duty" of the London billet, a position he had wanted for some time. What he did not want was another job in a pressure cooker, the Pentagon, where he foresaw that his counsel would be given little weight in the climate dominated by systems analysis—the creation of Secretary of Defense Robert S. McNamara.[10]

Another aspect of Admiral McDonald's philosophy counteracted his reservations about accepting the appointment as chief of naval operations. As a traditional military man, he believed that it was a naval officer's duty to express his views clearly to his seniors, and, when a decision had been reached, to carry it out to the best of his ability, whether he agreed with it or not.[11] President Kennedy apparently had decided that McDonald was to be his chief of naval operations. The admiral therefore acquiesced and set out to do his best.

The new CNO inherited a force of 664,647 naval personnel,[12] 870 ships, and 7,200 aircraft.[13] In addition, the Department of the Navy had a huge shore establishment manned by some of the naval personnel numbered above, and 343,970 civilians.[14] A massive reorganization of this establishment, which will be discussed below, was only one of the major issues that McDonald had to face immediately. Others were the specifications for the TFX (Tactical Fighter, Experimental), now called the F-111, threatened cutbacks in the number of attack aircraft carriers, and increasing civilian interference in the professional affairs of the navy, including the selection and assignment of flag officers. Permeating all these issues was the challenging task of establishing and maintaining a good working relationship with the Office of the Secretary of Defense (OSD). Under Robert McNamara, OSD was composed of many talented intellectuals, who firmly believed in the expediency of systems analysis and deprecated practical experience as being parochial. McDonald was an experienced man, but he had no firm grounding in systems analysis. This lack made the situation difficult for him, especially on questions pertaining to the development of hardware, notably the F-111.

Many believed that Anderson's tenure as CNO was abbreviated because of his attitude toward the F-111. Based on a conversation he had in April 1963 with Air Force Colonel George Brown, than an aide to Secretary McNamara, McDonald came to the same conclusion. In reply to a comment he made about the TFX being a hot issue, Brown said to him: "You know that thing's hot. Some service chief is going to get his throat cut on this if he doesn't watch out."[15]

McDonald knew very well that the F-111 was McNamara's pet project, and that it had been forced on the services. Shortly after McNamara's installation as secretary of defense, a committee had been formed from the three services to determine whether the TFX, which had been proposed by the air force, could meet projected requirements of the army and the navy. The committee's conclusions, reported on 3 March 1961, were threefold:

> The Army had no requirement for an aircraft remotely resembling the proposed TFX. In lieu thereof they needed a close support machine more closely akin to the A4D-5.[16]
>
> The Navy had no foreseeable requirement for the TFX unless its specifications were so drastically modified as to defy resemblance.
>
> Both the Army and the Navy would veto single-service development of the TFX by the Air Force.[17]

This result was deemed unsatisfactory by OSD and additional committees were formed and more studies were conducted, all of which reached basically the same conclusions. Nevertheless, on , June 1961, McNamara issued a memorandum in which it was stated: "The Air Force will be authorized to develop a new 'air superiority' aircraft to be used, when required, by both the Air Force and the Navy to replace the F-105 and the F4H."[18] Thus the new F-111 had its inauspicious start.

This decision was already two years old when McDonald assumed the office of CNO, and, because the dual-service development of the F-111 was a firm policy by that time, he acquiesced rather than fought, as Anderson had done. He turned the development of the F-111B (the carrier version) over to subordinates who had the technical expertise that he lacked. By this delegation of responsibility, which was part of the philosophical makeup he brought to his job from his earlier naval career, combined with another element of his philosophy, "Always tell the truth, and you'll never have to remember what you said," McDonald sought to avoid any confrontation with OSD over the potentially explosive F-111 issue. He simply told OSD he would carry out their orders, told his subordinates to try to make a carrier fighter out of the F-111, and let events take their course. He did not deceive or end-run OSD on this matter because he knew that the success or failure of the F-111 would ultimately depend on whether or not the aircraft could meet its performance requirements. He could simply tell OSD he was carrying out their directives and let the F-111 bring about its own downfall.

In the meantime, McDonald's technical experts determined that the F-111 was, indeed, a very poor design, overweight, and a marginal weapons platform.

In the words of Gerald E. Miller who, as a young rear admiral, was working on the F-111 at that time:

> We were all working to kill it [the F-111] but we had no suitable alternate that would sell until the F-14 concept came along. Those of us working the problem avoided any discussions with the CNO in order to protect him from higher authority. The less he knew about what we were doing, the better his position above. We knew we should kill the plane and we proceeded without much high level direction.[19]

In fact, the F-111B survived McDonald's tenure as CNO, and had to await Secretary McNamara's resignation in February 1968 to be put to rest, finally. At the authorization hearings for fiscal year 1969 before the Senate Armed Services Committee on 28 March 1969, Secretary of the Navy Paul R. Ignatius had just ended more than two hours of testimony on the requirement for the F-111B, when Senator John Stennis, chairman of the committee, asked the deputy chief of naval operations for air, Vice Admiral Thomas F. Connolly, for his personal opinion of the F-111B. Connolly replied, "Mr. Chairman, there is not enough thrust in all Christendom to fix that aircraft."[20]

By handling the F-111 problem as he did, McDonald avoided a confrontation with McNamara, such as had helped to topple his predecessor. He undoubtedly achieved a rapport with McNamara and his staff which helped him solve other problems facing the navy. There was little point in fighting the secretary of defense on his most sensitive project, for it was inevitable that the battle would be lost while the secretary was in power. By refusing to draw attention to the F-111B, a compromise substitute could be found, the F-14, and less than one month after McNamara stepped down, the F-111B program was terminated. In this instance, as at other times during his career, McDonald attempted to accomplish his objective in an undramatic, cautious fashion.

Many of the major issues that McDonald faced during his tour as CNO involved aircraft, the pilots who flew them, and the retention of the platforms from which they operated. In this last category in 1963 were fifteen attack aircraft carriers, nine antisubmarine support carriers, one training carrier, and three helicopter carriers. Maintaining the attack carriers at a minimum of fifteen was one of McDonald's primary objectives as chief of naval operations. It seemed to him that McNamara was determined to reduce that number as much as possible, and nothing that occurred during his tour caused him to change that view. In one of his first interviews as CNO he stated:

> I have to base an estimate of future need on past requirements, and it is difficult to justify such a thing on a purely mathematical basis, but during these last several years the Navy has been hard pressed to meet the carrier commitments actually imposed on it with the carriers we have had. I can foresee no lessening of the need, and no decrease in this requirement in the immediate or the foreseeable future.
>
> This is one reason, but I must emphasize it is only one of many reasons why I support the view that we must maintain our present attack-carrier capability.[21]

This definitive statement was not in keeping with McDonald's penchant for low-key, diplomatic handling of controversial matters, and may have been intended to demonstrate to OSD a policy position that was not negotiable.

The aircraft carrier that became the *John F. Kennedy* was written into the fiscal year 1963 budget before McDonald accepted the job of CNO. What type of propulsion she was to have had not yet been decided, however, and the battle lines were drawn from the outset between the proponents of nuclear power, including many congressmen, Vice Admiral Hyman G. Rickover, and the CNO, and their opponents in the Office of the Secretary of Defense. In fact, based on successful operating experience with the nuclear ships *Enterprise* and *Long Beach,* the navy wanted all ships of more than 8,000 tons to have nuclear propulsion. McNamara rejected this viewpoint and, on 9 October 1963, ordered that the new carrier be built with a conventional power plant. This action put McDonald in a very awkward position. Nevertheless, he was more concerned about maintaining the force of fifteen attack carriers and feared that if the navy, personified by the CNO, insisted on nuclear propulsion or nothing, it would get the latter. New carriers were vitally needed if fifteen attack flight decks were to be kept in the fleet, and even McDonald's concession as to the new carrier's propulsion plant was no guarantee that McNamara would not cancel the carrier outright. McDonald described the situation succinctly when nuclear-power advocate Senator John O. Pastore remarked: "Admiral, here we are trying to get you to go for a loaf of bread and you're willing to sell out for a slice." The admiral replied, "Senator, we're awful hungry."[22]

McDonald did, indeed, get his new attack carrier, with conventional power. However, McNamara changed his opinion about the value of nuclear propulsion two and one-half years later, when he requested for fiscal year 1967, the first of three nuclear-powered *Nimitz*-class attack carriers. These ships were to be built at two-year intervals for completion in 1971, 1973, and 1975, thereby maintaining a force of fifteen attack carriers for another decade. One of the concessions made by McDonald to get these carriers was that the navy would not seek to replace the antisubmarine carriers and would embark the new S-3 antisubmarine aircraft in the attack carriers.[23] Thus was a new concept born, the all-purpose aircraft carrier having the functions and the aircraft types, if not the total numbers, of both attack and antisubmarine carriers.

To relieve the carriers of some of their unnecessary responsibilities, McNamara had announced in the spring of 1962 that they would be taken out of the Single Integrated Operations Plan. This plan was implemented in early 1961 to allocate and coordinate the delivery of American strategic weapons against specific targets in the Soviet Union and the People's Republic of China. A child of the Eisenhower administration, it was designed to resolve the problem of the uncoordinated, nuclear-war plans of the 1950s, and, when created, the services scrambled to include their weapon systems under the plan. If a system were in the plan, its funding would be relatively secure, but if it were not, it might face an uncertain future. Burke had succeeded in placing the attack carrier force in the plan when it went into effect in 1961.

In his testimony before the House Appropriations Committee in support of the budget for fiscal year 1963, McNamara explained why he had removed the carriers from the Single Integrated Operations Plan:

> The principal use of the attack carriers in the years ahead will be in the limited war role. As we acquire larger forces of strategic missiles and Polaris submarines, the need for the attack carrier in the general war role will diminish. However, they will still maintain a significant nuclear strike capability which could augment our Strategic Retaliatory Forces. But in the Limited-War and Cold-War roles, the attack carrier force provides a most important and unique capability.[24]

That line of thinking was echoed by McDonald approximately eighteen months later:

> I should also emphasize that in the past, and in certain areas today, the aircraft carrier has made a necessary contribution to the nation's nuclear war deterrent. This contribution, though, has been a small one when measured as a percentage of the United States' over-all nuclear deterrent. This emphasizes that the primary role of the carrier is, as always, in something less than all-out-war, so that whether or not there comes a ban on nuclear weapons, and whether or not the carrier is removed from its role in nuclear deterrence will not have any large impact on the need for the carrier.[25]

Unlike so many of the secretary's other "innovations," this move was generally popular among naval officers. Admiral Horacio Rivero, vice chief of naval operations under McDonald, thought the decision was a good one: "It removed a restraint on CVA [attack] carrier operations and restored flexibility for conventional missions while retaining a nuclear capability against non-time-sensitive targets and tactical targets."[26]

To support and defend the fifteen attack carriers for which McDonald had fought so hard, escorts were needed, but most of the escorts then in service were fast becoming obsolete. Many of them were of World War II vintage and had already had their service lives extended through a modernization program. The navy kept submitting requests for modern, high-capability destroyers, and the secretary of defense kept approving only less-costly, low-performance escorts suitable for escorting slow-moving convoys across the Atlantic, but for little else. However, any surface combatants were better than none, so McDonald accepted as many of the DE-1052 escorts as OSD would approve and initiated the planning for the *Spruance*-class, 7,500-ton destroyers of the 1970s.[27]

This problem with escort ships points up the sometimes self-contradictory nature of McNamara's budget process. In the 1950s the Office of the Chief of Naval Operations drew up three different budgets: the first was what the navy considered it needed, without regard to cost; the second was what the CNO considered reasonable and therefore requested; and the third was what the navy could get without exceeding the ceiling figures set by OSD, usually considerably less than the amount requested. The changes brought about in the 1960s were described by McDonald in the following way:

> McNamara and company came along and we were told that ours was a rich country, so rich in fact that we could afford whatever was needed. We then would present a budget which contained what we thought was needed. If such required a monetary outlay which OSD thought excessive then instead of coming back to us and simply saying that this darn thing costs too much, please rearrange based on a specified reduction in cost, Mr. McNamara and his staff would do the same thing by simply saying that certain things weren't needed.[28]

Alain Enthoven and K. Wayne Smith, McNamara's assistants, complained that the navy argued for more nuclear-powered aircraft carriers and it was supported by the Joint Chiefs, "without having to specify whether the total defense budget should thus be increased . . . or whether the greater cost . . . should be paid from a reduction in the total number of carriers." Consequently, they argued, "the burden of choice in judging Service proposals rested almost entirely on the Secretary of Defense and his staff".[29] They failed to mention that the remedy they applied was inconsistent with the rules established by their own OSD, rules begotten by McNamara's reluctance to admit that costs really were one of the controlling elements in the defense budget.[30]

Basic misunderstanding and distrust generally permeated the relations between the civilians in the Office of the Secretary of Defense and all the services. McDonald, recognizing that this poisonous atmosphere was not one in which the navy's programs could be successful, cultivated the civilians whenever possible, using the tact he had polished in the Mediterranean. He relied on his staff to smooth the rough spots that inevitably appear whenever such disparate groups of individuals have to interact on important issues. His assistants, Admirals Miller and Rivero, established a good working relationship with Enthoven and prevented several confrontations from arising by the simple expedient of keeping OSD well informed on the navy's positions and the reasons for them.

This tense atmosphere was not confined to relations between the Office of the Secretary of Defense and the Office of the Chief of Naval Operations. Sometimes the politically appointed leadership of the services intruded in areas that professional officers regarded as their exclusive domain, notably the selection and assignment of admirals. This was a particular annoyance to McDonald, perhaps sensitized to the issue by what he perceived to be the abrupt treatment meted out to him at the time of his appointment as CNO. It was his contention that the uniformed naval seniors knew their subordinates far better than did any civilian secretaries who might have a brief association with them before they were up for promotion or reassignment. Such a brief association could alter the direction of a career that had been from twenty-five to thirty years in the making. Moreover, submitting the names of flag selectees to the politically appointed civilian secretaries for approval to some degree politicized the upper ranks, in addition to politicizing the billets to which these admirals were assigned. It was a problem that defied McDonald's solution, as it had his predecessors', and has his successors'.[31]

An historic reorganization of naval administration took place during McDonald's tenure as chief of naval operations. In 1966 the separate material bureaus that had reported to the secretary of the navy were unified under a Material Command, and the chief of that command, a full admiral, was subordinated to the CNO. This reshuffling was not accomplished overnight. It began in late 1962, when the secretary of the navy established the Dillon Board, which coordinated and integrated twenty studies as a basis for determining which areas might be better served by reorganization. General Order 5, which resulted from the work done by this board, was issued on 1 July 1963, and its most significant effect was the creation of the Naval Material Support Establishment (NMSE) under the command of the chief of naval material, who reported directly to the secretary of the navy. This new establishment had under its command the Bureau of Naval Weapons, the Bureau of Ships, the Bureau of Supplies and Accounts, and the Bureau of Yards and Docks. In McNamara's words: "The 1963 reorganization was accomplished within the existing statutory framework of the Department of the Navy and did not affect the traditional bilinear organization of the Department of the Navy; nor did it change the statutory bureaus which form the principal operating structure of the NMSE."[32]

Creation of the Naval Material Support Establishment was only the first step in the process leading to the reorganization of 1966. Unlike the 1963 reshuffle, this reorganization required legislative approval because it abolished bureaus set up by act of Congress. McNamara explained the plan while requesting congressional support:

> It is the belief of the Secretary of the Navy, which I share, that the Department of the Navy should be organized in such a fashion that the Navy's senior military officer, the Chief of Naval Operations, will have the same breadth of authority and responsibility for material, personnel, and medical support functions as he now has for the operating forces of the Navy. Additionally, the Secretary of the Navy believes that the organizations performing the Navy's material support functions should be so structured as to subject them to more effective command by the Chief of Naval Material *under the Chief of Naval Operations.* (Emphasis added.)[33]

In addition to subordinating the new Naval Material Command to the CNO instead of to the secretary of the navy, the plan called for the abolition of the four material bureaus and the establishment of their replacements along functional lines: air, ship, ordnance, electronic and supply systems commands, and facilities engineering command. Also, the bureaus of Naval Personnel and Medicine and Surgery were placed under command of the CNO. This restructuring seems to have been advocated and pushed more by civilians in OSD and the secretary of the navy than by McDonald or his staff, despite the fact that subordinating the material bureaus to the CNO was a major goal of many of his predecessors.

As McDonald's managerial and administrative responsibilities expanded, the number of his command prerogatives shrank. The CNO had, by law, been required to relinquish command of most of his forces to the joint commands established in 1958. Yet, by force of personality, Burke and Anderson had retained authority in virtual defiance of the statute. In the face of McNamara's growing dominance over the defense establishment and the political manipulation of military operations in the war in Vietnam, however, McDonald saw the last vestiges of the CNO's authority over the fleet slip away. This general trend was not limited to the navy, for McNamara seemed intent on substituting OSD for the Joint Chiefs and the service chiefs in the chain of command between the president as commander in chief and all the operating forces. Vietnam, McDonald's greatest frustration, provided the opportunity for OSD to make that substitution.

The Tonkin Gulf crisis of August 1964 exposed these new practices. On 31 July the *Maddox*, an unmodernized, World War II, *Sumner*-class destroyer, began the second "Desoto" patrol. These destroyer patrols into the Gulf of Tonkin were usually conducted within the twelve-mile territorial limit claimed by the North Vietnamese, but outside the three-mile limit recognized by the United States. Their primary purposes were to indicate American resolve to support South Vietnam and to collect intelligence. The mission of the *Maddox* was "to determine DRV [North Vietnamese] coastal activity along the full extent of the patrol track."[34] Unknown to the *Maddox*, South Vietnamese forces had made a raid on North Vietnamese islands on 30 July, and three North Vietnamese patrol boats were searching for the commandos responsible for the foray. On 2 August, the patrol boats mistook the *Maddox* for a South Vietnamese escort vessel and, in mid-afternoon, attacked her with torpedoes and machine guns. The *Maddox* avoided the torpedoes and returned fire with her 5-inch battery. F-8E Crusader fighters from the *Ticonderoga*, launched after the carrier had received word of the episode, also attacked the patrol boats with cannon and rockets. One boat was set afire by the *Maddox*'s guns and the other two were hit by the fighters' fire. The *Maddox* then retired to open waters, having suffered only one hit from a light machine gun.

These events took place early Sunday morning, Washington time. By the time Lieutenant Commander Winston Cornelius relieved the watch at the Defense Intelligence Agency, all the message traffic relating to the incident had been reviewed and filed by the air force watch-stander. He told Cornelius about the messages and recommended that he glance through them at his leisure. A short time later Cornelius was ordered to meet with the senior watch officer, who set up a briefing on the *Maddox* affair for General Earle G. Wheeler, chairman of the Joint Chiefs. Cornelius prepared the brief on his way to the general's home. Later, he briefed Acting Secretary of Defense Cyrus R. Vance, Secretary of State Dean Rusk, and finally, President Lyndon B. Johnson.

Cornelius was the only naval officer present at any of these briefings, but he was there in his capacity as a member of the Defense Intelligence Agency.[35] He had been unable to contact the duty captain in the Office of the Chief of Naval Operations to inform him of the incident and of this whirlwind of briefings, and so was acting without any guidance from his parent service.

Before briefing Johnson, Cornelius, on his own initiative, prepared a message ordering the *Maddox* back into the Gulf of Tonkin to reassert the doctrine of freedom of the seas. When Johnson asked for his recommendation, Cornelius showed him the message, which Johnson immediately approved. After leaving the White House, Cornelius finally was able to talk with the navy's duty captain, and informed him of the president's decision.[36] The message was sent to the commander in chief of the Pacific Fleet, who ordered the *Maddox,* accompanied by the *Turner Joy,* to return to the gulf. This patrol led to a second incident on 4 August, which caused Johnson to launch reprisal air strikes against North Vietnam and to push through Congress the Tonkin Gulf Resolution, giving him a mandate to conduct operations in Southeast Asia. The chief of naval operations was virtually excluded from the decision-making that surrounded these significant events. McDonald later remarked of the Tonkin Gulf incidents: "I don't know any more than what you read in the papers."[37]

"Desoto" patrols were terminated by the president shortly after the Tonkin Gulf incidents and, when the Joint Chiefs, as a group, strongly recommended that they be reinstated McNamara replied:

> I have noted the recommendation by the Joint Chiefs of Staff, as expressed in the referenced memorandum for the resumption of DESOTO Patrols. Their views were stated again in a subsequent memorandum (JCSM 902-64) as a proposed future course of action for Southeast Asia.
>
> This proposal of the Joint Chiefs of Staff, among other recommendations for courses of action in Southeast Asia, is under active consideration.[38]

By the time this memo was written, 20 November 1964, the secretary had managed to insert himself directly into the advisory and command channel between the president and the Joint Chiefs of Staff. McDonald and his colleagues thus became advisers to the secretary of defense, who apparently preferred the judgments of his systems analysts to those of military personnel. Bereft of his military commands and ignored, McDonald did little but watch the deepening quagmire in Vietnam and protest, unheard. The ultimate protest would have been for the admiral and the other chiefs to resign, but they chose to remain in office, virtually impotent. Vietnam was not the only issue facing McDonald, and he immersed himself in the others, preferring not to think about his ineffectiveness in resolving the war in Vietnam.

On 31 July 1967, McDonald retired and the next day, the successor he chose, Admiral Thomas H. Moorer, relieved him as chief of naval operations. McDonald was the first post-World War II CNO to serve a complete pair of two-year terms, no more, as Burke had, and no less, as had all the rest. He retired to Ponte Vedra, Florida, where he became active in the business community.

McDonald's tenure as CNO coincided with many important events in the evolution of the modern U. S. Navy. Most of these events were generated by forces outside his control, and he had to cope with them as best he could to ensure the well-being, as he saw it, of the service entrusted to his care. He was not a bureaucratic fighter, but a diplomat and negotiator, and his temperament was probably ideal for dealing with such a secretary of defense as Robert McNamara. McDonald's victories over OSD would probably not have been won had he attempted to fight for them, rather than negotiate; but at the same time his image as a leader would have been more dramatic and stronger had he engaged in a few confrontations, especially in association with his fellow Joint Chiefs over the war in Vietnam.

Most of the issues about which McDonald felt very strongly were resolved as he wished, the most notable exceptions being the war in Vietnam and civilian interference in the assignment and selection of flag officers. He maintained the strength of the attack carrier force at fifteen by getting Johnson and McNamara to approve the first of the *Nimitz*-class nuclear carriers. He pressed for, and received, a significant increase in the number of students entering flight training in order to relieve the load on the navy's pilots in Southeast Asia. In the face of unanimous opposition from the other members of the Joint Chiefs, McDonald succeeded in having Admiral Ulysses S. Grant Sharp, Jr., designated Commander in Chief, Pacific, in relief of Admiral Harry D. Felt. The other Chiefs wanted that position to be rotated amongst the services. He also succeeded in naming Admiral Thomas H. Moorer, a fellow naval aviator, as his successor.

The submarine force fared very well during McDonald's tenure, even without his special interest, for it had Rickover to champion its cause in OSD and the Congress. The surface fleet did not do as well, and greater emphasis by McDonald on the needs of the surface fleet might have overcome McNamara's reluctance to fund more capable escorts for task groups, but that is speculation. McDonald's successes in championing carrier aviation and the secondary status in which the surface fleet found itself may have been functions of the exigencies of the Vietnam War more than anything else.

Judgments on McDonald's tenure must, therefore, bear the caveat, "under the circumstances." The circumstances were not propitious for good relations between OSD and the navy, yet McDonald and his subordinates did well in that regard. They were not propitious for continued appropriations for major projects, but most major programs were funded. Therefore, given the conditions in which he worked, McDonald stood his watch well, oftentimes by relying heavily on his subordinates. But what of McDonald himself, the reluctant chief of naval operations. "If I had to do it over again, I don't know if I'd tell him I don't want the job. I might even go so far as not to take the job, but of course, if I'd done that I'd probably have been sent to Timbuktu."[39]

THOMAS HINMAN MOORER

1 August 1967–1 July 1970

J. KENNETH McDONALD

Thomas H. Moorer became the eighteenth chief of naval operations in August 1967 when he relieved Admiral David L. McDonald in ceremonies in Annapolis. Naval participation in the American escalation of the war in Vietnam was nearing its peak, and one-third of the seaborne forces were committed to the fighting in Indochina. As chief of naval operations, Moorer's first task was to ensure that the navy executed its assigned missions in that war. At the same time, he had to work constantly to limit the damage that the war did to the navy's ability to fulfill its other missions. Finally, in the face of an expanding Soviet Navy, Moorer had to initiate shipbuilding programs that would modernize the aged American fleet.[1]

William Howard Taft was president of the United States when Thomas Moorer was born on 9 February 1912 in Mount Willing, Alabama, a small country town some twenty-five miles southwest of Montgomery. His father, Richard Randolph Moorer, was a dentist, and named his eldest son after Thomas Hinman, his dean at the Southern Dental College in Atlanta. Thomas's mother, Hulda Hill Hinson Moorer, taught school until she married, and devoted herself thereafter to her family, the Baptist Church, and the United Daughters of the Confederacy. Both of his grandfathers served in the Confederate Army, and both fought in the Battle of Gettysburg. Mount Willing in the 1920s offered seven grades of elementary education from a single teacher in a one-room school. By listening to the grades ahead of him recite, Thomas learned his lessons early and finished seventh grade when he was only twelve years old. He was graduated from Cloverdale High School in Montgomery in June 1927, at the age of fifteen, and was valedictorian of his class.[2]

Being interested in everything mechanical, Moorer studied the catalogues of both the Military Academy and the Naval Academy, and came to the conclusion that the latter offered the more technical education. Indeed, he always considered the navy essentially a "technical service" and the army a "manpower service." Since he could not enter the Naval Academy until he was sixteen years old, he spent the interim working at his uncle's general store and sawmill, preparing for his entrance examinations, and enjoying life with his cousins, fishing, swimming and hunting coons. He passed the academy's tests in the required seven subjects and became the third alternate for an Alabama congressman's appointment for 1928. However, this appointment did not materialize, and worse, the congressman reneged on his promise to appoint Moorer in 1929. At the last moment, Richard Moorer, who had served in the Alabama legislature, persuaded Senator James T. "Cotton Tom" Heflin to appoint his son. The telegram of appointment arrived just in time for Thomas to join the plebes of the class of 1933 on 10 June 1929.[3]

At the Naval Academy Midshipman Moorer acquired the nickname "Dead Eye," and was described in the yearbook, the *Lucky Bag*, as "a true Johnny Reb if there ever was one." He played football for three years, and earned a reputation for both amiable astuteness and a sure grasp of all mechanical subjects. "He had the news from the beginning," the *Lucky Bag* commented, "in everything from answering questions of the upperclassmen as a Plebe to making 'big' leaves in foreign ports."[4]

Graduating in the depths of the Great Depression in June 1933, Moorer was in the upper half of his class, the only ones who were offered commissions. He began his career with the surface navy. After a few months in the cruiser *Salt Lake City*, he helped to fit out the *New Orleans* in the Brooklyn Navy Yard. He served in the gunnery and engineering departments of this new cruiser from her commissioning in early 1934 until he departed for aviation training in June 1935.

Moorer's technical competence and curiosity naturally led him to an interest in flying. His generation of midshipmen at the academy recognized the potential importance of naval air power. In 1933, for the first time, the *Lucky Bag* had a naval-aviation theme: open-cockpit biplanes diving around Moorer's photograph and brief student biography. He later disclaimed any special vision then of the future role of aviation in warfare: "I was just interested in flying," he recalled, "so I thought I would give it a try."[5] He took his flight training at Pensacola, Florida, and, while there, he married Carrie Ellen Foy in November 1935. The following July he earned his gold wings and a new assignment, while his bride organized the first of twenty-six moves they made before Moorer retired thirty-eight years later. Nonetheless, the marriage was successful and, upon his retirement, Moorer paid a warm tribute to Carrie as the perfect wife who had made him not only happy but successful.[6]

In 1936, when Ensign Moorer began his career as a naval aviator, he learned to fly all kinds of aircraft—fighters, bombers, and patrol planes—because there were then no specialties in naval aviation. His first assignment was with Fighting Squadron 1-B, flying from the *Langley* and, later, the *Lexington*. From 1937 until the eve of the war in Europe he flew from the *Enterprise* with Fighting Squadron 6.

When the Japanese attacked Pearl Harbor on 7 December 1941, Lieutenant Moorer was there, having been assigned to Patrol Squadron 22 of the Pacific Fleet since 1939. After the attack, his squadron was dispatched to the Southwest Pacific to participate in the desperate effort to stop the rapid Japanese advance into the Dutch East Indies. On 19 February 1942, he and his seven-man crew flew out of Darwin, Australia, in a PBY 5 on a reconnaissance mission and, when they were well out at sea, they were attacked by Japanese fighters. Moorer was wounded in the thigh, but he managed to put the burning flying boat down on the water. Everyone got onto a life raft and soon they were picked up by a Philippine merchant ship, which was promptly and accurately bombed by more Japanese aircraft. Moorer lost one of his crewmen in this attack, but as the ship sank he and forty other survivors abandoned her and rowed to a small, nearby island, from which they were rescued the next day. Moorer was awarded a Purple Heart and a Silver Star for "extremely gallant and intrepid conduct" both during and after the Japanese attacks.[7]

Back in the United States the following July, Moorer was sent to Britain for seven months' duty with the Royal Navy as a mine warfare observer. After this preparation he returned in the spring of 1943 to fit out and command an antisubmarine bombing squadron which, from its base at Key West, Florida, ranged from Cuba to Africa. This work, he later observed, gave him an opportunity to learn a great deal about surface operations. After this duty, he took up his last wartime assignment, on the staff of Admiral Patrick N. L. Bellinger, Commander, Air Force, Atlantic Fleet. It was in this billet that he earned his first Legion of Merit, for "meritorious conduct . . . as Force Gunnery and Tactical Officer."

When the war ended in August 1945, Commander Moorer emerged at the age of thirty-three with an enviable professional record. He had served in the Pacific, the Atlantic, and the Caribbean, as well as in Australia, England, and Africa. He was highly decorated for bravery, wounds, flying skills, and staff work. Perhaps most importantly, he had gained a remarkable variety of operational experience in combat. In the short term, his war record prepared and qualified him for continued advancement. In the long term, his wartime experience provided a standard against which he judged naval developments during the next three decades of his naval service.

Immediately after the war Moorer had an opportunity to assess the effectiveness of the air offensive against Japan. Assigned to the U. S. Strategic Bombing Survey in Japan in August 1945, he spent nine months working with other officers and civilians in interrogating Japanese officers and officials, examining Japanese records, and comparing enemy damage estimates with their own. The survey went beyond strategic bombing and assessed all American air operations in the Pacific war. Moorer dealt with the opening stage of the war and reported on Pearl Harbor, the Japanese invasions, and the Allied campaign in New Guinea. He found this one of the most revealing experiences of his naval career, because it answered so many questions raised by the wartime air effort.[8]

After his stay in Japan, Moorer had his first exposure to naval research and development. From 1946 to 1948 he served as executive officer of the Naval Aviation Ordnance Test Station at Chincoteague, Virginia, and, after two years of duty afloat as an operations officer, first in the carrier *Midway* and then on the staff of Vice Admiral Joseph "Jocko" Clark, Commander, Carrier Division 4, Atlantic Fleet, Captain Moorer returned to research and development. In August 1950, while the tremendous expansion of American armed forces to fight the Korean War got under way, he was sent to the Naval Ordnance Test Station at China Lake, California, in the navy's main missile-research center, as experimental officer—the senior naval officer. It was a widely sought-after billet: five of the first six experimental officers at China Lake from 1944 to 1955 attained flag rank.[9]

Moorer once claimed that World War II made him aware of the services' interdependence and the Korean War impressed upon him the close relationship between military strategy and national policy. In August 1952, he reported to Newport, Rhode Island, for the senior course at the Naval War College. During this year, while the stalemate in Korea dragged on, he first got the opportunity to develop his ideas about large military issues, especially American foreign policy and joint strategic planning.[10] He served a brief tour on the staff of Commander, Air Force, Atlantic Fleet, before reporting in 1955 to the Navy Department as an aide to Assistant Secretary of the Navy for Air James H. Smith. In 1956 he took command of the seaplane tender *Salisbury Sound;* this was a premier deep-draft command, because she deployed her own aircraft and often operated alone in the Pacific.

At this stage in his career, Moorer's prospects for selection to flag rank were superb because he had done well in a wide variety of billets. He was promoted in 1957 and became, at forty-five, the youngest officer yet selected for rear admiral. In October 1957 he came to Washington and—except for seventeen months in 1959 and 1960 when he went to sea in command of Carrier Division 6 in the Atlantic and Mediterranean—spent five years working in the Office of the Chief of Naval Operations as a special assistant in the Strategic Plans Division, as assistant CNO for war gaming, and, after his sea command, as the fourth director of the Long-Range Objectives Group. While Admiral Arleigh A. Burke was CNO this last was an enviable assignment for ambitious young admirals, its first four incumbents going on to achieve four-star rank.[11] Moorer held this post for most of the difficult first two years of the Kennedy administration, which instituted new military strategies and reorganized the Department of Defense. He found that these planning assignments in Washington forced him to spread out from his career experience in aviation and deal with the nontechnical problems of the other services as well as of the navy.

Leaving Washington for the Pacific, Vice Admiral Moorer took command of the Seventh Fleet in October 1962, and less than two years later he became a full admiral and commander in chief of the Pacific Fleet. He had hardly assumed command when, in August 1964, the Tonkin Gulf clashes occurred between North Vietnamese torpedo boats and two of Moorer's Pacific Fleet destroyers, the *Maddox* and the *Turner Joy*. After these incidents, President Lyndon B. Johnson authorized retaliatory bombing of North Vietnam and persuaded Congress to pass the Tonkin Gulf Resolution. Moorer still commanded the fleet in early 1965 when Johnson used the authority of that resolution, to begin systematic bombing of North Vietnam in February, and then, in March, to send American troops to fight in South Vietnam.

In the middle of the expanding American commitment in Vietnam, Moorer was sent halfway around the world to become, on 30 April 1965, commander in chief of the Atlantic Fleet and supreme allied commander in the Atlantic, NATO's top naval commander. When his assignment was announced, *Time* described him as "America's fastest-rising sailor," and his superior in the Pacific, Admiral Ulysses S. Grant Sharp, called him "an outstanding candidate for next Chief of Naval Operations." Moorer held these key posts for just over two years, dealing with the problems of President Charles de Gaulle's decision to withdraw France from NATO and the Six-Day War, as well as with the increasing Soviet naval threat.[12] To no one's surprise, in June 1967 President Johnson nominated him to succeed Admiral McDonald as chief of naval operations, and Moorer took office two months later.[13]

Moorer's experience as CNO convinced him that future historians would be unable to understand why the United States failed to use its immense military power to subdue the tiny country of North Vietnam. In his view, the key American decision was made in 1965—to intervene with combat forces in the war. Once the United States was committed to the fighting, Moorer wanted the country to seek a military victory and to do what was necessary to defeat North Vietnam. By contrast, the objective of the Johnson administration was not to achieve military victory, but rather to contain communism by preventing a communist victory in South Vietnam. Moorer clearly never agreed with this limited goal. Nor did he believe that either Johnson or his successor, President Richard M. Nixon, could achieve it by increasing the level of American ground forces in South Vietnam while ordering repeated halts to the bombing campaign against North Vietnam with the hope that Hanoi would respond to these signals. As did most senior American military officers, Moorer believed that Ho Chi Minh would respond only to military force, consistently applied. In 1965, when Johnson first ordered the execution of Operation Rolling Thunder, code name for the bombing campaign, Moorer advised Deputy Secretary of Defense Cyrus R. Vance that American forces should also mine Haiphong Harbor to cut the flow of seaborne military goods into North Vietnam. As chief of naval operations, Moorer pressed this strategy continually, but with no success. When it was finally undertaken by Nixon in 1972, Moorer felt a measure of satisfaction, despite the fact that by then it was part of an American strategy of withdrawal rather than victory.[14]

As CNO, Moorer strongly believed in the possibility of a military victory in the Vietnam War. He also thought that part of the difficulty in achieving this was the political leaders' interference in military decisions. He accepted the reality that the decision to intervene was strictly political; however, once that decision had been made, he felt that the Joint Chiefs of Staff should have been allowed to adopt strategies to defeat the enemy. In short, he held that civilian control of a war should stop once American combat forces have been committed. Of course, Johnson's policy of gradual escalation in order to "raise the cost of aggression" for North Vietnam failed. It is speculation as to whether the war could have been won—or how "winning" would have been defined—had the military been given a free hand in the conduct of the war. It will also never be known whether winning the war would have been worth the price that the professional military was willing to pay.

In fact, Moorer's role, as chief of naval operations and member of the Joint Chiefs of Staff, in deciding American policy and strategy during the escalation of the war appears to have been relatively limited. Indeed, he found it difficult to keep track of high-level thinking and decision-making about Vietnam during Johnson's administration. He believed that Johnson inherited Kennedy's distrust of the Joint Chiefs, which stemmed from the Bay of Pigs fiasco in 1961. Johnson did not rely on the Joint Chiefs or the National Security Council as his principal advisers on defense and foreign policy, rather he relied on an assortment of senior officials whom he invited to lunch at the White House every Tuesday. In this period, General Earle G. Wheeler, chairman of the Joint Chiefs, was not always invited to attend these vital meetings and therefore could not report the president's decisions to the service chiefs.

In any event, Moorer found that Johnson and his key advisers assumed that the war in Vietnam was primarily a land war, that the army had the primary mission, and the navy had only a small role. Although he received copies of telegrams from General William C. Westmoreland, the American commander in Vietnam, to Wheeler, Moorer felt that the other information he received, both as chief of naval operations and as a member of the Joint Chiefs of Staff, on the overall conduct of the war was sketchy and inadequate.

Moorer had been chief of naval operations for just six months when the Americans faced the Tet offensive of January 1968. In an unstinting effort to capture a major city, North Vietnamese and Vietcong units launched throughout South Vietnam bloody attacks which, at first, appeared to endanger the Saigon regime. In the opening phase, Moorer recalled, Westmoreland thought it would be a disaster for the United States, and demanded immediate troop reinforcements. Late in February the president sent Wheeler to Vietnam to estimate future troop needs. After consulting with Westmoreland, Wheeler suggested that he ask for 206,000 more men—above the existing limit of 525,000—and Westmoreland sent such a proposal to Washington. When the Joint Chiefs examined the recommendation, Moorer took the position that if the commander on the spot said he needed these reinforcements, he should either be given them, or be replaced as commander. Wheeler, who wanted to force Johnson to call the reserves to active duty, urged the service chiefs to approve Westmoreland's recommendation and they agreed.[15]

The Chiefs were surprised when this proposal for more troops, requiring the activation of about 250,000 reserves, precipitated a heated debate within the administration, as well as a national furor when it was leaked to and reported in the *New York Times.* Clark M. Clifford, who succeeded McNamara as secretary of defense on 1 March 1968, found that many men whose attitude had been "hawkish," including such key senators as Richard B. Russell and John C. Stennis, refused to agree to additional escalation of the ground war.[16] Former Secretary of State Dean G. Acheson, a tough cold warrior and a firm supporter of the commitment in Vietnam, had begun to lose confidence in American military leadership. During the Tet crisis, he warned Johnson "the Joint Chiefs of Staff don't know what they're talking about."[17] In March, at Clifford's urging, the president reluctantly decided against sending large reinforcements to Vietnam. And, at the end of the month, he announced that he would not seek another term as president, would halt most of the bombing of North Vietnam, and would attempt to negotiate peace with Ho Chi Minh's government.

It soon became evident to Moorer that Westmoreland's need for reinforcements had been exaggerated, because the Tet offensive soon proved to be a serious military defeat for North Vietnam and the Vietcong. Nevertheless, Moorer became convinced that Clifford had been appointed as secretary of defense by Johnson specifically to end the war. He believed this to be true despite Clifford's reputation as a "hawk," and the considerable evidence that he strained his relationship with Johnson by arguing against additional escalation of the war.[18] Moorer was also troubled by Clifford's preoccupation with the effect of the war on domestic politics. For instance, the admiral later claimed that Clifford insisted on a dramatic and popular halt in the bombing one week before the presidential election in November 1968, a move that most observers believed helped the Democratic candidate, Hubert H. Humphrey.

In many respects Moorer's most important concern as chief of naval operations was not the conduct of the war in Vietnam, but the effect that conflict had on the ability of American naval forces to respond to military crises elsewhere. He confronted one such crisis on the eve of Tet: the seizure by North Korea of the *Pueblo,* an intelligence-collection ship, in the Sea of Japan on 23 January 1968. The North Koreans claimed that the ship had violated their territorial waters, but Moorer insisted that she was in international waters when North Korean patrol boats, with air support, surrounded, boarded, and captured her. Convinced that this was piracy, which the United States could not tolerate, the chiefs had three plans to retaliate with military forces against North Korea. With the commitment in Vietnam, however, Johnson was unwilling to risk another war in Korea. He believed that the incident was designed to divert the attention of South Korea, which had deployed two divisions to South

Vietnam, and the United States from the Tet offensive that began only eight days after the seizure of the *Pueblo*. Thus, the JCS proposals to strike at North Korea were rejected and no retaliatory action was taken, although American forces in South Korea were modestly increased.[19] Moorer believed that, had the *Pueblo* crisis preceded the attacks in the Gulf of Tonkin in 1964, the United States would have retaliated against North Korea. And, in this view, the failure to retaliate severely weakened America's international prestige and encouraged a series of lesser incidents elsewhere which cost more American lives.

The captain of the *Pueblo,* Commander Lloyd M. Bucher, put up virtually no resistance and surrendered to the North Koreans without destroying the secret electronic gear aboard. In December 1968 the North Koreans released the crew of eighty-two, whose treatment by the navy upon their return home became a matter of controversy. Neither the navy nor the Joint Chiefs had any part in organizing the operations of the *Pueblo,* and Moorer concluded that the navy's only mistake in the whole affair was the assignment of Bucher to command the ship. Believing that Bucher should have resisted with all the means at his disposal and, if necessary, gone down with his ship, Moorer wanted to court-martial him, but Nixon decided against that and Secretary of the Navy John H. Chafee announced in May 1969 that charges against all the *Pueblo*'s officers had been dismissed on the grounds that "they have suffered enough."[20] This decision, in Moorer's view, established the unfortunate principle that a commanding officer is expected to resist force only when he has the power to overwhelm his assailant. He was especially concerned about the effect that Bucher's behavior had on younger officers and midshipmen. At that time, he recalled, there were bitter jokes at the Naval Academy, where midshipmen daily walk by the flag flown by Oliver Hazard Perry at the Battle of Lake Erie, which bears the words of the old American naval dictum, "Don't Give up the Ship."

The *Pueblo* incident demonstrated the degree to which the Vietnam War had limited the ability and will of the United States to initiate nonnuclear military action anywhere but in Southeast Asia. Moorer was forced to concentrate most of the navy's resources on the attack carriers, planes, and escort ships that were needed to deliver air strikes against targets in Vietnam and Laos. This meant that not only were the attack carriers over-committed to one theater, but also that everything that did not contribute to this limited mission was neglected. National preoccupation with the war in Vietnam posed a special problem for the navy because, while its global strength was declining, that of the Soviet Union was rapidly growing.

Moorer spent a good deal of time as chief of naval operations attempting to draw the attention of the administration, Congress, and the American public to the growing Soviet naval threat. He frequently quoted a radio broadcast that the chief of the Soviet Navy made to the Russian people in July 1969. "For the first time in its history," Admiral Sergei Gorshkov boasted, "the Soviet nation has acquired a powerful oceangoing navy. It has become the world's greatest naval power, capable of taking its line of defense out into the ocean."[21] Without accepting Gorshkov's claim of naval preeminence, Moorer emphasized that by any yardstick the Soviets had the world's second-largest and second-best navy. The Russian fleet was, he observed in late 1969, mostly new and very competent. The Soviets had applied their most advanced technology in both missile systems and electronic gear to their new fleet and were rapidly converting their submarines to nuclear propulsion. Moreover, they were developing the capacity to build rapidly both submarines and surface ships.[22] Nonetheless, in early 1970, Moorer still reassured those critics who charged that the "salt water Soviet bear . . . was towering over the remnants of a once-mighty American navy." The reason that image was false, he contended, was that the American fleet deployed aircraft carriers, whereas the Russians did not. Claiming that the attack carrier was the cornerstone of the American strategy of forward deployment, Moorer prophesied that the balance of naval power in the 1970s and 1980s would depend on whether or not the United States maintained a large carrier force.[23]

Not only Soviet naval strength but also strategy concerned Moorer, because he believed that Russia was "taking its line of defense out into the ocean." In December 1969, for example, a Soviet task force operated in the Philippine Sea, while Soviet ships, often present in the Indian Ocean and the Persian Gulf, visited Cuba. This maritime activity was in addition to the well-publicized Russian naval buildup in the Mediterranean. In the spring of 1970, in Operation Okean, the largest naval exercise in Russian history, Soviet units, all following a single plan, operated simultaneously in the Atlantic, Pacific, and Indian oceans, and in nine adjoining areas. More than 200 ships were deployed in this exercise, which Moorer termed "the widest in scope ever attempted by any navy." An additional concern for Moorer was the expansion of the Soviet merchant fleet, which was perhaps even more spectacular than that of her fighting navy.[24]

While the Soviet navy was growing, Moorer was presiding over an aging and shrinking fleet. In January 1969, he warned a congressional committee that 58 per cent of the ships in that fleet were at least twenty years old, while the comparable figure for the Soviet Navy was less than 1 per cent.[25] Indeed, under Moorer, the American navy began to face a severe problem of "block obsolescence." A large part of the American fleet had become over-age at the same time: between 1964 and 1969 the average age of its ships increased from fourteen to eighteen years.[26] And, because of the cost of the Vietnam War and the primacy of the army in that conflict, Moorer had great difficulty modernizing the fleet. He became embittered over the treatment of the navy by Secretary of Defense McNamara. He contended that McNamara, against his advice, organized the military budget so as to replace only material and weapons whose loss or deterioration resulted from the conduct of the war. Since American warships suffered little in this war, the navy was starved of funds to replace its aging ships. Although Moorer wanted, sensibly, to build new ships rather than repair and refit old ones, under McNamara's policy the navy received very little money for ship construction or conversion, and the fleet decayed. For fiscal year 1969, when inflation began to increase the costs of military procurement, the shipbuilding budget was the smallest since 1956; it actually fell below $1 billion. Although the navy's total budget increased from about $14 billion in 1964 to approximately $24 billion in 1969, most of the increase was spent fighting the war and the amount that could be invested in new ships, aircraft, and weapons declined during this period.[27]

In January 1969, President Nixon's defense secretary, Melvin R. Laird, told the Senate Armed Services Committee that improvement in American naval strength enjoyed a high priority in the new administration. In March, however, he told the same committee that he was recommending a reduction of $2.3 billion from the $80.6 defense budget proposed for fiscal year 1970 by Johnson. A month later, Moorer called for an accelerated and expanded naval shipbuilding program and Navy Secretary Chafee agreed that in the 1970s the service would require $3.5 annually (in 1969 dollars) for shipbuilding and conversions. Yet the 1970 military budget proposed by Laird allowed only $2.8 billion for that purpose and this was some $100 million less than the 1970 budget Johnson had proposed. In December 1969, after almost six months' consideration, Congress finally passed a $69.6 billion Defense Department Appropriation Bill for fiscal year 1970. Although Laird had already agreed to substantial cuts, this was some $5.6 billion less than he had requested, and was the biggest reduction in any annual military request since the end of the Korean War. The navy got a total of $20.8 billion, the least of the three services; and of this amount, only $2.49 billion went for ship-construction and conversion.[28] Moorer, who saw fleet modernization as the navy's primary problem, was deeply concerned by the continued cutbacks, which he considered paradoxical in view of the Soviet Navy's expansion. However, he was unable to reverse this trend, and during his term the navy's active fleet declined from more than 900 ships to about 760.[29]

Although the navy had increased its personnel strength very little as a result of the Vietnam War, the Nixon administration's policy of withdrawal from Indochina caused substantial reductions in force levels. During the war the navy had serious difficulty in retaining able, trained officers and skilled enlisted men. Under the pressure of the draft, it got what Moore described in 1969 as the highest quality of candidates, both enlisted and officer, it had ever had. But about half of these enlisted men joined simply to avoid being drafted into the army and obviously did not intend to stay in the navy beyond their required duty. Public opposition to the war, and the heavy pressure of continuous wartime operations, discouraged many from reenlisting, as did "back-to-back" deployments to the Western Pacific, which meant that many officers and men were at sea—and away from their families and the United States—for extraordinarily long periods of time.[30] These disturbing trends, which Moorer watched closely, were eased by the end of the war shortly after he left office.

Following the civil-rights movement, racial problems in the navy also emerged. The service had but four black officers when President Harry S. Truman ordered the armed forces to desegregate in July 1948. Twenty years later, the number of black naval officers was still only a modest 330. But, as Harvard and other leading private universities dropped Naval Reserve Officer Training Corps programs, Moorer in May 1968 established the first new NROTC unit in twenty-two years, at Prairie View Agricultural and Mechanical College, a predominantly black state institution in Texas.[31] Also, he suggested that councils on race relations be established at naval bases, and, in May 1970, he issued to commanders a personal letter dealing with the often-emotional subject of grooming—which had racial implications. Although emphasizing the necessity for neatness, Moorer reaffirmed naval policy permitting the wearing of sideburns, beards, and moustaches. Moreover, he discouraged commanding officers from attempting to regulate civilian clothing, and directed them to modify any of their regulations that conflicted with his letter. Moorer added, however, that no public announcement should be made on the matter. As his successor, Admiral Elmo R. Zumwalt, Jr., later noted, this last provision made it possible for recalcitrant officers to ignore Moorer's very reasonable directive.[32] Race relations in the navy did not reach a flashpoint under Moorer, and were but another smoldering problem that he left largely unresolved.

Of the three defense secretaries for whom he worked as chief of naval operations, the only one Moorer positively disliked was McNamara. He claimed that McNamara had instituted a pattern of civilian "meddling" in the selection and assignment of flag officers, which Moorer believed was the province of the chief of naval operations. He also objected to McNamara's "intellectual arrogance" and to the centralization that he imposed on the Department of Defense in which all major decisions were made by the secretary. Moreover, Moorer had little respect for most of the men McNamara brought into the department. He complained that they condensed complex military questions into one paper that offered, perhaps, three options, only one of which was remotely plausible, and ignored other, sounder, options. McNamara would then blithely accept his staff's predetermined choice. Moorer also felt that he and his fellow service chiefs were often "whipsawed" by the increasingly powerful office of the secretary of defense, which frequently offered them a choice of one policy—or none at all. This was Hobson's choice, since any chief would take something, however inadequate, rather than nothing. What Moorer especially resented, however, was the ensuing announcement from McNamara's office that this choice represented in fact the service chief's policy and preference. McNamara's successor, Clark Clifford, served slightly more than one year, and Moorer found him over-anxious to end the Vietnam War and too much preoccupied with the domestic political considerations of defense policy. Moorer was pleased that Laird backed away from McNamara's methods and allowed the Joint Chiefs more authority to make military decisions, but in the long run, he concluded resignedly, McNamara's system prevailed.

As CNO, Moorer also served under three secretaries of the navy: Paul H. Nitze, Paul R. Ignatius, and John H. Chafee. Nitze was promoted to deputy secretary of defense only a month after Moorer became chief of naval operations in August 1967, and in the following year Moorer enjoyed working with Ignatius, a competent administrator. When the Republicans took office in January 1969, Chafee, former governor of Rhode Island, became secretary. Moorer found him personally pleasant, but soon concluded that he was a "disaster" for the navy. His appraisal of Chafee was that he was weak, eager to cut defense spending, and "obsessed with liberal ideas"—all anathemas to Moorer. The two men clashed repeatedly. Chafee's interference in flag assignments did nothing to ease the strain between them, nor did his choice of Zumwalt to relieve Moorer in 1970.

In April, Nixon nominated Moorer to relieve Wheeler as chairman of the Joint Chiefs of Staff. Moorer recommended an aviator as his relief as CNO, but Laird and Chafee agreed on Zumwalt, a young, innovative, surface line admiral. Moorer later made no secret of his opposition to the choice or of his discontent with Zumwalt's policies as CNO. Not long before he relieved Wheeler, Moorer called on the general and found him bent over with his head in his hands. "You'll never survive!" Wheeler told Moorer. On 1 July 1970 Moorer left office as chief of naval operations and moved up to become chairman of the Joint Chiefs.

Over the next four years Moorer often worried that Wheeler's prophecy would prove accurate. In those difficult years, however, Moorer not only survived, but earned a reputation as a highly effective chairman. He managed to cope with the problems of "Vietnamization," the end of conscription, sharp cuts in defense spending, the strategic arms limitation talks and treaty (SALT-I), and the Arab-Israeli War of 1973. Highly respected by his professional colleagues, he kept a low public profile. A tall, affable man of imposing presence and relentless common sense, he worked hard to promote harmony and cooperation among the services. He demonstrated his conciliatory gifts by holding the confidence of such mutually antagonistic figures as Zumwalt and Secretary of State Henry A. Kissinger, as well as of key congressional leaders, senior officials of the Defense Department, and, not least, President Nixon. In 1972 the president appointed Admiral Moorer to a second two-year term as chairman of the Joint Chiefs.[33] The times in which Moorer served as chairman were not heroic. He took office as a divided nation was watching the slow and agonizing liquidation of the war in Vietnam. He left office as the Nixon administration was about to go under in the quagmire of Watergate. Moorer emerged from these somber years with great credit. When his term as chairman ended on 2 July 1974 he abundantly deserved the tribute paid him by Defense Secretary James R. Schlesinger in presenting him with an unprecedented second Distinguished Service Medal. "Tom Moorer," Schlesinger observed, "has always put his country's interest before anything else."[34]

Air Force General George S. Brown succeeded Admiral Moorer as chairman of the Joint Chiefs of Staff, and after forty-five years of naval service, from midshipman to admiral, Moorer retired to civilian life. He retreated no farther south than McLean, Virginia, just across the Potomac from Washington. Along with Kissinger he maintained an office at Georgetown University's Center for Strategic and International Studies, and took seats on the boards of directors of a number of corporations, including Texaco, Fairchild Industries, and Alabama Dry Dock and Shipbuilding Company. After his retirement, Moorer followed defense policy closely, and frequently appeared before congressional committees. A forceful opponent of the Panama Canal treaties, he testified in October 1977 before the Senate Foreign Relations Committee in direct opposition to testimony given the same day by two other noted retired officers, Admiral Zumwalt and General Maxwell D. Taylor. Moorer then warned: "Do not be surprised, if the treaty is ratified in its present form, to see a Soviet and/or a Cuban presence quickly established in the country of Panama."[35] He was also active in the organized opposition to the approval of the proposed SALT-II treaty. When the conservative American Security Council released an attack on the treaty in April 1979, Moorer described the SALT-II agreements as "heavily detrimental to the security and welfare" of the United States.[36]

Born before World War I, commissioned by President Franklin D. Roosevelt, battle-seasoned by World War II, and tested by the cold war and the war in Vietnam, Moorer served his country faithfully and well in a period of spectacular and accelerating change. On that sunny July morning in Annapolis in 1970 when Admiral Zumwalt saluted and said "Admiral Moorer, I relieve you," Moorer's record of naval service was already long and exceptional. He left the Navy Department only to undertake national service of even greater distinction, joining Fleet Admiral William D. Leahy and Admiral Arthur W. Radford, at that time the only naval officers who had served as chairman of the Joint Chiefs of Staff. For his service to the navy and the nation, Admiral Moorer deserved his place in their company.

ELMO RUSSELL ZUMWALT, JR.

1 July 1970–1 July 1974

NORMAN FRIEDMAN

When Elmo R. Zumwalt became chief of naval operations on 1 July 1970, he was the youngest man to hold the office. He will probably be remembered as the naval chieftain who tried to rock the boat, who sought to make fundamental changes in naval policy during an era dominated by generally conservative flag officers. As chief of naval operations, he appeared to offer the navy revolutionary solutions to its gravest problems, rather than the evolutionary changes with which most of the naval community felt comfortable. And, in contrast to his predecessors and contemporaries, Zumwalt was flamboyant: his style resembled the charismatic, vigorous military leader of the past, rather than the colorless, bureaucratic manager of modern armed forces. Whereas another admiral might have stressed continuity, Zumwalt preferred to sharpen the differences between his innovations and previous practices in an attempt to change underlying trends in naval policy and thought.

Elmo Zumwalt was born in San Francisco on 29 November 1920, the son of physicians who practiced in Tulare, California, where he was reared. He planned to become a doctor of medicine also, but his mother's terminal illness wiped out the family's savings and Elmo, a good student, decided to attend the Naval Academy, where he could get a free education, and to leave the navy after his required service in order to attend medical school. World War II delayed that plan. Zumwalt did well at the academy and stood seventh in the class of 1943, which, because of the war, was graduated one year early. He entered destroyer service and participated in several of the more dramatic engagements of the Pacific war, including the Battle of Savo Island and the classic sea fight in the Surigao Strait. After the war, Zumwalt applied both to medical and law schools and received acceptance notices, but he decided to stay in the navy because, he later claimed, he believed that the United States faced a serious postwar military threat from the Soviet Union. He had formed this view even before the end of the hostilities, but it was clearly reinforced by his contact in late 1945 in China with a community of White Russian emigrés. For several months after the surrender, he commanded a captured Japanese gunboat in Shanghai and it was there that he met his future wife, Mouza.[1]

Zumwalt continued to serve in destroyers and his postwar assignments included command of a destroyer escort, of a destroyer, and of the first American missile frigate, the *Dewey*. During the Korean War, Lieutenant Commander Zumwalt was navigator of the battleship *Wisconsin*, which saw action in the Far East. These conventional surface line billets were interspersed with study at the Naval War College from 1952 to 1953 and, later in his career, at the National War College from 1961 to 1962, and with a tour in Washington in the Bureau of Naval Personnel. His interest in Soviet affairs was constant and the thesis he presented at the National War College was on "The Problem of the Next Succession in the U. S. S. R." At that time Soviet studies was an especially fertile academic field, and Zumwalt came into contact with a number of specialists whose views refined his own ideas about Russian life and government.

He also met Paul H. Nitze, an important Democratic party public servant, who had written in 1950 the famous National Security Council Memorandum 68 which laid the groundwork for America's postwar rearmament program. Zumwalt agreed with Nitze's hard-line view of the implacability of the Soviet military threat to the United States. After John F. Kennedy returned the Democrats to office in 1961, he named Nitze to be assistant secretary of defense for international security affairs, and a year later Nitze brought Zumwalt into his office. Nitze was an important official during the Kennedy administration, and Zumwalt found himself near to the center of decision-making during the Cuban missile crisis of October 1962. Moreover, he participated in drafting some of the early studies on arms control that led to the Nuclear Test Ban Treaty of 1963, and he wrote papers on strategic arms limitation which laid the foundation for the American positions at the later SALT-I negotiations. When Nitze became secretary of the navy in November 1963, Zumwalt served as his executive assistant and senior aide. He recalled these years as particularly exciting, because Secretary of Defense Robert S. McNamara relied on his service secretaries "as assistant secretaries [of defense] for their departments." As Nitze's aide, Zumwalt became familiar not only with the inner workings of the Navy Department, but also with the development of naval policy and the terrible effects the Vietnam War was having on the navy's fleet-modernization and shipbuilding programs.[2]

In July 1965, he returned to sea as Commander, Cruiser Division 7, but Nitze and the chief of naval operations, Admiral David L. McDonald, cut this tour short one year later so that Zumwalt could return to Washington to become the first head of the navy's new Division of Systems Analysis. Early operations in the Vietnam War had already begun to strain the American fleet, most of which had been built in World War II, and one of Zumwalt's jobs in Systems Analysis was to find ways to replace these aging ships. In a report entitled "Major Fleet Escort Study," the division tried to establish sound, basic characteristics for a large class of replacement destroyers; these ultimately evolved into the *Spruances*. Unfortunately, as this class of ship increased in sophistication during the design and construction stages, the numbers that could be built fell far short of those required to replace the old destroyers. A competition for the design of the *Spruance* class was held just as Zumwalt left his post at Systems Analysis, and later, when he was chief of naval operations, he signed the production contract for that ship.

Under Zumwalt, the Division of Systems Analysis initiated other major studies which made recommendations on the improvement of the fleet's war-fighting capabilities. For example, he conducted a study of surface-to-surface missiles which led directly to the development of the Harpoon antiship missile. He also participated in the "Strat-X" study that led to the construction of the Trident-type submarine and ballistic-missile system. During his years in Washington, he became more keenly aware of the strategic balance between the United States and the Soviet Union and so, for a surface line officer, was unusually disposed to favor expenditures on naval strategic weapons, even at the cost of less money being available for general-purpose forces.[3]

After leaving the Pentagon, Zumwalt took command of American naval forces in South Vietnam. In this billet, he was responsible for riverine warfare which, unlike most American naval operations of the postwar period, did not involve the overwhelming superiority of U. S. forces against an inferior enemy. In addition, he had to fill an advisory role with the South Vietnamese Navy, which was an extraordinarily frustrating task. Whereas the carrier strike operations, which were under the commander of the Seventh Fleet, were fairly conventional, Zumwalt was forced to be tactically innovative in a combat environment that was hostile to the achievement of his mission. However, the navy believed that the experiment in riverine warfare was successful and Zumwalt received a large measure of credit for this.

In 1970 Secretary of Defense Melvin R. Laird persuaded President Richard M. Nixon to promote Admiral Thomas H. Moorer, the chief of naval operations, to be the new chairman of the Joint Chiefs of Staff. This meant that a relief for Moorer had to be found one year earlier than planned. Since the retirement of Arleigh Burke in 1961, all the CNOs had been aviators, but, ignoring Moorer's recommendation that this pattern be continued, Laird and Secretary of the Navy John H. Chafee picked Zumwalt, whom they believed would bring new ideas to the billet and a different perspective, given his background in the surface line. Zumwalt left Vietnam and became chief of naval operations on 1 July 1970.[4]

Zumwalt believed that he had become CNO at a time of a great military crisis for the United States. While America spent a large part of its defense budget on the limited war in Vietnam, at the same time the president and Congress refused to increase appropriations to match continuous Soviet military expansion. The Russians were greatly increasing the size and sophistication of their navy, and block obsolescence was simultaneously shrinking the number of ships in the American fleet. Not only that, but, as this went on, the Soviets began to approach parity with the United States in strategic nuclear forces. Thus, as chief of naval operations, Zumwalt faced the unhappy prospect of spending more on strategic nuclear forces while watching his navy's conventional units, which he believed would have to protect American interests in peacetime and in limited wars, fade in strength relative to those of the Soviet fleet.

One of Zumwalt's great frustrations when he became chief of naval operations was the complacency he found among government officials about the decline of American military power. Over the years, civilian leaders had become so accustomed to assuming that the United States was by far the strongest nation in the world that they made little attempt to calculate the true balance of military power. They maintained this view through a decade of growing Soviet power and gave no credence to claims of Russian advancement, partly because they did not want to face the politically unacceptable budget that a comparable American effort would require. Zumwalt began to try to turn things around: repeatedly during his tour as CNO he stated his belief that the U. S. Navy's fortunes had fallen to the point where the odds would favor the Soviets in a naval campaign. However, the antimilitary spirit of his time, generated by the opposition to the Vietnam War, suggested to many that the admiral was an alarmist.

In part, Zumwalt's persistent campaign for naval expansion was animated by the fear that American naval forces, which had been able to operate at sea almost without resistance since 1945, would be challenged successfully by the Soviets and their client states during an international crisis. For example, when he became CNO, he was convinced that the proliferation among Third World powers of Soviet-built antiship missiles might soon deny to American surface warships access during a period of tension to many of the world's coastal waters. Although he believed that the carrier task forces would be able to overcome such light opposition during a general war, in a crisis—before total war had broken out—the fact that unsupported American surface ships could not operate in these areas might have a devastating effect on the navy's ability to execute the nation's foreign policy. Complicating this problem, the Nixon Doctrine, which was enunciated before Zumwalt became chief of naval operations, mandated decreased American willingness to commit land forces outside Europe and, consequently, seemed to increase the demands on seaborne forces.[5]

In 1970 Zumwalt began to look towards a series of technical solutions to these difficulties, which he saw as only symptoms of a more basic disease: the lack of long-term strategic planning in the navy. He traced this lack to a subtle and generally unrecognized shift in the direction of the navy's mission following the end of World War II. Before that conflict, the American naval mission was clearly articulated within the service in terms of a general war with Japan; concentration on that mission was very important, for it provided a well-understood benchmark against which weapons, tactics, and strategies could be evaluated. After the war, an unprecedented aura of secrecy surrounded strategic planning for a nuclear war with the Soviet Union and debate over war planning in the navy became less and less realistic. More and more the navy explained its force levels in terms of capabilities applicable to a wide range of operational circumstances: antisubmarine warfare, strategic nuclear warfare, carrier-strike warfare, and amphibious assaults. These capabilities were increasingly dependent on specific technological developments not necessarily tied to an overall naval mission, and the practitioners of the technologies created unions within the navy. In this atmosphere, Zumwalt believed, the real strategist had become discredited. He concluded that the navy was confused about its justification for existence.

In addition, Zumwalt thought that naval strategic planning had become excessively defensive. The emphasis on advanced technology had produced ships and weapons of such complexity that they could be procured only in small numbers. At the same time, the Soviets had built an operationally impressive fleet, but they had not developed attack aircraft carriers, which many naval officers considered a prerequisite of modern sea power. Early in the cold war, American strategists, accustomed to viewing the Soviet fleet as a coastal defense force, intended to defeat it with longer-range aircraft from forward-deployed carriers. It seemed that the only Soviet oceanic threat was from her great force of torpedo-bearing submarines. However, in the 1960s, the Russians began to move large missile ships to sea, supporting them with long-range bombers intended specifically to attack American carriers. In Zumwalt's opinion, these developments had not been sufficiently appreciated within the U. S. Navy, in part because of the "unions" of surface, submarine, and aviation officers, which oriented naval thinking toward hardware. To regain the initiative at sea, the navy had to look again at its overall mission.

One important factor in this endeavor, Zumwalt believed, was to make long-range planning more effective. A Long-Range Objectives Group had been created in 1954 by Admiral Robert Carney during his tour as chief of naval operations. Carney's purpose had been to assign the unit to deal exclusively with very-long-term naval shipbuilding programs within the context of future naval missions. By 1970, however, the group had lost much of its influence within the navy, partly as a result of Secretary of Defense Robert S. McNamara's policy of planning in five-year cycles rather than for longer periods. Zumwalt sponsored instead a new long-range review of U. S. naval policy, Project 2000.[6]

Part of the problem, as Zumwalt saw it, was the lack of any clear measure of how well the navy could execute its missions. He observed that "there is no bottom line in the Defense Department. There have been only a few balance sheets worked out, and each has been minus from the start." The nearest thing to a bottom line there had been in the modern navy in peacetime was the combination of the Orange War Plans and the fleet problems of the 1930s, but they had vanished when the atomic bombs were dropped in 1945. In the absence of a bottom line, it was easy for the navy to become fragmented into unions, which tended to think only about their own part of the service. In an attempt to restore a balanced orientation toward the array of individual ships and weapons, Zumwalt created the Navy Net Assessment Group. Using many methods closely related to the systems-analysis techniques that Zumwalt had employed from 1966 to 1968, the work of this new unit was to give the American navy a gauge of its likely effectiveness against the Soviets in a number of situations: general war, limited wars at sea, and various kinds of crises in the Third World. He relied on these studies to develop his naval policies and strategies and tried to ensure that the group's classified reports, which were based on elaborate computer simulations of naval actions, were widely circulated and read. To Zumwalt, one great advantage of this work was that it forced him to keep in mind what the navy's net performance would be in what he considered realistic war scenarios against the Soviets.[7]

To achieve his goal of broadening strategic thinking in the service, Zumwalt resorted to other means. One was the courses at the Naval War College, traditionally the school of American naval tactics and strategy. He thought that the school's curriculum fell away from its real mission once it began to emphasize defense management. Moreover, the senior course was regarded by many naval officers as less than rigorous. In 1972, Zumwalt relieved the president of the college and named Vice Admiral Stansfield Turner to the billet. With Zumwalt's support, Turner revised the curriculum, made the course far more difficult, and emphasized the study of strategies and tactics—including Soviet tactics. At the same time, Zumwalt tried to make the fleet aware of the character of the Russian adversary. Believing that the Soviets took tactical studies very seriously and published their doctrines to educate their officers, Zumwalt had many of these writings reprinted in English. He constantly studied the works of Gorshkov and tried to see to it that they were widely circulated in the U. S. Navy. He also made sure that they were included in the new course of study at the Naval War College. Nonetheless, he was not satisfied that he had done enough to reverse the trend of strategic parochialism in naval thinking, particularly among the more junior officers.[8]

Of course, the instant operational problem that Zumwalt faced when he became chief of naval operations concerned the Vietnam War. He had to execute Secretary Laird's policy of "Vietnamization," that is, the transfer of combat responsibilities to South Vietnam's armed forces. Although he had, for some time, questioned the wisdom of American involvement and strategy in the war, he vigorously supported the new policy. Nonetheless, most of his concerns as CNO were not directly related to the Vietnam War because he had little influence on war policy. Instead, he concentrated on the dramatic effect of the conflict on the American fleet.[9]

In 1967, President Lyndon B. Johnson decided to fight the war in Vietnam with a restricted budget, often called his "guns and butter" budget. This meant that general-purpose forces had to be sacrificed in favor of a combination of limited-war forces, such as Zumwalt used in the riverine campaign, and modernization of the strategic arm. The net effect of this policy was to reduce the existing fleet by wearing out many of its older ships, while precluding their timely replacement. At the same time, the "guns and butter" budgets produced inflation, which increased the ultimate replacement costs of the general-purpose ships and made replacement of a large number of ships at once politically unattractive. The general malaise that settled on the United States after the experience in Vietnam appeared to prohibit such expenditures and left Congress extremely skeptical of claims—such as those made by Zumwalt—that the Soviets were on the march. It followed that, no matter what Zumwalt wanted to do, he would have to preside over a rapidly shrinking fleet.

Confronted by the high cost of replacements and the very high cost of maintaining tired ships, Zumwalt decided to accelerate the retirement of ships built in World War II, in order to set aside funds for vital new construction and for the improvement of younger ships. During his tour as chief of naval operations, ships were decommissioned at a furious rate, not so much because the Vietnam War was winding down as because he needed the monies for other projects. For example, Zumwalt placed great emphasis and urgency on attaining a high standard of antiship-missile defense in the fleet. This, in turn, required manufacturing a great deal of expensive electronic-countermeasures gear and placing high priorities on producing existing point-defense weapons such as Sea Sparrow.[10]

In fact, not every ship in the fleet was overdue for replacement during Zumwalt's tenure; part of the problem he faced was the way in which shipbuilding budgets had been skewed since 1945. They emphasized the most impressive and expensive manifestations of sea power: carrier strike forces and nuclear submarines. Zumwalt considered these ships as the upper, or "high," end of the spectrum of the fleet's capabilities, the "low" end of which included the large numbers of ships built to fight World War II. As the latter became over-age, he saw a need to replace that "low" end of what he believed had always been a "high-low" mix of ships. Many in the navy considered his concept of "high-low" radical and even dangerous, because it justified building new ships which were not the "best" of their types. In fact, the concept was hardly novel. For example, in World War II the navy operated "high-end" ships in its carrier task forces and "low-end" destroyer escorts for antisubmarine operations. After the war, few men in the navy sensed that, in fact, what was the "high end" during the conflict had slowly fallen towards the "low end" of the postwar mix. Zumwalt attempted to replace these "low end" units with ships such as the *Oliver Hazard Perry*-class frigates and the stillborn sea control ship. The capability of both these classes was deliberately limited and, for this reason, they met stiff opposition. Some of the officers who opposed Zumwalt's concept of "high-low" charged that it was simply a way of cutting shipbuilding costs by not procuring the first-class warships absolutely necessary to meet a first-class

Soviet threat. This charge was unfair in that the concept was not new, had been proven before, and was, in Zumwalt's opinion, the *only* practical way to get the ships necessary to maintain a fleet able to meet the Soviet challenge.[11]

Moreover, Zumwalt was not, as some suggested, concerned merely with the "low" end of the scale. He considered the approval for a fourth nuclear aircraft carrier, the *Carl Vinson,* to be vital to the maintenance of the strike forces and he fought for it in the Defense Department and before Congress. His victory in getting that ship approved was one of the most important achievements of his tour. In addition, he supported the Trident submarine and missile program, despite the fact that the "Strat-X" study, which led to it and of which he was a co-author, had earlier recommended smaller, less sophisticated boats.[12]

He argued that American sea power was the sum of many parts other than just the ships of the fleet. Like many of his predecessors, he came to see the merchant marine as a potential source of auxiliary tonnage in wartime. Escalating naval shipbuilding costs made the replacement of classes such as oilers and submarine and destroyer tenders more and more difficult, as the navy had to concentrate its limited funds on combatants. Indeed, the Maritime Commission had been created in the 1930s with exactly this goal of supporting the navy. However, by the 1970s the idea of cooperation between the navy and the Maritime Administration had been forgotten, and when Zumwalt raised it anew it was greeted as a radical notion. He lacked the legal machinery by which so much merchant tonnage was transferred to the navy during World War II and these laws were not going to be reenacted. Finally, he could do little because there was no money available and other issues were far more pressing.[13]

He also encountered major obstacles in his effort to improve the amphibious assault units intended to move the marines into combat on hostile shores. The postwar amphibious ships had been modernized and even the old amphibious flagships had been replaced, but little attention had been given to the requirements for fire support in landing operations. Moreover, by 1970 even the reserve fleet was losing its old cruisers and the reactivation of the battleship *New Jersey* for operations in Vietnam showed just how difficult the renovation of any major fire-support ship could be. The marines wanted Zumwalt to agree to build a new landing fire-support ship, designated LFS, but the cost was too high and the project came to nothing. All he could do was continue to allow the option of building one forward 8-inch gun into new destroyers, but he found this clearly less than satisfactory.

When Zumwalt took office in July 1970, he at once began what he called Project Sixty, an attempt to formulate an action program for the navy within sixty days. He intended the conclusions of this study to be his plan for his four-year tenure, evidently believing that, once he was well into his term, he would be spending so much of his time solving daily problems that never again would he be able to look at the navy as a whole. He wanted as his principal assistant Rear Admiral Worth Bagley, who was then commanding a destroyer flotilla, and until Bagley could be released his place was occupied by Stansfield Turner.

One of Zumwalt's first conclusions in Project Sixty was that a new escort program was needed. The previous program for mass replacement, called DX, was intended to provide about one hundred ships, but thirty *Spruance*-class destroyers were all that had been ordered. On 9 September 1970 Zumwalt initiated a study to devise a new class of ship which he wanted "optimized for essentially one mission of either antisubmarine warfare, antiaircraft warfare, or surface warfare, with common hull and propulsion configuration." He ordered that "equipments should be kept relatively simple and the use of complex integrated hardware and software systems should be avoided." This was "low" end with a vengeance. Zumwalt hoped to be able to buy enough ships to afford specialized types within a flexible force. The subsequent feasibility study emphasized cost constraints, and on 31 December Zumwalt issued a requirement for a $50-million escort ship. As work on the design progressed, Zumwalt became convinced that the antisubmarine escort might well be unnecessary, in view of the existing large force of newly built *Knox*-class frigates. Moreover, development of the Harpoon missile, which could be fired from an antiaircraft-missile launcher, made it possible to combine the antiaircraft and surface-warfare missions. The result was the single type of frigate which Zumwalt eventually ordered, the *Oliver Hazard Perry* class. Inflation affected the cost of building the *Perry* class—so much so that the price of each ship tripled within a few years after Zumwalt left office, but it seemed destined to become the most numerous postwar combatant class built by the navy. At least in terms of the numbers of ships the service was able to acquire, it vindicated the policy that Zumwalt pushed through the Defense Department and Congress against considerable opposition.[14]

Zumwalt's attempt to carry cost containment over to other types was less successful. For example, in 1970 a highly advanced antiaircraft-missile system, Aegis, was about ready to go into production. Zumwalt believed that it would be a counter to the emerging threat from Soviet ship-to-ship cruise missiles—if he could build enough ships to carry it. He wanted to build an inexpensive destroyer, which he called the DG, powered by cheap gas-turbine engines, eventually to replace very expensive nuclear-powered missile frigates as the primary escort for aircraft carriers. Believing that sheer numbers would count in a naval war with the Soviets, Zumwalt discovered that the navy could build from three to five conventional missile-carrying escort destroyers for every two that were nuclear-powered. However, Admiral Hyman G. Rickover, the legendary long-time head of the navy's nuclear-propulsion program, wanted all combatant ships to have nuclear power plants and, therefore, opposed Zumwalt's gas-turbine destroyers. An acerbic and elderly titan who did not get along with Zumwalt, Rickover had powerful allies in Congress and he persuaded them to disapprove the inexpensive destroyer and replace it with a program to build very costly nuclear-strike cruisers, whose primary equipment would be the Aegis. Zumwalt tried to bargain with Rickover by offering to support his "high" end nuclear-powered carriers and attack submarines, but Rickover—probably seeing that the deal was not a prerequisite to achieving his goals—refused. Thus, during his term as chief of naval operations, Zumwalt failed to curb Rickover's influence over the shipbuilding program. After he left office, however, Zumwalt had the satisfaction of watching Congress, convinced that the nuclear-strike cruiser was too expensive, replace it with another conventionally powered destroyer.[15]

Zumwalt's experience with the sea control ship was even less successful. When Project Sixty was completed, he ordered a study of a ship that would be capable of operating VSTOL (very short take-off and landing) aircraft and helicopters. His experts produced fifteen sketch designs of ships, displacing from 8,400 to 26,930 tons, fully loaded, one of which had nuclear propulsion. He selected a design for a 17,000-ton, 25-knot ship that could embark fourteen helicopters and three VSTOL aircraft. Zumwalt wanted to build several of these ships, and he ordered a test of the concept aboard the modified assault helicopter carrier *Guam*. The test, however, was inconclusive, mainly because there were ambiguities concerning the mission of the sea control ship. Zumwalt later claimed that the peacetime mission of the ship would be to show the flag in forward areas and so to remove from Soviet strategy any plan for a surprise ambush of American aircraft carriers. In wartime, he said, he wanted to use the sea control ship for antisubmarine operations in the sea lanes. However, many naval aviators opposed the ship on the grounds that Zumwalt overestimated its antisubmarine-warfare capabilities. They also charged that he wanted to deemphasize the need for heavy carriers and their strike aircraft. Again, Zumwalt lost and the Defense Department never authorized construction of the sea control ship. On the other hand, Zumwalt initiated a shift in the navy's thinking about VSTOL technology, which figured in many programs introduced after he left office and which many believed to be the key to less-expensive, sea-based air power.[16]

But low-cost solutions were not Zumwalt's only concern as chief of naval operations. For example, he believed American ships suffered from the fact that they no longer enjoyed significant advantages in speed over Russian vessels, particularly submarines. To some extent, his own experiences in destroyers probably shaped this view. Therefore, he sponsored a proposal for a surface-effects ship, capable of making 100 knots on an air cushion and displacing 3,000 tons. This was by no means an inexpensive piece of technology, but it was attractive to Zumwalt because he felt that it could perform several missions then assigned to much larger ships. In a similar vein, he supported the development of a hydrofoil combatant that displaced 240 tons, made 60 knots, and carried effective antiship missiles. He hoped that it would be a means of regaining the naval initiative in the Mediterranean since these craft were supposed to harry Soviet surface antiship forces. However, both the surface-effects ship and the hydrofoil ship were attacked as solutions in search of a problem. Critics charged that the advent of high-speed missiles with very long range had diluted the tactical value of speed. Moreover, they pointed out that the use of long-range acoustic sensors in antisubmarine operations had reduced the requirement for high speeds. Zumwalt promoted both ships during his term in office but, after his retirement, his successors gave them a low priority and they were often near cancellation. However, the value of high-speed platforms was unresolved, and the surface-effects ship and the hydrofoil ship had the potential to be one of Zumwalt's most important legacies to the navy.[17]

As CNO, Zumwalt undertook a number of projects that he hoped would regain the initiative for the U. S. Navy in its contest with Soviet naval forces. While he headed the Systems Analysis Division he began studies that led to the development of the Harpoon missile. Although Project Sixty emphasized missile defense, including significant improvements in electronic countermeasures, it also recommended acceleration of the Harpoon program, whose fruition was many years away, and other antiship missiles that would give American surface combatants on detached duty an "equalizer." Zumwalt not only accelerated the Harpoon program, but he also sought an interim solution in the form of a modified drone or antiaircraft weapon. That search produced a ship-launched version of the Standard antiradiation missile, small numbers of which were actually deployed while Zumwalt was chief of naval operations.

The Harpoon program symbolized the shift from an American navy so powerful it could ignore Soviet surface-ship interference and concentrate on carrier-strike warfare against land targets, to a force that might have to face the Russian fleet in sea battles and might not always be able to supply carrier aircraft to protect its surface ships against those of the enemy. Zumwalt believed that the U. S. Navy would never have enough aircraft carriers and that surface units often would have to operate in dangerous coastal areas, if only to show the flag. In those areas, the Soviets, their allies, and their clients could deploy a large number of missile boats quite capable of assaulting American destroyers and frigates. This explained the strategy behind his enthusiasm for the Harpoon.[18]

When Zumwalt took office as CNO in 1970 the navy also faced serious personnel problems, some of which had been untended by his predecessors. First and foremost, he had to deal with a very serious decline in morale. In part, this was a result of the age of the ships, since the older they became, the more maintenance they required, and this fact was especially true in wartime. Levels of exertion once considered extraordinary became the norm. This was compounded by the unusual character of fleet operations during the latter part of the cold war and the Vietnam War. During World War II the stress of operations at sea was balanced to some extent by a relaxation of regulations that crews found irksome. However, in the cold war, even in the war zone off Vietnam, there was little such relaxation. The Sixth Fleet in the Mediterranean in many ways operated at sea under wartime conditions, but those in command could not or would not allow the degree of informality common in combat circumstances.

Two points of annoyance often intersected. For example, by the early 1960s, space on the older carriers was so constricted that much of the maintenance on the aircraft had to be performed on the flight decks. This constant, exhausting work was caused by the fact that the aircraft had to remain on deck in bad weather. It was dirty, greasy work, but in the Sixth Fleet the rule that in port men on deck had to wear dress whites at all times was strictly enforced, and if they did not, or could not, produce clean white uniforms for liberty, they were not allowed ashore. Furthermore, carrier operations, always demanding, were more so during the Vietnam War than in World War II. Instead of steaming around the Pacific in search of the Japanese, carrying out occasional air strikes, launching planes for no more than a few weeks at a time and then going into port, in the Vietnam War the carriers took station off Vietnam and stayed there, launching their planes day and night, every day, for months at a time. For the crews, it was a grinding routine; moreover there was none of the usual exhilaration of combat operations since the enemy could not be seen from the offshore stations. All the armed forces had analogous problems, but the navy was particularly vulnerable because of the rigidity of the fleet's normal operating procedures, long overseas deployments which separated all of the men from their families, and aging ships. When Zumwalt became chief of naval operations, there was an undercurrent of discontent in the fleet that would soon erupt unless he paid attention to it.[19]

At the same time the navy in 1970, like the army and air force, was badly torn by the effects of more than a decade of unrest over civil rights and by the deepening sentiment in the United States against the Vietnam War. One of the reasons Secretary Laird chose Zumwalt to be chief of naval operations was because his views on the roles of blacks and women in the navy were more liberal than those of other senior admirals. He did not think that the navy had ever really tried to integrate blacks into the service and saw the general policy towards both blacks and women as tokenism. Not only did the navy lag behind national standards, it was far behind the other services in accommodating liberal reforms. But Zumwalt believed the personnel problem was even more complex and threatening than that. As the navy used more and more technologically sophisticated equipment, it became increasingly necessary that trained personnel be retained. Retention and, indeed, the entire problem of manning the navy was being exacerbated by the end of the draft. Although the navy was a volunteer force, it benefitted indirectly from the draft and, when conscription ended, retention in the navy would depend largely on the enlisted man's opinion of the service. Thus, Zumwalt quickly concluded that improving retention rates was one of his greatest tasks.[20]

He ascribed low morale in part to unnecessary regulations and in part to a caste structure justified on the grounds of military discipline, but actually repugnant to all but the most senior enlisted men. He realized that leadership might be more difficult in a less hidebound navy, but he considered this a price that had to be paid to foster retention rates sufficiently high to man the fleet. In a series of what he called "Z-grams" to the fleet, he ordered that regulations concerning dress, haircuts, and other "mickey mouse" matters be liberalized to make life easier and more tolerable for enlisted men. When it became clear that his initial instructions had been ignored, he made certain that the relevant "Z-grams" were posted on bulkheads and obeyed. At the same time, he instituted a number of measures designed to ensure the racial integration of the navy on an equitable basis. Some of these measures were significant: for example, he ordered that each ship designate an officer to deal with racial problems and complaints. Others concerned small things that had simply been overlooked: he ordered naval exchanges and ships' stores to carry cosmetics for blacks. The sum of the effects of the measures was less dramatic that was the reaction to them.[21]

Heralded by liberals and civil rights leaders, Zumwalt became anathema to conservatives in the navy who argued that the old practices embodied traditions and fostered a strong discipline which his measures threatened to erode. Moreover, Zumwalt's personnel reforms reduced morale among the senior enlisted men, who were bitter because their privileges and authority declined. Among their many complaints was that Zumwalt's decision to eliminate minor extrajudicial punishments made it more difficult to discipline junior enlisted men for small infractions of rules. Retention rates for the highest ratings plummeted. In effect, the navy was sacrificing some of its best-trained men in order to ensure that overall manning levels were acceptable.

Unfortunately, Zumwalt's reforms coincided with three race riots in the fleet: in the carrier *Kitty Hawk* on 12 October 1972; in the oiler *Hassayampa* on 16 October; and in the carrier *Constellation* on 3 November. Several former chiefs of naval operations roused their allies in Congress to investigate not only the riots but also Zumwalt's reforms and the general state of discipline in the navy. To many conservatives the episodes were proof that Zumwalt had fostered a climate of laxity, and they cited his seemingly lenient treatment of the black rioters as their main piece of evidence. However, Zumwalt had developed considerable liberal support in Congress, Nixon was trying to deal with the first hints of the Watergate scandal, and so the CNO emerged from the hearings little scathed. Zumwalt later claimed that the president, had he not been engulfed in Watergate during 1973, would have relieved him. And indeed, it is clear that Nixon was less than pleased with his CNO. Zumwalt survived the controversy and managed to save his programs, clearly the most forceful attempt at personnel reform by any chief of naval operations. Nonetheless, Zumwalt's liberalization policy was in reality little different from that undertaken by all the services at about the same time, partly as a result of the end of the draft and partly to catch up to the new habits of the society they served.

However, Zumwalt identified his changes in the navy with his regime, publicized them, and defended them publicly. In so doing, he personalized his reforms and made himself the object of controversy as well.[22]

Zumwalt entered office determined to save the navy from multiple potential disasters. He had a clear idea of the problems and specific notions as to how to solve them. Strategically, he believed that the position of the United States relative to the Soviet Union in military terms had fallen dangerously. He estimated that in a naval war the chance of an American victory was less than 50 per cent, and he urged war-planners to prepare for a conflict in which the United States would suffer a disastrous loss of allied forces and territory. In brief, he concluded that in any war, other than a complete exchange of strategic nuclear weapons, American naval units would be forced out of the Western Pacific and Eastern Mediterranean, Middle Eastern oil would be denied to the United States and NATO, and the U. S. Navy would be hard pressed to keep open the sea lanes to Europe. Unfortunately, as CNO, he was effectively prohibited from voicing such pessimism, and, without voicing it, he could not hope to mobilize public opinion behind a large program of naval expansion. Complicating Zumwalt's predicament was Secretary of State Henry A. Kissinger, who dominated foreign policy during the Nixon presidency and who believed that, since the United States was declining as a great power, the only realistic policy for Washington was to get the best possible terms from the ascendant power, the Soviet Union. Since Nixon and Kissinger saw the Strategic Arms Limitation accords as the greatest achievement of the administration, Zumwalt's voice arguing for a buildup of the American arsenal was fairly lonely and muffled.[23]

To assess Zumwalt's tenure is difficult at this early date because so much of what he tried to do concerned strategy or shipbuilding policies which take more years to bear fruit than are in the term of one CNO. His personnel reforms, heralded by the "Z-grams," clearly improved morale in the fleet, but they were detested by most senior ratings, many of whom retired in consequence. The turmoil was a high price to pay, but Zumwalt believed that the alternative was an explosion; if he was correct, and this is hard to measure, his policies were successful. The "high-low" concept for the fleet was likely to remain important for years, if only because any "all-high" policy was fiscally impractical if large numbers of ships were to be maintained. Lastly, Zumwalt wanted the navy to study the possibility of combat against the Soviet fleet in realistic terms and to encourage American naval officers to be patrons of a common mission and strategy rather than of discrete technologies. It is too early to say whether he achieved this, his most important aim.

Zumwalt left office on 1 July 1974, and retired from the navy. Two years later, he ran as a Democratic candidate for the Senate from Virginia and lost. His defeat was due to the fact that his opponent, Harry F. Byrd, Jr., belonged to an unbeatable political dynasty, and to opposition from the large number of military officers living in Virginia who resented his personnel reforms. Thereafter, Zumwalt accepted the presidency of the American Medical Building Corporation in Milwaukee, Wisconsin, a position offered to him because of his managerial ability. However, he retained his interest in national security, became a member of the executive committee of the bipartisan Committee on the Present Danger, and testified vigorously in 1979 against the ratification of the SALT-II Treaty. In his public activities after his retirement he tried to do for the nation what he had done for the navy as chief of naval operations: awaken it to the way in which the balance of power was changing in favor of the Soviets and to the need for America to reverse the trend.

NOTES

ABBREVIATIONS

Adm	Admiralty
AHR	*American Historical Review*
CCS	Combined Chiefs of Staff
CNO	Chief of Naval Operations
CominCh	Command in Chief, U.S. Fleet
FRUS	*Foreign Relations of the United States* (Washington, D.C.: GPO, 1864–)
GB	General Board of the Navy
GPO	U.S. Government Printing Office, Washington, D.C.
JB	Joint Board of the Army and the Navy
JCS	Joint Chiefs of Staff
LC	Manuscript Division, Library of Congress
MSS	Manuscript collection
NA	National Archives, Washington, D.C.
NHC	Operational Archives, Naval Historical Center, Navy Yard, Washington, D.C.
NI	U.S. Naval Institute, Annapolis, Maryland
NSC	National Security Council
NWCA	Naval War College Archives
NWCR	*Naval War College Review*
OH	Oral History
PRO	Public Record Office, London, United Kingdon
RG	Record Group
USNA	Nimitz Library, U.S. Naval Academy, Annapolis, Maryland
USNIP	*U.S. Naval Institute Proceedings*
WPD	War Plans Division

WILLIAM S. BENSON

1. Memorandum, undated, Box 46, William S. Benson MSS, LC.
2. Bradley A. Fiske, *From Midshipman to Rear Admiral* (New York: Century, 1919), pp. 584–85.
3. Fiske to Daniels, 26 August 1913, in U.S. Congress, Senate, *Naval Investigation: Hearings before the Subcommittee of the Committee on Naval Affairs*, 66th Cong., 2d Sess., Vol. I, p. 695. (Hereafter *Naval Investigation.*)
4. *Ibid.*, p. 731.
5. William R. Braisted, *The United States Navy in the Pacific, 1909–1922* (Austin: University of Texas Press, 1971), p. 178. For a brief summation of Daniel's reforms and his difficulties with naval officers, *see* Paolo E. Coletta, *American Naval Heritage in Brief* (Washington, D.C.: University Press of America, 1978), pp. 197–98; and Gerald E. Wheeler, *Admiral William Veazie Pratt, U.S. Navy: A Sailor's Life* (Washington, D.C.: GPO, 1974), pp. 109–11.
6. For an account of these negotiations, which took place between December 1914 and January 1915, *see* Fiske, *Rear Admiral*, pp. 569–76.
7. *Naval Investigation*, Vol. II, p. 2972. For Daniels's influence on the outcome, *see* pp. 2979–80.
8. For Daniels's explanation of the difference between the two versions, see *Naval Investigation*, Vol. II, pp. 2974–76. The report of the Hobson committee is on pp. 2976–79. E. David Cronon wrote that, while Daniels "favored some reorganization, he was instrumental in watering down the measure to insure that the Chief of Naval Operations would operate under the direction of the Secretary of the Navy, rather than as head of a largely autonomous general staff." E. David Cronon, ed., *The Cabinet Diaries of Josephus Daniels* (Lincoln: University of Nebraska Press, 1963), p. 93.
9. Braisted, *Navy in the Pacific*, p. 182.
10. Dr. Mary Klachko, who has been at work for a number of years on a biography of Benson, plans to analyze his early career in considerable depth. She kindly allowed me to read her draft chapters on Benson's life before he became chief of naval operations.
11. Memorandum, n.d., Box 46, Benson MSS.
12. Benson, memorandum, 3 March 1927, Box 46, Benson MSS.
13. *Naval Investigation*, Vol. II, p. 1948.
14. *Ibid.*, p. 1820.
15. *Ibid.*, pp. 2315–16. In 1920 Benson explicitly indicated his conviction that the chief of naval operations should be able to direct the activities of the bureau chiefs and should play an important role in their selection. *See Ibid.*, pp. 1864–65.
16. For Benson's report on these developments and others, *see Naval Investigation*, Vol. II, 3009–13; and Benson to Daniels, 30 September 1915, Box 41. Benson MSS.
17. Memorandum, n.d., Box 46, Benson, MSS.
18. David F. Trask, "The American Navy in a World at War, 1914–1919," in Kenneth J. Hagan, ed., *In Peace and War* (Westport, Conn.: Greenwood Press, 1978), Ch. 11.
19. Braisted, *Navy in the Pacific*, pp. 191–92, 197–99, 201.
20. For deficiencies at the outset of the war, *see* Coletta, *Naval Heritage*, p. 201; and Wheeler, *Pratt*, pp. 101–2. Most naval officers agreed that the U.S. Navy was not well prepared for the war, although they adduced different reasons for this fact and assessed blame variously. For representative views, *see Naval Investigation*, Vol. II:

statement by Benson on pp. 1830–31; by Captain Joseph K. Taussig on pp. 508–9; by Captain William V. Pratt on pp. 1594–95; and by Rear Admiral Henry T. Mayo on p. 614.

21. Benson to Polk, 4 October 1916, Box 2, Benson MSS.
22. For an analysis of Benson's opinions, *see* David F. Trask, *Captains and Cabinets: Anglo-American Naval Relations, 1917–1918* (Columbia: University of Missouri Press, 1972), pp. 47–49.
23. Wheeler, *Pratt,* pp. 93–96.
24. *Naval Investigation,* Vol. II, p. 1836.
25. *Ibid.,* p. 1864.
26. For an analysis of Wilson's diplomacy, especially its relation to the use of military power, *see* David F. Trask, "Woodrow Wilson and the Reconciliation of Force and Diplomacy: 1917–1918," *NWCR,* January-February 1975, pp. 23–31.
27. Wheeler, *Pratt,* p. 153.
28. For a summary of this episode, *see* Trask, *Captains and Cabinets,* p. 55. Benson's statement about Sims's indiscretion is in a memorandum, n.d., (c. 1920), Box 42, Benson, MSS. For the recollections of Benson and Sims about this affair, see *Naval Investigation,* Vol. I, pp. 268–71, and Vol. II, pp. 1881–85.
29. Trask, *Captains and Cabinets,* p. 64.
30. For a detailed analysis of the views of Sims, *see* Elting E. Morison, *Admiral Sims and the Modern American Navy* (Boston: Houghton Mifflin, 1942); Trask, *Captains and Cabinets,* pp. 61–101; and the insightful summary in Wheeler, *Pratt,* p. 99. American civilian leaders grasped early the potential of the convoy system and the use of destroyers in antisubmarine warfare. Wilson was interested in convoying as early as 25 February 1917. On 11 April 1917, Daniels cried out in his diary, "O for more destroyers! I wish we could trade money in dreadnaughts for destroyers already built." Cronon, ed., *Daniels,* pp. 105 and 133.
31. Trask, *Captains and Cabinets,* p. 95.
32. For Benson's offensive spirit, see *Ibid.,* p. 65. Wilson's speech of 11 August 1917 is in *Naval Investigation,* Vol. II, pp. 2022–24.
33. For the decision to suspend the building program, *see* Wheeler, *Pratt,* pp. 107–09. A summary of the modern scholarship on the submarine war from 1917 to 1918 is Holger H. Herwig and David F. Trask, "The Failure of Imperial Germany's Undersea Offensive Against World Shipping, February 1917-October 1918," *The Historian,* August 1971, pp. 611–36.
34. For the distinctions between the views of Sims and the policy of the Navy Department, *see* Trask, *Captains and Cabinets,* pp. 95–97.
35. *Naval Investigation,* Vol. II, p. 1917.
36. Dean C. Allard, "Admiral William S. Sims and United States Naval Policy in World War I," *American Neptune,* Summer 1975, pp. 103–04. For Sims's position, *see* Sims to Pratt, 28 January 1919, *Naval Investigation,* Vol. II, pp. 3285–88. On 7 January 1920, Sims sent a memorandum to Daniels that criticized the Navy Department and precipitated a full-scale investigation by Congress into the conduct—particularly in 1917—of the naval war. Sims's memorandum is *Ibid.,* Vol. I, pp. 1–9.
37. Wheeler, *Pratt,* pp. 103–05.
38. Benson's trip is summarized in Trask, *Captains and Cabinets,* pp. 181–82; *also see* Dean C. Allard, "Anglo-American Differences During World War I," a paper delivered at the annual meeting of the Organization of American Historians, 13 April 1978, pp. 17–18.

39. *Naval Investigation,* Vol. I, p. 226.
40. Trask, *Captains and Cabinets,* p. 197.
41. Wheeler, *Pratt,* p. 128. Benson was particularly exercised when the British sent a trade mission to Latin America during 1918. He believed that it went there "with the object of building up commercial relations and negotiating secret treaties, which if they had not been discovered and had been carried out, would have completely hampered any development of our trade in South and Central America." Benson, memorandum, 16 May 1921, Box 43, Benson MSS; and Mary Klachko, "Anglo-American Naval Competition, 1918–1922" (Ph.D. dissertation, Columbia University, 1962), pp. 26–32.
42. Trask, *Captains and Cabinets,* pp. 193–96.
43. Wheeler, *Pratt,* pp. 120–21. Technically, Sims fell under Mayo's command.
44. Allard, "Anglo-American Differences," p. 20. Allard notes the ironic fact that, despite the Navy Department's emphasis on troop transportation and protection, the British transported about 54 percent of the American Expeditionary Force to France. Because of limited shipping, the British faced a difficult problem: how to balance the need to ship food and supplies to the European Allies against the need to carry American reinforcements to the Western front. This conflict of interest was never resolved to the satisfaction of all parties. Trask, *Captains and Cabinets,* pp. 171–72.
45. For the organization, procedures, and accomplishments of the office of the Chief of Naval Operations during World War I, *see* Pratt to Daniels, 15 November 1918, *Naval Investigation,* Vol. I, pp. 1496–1505; and "Organization of the Office of Naval Operations," 1 August 1918, *Ibid.,* pp. 679–84.
46. *Ibid,* Vol. I, p. 681; and Braisted, *Navy in the Pacific,* pp. 469–70.
47. *Naval Investigation,* Vol. I, p. 398.
48. For Benson's high opinion of Pratt, *see* Wheeler, *Pratt,* pp. 126–27.
49. For a detailed analysis of the naval negotiations during the pre-armistice discussions, *see* Trask, *Captains and Cabinets,* pp. 313–55.
50. Stephen Roskill, *Naval Policy Between the Wars,* Vol. I: *The Period of Anglo-American Antagonism, 1919–1929* (2 Vols.; New York: Walker, 1968–1976), p. 72.
51. For the League of Nations navy, *see* Wheeler, *Pratt,* p. 129. Benson's statement on the subject is in Benson to American Commission to Negotiate Peace, 2 February 1919, Box 42, Benson MSS. For the view that Wilson thought of the proposed shipbuilding program for 1919 primarily as a bargaining chip at the peace negotiations, *see* Trask, "American Navy in a World at War," p. 214. Daniels entered in his diary on 20 November 1918 a statement of his reasons for urging a large building program on Congress: "We need to strengthen our Navy & as a good instrument to use at the Peace Conference." Cronon, ed., *Daniels,* p. 350.
52. Roskill, *Naval Policy,* p. 54; Cronon, ed., *Daniels,* pp. 380–81; and Benson, memorandum, 16 May 1921, Box 43, Benson MSS.
53. On the House-Cecil arrangement, *see* Braisted, *Navy in the Pacific,* p. 454; and Trask, "Navy in a World at War," p. 218.
54. Seth P. Tillman, *Anglo-American Relations at the Paris Peace Conference of 1919* (Princeton: Princeton University Press, 1961), p. 294.
55. *Ibid.,* p. 289.
56. Roskill, *Naval Policy,* pp. 92–93.
57. Benson, "Notes Relating to the International Conference on the Limitation of Armaments," 26 September 1921, Box 43, Benson MSS.

58. Braisted, *Navy in the Pacific*, p. 459; and Wheeler, *Pratt*, p. 142.
59. "Benson has sometimes been viewed as an Anglophobe, but he might more accurately be described as a nationalist who trusted no State's benevolent intentions." Allard, "Naval Differences," p. 2.
60. Jeffrey J. Safford, *Wilsonian Maritime Diplomacy, 1913–1921* (New Brunswick, N.J.: Rutgers University Press, 1978). Benson summarized his highly nationalist opinions about merchant marine policy—he remained enamored of the Mahanian outlook—in William S. Benson, *The Merchant Marine* (New York: Macmillan, 1923).

ROBERT E. COONTZ

1. Robert E. Coontz, *From the Mississippi to the Sea* (Philadelphia: Dorance, 1930), p. 66.
2. Coontz, *Ibid.*, p. 110; and Peter Karsten, *The Naval Aristocracy* (New York: The Free Press, 1972), pp. 285–87.
3. U.S. Department of thc Navy: Naval History Division, *The Chiefs of Naval Operations* (Washington, D.C.: GPO, 1974), article on Coontz.
4. Coontz, *From the Mississippi*, p. 149.
5. *Ibid.*, p. 172.
6. *Ibid.*, p. 287; and Karsten, *Naval Aristocracy*, p. 345.
7. Interview, Captain Robert J. Coontz, USN, (Admiral Coontz's grandson), Washington, D.C., 13 April 1978.
8. Coontz to Daniels, 17 September 1920, Special Correspondence, Box 73, Josephus Daniels MSS, LC; and Minutes, 5 October 1922, Sec Nav's Council Meetings, 1921–1923, Vol. II, p. 168, RG 80, NA.
9. Coontz, *From the Mississippi*, p. 324.
10. Karsten, *Naval Aristocracy*, p. 210.
11. Paper clipping and printed welcoming address (for Coontz's successor), n.d., Coontz MSS, held by Captain Coontz. The Coontz MSS consist of several scrapbooks, letter portfolios, photographs, etc., that cover his career, with the exception, unfortunately, of his term as chief of naval operations.
12. Coontz, *From the Mississippi*, p. 365.
13. *Ibid.*, p. 367–79.
14. *Ibid.*, p. 388.
15. *Ibid.*
16. Rogers to Newberry, 3 October 1919, Coontz MSS.
17. Interview, Captain Coontz.
18. Coontz, *From the Mississippi*, p. 400.
19. Memoranda, Items 22618–22724, SecNav General Correspondence; 1916–1926, Box 877, RG 80, NA.
20. Clipping, n.d., Coontz MSS.
21. Coontz, *From the Mississippi*, p. 406.
22. Admiral Harry W. Hill, OH, p. 71, Columbia University.
23. Items 22724–22750, Box 877, RG 80, NA.
24. Roosevelt to Denby, 19 November 1922, Diaries No. 1, Theodore Roosevelt, Jr. MSS, LC.
25. Coontz, "Military and Naval Policy," Box 3130, RG 80, NA.
26. William V. Pratt, "Autobiography," Ch. 4, p. 4, William V. Pratt MSS, LC.
27. Gerald E. Wheeler, "William Veazie Pratt, U.S. Navy; A Silhouette of an Admiral," *NWCR*, 1969, p. 45.

28. Entry, Diaries No. 1, p. 8, Roosevelt MSS.
29. Coontz, *From the Mississippi*, pp. 413–14.
30. *Ibid.*
31. *Ibid.*, pp. 418–29.
32. Coontz cautioned Daniels that a unified air service "would result in Army control." Minutes, 21 March 1921, SecNav Council Meetings, Vol. I, p. 19, RG 80, NA.
33. Clifford Lord, "The History of Naval Aviation, 1898–1939," p. 833, NHC.
34. U.S. Congress, House, Committee on Naval Affairs, *Sundry Legislation, Hearings*, 67th Cong., 1st Sess., pp. 82–83.
35. Coontz, *From the Mississippi*, pp. 408–09.
36. A.D. Turnbull and Clifford Lord, *The History of United States Naval Aviation* (New Haven, Conn.: Yale University Press, 1949), p. 253.
37. Stephen Roskill, *Naval Policy Between the Wars*; Vol. I: *The Period of Anglo-American Antagonism, 1919–1929* (2 vols.; New York: Walker, 1968–1976), pp. 55–56.
38. Coontz, *From the Mississippi*, p. 422.
39. *Ibid.*
40. Coontz to Daniels, 6 April 1922, Coontz MSS.
41. Coontz to Sims, 31 December 1921, Special Correspondence: R.E. Coontz, 1919–1922, William S. Sims MSS, LC.
42. Daniels to Coontz, 18 April 1923, Special Correspondence: No. 73, Daniels MSS.
43. Coontz, *From the Mississippi*, pp. 446–49.
44. *Ibid.*, p. 464.
45. Coontz to Drewry, 9 August 1927, Coontz MSS.
46. Roosevelt to Coontz, 23 May 1928, Coontz MSS.
47. The guided-missile frigate *Coontz* was built at the Puget Sound Naval Shipyard and was sponsored by Mrs. Robert J. Coontz, wife of the admiral's grandson, in November 1958.

EDWARD W. EBERLE

1. Material in this section was obtained from the Biographies Branch, U.S. Navy Office of Information; ZB file, NHC; an obituary in the *Washington Star*, 7 July 1929; and "Edward W. Eberle," *Dictionary of American Biography* (20 vols.; New York: Charles Scribner's Sons, 1928–1973), Vol. V, pp. 614–15.
2. Elting E. Morison, *Admiral Sims and the Modern American Navy* (Boston: Houghton Mifflin, 1942), pp. 292–93.
3. Sims to Mrs. Eberle, 6 January 1918, Box 55, William S. Sims MSS, LC.
4. William H. Standley, "Admiral Standley: Early Life and Naval Career," p. 321, Standley MSS, LC.
5. Morison, *Sims*, p. 498.
6. Edward W. Eberle, "Policy—Its Relation to War and Preparation for War," p. 6, Staff and Student Papers, RG 12, NWCA.
7. Eberle to Wilbur, ? April 1925, "Budget 1927. Estimate of the Situation and Base Development Program, 6 April 1925," p. 1, Secret & Confidential Correspondence: 1919–1926 (SCC), Box 22, RG 80, NA.
8. Gerald E. Wheeler, *Prelude to Pearl Harbor: The United States Navy and the Far East, 1921–1931* (Columbia: University of Missouri Press, 1963), pp. 116–17.
9. Jones to Eberle, 14 March 1922, Box 1, Hilary Jones MSS, LC.

10. Eberle, "A Few Reflections on Our Navy and Some of its Needs," *USNIP*, October 1925, p. 1403.
11. "Report of Special Board—Results of Development of Aviation on the Development of the Navy, January 17, 1925," pp. 13, 27, SCC, Box 22, RG 80, NA. (Hereafter "Eberle Board.")
12. *Ibid.*, pp. 153–54.
13. Eberle, "The Elements of Sea Power and the Future of the Navy," *USNIP*, October 1925, pp. 1833–34.
14. W. R. Shoemaker, "Budget 1926. Estimate of the Situation and Base Development Program, March 17, 1924," p. 14, SCC, Box 21, RG 80, NA.
15. "Eberle Board," p. 52.
16. *Ibid.*, p. 67.
17. Statement of Edward W. Eberle, *Hearings Before the President's Aircraft Board, September-October 1925*, Vol. I, p. 193, Printed Archives Branch, NA.
18. Shoemaker, "Budget 1926," p. 14.
19. "Eberle Board," pp. 153–54.
20. Eberle to Wilbur, 31 January 1925, "Policy with Reference to Upkeep of the Navy in its Various Branches," SCC, Box 45, RG 80, NA.
21. *Ibid.*
22. For example, *see* Charles McVay, Jr. to Wilbur, 25 June 1926, SCC, Box 22, RG 80, NA.
23. Eberle to Wilbur, 9 September, 1926, p. 3, SCC, Box 22, RG 80, NA.
24. *Ibid.*, p. 5.
25. Eberle to Chief of Bureau of Navigation, 16 and 23 July 1924, SCC, Boxes 2196 and 2542, RG 80, NA. *See also* Preston to Dudley W. Knox, 28 July 1924, Box 1, Dudley W. Knox MSS, LC.
26. Stephen Roskill, *Naval Policy Between the Wars*, Vol. I: *The Period of Anglo-American Antagonism, 1919–1929* (2 Vols.; New York: Walker, 1968–1976), pp. 498 –516; and Wheeler, *Prelude*, p. 131–58.
27. Jones to Eberle, 21 March 1927, Box 1, Jones MSS.
28. Eberle to Wilbur, 10 May 1927, SCC, Box 131, RG 80, NA.
29. Kellogg to Wilbur, 9 June 1927, SCC, Box 131, RG 80, NA.
30. Wilbur, Speeches: 1924–1927, Box 2, Curtis D. Wilbur MSS, LC.
31. Waldo H. Heinrichs, Jr., "The Role of the U.S. Navy," in Dorothy Borg and Shumpei Okamoto, eds., *Pearl Harbor as History: Japanese-American Relations, 1931–1941*, (New York: Columbia University Press, 1973), p. 197.
32. Eberle to Secretary of the Navy Josephus Daniels, 11 September 1913, "Report on Research on Mines and Mining," Box 707, RG 80, NA.
33. Jones to Eberle, 14 August 1926, Box 4, Jones MSS.
34. *Washington Star*, 7 July 1929.

CHARLES F. HUGHES

1. *Army and Navy Journal*, 20 September 1930.
2. Report by C.F. Adams, 17 September 1930, Naval Examining Board Records, Charles Frederick Hughes File, RG 125, Federal Records Center, Suitland, Md. I am indebted to Commander Charles E. C. Nimitz, USN (Ret.), for permission to examine Hughes's official records.
3. "I think of Him," *USNIP*, April 1974, pp. 92–93.

4. Standley "Autobiography," William H. Standley MSS, LC.
5. Information provided by Commander Nimitz.
6. Hughes to William E. Chandler, 15 April 1884, Applications to the U.S. Naval Academy, Charles F. Hughes, RG 24, NA.
7. Cadet and Conduct Books, Vol. 405, U.S. Naval Academy Records, RG 405, NA.
8. Report by Charles E. Clark, 1 July 1894–1 December 1894, Naval Examining Board Records, RG 125, NA. Clark later won fame as captain of the battleship *Oregon* during her famous dash around South America to join the Atlantic Fleet on the eve of the Spanish-American War. Hughes's wife was Caroline Russell Clark.
9. Report by Clark, 1 January 1897–1 July 1897, *ibid.*
10. Hilary A. Herbert to Hughes, 1 November 1894, with Board of Inquiry Findings, *Ibid.*
11. John D. Long to President McKinley, 17 June 1898, *ibid.*
12. Report on Hughes, 25 September 1899, *ibid.*
13. Report by Lieutenant L.H.C. Handley, 28 October 1901–1 November 1901, *ibid.*
14. Captain C.P. Eaton to secretary of the navy, 4 September 1903, *ibid.*
15. George Von L. Meyer to Hughes, 9 March 1909, *ibid.*
16. William W. Canada, Veracruz, to secretary of state, 8 October 1912, and Clarence A. Miller, Tampico, to secretary of state, 12 October 1912, *ibid.*
17. Reports by Charles J. Badger, 1 October 1913–31 March 1913, 1 April 1914–17 September 1914, *ibid.*
18. Report by Dewey, 28 September 1914–24 October 1914, *ibid.*
19. Hugh Rodman, *Yarns of a Kentucky Admiral* (Indianapolis: Bobbs-Merrill, 1928), pp. 56–57.
20. Rodman to SecNav, 12 February 1919, Bureau of Navigation File No. 3316/257, RG 24, NA. Records of the battleship *New York* indicate that the incident actually took place after Hughes's detachment. Naval Records Collection, Office of Naval Records and Library, OS File, RG 45, NA.
21. Ernest J. King and Walter Muir Whitehill, *Fleet Admiral King; A Naval Record* (New York: W.W. Norton, 1952), pp. 129–30.
22. Citation by the president, Naval Examining Board Records, RG 125, NA.
23. Gerald E. Wheeler, *Admiral William Veazie Pratt, U.S. Navy: A Sailor's Life* (Washington, D.C.: GPO, 1974), p. 217.
24. Clifford A. Lord, "The History of Naval Aviation, 1918–1939," NHC; and *New York Times*, 20 February 1925.
25. Adolphus Andrews, Jr., "Admiral with Wings, the Career of Joseph Mason Reeves," Term paper, 30 April 1943, School of Public Affairs, Princeton University, USNA.
26. Hughes to CinCus, 1 July 1926, and Hughes to SecNav, 25 September 1929, Microcopy # 971, Annual Reports of the U.S. Fleets, Rolls 5 and 6, Microcopy No. 971, NA.
27. Yates Stirling, Jr., *Sea Duty: The Memoirs of a Fighting Admiral* (New York: G.P. Putnam's Sons, 1939), pp. 201–05.
28. *Army and Navy Journal*, 28 November 1927.
29. For a picture of Hughes leading the navy line at the White House reception in 1930, *see* Peter Karsten, *The Naval Aristocracy* (New York: Free Press, 1972), p. 167.
30. Thomas P. Magruder, "The Navy and Economy," *Saturday Evening Post*, 24 Sep-

tember 1927, pp. 6 ff. For extensive naval materials on the Magruder affair, *see* SecNav Confidential Correspondence, 1926–1940, File A7-2 (1), RG 80, NA.
31. King, *Record,* pp. 195–204.
32. For the *S-4* tragedy and Hughes's connection therewith, *see* OS File, Naval Records and Library Collection, RG 45, NA; and SS 109 File, General Records of the Navy Department, 1926–1940, RG 80, NA.
33. Hughes to Bureau of Navigation, 2 April 1928, General Records, SS 109, RG 80, NA.
34. *Army and Navy Journal,* 22 March 1929.
35. Schofield to CNO, 13 April 1928, File L1-1, SecNav's Confidential Correspondence, RG 80, NA.
36. Hughes to SecNav, 1 April 1928, with approval by Wilbur, *ibid.*
37. Story provided by Commander C. E. C. Nimitz.
38. William R. Braisted, "The United States Navy's Operational Outlook in the Pacific." Paper presented at conference on Japanese-American relations, Kawai, Hawaii, January 1976; printed as "Amerika Kaigun to Oranji Sakusen Keikaku," in Hosoya Chihiro and Sato Makoto, eds., *Washinton Seitai to Nichibei Kankei* (Tokyo: 1978), pp. 415–40.
39. Joint Army and Navy War Plan Orange, 1929, JB Records, JB 325, Ser. 228, RG 225, NA.
40. Hughes to SecNav, 14 June 1928, JB 303, Ser. 298, *ibid.*
41. Hughes to Navy Basic War Plan Orange Distribution List, 1 March 1929, NHC.
42. Joint Army and Navy War Plan Red, 1930, JB Records, JB 325, Ser. 435, RG 225, NA; and William R. Braisted, "On the American Red and Red-Orange Plans, 1919–1939," in Gerald Jordan, ed., *Naval Warfare in the Twentieth Century* (London; Croom Helm, 1977), pp. 167–85.
43. Wilbur to Budget Director, 14 September 1927, File L1-1/EN, General Records of the Navy Department, 1926–1940, RG 80, NA; and Wilbur to GB, 20 September 1927, GB 420–1, Ser. 1358, NHC.
44. Jones to SecNav, 27 September 1927, *ibid.*
45. H.M. Lord to SecNav, 14 December 1927, Bureau of the Budget Central File 21.1, RG 51, NA, and *FRUS: 1927,* Vol. I, pp. vii–viii.
46. Testimony by Hughes, 11, 13, 16, 17, and 18 January 1929, U.S. Congress, House, Committee on Naval Affairs, *Hearings on H.R. 7359, An Act to Authorize the Construction of Certain Naval Vessels,* 70th Cong., 1st Sess., pp. 511–867.
47. Report reproduced in *Army and Navy Journal,* 10 March 1928.
48. *Ibid.,* 28 May 1928.
49. Editorial, *Army and Navy Journal,* 4 August 1928.
50. Kellogg to Wilbur, 16 August 1928, Coolidge to Kellogg, 2 August 1928, 3 August 1928, telegrams, Kellogg to Coolidge, 9 August 1928, State Department Decimal File 500.A15/Franco-British, RG 59, NA.
51. Everett Sanders to Hughes, 10 August 1928, telegram, File 28, Calvin Coolidge MSS, LC; and *Army and Navy Journal,* 18 August 1928.
52. Kellogg to Norman Armour, 25 September 1928, *FRUS*: *1928,* Vol. I, pp. 282–86; and Wilbur to Kellogg, n.d., indexed 1 October 1928, State Department Decimal File 500.A15/Franco-British, RG 59, NA.
53. Kellogg to Coolidge, 9 August 1928, *ibid.*

54. Hughes to Wilbur, 9 June 1928, with Fundamental Naval Policy approved by Wilbur, 6 October 1928, GB 420–1, Ser. 1183, NHC.
55. An Act for the Increase of the Navy, 13 February 1929, *U.S. Statutes at Large*, Vol. 45, Part 1, p. 1165; Hughes to SecNav, 10 April 1929, File L1-1, SecNav's Confidential Correspondence, RG 80, NA; and *Army and Navy Journal*, 9 February 1929.
56. Testimony by Hughes, 20 June 1930, U.S. Congress, House, Committee on Naval Affairs, *A Hearing on H.R.* 12964 and 12965 *for the Modernization of the Battleships "New Mexico," "Idaho," and "Mississippi,"* 71st Cong., 2nd Sess., pp. 3109–15; and Central File, 21–1, Bureau of Budget Records, RG 51, NA.
57. *Army and Navy Register*, 27 April 1930, with pencil note, *ibid.*
58. U.S. Congress, Senate, Committee on Foreign Affairs, *Hearings on the London Naval Treaty of 1930*, 71st Cong., 2nd Sess., pp. 301–03.
59. Memorandum on Organization of the United States Fleet, 27 September 1927, File A7-2: SecNav's Confidential Correspondence, RG 80, NA; and Gerald E. Wheeler, *Prelude to Pearl Harbor, The United States Navy and the Far East, 1921–1931* (Columbia: University of Missouri Press, 1968), pp. 73–75.
60. Wiley to CNO, 28 September 1928 and 21 May 1929, File A9-1/FF1, SecNav's Confidential Correspondence, RG 59, NA.
61. Henry A. Wiley, *An Admiral from Texas* (Garden City, N.Y.: Doubleday, Doran, 1934), pp. 303–04.
62. Comment by Office of the Chief of Naval Operations, 5 November 1927, Annual Reports of United States Fleets, Roll 7, Micro 971, NA.
63. Pratt to Wiley, 20 September 1928, William V. Pratt MSS, NHC; and Pratt to Hughes, 1 August 1930, File A-9/FF1, SecNav's Confidential Correspondence, RG 80, NA.
64. The *Langley* was actually the first carrier, but she was termed "experimental."
65. Wheeler, *Pratt*, 274–75; and Materials on Fleet Problem IX, SecNav's Confidential Correspondence, File A-16-3, RG 80, NA.
66. U.S. Congress, House, Subcommittee of the Committee on Appropriations, *Hearings. . . on Navy Department Appropriation Bill for 1931*, 71st Cong., 1st Sess., pp. 45–48.
67. King, *Record*, pp. 210–11.
68. John Towers to Moffett, 24 January 1930, William A. Moffett MSS, USNA.
69. Moffett to William Wrigley, Jr., 13 October 1928, 26 October 1929, *ibid.*
70. Moffett to Lieutenant Commander Claude Bailey, 3 April 1929, *ibid.*
71. Moffett to Emory S. Land, 7 July 1930, *ibid.*; and Memorandum of Conversation with Admiral Hughes, 22 October 1929, State Department Decimal File No. 500A15a3/334, RG 59, NA.
72. *Hearings . . . on Navy Department Appropriation Bill for 1931*, p. 51; and Towers to Moffett, 24 January 1930, Moffett MSS.
73. Andrew T. Long to SecNav, 25 November 1929, GB 449, Ser. 1458, NHC.
74. *Army and Navy Journal*, 30 March 1929.
75. Director of Fleet Training Luke McNamee to CNO, 25 March 1930, Bureau of the Budget Central Files, File 21.1, RG 51, NA; and *Hearings . . . on Navy Department Appropriation Bill for 1931*, p. 51.
76. Moffett to Porter Adams, 14 November 1929, Moffett MSS.
77. Memorandum for the President by Lord, 19 April 1929, File 21.1, Bureau of the Budget Records, RG 51, NA.

78. Memorandum by Stimson, 6 June 1929, State Department Decimal File 500.A15a3/21, RG 59, NA. The best account of the preliminary negotiations is Raymond G. O'Connor, *Perilous Equilibrium: The United States and the London Naval Conference of 1930* (New York: W.W. Norton, 1969), pp. 20–46.
79. Address by Gibson, 22 April 1929, *FRUS: 1929*, Vol. I, pp. 91–96.
80. Text, Hoover Memorial Day Address, 30 May 1929, *ibid.*, p. 115.
81. Adams to GB, 31May 1929, SecNav's Confidential Correspondence, File A-19, RG 80, NA.
82. Hughes to SecNav, 10 June 1929, GB 438, Ser. 1427, NHC. Hughes's attendance at GB meetings is recorded in the board's minutes.
83. Adams to GB, 14 June 1929, SecNav's Confidential Correspondence, File A-19, RG 80, NA.
84. Long to SecNav, 1 August 1929, *ibid.*
85. Hughes to SecNav, 23 August 1929, GB 438–1, Ser. 1444, NHC.
86. Dawes to secretary of state, 31 August 1929, 10 September 1929, *FRUS: 1929*, Vol. I, pp. 214–23.
87. Hughes to SecNav, 11 September 1929, with unsigned memorandum of events, 11 September 1929, GB 438–1, Ser. 1444-A, NHC.
88. Unsigned memorandum, *ibid.*
89. Adolphus Andrews, Jr., "Admiral with Wings," pp. 80–81. Apparently relying on Admiral Reeves's memory, Andrews described a White House meeting in April 1930 at which Hughes told the president, when the latter refused to accept the board's demand for twenty-three heavy cruisers, that the board had completed its last study of the cruiser question. Since the board had already come down to twenty-one heavy cruisers and since Hoover apparently did not consult it regarding cruisers after September 1929, it would appear probable that, although Reeves correctly recalled the collision between Hoover and Hughes, he was mistaken about the date and details. For Stimson's version of the events on 11 September as told to Charles G. Dawes, *see* Dawes, *Journal as Ambassador to Great Britain* (New York: Macmillan, 1939), pp. 95–96.
90. Hoover to Stimson, 11 September 1929, Presidential Papers, Herbert Hoover MSS, West Branch, Iowa.
91. Unsigned memorandum, 11 September 1929, GB 438-1, Ser. 1444-A, NHC.
92. Wheeler, *Pratt*, pp. 296–97.
93. U.S. Congress, Senate, Committee on Naval Affairs, *Hearings on the London Naval Treaty of 1930*, 71st Cong., 2nd Sess., pp. 304–05.
94. Hughes to Frances Lovering Adams, 3 November 1930. Letter provided by Charles Francis Adams IV.
95. Hoover to Stimson, 1 October 1929, Hoover MSS; Hughes to Hoover, 8 October 1929, GB 438–1, Ser. 1455, NHC; and O'Conner, *Perilous Equilibrium*, p. 49.
96. Senate Committee on Naval Affairs, *Hearings on the London Naval Treaty*, p. 304.
97. U.S. Congress, House, Subcommittee of the Committee on Appropriations, *Hearings . . . on Navy Department Appropriation Bill of 1931*, 71st Cong., 2nd Sess., pp. 45–85.
98. Standley, "Autobiography;" Leigh to Hughes, 26 March 1930, and Leigh to ComDesRons BattFlt, 7 April 1930, telegram, Personnel File 3316, Bureau of Navigation, RG 24, NA.
99. Minutes, GB meeting, 30 April 1930, NHC.

100. Senate Committee on Naval Affairs, *Hearings on the London Naval Treaty*, pp. 297–307; and Senate Committee on Foreign Affairs, *Hearings . . . on the London Naval Treaty of 1930*, pp. 281–82.
101. Hughes to Lord, 27 May 1929, File 21.1, Bureau of the Budget Central Files, RG 51, NA; and Act to Provide for an Assistant to the Chief of Naval Operations, 27 May 1930, *U.S. Statutes at Large*, Vol. 46, Pt. 1, pp. 430–31.
102. Pratt, Memoirs; Standley, "Autobiography."
103. Adams to Hoover, 9 September 1930, Hoover MSS; and Hughes to Hoover, 15 September 1930, and Hoover to Hughes, 16 September 1930, reprinted in *Army and Navy Journal*, 20 September 1930.
104. Hughes to McVay, 16 September 1930, Charles B. McVay MSS, LC.
105. Adams to Hughes, 1 November 1930, copy provided by Commander Nimitz; and Wheeler, *Pratt*, pp. 319–20.
106. Reeves to Hughes, 1 July 1934, copy provided by Commander Nimitz.

WILLIAM V. PRATT

1. Parts of this paper were delivered at the Citadel Conference on War and Diplomacy in Charleston, S.C. on 9 March 1978. The quotation is from Pratt's unpublished "Autobiography," manuscript copies of which are in the Pratt MSS, in NHC and NWCA.
2. Pratt, "Autobiography," p. 260.
3. *Ibid.*, p. 24.
4. *Ibid.*, pp. 169–70, 172.
5. *Ibid.*, pp. 203, 204.
6. *Ibid.*, p. 228.
7. Gerald E. Wheeler, *Admiral William Veazie Pratt, U.S. Navy: A Sailor's Life* (Washington, D.C.: GPO, 1974), p. 167.
8. *Ibid.*, pp. 176–81.
9. Harold and Margaret Sprout, *Toward a New Order of Sea Power* (reprint; Westport, Conn.: Greenwood Press, 1940); and Thomas H. Buckley, *The United States and the Washington Conference, 1921–1922* (Knoxville: University of Tennessee Press, 1970).
10. William V. Pratt, "Some Considerations Affecting Naval Policy," *USNIP*, November 1922, pp. 1845–62.
11. William V. Pratt, "Naval Policy and the Naval Treaty," *North American Review*, May 1922, p. 593.
12. William V. Pratt, "Our Naval Policy," *USNIP*, July 1932, p. 963.
13. Pratt's Fitness Report, 15 November 1919, in Wheeler, *Pratt*, p. 166.
14. Pratt to Louise Pratt, 16 September 1929, Box 13, Series III, Pratt MSS, NHC.
15. Pratt, "Autobiography," p. 312.
16. Raymond G. O'Connor, *Perilous Equilibrium: The United States and the London Naval Conference of 1930* (New York: W. W. Norton, 1969).
17. Pratt, "Autobiography," p. 318–19.
18. Wheeler, *Pratt*, p. 314.
19. Pratt, "Autobiography," p. 303.
20. *Ibid.*
21. *Ibid.*, p. 325.
22. *Ibid.*, p. 326.

23. Russell F. Weigley, *The American Way of War* (New York: Macmillan, 1973), p. 264; and Waldo H. Heinrichs, Jr., "The Role of the U.S. Navy," in Dorothy Borg and Shumpei Okamoto, eds., *Pearl Harbor as History: Japanese-American Relations, 1931–1941* (New York: Columbia University Press, 1973), p. 207.
24. Pratt, "Autobiography," p. 332.
25. U.S. Congress, *Congressional Record*, LXXII, p. 8784.
26. *Ibid.*, p. 8690.
27. Wheeler, *Pratt*, pp. 309–10.
28. *Ibid.*, pp. 332–34.
29. U.S. Department of the Navy, *Annual Report of the Secretary of the Navy, 1930* (Washington, D.C.: GPO, 1931), "Annual Report of the Chief of Naval Operations," p. 93; and *Ibid.*, 1931, p. 109.
30. CNO to SecNav, 12 October 1931, Pratt MSS, NHC. Wheeler interprets this memorandum somewhat differently. He claims Pratt approved the idea of a building holiday with some reservations; however, those reservations were extensive enough to imply complete rejection of the basic idea of a holiday. Wheeler, *Pratt*, pp. 340–44. *See also* Christopher Thorne, *The Limits of Foreign Policy: The West, the League, and the Far Eastern Crisis of 1931–33* (New York: Putnam & Sons, 1972), p. 80.
31. U.S. Department of the Navy, Office of the Secretary, Confidential Correspondence, 1927–1939: "Annual Estimate of the Situation, 1931," pp. 3–4, File L1-1, RG 80, NA.
32. Ernest Andrade, "United States Naval Policy in the Disarmament Era, 1921–1937," (Ph.D. dissertation, Michigan State University, 1966), pp. 261–62.
33. U.S. Department of the Navy, *Annual Report of the Secretary of the Navy, 1932*: "Annual Report of the Chief of Naval Operations," p. 97; *Washington Post*, 5 July 1932, p. 6; and Pratt to Robert Hopkins, 17 February 1933, Series I, Box 3, Pratt MSS, NHC.
34. Stephen S. Roberts, "The Decline of the Overseas Station Fleets: The United States Asiatic Fleet and the Shanghai Crisis, 1932," *American Neptune*, July 1977, pp. 185–202.
35. Dorothy Borg, *The United States and the Far Eastern Crisis of 1933–1938* (Cambridge: Harvard University Press, 1964); Robert H. Ferrell, *American Diplomacy in the Great Depression: Hoover-Stimson Foreign Policy* (New Haven: Yale University Press, 1957); Armin Rappaport, *Henry L. Stimson and Japan* (Chicago: University of Chicago Press, 1968); and Thorne, *Limits of Foreign Policy*.
36. Pratt, "Autobiography," pp. 335–36.
37. Thorne, *Limits of Foreign Policy*, pp. 78–89.
38. William V. Pratt, "Lest They Forget," *USNIP*, April 1933, pp. 496, 493, 499.
39. Pratt, "Autobiography," p. 243.
40. Wheeler, *Pratt*, pp. 362–64.
41. U.S. Department of the Navy, *Annual Report of the Secretary of the Navy, 1931* (Washington, D.C.: GPO, 1932) "Annual Report of the Bureau of Yards and Docks," p. 173, 175; and *Ibid.*, 1933, p. 25. Hoover first recommended "an emergency construction fund to increase employment" on 4 December 1930. By the end of the fiscal year, 1 July 1931, $3.6 million had been spent to employ 2,295 people in new government jobs, and 546 more with civilian contractors to the navy.
42. Pratt, "Lest They Forget," p. 499.
43. *Ibid.*, pp. 484, 487, 492–93.

44. *Ibid.*, p. 493.
45. Pratt to Louise Pratt, 10 February 1937, Series III, Item 4, Pratt MSS, MHC.
46. Pratt, "Some Considerations," pp. 1848–49.

WILLIAM H. STANDLEY

1. Standley to Wayne F. Tolliver, memorandum, n.d., William H. Standley MSS, Library, University of Southern California, Los Angeles, California.
2. William H. Standley, "Autobiography," p. 16, William H. Standley MSS, LC.
3. *Ibid.*
4. Citation in Standley MSS, LC.
5. William H. Standley, "Principles of Command," Thesis for Class of 1920, Naval War College, Standley MSS, LC.
6. Standley, "Autobiography," p. 165.
7. *Ibid.*, p. 181.
8. *Ibid.*, p. 183.
9. *Ibid.*, pp. 192–97.
10. Pratt to Standley, 31 May 1933, Standley MSS, LC.
11. Standley, "Autobiography," p. 199; and William H. Standley and Arthur A. Ageton, *Admiral Ambassador to Moscow* (Chicago: Henry Regnery, 1955), pp. 27–28.
12. Captain Harold R. Stark to all departments, 11 July 1933, Box 2087, RG 80, NA. This letter refers to Swanson's plan to take an extended fall cruise for health reasons.
13. Ernest J. King and Walter Muir Whitehill, *Fleet Admiral King: A Naval Record* (New York: W.W. Norton, 1952), pp. 262–63.
14. Standley, "Autobiography," p. 202.
15. Rear Admiral William D. Leahy, "Annual Report of the Chief of the Bureau of Navigation, Fiscal Year 1934," Box 2086, RG 80, NA.
16. Leahy to Swanson, 9 August 1933, Box 2087, RG 80, NA.
17. *Ibid.*
18. Standley, "Annual Report of the Chief of Naval Operations, Fiscal Year 1934," Box 12092, RG 80, NA.
19. Standley to Kalbfus, 12 October 1933, Standley MSS, U.S.C.
20. Text, speech over Columbia Broadcasting System, 26 October 1933, Standley MSS, U.S.C.
21. Stephen E. Pelz, *The Race to Pearl Harbor* (Cambridge: Harvard University Press, 1974), pp. 77–81, 202–03.
22. Standley, "Autobiography," p. 215.
23. Standley to Leahy, 12 November 1934, Standley MSS, U.S.C.
24. Standley to Upham, 15 April 1935, Standley MSS, U.S.C.
25. "Conversation between American and British Naval Delegations," 23 February 1936, Standley MSS, U.S.C.
26. Standley to Taussig, 27 January 1936, Standley MSS, U.S.C.
27. *Ibid.*
28. "General Board Hearings on the Characteristics of Capital Ships," 30 October 1936, p. 141, GB Records, NHC.
29. Standley to Swanson, 26 August 1936, Box 889, RG 80, NA.
30. Standley to Rear Admiral Adolphus Andrews, 30 December 1935, Standley MSS, U.S.C.

31. Standley to Hepburn, 30 December 1935, and Hepburn to Standley, 16 January 1936, Standley MSS, U.S.C.
32. Standley to Taussig, 15 September 1936, Standley MSS, U.S.C.
33. *Ibid.*
34. Standley to King, 22 October 1936, Standley MSS, U.S.C.
35. Captain Paul Bastedo to Roosevelt, 30 December 1936, File 18-R, President's Office File, (POF), Franklin D. Roosevelt MSS, Hyde Park, New York.
36. Printed dinner program, File 18-R, POF, Roosevelt MSS.
37. Roosevelt quoted in Standley to Roosevelt, 10 January 1937, File 18-R, POF, Roosevelt MSS.
38. *New York Times*, 26 October 1963, p. 27.

WILLIAM D. LEAHY

1. For Leahy's career before he became chief of naval operations, *see* Gerald Thomas, "Admiral Leahy and America's Imperial Years" (Ph.D. dissertation, Yale University, 1973); and Winston Lewis and Robert William Love, Jr., "William D. Leahy," *Dictionary of American Biography: 1950–1959 Supplement* (New York: Charles Scribner's Sons, 1980).
2. *The New York Times*, 9 January 1937, and 17 and 18 February 1937; Robert Levine, "The Politics of American Naval Rearmament, 1930–1938," (Ph.D. dissertation, Harvard University, 1972), pp. 414–33, 477–83; John C. Walter, "The Navy Department and the Campaign for Expanded Appropriations, 1933–1938" (Ph.D. dissertation, University of Maine, 1977), pp. 13–17; and John C. Walter, "Myths and Realities: F.D.R. and the U.S. Navy, 1933–1938" (Paper presented at the Third Naval History Symposium, U.S. Naval Academy, Annapolis, Md., 26 October 1977), pp. 13–17.
3. Sumner Welles, *Seven Major Decisions* (London: Hamish Hamilton, 1951), p. 81; and Entry, 24 August 1937, William D. Leahy Diary, LC.
4. Entries, 28 August 1937, and 2 and 24 September 1937, Leahy Diary; Yarnell to Leahy, 12 September 1937, Box 78, President's Secretary File (PSF), Franklin D. Roosevelt MSS, Hyde Park, N.Y.
5. Yarnell to Leahy, 15 October 1937, Box 78, PSF, Roosevelt MSS; Dorothy Borg, *The United States and the Far Eastern Crisis of 1933–1938* (Cambridge, Mass.: Harvard University Press, 1964), pp. 405–08, 422–32; and Waldo H. Heinrichs, Jr., "The Role of the U.S. Navy," in Dorothy Borg and S. Okamoto, eds., *Pearl Harbor as History* (New York: Columbia University Press, 1973), pp. 211–18.
6. James R. Leutze, *Bargaining for Supremacy: Anglo-American Naval Collaboration, 1937–1941* (Chapel Hill: University of North Carolina Press, 1977), pp. 16–17; and John McVickar Haight, Jr., "Franklin D. Roosevelt and a Naval Quarantine of Japan," *Pacific Historical Review*, May 1971, p. 207.
7. Entries, 12 and 13 December 1937, Leahy Diary; Harold L. Ickes, *The Secret Diary of Harold L. Ickes*, (2 vols.; London: Weidenfeld and Nicolson, 1955), Vol. II, p. 274; and Welles, *Seven Major Decisions*, p. 83.
8. Leutze, *Bargaining*, pp. 19–24, 27; Admiral Royal E. Ingersoll OH, Columbia University, New York; and L. R. Pratt, "The Anglo-American Naval Conversations on the Far East of January 1938," *International Affairs*, 1971, p. 745ff.
9. Leutze, *Bargaining*, pp. 24–26; and Entry, 10 January 1938, Leahy Diary.
10. Leahy to Roosevelt, 9 January 1937, File A16–3, WPD, NHC.

11. Haight, "Quarantine," p. 207; and Louis Morton, *The War in the Pacific: Strategy and Command, The First Two Years* (Washington, D.C.: GPO, 1962), p. 39.
12. Ingersoll to Leahy, 12 July 1937, File A16-3FF, WPD, NHC; and Army Plan of 30 November 1937, pp. 1–6, JB File 325, Serial 617–8, RG 225, NA.
13. Army Plan of 30 November 1937, pp. 1–6, JB File 325, Serial 617–8, RG 225, NA; and Morton, *Strategy and Command*, p. 40.
14. File A1–3, SecNav Secret Correspondence, RG 80, NA; Davis to Roosevelt, 30 July 1937, Box 78, President's Safe File (PSF), Roosevelt MSS; and Leahy to Roosevelt, Box 18, President's Official File (POF), Roosevelt MSS.
15. U.S. Congress, House, Committee on Naval Affairs, *Hearings . . . on H.R. 9218*, 75th Cong., 2nd Sess., pp. 1943–46, 2070, 2072–73; (hereafter cited as *House Hearings*); and U.S. Congress, Senate, Committee on Naval Affairs, *Hearings . . . on H.R. 9218*, 75th Cong., 2nd Sess., p. 34 (hereafter cited as *Senate Hearings*).
16. Haight, "Quarantine," p. 224; *House Hearings*, pp. 1948, 1979, 1956; and Walter, "The Navy Department," p. 324.
17. *House Hearings*, p. 1943.
18. *Ibid.*, pp. 2070–72; and Entries, 2 and 30 March 1938, Leahy Diary.
19. Entries, 14 April and 24 September 1937, 8 April 1938, and 24 March 1939, Leahy Diary; Gibbs to Hull, 22 April 1938, File EF6/BB, SecNav Secret Correspondence, RG 80, NA; Thomas R. Maddux, "United States–Soviet Naval Relations in the 1930s: the Soviet Union's Efforts to Purchase Naval Vessels," *NWCR*, Spring 1976, pp. 28–37; and *FRUS: The Soviet Union, 1933–1939*, pp. 457–91, 670–708, 869–903.
20. *House Hearings*, pp. 1943, 1971, 2033–39.
21. Admiral Charles M. Cooke, Jr. "Memoirs," Box 24, Cooke MSS, Hoover Institution, Stanford University, Palo Alto, Calif. (I am obliged to Robert William Love, Jr., for allowing me to see this material). Leahy to Bloch, 18 March 1938, File NB, WPD, NHC.
22. Knerr to Andrews, n.d., (c. March 1939), "Data for Final GHQ Air Force Report," Major General Frank M. Andrews, USA, Official MSS, LC; and Envelope 11, Box 3, Confidential Correspondence: 1936–1942, RG 18, NA.
23. King to CinCUS, 20 November 1937, File A16–3/A21, WPD, NHC; and Cooke to Leahy, 8 January 1938, File A16–3(3)VP, SecNav Secret Correspondence, RG 80, NA.
24. Woodring to Lister Hill, 16 April 1937, "Wilcox Bill, 1926–1936," Andrews MSS; Eichelberger to WPD, 21 July 1937, File 3807–17, WPD, RG 165, NA; Woodring and Swanson to Roosevelt, 19 October 1937, File 354–2, Box 3, RG 18, NA; and Office of Chief of Staff to Adjutant General, 18 October 1937, File AG 111 (10–14–36), RG 94, NA.
25. Entries, 25 February and 27 June 1938, Leahy Diary; and *Senate Hearings*, pp. 11, 62.
26. Mins, 19 November 1938, "Minutes of Standing Liaison Committee: 15 February 1938 to 23 December 1940," Series 30, Box 912, RG 165, NA.
27. Arnold, memorandum, 21 November 1938, Andrews MSS, LC; and Cooke to Leahy, 22 November 1938, File A1–3/VV, SecNav Confidential Correspondence, RG 80, NA.
28. Entry, 4 November 1938, Leahy Diary; Strong to Andrews, 18 January 1939, File 354–2, RG 18, NA; and WPD to Chief of Staff, 8 August 1939, File 3748–17, WPD, RG 80, NA.

29. The full text of the Hepburn Board's report was published in U.S. Congress, House, Document No. 65, 76th Cong., 1st Sess. *See in particular* paragraphs 10, 112–118, and 151. *House Hearings*, p. 2023; NY to QT, 29 June 1939, SecNav Secret Correspondence, RG 80, NA; and Cooke to WPD, 19 January 1939, File A16–3/EG54, WPD, NHC.
30. Roosevelt to Edison, 12 December 1938, Box 11, PSF, Roosevelt MSS; and Entries, 5, 6, and 30 January 1939, Leahy Diary.
31. Cooke to WPD, 20 October 1938, Cooke MSS; Entry, 28 November 1938, Leahy Diary; Crenshaw, memorandum, 28 June 1939, File BB, WPD, NHC; and Entries, 30 August and 26 October 1938, Leahy Diary.
32. Cooke Memorandum, 7 October 1938, File A16–3, WPD, NHC; and JB File 325, Serial 634, RG 225, NA.
33. Ghormley to Leahy, 15 February 1939, File L1–1(1941), SecNav Secret Correspondence, RG 80, NA; Cooke to Ghormley, 2 February 1939, File SecNav Secret Correspondence, RG 80, NA; Items III-24, V-1 and 2, and IV-14, JB File 325, Serial 634, RG 225, NA; and Entry, 24 April 1939, Leahy Diary.
34. "Annual Estimate of the Situation of the Chief of Naval Operations for the Fiscal Year 1941," pp. 3–1, III-12, 3–2, NHC; and Ghormley to Leahy, 12 April 1939, File A16–3/FF, WPD, NHC.
35. L. R. Pratt, *East of Malta, West of Suez: Britain's Mediterranean Crisis, 1936–1939* (Cambridge: Cambridge University Press, 1975), pp. 176–79; Entries, 11, 14, and 15 April 1939, Leahy Diary.
36. John Morton Blum, *From the Morgenthau Diaries*, (3 vols.; Boston: Houghton Mifflin, 1965), Vol. II pp. 90–91; Entries, 13 May 1938 and 17 July 1939, Leahy Diary; and Leutze, *Bargaining*, pp. 43–45.
37. Leutze, *Bargaining*, pp. 37–40.
38. Maurice Matloff and Edwin M. Snell, *The War Department: Strategic Planning for Coalition Warfare, 1941–1943* (Washington, D.C.: GPO, 1953), pp. 6–8; and Robert William Love Jr., "Admiral Leahy and American Naval Leadership in the Second New Deal, 1937–1939" (Paper presented at the Conference on War and Diplomacy, The Citadel, Charleston, South Carolina, 10 March 1978), p. 15.
39. Heinrichs, "Role of the U.S. Navy," pp. 216–17.
40. Entry, 12 April 1939, Leahy Diary; William D. Leahy, *I Was There* (New York: Whittlesey House, 1950); and Forrest C. Pogue, *George C. Marshall*, Vol. II: *Ordeal and Hope, 1939–1942* (4 vols.?; London: McGibbon and Kee, 1963–) pp. 298–300, 473.
41. Grace G. Tully, *F.D.R., My Boss* (New York: Charles Scribner's Sons, 1949). Information on Leahy's wartime career may be gleaned from Kent Roberts Greenfield, ed., *Command Decisions* (New York: Harcourt, Brace, 1959); Maurice Matloff, *The War Department: Strategic Planning for Coalition Warfare, 1943–1944* (Washington, D.C.: GPO, 1959); Pogue, *George C. Marshall*, Vol. III: *Organizer of Victory*; and Christopher G. Thorne, *Allies of a Kind: the United States, Britain, and the War Against Japan, 1941–1945* (London: Hamish, Hamilton, 1978).
42. For Leahy's career after World War II, *see* Robert J. Donovan, *Conflict and Crisis: The Presidency of Harry S. Truman, 1945–1948* (New York: W. W. Norton, 1977); and Daniel Yergin, *Shattered Peace: The Origins of the Cold War and the National Security State* (Boston: Houghton, Mifflin, 1977). A popular view of Leahy as he neared retirement is given in Frank Gervasi, "Watchdog in the White House," *Colliers*, 9 October 1948.

HAROLD R. STARK

1. *New York Times*, 21 *August* 1941, p. 42.
2. File: "Fitness Reports," Box 23, Series III, Harold R. Stark MSS, NHC.
3. *New York Times*, 30 July 1939, p. 16.
4. Stark "Fitness Reports," Box 23, Series III, Stark MSS, NHC.
5. Leahy recommended to Roosevelt that Stark succeed him as CNO. Rear Admiral William Harrington Leahy to Robert William Love, Jr., 11 August 1973.
6. Tracy B. Kittredge, *Naval Lessons of the Great War* (Garden City, New York: Doubleday, Page, 1921).
7. These hearings started on 8 January 1940 and were concluded on 14 February. U.S. Congress, House, Committee on Naval Affairs, *Hearings to Establish the Composition of the U.S. Navy*, 76th Cong., 3d Sess., pp. 1709–2187; and *New York Times*, 9 January 1940, p. 8.
8. U.S. Congress, House, Committee on Naval Affairs, *Establishing the Composition of the United States Navy and Authorizing the Construction of Certain Vessels*, 76th Cong., 3d Sess., Report No. 1593.
9. Stark to Roosevelt, 9 March 1940, Box 79, President's Safe Files (PSF), FDR MSS.
10. U.S. Congress, House, Committee on Naval Affairs, *Hearings on HR* 10100 *To Establish the Composition of the United States Navy, To Authorize the Construction of Certain Naval Vessels, and for Other Purposes*, 76th Cong., 3d Sess., pp. 3551–3616 and Report No. 2641.
11. Naval History Division, *Dictionary of American Naval Fighting Ships* (2 vols.; Washington, D.C.: GPO, 1959–63), Vol. I, pp. 189–330 and Vol. II, pp. 461–86.
12. James R. Leutze, *Bargaining for Supremacy* (Chapel Hill: University of North Carolina Press, 1977), pp. 72–97.
13. Stark to Knox, 17 August 1940, File: DD/EF13, CNO Classified Records, NHC.
14. Stark to Roosevelt, 21 August 1940, Box 74, PSF, FDR MSS. Stark added the handwritten comment, "This is the time a 'feller' needs a friend." Also, *see* Patrick Abbazia, *Mr. Roosevelt's Navy* (Annapolis, Md.: Naval Institute Press, 1975), pp. 97–106.
15. U.S. Congress, Joint Committee, *Hearings on the Investigation of the Pearl Harbor Attack (PHAH)*, 79th Cong., 1st Sess., Part 5, p. 2189.
16. George C. Dyer, *On the Treadmill to Pearl Harbor: the Memoirs of Admiral J.O. Richardson* (Washington, D.C.: GPO, 1973), pp. 307–33.
17. Tracy B. Kittredge, "United States-British Naval Cooperation 1937–1942," NHC, Chs. 7 and 8. This navy monograph provides the best account of the development of war plans in 1940 and is more balanced than the U.S. Army official histories of World War II, which reflect an understandable but unfortunate bias.
18. Stark to Knox, 12 November 1940, Box 5, Series III, Stark MSS; and Kittredge, "Naval Cooperation," Ch. 13.
19. Harold C. Ickes, *The Secret Diary of Harold L. Ickes*, Vol. III: *The Lowering Clouds* (3 vols.; New York: Simon and Schuster, 1954–1955), pp. 388–89.
20. Leutze, *Bargaining*, p. 205. Leutze concluded on the basis of the same evidence that I have used that Stark attempted to protect Roosevelt by saying that he had invited the British on his own initiative. However, to support this contention one must conclude that Stark perjured himself before the joint committee that investigated the Pearl Harbor attack in 1946. *PHAH*, Part 5, p. 2332. Stark remained loyal to Roosevelt, but to imply perjury on his part because of such loyalty is both incredible and wholly

out of character. Roosevelt was certainly devious, and he may have learned of the invitation from some source other than Stark.

21. Leutze, *Bargaining*, pp. 216–52.
22. Kittredge, "Naval Cooperation," Ch. 14.
23. James H. Herzog, *Closing the Open Door* (Annapolis, Md.: Naval Institute Press, 1973).
24. *PHAH*, Part 5, pp. 2293–96; and Kittredge, "Naval Cooperation," Ch. 19.
25. Theodore A. Wilson, *The First Summit* (Boston: Houghton Mifflin, 1969).
26. *PHAH*, Part 5, p. 2395; and Samuel Eliot Morison, *History of United States Naval Operations in World War II*, Vol. III: *The Rising Sun in the Pacific* (15 vols.; Boston: Little, Brown, 1947–1961), p. 47.
27. Stark to Kimmel, Box 78; and Stark to Hart, Box 79, Series XIII, Stark MSS.
28. *PHAH*, Part 14, pp. 1396–1400.
29. Stark to Kimmel, 17 October 1941, Box 2, Series I, Stark MSS.
30. Stark and Marshall to Roosevelt, 27 November 1941, Box 28, Series IV, Stark MSS; Herzog, *Closing*, p. 207; and *PHAH*, Part 5, p. 2290.
31. Stark to Kimmel, 25 November 1941, Box 2, Series I, Stark MSS.
32. *PHAH*, Part 14, p. 1406, and Part 5, pp. 2323–24.
33. *Ibid.*, Part 14, pp. 1407–08.
34. *Ibid.*, Part 5, pp. 2302–03; and Robert E. Sherwood, *Roosevelt and Hopkins* (New York: Harpers, 1948), p. 425.
35. U.S. Congress, Joint Committee, *Report of the Joint Committee on the Investigation of the Pearl Harbor Attack (PHR)*, 79th Cong., 2d Sess., 1946, pp. 42–43.
36. *PHAH*, Part 32, p. 160, Part 5, pp. 2132–33, and Part 39, p. 330.
37. Martin V. Melosi, *The Shadow of Pearl Harbor* (College Station: Texas A&M University Press, 1977), pp. 22–27; and *PHAH*, Part 24, pp. 1749–56.
38. Entry, 7 March 1942, Stark Diary, Stark MSS; and Stark to Roosevelt, 7 March 1952, Box 59, Official Files, FDR MSS; and Ernest J. King and Walter Muir Whitehill, *Fleet Admiral King* (reprint; New York: Da Capo, 1976), pp. 349–59.
39. Anne H. Sims to Stark, 30 April 1942, Box 1, Series I, Stark MSS.
40. "Administrative History, United States Naval Forces in Europe, 1942–1945," pp. iv–vii, NHC.
41. B. Mitchell Simpson, III, "Political Consultations Between the United States and the French National Committee, 1942–1943: the Embassy of Admiral Harold R. Stark, USN" (Ph.D. dissertation, Fletcher School of Law and Diplomacy, 1968).
42. *PHAH*, Part 39, pp. 318–21.
43. *Ibid.*, Part 39, p. 344.
44. *Ibid.*, Part 5, pp. 2261–62.
45. *PHR*. pp. 181–91. The Joint Committee was unable to conclude that requests for information on berthing plans pointed directly to an attack on Pearl Harbor, but it felt that these requests should have received greater attention in Washington.
46. *Ibid.*, p. 192.
47. King to Sullivan, 14 July 1948, Service Record of Harold R. Stark, NHC.
48. Stark Diary, Stark MSS.

ERNEST J. KING

1. I am indebted to Dr. Richard Mathieu, Director of Research, U.S. Naval Academy,

and the Naval Academy Research Council, for providing grants to support research for this essay.

2. For an examination of King's role in the broader context of American naval history, *see* Robert William Love, Jr., "Fighting a Global War, 1942–1945," in Kenneth J. Hagan, ed., *In Peace and War* (Westport, Conn.: Greenwood Press, 1978), Ch. 14.
3. The principal sources for King's early life are Ernest J. King and Walter Muir Whitehill, *Fleet Admiral King: A Naval Record* (New York: Norton, 1952), Chs. 1 and 2; and various memoranda and items of correspondence in Ernest J. King MSS, LC. For a typical episode illustrating King's ideas about command, *see* King, notes, n.d. (c. 1947), Box 35, King MSS, LC.
4. King, *Record*, Ch. 3–7.
5. *Ibid.*, Ch. 8–12; Emory S. Land, *Winning the War with Ships: Land, Sea, and Air—Mostly Land* (New York: R.M. McBride, 1958), p. 126; various letters between King and Moffett in King MSS, LC, and in William Moffett MSS, Nimitz Library, USNA; and George Van Deurs, ltr to editor, *USNIP*, June 1975, p. 82.
6. King, *Record*, Ch. 13–16; and Taussig to Standley, 20 August 1936, William S. Standley MSS, University of Southern California Library, Los Angeles, California.
7. Confidential interviews; Cato Glover, *Command Performance—with Guts*! (privately printed; New York: Greenwich Publishing, 1969), p. 36; and Thomas B. Buell, "The Prewar Career of Ernest J. King," in Robert William Love, Jr., ed., *Changing Interpretations and New Sources in Naval History* (New York: Garland, 1980), Ch. 30.
8. Harry Sanders, "King of the Navy," *USNIP*, August, 1974, p. 57; J. J. Clark and Clark G. Reynolds, *Carrier Admiral* (New York: David McKay, 1967), p. 64; and Admiral Bernard Bieri OH, NI, pp. 334–35.
9. King, *Record*, pp. 291–93; and Rear Admiral William Harrington Leahy, USN (Ret.) (Admiral William D. Leahy's son) to author, 12 January 1974.
10. King, *Record*, p. 294.
11. Philip Goodhart, *Fifty Ships that Saved the World* (Garden City, New York: Doubleday, 1965).
12. Charles M. Cooke OH, untranscribed tape recordings, privately held.
13. *Ibid.*; Edison to Roosevelt, 30 June 1940, FDR MSS; and Richard Connolly OH, NI, pp. 278–79. Earlier, Stark had planned to have King replace Admiral James O. Richardson, commander in chief of the U.S. Fleet, whom the president wanted to relieve. Rear Admiral Chester W. Nimitz to Richardson, 29 October 1940, in George C. Dyer, ed., *On the Treadmill to Pearl Harbor: The Memoirs of James O. Richardson* (Washington, D.C.: GPO, 1973), p. 402. Also, Ambassador Kichisaburo Nomura to Foreign Office, Tokyo, 25 July 1941, in U.S. Department of Defense, *The 'Magic' Background to Pearl Harbor* (Washington, GPO, 1979), Vol. II, p. A-101.
14. Holland M. Smith, *Coral and Brass* (New York: Scribners, 1949), pp. 74–80; and Sanders, "King," p. 55.
15. King, *Record*, p. 346.
16. Indeed, King was in Washington on 26, 27, and 28 November 1941. He briefly chatted with Roosevelt at 3:45 p.m. on 27 November. Edwin M. Watson (president's military aide) to Roosevelt, 26 November 1941, Box 166, President's Personal File (PPF), FDR MSS, Hyde Park, N.Y.
17. King, *Record*, p. 346; Knox to Roosevelt, 14 December 1941, File: Navy Department—July to December 1941, Box 80, President's Safe File (PSF), FDR MSS; Knox to Raleigh Warner, 23 December 1941, in George Lobdell, "Frank Knox," in

Paolo E. Coletta, ed., *American Secretaries of the Navy* (Annapolis, Md.: Naval Institute Press, forthcoming), manuscript copy, p. 76; Cooke to Stark, 13 December 1941, Box 6, Charles M. Cooke MSS, Hoover Institute, Stanford, California.

18. King, *Record*, pp. 350–51, 357*n*.
19. Entry, 18 December 1941, Henry L. Stimson Diary, Yale University Library, New Haven, Conn.; *FRUS: Conferences at Washington and Casablanca, 1941–1943*, pp. 61–208; "Brief Joint Estimate of the Military Situation of the Associated Powers," 20 December 1941, JB 325 (Serial 729), RG 225, NA; and Grace P. Hayes, "The Joint Chiefs of Staff and the War Against Japan," unpublished manuscript, pp. 47–48, NHC; and Memorandum, British Chiefs of Staff (COS) 24 December 1941, in *FRUS: Washington and Casablanca*, pp. 210–14.
20. Stark to Marshall, 11 December 1941, in Louis Morton, *The War in the Pacific: Strategy and Command, the First Two Years* (Washington, D.C.: GPO, 1962), p. 146; and Stark to Pye, 16 December 1941, msg 160050, NHC.
21. Stark to Pye, 22 December 1941, msg 221706, NHC.
22. Stark to Hart, 10 December 1941, msg 101958, NHC; Henry L. Stimson and McGeorge Bundy, *On Active Service in Peace and War* (New York: Harper Bros., 1948), p. 376; Mins, Roosevelt and JB meeting, 28 December 1941, in *FRUS: Washington and Casablanca*, pp. 129–130; and King to Rear Admiral C. S. Freeman, 5 January 1942, King MSS, NHC.
23. *FRUS: Washington and Casablanca*, pp. 103 and 117; Robert Sherwood, *Roosevelt and Hopkins* (New York: Harper, 1948), p. 467; Roger Parkinson, *Blood, Toil, Tears, and Sweat* (New York: David McKay, 1973), pp. 344–45; and Maurice Matloff and Edwin M. Snell, *The War Department: Strategic Planning for Coalition Warfare*, Vol. I: *1941–1942* (2 vols.; Washington, D.C.: GPO, 1953–59), p. 124.
24. Mins, Roosevelt, Churchill, Chiefs of Staff, and JB meeting, 1 January 1942, *FRUS: Washington and Casablanca*, pp. 152–56; Mins, King and Pound meeting, 4 January 1942, Adm 205/19, PRO; King to Pound, 8 January 1942, "Anzac" File, WPD, CNO MSS, NHC.
25. Stimson, *Service*, p. 398; and Sherwood, *Roosevelt and Hopkins*, p. 492. During the war, Roosevelt asked Samuel Eliot Morison to write a semi-official account of the navy in the war, which was published as *History of United States Naval Operations in World War II* (15 vols.; Boston: Atlantic, Little, Brown, 1947–62). In 1947, Morison asked King to tell him why Hart had been relieved. "I would not necessarily use the real reason in the Naval History," Morison confided, "but would like to know it." Morison to King, 27 September 1947, Box 18, King MSS, LC.
26. King to Stark, 20 January 1942, CominCh Records, NHC; Stark to Roosevelt, 23 October 1944, Box 166, PPF, FDR MSS; Roosevelt to Marshall, 5 March 1942, and Stark to Roosevelt, 7 March 1942, File: 18-R, Box 59, President's Office File (POF), FDR MSS; Entry, 6 March 1942, Stimson Diary; and Dyer, *Richardson*, pp. 441–42.
27. King to Cooke, 23 February 1942, Cooke MSS; Admiral John H. Hoover OH, NI, p. 215; and King, *Record*, pp. 628–29. Turner later claimed that King told him that he had been replaced by Cooke at the insistance of Marshall. Forrest C. Pogue, Marshall's biographer, agrees with me that Marshall lacked that sort of influence with King. Conversation, Pogue with author, 28 December 1979.
28. Forrest C. Pogue, *George C. Marshall*, Vol. II: *Ordeal and Hope, 1939–1942* (4 vols.?; New York: Viking, 1962–?), pp. 298–300; King to Robert Albion, n.d. (c. 1948), "Albion" File, Box 35, King MSS, LC; and Entries, 5 and 6 June and 6, 7, and 18 July 1942, William D. Leahy Diary, LC.

29. King to Nimitz, 28 January 1942, msg 272333, NHC; King, *Record*, pp. 353–54; and King to Nimitz, 15 January 1942, msg 152048, NHC.
30. King to Nimitz, 31 January 1942, msg 311606, NHC.
31. King, *Record*, pp. 377 and 382; Morton, *Strategy*, p. 218; and Roosevelt to Churchill, 18 February 1942, Roosevelt-Churchill Messages, FDR MSS; King to JCS, 2 March 1942, CominCh Records, NHC.
32. Wesley Frank Craven and James Lea Cate, eds., *The Army Air Forces in World War II* (7 vols.; Chicago: University of Chicago Press, 1949–1958), Vol. I, pp. 438–44; Francis S. Low, "A Personal Narrative of Association with Fleet Admiral Ernest J. King. U.S. Navy," (privately printed, 1961), pp. 25–26; King to Ingersoll, 8 February 1942, msg 081615, CominCh Records, NHC; and Ghormley to Pound, 21 February 1942, Adm 205/19, PRO.
33. John B. Lundstrom, *The First South Pacific Campaign* (Annapolis, Md.: Naval Institute Press, 1976), pp. 121–22.
34. King to Nimitz, 19 April 1942, msg 191012, NHC; Mins, King and Nimitz meeting, 25–26 April 1942, King MSS, NHC.
35. King to Marshall, 12 May 1942, CominCh Records, NHC; King to Nimitz, 15 May 1942, msg 152130, NHC.
36. King to Nimitz, 17 May 1942, msg 170231, NHC; King to Pound, 19 May 1942, Adm 205/19, and Pound to King, 19 May 1942, Adm 205/19, PRO; and King to Pound, 21 May 1942, King MSS, NHC. The justification brought forward by the official British naval historian for the failure of the Admiralty to provide any aid is rather weak. Stephen W. Roskill, *The War at Sea, 1939–1945*, Vol. II: *The Period of Balance* (3 vols.; London: Her Majesty's Stationery Office, 1954–1961), p. 37.
37. Mins, CCS meeting, 2 March 1942, Records of the Combined Chiefs of Staff (and Joint Chiefs of Staff), RG 218, NA; Cooke to Hoover, 18 May 1958, Cooke MSS; and Henry H. Arnold, *Global Mission* (New York: Harper, 1949), p. 305. Pound and the Admiralty thoroughly opposed Sledgehammer. Marshall to Roosevelt, 1 May 1942, File: Marshall, Box 5, PSF, FDR MSS; and Pound to Director (Plans), 27 May 1942, Adm 205–19, PRO.
38. Matloff, *Strategic Planning*, pp. 192–93; George E. Mowry, *Landing Craft and the War Production Board* (Washington, D.C.: GPO, 1946), pp. 10 and 72; Rear Admiral J. W. S. Dorling, RN, "Report of British Admiralty Delegation," pp. 25–37, Adm 199/1236, PRO; and Mins, War Production Board meeting, 12 May 1942, King MSS, NHC.
39. John Terraine, *The Life and Times of Lord Mountbatten* (London: Hutchison, 1968), p. 94; Albert W. Wedemeyer, *Wedemeyer Reports!* (New York: Devin-Adair, 1958), pp. 136–39; Cooke OH; and Hewitt OH, p. 260.
40. King to Marshall, 11 June 1942, WPD, NHC; Matloff, *Strategic Planning*, pp. 259–60; King to Nimitz, 26 June 1942, msg 271415, NHC; notes, King, n.d. (c. 1947), Box 35, King MSS, LC; King to Marshall, 2 July 1942, King MSS, NHC; and Mins, King and Nimitz meeting 4 to 6 July 1942, King MSS, NHC. King clearly discussed the Guadalcanal operation with Roosevelt *before* he revealed his plan to Marshall. He also apparently had the president's approval for the plan. Mins, Pacific War Council meeting, 10 June 1942, File 168, Map Room (MR), FDR MSS.
41. King, *Record*, p. 398; and Entry, 28 July 1942, Leahy Diary. In February and March 1942, King and Eisenhower, then head of the Army's War Plans Division, frequently clashed. On 23 February 1942, Eisenhower wrote in his diary that King "is an arbitrary, stubborn type, with too much brains and a tendency toward bullying

his juniors!" On 10 March 1942, he scribbled, "One thing that might help win this war is to get someone to shoot King. He's the antithesis of co-operation—a deliberately rude person—which means he's a mental bully." *Baltimore Sun*, 4 October 1979. However, in his retirement Eisenhower revealed that King had first proposed to put Eisenhower in command of the Torch operation. Dwight D. Eisenhower, *At Ease: Stories I Tell to Friends* (Garden City, N.Y.: Doubleday, 1967), p. 252.

42. King and Marshall to Roosevelt, 4 August 1942, Cooke MSS. Cooke pressed for the guarantees to Franco. Cooke to King, 29 August 1942, Cooke MSS. King later asserted that he "was always afraid that U-boats could concentrate a force that would block the Straits of Gibraltar for days, even weeks, and render 'Gymnast' [the early code-name for Torch] a bust." King to Tracy B. Kittredge, 26 April 1950, Box 35, King MSS, LC.
43. Assistant Chief Naval Staff (T) to Pound, 14 June 1942, Adm 205/19, PRO.
44. Captain Charles Lambe, RN, "British-American Conversations," 12 December 1941, Adm 205/19, PRO; King to Pound, 2 February 1942, msg 022335, NHC; Dorling, "Report," p. 17, Adm 199/1236, PRO; and Lambe to Pound, 8 January 1942, Adm 205/19, PRO. Roosevelt supported King's position on the command issue. Draft, Churchill to Clement Atlee (Deputy Prime Minister), 28 December 1941, in *FRUS: Washington and Casablanca*, pp. 277–78.
45. King to Pound, 13 February 1942, CominCh Records, NHC; King to Pound, 7 February 1942, msg 071705, NHC; Churchill to Hopkins, 6 February 1942, Adm 199/1935, PRO; King to Andrews, 12 February 1942, "Eastern Sea Frontier War Diary," Ch. IV, p. 12, NHC; and Roosevelt to Churchill, 17 March 1942, Roosevelt-Churchill Correspondence, FDR MSS.
46. I am grateful to Midshipman First Class Thomas Belke, USN, who undertook the stratistical studies that proved King's assertion to be correct.
47. Roosevelt to Churchill, 18 March 1942, Roosevelt-Churchill Correspondence, FDR MSS; King, *Record*, p. 447; and Pound to King, 18 March 1942, Adm 205/13, PRO.
48. ACNS (T) to Pound, 14 June 1942, Adm 205/21, PRO.
49. Roosevelt to Knox, ? January 1942, File: Navy, Box 5, PSF, FDR MSS; Dorling, "Report," p. 36, Adm. 199/1236, PRO; Entry, 3 September 1942, Leahy Diary, LC; and King to Knox, 6 June 1942, Cooke MSS.
50. Potter, *Nimitz*, pp. 183–85.
51. King to Marshall, 3 September 1942, King MSS, NHC; and Mins, King and Nimitz meeting, 7 to 8 September 1942, King MSS, NHC. Arnold complained to Stimson about King: "He never lets up. He has not receded one inch from any of his demands upon us and I prophecy that he will eventually get them all." Pogue, *Marshall*, Vol. II, p. 385.
52. Mins, Pacific War Council meeting, 15 September 1942, Box 178, MR, FDR MSS; Entry, 30 October 1942, Stimson Diary; Connolly OH, NI, p. 112; King to Marshall, 3 October 1942, King MSS, NHC; and Potter, *Nimitz*, p. 195.
53. Potter, *Nimitz*, pp. 196 and 211. King later discovered that Ghormley had little experience at sea in command billets. King to Tracy B. Kittredge, 1 February 1950, Box 35, King MSS, LC.
54. Roosevelt to King and Marshall, 24 October 1942, King MSS, NHC.
55. King to Roosevelt, 26 October 1942, King MSS, NHC; Potter, *Nimitz*, pp. 200–06; and Mins, JCS meeting, 20 December 1942, RG 218, NA.

56. Mins, King and Nimitz meeting, 9 to 10 December 1942, King MSS, NHC.
57. King had always been over-optimistic about the South Pacific operation. Cooke OH; and Cooke to Captain J. G. Corn, 6 July 1942, and Cooke to Corn, 28 July 1942, WPD, NHC.
58. CCS to Roosevelt and Churchill, 23 January 1943, Record of the Casablanca Conference, RG 218, NA.
59. Briefing notes, Cooke to King, 9 January 1943, Cooke MSS; Entry, ? January 1943, Cooke War Diary, privately held; and King, *Record*, pp. 420–21. Cooke persuaded King that Roundup "was not practicable." In Cooke's opinion, the Allies simply could not "finish the campaign in Africa and then turn around a million men, their supplies, and equipment, and land them in England in time for the preparation and execution of a landing in Northern France in 1943. King agreed after some delay, but it was some days before Marshall and Wedemeyer allowed themselves to be convinced." Cooke OH.
60. Mins, CCS meeting, 14 January 1943, RG 218, NA. After the war, King wrote, "We always had trouble with the British whenever we tried to improve the situation in the Pacific." King to Morison, 27 October 1948, Box 18, King MSS, LC.
61. Mins, King and Nimitz meeting, 22 February 1943, and King to Marshall, 6 January and 8 January 1943, King MSS, NHC; and Potter, *Nimitz*, p. 210.
62. Matloff, *Strategic Planning*, Vol. II, pp. 90–93; Mins, JCS meeting, 16 and 19 March 1943, RG 218, NA; Norton, *Strategy and Command*, pp. 390–95; and Cooke and Wedemeyer to JCS, 16 March 1943, Cooke MSS.
63. *New York Times*, 6 September 1943, Cooke OH; Vice Admiral Bernhard Bieri OH, NI, pp. 334–35; King to Secretary of the Navy John L. Sullivan (draft), 9 June 1948, Box 35, King MSS, LC; and Sanders, "King," p. 56.
64. Wilfred Jasper Holmes, *Double-Edged Secrets* (Annapolis, Md.: Naval Institute Press, 1979), p. 83; Glover, *Command Performance*, p. 32; Connolly OH, p. 280; Bieri OH, p. 340; King to Cooke 7 January 1942, Cooke MSS; King to Halsey, 3 August 1943, King MSS, NHC; Cooke OH; and U.S. Congress, Joint Committee to Investigate the Pearl Harbor Attack, *Hearings on the Investigation of the Pearl Harbor Attack*, 79th Cong., 1st Sess., Part 39, p. 344.
65. Years later the president's son, James Roosevelt, wrote of his father, "I knew he thought Admiral King the wisest of his staff of military men. I remember him being asked why he kept King in the White House instead of sending him up front to take command. 'The president has to have close to him the shrewest of strategists. Most critical decisions must be made here. You don't send these men into the front lines where their lives may be endangered.'" James Roosevelt, *My Parents: A Differing View* (Chicago: Playboy Press, 1976), p. 166. *See also* Roosevelt to Andrews, 24 June 1942, King MSS, NHC; *Nation*, 9 December 1943, p. 37; Robert G. Albion and Robert H. Connery, *Forrestal and the Navy* (New York: Columbia University Press, 1962), pp. 96–103; and Roosevelt to Marvin McIntyre (presidential appointments secretary), 30 July 1942, File 18-R, Box 59, POF, FDR MSS.
66. W. C. Ament (Pathé News) to King, 27 May 1942, Admiral Arthur J. Hepburn to King, 4 June 1942, and King to Ament, 7 June 1942, King MSS, NHC; Potter, *Nimitz*, pp. 82 and 103; Nicholas Roosevelt, *Front Row Seat* (Norman: University of Oklahoma Press, 1953), p. 258; and Entry, 21 July 1942, Stimson Diary.
67. King, *Record*, pp. 618–37; and Cooke OH.
68. Connolly OH, pp. 278–79; Bieri OH, p. 332; Forrest C. Pogue, "George C. Marshall and His Commanders, 1942–1945," in B. Franklin Cooling, ed., *Essays in*

Dimensions of Military History (Carlisle Barracks, Penn.: U.S. Army War College, 1976), p. 89; *New York Times*, 6 September 1943; and Pogue, *Marshall*, Vol. II, pp. 372–73.

69. Entries, 2 and 8 May 1943, William D. Leahy Diary, Leahy MSS, LC. There are no other records of these meetings.
70. CCS 242/6, 25 May 1943, RG 218, NA; and Annex, Mins, CCS meeting, 13 May 1943, RG 218, NA.
71. Mins, CCS meeting, 21 May 1943, and CCS 242/6, 25 May 1943, RG 218, NA.
72. Mins, King and Nimitz meetings, 1 June 1943, King MSS, NHC.
73. Major General Lawrence Kuter to Cooke, 10 July 1943, Cooke to Kuter, 26 July 1943, Cooke MSS.
74. King to Halsey, 3 August 1943, King MSS, NHC; and Pogue, *Marshall*, Vol. III, p. 626.
75. Mins, King and Nimitz meetings, 30 July to 1 August 1943, King MSS, NHC.
76. Matloff, *Strategic Planning*, Vol II, pp. 158–59; and Cooke to King, 19 July 1943, Cooke MSS.
77. Mins, Roosevelt and JCS meeting, 10 August 1943, and Mins, Joint Planning Staff meeting, 12 August 1943, RG 218, NA.
78. King to Commander Reuthven Libby, 31 August 1943, King MSS, NHC; Winston S. Churchill, *The Second World War*, Vol. V: *Closing the Ring* (6 vols.; Boston; Houghton Mifflin, 1949–1960), p. 85: CCS 419/5, 24 August 1943, RG 218, NA; and Mins, CCS meeting, 15 August 1943, RG 218, NA; and Cooke to King, 8 October 1943, Cooke MSS. The opportunity costs of the landing craft program for Overlord were significant. Cooke to King, 30 October 1943, Cooke MSS.
79. Mins, King and Nimitz meetings, 25 to 27 September 1943, King MSS, NHC.
80. George E. Mowry, "Landing Craft and the War Production Board, April 1942 to May 1944," USNA; King to Roosevelt, 13 December 1943, "Status of DE's," Cooke MSS; Dorling to Pound, 10 February 1943, Adm 205/19, PRO; and "Admiralty Review of Anti-U-boat Warfare Committee," Adm 205/19, PRO.
81. Terry Hughes and John Costello, *The Battle of the Atlantic* (London: Collins, 1977), pp. 275–90; and Patrick Beesly, *Most Secret Intelligence* (London: Hamish Hamilton, 1977).
82. King, *Record*, Ch. 35.
83. OP-20-G report, "Radio Intelligence and the Battle of the Atlantic," May 1945, USNA; and Interview, Captain Kenneth J. Knowles, USN and Vice Admiral Norman Denning, RN, 25 October 1977.
84. *FRUS: The Conferences at Cairo and Tehran, 1943*.
85. Theodore H. White, ed., *The Stilwell Papers*, (New York: William Sloan, 1948), p. 245: Entries, 3 to 5 December 1943, Leahy Diary, Leahy MSS; and notes, n.d. (c. 1947), Box 35, King MSS, LC.
86. Cooke OH.
87. CCS 417/Annex II, 2 December 1943, RG 218, NA; King to Stark, 5 November 1943, King MSS, NHC; *FRUS-Cairo*, pp. 765–73, 809, and 828–31; and Bieri OH, p. 334.
88. King, *Record*, pp. 523–25; and notes, n.d. (c. 1947), Box 35, King MSS, LC.
89. Mins, King and Nimitz meetings, 3 to 4 January 1944, King MSS, NHC.
90. *Ibid.*
91. Cooke OH; Potter, *Nimitz*, pp. 282; and Mins, JCS meeting, 8 February 1944, RG 218, NA.

92. King to Nimitz, 17 February 1944, King MSS, NHC.
93. Potter, *Nimitz,* 287–88; MacArthur to Marshall, 5 March 1944, Cooke MSS; Mins, JCS meetings, 7 and 11 March 1944, RG 218, NA; and JCS to Nimitz and MacArthur, 12 March 1944, CominCh Records, NHC. Sutherland believed that Nimitz agreed with MacArthur but was afraid to oppose King on the issue. Matloff, *Strategic Planning,* Vol. II: *1943–1944,* p. 457.
94. Cooke to King, 30 January 1944, Cooke MSS; Matloff, *Strategic Planning,* Vol. II, pp. 43–44; Arthur Bryant, *Triumph in the West* (New York: Doubleday, 1959), pp. 107–09; Harry C. Butcher, *My Three Years with Eisenhower* (New York: Simon and Schuster, 1946), pp. 491 and 494; Cooke OH; Cooke to King, 8 March 1944, Cooke to Stark, 14 March 1944, and Cooke to Stark, 10 April 1944, Cooke MSS.
95. Cooke War Diary; Mins, King and Nimitz meeting, 6 May 1944, King MSS, NHC; Mins, CCS meetings, 10 to 15 June 1944, RG 218, NA; and King, *Record,* pp. 547–553. The reasons for King's momentary agreement to the Istrian operation are obscure.
96. Mins, King and Nimitz meetings, 13 to 22 July 1944, King MSS, NHC; Captain Arthur C. Davis to Cooke, 24 July 1944, Cooke MSS; and CCS 417/3, RG 218, NA. No documentation exists in the Roosevelt MSS, King MSS, LC and NHC, or the Cooke MSS, to suggest that FDR directed the JCS to select Luzon over Formosa. Indeed, all the records indicate quite the contrary. However, after the war King wrote that "Mr. Roosevelt was fated to decide for the 'poor' Philippines although in the long view he was misled." King, notes, n.d. (c. 1947), Box 35, King MSS, LC. And, in 1950, he noted that "Roosevelt decided (with MacArthur and the Army) to go up through the Philippines. . . . " King to Edwards, 30 January 1950, Correspondence File: Edwards, Box 17, King MSS, LC. It is possible that Leahy's position—preferring Luzon over Formosa—misled King into thinking that FDR also favored this course.
97. Cooke OH; King to Marshall and Arnold, 9 August 1944, King MSS, NHC; and Mins, JCS meeting, 8 September 1944, RG 218, NA.
98. King to Roosevelt, 3 June 1944, File: "Halsey," PPF, FDR, MSS; and Cooke OH.
99. King to Kinkaid, n.d. (c. late October 1944), and Kinkaid to King, 16 December 1944, King MSS; Cooke OH; and King, *Record,* p. 580.
100. JCS meeting, 1 September 1944, RG 218, NA; and Mins, King and Nimitz meeting, 29 September to 1 October 1944, King MSS, NHC.
101. King to Stark, 5 November 1943, Mins, King and Nimitz meeting, 4 January 1944, Cooke to King, 14, 23, and 24 January 1944, King MSS, NHC; King to Nimitz, 24 January 1944, msg 251303, NHC; and Mins, King and Nimitz meeting, 6 March 1944, and King to MacArthur, 21 July 1944, King MSS, NHC.
102. Churchill to Roosevelt, 4 and 14 April, and 10 August 1944, and Roosevelt to Churchill 13 April 1944, Roosevelt-Churchill Messages, FDR MSS; CCS 452/18, RG 218, NA; Sherwood, *Roosevelt and Hopkins,* pp. 814–17; and Winston S. Churchill, *The Second World War,* Vol. V: *Closing the Ring* (6 vols.; Boston: Houghton Mifflin, 1948–53), p. 154.
103. "The Role of Communications Intelligence in Submarine Warfare in the Pacific, January 1943–October 1944," SRH-001, RG 457, NA; *FRUS: Conference at Yalta;* King to Senator William Knowland, 21 June 1951, Box 13, King MSS, LC; Leahy to Richard Korvola, 25 February 1953, Leahy MSS, Wisconsin Historical Society, Madison, Wisc.; King, *Record,* pp. 587–95; Cooke OH; and Vice Admiral Oscar C. Badger OH, NI.

104. Mins, King and Nimitz meeting, 6 March 1945, King MSS, NHC; Mins, Joint Planning Staff meetings, 10 March 1945, and JCS 1331/3, 25 May 1945, RG 218, NA; and King, *Record*, pp. 620–21. In 1943, King forecast that the Germans, whom he believed were "realists," would "surrender when they realize they are outclassed in men and equipment." However, he believed that the Japanese "will kill themselves before they surrender and we will have to kill everyone along the route to Tokyo." *New York Times*, 6 September 1943.
105. Harry S. Truman, *Mr. Citizen* (New York: Bernard Geis, 1960), pp. 186–87; Cooke War Diary; and John Toland, *The Rising Sun* (New York: Random House, 1970), pp. 763–65.
106. Mins, JCS meeting with Truman, 18 June 1945, RG 218, NA.
107. *New York Times*, 26 June 1956.
108. Land, *Winning the War*, pp. 63–64; and *New York Times*, 23 November 1952.

CHESTER W. NIMITZ

1. Julius A. Furer, *Administration of the Navy Department in World War II* (Washington, D.C.: GPO, 1959), pp. 113–14, 126, 133–34, 168, 949–50.
2. E. B. Potter, *Nimitz* (Annapolis, Md.: Naval Institute Press, 1976), pp. 22–26.
3. *Ibid.*, pp. 28–29.
4. *Ibid.*, Ch. 8.
5. *Ibid.*, pp. 129–31.
6. Nimitz to Admiral John Nelson, USN, ? September 1965, President's File, NWCA.
7. Nimitz, lecture at Naval War College, 12 October 1961, NWCA.
8. Potter, *Nimitz*, Chs. 9–12.
9. *Ibid.*, pp. 169–71.
10. John C. Lundston, *The First South Pacific Campaign* (Annapolis, Md.: Naval Institute Press, 1976).
11. Potter, *Nimitz*, p. 323; and Thomas B. Buell, *The Quiet Warrior: A Biography of Admiral Raymond A. Spruance* (Boston: Little, Brown, 1974), pp. 307–08.
12. Entry, 6 October 1945, Forrestal Diary, NHC; Robert G. Albion and Robert H. Connery, *Forrestal and the Navy* (New York: Columbia University Press, 1962), pp. 91–92 and 138; Potter, *Nimitz*, p. 407; Ernest J. King and Walter Muir Whitehill, *Fleet Admiral King: A Naval Record* (New York: Norton, 1952), p. 636.
13. Vincent Davis, *The Admiral's Lobby* (Chapel Hill: University of North Carolina Press, 1967), pp. 29, 32, 75, 89–90, and 99–101.
14. Demetrios Caraley, *The Politics of Military Unification* (New York: Columbia University Press, 1966), pp. 25–30.
15. Lawrence Legere, "The Unification of the Armed Forces" (Ph.D. dissertation, Harvard University, 1950), p. 299.
16. Harry S. Truman, *Memoirs*, Vol. II: *Years of Trial and Hope* (2 vols.; New York: Doubleday, 1956), pp. 46–49; Caraley, *Politics*, pp. 48–49; Legere, "Unification," p. 418; Davis, *Admiral's Lobby*, p. 196; and Walter Millis, ed., *The Forrestal Diaries* (New York: Viking, 1951), p. 151.
17. Various speeches and statements, Fleet Admiral Chester W. Nimitz MSS, Immediate Office Files, NHC.
18. *Ibid.*, Nimitz, "Reasons for Opposing Proposed Merger of War and Navy Departments."

19. Chester W. Nimitz, "Your Navy as Peace Insurance." *National Geographic Magazine*, June 1946, pp. 719–20; and Chester W. Nimitz, "Is the Navy Obsolete?", *Sea Power*, November 1946, p. 12.
20. Copy of testimony, 3 May 1946, Folder 34, Series 13, Nimitz MSS.
21. J. J. Clark and Clark G. Reynolds, *Carrier Admiral* (New York: David McKay, 1967), p. 250; and Millis, ed., *Forrestal Diaries*, pp. 163–64, 225–26.
22. Potter, *Nimitz*, Ch. 25.
23. Millis, ed., *The Forrestal Diaries*, pp. 163–64.
24. Albion and Connery, *Forrestal and the Navy*, pp. 281–83.
25. Millis, ed., *Forrestal Diaries*, p. 295.
26. Office Report of the Chief of Naval Operations to the Secretary of the Navy covering the period 1 October 1945 to 30 June 1946, pp. 4 and 23, NHC.
27. *Annual Report of the Secretary of the Navy for the Fiscal Year 1947* (Washington, D.C.: GPO, 1948), p. 10.
28. Joint War Plans Committee (JWPC) 432/7, ? June 1946, and assorted correspondence and drafts, File A16–3(5), Series V, WPD, CNO Records, NHC.
29. David A. Rosenberg and Floyd Kennedy, "History of the Strategic Arms Competition, 1945–1962: Supporting Study: U. S. Aircraft Carriers in the Strategic Role" (Arlington, Va.: Lulejian Assoc., 1975), p. 35.
30. JCS 1725/1, "Strategic Guidance for Industrial Mobilization," 13 February 1947, CCS Records, RG 218, NA.
31. Various items, A16–3 (5), Box 111, Series V, WPD Records, and 00 Files: 1942–47, Carton 1, CNO Records, NHC.
32. Rosenberg, "Aircraft Carriers," pp. 30 and 48; items in A16–3(5), Box 111, Series V, WPD Records, NHC; Forrestal to Truman, 16 (or 20) December 1948, "Atomic" File, Box 4, President's Safe File, Harry S. Truman MSS, Independence, Missouri; and Office of CNO, "Estimate of the Effect on the Nature of War of Future Technical Developments in Weapons," 22 November 1946, CNO Records, NHC.
33. Dennis M. Pricolo, "Naval Presence and Cold War Foreign Policy: A Study of the Decision to Station the 6th Fleet in the Mediterranean, 1945–1948," Trident Scholar Report No. 85, 1 June 1978, USNA.
34. For background on the navy's role in the program, see various letters and memoranda, 1939–1946, Series II, "Selected Records on the Navy's Role in the Atomic Energy Program," NHC.
35. *Ibid.*
36. "Official Report of the Chief of Naval Operations to the Secretary of the Navy . . ., 1 October 1945 to 30 June 1946," pp. 21–22, NHC: and Richard G. Hewlett and Francis Duncan, *Nuclear Navy, 1946–1962* (Chicago: University of Chicago Press, 1974), pp. 31–32.
37. Nimitz, memo, 10 January 1947, Letters and Memoranda: 1939–1946, Series II, "Selected Records on the Navy's Role in the Atomic Energy Program," WHC.
38. Nimitz to Sullivan, 5 December 1947, CNO Serial 00–26–P36(SC) S1–1 and CNO Serial 0027P36(SC) SS1–1/SS, Central Security Classified Records of the SecNav and CNO, NHC.
39. Nimitz to Sullivan ? 1947, "The Future Employment of Naval Forces," pp. 1–7, NHC.
40. Potter, *Nimitz*, pp. 438–39, 445–48, and 452.

LOUIS E. DENFELD

1. Rear Admiral William Harrington Leahy, USN (Ret.), to Robert Wm. Love, Jr., 11 August 1973, courtesy of Dr. Love.
2. Walter Millis, ed., *The Forrestal Diaries* (New York: Viking, 1951), p. 325.
3. *New York Times; Worcester Telegram* (Mass.); *Washington Post*; and *Washington Star*; Admiral Charles D. Griffin, USN OH, NI, p. 183. A comment similar to Griffin's remark can be found in Hanson W. Baldwin OH, NI, p. 465.
4. U. S. President's Air Policy Commission, *Survival in the Air Age: A Report by the President's Air Policy Commission* (Washington, D.C.: GPO, 1948).
5. U. S. Congress, House, Subcommittee on Appropriations, *Hearings: National Security Establishment*, 80th Cong., 2d Sess., 16 March to 22 May 1948; and *New York Times*, 24 June 1948.
6. Drew Pearson, "Washington Merry-Go-Round," *Philadelphia Bulletin*, 10 April 1948; Carl W. Borklund, *Men of the Pentagon: From Forrestal to McNamara* (New York: Praeger, 1966), pp. 75–76; Daniel V. Gallery, *Eight Bells and All's Well* (New York: Norton, 1965), pp. 221–22; Paul Y. Hammond, "Super Carriers and B-36 Bombers: Appropriations, Strategy and Politics," in Harold Stein, ed., *American-Civil-Military Decisions: A Book of Case Studies* (University, Ala.: University of Alabama Press, 1963), pp. 472, 480.
7. Walter Poole, "The Joint Chiefs of Staff, 1947–1949," unpublished manuscript, RG 218, NA.
8. H. C. Beauregard to SecNav, 27 February 1948, "Mins, mtg of Sec Nav," Records of the Secretary of the Navy (SNP), RG 80, NA.
9. Beauregard to SecNav, 5 March 1948, "Mins, mtg of SecNav," SNP, RG 80, NA; *New York Times*, 27 May 1948; and Millis, ed., *Forrestal Diaries*, pp. 390–91.
10. U.S. Department of Defense, Memo to the Service Secretaries and the JCS, "Functions of the Armed Services and the Joint Chiefs of Staff," 21 April 1948, SNP, RG 80, NA. The text of this paper appeared in the *Army Navy Journal*, 20 March 1948, pp. 807–09.
11. Beauregard to SecNav, 7 April 1948, "Synopsis of Air Force and Army Presentation to Executive Session Yesterday"; Beauregard to SecNav, 12 April 1948, "Testimony of Secretary Royall and General Bradley in Executive Session of the Senate Armed Services Committee on Monday, 12 April 1948"; Vice Admiral Robert B. Carney (DCNO, Logistics) to SecNav, 3 June 1948; Vice Admiral Fitzhugh Lee to John L. Sullivan, 14 May 1948; and Sullivan to W. Stuart Symington, 7 April 1948; all in SNP, RG 80, NA.
12. "Statement by Admiral Louis E. Denfeld, CNO, before the Senate Armed Services Committee," 1 June 1948, SNP, RG 80, NA.
13. Beauregard to SecDef, 15 May 1948, SNP, RG 80, NA.
14. Spaatz to Senator Chan Gurney, 24 May 1948, SNP, RG 80, NA; Hammond, "Super Carriers," p. 481; "Super Carrier," *Aviation Weekly*, 24 May 1948, p. 12; and "Carrier War," *Aviation Weekly*, 31 May 1948, p. 9.
15. Frank R. Futrell, *Ideas, Concepts, Doctrine: A History of Basic Thinking in the United States Air Force, 1907–1964* (Montgomery, Ala.: Air University, 1971), pp. 99–100; Millis, ed., *Forrestal Diaries*, pp. 462–68, 476; and Hammond, "Super Carriers," pp. 451–54.

16. Futrell, *Ideas*, pp. 124–26; and Millis, ed., *Forrestal Diaries*, p. 467.
17. Vice Admiral Fitzhugh Lee OH, NI, pp. 190–91; Vincent Davis, *The Admiral's Lobby* (Chapel Hill: University of North Carolina Press, 1967), pp. 251–85.
18. Tyler Abell, ed., *Drew Pearson Diaries, 1949–1959* (New York: Holt, Rinehart and Winston, 1974), p. 9.
19. Denfeld to Sullivan, 18 December 1948, SNP, RG 80, NA.
20. Abell, ed., *Pearson Diaries*, p. 9.
21. Admiral Robert L. Dennison OH, Harry S. Truman Library, Independence, Mo., pp. 17, 21, 28; Vice Admiral Herbert T. Riley OH, NI, pp. 310, 315–16; General Oliver P. Smith, USMC, OH, Historical Division, Headquarters, USMC, p. 185.
22. *New York Times*, 24 and 26 April 1949.
23. Sullivan to Truman, 26 April 1949, SNP, RG 80, NA; *New York Times*, 27 April 1949; and Burke to Denfeld, 28 April 1949, Op-23 Files, NHC.
24. "National Military Establishment Order to the JCS," *Army Navy Journal*, 28 May 1949, p. 1117; and Ad Hoc Committee, Report to the JCS, 11 May 1948, "Evaluation of Effect on Soviet War Efforts Resulting from the Strategic Air Offensive," Op-23 Files, NHC.
25. Matthews to Vinson, 20 July 1949, CNO Records, NHC.
26. Matthews to Truman, 12 July 1949, SNP, RG 80, NA.
27. *New York Times*, 17 May 1949; *Washington Post*, 12 August 1949; Chairman, General Board, to Matthews, 27 July 1949, and Denfeld to Matthews, 27 July and 11 August 1949, SNP, RG 80, NA; and Matthews to Vinson, 20 July 1949, CNO Records, NHC.
28. Hanson Baldwin column, *New York Times*, 15 October 1949; Hammond, "Super Carriers," p. 505–07; and Vice Admiral Charles Wellborn, Jr., OH, NI, p. 292.
29. Bogan to Matthews, 20 September 1949, CNO Records, NHC.
30. "Texts in Naval Discussion," *Army Navy Journal*, 8 October 1949, p. 193.
31. Baldwin OH, p. 468; Wellborn OH, p. 293; Joseph J. Clark and Clark G. Reynolds, *Carrier Admiral* (New York: David McKay, 1967), p. 263; "Captain Crommelin's Statement," *Army Navy Journal*, 17 September 1949, p. 51; Borklund, *Pentagon*, p. 78; and Admiral Richard L. Conolly OH, NI, pp. 393–98.
32. U.S. Congress, House, Committee on Armed Services, *The National Defense Program: Unification and Strategy*, 81st Cong., 1st Sess., pp. 2–35; and *New York Times*, 8 October 1949.
33. *Unification and Strategy*, pp. 39–53; and Griffin OH, p. 275.
34. Borklund, *Pentagon*, p. 81; Hammond, "Super Carriers," p. 528; Dennison, OH, p. 140; Wellborn OH, p. 289; Baldwin OH, p. 470; and Griffin OH, p. 193.
35. Wellborn OH, p. 289.
36. Baldwin OH, pp. 471–72; Griffin OH, pp. 187–90.
37. Dennison OH, p. 141; *Unification and Strategy*, pp. 349–64; Griffin OH, p. 190.
38. Prof. E. B. Potter (Nimitz's biographer) to author, 24 September 1975; and manuscript copy of Potter, "Nimitz: A Biography," Ch. 24.
39. Harry S. Truman, *Memoirs*, Vol. II: *Years of Trial and Hope* (2 vols.; Garden City, N.Y.: Doubleday, 1955–56), p. 53.
40. Armin Rappaport, *The Navy League of the United States* (Detroit: Wayne State University Press, 1952), p. 197; "Contempt of Congress," *U.S. News and World Report*, 4 November 1949, pp. 34–36; "Ax for the Admiral," *Newsweek*, 7 November 1949, p. 27; Ernest K. Lindley, "Denfeld Firing: A Turning Point," *Newsweek*, 7 November

1949, p. 26; and newspaper opinion cited in *Army Navy Journal*, 5 November 1949, p. 250.

41. Matthews to Johnson, 3 November 1949, SNP, RG 80, NA; "House B-36 Report May Stir New Laws," and "Report Urges Restudy of Defense Concepts, Scores Denfeld's Relief," *Army Navy Journal*, 4 March 1950, pp. 693, 708–13, and 723–24.
42. Louis E. Denfeld, "Reprisal: Why I Was Fired," *Colliers*, 25 March 1950.
43. Louis E. Denfeld, "The Only Carrier the Air Force Ever Sank," *Colliers*, 2 April 1950.

FORREST P. SHERMAN

1. Jack Alexander, "They Sparked the Carrier Revolution," *Saturday Evening Post*, 16 September 1944, pp. 49–53 and *passim; New York Times*, 23 July 1951; Clark G. Reynolds, *Famous American Admirals* (New York: Van Nostrand Reinhold, 1978), pp. 306–08; *Dictionary of American Biography* (5th Suppl.; New York: Charles Scribner's Sons, 1977), pp. 620–22; and "Admiral Forrest P. Sherman," official navy biography, Biographies Branch, NHC.
2. *Lucky Bag, 1918* (Annapolis, Md.: U.S. Naval Academy, 1917), p. 104.
3. Reynolds, *American Admirals*, pp. 306–08.
4. *Current Biography: 1948*, p. 577.
5. "Records of the U.S. Naval Members, Permanent Joint Board on Defense, Canada-United States, 1940–1947," Series XIII p. 4, WPD, NHC.
6. Samuel Eliot Morison, *History of United States Naval Operations in World War II*, Vol. V: *The Struggle for Guadalcanal* (15 vols.; Boston: Atlantic, Little, Brown, 1947–1962), pp. 130–38.
7. Clark G. Reynolds, *The Fast Carriers* (2d ed., rev.; New York: Robert Krieger, 1978), pp. 69, 89–90.
8. *Ibid.*, pp. 104–05, 115–21, and 389; and Captain G. Willing Pepper, USNR (Ret.) to author, 16 August 1966. Pepper served on Nimitz's wartime staff.
9. Vincent Davis, *Post-War Defense Policy and the U.S. Navy, 1943–1946* (Chapel Hill: University of North Carolina Press, 1966), pp. 146, 230–31, 238; and Demetrios Caraley, *The Politics of Military Unification* (New York: Columbia University Press, 1966), pp. 78, 189.
10. Caraley, *Unification*, pp. 150–55.
11. *Ibid.*, pp. 226, 257–58; and Davis, *Defense Policy*, pp. 250–56.
12. *Current Biography, 1948*, pp. 578–79; Walter Millis, ed., *The Forrestal Diaries* (New York: The Viking Press, 1951), pp. 222–29, 249; Sherman, "Presentation to the President," 14 January 1947, Chronological File, Command File, CNO Records, NHC; and Rear Admiral Cato D. Glover to Nimitz, "Resume of PINCHER Planning," 21 January 1947, File A16–3, Series 0005P30, Op-30 Files, WPD, NHC.
13. Sherman to Nimitz, 1 January 1948, and Lt. General James A. Van Fleet to Cedric Foster (Yankee Radio Network), 8 November 1949, appended to Foster to Sherman, 5 December 1949, in "00" and "Blue Flag" Files, Admiral Forrest P. Sherman MSS, NHC.
14. Paolo E. Coletta, ed., *American Secretaries of the Navy* (Annapolis Md.: Naval Institute Press, forthcoming). Professor Coletta generously lent me a draft copy of the chapter on Matthews. Also, interview, author with W. John Kenny, ? June 1963.
15. Cole to All Members, House Committee on Armed Services, 8 December 1949, Papers of the SecNav, RG 80, NA. This document includes the original telegram

plus excerpts of replies by selected, but unidentified, admirals. Sherman initialed his reply on his own copy of the Cole questionnaire.

16. E. B. Potter, *Nimitz* (Annapolis, Md.: Naval Institute Press, 1976), pp. 466–48; Coletta, *Secretaries of the Navy* draft; and Lawrence J. Korb, *The Joint Chiefs of Staff* (Bloomington: Indiana University Press, 1976), pp. 56–57.
17. Sherman to Towers, 11 November 1949, Sherman MSS; and Coletta, *American Secretaries of the Navy* draft.
18. Towers to Sherman, 2 November 1949, and Sherman to Towers, 11 November 1949, Sherman MSS.
19. Coletta, *American Secretaries of the Navy* draft; *New York Herald Tribune*, 18 November 1949; and Sherman to Rear Admiral John J. Ballentine, 22 November 1950, Sherman MSS. In this letter Sherman referred to a lesser matter when he wrote, "I see no justice in doing it on a rank basis or a friendship basis. When the question is referred to me, I must face up to it as a matter of policy applying to all concerned."
20. *Public Papers of the Presidents of the United States: Harry S. Truman, 1950* (Washington, D.C.: GPO, 1964), p. 502; *Washington Post*, 13 January 1950; and *New York Times*, 17 March 1950.
21. Clippings, syndicated columns by David Lawrence, July 1951, and Sherman to Matthews, 16 December 1949, Sherman MSS; Interview, Bogan with author, 1964; and *New York Times*, 3 December 1949.
22. Sherman to Matthews, 31 May 1950, Sherman MSS; and Robert S. Allen and William V. Shannon, *The Truman Merry-Go-Round* (New York: Vanguard Press, 1950), p. 482.
23. Joseph C. Harsch, "Admiral Sherman and the JCS," *The Christian Science Monitor*, 23 July 1951. Unfortunately, the navy's image suffered a slight blow in January 1950, when the "Mighty Mo" ran aground while leaving the Norfolk, Virginia, navy yard and remained ignominiously stuck for two weeks.
24. Sherman to Vinson and Cole, 14 November 1950, Vinson to Sherman, 15 November 1950, and memo Op-003 to Op-212, 16 April 1951, Sherman MSS.
25. Draft, Truman to Cates, n.d., Sherman MSS; and *New York Times*, 18 April and 24 May 1951. My use of newspaper accounts for many of Sherman's important decisions is justified by his practice of carefully keeping files of all statements he made to reporters and published by the press.
26. Clippings, syndicated columns by David Lawrence, Sherman MSS; *Bedford-Standard Times*, 25 July 1951; *New York Times*, 23 July 1951; and Sherman to Conolly, 23 May 1950, Sherman MSS.
27. Hanson Baldwin, "Admiral Sherman Weathers the First Storm," *New York Times Magazine*, 19 March 1950, p. 12.
28. JCS 2079/4-8 and JCS 1800/68, cited in Op-003, memo for file, "Increase in Naval Forces," 13 July 1951, Sherman MSS; R. Earl McClendon, *Army Aviation, 1947–1953* (Maxwell, Ala.: Air University Documentary Study, 1954), pp. 12, 15; and Sherman to Conolly, 10 July 1950, Sherman MSS.
29. *Boston Herald*, 13 December 1945: *New York Times*, 17 March, 27 April, and 2 May 1950; and Richard G. Hewlett and Francis Duncan, *Nuclear Navy, 1945–1962* (Chicago: University of Chicago Press, 1974), pp. 162–63.
30. JCS 1800/96 and 99 and JCS 1906/20, Sherman MSS.
31. *New York Times*, 1, 3, and 24 May 1951; Sherman to Chiefs of the Bureaus of Ships, Ordnance, and Aeronautics, 6 July 1951, Serial 1019P43, Sherman MSS; *New York*

Herald Tribune, 14 December 1950; "The Naval Aeronautical Organization," Op 502B/mg, n.d. (probably summer 1951), Sherman MSS; Hewlett and Duncan, *Nuclear Navy*, pp. 196–97; "Operational Experience of Fast Carrier Task Forces in World War II," Weapons System Evaluation Group Study No. 4, 15 August 1951, NHC; and Sherman to Sen. Harry F. Byrd, 8 February 1951, Sherman to Bureau Chiefs, 6 July 1951, Rear Admiral Homer N. Wallin to Sherman, 12 June 1951, and Byrd to Sherman, 26 February 1951, Sherman MSS.

32. *New York Times*, 24 May 1951. Sherman made this statement to the House Armed Services Committee.
33. Coletta, *American Secretaries of the Navy* draft; and *London Daily Mail*, 23 July 1951.
34. Sherman to Rear Admiral James L. Holloway, Jr., 4 January 1950, Sherman MSS.
35. *New York Times*, 22 December 1949; *Washington Post*, 30 April 1950; Davis, *Defense Policy*, p. 256; Baruch to Sherman, 14 March 1950, and Sherman to Baruch, 16 March 1950, Sherman MSS. After another exchange, an admiring Baruch sent Sherman a number of quail for his table.
36. Johnson to Conolly, 23 May 1950, Conolly to Sherman, 20 and 28 May 1950, Sherman to Conolly, 10 June 1950, Sherman MSS.
37. *New York Times*, 8 December 1949; and Sherman to Conolly, 10 June 1950, Conolly to Sherman, 3 July 1950, Sherman to Ballentine, 30 June, 5 August, and 22 November 1950, Ballentine to Sherman, 31 May, 29 July, and 17 August 1950, Sherman MSS.
38. Douglas MacArthur, *Reminiscences* (New York: McGraw-Hill, 1964), p. 350.
39. "JCS Visit to the Pacific, February 1950," prepared by Pacific Fleet Staff, Sherman MSS. This document cites JCS 1380/75, NSC 13/3, and NSC 49.
40. *Ibid.*, citing JCS 1483/50; and *New York Times*, 14 February 1950.
41. *Ibid.*
42. Cooke to Sherman, 14 April, 23 May, and ? (received 19) July 1950, Sherman to Cooke, 29 May 1950, Sherman MSS. Sherman cautioned Cooke that he was acting as a private citizen. Also, Sherman to JCS, 1 May 1950, Serial 0004P00, General of the Army Omar Bradley MSS, LC; *New York Times*, 17 and 19 March, 1950; Malcolm W. Cagle and Frank A. Manson, *The Sea War in Korea* (Annapolis, Md.: Naval Institute Press, 1957), pp. 24, 31–32;
43. David Rees, *Korea: The Limited War* (Baltimore: Penguin Books, 1964), pp. 22–23; Richard F. Haynes *The Awesome Power: Harry S. Truman as Commander in Chief* (Baton Rouge: Louisiana State University Press, 1973), p. 167; and Sherman, "Memorandum for the Record," 25 June 1950 to 11 April 1951, Sherman MSS. The latter document recorded all JCS actions and was actually a diary. Sherman probably borrowed the practice of keeping such a running account from Towers, whose war diary Sherman often maintained while he served as Towers' chief of staff.
44. Sherman Memorandum, Sherman MSS.
45. *Ibid.*; and Cagle and Manson, *Sea War in Korea*, p. 142.
46. Sherman Memorandum, and Sherman to Nimitz, 6 July 1950, Sherman MSS; and U.S. Congress, Senate, Armed Services and Foreign Relations Committees, *Hearings on the Military Situation in the Far East* (Washington, D.C.: GPO, 1951), Part II, p. 1650.
47. Rear Admiral James H. Thach, Jr. (Director, International Affairs) to Sherman, n.d. (probably April 1951), Serial 000194P35, Sherman MSS; *New York Times*, 3 October 1950; and Cagle and Manson, *Sea War in Korea*, p. 281.

48. Entries, 1, 8, 10, 15, and 21 August 1951, Sherman Memorandum, Sherman MSS.
49. Entries, 15 July and 9 and 10 August 1950, Sherman Memorandum, Sherman MSS.
50. Entries, 21 and 22 August 1950, Sherman Memorandum, Sherman MSS; Cagle and Manson, *Sea War in Korea*, pp. 75–79; and MacArthur, *Reminiscences*, pp. 347–48.
51. MacArthur, *Reminiscences*, p. 350.
52. Cagle and Manson, *Sea War in Korea*, p. 76; and Rees, *Korea*, pp. 82–83.
53. Entry, 23 August 1950, Sherman Memorandum, Sherman MSS.
54. Cagle and Manson, *Sea War in Korea*, p. 76.
55. Sherman to MacArthur, 25 August 1950, and Entry, 25 August 1950, Sherman Memorandum, Sherman MSS.
56. Sherman to Conolly, 16 October 1950, Sherman MSS.
57. Entries, 26 August to 21 November 1950, Sherman Memorandum, Sherman MSS; Cagle and Manson, *Sea War in Korea*, pp. 112, 142; and Rees, *Korea*, pp. 115ff.
58. Entries, 23 to 30 November and 2 December 1950, Sherman Memorandum, Sherman MSS; and Cagle and Manson, *Sea War In Korea*, pp. 180, 186.
59. Thach to Sherman, ? April 1951, Sherman MSS. This document cites in detail Matthews to Marshall, 2 November 1950, NSC 91/1, JCS 2004/18 of 22 November 1950, Matthews to Marshall, 7, 8, and 20 December 1950, NSC 92, Sherman to Matthews, 7 December 1950, and Department of Transportation Order No. 2, 16 December 1950. Also, entries, 3, 16, and 19 December 1950, Sherman Memorandum, Sherman MSS.
60. Thach to Sherman, ? April 1951, Sherman MSS. This document cites JCS 2118/5, 3 January 1951. Also, MacArthur to JCS, 30 December 1950, JCS to MacArthur, 9 January 1951, and entries, 22 December 1950 and 2, 9, and 10 January 1951, Sherman Memorandum, Sherman MSS; and Rees, *Korea*, pp. 179–81.
61. Haynes, *Awesome Power*, p. 225; Rees, *Korea*, pp. 182–84; entries, 10 to 24 January 1951, Sherman Memorandum, Sherman MSS.
62. Sherman, paper on blockade of China, n.d., Thach to Sherman, ? April 1951, Sherman MSS. The latter document cites JCS 2118/16, 5 February 1951. Also, Sherman to SecNav, 21 February and 10 April 1951, and JCS DM-87–51, 31 May 1951, Sherman MSS. The latter document is the originally classified parts of Sherman's testimony in the May 1951 hearings on the relief of MacArthur.
63. Entries, 19, 20, 23, 24, and 28 March 1951; and Rees, *Korea*, pp. 208–11.
64. Entries, 2 to 8 April 1951, Sherman Memorandum, and Bradley's statement, JCS meeting, 23 April 1951, Sherman MSS.
65. Entry, 8 April 1951, Sherman Memorandum, Sherman MSS.
66. Entries, 8 and 11 April 1951, Sherman Memorandum, Bradley, statement to JCS meeting, 23 April 1951, and Bradley to JCS, No. 71321, 16 May 1951, Sherman MSS.
67. Evelyn Peyton Gordon, "About MacArthur—And Nobody in Washington Talks About Anything Else," *Washington News*, 18 April 1951.
68. Copy, Sherman testimony in MacArthur hearings, Sherman, MSS. *See* note 46.
69. Entries, CNO Appointments Log: 24 March to 1 August 1951; DM–87–51, JCS meeting, 31 May 1951; news clippings, including editorial, *Los Angeles Times*, 1 June 1951 ; letters of congratulations, including Senator Harry F. Byrd to Sherman, 31 May 1951; all in Sherman MSS. Byrd wrote, "I was with a group of senators at the luncheon table today and all agreed that your testimony was the best yet given." Also, David S. McLellan, *Dean Acheson: The State Department Years* (New York: Dodd, Mead, 1976), pp. 315–16; and Rees, *Korea*, pp 275–83.

70. JCS to Radford, 1 June 1951, msg 92847, Sherman MSS; and Speech, Sherman before the Pendennis Club, Louisville, Kentucky, 19 May 1951, in *New York Times*, 20 May 1951.
71. Entries, CNO Appointments Log: 24 March to 1 August 1951, Sherman MSS; Rees, *Korea*, pp. 262–63, 284–85; Conolly to Sherman, 17 August 1950, Sherman to Conolly 10 July and 26 August 1950, and Sherman to Captain George W. Anderson, Jr., 3 May 1951, Sherman MSS; and *New York Times*, 20 February 1951.
72. Sherman to Conolly, 16 October 1950, and Sherman to Anderson, 22 June 1951, Sherman MSS; and *Current Biography, 1951*, pp. 98, 196.
73. Carney to Admiral Sir George Creasy, RN (vice chief of naval staff), 25 February 1951, Sherman to Anderson, 5 May 1951, Carney to Eisenhower and Sherman, 8 March 1951, Serial 00097, Carney to Eisenhower, 8 March 1951 (no serial), Carney to Sherman, 30 March 1951, and Sherman to Carney, 10 May 1951, Sherman MSS.
74. *Ibid.*
75. Carney to Sherman, 7 July 1951, Sherman to Carney, 7 July 1951, and Sherman to Eisenhower, 3 July 1951, Sherman MSS.
76. Acheson to Marshall, 1 May 1951, Griffis to Sherman, 26 April 1951, Assistant Secretary of State (European Affairs) George W. Perkins to Sherman, 21 May 1951, Ambassador Walter S. Gifford to Acheson, 8 July 1951, and DM–89–51, JCS meeting, 31 May 1951, Sherman MSS; *London Daily Mail*, 23 July 1951; and *Manchester Union Leader*, 25 July 1951.
77. Chief, Bureau of Medicine and Surgery, to Sherman, 30 October 1950, Sherman MSS. Sherman was examined on 11 October 1950. Also, *Spokane Spokesman Review*, 24 July 1951.
78. Memorandum of conversation, Sherman with Franco, 16 July 1951, and Sherman to JCS, 17 July 1951, Sherman MSS.
79. Commander Richard G. Colbert (special assistant to the CNO) to Admiral Lynde D. McCormick, 25 July 1951, Carney, Record of Conference Held in Naples on 21 July between Admirals Carney and Sherman, Major Sherman A. Smith, USMC (personal aide to the CNO) to McCormick, "Sequence of events leading up to and immediately following the death of Admiral Forrest P. Sherman . . . ," 27 July 1951, Sherman MSS. The first attack was angina pectoris, the second a coronary thrombosis.
80. *London Daily Telegraph & Morning Post*, 23 July 1951; *London Daily Mail*, 23 July 1951; *Time*, 30 July 1951; *Oakland Tribune*, 27 July 1951; *Washington Post*, 20 June 1951, *Washington Star*, 29 May 1951: *Detroit News*, 24 July 1951; *Portland Oregonian*, 24 July 1951; and *Muncie Press*, 24 July 1951.

WILLIAM M. FECHTELER

1. *The Lucky Bag*, 1916, p. 152; and *Army-Navy-Air Force Register*, 11 August 1951, p. 9.
2. Fechteler, OH, Columbia University.
3. *Generals of the Army and Air Force and Admirals of the Navy*, Vol. 3, May 1955, pp. 14–15; and *Register*, 4 August 1951, pp. 1, 23.
4. Fechteler OH, pp. 53–54.
5. *Register*, 4 August 1951, pp. 1, 23.
6. *Ibid.*; Fechteler OH, pp. 64–66; *New York Times*, 2 August 1951; *Register*, 11 August 1951, p. 5; and U.S. Congress, *Congressional Record*, 82d Cong., 1st Sess., Vol. 97, Part 7, p. 9717.

7. *U.S. News and World Report*, 10 August 1951, p. 49.
8. Fechteler OH, pp. 53, 88.
9. *Ibid.*, p. 75.
10. *Ibid.*, p. 100; *New York Times*, 10 May 1952; *Time*, 26 May 1952, p. 47; and *USNIP*, September 1950.
11. U.S. Congress, Senate, Committee on Armed Services, *Hearings, Task Force of the Preparedness Subcommittee (Incentive Pay and Overseas Allowances)*, 82d Cong., 2d Sess., pp. 23–26; U.S. Congress, House, Committee on Armed Services, *Hearings, Sundry Legislation Affecting the Naval and Military Establishments*, 83d Cong., 1st Sess., p. 846; and *Register*, 23 May 1953, pp. 1, 7.
12. U.S. Department of the Navy, Office of the Chief of Naval Operations, *History of Administrative Problems, Korean War* (n.p., n.d.), Vol. 2, pp. IV-1.
13. *New York Times*, 5 July 1967; Fechteler OH, pp. 98–99; U.S. Congress, House, Subcommittee of the Committee on Appropriations, *Hearings, Department of the Navy Appropriation, 1954*, 83d Cong., 1st Sess., pp. 1–99.
14. *Register*, 12 July 1952; *Our Navy*, mid-August 1952, p. 6; and Fechteler OH, pp. 105–20.
15. *New York Times*, 14 and 15 May 1953; *Navy Times*, 16 May 1953; and *Register*, 16 May 1953, pp. 1, 23.
16. Fechteler OH, pp. 123–29; *Our Navy*, mid-May 1952, p. 24; *All Hands*, August 1953, p. 39; and *Navy Times*, 22 August 1953, p. 4.
17. Fechteler OH, pp. 132–35, 174, 265; and *USNIP*, October 1952, pp. 1123–24.

ROBERT B. CARNEY

1. Biographical data on Carney from NHC; and Interview, author with Carney, 3 May 1978, Washington, D.C.
2. Glenn Snyder, "The New Look of 1953," in Thomas Schilling, et al., eds., *Strategy, Policy, and Defense Budgets* (New York: Columbia University Press, 1962).
3. *Congressional Record*, 83d Cong., 2d Sess., Part 2, p. 1885.
4. Snyder, "New Look," p. 442.
5. Paul Y. Hammond, *Organizing for Defense* (Princeton, N.J.: Princeton University Press, 1961), pp. 333–34.
6. Snyder, "New Look," p. 510.
7. Hanson W. Baldwin OH, NI, p. 454.
8. U.S. Department of Defense, *Statements by Secretaries and Chiefs of Staff, Congressional Committees* (Washington, D.C.: GPO, 1955), p. 38.
9. *Ibid.*, p. 50.
10. Edwin B. Hooper, et al., *United States Navy and the Vietnam Conflict*, Vol. I: *The Setting of the Stage to 1959* (? vols.; Washington, D.C.: GPO, 1976–?), p. 230.
11. *Ibid.*, p. 258.
12. *Ibid.*, p. 235.
13. *Ibid.*, p. 236.
14. *Ibid.*, p. 247.
15. *Ibid.*, pp. 243–49.
16. *Ibid.*, p. 253.
17. *Ibid.*, pp. 256–69.
18. *Ibid.*, p. 272.
19. Davis, *Admiral's Lobby*, p. 184.

20. *Ibid.*
21. CNO Instruction 5430.3, 23 February 1955, NHC.
22. Interview, author with Carney, 3 May 1978, Washington, D.C.
23. *Ibid.*
24. *Ibid.*
25. Just before he retired, Carney was preparing his statutory report to the president. Wilson asked Carney not to leak his report to the press, as Ridgway had done. Carney replied, "No, I'm not even going to leak it to you."
26. Robert B. Carney, "The Role of the Navy in Future War," *NWCR*, June 1954.
27. Townsend Hoopes, *The Devil and John Foster Dulles* (Boston: Little, Brown, 1973), p. 267.
28. Dwight D. Eisenhower, *Mandate for Change, 1953–56* (New York: Doubleday, 1963), p. 472.
29. Peter Lyon, *Eisenhower: Portrait of a Hero* (Boston: Little, Brown, 1973), p. 640.
30. Interview, author with Carney, 3 May 1978, Washington, D.C.
31. Lyon, *Eisenhower*, p. 462.
32. James M. Gavin, *War and Peace in the Space Age* (New York: Harpers, 1958), p. 155.
33. Address text, Robert B. Carney, "The Foundations of Future Navy Planning," Naval War College, 13 September 1949, NWCA.

ARLEIGH A. BURKE

1. The author would like to acknowledge the considerable assistance of the following individuals: Admiral Arleigh A. Burke, USN (Ret.); Vice Admiral William I. Martin, USN (Ret.); Vice Admiral Thomas Weschler, USN (Ret.); Rear Admiral George H. Miller, USN (Ret.); Captain Lionel Krisel, USN (Ret.); Mr. John P. Coyle; Dr. Dean C. Allard; Mrs. Jeannette Koontz; and Ms. Deborah L. Haines. Burke, "Memorandum for Record," n.d., Subject: Trip to Washington, 10 May [1955], in black notebook marked "Return to Op-oo's Office," pp. 1–23, and "Transcript of interview with Admiral Robert B. Carney by Stan Smith," n.d. (c. 1965), both in Arleigh A. Burke MSS, NHC; and Interview, author with Burke, Washington, D.C., 4 January 1978.
2. Interview, author with Mrs. Ruth [Burke] Weaver and Mr. Victor G. Burke, Boulder, Colorado, 22 October 1978; Interview, author with Arleigh Burke, Washington, D.C., 31 October 1978; *Boulder* [Colorado] *Daily Camera*, 13 August 1955, p. 3.
3. Burke to author, January 1973, p. 43. For a more complete discussion of Burke's early life and career, *see* David Alan Rosenberg, "Officer Development in the Interwar Navy; Arleigh Burke—The Making of a Naval Professional, 1919–1940," *Pacific Historical Review*, November 1975, pp. 503–26.
4. U.S. Department of the Navy, *Annual Report of the Secretary of the Navy, 1923* (Washington, D.C.: GPO, 1923), p. 596.
5. Fitness Report on Lieutenant Commander A.A. Burke, 1 October 1939–9 May 1940, by Captain F.E.M. Whiting, Burke MSS.
6. Burke to Whiting, 6 December 1946, Personal File (PF), Burke MSS.
7. Burke to Chief, Bureau of Navigation, 8 December 1941, PF, Burke MSS; and transcript of taped narrative by Commodore Arleigh A. Burke, USN, 31 July 1945, on Destroyers, South Pacific, Film No. 441, p. 1, Burke MSS.

8. Transcript of narrative, 31 July 1945, pp. 7–14; *see also* E.B. Potter and Chester W. Nimitz, eds., *Sea Power, A Naval History* (Englewood Cliffs, N.J.: Prentice-Hall, 1960), p. 721*n*.
9. Ken Jones, *Destroyer Squadron Twenty Three* (Philadelphia: Chilton Books, 1959); Ken Jones and Hubert Kelley, Jr., *Admiral Arleigh (31-Knot) Burke, the Story of a Fighting Sailor* (Philadelphia: Chilton Books, 1962), pp. 93–110; Samuel Eliot Morison, *History of United States Naval Operations in World War II*, Vol. VII: *Breaking the Bismarcks Barrier, July 1942–May 1944* (15 vols.; Boston: Little, Brown, 1950), pp. 305–22, 352–59; Fletcher Pratt, *Night Work, The Story of Task Force 39* (New York: Henry Holland, 1946), pp. 181–256; and the four transcripts of narratives by Burke, 31 July–8 August 1945, Film Nos. 411 to 411-III, Burke MSS. Pratt provides the only full published story of how the nickname "Little Beavers" was chosen. "Little Beaver" was a small, pot-bellied Indian boy who was cowboy Red Ryder's constant companion in the popular newspaper comic strip "Red Ryder," drawn by Colorado cartoonist Fred Harmon. Coloradoan Burke, who followed Harmon's strip, noted that his destroyers were "the Little Beavers for those cruisers" of Task Force 39, and decided so to name his squadron. Pratt, *Night Work*, 185-86.
10. For a complete description of these battles, *see* United States Fleet, Headquarters of the Commander in Chief, Secret Information Bulletin No. 14, Battle Experience, Naval Operations, South and Southwest Pacific Ocean Areas, 6 October–2 November 1943, and Secret Information Bulletin No. 16, Battle Experience, Battle of Cape St. George, New Ireland, 24–25 November 1943. Both are compendia of the original action reports. Copies may be found in the Naval War College Library and NHC. *See also* Morison, *Breaking the Bismarcks Barrier*, p. 358, for the comment by Naval War College president Vice Admiral William S. Pye.
11. Burke to Rear Admiral J. L. Kauffman, 24 May 1944, PF, Burke MSS. For Burke's wartime service with Mitscher, *see* Arleigh Burke, "Admiral Marc Mitscher, A Naval Aviator," *USNIP*, April 1975, pp. 54–63; Theodore Taylor, *The Magnificant Mitscher* (New York; W.W. Norton, 1954); and the four transcripts of narrative by Burke, 20 and 21 August 1945, Film Nos. 417 to 417-3, Burke MSS.
12. Burke to Kauffman, 12 August 1944, and Mitscher to Chief of Naval Personnel, Serial No. 334, 22 June 1945, PF, Burke MSS.
13. Fitness Report on Commodore A. A. Burke, 1 March–6 July 1945, by Mitscher, Burke MSS.
14. Burke entry in *Your 25th Reunion Class Record* (Annapolis: Privately Printed, 1948), p. 40, Class of 1923 Folder, PF, Burke MSS; and Jones and Kelley, *31-Knot Burke*, pp. 136–45.
15. Burke, "Admiral Marc Mitscher," pp. 62–63.
16. Burke to Mitscher, 15 January 1947, Subject; Naval Policy, PF, Burke MSS.
17. Forrestal to Real Admiral J. Foskett, 6 February 1947, attached to W.R. Smedberg to Burke, n.d., [c. February 1947], PF, Burke MSS.
18. The full range of matters Burke dealt with on the General Board may be found in a series of working folders labeled "General Board, 1947–1948," PF, Burke MSS.
19. "National Security and Navy Contributions Thereto, A Study by the General Board," 25 June 1948, GB 425, Serial 315, GB Folder, Enclosure (D) 6–7, Covering Letter 4, PF, Burke MSS. For reactions to this study, *see in particular* C.A. Buchanan to Forrestal, 4 June 1948, Folder CD 23-1-10, Records of the Office of the Secretary of Defense, RG 330, NA.

20. Walter Millis and Eugene Duffield, eds., *The Forrestal Diaries* (New York: Viking Press, 1951), p. 450.
21. Chief of Naval Operations to All Bureaus, Boards and Offices, Navy Department, and Headquarters, Marine Corps, Serial 1P23, 23 December 1948, Subject: Organizational Research and Policy Division; Establishment of as Op-23, PF, Burke MSS.
22. Lieutenant Commander R.T. Swenson, Memorandum for Record, 22 June 1949, Subject: Notes on First Meeting of the Under Secretary's Task Force, Folder A1/Chronology, Section III, Papers of the Organizational Research and Policy Division (Op-23), NHC. *See also* draft paper "A History of the Investigation of the B-36," n.d. [c. November 1, 1949], PF, Burke MSS.
23. U.S. Congress, House, Committee on Armed Services, Hearings: *The National Defense Program: Unification and Strategy,* 81st Cong., 1st Sess., pp. 255–72. *See also* set of papers dealing with major issues in the unification and strategy hearings in B-9 Agenda Manual Folder, and the short paper "Points to Prove in Testimony," n.d. [c. October 1, 1949] in C-1, Briefing of Witnesses Folder, both in Section III, Op-23 Papers, NHC.
24. Interview, Stan Smith with Admiral Robert B. Carney, Burke MSS; and Fitness Reports on Burke for period 1945–1949 by Vice Admiral Marc A. Mitscher, Admiral W.H.P. Blandy, Vice Admiral Charles H. McMorris, and Rear Admiral Charles Wellborn, Burke MSS.
25. Burke's removal from the flag selection list was covered in detail in front-page articles in, among other papers, *The Washington Star,* 16 December 1949, *The New York Herald Tribune,* 13 December 1949, and *The New York Times,* 16 December 1949, while strong protests against the action were registered by columnist David Lawrence in *The Washington Star,* 16 December 1949, and later columns, and in editorials in Washington papers and the *Christian Science Monitor.* The story of Burke's reinstatement on the selection list is based on information in Admiral Robert L. Dennison (former naval aide to President Harry S. Truman) OH, Harry S. Truman Library, Independence, Missouri, pp. 136–38, and on a comparison of the information in that oral history with President Truman's appointments between 1 December and 30 December 1949. Truman's schedules are in the President's Secretary's File, Harry S. Truman Library. For the reaction to Burke's reinstatement, *see* front-page headlines in *The Washington Post, Washington Daily News,* and *Washington Times Herald* for 30 December 1949.
26. For a discussion of Burke's feelings on retirement and on the need for politically aware officers, *see* Burke to Radford, 21 December 1949, and Burke to Alvin Herzig, 9 November 1949, PF, Burke MSS. *See also* Vincent Davis, *The Admirals' Lobby* (Chapel Hill: University of North Carolina Press, 1967), pp. 286–303.
27. James E. Auer, *The Postwar Rearmament of Japanese Maritime Forces, 1945–1971* (New York: Praeger, 1973), pp. 63–83, and Burke's foreword to the book, pp. vii–viii.
28. Burke to Mrs. A. A. Burke, 27 July 1951, PF, Burke MSS. For a detailed look into the problems and frustrations that Burke faced while serving on the truce delegation, *see* Allen E. Goodman, *Negotiating While Fighting: The Diary of Admiral C. Turner Joy at the Korean Armistice Conference* (Stanford, Calif.: Hoover Institution Press, 1978), pp. 11–111.
29. Burke to Mrs. Burke, 20 November 1951, PF, Burke MSS.
30. Burke to Captain C. D. Griffin, 8 October 1951, PF, Burke MSS.

31. Burke's meeting with Truman is described in Burke to Joy, 17 December 1951, PF, Burke MSS.
32. For examples of Burke's work as director of the Strategic Plans Division, *see* Memorandum, Op-30 to Op-30B, Op-30C, Branch Heads, Op-30, 19 February 1953, Subject: Naval Strategic Planning, A-1 Plans, Programs, Developments, 1953 Folder, Papers of the Strategic Plans Division (Op-30/60), NHC; JCS 2101/76, 28 October 1952, (an Op-30 paper prepared for the Joint Chiefs of Staff on "Re-examination of Programs for National Security"), CCS 381, U.S. (1–31–50), Sec. 21, Records of the JCS, RG 218, NA. For Burke's efforts to reorient attention to the Pacific, *see* Burke to Joy, 19 December 1951, PF, Burke MSS.
33. JCS 2101/112, 7 December 1953, CCS 381, U.S. (1–31–50), Sec. 31, RG 218, NA. This is an Op-30 paper, evidently written by Burke as a critique of the newly evolved Eisenhower defense policy of "Massive Retaliation."
34. Interview, Stan Smith with Carney, Burke MSS.
35. Burke Memorandum for the Record, Trip to Washington, 10 May 1955, pp. 42–59, Burke MSS.
36. Interview, author with Burke, 4 January 1978; and interview, author with Vice Admiral Thomas R. Weschler (personal aide to Burke, 1955–1957), Newport, R.I., 28 April 1978.
37. Interview, author with Vice Admiral William I. Martin (executive aide to Burke, 1956-1957), Mt. Vernon, Va., 7 November 1978; and interview, author with Weschler, 21 April 1978. *See also* Burke to Admiral Jerauld Wright, 8 August 1955 and 23 January 1956, Burke to Admiral W.M. Fechteler, 10 September 1955 and 24 January 1956, and Burke to Rear Admiral George W. Anderson, 5 January 1956, all in Chief of Naval Operations Personal File (hereafter cited as CPF), Burke MSS.
38. Interview, author with Martin, 7 November 1978; and Admiral J. J. "Jocko" Clark, "31-Knot Burke," *Flying*, (January 1956, pp. 22–23, 53, 54, 56.
39. Interview, author with Burke, 4 January 1978; and Burke OH, NI, pp. 25–27.
40. Daily Record, 19 August 1955, in black notebook marked "Return to Op-00's Office," Burke MSS; Burke OH, NI, pp. 28–34; and Interview, author with Burke, Washington, D.C., 31 October 1978.
41. This overview of the U.S. Navy in 1955 is drawn from the following sources: Chief of Naval Operations Report to the Secretary of the Navy, Fiscal Year 1955, Post 1946 Command File, NHC; JSPC 851/134, 18 January 1955, (Report by Joint Strategic Plans Committee on Command and Organizational Structure of U.S. Forces: Forces and Manning Levels), CCS 370 (8–19–45), Sec. 49, RG 218, NA; and *Semiannual Report of the Secretary of the Navy, January 1 to June 30, 1956* (Washington, D.C.: GPO, 1957), (hereafter *SecNav Report* with appropriate date), pp. 163–71.
42. In addition to the sources cited above, *see* David Alan Rosenberg, "The Search for Maturity in American Postwar Air Doctrine and Organization: The Navy Experience," in Alfred F. Hurley and Robert C. Ehrhart, eds., *Air Power and Warfare: The Proceedings of the Eighth Military History Symposium, U.S. Air Force Academy, 18–20 October 1978* (Washington D.C.: GPO, 1979); Director, Long Range Objectives Group to Distribution List, Serial 007P93, 18 May 1955, forwarding Second Interim Report on Long Range Shipbuilding Plans and Programs, L1-1 Folder, 1955, Strategic Plans Division Files, NHC; and Norman Polmar, "Building the United States Fleet, 1947–1967," in J. L. Moulton, et al., eds., *Brassey's Annual, The Armed Forces Yearbook 1966* (New York: Praeger, 1966), pp. 68–81.

43. Estimate of the Situation in NSC 5602, Basic National Security Policy, 8 February 1956, National Security Council Papers File, Modern Military Branch, NA; Burke to Nimitz, 11 February 1956; Burke to Rear Admiral J. C. Daniel, 18 March 1956; and Commander in Chief, Atlantic, to CNO, Serial 00667, 12 September 1956, Post 1956 Command File, NHC.
44. Richard G. Hewlett and Francis Duncan, *Nuclear Navy, 1946–1962* (Chicago: University of Chicago Press, 1974), pp. 220–25, 259–60, 265–67.
45. For general overviews on Burke and his role in the development of a sea-based IRBM, *see* Hewlett and Duncan, *Nuclear Navy*, pp. 223, 266–67; James R. Killian, Jr., *Sputniks, Scientists and Eisenhower* (Cambridge: Harvard University Press, 1972), pp. 14–41; Vincent Davis, *The Politics of Innovation: Pattern in Navy Cases* (Denver, Colo.: University of Denver, 1967), pp. 31–41; and Harvey M. Sapolsky, *The Polaris System Development, Bureaucratic and Programmatic Success in Government* (Cambridge: Harvard University Press, 1972), pp. 14–41.
46. Rear Admiral J. H. Sides, Director, Guided Missiles Division, to CNO, Serial 00266P31, 7 October 1955, with first endorsement by Vice Admiral Thomas S. Combs, Deputy CNO (Air) Serial 009P05, 11 October 1955, and second endorsement by Vice Admiral R. P. Briscoe, Deputy CNO (Fleet Operations and Readiness), Serial 0076P03, 14 October 1955, in Ballistic Missiles to 1955 Folder, Box 66, Guided Missiles Division (hereafter Op-51 Papers), Accession No. 38–76–81, Washington National Records Center (hereafter WNRC), Suitland, Maryland.
47. Interview, author with Burke, Washington D.C., 12 December 1975; Interview, author with Weschler; Burke to H. H. Porter, Applied Physics Laboratory, Johns Hopkins University, 26 September 1955, and Burke to Sam P. Ingram, General Electric Company, Electronics Division, Syracuse, N.Y., 17 October 1955, both in CPF, Burke MSS.
48. Burke to Admiral D. B. Duncan, 19 October 1955, "Ballistic Missiles—to December 1955" Folder, Box 66, OP-51 Papers, WNRC; *See also* Daily Record, 10 to 11 July 1955 in black notebook marked "Return to Op-00's office," Burke MSS; Commander Ted Wilbur, "Rocket Politics—and Robert F. Freitag," *Space and the United States Navy*, a special issue of *Naval Aviation News* (Washington, D.C.: GPO, November 1970), pp. 53–58; and Burke to Porter, 26 September 1955, PF, Burke MSS.
49. Hewlett and Duncan, *Nuclear Navy*, p. 266; Sapolsky, *Polaris System Development*, pp. 23–26. *See also* pamphlet "Polaris Chronology, History of the Fleet Ballistic Missile Weapon System Development Program, 1955–1963" (Washington, D.C.: Special Projects Office, Department of the Navy, 1963), pp. 1–2.
50. "Polaris Chronology," pp. 2–3; Information on NAVWAG 1, "The Introduction of the Fleet Ballistic Missile into Service," January 1957, is taken from author's Interview with John P. Coyle, author of NAVWAG 1, and authority on U.S. Navy strategic missile systems, Washington, D.C., 29 March 1978, and from Norman C. Polmar, *History of the US-USSR Strategic Arms Competition, Supporting Study: U.S. Strategic Missile Submarines, Part III, the Ascendancy of Submarine Launched Missiles (1955–1972)* (Falls Church, Va: Lulejian and Associates, Inc., Contract No. N00014–75–C–0237 for Deputy Chief of Naval Operations [Plans and Policy], October 1975). pp. 13–14.
51. Burke, Memorandum for Record, n.d., Subject: Trip to Washington, 10 May [1955], pp. 44–51 (covering meeting with President Eisenhower, 17 May 1955; JCS Policy Memo 84, Joint Program for Planning, 27 July 1955, CCS 381 (11–29–49),

Sec. 24, RG 218, NA; and Interview, author with Weschler, 21 April 1978. For an example of the time Burke allotted to JCS business, *see* Schedule, 17 August–15 September 1956, in CPF, Burke MSS.

52. Information on Eisenhower's Basic National Security Policy is derived from the following three consecutive statements of that policy: NSC 162/2, 30 October 1953; NSC 5501, 6 January 1955; and NSC 5602/1, 15 March 1956, all in the NSC Papers File, Modern Military Branch, NA; from Douglas Kinnard, *President Eisenhower and Strategy Management, A Study in Defense Politics* (Lexington: University of Kentucky Press, 1977), pp. 1–36; and from Maxwell D. Taylor, *The Uncertain Trumpet* (New York: Harper and Brothers, 1960), pp. 11–46.
53. Taylor, *The Uncertain Trumpet*, pp. 36–42; Kinnard, *President Eisenhower and Strategy Management*, pp. 54–57; and JCS 2143/56, 12 April 1956 (Memo by Taylor to the JCS on the development of the JSOP for July 1960), and JCS Decision on JCS 2143/56, 17 April 1956, CCS 381 (11–29–49), Sec. 30, RG 218, NA.
54. JCS 2101/112, 7 December 1953, CCS 381, U.S. (1–31–50), Sec. 31, RG 218, NA.
55. Interview, author with Burke, Washington D.C., November 1978.
56. Captain Richard H. Phillips, Memo for Joint Strategic Plans Committee et al., SM 423–56, 23 May 1956, enclosing Strategic Concepts for General War and for Cold War or Military Conflicts Short of General War for JSOP for 1 July 1960, CCS 381 (11–29–49), Sec. 30, RG 218, NA. *See also* Colonel R. D. Wentworth, USA, Memo for Commander in Chief, Atlantic, et al., SM-763–56, 19 September 1956, Subject: Atomic Support of Allied Forces, CCS 381 (1–31–50), Sec. 66, RG 218, NA.
57. U.S. Congress, Senate, Hearings before the Subcommittee on the Air Force of the Committee on Armed Services, *Study of Air Power*, 85th Cong., 1st Sess., Part XVIII, p. 1341.
58. CNO to SecDef, Subject: 1958 New Obligational Authority, Navy, Serial 012P00, 6 November 1956, Originator's File (OF), Burke MSS. This paper was well circulated. Copies are also in Folder L1, SecNav Papers, 1956, Box 3, Accession No. N59-1443, WNRC.
59. Burke to Vice Admiral C. R. "Cat" Brown, Commander, Sixth Fleet, 22 August 1956, OF, Burke MSS; Dwight D. Eisenhower, *The White House Years, Waging Peace, 1956–1961* (Garden City, N.Y.: Doubleday, 1965), p. 40. *See also* Burke to Admiral W. F. Boone, Commander in Chief, U.S. Naval Forces, Eastern Atlantic and Mediterranean, 2 August 1956, CPF, Burke MSS.
60. Burke OH, pp. 13–15, John Foster Dulles Oral History Project, Princeton University Library.
61. This exchange of messages is described in *New York Times*, 15 November 1956, pt. 4, p. 1, and Admiral Arleigh Burke, "The Lebanon Crisis," in Lieutenant Arnold R. Shapach, ed., *Proceedings, United States Naval Academy: Naval History Symposium* (Annapolis, Md.: USNA, 1973), p. 90.
62. Burke to Vice Admiral Friedrich Ruge, FGN, 14 November 1956, CPF, Burke MSS. For a description of naval operations in connection with the Suez crisis, *see* Richard K. Smith, *Cold War Navy* (Falls Church, Lulejian and Associates, Inc., Contract N00014–75-C1001 for Chief of Information, U.S. Navy, March 1976), Ch. 13.
63. This was an exercise known as "Project Budapest." Interview, author with John P. Coyle, 29 March 1978.
64. Burke, Memo for Self (Eyes Only), Op-00/jjb, 15 March 1957, Subject: Reappointment as CNO, OF, Burke MSS.

65. "Polaris Chronology," pp. 4–5; and Hewlett and Duncan, *Nuclear Navy,* pp. 300–11. On Burke's Pacific tour, *see* Harold H. Martin, "On the Prowl with '31 Knot' Burke," *Saturday Evening Post,* 18 January 1958, pp. 36–37, 86–88.
66. Hewlett and Duncan, *Nuclear Navy,* p. 313; "Deterrence and Survival in the Nuclear Age." Report to the President by the Security Resources panel of the Science Advisory Committee, 7 November 1957. Printed for the use of the Joint Committee on Defense Production, 94th Cong., 2nd Sess. (Washington, D.C.: GPO, 1976).
67. "Polaris Chronology," pp. 5–6; Hewlett and Duncan, *Nuclear Navy,* p. 314; Polmar, *U.S. Strategic Missile Submarines, Part III,* pp. 22–29; Burke to Vice Admiral Frank T. Watkins, Commander, Antisubmarine Defense Force, Atlantic Fleet, 16 January 1958, CPF, Burke MSS.
68. Burke Memo to Op-31, Subject: Urgency for Improvements in ASW, Op-00 Memo 000677–57, 11 December 1957; Burke, Memo for the Record, Subject: Russian General War Capabilities, Op-00 Memo 0021–58, 13 January 1958; R. L. Shifley, Memo to Burke, 20 February 1958, with Burke's comment thereon, all in OF, Burke MSS; *SecNav Report, January 1 to June 30, 1958,* pp. 214–16; Gordon Swanborough and Peter M. Bowers, *United States Navy Aircraft Since* 1911 (New York: Funk and Wagnalls, 1968), pp. 268–69, 352–53; and "Meeting the Soviet Submarine Threat" in Tom Compere, ed., *The Navy Blue Book* (Indianapolis, Ind.: Bobbs Merrill, 1960), pp. 28–32.
69. L. M. Mustin (Op-001) to Op-60, Subject: Estimated Capabilities of USN Antisubmarine Forces, Serial 00101–61, 17 August 1961, copy courtesy of Norman C. Polmar.
70. Burke to Rear Admiral Walter G. Schindler, 14 May 1958, CPF, Burke MSS. This 22-page letter is a succinct statement of Burke's—and the navy's—philosophy of command. *See also* Burke, address before the National Press Club, Washington, D.C., 6 January 1958, reported in *New York Times,* 7 January 1958.
71. Eisenhower, *Waging Peace,* pp. 244–53; and John C. Ries, *The Management of Defense, Organization and Control of the U.S. Armed Forces,* (Baltimore, Md.: The Johns Hopkins University Press, 1964), pp. 167–88.
72. Burke testimony, 30 April 1958, U.S. Congress, House, Committee on Armed Services, *Hearings on Sundry Legislation Affecting the Naval and Military Establishments, 1958,* 85th Cong., 2nd Sess., p. 6347.
73. Burke to Captain George H. Miller, 10 July 1958, describes the "rebuke" incident in detail. Copy of the letter courtesy of Rear Admiral Miller. *See also* Burke to Vice Admiral Austin K. Doyle, 8 July 1958, CPF, Burke MSS; Eisenhower, *Waging Peace,* p. 250; and Burke to Miller, 19 April 1958, copy courtesy of Admiral Miller.
74. Burke, "The Lebanon Crisis," p. 74; and Smith, *Cold War Navy,* Ch. 14.
75. Burke, "The Lebanon Crisis," pp. 74–80; and Smith, *Cold War Navy,* Ch. 15. *See also* Eisenhower, *Waging Peace,* pp. 262–91.
76. Burke, "The Lebanon Crisis," p. 73.
77. On the Taiwan Strait crisis, *see in particular,* M. H. Halperin, *The 1958 Taiwan Straits Crisis: A Documentary History* (Rand Corporation Research Memorandum RM-4900-ISA, December 1966 Top Secret Study, Sanitized and Declassified, 18 March 1975), copy courtesy of the Center for National Security Studies, Washington, D.C.; Eisenhower, *Waging Peace,* pp. 292–304; Jonathan Trumbull Howe, *Multicrises, Sea Power and Global Politics in the Missile Age* (Cambridge, Mass.; MIT Press, 1971), pp. 161–282; and Smith, *Cold War Navy,* Ch. 16.

78. "The Important Things Are Intangible," Interview, Robert J. Donovan with Burke, 2 October 1958, in *ONI Review*, November 1958, pp. 517–20.
79. Burke to Rear Admiral J. L. Holloway, Jr., 3 October 1958, CPF, Burke MSS. Burke went to great lengths to explain the rationale behind American policy during the Taiwan Strait crisis. *See* two Memoranda for Distribution List by Captain Harvey P. Lanham, Executive Assistant and Senior Aide to the CNO, 3 and 6 October 1958, with CNO papers on Taiwan and "The United States in World Events" appended, respectively, Miscellaneous Folder, Box 94, Op-51 Papers, WNRC.
80. Halperin, *The 1958 Taiwan Straits Crisis*, pp. 109–12, 118–19, 183–92, 199–210; and Burke OH, Princeton University, pp. 23–28.
81. Halperin, *The 1958 Taiwan Straits Crisis*, pp. 256, 258–59, 268–78, 285–88, 294–491; and Smith, *Cold War Navy*, pp. 16–6, 16–15.
82. Taylor, *The Uncertain Trumpet*, pp. 57–65; Townsend Hoopes, *The Devil and John Foster Dulles* (Boston: Little, Brown, 1973),pp. 425–30. *See also* Memo, Rear Admiral Roy L. Johnson to Director, Strategic Plans Division (Op-60), Subject: National Security Policy, Serial 00014P93, 29 October 1958, in A8 (5500) Folder, 1959, Strategic Plans Division Papers, NHC.
83. For a general description of Op-93's role, *see* David A. Rosenberg, "History of Navy Long Range Planning, An Overview," Appendix A to *The Maritime Balance Study, A Strategic Planning Experiment in the Maritime Balance Area* (Washington, D.C.: Office of the CNO, 1979).
84. Rear Admiral Roy L. Johnson, Memo for the Distribution List, Subject: Adaptation of a National Military Posture to the Era of Nuclear Parity, A Suggested Navy Position, Serial 0008P93, 3 December 1957, with paper, same subject, appended, A16–10 Folder, 1957, Strategic Plans Division Papers, NHC.
85. "The Navy of the 1970 Era," study transmitted by CNO to the Distribution List, Serial 04P93, 13 January 1958. Declassified copy in Naval War College Library under call no. NA50.062; Telephone interview, author with Burke, Washington, D.C., 1 December 1974.
86. "Views on Adequacy of U.S. Deterrent/Retaliatory Forces as Related to General and Limited War Capabilities," paper appended to Director, Strategic Plans Division, to Distribution List, Serial 0130P60, 17 June 1959, 3010 Folder, 1959, Strategic Plans Division Papers, NHC; and Burke, Memo to Op-60, Subject: Overemphasis on Large Numbers of High Yield Atomic Weapons, Op-00 Serial 000291–59, 26 June 1959, OF, Burke MSS. *See also* "Adaptation of National Military Posture to the Era of Nuclear Parity" paper, December 1957. On air force strategic nuclear planning, *see* Robert Frank Futrell, *Ideas, Concepts, Doctrine: a History of Basic Thinking in the United States Air Force* (Maxwell Field, Ala.: Aerospace Studies Institute, June 1971), Vol. II, pp. 551–52, 564–67, 570–73.
87. Interview, author with John P. Coyle, 29 March 1978.
88. "Views on Adequacy of U.S. Deterrent/Retaliatory Forces. . . . " Paper, June 1959; Commander Paul H. Backus, "Finite Deterrence, Controlled Retaliation," *USNIP*, March 1959, pp. 23–30; and Futrell, *Ideas, Concepts, Doctrine*, pp. 561–62.
89. Burke, Memo for Op-51, Subject: Study by WSEG of Minuteman, Op-00 Serial 0084–58, 24 February 1958; Burke, Memo for Op-06, Subject: ICBMs in the U.S., Op-00, Serial 000250–59, 3 June 1959, both in OF, Burke MSS; and Director, Long Range Objectives Group, to Distribution List, Subject: The Coming Crisis in Deterrence, Serial 00012P93, 1 August 1958, A16–1 Folder 1958, Strategic Plans

Division Papers, NHC. For Burke's views on maintaining both land- and sea-based deterrent systems, *see* his green-pencil comments on Memo, James S. Russell to Op-00, Subject: "Dependable Striking Power" paper attached, 24 January 1961, as well as Memo, Op-60 to Op-06, 2 February 1961, all in Folder 3060, Military Prepations for National Defense, 1961, Strategic Plans Division Papers, NHC.

90. Burke to SecDef, Serial 012P00, 6 November 1956; Burke to SecNav, Subject: Shipbuilding Programs to Meet Long Range Objectives, Serial 0026P03, 30 April 1958, CPF, AAB, NHC; and "Cancellation or Delay of Guided Missile Programs," 8 January 1958, Guided Missiles General 1958 Folder, Box 98, and Director, Guided Missiles Division, to Chief of Naval Operations, Subject: Regulus II Cancellation, Serial 047851, 19 December 1958, Regulus II Folder, Box 96, both in Op-51 Papers, WNRC.

91. On Burke's interest in the P-6M, see "H Bomb Cannot Wipe Out U.S. Navy, Interview with Admiral Arleigh A. Burke," *U.S. News and World Report,* 4 May 1956, p. 86; and Burke, Memo for Record, Subject: Conversation with Admiral Radford re Attack Seaplane, 20 February 1957, OF, Burke MSS. On the P-6M cancellation, *see* Bill Gunston, "Martin Sea Master," *Aeroplane Monthly,* November 1974, pp. 948–53: and Director, Aviation Plans Division, to Chief of Naval Operations, Subject: P6M Termination, Serial 002024P50, 6 November 1959, in Department of the Navy, P6M Termination Report, 24 August 1959–31 December 1960. Paper courtesy of Floyd D. Kennedy, Jr.

92. Polmar, "Building the United States Fleet, 1947–1967," pp. 72–77; "Active and Reserve Fleet Force Levels, 1908–1973," in Files of Op-965, Extended Planning Branch, Systems Analysis Division, Office of the Chief of Naval Operations; "Toward the Nuclear Fleet," in Tom Compere, ed., *The Navy Blue Book,* pp. 33–37; and "Polaris Chronology," pp. 6–9.

93. Burke OH, NI, pp. 189–207; *See also* Burke, "Remarks," *NWCR,* Winter 1977, pp. 70–73; and "Fred Ruge, My Friend," in *Seemacht und Geschichte, Festschrift zum 80. Geburtstag von Friedrich Ruge* (Bonn, West Germany: Deutsches Marine Institut, 1975), pp. 29–38.

94. Burke, Speech, Chamber of Commerce, Charleston, S.C., 20 February 1959, Burke MSS. For another statement of Burke's thinking on this matter, *see* Bruno Shaw, "Admiral Burke Charts the Challenge," in Compere, ed., *The Navy Blue Book,* pp. 39–45.

95. For an example of the nature of Burke's relationship with Eisenhower, *see* John S. D. Eisenhower, *Strictly Personal* (Garden City, N.Y.: Doubleday, 1974), pp. 200–201; and Burke OH, NI, pp. 34–36, 83–84. On Burke and Dulles, *see* Burke OH, Princeton University, pp. 16–19.

96. Burke OH, NI, pp. 208–9.

97. *Ibid,* p. 210.

98. Polmar, "Building the United States Fleet, 1947–1967," pp. 72–77; *SecNav Report, January 1–June 30, 1958,* pp. 209–18, and *Fiscal Year 1959,* pp. 214–21, 239–45; Raymond V. B. Blackman ed., *Jane's Fighting Ships, 1959–1960* (New York: McGraw Hill, 1959), pp. 348–456; and "Random Recollections of Admiral Arleigh Burke of projects started while he was CNO in which he had some participation," enclosed in Burke to author, 9 April 1970.

99. This evaluation is based on examination of the class years of naval officers in senior positions in the navy in Washington and in the fleet, with the rank of vice admiral and above. Information was taken from the *Register of Commissioned Officers in the*

U.S. Navy and Marine Corps for the years 1955–1959, as well as the regular listings of naval officers in the Office of the CNO and in fleet commands maintained by the Bureau of Naval Personnel.

100. Burke, "Random Recollections," 1970; "The Admiral and the Atom," *Time*, 21 May 1956, p. 32.
101. John G. Hubbell, "Moral Buildup Gives New Strength to the Navy," in Tom Compere, ed., *The Navy Blue Book*, pp. 129–33; *SecNav Reports, Fiscal Year 1961*, pp. 226–27; Fitness Report on Admiral Arleigh Burke, 17 August 1955–1 August 1961, by Secretary of the Navy John B. Connally, Burke MSS.
102. For a discussion of the "Missile Gap" and its impact, *see* Kinnard, *President Eisenhower and Strategy Management*, pp. 66–122; Richard A. Aliano, *American Defense Policy from Eisenhower to Kennedy, The Politics of Changing Military Requirements, 1957–1961* (Athens: Ohio University Press, 1975); and Edgar A. Bottome, *The Missile Gap, A Study of the Formulation of Military and Public Policy* (Cranbury, N.J.: Fairleigh Dickinson University Press, 1970).
103. Norman C. Polmar, *Aircraft Carriers, A Graphic History of Carrier Aviation and its Influence on World Events* (Garden City, N.Y.: Doubleday, 1969), pp. 615–16.
104. George B. Kistiakowsky, *A Scientist at the White House* (Cambridge: Harvard University Press, 1976), pp. 112–13, 127, 157–59, 162, 284–85, details the development of opposition to carriers in the Executive Branch, including Eisenhower's dissatisfaction in October and November 1959. For an example of Burke's arguments in favor of the carrier, *see* his Reclama Statement before the Defense Subcommittee, Senate Appropriations Committee, 11 June 1959, appended to Director, Strategic Plans Division, to Distribution List, Serial 0130P60, 17 June 1959, Folder 3010, 1959, Strategic Plans Division Papers, NHC.
105. Polmar, *U.S. Strategic Missile Submarines, Part III*, pp. 54–57; Paul H. Backus, "In Retrospect: Polaris in the Pentagon" (unpublished article of June 1970, supplied courtesy of John P. Coyle), pp. 34–36; and the March 1960 testimony by Burke and Raborn, in U.S. Congress, House, Committee on Government Operations, *Civil Defense Part III, Relation to Missile Programs*, 86th Cong., 2nd Sess., pp. 184, 196–97.
106. Burke, Memorandum, no subject, no serial, 22 April 1959, OF, Burke MSS; Polmar, *U.S. Strategic Missile Submarines, Part III*, pp. 62–71; and Raborn testimony, *Civil Defense, Part III*, pp. 196–97. The original concept was to put Regulus-II missiles on ships, but this was changed to Polaris following the December 1958 cancellation of Regulus-II. *See* Blackman, ed., *Jane's Fighting Ships, 1959–1960*, pp. 377–79.
107. Hanson W. Baldwin, "Pentagon Bars Navy Plan for Missile Cruiser Fleet," *New York Times*, 31 July 1959, pt. 1, p. 5; Burke to Miller, 22 June 1959, copy courtesy Admiral Miller; Interview, author "Originator's File," with Burke, November 1978.
108. Information on the air force's push to control the operations and targeting of nuclear forces may be found in the declassified sections of the JCS 2056 series from 1950 to 1957, CCS 373.11 (12–14–48), RG 218, NA; Thomas S. Power, *Design for Survival* (New York: Coward-McCann, 1962), pp. 185–87; Futrell, *Ideas, Concepts, Doctrine*, Vol II, pp. 528–29.
109. Burke, Memo for Op-06, Subject: Command of Polaris Submarines, Op-00 Memo 0151–59, 10 April 1959, OF, Burke MSS.
110. L. Edgar Prina, "AF Acts to Strip Navy of Polaris Sub Control," *Washington Star*, 17

April 1959. *See also* Hanson W. Baldwin, "New Role Sought for Submarines," *New York Times,* 17 April 1959.

111. Burke, Memo to All DCNOs, Subject: SAC Control of the FBM, Op-oo Memo 0259–58, 8 December 1958, OF, Burke MSS. *See also* Polmar, *U.S. Strategic Missile Submarines,* III, pp. 38–41.

112. Polmar, *Ibid.*, pp. 42–46.

113. Power, *Design for Survival,* pp. 187–92; and Henry S. Rowen, "Formulating Strategic Doctrine" in *Commission on the Organization of the Government for the Conduct of Foreign Policy, June 1975, Vol. 4, Appendix K: Adequacy of Current Organization: Defense and Arms Control* (Washington D.C.: GPO, 1975), pp. 219–34.

114. Polmar, *U.S. Strategic Missile Submarines, Part III,* pp. 46–48; Burke, Memo for Vice Admiral Smedberg, Subject: Deputy of CinCSAC, Op-oo Memo 0380–60, 10 July 1960, OF, Burke MSS; and Hanson W. Baldwin, "Problems of Command," *New York Times,* 6 August 1960.

115. Rowen, "Formulating Strategic Doctrine," pp. 220–21, 225.

116. Burke, Memo for Admiral Blackburn, Subject: Political Aspects of the SIOP, Op-oo Memo 0653–60, 9 November 1960, OF, Burke MSS; and Interview, author with John P. Coyle, 29 March 1978.

117. Kistiakowsky, *A Scientist at the White House,* pp. 396, 399–400, 405–7, 413–16, 421.

118. *SecNav Report, Fiscal Year 1959,* pp. 209–14, *Fiscal Year 1960,* pp. 233–39, 267–68; *Fiscal Year 1961,* pp. 197–205; Hewlett and Duncan, *Nuclear Navy,* pp. 370–76; Polmar, *Aircraft Carriers,* pp. 616–17; U.S. Congress, Senate, Select Committee to Study Governmental Operations with Respect to Intelligence Activities, *Interim Report: Alleged Assassination Plots Involving Foreign Leaders* (Washington D.C.: GPO, November 1975), pp. 93, 115–16.

119. Burke OH, NI, pp. 13–14, 62–65, 233–34, 239, 243–44; Interview, author with Rear Admiral George H. Miller, Washington, D.C., 31 March 1978; Interview, author with Burke, Washington, D.C., 5 January 1978; Interview, Stan Smith with Commander C.R. Wilhide, n.d. [c. 1964], Burke MSS.

120. Interview, author with Burke, 5 January 1978; Burke OH, NI, pp. 216–18; Burke OH, John F. Kennedy Library, Boston, Mass.

121. Interview, author with Burke, 5 January 1978.

122. *Ibid. See also* Henry L. Trewhitt, *McNamara, His Ordeal in the Pentagon* (New York: Harper and Row, 1971), p. 96.

123. Burke, Memo for the Record, Subject: Record of Clearance of Silver Quill Speech, Op-oo Memo 089–61, 23 February 1961; and Burke, Memo for the Record, Subject: Discussion with the President after JCS Meeting, 23 February 1961, Op-oo Memo 0120–61, 23 February 1961, both in OF, Burke MSS. *See also* U.S. Congress, Senate, Committee on Armed Services, Special Preparedness Subcommittee, *Hearings, Military Cold War Education and Speech Review Policies,* 87th Cong., 2nd Sess., Part 1, pp. 13–26, 144–76, Part 7, pp. 3241–46, and Report, pp. 94–95.

124. Theodore Sorenson, *Kennedy* (New York: Harper and Row, 1965), pp. 603–4; William W. Kaufmann, *The McNamara Strategy* (New York: Harper and Row, 1964), pp. 29–46; Alain C. Enthoven and K. Wayne Smith, *How Much is Enough?* (New York: Harper and Row, 1971), pp. 1–30. The conclusion on naval programs in this paragraph is based on the fact that none of these critical studies of Eisenhower's defense policies indicts the navy for lack of readiness.

125. Enthoven and Smith, *Ibid,* pp. 31–101.

126. Interview, author with Burke, 5 January 1978.
127. Enthoven and Smith, *How Much is Enough?* pp. 16–17; "Record of Actions by the National Security Council at its 475th Meeting, 1 February 1961," NSC Papers File, Modern Military Branch, NA, particularly Action No. 2398; and Interview, author "Originator's File" with Burke, November 1978.
128. U.S. Congress, House, Committee on Armed Services, *Hearings: Military Posture Briefings*, 87th Cong., 1st Sess., pp. 899–901.
129. The statistics for 1979 are taken from "Summary of Major Military Forces," in *USNIP*, May 1979, p. 255. The active fleet was composed of 398 ships, plus 22 fleet auxiliary ships. There were also 41 fleet ballistic-missile submarines, and 59 naval reserve ships.
130. Information on the Bay of Pigs invasion was taken from the following sources: Report of the Cuban Study Group, 13 June 1961, transmitted by letter, Maxwell D. Taylor to the President, 13 June 1961; and the associated sanitized Memorandums for Record of Paramilitary Study Group Meetings, 1961, particularly First Meeting, 23 April 1961; Second Meeting, 24 April 1961 (Parts I and II); Seventh Meeting, 1 May 1961 (testimony of Rear Admiral John Clark, and letter from McGeorge Bundy); Ninth Meeting, 3 May 1961 (testimony of Secretary of Defense McNamara); Tenth Meeting, 4 May 1961 (testimony of Brigadier General David W. Gray); Twelfth Meeting, 8 May 1961 (testimony of General Thomas D. White, General George H. Decker, and General David M. Shoup,); Seventeenth Meeting, 18 May 1961 (testimony of General Lyman L. Lemnitzer), and Eighteenth Meeting, 19 May 1961 (testimony of Admiral Arleigh Burke), all in the Zapata Folder, NSC File, Modern Military Branch, NA. These papers were originally released by the John F. Kennedy Library. *See also* Peter Wyden, *Bay of Pigs, The Untold Story* (New York: Simon and Schuster, 1979); Burke OH, NI, pp. 216–23; and Telephone interview, author with Captain Lionel Krisel, 21 August 1979.
131. Karl E. Meyer and Tad Szulc, *The Cuban Invasion* (New York: Praeger, 1962), pp. 22, 104–5; and Herbert S. Dinerstein, *The Making of a Missile Crisis, October 1962* (Baltimore, Md.: The Johns Hopkins University Press, 1976), p. 101.
132. Wyden, *Bay of Pigs*, pp. 87–92.
133. McNamara testimony, Memo for the Record, Ninth Meeting, 3 May 1961.
134. For the background of the Laos crisis, *see* Charles A. Stevenson, *The End of Nowhere, American Policy Toward Laos Since 1954* (Boston: The Beacon Press, 1973), pp. 72–154; and Arthur M. Schlesinger, Jr., *A Thousand Days, John F. Kennedy in the White House* (Boston: Houghton Mifflin, 1965), pp. 320–42.
135. On Burke and the Laos crisis, *see* Burke to Walter S. Robertson, Assistant Secretary of State for Far Eastern Affairs, 9 December 1958, CPF, Burke MSS; Burke, Paper, "Estimate of the Situation, Laos," 31 December [1960], OF, Burke MSS; and, most important, Burke OH, NI, pp. 164–78.
136. In addition to the sources cited in Note 130, *see* Maxwell D. Taylor, *Swords and Plowshares* (New York: W.W. Norton, 1972), pp. 184–94.
137. Report of the Cuban Study Group, 13 June 1961, Memorandum No. 3, Conclusions, 1–3, and Memorandum No. 4, Relations of the JCS to the President in Cold War Operations, pp. 6–7.
138. Taylor, *Swords and Plowshares*, p. 189; and National Security Action Memorandum No. 55, President Kennedy to the Chairman, JCS, Subject: Relations of the JCS to the President in Cold War Operations, 28 June 1961, in National Security Action Memorandums Folder, NSC Papers File, Modern Military Branch, NA.

139. Interview, author with Burke, 5 January 1978.
140. Interview, author with Burke, 5 January 1978; and Burke OH, Kennedy Library.
141. Information on Burke's postretirement activities is taken from his postretirement resume/autobiography; and Interview, Stan Smith with Burke (Retirement: directorships, public service), n.d. [c. mid-1960s], both in Burke MSS.
142. Arleigh Burke, "Power and Peace," *Orbis*, Summer 1962, pp. 187–204.

GEORGE W. ANDERSON

1. Background information on Anderson's life can be found in *Current Biography*, 1962, pp. 11–13.
2. Arleigh Burke OH, NI.
3. Sources for this essay include author's interviews with: Admiral Anderson, 5 September 1968; Admiral Arleigh A. Burke, 6 September 1968; General George H. Decker, 4 September 1968; Admiral David L. McDonald, 27 August 1968; Wilfrid J. McNeil (former Comptroller, Department of Defense), 13 December 1968; Admiral Arthur W. Radford, 4 September 1968; General Maxwell D. Taylor, 4 September 1968; and General Earle G. Wheeler, 8 October 1971.
4. *Time*, 30 June 1961, p. 77.
5. Author's interviews.
6. *See*, for example, Charles Hitch, *Decision-Making for Defense* (Berkeley: University of California Press, 1966), p. 27.
7. *See*, for example, U.S. Congress, House, Committee on Appropriations, *Hearings on the FY 1965 Defense Budget*, 89th Cong., 2nd Sess., Part IV, pp. 447–95.
8. The best sources on McNamara's decision-making style are Alain Enthoven and K. Wayne Smith, *How Much Is Enough?* (New York: Harper, 1977); William Kaufman, *The McNamara Strategy* (New York: Harper, 1969); and James Roherty, *Decisions of Robert McNamara* (Coral Gables: University of Miami Press, 1970).
9. Anderson's views on civil-military relations were well summarized in two public speeches: "Address," Navy League Convention, San Juan, Puerto Rico, 3 May 1963, and "Address," National Press Club, Washington, D.C., 4 September 1963.
10. "Address," National Press Club.
11. For an analysis of this point, *see* Laurence J. Korb, "Service Unification: Arena of Fears, Hopes and Ironies," *USNIP*, May 1978, pp. 170–83.
12. Author's interviews.
13. U.S. Congress, House, Committee on Armed Services, *Hearings on Military Posture*, 87th Cong., 2nd Sess., pp. 3630–31.
14. For an analysis of this issue from McNamara's perspective, *see* Enthoven and Smith, *How Much Is Enough?*, pp. 243–51.
15. Author's interviews.
16. Author's interviews.
17. For an excellent summary of this issue from the congressional perspective, *see* Edward Kolodiej, *The Uncommon Defense* (Columbus: Ohio State University Press, 1965), pp. 411–17.
18. This discussion is drawn primarily from Enthoven and Smith, *How Much Is Enough?*, pp. 263–66; Robert Art, *The TFX Decision* (Boston: Little, Brown, 1968); and Robert Coulam, *Illusions of Choice* (Princeton: Princeton University Press, 1977).
19. Art, *TFX*, p. 48.
20. Since TFX was a biservice program, there were naval representatives on each of these boards.

21. Art, *TFX*, p. 70.
22. *Ibid.*, p. 73.
23. *Ibid.*, p. 77. Boeing's plane had 61 per cent commonality while that of General Dynamics had 84 per cent.
24. U.S. Congress, Senate, Permanent Subcommittee on Investigations of the Senate Committee on Government Operations, *TFX Contract Investigation*, 88th Cong., 2nd Sess., Part III, p. 781.
25. *Ibid.*, pp. 774–92.
26. This discussion is drawn from Graham Allison, *Essence of Decision* (Boston: Little, Brown, 1971), pp. 127–32; Elie Abel, *The Missile Crisis* (Philadelphia: Lippincott, 1966), pp. 154–56; and Henry Trewhitt, *McNamara* (New York: Harper and Row, 1971), pp. 107–08.
27. There is some dispute about the exact words exchanged by the two men. However, there is no doubt that McNamara and Anderson engaged in a heated exchange.
28. Abel, *Missile Crisis*, p. 156; and Trewhitt, *McNamara*, p. 108.
29. Richard Betts, *Soldiers, Statesmen and Cold War Crises* (Cambridge: Harvard University Press, 1977), p. 71. Betts's sources are two interviews, one with a civilian and one with a military officer.
30. Author's interviews.
31. Elmo Zumwalt, *On Watch* (New York: Quadrangle, 1976), pp. 233, 464.

DAVID L. MCDONALD

1. David L. McDonald, OH, NI, pp. 319–20. This is the primary source for McDonald's pre-CNO years.
2. *Ibid.*, p. 321.
3. *Ibid.*, p. 322.
4. *Ibid.*, p. 6.
5. Shortly after reporting for this duty, McDonald took part in an odd operation for a neutral. A small task force composed of the aircraft carrier *Ranger*, the light cruiser *Savannah*, and some destroyers provided an escort for six U.S. transports loaded with more than 20,000 British troops bound for Calcutta. The *Ranger*, the *Savannah*, and an oiler broke off from the formation just south of the equator and returned home. Eight destroyers continued with the convoy beyond Capetown, where half the escorts turned around for home and the remainder proceeded toward Calcutta. It was upon returning from this operation that McDonald learned of the Pearl Harbor attack. *Ibid.*, pp. 79–80.
6. *Ibid.*, pp. 84, 87, 96.
7. *Ibid.*, pp. 34–35.
8. *Ibid.*, p. 139.
9. *Ibid.*
10. McDonald to author, 12 June 1978.
11. McDonald to author, 27 April 1978.
12. U.S. Department of Defense, *Department of Defense Fact Sheet* (Washington, D.C.: Office of Assistant Secretary of Defense for Public Affairs, February 1971), p. 16. (Hereafter, DOD Fact Sheet.)
13. Mark S. Watson."New Naval Concepts for Nuclear Age, *BuWepsLog*, 10 September 1963. In the files of the Naval Air Systems Command Historian, Washington, D.C.
14. DOD Fact Sheet, p. 17.

15. McDonald OH, p. 316.
16. The A4D-5 (later redesignated A-4E) was a lightweight attack aircraft formerly used by the navy. A later variant of this aircraft, the A-4M, was used by the marine corps.
17. Memorandum from "R to A," "Current Status of the Air Forces' proposed program for the development of a variable geometry fighter/bomber," 3 March 1961. In the F-111 file of the Naval Air Systems Command Historian.
18. McNamara memorandum, 7 June 1961. In the F-111 file of the Historian.
19. Vice Admiral Gerald E. Miller, USN (Ret.), to author 24 May 1978.
20. Gerald E. Miller, "High-Low," *USNIP*, December 1976, pp. 84–85.
21. Watson, "Naval Concepts," p. 2.
22. McDonald OH, p. 358.
23. Admiral Horacio Rivero, USN (Ret.), to author 23 June 1978.
24. U.S., Congress, House, Appropriations Committee, *Hearings on the Fiscal Year 1963 Defense Budget*, 87th Cong., 2nd Sess., 1962, p. 66.
25. Watson, "Naval Concepts," p. 2.
26. Rivero to author, 23 June 1978.
27. *Ibid.*
28. McDonald to author, 27 April 1978.
29. Alain C. Enthoven and K. Wayne Smith, *How Much Is Enough*? (New York: Harper & Row, 1971), p. 325.
30. McDonald to author, 27 April 1978.
31. DOD Fact Sheet, p. 17.
32. U.S. Congress, House, *Communication from the President of the United States Transmitting a Plan for the Reorganization of the Department of the Navy, Pursuant to the Provisions of Section 125, Title 10, United States Code*, House Document No. 409 (Washington, D.C.: GPO, 1966), p. iv.
33. *Ibid.*
34. Leslie Gelb et al., *The Pentagon Papers: The Defense Department History of United States Decisionmaking on Vietnam* (Boston: Beacon Press, n.d.), Vol. 3, p. 182.
35. "Purple Suit" was a euphemism used by members of the armed forces to indicate a service member assigned to a Department of Defense billet in which he was not the representative of a single service, but of the entire Defense Department. Theoretically, a "purple suiter" took his directions from DOD officials rather than from his parent service.
36. Interview, Commander Winston Cornelius, USN (RET.), 7 March 1978.
37. McDonald OH, p. 384.
38. Gelb, *Pentagon Papers*, Vol. 3, p. 641
39. McDonald OH, p. 333.

THOMAS H. MOORER

1. Harold S. Torrance, "Naval and Maritime Events, 1 July 1967–30 June 1968," in Frank Uhlig, Jr., ed., *Naval Review 1969* (Annapolis, Md.: Naval Institute Press,1969), p. 285; Townsend Hoopes, *The Limits of Intervention* (New York: David McKay, 1969), p. 57.
2. Unless otherwise noted, the information in this article is from: Interviews, author with Moorer, Washington, D.C., 14 and 18 December 1978, and 4 January 1979; and biographical data provided by Moorer's office.

3. *Ibid.*
4. *The Lucky Bag, 1933* (Annapolis, Md.: U.S. Naval Academy).
5. Transcript, Thomas H. Moorer, U.S. Naval Institute Lecture-Discussion, n.d. (1967?), NHC.
6. Thomas H. Moorer, *Speeches and Statements . . . as Chairman Joint Chiefs of Staff* (Washington, D.C.: GPO, 1974), pp. 319–20.
7. *Time*, 26 February 1965, p. 21.
8. U.S. Strategic Bombing Survey (Pacific), Naval Analysis Division, *The Campaigns of the Pacific War* (Washington, D.C.: GPO, 1946), pp. 1–51; Moorer, Naval Institute Lecture.
9. J. D. Gerrard-Gough and Albert B. Christman, *The Grand Experiment at Inyokern* (Washington, D.C.: GPO, 1978), p. 96*n*.
10. Moorer, Naval Institute Lecture.
11. David A. Rosenberg, "The Maritime Balance Study: Appendix A: History of Navy Long Range Planning: An Overview," (Draft typescript prepared for the Office of the SecNav, March 1979), p. 9.
12. *Time*, 26 February 1965, p. 21.
13. Clark M. Gammell, "Naval and Maritime Events, 1 July 1966–30 June 1967," in Frank Uhlig, Jr., ed., *Naval Review 1968*, (Annapolis, Md.: Naval Institute Press, 1968), p. 270.
14. Interviews, Moorer.
15. Johnson, *Vantage Point*, pp. 388–89; for the view from Saigon, *see* William C. Westmoreland, *A Soldier Reports* (Garden City, N.Y.: Doubleday, 1976), pp. 350–59.
16. Hoopes, *Limits*, p. 149; Naval Review, 1969, p. 303; Westmoreland, *Reports*, p. 358.
17. Hoopes, *Limits*, p. 204.
18. *Ibid.*, pp. 150–51; Johnson, *Vantage Point*, p. 412; Westmoreland, *Reports*, p. 358.
19. Johnson, *Vantage Point*, pp. 532–37; D. L. Strole and W. E. Dutcher, "Naval and Maritime Events, 1 July 1968–31 December 1969," in Frank Uhlig, Jr., and Jan Snouck-Hurgronje, eds., *Naval Review 1970*, (Annapolis, Md.: Naval Institute Press, 1970), 14 May 1969 entry; and Johnson, *Vantage Point*, p. 535.
20. Trevor Armbrister, *A Matter of Accountability* (New York: Doubleday, 1969). This is the standard account of the *Pueblo* incident.
21. Thomas H. Moorer, Speech extract in U.S. Air Force (SAFAA), Executive Agent for the Dept. of Defense, *Selected Statements by Department of Defense and Other Administration Officials, January 1–June 30, 1970* (Washington, D.C.: GPO, 1970), p. 310.
22. "How Good Are U.S. Defenses?: Interview with Admiral Moorer, Chief of Naval Operations," *U.S. News and World Report*, 1 December 1969, p. 76.
23. Thomas H. Moorer, "The Attack Aircraft Carrier," *Vital Speeches of the Day*, 15 April 1970, p. 394.
24. "How Good Are U.S. Defenses?" pp. 76–77; Moorer, *Selected Statements*, p. 287.
25. *Naval Review, 1970*, 21 January 1969 entry.
26. Charles A. Bowsher, Speech extract in U.S. Air Force, *Selected Statements*, p. 67.
27. *Ibid.*
28. *Naval Review, 1970*, 15 January, 19 March, 1 April, 19 and 30 December 1969 entries.
29. Moorer, "Attack Aircraft Carrier," p. 393.
30. "How Good Are U.S. Defenses?," p. 74.
31. *Naval Review, 1970*, 19 May, 16 and 25 July 1968, and 7 May 1969 entries.

32. Elmo R. Zumwalt, Jr., *On Watch* (New York: Quadrangle 1976), pp. 191 and 209.
33. Moorer is rarely mentioned in the memoirs and principal studies of the Johnson-Nixon period. Johnson's memoirs, *The Vantage Point*, mention Moorer not at all, while Richard M. Nixon, *The Memoirs of Richard Nixon* (New York: Grosset and Dunlap, 1978), contains only a few incidental references to Moorer, as chairman of the Joint Chiefs of Staff.
34. Transcript, speech by James R. Schlesinger, Washington, D.C., 2 July 1974.
35. John M. Goshko, "Retired Brass Disagree on Canal Pacts," *Washington Post*, 11 October 1977, p. A1.
36. Don Oberdorfer, "SALT Would Lock U.S. Into Inferiority, Military Men Warn," *Washington Post*, 12 April 1979.

ELMO R. ZUMWALT, JR.

1. Much of the material in this essay is taken from Elmo R. Zumwalt, *On Watch: A Memoir* (New York: Quadrangle, 1976); two interviews with Zumwalt, May and September 1978; Zumwalt's comments on a draft of this essay; and interviews with several senior and junior naval officers, all of whom have asked for anonymity.
2. Zumwalt, *On Watch*, p. 33.
3. "Major Fleet Escort Study," 1971, NHC; Naval Engineering Center, "Report on the Patrol Frigate Conceptual Design," Navy Department, 1971; and Norman Friedman, "U.S. Destroyers," (Annapolis, Md.: Naval Institute Press, forthcoming)
4. Interview, author with Zumwalt, September 1978.
5. Zumwalt's briefing materials for Project Sixty; and *On Watch*, pp. 66–84.
6. This is based on a reading of the surviving long range objectives (LRO) studies, and an interview in December 1978 with David A. Rosenberg, who is writing a study of naval long range planning. The contrast between LRO studies and Systems Analysis reports—such as the "Major Fleet Escort Study" (MFE)—is striking; in earlier years, MFE would have been fed into an LRO as a source of future desirable force levels, but the LROG would have balanced the differing naval requirements in evaluating the levels recommended in the MFE.
7. Interview, author with Zumwalt, May 1978.
8. *Ibid.*
9. For the origins of the Long-Range Objectives Group, *see* chapter by Paul Schratz on Admiral Robert Carney, pp. 243–261.
10. Zumwalt, *On Watch*, Ch. 4.
11. Another earlier one is provided by R.H. Smith, "A United States Navy for the Future, " *USNIP*, March 1971. This essay won the Naval Institute Prize.
12. Zumwalt, *On Watch*, pp. 73–74, 101–07, 140–41, 157–63, and 495–503.
13. *Ibid.*, p. 71.
14. Zumwalt had been concerned with destroyer development long before he became CNO. *See* Elmo R. Zumwalt, " A Course for Destroyers," *USNIP*, November 1962.
15. Zumwalt, *On Watch*, Ch. 5.
16. The sea control ship idea was actually somewhat older. For example, in 1969 in its last major study, LRO-81, the Long Range Objectives Group proposed construction of anti-submarine helicopter ships: As head of Systems Analysis at the time, Zumwalt had a hand in this study.
17. Zumwalt, *On Watch*, pp. 76–77.
18. *Ibid.*, pp. 74–75 and 81–82.

19. *Ibid.*, Ch. 10.
20. *Ibid.*, pp. 210–14.
21. *Ibid.*, pp.172–96.
22. *Ibid.*, pp. 217–47.
23. *Ibid.*, Ch. 18.

THE AUTHORS

DAVID F. TRASK (B.A., Wesleyan University; A.M., Ph.D., Harvard University) is director of the Office of the Historian, Bureau of Public Affairs, in the U. S. Department of State. He has taught at Boston University, Wesleyan University, and the University of Nebraska, and served as the chairman of the history department at the State University of New York at Stony Brook. A specialist on the relationship between force and diplomacy during World War I, his books include *The United States in the Supreme War Council, General Tasker H. Bliss and the "Sessions of the World", Victory without Peace,* and *Captains and Cabinets.* He is also the coauthor of *A Bibliography of United States-Latin American Relations Since 1910* and *The Ordeal of World Power.* He has just completed *The War with Spain in 1898* and is beginning a general study of the relationship between force and diplomacy in American history.

LAWRENCE H. DOUGLAS (B.S., State University of New York at Oswego; Ph.D., Syracuse University) is associate dean for academic affairs and associate professor of history at Plymouth State College of the University System of New Hampshire. He has taught at the University of Rochester and Nazareth College of Rochester, New York. He has published several articles dealing with international disarmament and the submarine.

RICHARD W. TURK (B.A., Albion College; M.A., Ph.D., Fletcher School of Law and Diplomacy) is an associate professor of history at Allegheny College, Meadville, Pennsylvania. His publications include "Defending the New Empire, 1900–1914" in *In Peace and War.* He is currently engaged in a study of the Mahan-Roosevelt relationship and its impact on American foreign and naval policy.

WILLIAM R. BRAISTED (B.A., Stanford University; M.A., Ph.D., University of Chicago) is professor of history at the University of Texas at Austin, where he teaches Japanese and naval history. His books include *The United States Navy in the Far East, 1897–1909, The United States Navy in the Far East, 1909–1922,* and

Meiroku Zasshi: Journal of the Japanese Enlightenment. A specialist in the age of the battleship, he is now continuing his study of the American Navy through to the attack on Pearl Harbor.

CRAIG L. SYMONDS (B.A., University of California, Los Angeles; M.A., Ph.D., University of Florida) is an associate professor of history at the U. S. Naval Academy. He taught previously in the Strategy and Policy Department at the U.S. Naval War College. He is the author of several articles on American naval history as well as *Charleston Blockade* and *Navalists and Antinavalists.* He is currently working on a study of the steam navy of the nineteenth century.

JOHN C. WALTER (B.S., Arkansas State College, Pine Bluff; M.A., University of Bridgeport; Ph.D., University of Maine) is an assistant professor of history and director of Afro-American Studies Program at Bowdoin College, Brunswick, Maine. He previously taught at Purdue University and the City University of New York. A specialist in Afro-American history and American naval history during the New Deal, he is currently writing a book on FDR and naval rearmament from 1933 to 1939.

JOHN MAJOR (B.A., M.A. (Cantab.), Cambridge University) is a lecturer at the University of Hull, where he teaches the history of American foreign policy. His publications include *The Oppenheimer Hearing, The New Deal,* and *The Contemporary World.* In addition, he coauthored *Send a Gunboat.* Currently, he is writing a history of the Panama Canal.

B. MITCHELL SIMPSON III (B.A., Colgate University; Ll.B, University of Pennsylvania; M.A., M.A.L.D., Ph.D., Fletcher School of Law and Dipolmacy) is a retired career naval officer. Following extensive sea duty in destroyers, amphibious ships, and carriers, he taught at the U. S. Naval War College as professor of strategy and edited the *Naval War College Review.* He is the author of *War Strategy, and Maritime Power* and editor of Herbert Rosinski's *The Development of Naval Thought.* Currently, he is serving as executive director of the Newport Institute, a nonprofit, public interest organization for the study of national security and defense issues. He is also writing a full-length biography of Harold R. Stark and collaborating on the centennial history of the U. S. Naval War College.

ROBERT WILLIAM LOVE, JR. (B.A., University of Washington; M.A., California State University at Sonoma; Ph.D., University of California, Davis) is an assistant professor of history at the U. S. Naval Academy, where he teaches American naval history and British history. He is the editor of *Changing Interpretations and New Sources in Naval History* and the author of several articles on Anglo-American naval diplomacy. He is currently completing the first volume of *From Pearl Harbor to Tokyo Bay,* a history of American naval policy and strategy in World War II.

STEVEN T. ROSS (B.A., Williams College; M.A., Ph.D., Princeton University) is professor of strategy at the U. S. Naval War College. He previously taught at the University of Nebraska and the University of Texas at Austin. A specialist in military history, he has written several books and numerous articles on military affairs, particularly in the age of Napoleon. He is currently studying post-1945 American war plans.

PAOLO E. COLETTA (B.S.Ed., M.A., and Ph.D., University of Missouri) is professor of history at the U. S. Naval Academy where he has taught since 1946. His books outside the field of naval history include a three-volume biography of William Jennings Bryan, while his publications in naval history are: *The American Naval Heritage in Brief, The U. S. Navy and Defense Unification, 1947–1953, Bowman Hendry McCalla: A Fighting Sailor, French Ensor Chadwick: Scholarly Warrior,* and *Admiral Bradley A. Fiske and the American Navy*. He is the coeditor of a two-volume study of the *American Secretaries of the Navy* and has published more than fifty articles in historical and military journals. His *Bibliography in American Naval History* will soon be published. Currently, he is studying the naval phase of World War I on the Western Front, including the Atlantic and Adriatic areas of operations.

CLARK G. REYNOLDS (B.A., University of California, Santa Barbara; M.A., Ph.D., Duke University) is curator and historian of Patriots' Point Naval and Maritime Museum, Charleston, South Carolina. He has taught at the U. S. Naval Academy and at the University of Maine, and chaired the Humanities Department at the U. S. Merchant Marine Academy. In addition to several articles on American naval history, his publications include *The Fast Carriers, Command of the Sea,* and *Famous American Admirals*. He is currently studying the career of John Towers.

GERALD KENNEDY (B.S., M.Ed., M.S.A., Loyola University; M.B.A., University of Pennsylvania; M.A., University of Chicago; M.S.L.S., Catholic University; Ed.D., University of Maryland; Ph.D., University of Minnesota) is an archivist with the Adjutant General's Office, Department of the Army. He has served in a variety of administrative and faculty positions at the U. S. Naval Academy, the University of Maryland, and the University of Minnesota. A specialist in American military and naval participation in World War I and in professional military education and training, his articles have appeared in military and education journals.

PAUL R. SCHRATZ (B.S., U. S. Naval Academy; M.A., Boston University; Ph.D., Ohio University) is professor of military strategy at the Air War College, U. S. Air University. He has also taught at Georgetown University, was director of international studies for the University of Missouri, and served on the White House-Congressional Commission on the Organization of the Government for Foreign Policy. He has published widely on professional military subjects, is the editor of *The Evolution of American Defense Policy Since World War II,* and is currently preparing a book on *The Evolution of Modern Strategic Thought.*

DAVID ALAN ROSENBERG (B.A., American University; M.A., University of Chicago) is currently an independent historian and consultant. He taught previously at the University of Wisconsin-Milwaukee, prepared a study of early naval atomic strategy for the Office of the Chief of Naval Operations, and wrote a history of long-range planning in the navy for the Naval Research Advisory

Committee of the Office of the Secretary of the Navy. His articles on nuclear strategy and naval history have appeared in *The Journal of American History, Pacific Historical Review,* and the *Naval War College Review.* He is completing a book on the development of American atomic strategy from 1945 to 1953 and is working on a full-length biography of Arleigh Burke.

LAWRENCE KORB (B.A., Atheneum of Ohio; M.A., St. Johns University; Ph.D., State University of New York at Albany) is professor of management at the U. S. Naval War College and an adjunct scholar of the American Enterprise Institute, where he specializes in budgetary analysis and national security policy. He has served as a consultant to the Office of the Secretary of Defense, the National Security Council, and the U. S. Office of Education. He is the author of *The Joint Chiefs of Staff, The Rise and Fall of the Pentagon: Defense Policies of the 1970s, The Price of Preparedness: the FY 1978–82 Defense Program, The FY 1979–83 Defense Program: Issues and Trends,* and *The FY 1980–84 Defense Program: Issues and Trends.* He is the coauthor of *Public Claims on U. S. Output: Federal Budget Options for the Last Half of the Decade* and has written more than fifty articles on national security affairs.

FLOYD D. KENNEDY, JR. (A.B., University of Illinois; M.A., Ph.D. cand., American University) is senior naval analyst with the BDM Corporation, McLean, Virginia. A specialist in postwar American and Soviet naval and aviation developments, he contributed to *In Peace and War* and was coeditor of *World Combat Aircraft Directory.* He has published articles on the Soviet Navy in *Naval War College Review, National Defense,* and *Naval Intelligence Quarterly,* and is the maritime columnist and a contributing editor of *National Defense.* He is currently preparing a comprehensive history of military and naval helicopter development.

J. KENNETH MCDONALD (B.A., Yale University; B.Litt., D.Phil., Oxford University) is professor of strategy at the U. S. Naval War College while on leave from his post at George Washington University. At the Naval War College he previously held the King and Nimitz chairs and served as chairman of the Strategy Department. His research focuses on twentieth century British and American naval policy and he is now completing a book, entitled *From Disarmament to Rearmament,* on the impact of the interwar naval treaties on the origins of World War II in the Pacific.

NORMAN FRIEDMAN (B.A., Ph.D., Columbia University) is a defense analyst and naval historian at the Hudson Institute. His publications include *Modern Warship Design and Development* and *Battleship Design and Development, 1905–1945.* His principal area of professional study is the Soviet-American naval balance, and he is currently preparing a history of U. S. destroyer design in which the interaction between national policy and naval technology is examined.

INDEX